VEIL

ALSO BY BOB WOODWARD

ALL THE PRESIDENT'S MEN
(with Carl Bernstein)

THE FINAL DAYS
(with Carl Bernstein)

THE BRETHREN
(with Scott Armstrong)

WIRED
The Short Life and Fast Times of John Belushi

VEIL: The top-secret code word
for covert operations
undertaken in the latter years
of the Reagan Administration
to influence events abroad

VEIL

The Secret Wars of the CIA 1981-1987

Bob Woodward

SIMON & SCHUSTER
LONDON

FIRST PUBLISHED IN GREAT BRITAIN BY
SIMON & SCHUSTER LIMITED 1987

**SIMON & SCHUSTER LIMITED, WEST GARDEN PLACE,
KENDAL STREET, LONDON W2 2AQ**

SIMON & SCHUSTER AUSTRALIA PTY LIMITED,
SYDNEY

BRITISH LIBRARY CATALOGUING IN PUBLICATION DATA AVAILABLE

ISBN 0-671-65543-4

PRINTED AND BOUND IN THE UNITED STATES OF AMERICA

To Elsa

CONTENTS

AUTHOR'S NOTE

THIS BOOK WAS POSSIBLE because of the tireless and diligent work of Barbara Feinman, a 1982 graduate of the University of California at Berkeley, who assisted in every step—conducting interviews, locating people and facts, thinking, scrutinizing, writing, editing, organizing, correcting misjudgments and spelling. Her friendship and sense of fairness guided the daily enterprise; the book is as much hers as mine.

A NOTE TO READERS

MOST OF THE INFORMATION in this book was obtained from interviews with more than 250 people involved directly in gathering or using intelligence information. I conducted multiple interviews with more than one hundred of these people; about fifteen key sources were each interviewed a half-dozen or more times. I would prefer sharing the name and position of each source with the reader. But because of the topic's sensitivity, nearly all the interviews were conducted on "background," which means that I have promised that these sources will not be identified. The simple reality is that people will not discuss intelligence and security matters without this protection. A number of sources also provided access to documents, memoranda, notes, calendars, other written chronologies, letters, transcripts and diaries. Where quoted directly, the documentation is identified in the text. I found, however, that the discussions with well-placed sources were generally more illuminating than reading stacks of documents.

The various investigations of the Iran-contra affair, including those of the Senate Select Committee on Intelligence, the Tower review board, the joint Senate-House select committees, and independent counsel Lawrence Walsh, provided additional information and documentation, especially for the years 1985 and 1986.

The use of dialogue in meetings or conversations comes from at least one participant or written memos or contemporaneous notes. In the narrative when someone is said to have "thought" or to "believe," that point of view has been obtained from that person or from some source who gained direct knowledge of the person's conclusions from a conversation with that person. I have attempted to preserve the language of the main characters and sources as much as possible, using their words even when they are not directly quoted, reflecting the flavor of their speech and attitudes as best I could. In those cases where the memories of sources or the documentation was not absolutely clear no quotations were used.

Ken Auletta wrote in his most recent book, "No reporter can with 100 percent accuracy re-create events that occurred some time before. Memories play tricks on participants, the more so when the outcome has become clear. A reporter tries to guard against inaccuracies by checking with a variety of sources, but it is useful for a reader—and an author—to be humbled by this journalistic limitation." I subscribe fully to this important observation.

Work on this book began in late 1984. My purpose was initially to cover only the first four years of the CIA under Reagan and Casey. But during the reporting and writing of this book, I worked daily as a reporter and an editor at *The Washington Post,* and it soon became clear from events relating to Nicaragua, Libya and Iran that the book would have to cover 1985, 1986 and a portion of 1987. Since this book is one of the first to treat the subject, I realize that it will by no means be the last word or even come close to it. Accordingly, this book is much closer to journalism than to history, particularly as the Iran-contra hearings and the various investigations continue.

In half a dozen scenes in this book, the editors at the *Post* and I were involved in making decisions about publishing national-security stories. In these cases, I was my own source and reluctantly I enter the narrative in an attempt to describe as precisely as possible what happened. I also describe several of my meetings with William J. Casey.

I have attempted to tell the story of intelligence from three main perspectives: (1) Director of Central Intelligence Casey, (2) the White House, (3) the Senate Select Committee on Intelligence.

I had more than four dozen interviews or substantive discussions with Casey from 1983 to 1987. We talked at his house, at his office, on plane rides, in corners at parties, or on the phone. At times he spoke freely and explained his views. At other times he declined. Overall, I was able to obtain his perspective on the major intelligence topics discussed in this book. He once said, "Everyone always says more than they're supposed to." It was a maxim he clearly accepted both in others and in himself. He rarely was willing to be identified by name or as a source for my newspaper writing. He also knew I was gathering information for this book on his CIA, and on a number of occasions he stipulated that information was not to appear in the next day's newspaper but was for the book. Among many other things, Casey thought of himself as a historian. In fairness to him, I am sure that if he had lived to write his own account, this is not the way he would tell it. He would disagree vehemently with me, as he often did while he was alive. I, nonetheless, am certain he would recognize all or nearly all of what is assembled here. So this is in no sense an "authorized" version of his CIA years, but he was a participant. It was perhaps his way of playing defense, or shaping the story, or out of curiosity.

The White House and the National Security Council are the most important users of intelligence. Dozens of members of President Reagan's staff assisted me. The President was not interviewed.

In 1971, Senator John C. Stennis, a strong supporter of the CIA, said on the Senate floor, "Spying is spying . . . You have to make up your mind that you are going to have an intelligence agency and protect it as such, and shut your eyes some and take what is coming." After the intelligence abuses were exposed in the 1970s, the Senate Select Committee on Intelligence was probably the most visible congressional overseer of intelligence activities, designated to watch and monitor. By law, it and its counterpart in the House were to insure that congressional eyes were open. In the Reagan years, legislative oversight of intelligence stumbled along and finally failed, and many Senate committee members and their staffs assisted me in recording that story.

A word is in order about secrets. It is easy on one hand to adopt a stance of reverence about classification and assume that because someone has stamped a document SECRET or TOP SECRET that actually means it was so sensitive that it had to be kept classified. On the other hand, it is easy to become skeptical and assume that classification has no meaning, that it is a ritual designed to conceal bad policy and embarrassment. Guided by my best sources, I have attempted a middle course in choosing what to disclose. But there is no sterilized version of this story that could have much meaning, and this is not one.

BOB WOODWARD

CAST OF CHARACTERS

Director of Central Intelligence (DCI)	
William J. Casey	January 28, 1981–January 29, 1987
Deputy Director of Central Intelligence (DDCI)	
Bobby R. Inman	February 12, 1981–June 10, 1982 (NSA Director, 1977–81)
John N. McMahon	June 10, 1982–March 29, 1986 (DDO, 1978–81)
Robert M. Gates	April 18, 1986–
Deputy Director for Operations (DDO)	
Max C. Hugel	May 11, 1981–July 14, 1981
John H. Stein	July 1981–June 1984
Clair George	June 1984–
CIA General Counsel	
Stanley Sporkin	May 18, 1981–February 7, 1986
Former DCIs	
Richard M. Helms	June 30, 1966–February 2, 1973
James R. Schlesinger	February 2, 1973–July 2, 1973
William E. Colby	September 4, 1973–January 30, 1976
George Bush	January 30, 1976–January 20, 1977 (Vice-President, January 20, 1981–)
Stansfield Turner	March 9, 1977–January 20, 1981
President of the United States	
Ronald Reagan	January 20, 1981–

National-Security Adviser

Richard V. Allen	January 21, 1981–January 4, 1982
William Clark	January 4, 1982–October 17, 1983
Robert C. McFarlane	October 17, 1983–December 4, 1985
John M. Poindexter	December 4, 1985–November 25, 1986
Frank C. Carlucci III	January 2, 1987– (DDCI, 1978–81) (Deputy Secretary of Defense, 1981–82)

Assistants to the President

James A. Baker III, chief of staff	January 21, 1981–February 2, 1985 (Secretary of the Treasury, February 3, 1985–)
Edwin Meese III, counselor	January 21, 1981–February 24, 1985 (Attorney General, February 25, 1985–)
Michael K. Deaver, deputy chief of staff	January 21, 1981–May 10, 1985
Donald T. Regan, chief of staff	February 4, 1985–February 27, 1987

Secretary of State

Alexander M. Haig, Jr.	January 22, 1981–June 25, 1982
George P. Shultz	July 16, 1982–

Assistant Secretary for Inter-American Affairs

Thomas O. Enders	June 23, 1981–June 27, 1983
L. Anthony "Tony" Motley	July 12, 1983–July 3, 1985
Elliott Abrams	July 17, 1985–

Secretary of Defense

Caspar W. Weinberger	January 21, 1981–

Senate Select Committee on Intelligence

Barry M. Goldwater, chairman, 1981–85
David Durenberger, chairman, 1985–86
Daniel P. Moynihan, vice-chairman, 1981–84
Patrick J. Leahy, vice-chairman, 1985–86

INTELLIGENCE ACRONYMS, TITLES AND DEFINITIONS

BIGOT LIST—A narrow, select group of people with access to the reports from a particularly sensitive agent or espionage operation.

CIA—Central Intelligence Agency, which conducts foreign-intelligence operations and intelligence-gathering abroad; has no authority to operate domestically and no arrest power.

CLASSIFICATION—The systematic division of sensitive military, intelligence or policy information.

Confidential is the lowest level of classification and consists of material the disclosure of which could reasonably be expected to cause some form of damage to the national security.

Secret information consists of material the disclosure of which could be reasonably expected to cause "serious damage" to the national security.

Top-Secret information includes material the disclosure of which could be expected to cause "exceptionally grave" national-security damage.

COUNTERINTELLIGENCE—Activity designed to neutralize, thwart or capitalize on the intelligence activities of foreign intelligence services, including the penetration of a foreign service with a "mole," or agent who reports back on the work or on agents of the hostile service.

COVERT ACTION—Clandestine activity designed to influence events in foreign countries without the United States or CIA role being known; action can range from low-level placement of propaganda to an attempt to overthrow a government deemed to be unfriendly.

DCI—Director of Central Intelligence, the overseer and coordinator of all U.S. intelligence agencies, and simultaneously the head of the Central Intelligence Agency; also the President's chief intelligence adviser.

DDCI—Deputy Director of Central Intelligence, the deputy to the DCI and No. 2 at the CIA.

DDI—Deputy Director for Intelligence, the head of the CIA's analytic directorate, which evaluates, weighs and summarizes raw intelligence reports.

DDO—Deputy Director for Operations, the head of the CIA's clandestine or espionage branch, called the Directorate of Operations (DO), which manages the CIA stations abroad and conducts covert action, recruits and manages human intelligence sources and assists in other sensitive intelligence-gathering abroad.

DIA—Defense Intelligence Agency, the coordinating intelligence agency in the Defense Department that reports to the Secretary of Defense, but is subject to the coordinating authority of the DCI.

DO—Directorate of Operations. See DDO.

FINDING—The presidential authorization for covert action, almost always in writing; a short directive in which the President states that he "finds" that a certain "covert action" is important to the national security.

INR—Bureau of Intelligence and Research, the State Department intelligence office.

INTELLIGENCE COMMUNITY—a term used to refer to all the U.S. intelligence agencies and employees; the DCI is the most senior member.

NFIB—National Foreign Intelligence Board, the heads of all U.S. intelligence agencies, that acts as a board of directors for U.S. intelligence and approves the formal estimates, NIEs and SNIEs. It is chaired by the DCI, and members include representatives from the CIA, the NSA, the DIA, the NRO and the intelligence services of the Navy, the Army, the Air Force, the Marine Corps, the FBI, and the Departments of State, Energy and the Treasury.

NID—National Intelligence Daily, a top-secret UMBRA (see SCI) summary of the main intelligence items from the previous day; about 150 copies are printed and circulated.

NIE—National Intelligence Estimate, a formal written forecast of future events in countries, of leaders or of various intelligence, military or economic problems, representing the best collective judgment of all the U.S. intelligence agencies and the DCI.

NIO—National-intelligence officer, a senior analyst responsible for a region or a special intelligence area, who reports to the DCI.

NRO—National Reconnaissance Office, the low-profile agency responsible for satellite and other aerial overhead intelligence-gathering; it also reports to the Secretary of Defense, but its activities are coordinated by the DCI.

NSA—National Security Agency, the largest and most secret intelligence agency; it intercepts worldwide signals intelligence (SIGINT) and conducts eavesdropping operations abroad, using listening posts, satellites and other sophisticated collection technology. Military and diplomatic codes of some foreign nations are broken; the NSA is also charged with protecting the communication and cryptographic systems and codes of the United States.

NSC—National Security Council, the President and his senior foreign-policy-makers, including the Vice-President and the Secretaries of State and Defense. The DCI and the Chairman of the Joint Chiefs of Staff serve in advisory roles. The NSC staff is headed by the President's Assistant for National Security Affairs, or national-security adviser, who reports to the President.

NSDD—National Security Decision Directive, a formal written order from the President directing his senior advisers and departments on major foreign-policy matters or procedures; the orders are usually classified and are numbered in sequence.

NSPG—National Security Planning Group, the key gathering in the Reagan Administration of the President and his top foreign-policy advisers, including the Secretaries of State and Defense and the DCI; for practical purposes the NSPG replaced the NSC as the chief decision-making body in the Reagan Administration.

OSS—Office of Strategic Services, the American intelligence service during World War II, headed by William J. "Wild Bill" Donovan.

PDB—President's Daily Brief, the most sensitive and exclusive intelligence items, which are summarized and sent to the President, the Vice-President, the Secretaries of State and Defense, the DCI, the national-security adviser and a few other senior White House aides.

PFIAB—President's Foreign Intelligence Advisory Board, a nonpartisan group of fourteen senior Americans who monitor intelligence performance for the President; a largely honorary body which at times, however, becomes involved in intelligence controversies.

SCI—Sensitive Compartmented Information, the process of further restricting access to the most sensitive information by imposing special controls and handling. *Compartments* of such information for a particular operation or sensitive source or method of collecting intelligence are generally given *code words*. Individuals in the government from the President on down must be granted specific code-word access to each compartment. Code words are selected at random. Some employed by the NSA for signals intelligence include RUFF, ZARF, SPOKE, MORAY and two of the most restrictive involving decoded messages, UMBRA and GAMMA. VEIL was the code word for the covert action compartment during the last several years of the Reagan Administration.

SNIE—Special National Intelligence Estimates, shorter formal evaluations completed in weeks or days on topics deemed to be of unexpected or urgent national-security interest.

Prologue

THE ALARM WOKE the Director of Central Intelligence, Admiral Stansfield Turner. He hated getting up in the morning, and he had set the alarm for the last possible minute—7 A.M.—this Thursday, November 20, 1980. It was the 383rd day of the Iran hostage crisis; the fifty-two Americans held captive in Tehran had sunk Jimmy Carter's presidency earlier that month. Turner was to give an intelligence briefing to President-elect Ronald Reagan later that day.

Earlier in the year, a twenty-four-hour-a-day security guard had been placed on the ground floor of Turner's house for several weeks, after the Federal Bureau of Investigation found some Iranians holding target practice with high-powered rifles on the outskirts of Washington. But the security was gone now, and the house was quiet.

At fifty-six, a retired four-star admiral, Turner was in his prime. A systems analyst, a Navy "thinker" and a Rhodes Scholar, he tried always to look beyond the day to the larger issues. But he was an emotional man, and now, caught between old and new bosses, he was pulled by a range of contradictory feelings about the transition period.

First, he had to gauge when and how to pass on the real secrets to Reagan—the potentially explosive and dangerous operations and spying techniques that the new President would need to understand. This was the stuff at the bottom of the barrel that had not leaked to the news media or been lost to Soviet espionage. The passing of this knowledge would have to be man to man, just the two of them, until Reagan designated those he was going to trust with it. Turner could not divulge the secrets in front of the political hangers-on who had hovered at two earlier briefings and who could be expected to be in attendance at today's briefing. In one of the most secret intelligence operations that Turner would eventually have to explain to the President-elect, the lives of more than a hundred men were regularly at risk.

Turner also needed to direct Reagan's attention to the broad philosophical issues involved—the opportunities and hazards of spying and covert action. This was where a President could make real choices, and Reagan had promised a reinvigoration.

Turner wanted to improve his own read on Reagan. In the previous briefings, Reagan had been ostensibly outgoing but ultimately inaccessible. There had been a lightness and a detached congeniality as Reagan waved Turner on, seeming to bat away the problems of the world with a laugh, a Hollywood story, a line of conservative dogma. What a contrast to the grave, almost ruthless grillings Turner had endured with Carter. The more he was exposed to Reagan, the more Turner had come to doubt the man's basic thoughtfulness. He had described him privately as "stupid."

The last matter Turner had to consider was his own future. He wanted to convey his willingness, his desire even, to stay on as DCI. Reagan and the Republican platform had charged that Carter had bottled up the Central Intelligence Agency, making it virtually impossible for the agency to conduct effective espionage. The Republicans had argued that Turner, as director, was overly responsive to the Carter human-rights campaign, and that he was so enamored of the latest satellite and electronic eavesdropping technology, which was clean, passive and comparatively safe, that he took no chances. The word "debilitated" had been used about the agency. Turner thought he could rebut this if the President-elect gave him a hearing. His CIA had run some operations that would knock the socks off Ronald Reagan.

"Reagan doesn't want to politicize the agency and will see we're on the right track," Turner had told his top aides. They had scoffed at the Director's suggestion that he was not finished. His old Navy friend Herb Hetu, a retired captain and the agency's public-affairs chief, thought Turner needed some reality therapy.

"No way will they keep you," Hetu told him, "no way. They spent the campaign shooting your nuts off."

Turner stuck to his optimism. It was hard at times. Just before the presidential election, he had gathered his fifteen top deputies for a management seminar at Camp Peary, "the farm," the agency's secret training facility and academy in the Virginia countryside. Half joking, he had asked for a secret straw vote. It was a glass of cold water in the face as the vote was tallied on a blackboard: Carter 2; Reagan 13. That would just about reflect Reagan's 489-to-44 Electoral College victory.

The morning after the election had been particularly bad. The joy in the corridors at CIA headquarters at Langley was palpable. CIA people weren't quite hanging out of the windows cheering, but many had treated Reagan's victory like Liberation Day in Paris.

After a shower, Turner dressed and sat down to read for a few minutes. He picked up the weekly Christian Science lesson. If he didn't pause now, there would be no other opportunity during the day. He liked to think that his was the intellectual branch of Christianity—the mind and the spirit over all else.

The lesson for the next Sunday said: ". . . vehemently tell your patient that he must awake. Turn his gaze from the false evidence of the senses . . ." Look inward, the message said. It was, Turner conceded, an odd point, perhaps, for the head of the largest and most sophisticated intelligence service in the world. But he had witnessed the power of these teachings. His mother had survived the 1920s when her father lost his money in the stock market and took his own life. Later, when Turner's only brother died in an automobile accident, Turner had immersed himself in his religion to deal with the unexplainable tragedy and the pain. With a red pen Turner had underlined "Trials are proofs of God's care."

There wasn't any time left, and he rose, knowing he was neglecting the lesson. A solid, compact five feet nine and a half inches, Turner bounded down the stairs to breakfast—"ramming speed," his aides called it. His thick gray hair was usually slightly windblown in the breeze he created as he moved along. The pale-blue eyes, the beaming brief smile and the Rotary Club manner suggested anything but CIA.

At the breakfast table, he drank juice and hot water with lemon. Christian Science meant no stimulants, no coffee. Turner didn't even like the taste of coffee ice cream.

The Washington Post was there: "Casey Is Reported in Line for Directorship of CIA." Turner grabbed the paper. He had heard nothing whatsoever about that possibility. The "Casey" was William J. Casey, the sixty-seven-year-old Reagan campaign chairman. Turner felt that such a choice would be a step backward, absolutely wrong. Richard Nixon had appointed his 1968 campaign manager, John N. Mitchell, Attorney General. Was the CIA this year's political war trophy?

Turner read: "Casey worked for the Office of Strategic Services (OSS) —the CIA's organizational ancestor—during World War II." He thought that was irrelevant, like getting some old World War II admiral to head the Fleet. The OSS was the old-hand, old-boy network as far as Turner was concerned. OSS remnants and OSS attitudes still endured at the agency and had created major troubles for Turner. These men were the operators, the inner agency, the band of brothers. In a crunch with the White House or the Congress, the band of brothers might get it in the neck, as had happened during the CIA investigations in the mid-1970s. But the old-timers survived because they were needed. Every President, every DCI needed the dedicated secretive operatives who did the dirty work. They formed a club that didn't meet. They were gung-ho in the service of secret projects, the sort of people who could thrive in an environment where even the rewards were secret. They were both a strength and a weakness in the CIA. And here was a brother apparently emerging from the woodwork. The *Post* said Casey had been in charge of dropping spies behind German lines during the last six months of World War II. That was thirty-five years ago.

Turner had expected they would extend him the courtesy of informing him that he was going to be replaced before they told the newspapers. The story might be a trial balloon or simply wrong. He had not even heard of Casey until the presidential campaign. Reagan had announced at his first press conference as President-elect, two weeks before, that Casey would be returning to his private law practice.

The prospect of dismissal only strengthened Turner's conviction that he had guided the CIA out of the dark, turbulent period of the mid-1970s —the upheavals that came in the aftermath of Vietnam and Watergate, the congressional investigations that had dug deeply into the secret CIA past: plots to assassinate foreign leaders, the feeding of dangerous experimental hallucinogenic drugs to the unsuspecting, the stockpiling of small amounts of poison and venom banned by presidential order, clandestine mail openings, and spying on Americans who opposed the Vietnam War. He had brought the CIA out of the cowboy era, countered what he felt was a warped, obsessively secretive culture, and demonstrated that the agency could operate effectively under reforms that required strict accounting to congressional intelligence committees, even for the most sensitive operations. The operations of his CIA were sound, they had the support of Congress. If they were understood, they would have the support of Reagan and of the American people, Turner believed.

A month before the election, Turner had taken a week at home to shut out the daily routine and write a report on his stewardship of the last four years and his plan for the next four. Dated October 17, 1980, stamped "DCI EYES ONLY," the seven-page outline was more than top secret. "Goals–/Turnover Notes" told a story that would surprise the President-elect and his team. Yes, Turner had had trouble controlling some of the wilder impulses of the cowboys and the brothers, but he had finally gained control and many of those old hands were now gone. But there was a larger problem. The CIA had frayed nerves. Resistance and timidity often marked the Directorate of Operations, the espionage branch, the secretive and exclusive arm that ran the CIA stations and spying abroad and undertook covert actions when the President authorized secret interference in the affairs of other countries.

Turner had suggested new covert operations on a number of occasions, and the directorate had balked. In one instance, on his own, without consulting the White House, Turner had sent a testing-the-waters note to the Deputy Director for Operations, the DDO, inquiring what might be done to oust three leaders who were troublesome to U.S. interests—Cuba's leader Fidel Castro, Iran's leader Ayatollah Ruhollah Khomeini, and Libya's Muammar Qaddafi. The response from the DDO was: No, please; there wasn't a viable political opposition in any of the three countries, or the CIA didn't know enough about it to support a movement or a party or a leader. All Turner had been looking for was some way to funnel covert money or assistance to some groups or individuals inside these countries. Assassination was banned by executive order, signed by President Ford in 1976 and reaffirmed by Carter. Turner agreed with the ban entirely, but even so, somehow the operatives had feared that he was going to take them down a dangerous road. Turner had been surprised at the depth of their reluctance. No matter how he had explored the matter, however, the DDO had come up blank. They were uncomfortable at the prospect of serious meddling in other nations' affairs, even though that was their job. True, some money was being passed to anti-Khomeini forces outside Iran, but that was, at least in the view of the White House, designed to punish Khomeini or to establish some contacts in the event of a counterrevolution.

Turner had also proposed to the directorate that the agency devise a limited covert action plan to find and assist some centrist politician in Guatemala, perhaps even to get some up-and-coming Guatemalan onto the CIA payroll. Political violence was rampant in Guatemala. It was classic Central American standoff: a rightist military government versus leftist-Marxist guerrillas. Hundreds had died that year. In Turner's opinion this was precisely the kind of situation where covert political support of moderates could serve U.S. interests.

The directorate had reacted as if he had proposed inviting the KGB to his 9 A.M. senior-staff meetings. The covert operators argued that such an operation would run a great risk of putting the CIA out ahead of Administration policy, which in any case was not at all clear. Suppose the guy they picked didn't work out. Suppose he became a Frankenstein's monster. Suppose they built him up and then President Carter or some other President wanted to go in another direction. It was too easy to be wrong. The outcry had been unanimous, and Turner had not dared even raise the suggestion at the White House. National-security adviser Zbigniew Brzezinski would almost certainly have supported some covert program, but Carter would likely have engaged in a hesitation waltz. A fact of life of the Carter presidency was that the President had vacillated between the "tough" view of the world provided by Brzezinski and the "soft" view of Secretary of State Cyrus Vance. Turner had once referred privately to Carter as a "peacenik."

Earlier that month, on November 14, Turner had put additional views and private thoughts into another memo. Under the heading "White House" he had written, "Sources of conflict." The list was long, but many of the problems flowed to and from national-security adviser Brzezinski, who seemed to think that the CIA worked for him. On one arms control intelligence issue, when Turner dug in his heels, Brzezinski had told him, "You're not the Supreme Court. You're not a fourth branch of government. You've got to decide who you work for."

Brzezinski loved raw intelligence. The National Security Agency, which intercepted foreign communications, often provided him with transcripts of some head of state talking, or with the decoded political analysis that some foreign embassy in Washington had sent back to its capital. "Did you see that intercept?" Brzezinski would ask. Turner felt that Brzezinski made the typical junior analyst's mistake, believing that it was possible to explain large events by isolated cables or intercepts. Too often the NSA picked up some blowhard, or a misinformed and self-important official, or an ambassador reporting more than he knew. Turner had written under the heading "NSA": "Uni-source analysis is dangerous."

There had been a constant struggle with Brzezinski, who was at times predatory. "You haven't got a single asset in the Soviet Union," he once charged at a meeting with Turner's senior deputies. In fact Turner had developed several Soviet assets, though there had been only one he was sure was genuine, and two had been lost, probably killed—he could not be certain.

What had started out in 1977 as Turner's thrice-weekly intelligence briefings for the President had been cut to once a week, and then to once every two weeks. He blamed that on Brzezinski, who once offered the opinion that his former graduate students at Columbia University turned out better analysis than the CIA.

When the Shah of Iran came to the United States for medical treatment in October 1979, two weeks before the American hostages were taken in Tehran, the White House had wanted the CIA to bug the deposed Iranian ruler's hospital room to discover what the mercurial, cancer-stricken man intended to do. Turner had argued that the Shah had the same rights as a U.S. citizen and that, by law, the CIA couldn't gather intelligence in the United States. But he was given a written order. He swallowed hard and authorized the electronic surveillance of the Shah's three private rooms on the seventeenth floor of a New York City hospital, though he still thought it improper.

Carter and Brzezinski regarded intelligence as a tool, like the plumbing. When it didn't work, when the "bug" was not instantly in place, or when the CIA could not foresee the future, there was hell to pay. Turner realized, dimly at times, starkly at other times, that he was isolated both from his own agency and from the President he served.

In an attempt to reach out to the President-elect, Turner had given a copy of his second memo to a member of the transition team that was looking at the CIA for the new Administration. It had been returned to him marked up in pencil with suggestions that called for an abrupt conversion of the agency into an arm of anti-Soviet analysis and covert action. Where Turner had listed some positive attributes of the CIA, he had found the scrawled comment "Too liberal, afraid of political controversy." On the congressional intelligence oversight committees and their staffs, the Reagan team member had written: "Left wing must go to extent possible." Turner had also noted in his outline that the CIA could not "withstand another scandal." A handwritten note said, "Climate has changed. Will change more. If we operate on fear basis, will do very little." Where Turner had referred to the paramilitary capability of the CIA—the most activist, most interventionist arm—the scrawled comment was: "Must rebuild." Well, good luck on that, Turner thought.

As Turner finished breakfast, his driver, Ennis Brown, appeared in the driveway to take him downtown to the Reagan briefing. He climbed into the back, where the overnight and morning messages were in a folder for him. The dark government Oldsmobile went down Skipwith Road, onto Route 123 and into the morning traffic. Brown weaved in and out, darting professionally around the slower cars, speeding creatively, taking advantage of each passing opportunity.

A lone CIA security guard, one of four who rotated as the Admiral's protection, rode shotgun in the front seat. His eyes swept over the landscape, looking for the unusual. It was a beautiful sunny fall day, but the bulletproof windows in the Oldsmobile didn't roll down, so no one inside could enjoy it. The car had full high-security accessories, armor-plating and anti-mine flooring.

Turner shuffled and fidgeted in the back. He wanted to focus on the positive, the most creative, imaginative and gutsy undertakings. An intelligence outsider like Reagan, who had never held a full-time federal post, would probably not have a clue about what was involved. Turner's presentations over the next month might still help him keep his job.

One of the most secret operations was the SNCP, the Special Navy Control Program—"Navy Special," as it was called—in which U.S. submarines trailed Russian subs and also conducted high-risk surveillance and intelligence-gathering around the Soviet Union, at times inside Soviet territorial waters or in its harbors. Its activities included the planting of sophisticated electronic recording devices, or "pods," to tap into communications channels in an array of key Soviet undersea cables. These were probably the most sensitive operations of all. They risked the lives of all on board, putting the submarine, its crew and an assigned NSA team in jeopardy. It was the pride of the Navy, which loved the macho, daring exploits. Each mission had to be approved by the President. A nuclear sub went to sea, placed the tap pod, left the area and waited for weeks before coming in to retrieve the tapes from the recording device that had been installed on the cable. The tapes then had to be brought back to the NSA, and the information was distributed to only a few in the CIA, the Defense Department and the White House. At times Turner thought the information was of marginal value given the dangers.

Yet he conceded that sometimes the submarine returned with a rich harvest of data about the Soviet military. It was one of the few operations that acquired large amounts of high-quality hard intelligence out of the Soviet Union. On occasion, the "take" included Soviet officials talking to one another, revealing their uncertainties, their lies and their weaknesses. Like many successful intelligence operations, the opportunity was based on the other side's mistake. The Soviets had assumed that these undersea cables couldn't be tapped, so the communications links used comparatively unsophisticated coding systems, or in some cases no coding at all.

Another project was Indigo, a new highly secret satellite system in development that could be the key to verifying future arms control agreements with the Soviets. Using radar-imaging, Indigo would see through clouds and work at night, when photographic satellites were blind. This would be particularly important over Eastern Europe, where the so-called "demon cloud cover" could sit for days or weeks.

Some of the best intelligence-gathering operations were conducted abroad by Special Collection Elements (SCE), elite CIA and National Security Agency teams that ran eavesdropping operations with the latest gadgets in many foreign capitals. The SCEs could perform espionage miracles, delivering verbatim transcripts from high-level foreign-government meetings in Europe, the Middle East and Asia, and phone conversations between key politicians. It supplemented the regular CIA officers who spied undercover from the U.S. embassies.

In his "DCI EYES ONLY" memo, Turner had written, "Greater need for intelligence on allies and friends." Spying on friends, Turner believed, was sticky but essential business. The Shah of Iran had been a great friend of the United States and the CIA, and his intelligence service, the dreaded SAVAK, had been the agency's main pipeline in Iran. What a mistake, Turner had come to realize. He and his CIA had studiously misread Khomeini as a benign, senile cleric, and now he held the United States hostage. No one, Turner concluded, could surprise like a friend. It was almost easier with unfriendly nations; the CIA knew what to expect.

Since the shock of the Iranian revolution, Turner had attempted to increase the network of paid agents in foreign governments and foreign intelligence services, including some allies and friends. Egypt was an example. A CIA security operation in Egypt, designed to provide President Anwar Sadat with protection and with warnings of coup and assassination plots, also provided the CIA with electronic and human access to Egypt's government, its society and its leader. Sadat smoked dope and had anxiety attacks, but Turner never paid any attention to this palace gossip. The CIA, however, was not likely to be surprised by Sadat or by events in Egypt. The place was wired.

From intelligence reports, Turner knew that Crown Prince Fahd of Saudi Arabia did a good deal of drinking, contrary to the strict proscriptions of his Muslim religion. Turner also had top-secret reports on the health of Soviet Premier Leonid Brezhnev that were helpful to the White House, particularly on the eve of negotiating sessions. Intelligence support on arms control was very good; the NSA was able to decode some information from Soviet missile tests. But political intelligence about the goings-on in the Politburo, the highest council of the Soviet Union, was weak to nonexistent. It was what Carter and Brzezinski had wanted most, and Turner had been unable to deliver much.

In his time at the CIA, Turner had never once seen an intelligence report that was worth risking someone's life. Nonetheless, he had pushed for more. It was his job. Only once in four years had he turned down a proposal for a sensitive collection operation overseas to gather intelligence; it was to have been a repeat of an earlier, successful operation, and Turner had thought going in a second time too risky.

Over the next two months, it would be Turner's job to introduce the new President to these realities and to much more. Reagan would have to see the entire floor plan of intelligence operations, how they fit together, what their limitations were.

For instance, in an operation called Cervical Rub, a code name selected at random, a sophisticated electronic device disguised and constructed to look like a tree limb, complete with bark covering, was to be "planted" in a tree outside a Soviet air base in Eastern Europe to collect data on advanced Soviet MiG radars. The base was next to a park frequented by picnickers, and an agent had only to go over a fence some Sunday, climb a tree and screw the device into place. But Cervical Rub had been delayed because the only available CIA operative was a non-European, and it was considered too risky to send him among the Sunday picnickers, where he would stand out.

The point was that operations were chancy. A great many things had to fall into place. Intelligence on Soviet radar might be more important than certain Politburo information. But the CIA could not keep tabs on the whole world.

Turner's Oldsmobile approached Lafayette Park, across from the White House, and turned down one-way Jackson Place. It stopped before No. 716, a government-owned brick town house where Reagan was staying. Turner stepped out and charged up the six steps.

Reagan's temporary residence was a nondescript twenty-two-foot-wide four-story 113-year-old building. Six years earlier, Vice-President Nelson A. Rockefeller had used the high-security town house as headquarters for a commission he headed that was investigating the CIA's questionable domestic activities. Reagan had been one of the eight members, though he had not been very active, attending only ten of the commission's twenty-six meetings. When its final report was issued, Reagan had defended the CIA, saying, "In any bureaucracy of about sixteen thousand people there are going to be individuals who make mistakes and do things they shouldn't do."

Soon after Turner entered, Reagan came down and greeted him warmly. The President-elect showed no anxiety, no impatience, only a natural kindliness. His retinue included George Bush, the Vice-President-elect, who had been the DCI Turner had succeeded. Reagan's top aide, Edwin Meese III, an amiable lawyer, stood to the side. Three other aides were present. And Bill Casey.

Turner briefed them on the European military balance and Central

America. He gave an update on Poland, where the Soviets were threatening an invasion to crush the independent Solidarity trade union. Overhead satellite reconnaissance photographs and electronic communications intercepts picked up from places like Berlin—the intelligence collection capital of the world—provided a good account.

There was also human intelligence, Turner added suggestively.

Casey cocked his head.

Turner was tempted to disclose, but he did not, that the CIA had a deep-penetration spy, a colonel on the Polish General Staff, who provided a steady flow of intelligence out of Warsaw on the intentions of the Poles and the Soviets. The colonel's sensitive reports were circulated on a BIGOT list only to the most senior U.S. officials who had an absolute need to know. The reports were hand-carried to each official in a folder with a distinguishing blue border or a wide blue stripe denoting a sensitive human source. Carter, Vice-President Walter F. Mondale and Brzezinski were the only ones from the White House with regular BIGOT-list or "blue-stripe" access. The colonel's name, Kuklinski, was never included in these reports, and only a few CIA officers knew it.

As Turner guided the tour of the world's hot spots, he glanced periodically at Casey. There was something about Casey that was not zestful. He slurred his words, and his speech was like a shortwave broadcast, fading in and out. The few strands of wiry white hair on the edges of his bald head each embarked on its own stubborn course, further contributing to the appearance of the absent-minded professor. His ears were overlarge, even flappy. Deep facial wrinkles shot down from each end of his flat nose, passing his mouth on either side to fall beyond his chin and lose themselves in prominent jowls. He seemed in disarray. Even so, Turner sensed that Casey was listening attentively.

Afterward, Casey walked over. He looked vaguely hunchbacked as he extended a personal welcome with exaggerated but, Turner felt, genuine bonhomie, his elbow high in the air, his large mitt flying to catch Turner's.

"Hello, Stan," Casey said loudly, with a big smile. He drew Turner aside.

"The story about me taking over," Casey said, mushing his words. "It's not true. Nothing has been decided yet." It was hardly an absolute knockdown of the story. Perhaps detecting Turner's concern, Casey added, "I'm not bucking for your job."

Turner left deeply uncertain about his future and the CIA's. There were signs that he was out, but not for sure.

Later that day Meese passed a message through the Carter White

House to Turner. Meese was generally viewed as the voice of authority on key senior appointments for the incoming administration and already was considered a kind of deputy President-elect. Meese wanted it known that he had not put out the Casey story that day. But he also left the impression that Casey's appointment was not out of the question.

1

ALTHOUGH CASEY WASN'T bucking for DCI, he thought Turner probably didn't believe him. In fact Casey wanted Secretary of State or Defense. State and Defense counted. They would, by all reasonable anticipation, be the instruments for a new Reagan foreign and military policy. But Casey understood that he might have to settle for less, or for nothing. He was not one of the President-elect's California intimates, and clearly the Californians were going to dominate. He had come late to the Reagan campaign, and his final role as campaign manager, exalted at least in theory, was partly accidental. He had not been a longtime, committed Reaganaut.

Earlier the previous year, 1979, Casey had received a call out of the blue from candidate Reagan, soliciting help. Casey was a dedicated lifelong Republican who practiced a rich man's law from his office at 200 Park Avenue in New York. He had made millions from a string of highly speculative investments, from good luck and intuition with the stock market, and from his authorship or editorship of some two dozen tax, investment and legal books. Money gave him the time to play in his favorite game of politics. Having served as campaign worker, organizer, speech writer and Republican convention-goer dating back to 1940, he had had several senior federal posts in the Nixon and Ford administrations, the most prominent being chairman of the Securities and Exchange Commission in 1973–74.

"It's too early to join your campaign," Casey told Reagan during that phone solicitation. He explained that his reluctance to sign up now should not be taken as a lack of sympathy. On the contrary.

He grabbed his checkbook and hastily filled in $1,000 to the Reagan candidacy, as he had done for all the other Republican hopefuls. It was the maximum allowable individual contribution. He scrawled his name at the bottom of the check, the *W* in "William" a slashing parody of the grammar-school penmanship he had learned at Public Schools 13 and 89 six decades earlier in the lower-middle-class Queens community of Elmhurst in New York. The *y* at the end of "Casey" was a strong textbook *y* with a nearly straight, long downstroke and a beautiful, exquisitely curled loop, as if he had created a signature that was self-confident but not self-important.

There had been nine "Tardy" marks and a letter-grade C in conduct on his report card in the second half of sixth grade at P.S. 89, his only grammar-school grade lower than a B. His academic work had been graded A. His classmates called him "Volcano." Since that year, 1924, his life had been a steady march to the other, better side of the tracks. He learned to play golf by caddying, and now he belonged to a good club. In 1934–35, he attended the Catholic University School of Social Work, where most students were priests, nuns and others with strong religious convictions. At the bottom of his scholastic record someone scrawled, "Very good." But Casey concluded that social work was for women, and left for law school. This very year he had given away the equivalent of a social worker's annual salary in charitable contributions, $21,970, through a foundation he had set up in 1958. He was a common man of uncommon wealth. He hoped he was a heavyweight, a man of means, a man of affairs who had learned the art of advancement on two tracks: first through personal wealth and business; second through experience in government, boards, commissions and political involvement. All this had been earned, he realized, at the partial expense of his reputation. Many saw him as an unsavory businessman, a corner-cutter who had made quick money through a string of opportunistic investments and countless business aggressions, a magnet for controversy. He was known as a man who astutely played the stock market he had once regulated. At times he appeared indifferent to criticism, accustomed to lawsuits, but underneath Casey craved acceptance and respect. With all his devotions, his church, his Republicanism, his stock portfolio, he could appear flexible about ideas, but not about people. His friends received his total loyalty. But Casey showed a hundred different faces to a hundred different worlds.

Reagan had called Casey again. He wanted more than the $1,000. He was coming east for a fund-raiser on Long Island, Casey's home. Could they meet? Casey agreed. The two had breakfast at a motel near Casey's home, a large Victorian-era estate named Mayknoll.

The two men schmoozed easily over the Republican election prospects for an hour and a half. Casey had heard that Reagan was shallow, but found him knowledgeable enough about economics and national-security issues. Reagan didn't delve deeply, but his instincts on these matters seemed sound, and they conformed with Casey's convictions about a free market, strong defense and active anti-Communism. Reagan was only two years older, and the two men shared a generational view. Both had been poor as children. Casey was attracted to the variety in Reagan's life—as sportscaster, actor, labor union officer, governor, and conservative spokesman with stamina. It mirrored somewhat the variety in Casey's own—lawyer, author, OSS spymaster, amateur historian (he was presently writing a book on the OSS) and former government official. They had both seen the Depression and four wars. They both found genuine satisfaction in a well-told story and a good, hearty laugh. More important, though, both had contempt for Jimmy Carter and what they thought was his weakness, his indecisiveness and his unhealthy, hand-wringing anxiety.

Soon Casey was invited to California to be on the executive committee of the Reagan campaign task force on issues. It was a bone, he knew, but it was involvement. He flew out, looked at the issue books and met Meese and the Reagans' closest friend, a small, pleasant man named Michael Deaver.

"I want you to come into town and have lunch with Ron and Nancy Reagan," Casey was soon saying to his rich Republican friends, inviting them to a fund-raiser. If they hesitated, he added, "Listen, you don't want to be out of it, do you? This fellow's going to win. This fellow's going to be President." Casey knew how to squeeze out the New York Republican money. Working the phone persistently, he was instrumental in collecting $500,000 for the Reagan campaign in late 1979. When Reagan's campaign manager, John P. Sears, was fired, in early 1980, the candidate asked Casey to take over.

It was something Casey had worked for all his life. Politics was his first love.

Back at the 1952 Republican convention, Casey, then only thirty-nine, had watched with disappointment as the conservative Senator Robert A. Taft was beaten out by Dwight D. Eisenhower for the Republican presidential nomination. Shortly after, Casey shared his view of this with twenty-six-year-old William F. Buckley, Jr., already launched on his highwire act as the conservative boy wonder with his book *God and Man at Yale*. Casey and Buckley were members of the anti-Communist, antiliberal fraternity in New York City. It was a very small club, maybe fifty members. There was practically a secret handshake, Buckley used to joke. Casey told Buckley, "If I had managed that campaign, Taft would've won the nomination," and Buckley remembered the remark for years. So in 1980, when Reagan called his friend Buckley to tell him,

"I've fired John Sears and I've hired Bill Casey," Buckley was delighted. As far as Buckley was concerned, Casey was a true believer with only one minor, forgivable deviation. In 1966, two years after Barry Goldwater's disastrous run for the presidency, Casey had launched his first and, thank God, only campaign for public office. He had sought the Republican congressional nomination from his district on the North Shore of Long Island with the backing of the Nelson Rockefeller–Jacob K. Javits wing of the party. Steven B. Derounian, a Goldwaterite, won the Republican nomination, and Casey returned to behind the scenes, where Buckley and many New York Republicans thought he belonged.

As the new Reagan campaign manager, Casey had to assess the power centers around Reagan. The looks, the voices, the glances, the subtle deference told one story: Nancy. Actor James Stewart had once remarked, "If Ronald Reagan had married Nancy the first time, she could've got him an Academy Award." Casey could see that Nancy Reagan was the premier student in identifying her husband's interests.

But Casey was not always comfortable with the hard right-wingers in the campaign. "There're some crazies around us and I'm a member of the Council on Foreign Relations," he told a campaign associate. He didn't add that he had initially been rejected for membership and was furious that only when he became undersecretary of state in 1973 had he been invited to join. Casey had been tempted to throw the invitation in the toilet and tell them to go to hell, but had calmly accepted. It was a useful if pretentious credential.

Certain campaign members and some reporters described Casey as "spacey." He abandoned laundry all over Washington and Los Angeles. Sometimes he traveled without a suitcase and just bought clean clothes when he needed them. On one occasion Deaver sat next to him at a meeting and, from his body odor, concluded that Casey had not had time to shop. The next day Casey was scrubbed clean, apparently having been made aware of his oversight. But Deaver realized that when Casey was on a mission he let nothing get in his way. He worked nights, weekends. It was a single-mindedness that had to be admired.

One month before the election, anticipating a Reagan victory, Casey created a little-noticed interim foreign-policy advisory board, selecting a group of seventeen senior experts, including former President Ford and other Republican and Democratic high-profilers. He chaired the group, assigning papers and studies. Some thought he was placing himself center stage as a potential Secretary of State. When he had served briefly as undersecretary of state for economic affairs in 1973–74, he had been forced out by the then Secretary, Henry A. Kissinger. Casey had left little impact and had merited a single perfunctory reference in Kissinger's 2,690-page two-volume memoir, but he placed Kissinger on Reagan's advisory board.

The group identified an immediate and important challenge to the incoming Administration. It was the Communist insurgency in a tiny Central American country. Casey decided that El Salvador was, symbolically, the most important place in the world. If the United States could not handle a threat in its backyard, Reagan's credibility would be at risk in the rest of the world. Casey was dumbfounded to learn that the CIA had closed its station in El Salvador in 1973 to save money and had reopened it only in 1978. That left a five-year gap. How could that be? What was going on at the CIA? Intelligence was supposed to be a first line of defense. It would have no role in defense or offense if there was no effort to get information.

The day after Turner's November 20 briefing, Reagan flew back to California. While he was waiting to take office, the soul of the Reagan Administration was up for grabs. No one recognized this more than his conservative friends in California and elsewhere. They had arranged for Reagan to receive an important visitor from abroad. He was Colonel Alexandre de Marenches, the head of the French equivalent of the CIA, the Service of External Documentation and Counterespionage, the SDECE. Marenches was a well-known figure in European conservative circles. A large, mustached patrician with an American wife, he had headed the SDECE for ten years. The SDECE, nicknamed the "Swimming Pool" because its headquarters buildings are located near the Tourelles swimming pool on the outskirts of Paris, had played heavily in French internal politics. Marenches had in his office a map of the world that showed the spread of Communism in red. Small versions of the map were handed out to official visitors. Several years earlier he had given one of his maps to Admiral Turner during an official liaison meeting between the two intelligence chiefs.

On his California trip, Marenches had more than a colored map to offer. For the French official, spying was a most serious business, one to be undertaken at great risk, with expectations of great return. He held in low esteem the CIA habit of hiding its agents abroad undercover as diplomats in American embassies; the CIA station chief and the senior officers—often all CIA officers—were quickly identifiable, making a mockery of their espionage. It was more effective, if more difficult, to operate undercover as an airplane salesman or someone simply out in society. Real spying involved total immersion; it was strenuous exercise. European intelligence services at times used journalists as cover for spying, but the Americans shunned this. Free speech was valued over national security. Spies posing as diplomats were, in Marenches' eyes, pretenders.

Marenches talked to the President-elect about shared conservative principles—the menace of Communism, the danger of weakness in military and intelligence matters. But he spoke in general themes.

"Aren't you going to give me advice?" Reagan asked. "Everyone has advice for me."

"I can only tell you about people," Marenches replied. (He spoke perfect English; he believed that languages were a must for an intelligence officer.) He could only tell the President-elect about "people you should see and people you shouldn't see."

"Who should I see?"

Marenches mentioned Alexander Solzhenitsyn, the Soviet author. He understood the nature of the Soviet evil. Also Reagan should see Jonas Savimbi, the resistance leader in Angola who was fighting the Communist regime in that key southwest-African nation. The United States had given covert CIA support to Savimbi, but it had been cut off when Congress in 1976 passed the so-called Clark Amendment banning covert action in Angola.

"When you want to learn about hell, you should talk to people who have been there," the French chief declared.

"Who shouldn't I see?" Reagan said.

"Many," Marenches said. "But I will give you one who stands for them all—Armand Hammer." Hammer was the chairman of Occidental Petroleum and longtime friend of many Soviet leaders. He was the symbol of détente.

"Funny," Reagan said, "I see him often. Every time I go the barbershop, he's there."

"See what I mean?" Marenches said.

Hammer had recently made a standing request: Every time Reagan scheduled a haircut at Drucker's in Beverly Hills, Hammer wanted an appointment in the next chair.*

Marenches had an additional thought. "Don't trust the CIA. These are not serious people." The French intelligence chief did not mean that the

* Harry Drucker confirmed that both men were regular customers but denied that Hammer ever arranged to be seated next to Reagan.

CIA had a mole or lax security or that it leaked to newspapers. He was referring to its lack of purposefulness.

Reagan repeated Marenches' warning—"Don't trust the CIA"—to George Bush, who had been CIA chief in 1976–77. Bush thought it was hogwash, but all the same it obviously left a deep impression on Reagan. Bush had already told one of his CIA friends that, given Reagan's detached management style and his unfamiliarity with intelligence matters, it was important that the President have a CIA director he felt close to, someone he trusted fully, particularly on the issue of purposefulness. Now, after the Marenches warning, that was even more important.

Casey watched with some dismay as the Reagan Cabinet selection went forward. There was a list of three names for each Cabinet post, and he was on for State and Defense, but there was no overall coordinator. Instead, as in the campaign, there were pockets of authority, none of them absolute. There were Meese and the California Kitchen Cabinet, there were the individual ambitions of the hopefuls, and there was Reagan himself, now back at his Palisades home in California. Things got screwed up terribly and quickly. Reagan had decided finally that George P. Shultz, the former Nixon and Ford Cabinet member (Labor Secretary, Office of Management and Budget director, Treasury Secretary) was his first choice for State. Apparently thinking the groundwork had been laid, Reagan had called Shultz. The trouble was, Shultz had been told that he was on the Treasury list.

"I'm interested in having you join my Cabinet," the President-elect told Shultz with unintentional ambiguity.

Shultz, assuming that it was Treasury, turned it down.

Deaver, who was in the room when Reagan made the call, didn't learn until months later what had happened. Shultz would have accepted State.

Reagan's second choice, Alexander M. Haig, Jr., emerged as the front-runner for State, and Nancy Reagan favored him. She thought Haig had star quality—he was handsome, forceful, had military bearing, was charming and warm. A leading man. It became clear that the gap in Reagan's foreign-policy background could not be bridged by Casey's foreign-policy advisory board and Haig had it all. He was a four-star general who had commanded NATO forces in Europe, he had White House experience as Kissinger's deputy and as Nixon's chief of staff.

"I won't get State," Casey told a friend. "We all supported Haig. We need the prestige."

And Caspar W. Weinberger, an old Reagan California friend, landed Defense.

Casey, miffed, went home to New York to catch up on the rest of his life, but it was not nearly as exciting as what was going on in Washington and California, where the rest of the Cabinet was being selected. He kept in touch with Meese. Casey let it be known that he wanted to serve in the Cabinet, but there were not many positions left. DCI, the natural slot, was not Cabinet. Meese, aware of Casey's wounded feelings, told him that DCI could easily be made Cabinet rank. There was more discussion.

Meese told Deaver, "Bill Casey wants to be head of the CIA."

"I think that's a mistake," Deaver replied. "I don't think we can give that kind of a job to a political hack."

Meese made it clear that the deal was about to be cut. Casey was a good man, he knew intelligence, and he deserved a senior post if he wanted it. Deaver said no more. Meese went to Reagan and proposed Casey for CIA, and that the DCI be made a Cabinet post.

"It's fine with me," Reagan said. That was the extent of his involvement, other than to call Casey with the offer.

Casey's response was cool. He told the President-elect that he wanted to think it over and consult his wife, Sophia.

Fine, Reagan said patiently, but he later expressed his surprise. What had happened? He had thought it was all set. Did Casey want CIA or not?

In a small, spare fourth-floor office on K Street in the middle of downtown Washington, a lean, well-preserved man who had a kind of enduring dignity and polish watched the Reagan victory with great though detached interest. He was squinting, which meant he was thinking. He was a hard thinker. He wore a neatly pressed dark suit, the mandatory handkerchief, dark socks held up by old-fashioned garters, well but not conspicuously polished shoes. His gray hair was slicked back with some thick tonic from a previous era, but not in such great quantities as to prevent a few strands from curling up above his collar.

The sign on the door said "Safeer Company." It was an international consulting firm. Safeer was the Farsi word for "ambassador." He had been U.S. ambassador to Iran from 1973 to 1976. To someone unfamiliar with his manner, the man might have seemed nervous. But to acquaintances this edginess was recognized as attentiveness. He was all ears and all eyes as he made calls, took long lunches with old friends, weighed new arguments, read the newspapers carefully, including the odd items —one paragraph on a new Defense Minister in Greece, a vote in the

Norwegian Parliament, the Japanese trade surplus. He was an intelligence officer, if not now by position, by temperament—an obsessive sifter of information.

Richard Helms, one of the enduring symbols, controversies and legends of the CIA, turned his analytic power on the succession. Helms's ties, affections, convictions and past were all agency. He had been OSS in World War II; he had joined the CIA in 1947 when it was formed; he had taken over the Operations Directorate after the Bay of Pigs (at that time the Operations job was called DDP—deputy director for plans); and he had been DCI from 1966 to 1973 during Vietnam—not the beginning or the end, but the tormenting middle years. Helms's era also had included the beginnings of Watergate, though he had been shuffled off as ambassador to Iran by Nixon before the end.

Now, in 1980, the CIA was certainly about to turn another corner, to be jostled, redeemed or demeaned once again by a new President. Helms's candidate was Bill Casey. Casey could protect the traditions. Helms had known him for thirty-five years, going back to the days when they had both served in the OSS in London. When he arrived there in 1945, Helms was assigned to work for Casey and didn't have a place to live. "Hell, come stay with us," Casey said. He invited Helms to share an apartment on Grosvenor Street. Indeed, "Hell, come stay with us" summed up for Helms the Casey approach: quick, direct solutions; warm, friendly, accommodating, no formality, profane, convention-defying. Helms had rarely seen Casey in the last year of the war, because they were both so busy. He thought that Casey's OSS background gave him a fundamental understanding of intelligence work. They had been trained by the British, and CIA traditions were British traditions. The secret service and the silent service. As Helms often said, "We are the silent service, and silence begins here." Casey understood the shock and betrayal that Helms and his followers had felt by the disclosures during recent investigations of the CIA—the Church and Pike committees in Congress, and the Rockefeller Commission. Helms thought there was no necessity for such testimony as had been demanded, all those papers going up to the Congress. There was a time when no one from the CIA would have thought of writing a book. In the last decade there had been a number. It was almost inconceivable to him.

At the CIA, one was prepared to take the risks associated with intelligence work. But no one had imagined that the peril would come from one's own government, that one's own government would turn on him. Helms said he had worn his ass nearly raw sitting on the flights coming back from Iran for the inquisitions, including the one that had finally engulfed him. He had, three years before, pleaded no contest to a misdemeanor charge in criminal case 77-650, *United States of America* v. *Richard M. Helms,* for not testifying "fully and completely" to a Senate committee about CIA covert operations in Chile during the Nixon presidency. The sentence was a $2,000 fine and a suspended two-year jail term, delivered with a lecture from the judge, who had accused Helms of "dishonor" in open court. Helms's lawyer, Edward Bennett Williams, had told the press that his client would "wear this conviction like a badge of honor, like a banner." And Helms had tried. There were thoughtful people who considered the charges unjust. Helms had attempted to save a secret, to keep a covert operation ordered by the President from unnecessary ears. The criterion in disseminating information about sensitive intelligence had always been whether those brought into the circle of secrets truly had to know in order to do their job. Need to know had to be absolute. Presidents and DCIs frequently didn't need the nitty-gritty details, the names of sources, the exact technology. It had been simple common sense to dodge the questions about Chile.

The memory of his no-contest plea still stung. It was a stain in spite of the widespread support he had received. (Afterward he had been given a standing ovation by four hundred retired intelligence officers at the Kenwood Country Club in Bethesda, Maryland, where two wastebaskets were stuffed with cash and checks to pay the $2,000 fine.) There was something not tidy about the outcome. There was a conflict between the pledge to keep secrets and the meddling and pursuit of secrets by the Congress. What were the new rules? Did the new rules jeopardize important secrets?

Casey was a street-smart, tough New Yorker, and New York, in Helms's view, was a mean, lonesome town. You survived or went down. And Casey had outlasted most. Casey was no prissy boy; you couldn't be a priss and survive as DCI. Helms had learned from the Kennedys at the Bay of Pigs. The Kennedys wanted results. They wanted Castro out—dead, though they never said it in as many words. If Helms, who was running covert operations then, had said it couldn't be done, he would have been out.

The tradecraft of spying had changed since World War II. There would be a lot for Casey to learn. Reconnaissance satellites meant, as Helms once put it, "We are going to spy, not by looking up your asshole, but we are going to spy by looking down on your head."

Helms knew enough to say nothing, not indirectly, not behind the scenes, not a word for his old roommate. He might kill Casey's chances, certainly not help them. He did what he had done best for so many years. He remained silent.

Senator Barry M. Goldwater, the crusty conscience of the Republican Party, had almost whooped with delight at the Reagan victory. Goldwater felt a special bond with Reagan. Reagan's political career had been launched in 1964 when he delivered a stirring nationally televised government-bashing half-hour speech supporting Goldwater's presidential candidacy. The 1980 presidential election was as sweet a vindication as a man gets, Goldwater thought. It was as if a younger brother were moving into the White House. And with the Reagan landslide the Republicans had finally gained control of the Senate, making Goldwater's political world even sweeter.

Vice-chairman of the Senate Select Committee on Intelligence during the Carter-Turner years, Goldwater, at seventy-one, was now moving up to be chairman of the committee, a powerful new instrument born of the investigations of the 1970s. As a member of the Church Committee that had investigated the CIA in 1975–76, he had flatly refused to sign its final reports because of what he considered their unbearably self-righteous, moralizing tone. The CIA, he felt, had had much too much shit kicked its way.

This was a moment in history to do the absolute right thing—no compromises. Goldwater, a tanned, well-groomed man of commanding presence, was reinvigorated. Despite some problems with his hips, there was a new energy as he moved around, a new iron in his voice.

And he had a solution: find a man for DCI who was totally trustworthy, and let him keep the secrets and get Congress out of the agency's goddamn hair.

One of Goldwater's first steps as the new Intelligence Committee chairman was to bring his best friend, Lieutenant General William W. Quinn, U.S. Army retired, onto the staff of the committee as an unpaid consultant. West Point class of 1933, World War II intelligence officer and the first deputy director of the Defense Intelligence Agency, Quinn was a jovial, laid-back but determined man. He was both family and a drinking buddy to Goldwater, whose wife hated Washington and wasn't around much. Goldwater had cocktails and dinner with Quinn and his wife, Bette, about twice a week and regularly spent the weekend at their farm on the Maryland Eastern Shore.

Quinn had filled an important but unsung role in U.S. intelligence. After the war, Lieutenant Colonel Quinn had been in charge of the Strategic Services Unit (SSU), whose job it was to wind down OSS operations. Goldwater admired the way he had marched up to Congress in 1946, requested a closed committee session for five minutes on his meager budget, and finagled an additional $8 million in unvouchered funds to pay his secret sources. Aware that legislators love to hear secrets, Quinn had shared with the committee some information about his sources. One was a maid at the Russian headquarters in Berlin who lifted vital intelligence from wastebaskets; a second was an embassy code clerk who allowed the U.S. to read all the messages of another major country; a third, in yet another embassy, had been paid ten thousand dollars for the Soviet Baltic fleet's war plan. The closed session had lasted twenty minutes, and Quinn had used the $8 million to preserve a nucleus of agents and sources for the CIA, which was formed the next year, in 1947.

Though a report that Casey would be the new DCI had been in the newspapers, Goldwater disagreed with the choice. He had his own candidate. "Bobby," he told Quinn. "It's got to be Bobby."

Bobby was Admiral Bobby Ray Inman, who had headed the National Security Agency for the preceding four years under Carter. The NSA was the largest and most secretive of the intelligence agencies and had a budget several times the size of the CIA's. The sprawling headquarters at Fort George Meade in the Maryland suburbs ran listening posts worldwide on land and from orbiting satellites. It broke the codes of both enemies and friends, and was on the frontier of new technology. NSA had no human spies and had escaped relatively unexamined during the investigations into the CIA.

Goldwater thought that Inman was an intelligence genius, a man who understood science, politics and human nature. He was also a skilled congressional hand-holder.

In twenty-eight years of naval service, Inman had risen through the officer ranks to three-star admiral, the only intelligence specialist to serve as executive assistant and senior aide to the Vice-Chief of Naval Operations (1972–73)—a post normally reserved for officers who have held ship commands. He had gone on to be the director of Naval Intelligence (1974–76) and the No. 2 at the Pentagon's Defense Intelligence Agency (1976–77) before heading the NSA. Inman knew the intelligence business cold. He was the best source on everything from the latest spy satellite to the bureaucratic maneuvering required to get intelligence programs going. He had a fabulous memory.

With his boyish, toothy smile, large head, thick glasses, Inman looked like a grown-up whiz kid. He was one of the few intelligence officials who would talk to reporters and get them to hold off on stories that compromised intelligence. He had nurtured all the important relationships in the Congress. Goldwater could not recall an instance in which Inman had failed to return a phone call or to track down an answer on the rare occasion when he didn't know it.

Goldwater worried over Inman with Quinn. He wanted to make sure he got Inman the job. "I have an input on this," he said. "The security of the country should be above politics. Bobby is in the saddle. He's apolitical. He's a dedicated sailor, an absolute natural for the job."

Quinn loved Goldwater and he felt free to tell him when he was off base, but he agreed about Inman. "I'm going to see the head man on this," Goldwater told him.

It was easy for Goldwater to slip in to see the President-elect and explain his unqualified enthusiasm for Inman. The most capable man in the field, he said, a man in a category by himself. Reagan listened but seemed unconvinced. Goldwater banged the drum very hard, making it clear that the new Administration would have a lock on the Hill for intelligence matters if Inman were DCI.

Reagan replied that he preferred an outsider, and it was going to be Bill Casey.

Perhaps, Goldwater suggested, this was the one appointment he was owed.

Jovially, avoiding confrontation, Reagan dismissed the issue. "You are going to get Casey."

Goldwater went back to his friend Quinn.

"Barry," Quinn said, "don't underestimate Bill Casey. He was not born yesterday."

Goldwater had had so many political disappointments. This was minor, but he couldn't see the reasoning and was irked.

Quinn told him that Casey had always been an advocate for intelligence, keeping lines of communication open, calling often, following the Defense Intelligence Agency during its formative years in the early 1960s. Back in 1964, he had been instrumental in seeing that Quinn received the William J. Donovan Award, named after the founder of OSS and the father of American intelligence.

Goldwater wasn't any happier.

Quinn said that Casey appreciated the art of intelligence, the power of facts and information, what's expected of intelligence officers, the dedication and application. Casey was fascinated by intrigue, Quinn said. "He loves mystery. He loves the cloak, and he loves a little of the dagger."

Goldwater told Quinn, "They're fucking it up."

• • •

Inman watched the early transition wars from the other side of the world. He was in New Zealand at one of the NSA's listening posts. He relished the possibility of becoming Reagan's DCI and was keenly aware that he had a powerful patron in Goldwater. Cool and mild on the outside, Inman was within a very passionate man, restless and ambitious.

Every day but Sunday, Inman rose at 4 A.M. In those early-morning hours, uninterrupted, he did his careful thinking and reading. The essence of good intelligence work was anticipation. There was no way to figure everything, but you had to be there and ready, even in New Zealand.

The NSA stood as an island. Though basically a military institution and part of the Defense Department, it had responsibilities to the DCI, whose job included the coordination of intelligence budgets, priorities and targets. Because the NSA was something of a stepchild, Inman felt he had to be its link to the rest of the world, so he worked the White House, the Congress, the Pentagon and the news media like a lobbyist. He had access and he gave access.

Inman had kept DCI Turner out of the NSA's hair through his alliances with powerful figures in the Carter Administration. He made sure that national-security adviser Brzezinski received the raw communications intercepts he coveted so much, but at the same time he felt strongly that the NSA should remain within the Defense Department in order to keep its focus on military information—the key to early warning, the key to preventing war.

In New Zealand, Inman took a call from J. William Middendorf II, who was heading the CIA transition team for Reagan. Middendorf had been the Secretary of the Navy when Inman was the Navy's intelligence chief.

It looked as though Casey was going to become DCI, Middendorf said. It had not been announced, and there seemed to be some uncertainty in Middendorf's voice. But he was calling to inquire whether Inman was interested in the No. 2 spot at the CIA—the job of DDCI, the Director's deputy and alter ego in the intelligence community.

Inman said he had no interest. He was set to retire from the military next summer, and, as an intelligence specialist, by tradition he normally could not rise higher than three stars.

This was an easy no for him. Deputy was not enough. He saw the Reagan Administration as a necessary counterweight to the Carter years. Carter had perhaps too many illusions about the Soviets, but Reagan had too few. Neither had the sense of balance Inman preferred.

Several days later, when Inman was back in Washington, Middendorf renewed the invitation. Politely, Inman pushed it away again. He would soon be fifty, and at that age he still had a chance to start a new career, perhaps make some money in business.

Helms was hearing all the talk about Inman and he wanted to see for himself. He did not really know Inman, having left the CIA in 1973, the year before Inman became head of Naval Intelligence. Helms asked Jack Maury, a former CIA Soviet specialist, to arrange a lunch. Maury, a beloved, tweedy, cheerful old boy from an established Virginia family, had served twenty-eight years with the CIA, the last six as Helms's liaison with Congress just before the investigations.

Inman felt that he was being courted for membership in an elite club. These were the covert operators with whom he felt ill at ease. There was a running feud between the CIA and the NSA—human operations versus machines, daring actions against systematic method, James Bond as opposed to the cipher clerk in wire-framed glasses. But they were going out of their way, almost soliciting his views.

As they lunched, it was clear that Inman and Helms shared an overriding conviction about the purpose of the intelligence agencies. Mistakes had been made—including some on Helms's watch—because of a failure to warn the President or the Congress that some trouble was brewing. Early warning, preventing surprises, was everything, they agreed. ("It's everything and underline everything," Helms once said in his elegant voice, jiggling a thin finger with determination.) It was a fact that the President and the Congress would go the distance with the CIA or the NSA if they had prior warning, even if there was a screw-up.

Helms left convinced that Inman was bright and sensible and would make a good addition to the Reagan intelligence team.

Inman saw more signs of trouble. Richard Allen was going to get national-security adviser, the old Brzezinski and Kissinger post. Allen was a deeply suspicious right-winger, who had privately charged that the NSA and Inman were intercepting his telephone conversations during the transition and reporting them to the Carter White House. It was a false and outrageous charge, Inman knew. He had made sure that the NSA didn't collect intelligence in the United States, and that when it did pick up an overseas communication by a U.S. citizen the rules were strictly obeyed. Those rules meant that the intercept would not be used or circulated unless there was reason to believe the communication involved espionage or a crime. Inman felt he could only deflect Allen's charge. He didn't want a fight with the new national-security adviser. But Allen's paranoia startled Inman. Allen was close to some members of the CIA transition team who were pushing some hysterical nonsense that the regulations resulting from the Church Committee investigation, which were in force during the Carter Administration, made it impossible to track down spies and for the intelligence agencies to gather information.

Vice-President-elect George Bush had passed a worried warning to Inman that Reagan was falling under the spell of the extremists. Most alarming was the well-poisoning visit that the French intelligence chief had made to the President-elect telling him that the CIA could not be trusted.

Inman felt caught in the crossfire. Defense Secretary–designate Caspar Weinberger asked him to come by and offered him a fourth star to head Pentagon intelligence, as a kind of overall chief of the NSA and the DIA. Inman suspected that it would be a nothing job, just another layer between the top and the real power. Soon this offer became a request that he retire from the Navy and take a post as assistant secretary of defense for Pentagon intelligence—the same job in different wrapping. Inman said no again.

Casey was still contemplating Reagan's offer of DCI. He moved about the streets of New York, once again appreciating real city life. The fall air was bracing, but reentry was less than satisfying. Casey normally did not fret over decisions, but he was going to take a couple of days on this one. In 1975, when he resigned as head of the Export-Import Bank, a post which admitted him to the central bankers' club, he had not expected or planned to come back to Washington to live and work. His years of government service, 1971 to 1975, had been the scandal years.

He felt that his mere presence in the Nixon Administration had sucked him into the whirlpool of investigations. Because of a dispute over the handling of some International Telephone and Telegraph Company files during the 1972 election year, when he headed the SEC, he had been subject to a perjury investigation. "The main focus in the perjury investigation was William Casey," said a confidential memo from the Watergate Special Prosecutor's Office that was never made public. Casey had arranged to ship to the Justice Department thirty-four boxes of ITT documents and thirteen "politically sensitive" interoffice memos and letters, out of the hands of a congressional subpoena. The deputy attorney general had sworn that it was Casey's idea. Casey had denied this and testified that Justice had requested the files. The prosecutor's memo added, "Casey's entire statement here is deceptive, both as to his dealings with Justice and Dean"—a reference to then Nixon White House counsel

John W. Dean. Casey was never charged. He was a small fish. While the memo repeatedly described his testimony as "evasive," it concluded that conviction of Casey "simply had such a low chance of success that it could not be brought." Casey thought it was stupid, but it had made him wary.

There had been other brushes with investigations. Nixon Attorney General Mitchell and chief Nixon campaign fund-raiser Maurice H. Stans were indicted—and later acquitted—for accepting a $200,000 campaign contribution from international swindler Robert Vesco, who was trying to influence one of Casey's SEC cases. Casey wasn't bothered by any of this, he assured friends. He had been a prosecution witness, waving to defendant Mitchell as he took the stand. He was clean. But those Watergate times had not been the happiest. Casey and Sophia had returned to New York, and one of Casey's favorite two-liners became "You know the best thing about Washington? It's only an hour to New York."

Two years later, they sold their house at 2501 Massachusetts Avenue, the Embassy Row of Washington, to the People's Republic of Bangladesh for $550,000. Sophia, his wife of forty years, a small, white-haired loyal and intense fixture of support at his side, would never forgive him for selling that house if they went back to Washington.

Their New York life now centered around their family compound, Mayknoll, the Victorian waterfront landmark on the North Shore of Long Island. He coveted time there, especially the weekends, among his books or at The Creek golf course a quick drive away. Casey was a double-bogey golfer shooting about two strokes over par on each hole; it was a fabulous day if he broke 100 for eighteen holes. But he loved the walk over the course, the outdoors. He had many old friends, and the Caseys' only child, Bernadette, who was now in her mid thirties, was very close to her parents. Three years earlier they had bought a $350,000 home on Ocean Boulevard in West Palm Beach, Florida, for the winter months. He was not discontent with his life.

In the couple of years before he joined the Reagan campaign, Casey had started another book, his best, he believed. Tentatively entitled "The Clandestine War Against Hitler," the six-hundred-page manuscript recounted the OSS spying in World War II and had two main characters. The first was Casey. The second was Casey's mentor and surrogate father, General William "Wild Bill" Donovan. Casey drew a loving portrait of the OSS founder, a roly-poly man with soft blue eyes and an unrelenting curiosity and drive. Donovan had been twice the age of the thirty-year-old Lieutenant (junior grade) Casey when they met in Washington in 1943, but he had closed the multiple gaps of generation, military rank, education and social background. Donovan wanted to know what someone could do. Results counted. "The perfect is the enemy of the good," Donovan said often. Casey would have walked through fire for him. Donovan always visited the scene of the action, showing up at nearly every Allied invasion as if it were opening night on Broadway.

Donovan had bestowed great responsibility on Casey during the last six months of the war. Casey had written a memo saying, "OSS must be ready to step up the placing of agents within Germany." Donovan wanted an instant spy network behind German lines, and he named Casey "Chief of Secret Intelligence for the European Theatre." As best Casey could remember, Donovan's command was no more than "Get some guys into Germany." What was lacking in detail was made up in authority. Casey, by then a thirty-one-year-old full lieutenant, commanded colonels and dealt with British and American generals more or less as equals. Ordered out of uniform, he was sent to Selfridge's on Oxford Street in London to buy a gray suit that would blur, if not conceal, the distinctions in rank.

Casey had thrown himself into every detail of spy-running. Selecting credible spies was difficult. Americans just wouldn't cut it at Gestapo headquarters in downtown Berlin. Some forty anti-Nazi POWs were chosen—a violation of the Geneva Convention. Casey didn't blink. Necessity.

Creating cover was an art. An attic archive in London provided newspaper clippings about what was going on inside Germany so that the spies would know the latest news. Documents were forged and clothes with German labels obtained. Casey begged for the planes for agent drops. Without a secure communications system the spies would not be able to get their information out, so a low-power transmitter, called a "Joan Eleanor," which could broadcast to a circling plane was developed and put into service. Casey checked drop times, maps and even moon tables. He established a Division of Intelligence Procurement to determine what exact information was wanted from the spies. The answers weren't obvious and it required balancing the needs of the senior Allied commanders (who would have loved to have Hitler's General Staff's morning meeting minutes) with what was obtainable. The first priority was German troop movements in and out of major railroad centers, the most visible clue to Hitler's plans and troubles. The second was potential bombing targets. Casey always saw his agents off.

By February 1945 there were two agents inside Berlin. By the next month, Casey had thirty teams. "A chess game against the clock," he had written in his manuscript. By the next month, he had fifty-eight teams inside Germany. One team, code-named Chauffeur, used prostitutes as spies. It was war.

Now as he contemplated the post of DCI, Casey tried to summarize his conclusions about intelligence. He called it "the complex process of mosaic-making." Bits and pieces comprised the intelligence puzzle. Things didn't turn out as you expected. It was possible to infer if you had many pieces, but to infer with a few was a mistake. After the liberation of Germany he had been thunderstruck on a drive from Munich through southern Germany to Pilsen when all he could see were white flags. A sheet here, a towel, a shirt. No one had asked the Germans for this abject display. It mocked the idea that this had been a master race. The Germany he had imagined when he sat in London headquarters creating a spy network didn't exist.

"Intelligence," he wrote in this latest book, "is still a very uncertain, fragile and complex commodity." Besides gathering the information, evaluating its accuracy, seeing how it fit into the rest of the information—the "mosaic"—and determining meaning, he wrote that intelligence included attracting powerful attention and then forcing a decision. The intelligence person was not passive. It would be a giant miscalculation, Casey felt, to limit the role of intelligence or the intelligence-gatherer. Getting, sifting, distributing intelligence was only the start.

"Then you have to get him to act," he wrote.

He could not help but write a few unkind words about the Carter Administration: "Right now as we crusade for human rights in countries which do not threaten us, we conceal from public view the photos we take of slave labor camps in Siberia." There was a moral dimension to intelligence that could not be escaped. There was, too, Casey figured, a moral dimension to life that could not be escaped. He had gone to Dachau a few days after it was liberated in April 1945. And he would never forget the piles of shoes, the bones and the decaying human skin. People had done this to people? It was unthinkable. There was verifiable evil in the world. There were sides, and a person had to choose.

And as he reflected, Casey came to realize that he yearned to go back to intelligence work. The Reagan sweep had to go forward and not bounce back—surge on past the inevitable counterforces. Accepting DCI would give him a chance to plead for an understanding of the world of secrets. Admiral Turner had been an intruder. Casey would go in as a brother. His talk with Sophia lasted only ten minutes. She called it a "love-story" job for him. He told Reagan yes.

2

CASEY MOVED INTO A SUITE at the Jefferson Hotel in downtown Washington several weeks before the formal announcement of his appointment. These would be important weeks to move behind the scenes and quietly do his homework. He had a good general idea of what the CIA did, but he lacked the details which, of course, were everything. His understanding of post–World War II secrets was limited. In 1969, President Nixon had named him to an advisory council for the Arms Control and Disarmament Agency. Casey had, as required, signed a document swearing him to secrecy and granting him access to Sensitive Compartmented Information for a top-secret arms-control-verification satellite reconnaissance program. He knew that the satellites were one of the new wonders, and he wanted to learn as much as possible. Several years earlier, he had served for a year on the President's Foreign Intelligence Advisory Board (PFIAB), a high-powered nonpartisan community of elders to whom the White House owed a favor. PFIAB was told some of the secrets and in return was supposed to audit the performance of U.S. intelligence agencies for the President.

The Jefferson Hotel's owner, Edward Bennett Williams, one of the city's most celebrated criminal lawyers, the man who had defended Helms, stopped by to see him. Casey enjoyed Williams' booming, back-slapping prattle, his playing the rogue Democrat to Casey's rogue Republican. Williams had served on the PFIAB with Casey, and, like everyone else Casey encountered, he had strong opinions about Casey's new task. Williams was a powerful figure in Washington; his clients ranged from the late Teamsters Union president Jimmy Hoffa to *The Washington Post*.

Williams argued vehemently to Casey that U.S. intelligence had been reduced to rubble not just by Carter but earlier by President Ford. Banging the air with a large fist, Williams used the word "dismantled," the very description employed in the 1980 Republican platform. During the

Ford Administration, the Soviets had intercepted phone calls from nearly half a dozen places in the Washington area. U.S. intelligence had read some of the Soviet "take" from these phone calls, including some of what went back to Moscow, but Ford's Justice Department had instituted a rule that inhibited the FBI and the NSA from continuing this practice, in order to protect the privacy of the U.S. citizens. Williams thought it ridiculous—the Soviets could tap calls, but not the U.S. intelligence agencies.

"They were stealing and we couldn't look in our pockets to see what had been taken," Williams said.

Casey nodded.

Intelligence, knowledge of the other side's plans and capabilities, is the most important thing in winning, Williams said. "You have got to know," he said in his head-coach style. "If you don't, you're dead."

As for the CIA, Williams said in classic overstatement, "The CIA is like a great dog that got hit by a truck. You can only say, 'He was a great dog until he got hit by a truck.' " He threw an arm around Casey as if to say, "Go get 'em, boy."

Casey was determined that Williams' great dog was going to be revived.

Casey next phoned up his old OSS roommate, Richard Helms, to say it was official.

Good, thought Helms. Damn good. Perfect. They agreed to lunch on Monday, December 1.

Helms had had several years since Iran to reflect on his tenure in the CIA, particularly as director. He frequently huddled with former colleagues and old memories, and he conducted a continuous seminar on the subject with himself. The year before, Thomas Powers' book called *The Man Who Kept the Secrets: Richard Helms and the CIA* had been well received. Some of the reviewers had said the book told what it was really like to be DCI. Not possible. No one could know. Even when his wife, Cynthia, and three leading conservative columnists, Buckley, William Safire and George Will, each told him it was brilliantly written, Helms could not bring himself to accept that. He was working it out in his own mind, mind-writing a continuously revised and updated memoir to himself, in which he was piercing the shades and screens of his life. There was much to learn—fragments of recollection, snatches of dialogue from White House meetings, and the elusive meanings. He'd never get it all back. Nor was the answer in any file; the records and the paper trails could lie.

Helms calculated that his problem as DCI had sprung from the simple fact that he had had no real, personal relationship with the Presidents he had served. His no-contest plea to the misdemeanor charge was a case in point.

Helms had produced his notes from the September 15, 1970, meeting with Nixon at which the covert action in Chile had been ordered directly by the President. Nixon had been insistent: Marxist candidate Salvador Allende had to be prevented from taking office. How many people had ever seen a President of the United States on fire? It was a sight. There was no choice but to carry out the order. Helms's notes quoted Nixon: "One in 10 chance perhaps, but save Chile! . . . $10 million available, more if necessary. . . . make the economy scream."

Helms knew what was missing from the notes: he had not written down what *he* had said. His recollection was that he had replied, "You are giving me almost an impossible job." It was a doomed covert plan—too little, too late, inadequate preparation.

Helms's good friend Kissinger had told him later that much of what Nixon said was not to be taken literally, let alone seen as an order. Often Nixon was merely expressing his frustration—"Do something, Henry!" Kissinger said Nixon didn't always mean what he said. To Henry, this was a simple truth. He knew it from experience. Unfortunately Helms hadn't known. Nixon was not available in an important, personal way to his Director of Central Intelligence. He distrusted the agency, thought of it as an institution filled with Ivy Leaguers and Eastern-establishment liberals. And not knowing his chief very well or understanding him, Helms had left the Oval Office that day in 1970 with a mission. As he later testified, "If I ever carried the marshal's baton in my knapsack out of the Oval Office, it was that day." It was a choice of words he would regret.

Helms, of course, knew even more. The key to the order was Nixon's relationship to Donald Kendall, chairman and chief executive officer of PepsiCo, which had a Pepsi-Cola bottling plant in Chile. Kendall had given his firm's corporate account to Nixon when Nixon began practicing law in New York. The anti-Allende operation was essentially a business decision; Kendall and other U.S. firms didn't want a Marxist leader in Chile. Helms and the CIA had been misused, and his silence before the Senate committee had been partly out of embarrassment for the CIA, the President and himself. He had failed to prevent the worst covert action since the Bay of Pigs. He had broken his own law: "Covert action is like a damn good drug. It works, but if you take too much of it, it will kill you." Allen Dulles, the DCI in the Eisenhower years, had said, If you want a little CIA, some agency in a remote, dusty corner, get out of covert operations. Presidents always want a hidden way of doing things. That's how the CIA gets its clout with the White House, Dulles said.

Helms was pro-President—all Presidents. Even though trying to argue with Richard Nixon was like "talking into a gale," as he once said, he wanted to comply. And Helms had agreed when Nixon told him, "I don't want the goddamn CIA to make policy anymore." The agency is to serve Presidents who are the makers of foreign and military policy. Those of Helms's generation, including Casey, knew that orders were to be obeyed.

"Maybe we took too many orders from Presidents," Helms once remarked, adding proudly, "but we obeyed them."

And if that meant that intelligence had to take the heat, then so be it. If that meant that intelligence officers had to fry, and many of them did just that, then so be that too. There was no other way to run things. So Helms had taken the heat. It was his turn. And it was only a testimonial parking ticket, wasn't it? Former DCI James R. Schlesinger had seconded Ed Williams' "badge of honor" accolade, calling the plea "a kind of dueling scar."

Casey, as DCI, was going to have some protections, Helms figured. Casey knew "the Company's" history and he knew his President. There was no need to go over it at their lunch. Helms had always hated it when a former DCI looked over his shoulder. He vowed never to do it, even in advance. So as Helms prepared for the lunch with Casey he was determined to avoid anything that resembled a lecture. He did not want to teach Casey how to suck eggs, and certainly he did not want to sound that way. Better to say too little.

But there was one matter Helms felt he could help with, without sounding patronizing. That was the people. His son, Dennis, had interned at the agency for a summer while in college. One evening Dennis had told his father that he was very lucky to have worked at the CIA. Why? Helms had asked. He never forgot the answer: "Because the people there are so civilized." That was it. There was a sense of decency out there; it was the great barrier reef to the toughness, the deception, the impossibility of playing by the Marquess of Queensberry rules on the world stage. Inside the agency, among themselves, they were all Caesar's wife—no lies, straight dealing.

On Monday, December 1, at the lunch hour, Helms appeared at the door of Casey's small suite at the Jefferson. They shook hands warmly. Casey was still basking in the afterglow of the election victory. He was pleased and elated to be riding a tidal wave of history, to be an instrument of the Reagan revolution.

Bill, you're a natural and it's wonderful, Helms said, smiling. His eyes almost closed when he smiled or laughed, as if Helms had discovered some cosmic irony in the joy or fun of the moment.

The waiter took their order.

Helms didn't need to remind Casey that the CIA had had a rough time in the last decade—Watergate, the investigations, Admiral Turner. The result, Helms felt, was that no one was willing to take chances anymore, let alone risk his life. Well, as they knew, great intelligence operations involved both.

Casey agreed heartily. Since the senior appointments in the agency would be key, he asked whether Helms thought Inman would be the right fellow as deputy.

Congress would not be an easy road, Helms said. It was not the same as before the investigations. Some collaboration had to be worked out. Helms said that he had met Inman just once several weeks before. He had seemed sound and might provide a good fit: a ready-made relationship with Goldwater, a background with the NSA, the technical side that Casey couldn't know that well. Inman also knew military intelligence, which was important; the Pentagon always, eternally, had its hand in every intelligence pie in town. It would be rational to pick Inman.

Casey said he wasn't sure; he would have to think about it.

Helms felt he couldn't say more. It would not be plausible for him to push a man he had met just once for such a key post. He sensed Casey's resistance.

"Look," Helms continued, "why don't you get some people who can help you, that you can consult with?" The various factions would be warring for Casey's attention. Too easy to misstep, get the wrong advice. Casey could use a good guide. The way Casey came to understand the past would, in large measure, determine his course.

Casey seemed agreeable.

Someone with a historical perspective, Helms said.

Yes, exactly.

And Helms had just the man. One good guy, someone Casey knew during the war, someone sound, someone who would not leak on Casey. John Bross.

Casey's face lit up. The perfect man. Casey had known Bross in his OSS days. In his just-completed manuscript on the clandestine war against Hitler he had described Bross as a gentle, urbane man who was a parachutist and an expert in sabotage and hand-to-hand combat.

Helms suggested Bross because he had been with the agency for twenty years, had been a division chief in the Directorate of Operations, the comptroller, had handled the intelligence community, was low-key, didn't flap and was a lawyer. As important, Bross was a man neither of the right nor of the left. Helms had calculated carefully. The danger, the threat to the CIA, came from both the right and the left. Maybe the left had had its way in the 1970s and the investigations, causing their trouble. But the right could do its own mischief. Helms had another concern, one he didn't voice because he didn't want to lecture and he hadn't been asked a specific question. But in 1966, when he was appointed DCI from the ranks, Lyndon Johnson had told Helms to go out there to Langley and break some crockery, shake things up, kick some ass. Helms had found that unnecessary. Too much faith was placed in reorganization schemes. In 1966 reorganization was bullshit, and Helms suspected that it would be bullshit in 1980. Bross would see that. Bross would also have the time; he was independently wealthy and lived on the Potomac River several miles from the agency.

Casey jotted Bross's name on a napkin and said he would contact him at once.

They had not really touched on sensitive matters, but the lunch was over.

Helms felt that Casey was a jumble of contradictions. He had detected an absence of excitement on Casey's part. For reasons Helms could not clearly identify, he had the impression that Casey really wanted to be Secretary of State.

Later Casey moved out of the Jefferson Hotel at the urging of CIA security. The Soviet Embassy was half a block down Sixteenth Street, and they had the technology to aim electronic sensors in parabolic antennas and eavesdrop on Casey's conversations.

Williams thought the alarm laughable. There was no way, he joked in front of Casey, that the Soviets would have any more luck deciphering his mumbles than anyone else.

In his old rambling house on the Potomac, John Bross received Casey's call. Casey confirmed that he was going to be Reagan's DCI and invited Bross to join the CIA transition team and assist during the months ahead. Bross was sixty-nine, and this was perhaps his final call to serve his agency; he accepted at once. The assignment might be among his most important: a new administration always had new ideas, and some could be dangerous.

Bross had a jovial manner and he was a charter member of the old boys' intelligence-oversight club, a powerful alumni association that kept its hands unofficially in agency business, seeing to its well-being whenever possible. He also dabbled within the foreign-policy establishment of ex-officials. Bross was often included in the boards, the commissions, the private lunches.

In Bross's view, Casey was a solid choice. He had known him since 1943, and the two had kept in touch. In the 1960s, Bross had had a couple of foreign-policy heavyweights to dinner with Casey. One, a classic Soviet-basher, had taken Bross aside and said of Casey, "That man really understood what I was saying." The next day the other guest, a moderate, had told Bross he'd been pleased that Casey had understood his arguments. Casey was not a fanatic. Bross could capitalize on that, though he knew that he would be talking across a divide. Harvard '33, Harvard Law '36, Bross was Eastern establishment and Casey was fighting Irishman, but the connection was Donovan, their dear old leader. Bross could see that Casey was modeling himself after Donovan. And among Donovan's traits were loyalty and intense personal relations. Bross decided to make himself completely available to Casey. And he knew that Casey would open up. It was Donovan's way: establish and nurture.

Bross dropped around to assess the transition team. He found its leader, Middendorf, useless. The three Republican aides from the Senate Intelligence Committee, including an extremely conservative fire-thrower named Angelo Codevilla, had been assigned to the team and were writing attack documents. Their plan called for the CIA to be divided into three parts. The first would be an elite, hardball covert-operations division that would launch secret wars to thwart the Soviets, would increase the number of spies dramatically and would get the agents out of the embassies and into nonofficial cover—businesses and consulting firms. The second would be a crack analysis division that would pit groups and agencies against one another to insure tough-mindedness. The third, supported by Middendorf, would be a new superagency combining FBI and CIA counterintelligence functions. This last, Bross felt, would be particularly disastrous, dragging the CIA into domestic intelligence.

The right-wing aides on the transition team had been in opposition too long and were not used to getting their way, Bross concluded. They overstated their case; they created plans that would destroy the CIA's integrity. Bross was also aware that he was not welcome, that he came across as the old veteran steeped in the 1950s view that the Cold War was a perpetual engagement. The transition team was plotting a way to win it, with no sense of the risk of going too far. There was no balance. Lots of missionary work with Casey would be required to ensure that the new DCI was not captured by the right wing.

Casey next contacted William E. Colby, who had been DCI during the most turbulent thirty months at the CIA, 1973 to 1975. The final days of Watergate, the end of Nixon, a full year of investigations. Colby was a pariah in many intelligence circles, where he was thought to be the only politically liberal DCI. He had presided over a hemorrhage of CIA documents and secrets to the Congress. He may have had little choice, but he was perceived to have betrayed the code of silence, omertà, and to have committed the cardinal sin of turning in a colleague. Faced with official investigations and what he considered near-hysterical public and media pressures, Colby had forwarded information to the Justice Department that had triggered the Helms perjury investigation. To the old boys, this was unnecessary. It was as if a Pope had betrayed his predecessor.

Casey had never met Colby during the war, but they knew each other through the OSS veterans' organization, and there were no casual acquaintances among the OSS vets. They had been in it together. Colby had parachuted behind enemy lines after D-Day as a member of one of the Jedburgh Teams, whose job it was to stir French resistance behind German lines. (Jedburgh was a town in Scotland famous for its border wars, and Jedburgh justice meant "Hang them first, try them afterward.")

Casey told Colby that he was "going to take the job" and wanted to chat. Colby agreed to come over to the Reagan transition offices on M Street. He planned to be blunt. He had been out of the CIA for five years, ever since he was fired by President Ford for being the captain on the bridge when the CIA collided with the "investigations" and secrets were spilled. Colby was a courteous man who returned phone calls, opened doors, moved around smiling with deference to all. A small, lean man with plain, military-issue spectacles, Colby in no way looked CIA, let alone a director. Give him a smock, a comb and a pair of scissors and he would fit into a Norman Rockwell painting of a small-town barber. He was smart (Phi Beta Kappa, Princeton class of '40 and a Columbia Law degree in 1947), and when he removed his glasses his appearance changed. There was a toughness, a hard edge to the eyes, imperturbable, almost cold. There was a Jedburgh Justice side to this man.

To a question about CIA secrets from someone without the proper security clearance or the need to know, Colby's face would grow small and seem to disappear, running for cover behind his glasses and into his eye sockets. His palms would turn out and his shoulders fly toward his ears. He didn't remember. He couldn't say. He didn't care. It was the great universal disavowal, and to those who knew him it meant: go no further, No Trespassing. To an artful question, his dodge was even better. When body and facial language might provide a clue, Colby would slip into silence. Feelings were the natural enemy of the CIA operative. In his autobiography, *Honorable Men,* published in 1978, he included himself among the CIA's "gray men," those who drew little or no attention to themselves but who could perform their assigned tasks with precision and spine.

In dealing with all the investigations of the intelligence agencies, Colby had taken special care to protect the National Security Agency by sharply narrowing inquiry into its work. The NSA broke more codes and intercepted more communications than anyone on the outside could imagine. It had become the heart of "the product," as Colby called the work of the intelligence agencies. If there was any sleight-of-hand in the way he had opened things up, that was it. Protection of the NSA was the unwritten chapter in the investigations, and Colby was happy to keep it that way. The NSA played by tight rules, but the degree of its intrusion into the world's privacy was not fully comprehended. Colby thought that Casey probably had the best chance of succeeding at CIA; he had better credentials than "any of us," meaning the real insiders. Casey was a good mix: historian (Colby had read his little-known book on the American Revolutionary War battles, *Where and How the War Was Fought*), a lawyer (Colby had a desk manual for lawyers that Casey had authored), a man with an apparently broad acquaintance with foreign affairs, and a risk-taker in business. In his endless hours and years of self-examination since leaving the CIA, Colby had come to feel that perhaps he had not taken enough risks. Casey would. And Casey would have that crucial political and personal connection with the President that meant access.

At the Reagan transition office, in a shabby and beat-up room, Colby greeted Casey exuberantly. The torch was passed in their handshake.

"You're a natural for it," Colby said. "Your relationship with the President is a big plus." His tone was wistful. "It's a great job."

Casey seemed to want to listen. What were Colby's mistakes? His assessment? His advice?

"Look," Colby began, "you organize the bloody place any way you want. It's there to serve you." The whole job was advising the President. "You'll be at the NSC meetings in the White House and you're all by yourself. You've got to know what's happening—you've got to come up with instant estimates on the spot.'' Good advice in a crisis was the ball game. Analysis in a pinch was ''everything.''

Casey seemed a little taken aback, but he concentrated his entire attention on Colby.

''You are the President's intelligence officer,'' Colby said. That is the job. Do that well and the rest should be easy. All the bureaucratic stuff can be handled by others. Intelligence should not sit still at the White House when policy options come up for discussion. The DCI is not a main player in determining policy, but it is important to speak up if there is a clear, desirable course.

''You need an analytic center that asks the right questions,'' Colby said. And that directorate is presently organized all wrong, by disciplines —politics, economics, the military, nuclear strategic questions, like a university.

''I'm not going to tell you how to run your railroad,'' he said, but if he were back as DCI he would reorganize the analysis division by geography. Then there would be experts who could weigh and analyze the whole situation in a country or a region. He once had had a meeting with sixteen CIA experts in the room, each with his special area or discipline, and he was the only one who was looking at the entire picture. That made no sense at all. Those brainy people weren't encouraged to let their good minds roam beyond their narrow corridors.

The quality of advice to the President hinges on having good analysis, Colby said. Many of the elements necessary to it are public and in the press. Coupled with intelligence, a lot can be deduced. Those deductions have to be the best, requiring the best minds and as many as possible. The system is not set up to do that well. If intelligence did its job, ironically it would be proven wrong. Good intelligence and accurate projections would trigger steps by policy-makers that would avert problems and catastrophes. They say you can't predict the future, but it is the CIA's job to do it every day.

''The staff is really pretty good,'' Colby said. ''Very high talent. They are loyal and will serve you. But don't get confused, you can override the staff.''

Colby said there was fragmentation among the directorates—analysis, operations and technical. The heads of those directorates ran their own shows. He had moved against it, but not enough.

Particularly in the Directorate of Operations. He had come from there, had run it for a while. It's a closed culture, very inward, Colby said. Group loyalty runs very high. But the strength of the CIA comes from the stations abroad run by the DO. Young people abroad, often in their thirties, become chiefs of station and have to handle all the management, security, secret operations, occasional diplomacy, and the risks. They are in charge, not like State Department Foreign Service officers, who oversee only their secretaries and whose every move is dictated by a State Department cable.

Covert action is necessary and can be helpful, Colby said. A propaganda operation or covert political support to a struggling centrist leader often makes sense. A covert plan in basic conformity with publicly stated Administration policy can work. If it leaks, it will not come as any great surprise and criticism will be minimal. But there must be a natural political base of support in the country where the covert operation is carried out—a true resistance or political opposition. The CIA cannot create one.

He wasn't a great advocate of covert action. It had been a dirty word during his time as DCI. In the 1950s, covert action had taken up 50 percent of the CIA budget. When he left, it was down to about 4 percent. Casey and Colby shared the same impression that the outgoing Carter Administration had become more activist with covert operations in the last year or two.

Colby turned to the Congress, which he had come to know only too well; in his last year it had occupied half his time. The new intelligence committees were all right. The arrangement was workable. It was now important that Congress, through those committees, understand what intelligence work was all about. That could be done only by sharing the secrets. It was possible to calibrate the process to minimize the risk and still get the understanding.

One subject remained, the most important—the Soviet Union, the "hard" intelligence target. Colby remarked that the Soviets couldn't keep their country and their society closed up as tight as in the past. Though there was, regrettably, no Moscow counterpart to *Aviation Week,* the U.S. magazine that regularly published vital technical and military secrets, opportunities were opening up in Russia.

"Don't forget," he said, "though you've got magnificent technology, work to get real penetrations there. It's tough." Get to the sacred circle of Soviet leadership. No one has been able to, but you might do it. Speaking to a man he knew to be famous for taking financial and business risks, Colby baited Casey, "It's worth taking a few losses."

Casey seemed to know what that meant.

Any penetration of the Soviet Union by the CIA could turn out to be a double agent, Colby stated. "If you get a bad one on occasion," he advised, "you'd get five good ones in the meantime—you get burned once in a while but continue.'' Such intelligence was vital and could make the difference. Casey was the man and this was the time.

Casey nodded, sitting still, his eyes intent and fixed on Colby as if the two were in a therapy session.

''Don't worry about the midseventies anymore,'' Colby said. He felt he had got the past out of the way, perhaps atoned for it for all of them, exorcised it. ''Go to work,'' he said.

Casey replied that he might need to call on Colby at some time in the future. Casey was friendly, charming. There was no distance. Only, he had said very little.

Colby left with a strong, even intense feeling of goodwill. Casey was a good shrink.

Casey figured he owed Stan Turner a phone call.

''Stan,'' Casey said, ''the rumors about me taking over that were not true a couple of weeks ago are now true. It's come to pass—I'll be the new DCI.''

Fine, Turner said. He offered no congratulation. One of Turner's deputies was in the office and he wanted to keep Casey's news secret, hoping to tell his people himself, on his own schedule.

Casey was a little put off by the chilly reply, but the two agreed to meet soon. Turner was a strange man, Casey felt. It would be best to bypass him as much as possible during the transition.

On December 9, Casey arrived at Turner's office at the Old Executive Office Building, fourth deck. He took short, unsure steps as if his feet were sore or someone had put a handful of gravel in each shoe. But he was in great, high spirits.

''Ronald Reagan may want to be President at age sixty-nine,'' Casey opened, ''but I sure don't want to be Secretary of State at age sixty-seven—have to do all that travel and diplomacy.'' He waved his hand, letting it flutter in the air. This was the unwieldy flap of an old man, suggesting more than the ten years' age difference with Turner.

''Well,'' Turner replied, ''you will find that as DCI you're going to have to meet a lot of people. All the traveling intelligence chiefs that come through town are going to want to talk to you.''

Casey wondered how many that could be.

''In the case of the French,'' Turner said, ''there is no chief of intelligence as such.'' Marenches, as head of the SDECE, is the closest, but there is no DCI equivalent, no overall coordinator. ''So the chief of counterintelligence is going to want to meet you, the French FBI is going to want to meet you, and they are all going to think of themselves as your peer."

Casey had brought no notes, no list of questions, so Turner hoped to direct the agenda. Casey seemed only mildly interested, but now and then a penetrating glance would flash from behind his glasses.

"Do you see any objection to me being put in the Cabinet?" Casey asked flatly. Elevation to the Cabinet had been a condition of his accepting, though he didn't mention this to Turner.

Turner said that even though the DCI was not currently a Cabinet post, Reagan could easily do it. The salary level, however, would be one step below a Cabinet secretary's, about $10,000 less, unless the Congress increased it.

Under no circumstances did Casey want less than Cabinet status, but the $10,000 clearly made no difference.

As they talked, a call came in from national-security adviser Brzezinski. Turner did not wish to air dirty Carter Administration linen in front of Casey, so he excused himself and stepped out to take the call.

Casey found this odd. Clearly there was bad blood between Turner and Brzezinski when there should have been a natural alliance between the Admiral and the hard-line national-security adviser. Casey had been able to piece together from the briefings some of what had been going on.

Turner had been predicting that the Soviets would invade Poland under the guise of a military exercise. He had good satellite photography showing a massing of Soviet forces on the border, and he had some supersecret human source inside Poland. Everyone was on high alert. Brzezinski had launched a public campaign to warn the world and to try to scare off the Soviets. He had sprayed the Soviets with back-channel, secret diplomatic warnings through France and India. But he wanted to put out still more information, and Turner was resisting. Each time Brzezinski released a detail or sounded as if he was certain, some source or some method of intelligence-gathering was at risk. But Brzezinski was insisting that the claims must be made credible and that the President would not allow a passive stance on this. The Soviets had to be deprived of secrecy and surprise. (The banner headline in *The Washington Post* the previous morning had read: "Concern Grows on Soviet Plans in Poland.")

Brzezinski had arranged for the leaders of the Solidarity labor union in Warsaw to get phone calls warning them. Internal resistance was surfacing as union members started shutting down plants, cutting off communications lines, flooding mines.

Casey waited a long time in Turner's office, and both men felt awkward when Turner finally returned. They were not being candid with each other.

You can make yourself an absolute hero at the CIA, Turner said. Get the Reagan transition team out of the building. They are talking about a purge of the civil-service ranks. And this, Turner said, is, as you might expect, very much feared.

Casey was unreceptive. He made it clear that he knew a lot about intelligence—from his OSS background, from his year on the President's Foreign Intelligence Advisory Board.

Turner smiled to himself. He was surprised that Casey had no inclination to get into the philosophy, the things Turner had dwelled on in his memos. Didn't Casey want to know that covert action would be resisted by the operations arm?

Casey had a few questions about the average work day and the mechanics of the job. After an hour and twenty minutes, he stood up to leave. He had been caught short by Turner's demeanor—all steamy, tightly wound anxiety and frustration.

Two days later, Thursday, December 11, Turner went over to give another intelligence briefing to Reagan and Casey. Reagan had moved to Blair House, the presidential guest house, diagonally across Pennsylvania Avenue from the White House. Turner was directed to a large ground-floor room. The Soviet–U.S. strategic balance was on the agenda; this was certainly the major issue of the day; it involved a long, detailed examination of the Soviet war-fighting capacity. Meese asked Turner to drop the whole subject. It was a political hot potato, because Reagan had implied and stated throughout his campaign that the Soviets had nuclear superiority or were on the verge of achieving it. Turner agreed; a replay of the campaign would serve no purpose.

Therefore, the first subject was the Soviet economy. Turner said it was in trouble. The Soviets had a demographic problem and insufficient numbers of new workers; they had not licked inefficiency; annual overall economic growth was expected to decline from around 5 percent to about 2 percent—a stunning slump. Next, as he charged through issues relating to the Soviet Union and China, Turner was still itching to make his pitch on the Soviet–U.S. strategic balance. It was too important to skip, and he was deeply involved in drafting the annual top-secret National Intelligence Estimate (NIE) on Soviet intentions and capabilities, called NIE 11-3-8. Since he had both Reagan and Casey listening, Turner decided without missing a beat to restore the topic to the agenda.

The overriding issue in the strategic balance, he told the President-elect, is not the number of missiles or bombs, or the brute force of the Soviet missiles. It's not how many weapons that matters, it's what they can do. And that means not just counting—not just the numbers, but going the next step and attempting to project what might happen in a nuclear exchange. Generally, if the Soviets launched a first strike, and we retaliated, the remaining forces on both sides would be roughly equivalent. There would be a standoff.

In fact, he said with a studious air, after a Soviet first strike the United States would have enough strategic nuclear weapons to destroy all Soviet cities with populations over 100,000.

This meant that the Soviet advantage was not real. The only weakness in this judgment was whether the analysts had underestimated how much the Soviets could destroy in a first strike. But Turner felt they had it about right. That was the message: worry about the vulnerability of our strategic nuclear forces, not the numbers.

This was heresy to Reagan, who had campaigned on the charge that the United States was dangerously behind, that more military spending and new weapons systems were essential. Reagan, Meese and Allen sat mute.

And Casey kept quiet, too. Arms control that might cut the number of nuclear weapons in half was bullshit. What difference would it make, he thought. There would still be enough to destroy the world.

Turner brought up civil defense, a Reagan hobbyhorse. Reagan had suggested during the campaign that the Soviets were sheltering their population and preparing for nuclear war.

"Yes," Reagan now said as Turner broached the subject, "we need more of that."

"No, sir," Turner said, "I disagree." The CIA had just concluded that less than 10 percent of the Soviet urban population could be sheltered. And alleged Soviet plans to evacuate were untested. Imagine trying to get eight million people out of Moscow during a Russian winter.

After the briefing, Reagan got up to leave and headed toward the stairs. Turner followed him.

"Could I have a private word with you, sir?"

"Yes," Reagan said, smiling, pausing on the stairs. He was always willing to listen. The others, including Casey, seemed to fade away, abiding naturally by his wish.

"Sir," Turner began, standing on the stairs, "there are some things that are so sensitive that we are doing." He stopped for emphasis, catching Reagan's eye. This was it. Every person, certainly any President-elect, had to imagine that these things existed. The bottom of the secrets barrel.

Reagan was looking at him intently, as if he had half anticipated this, half feared it.

"President Carter restricted these in the White House to two or three people," Turner said to underline the seriousness. "For instance, Hamilton Jordan did not know these things." Jordan had been Carter's top political strategist and his White House chief of staff. "Sir, I have not touched on them yet. I would like to give you and Vice-President Bush —just among the three of us—a briefing on the eight most sensitive things that we are doing."

Sure, Reagan said.

Turner said that these were not necessarily the most important, but were the most sensitive and would be the most harmed by a leak or a compromise. "Then," Turner continued, "you will be able to decide who in the White House staff, in your staff, you want to have access to this material."

Reagan agreed, and Turner walked away.

Casey came up to him. "My appointment is going to be announced."

"When?"

"In three hours."

Three hours?

Casey said he'd forgotten to pass the word along.

Turner raced out to his Oldsmobile and back to the agency. He was furious that they had given him only several hours' notice—an unthinkable slight. He felt it was important that his staff get the news from him. Once at headquarters, he called together the fourteen top deputies and assistants who were normally at the thrice-weekly 9 A.M. meeting. They gathered in the small, cramped conference room across from his office. Turner was not fond of that conference room. So many bad memories, bad times, the countless occasions when the staff had presented him with difficult decisions on important matters, or requests to do something. And rarely was there anyone present who knew enough about the subject, who had the in-depth knowledge to answer his questions.

Turner walked over to the conference room and made the announcement. He was somber and sad.

That afternoon, Casey came onto the ballroom stage at the Mayflower Hotel in downtown Washington and stood with seven other Reagan Cabinet-level appointees before a blue curtain. James Brady, the affable spokesman of the Reagan transition team, made the announcements for the President-elect.

That evening, Katharine Graham, chairman of the Washington Post Company, gave a dinner in Reagan's honor at her home in Georgetown. Bill and Sophia Casey were among the seventy guests. Casey was seated with Mary Graham, wife of *Post* publisher Donald Graham, on one side, and Nancy Kissinger, wife of the former Secretary of State, on the other. He was exuberant, a little tipsy, and talked a lot about the campaign.

3

CASEY WENT TO SEE NSA Director Bobby Inman. The NSA was the inner circle of secrets—the communications intercepts and breaking of codes. It was apparent to Casey from his briefings that it frequently delivered the goods. And after four years of erecting walls and protecting his turf from Turner, Casey was aware that Inman had his back up a bit.

Look, Casey said at the beginning of their meeting, I know that you were approached about becoming the deputy and that you turned it down. "I regret that."

Inman relaxed. He said that the weeks after the election had been particularly uncomfortable for him personally and professionally, because Goldwater and others were pushing him for DCI.

Casey grunted.

Inman praised the NSA. The agency had forty thousand people spread all around the world at listening posts and at Fort Meade headquarters in Maryland. A key part was the Directorate of Operations and within it the Soviet group of one thousand, mostly civilians, at Fort Meade. Most of them spoke or read some Russian. Intercepted communications provided some of the best intelligence on the Soviets. It was less than anyone wished, but, taking it as a whole, the NSA should be able to tell whether the Soviets were planning a major military move. Another group managed communications intercepts from Asia, and a third group all "other" countries. The list of "other" target countries was growing. Every Secretary of State and every national-security adviser wants more, insists on knowing what the other guy is doing, Inman said.

Inman's central concern was the need for massive investment. Areas of the world were uncovered. The NSA was confronting new, sophisticated coding methods being used by the Soviets and others. And there were more signals out there. They had to focus on *timeliness,* he said. Getting, sorting, decoding if possible and routing the intelligence to the users. Listening equipment mounted on orbiting satellites could relay intercepted communications instantly, but again the question was the amount of time it took to process it. It was too long.

Casey was in agreement.

Inman said that in a crisis the intelligence might be sitting on some tape, or in some computer, or awaiting translation. For example, of the various room or office eavesdropping devices placed around the world, there was, at that time, no case where the NSA had real-time listening—a person in place with earphones at all times, ready to pass on an urgent intercept. There were not enough people, and it would be a mind-numbing task to maintain such a watch. Information had to be culled from the massive influx of intercepts by computers programmed to pick out key words or names.

Casey asked lots of questions. Despite his thrown-together appearance, Inman found Casey to be alert, not sleepy. His questions had no CIA turf angle or CIA spin on them, as Inman had come to expect from Turner.

Casey left the meeting concerned that Inman thought there could be another intelligence failure similar to that at Pearl Harbor when the decoded Japanese messages had not made it to the proper people.

On December 18 Casey went over to F Street, where Turner had his offices to supervise the intelligence community. Turner had indicated that he had some really important subjects to discuss, and though Casey thought Turner seemed still to be fighting his own, lost battles, he figured he had better hear him out.

Turner said he wanted to talk about code words. The system of compartmentalizing the most sensitive information with individual code words was a mess, he said. It was the primary means of controlling classified information. There were dozens of code words both for operations and for capabilities. The NSA, the Navy and even the Operations Directorate of the CIA ran their own code-words systems. On one satellite system of great importance, Turner explained, about fifty thousand people had the code-word clearance. He had added it up himself: everyone on the manufacturing floor, from the ten contractors involved in building the system; all the communications people; even the President's personal secretary. The fifty thousand did not include all the alumni who once had had the code-word clearance and had moved on.

Turner explained with excitement that he had a way of reducing compartmented information to five code words for all information above top secret. He had a name, "Apex." The five code words would be PHOTINT, all overhead satellite and spy-plane photography; COMINT, all communications intercepts; HUMINT, all human sources; TECHINT, all technical matters; and ROYAL, a new code word for special techniques or operations that were particularly sensitive—which could be limited to fewer than a hundred of the most senior people.

Casey nodded politely. He wondered how this would cut back access to sensitive information. Would someone who dealt with human sources in one country be granted access to all human sources in all countries? He didn't ask. Turner was fired up, presenting Apex as if he had discovered the Ten Commandments.

Turner said that the NSA was resisting, it was fighting him because Apex would give the DCI control of communications intercepts.

Casey saw a man who made life hard for himself. Turner radiated defeat and seemed unsettled, advertising the fact that he had never gotten a handle on things and that after four years he was still slugging it out with the NSA. It seemed to be about labels and turf. Casey just didn't give much of a shit about labels, but didn't want to say so. Those weren't intelligence issues. If anything, Casey figured he would need more compartments and code words, since that was the main instrument for keeping secrets. Turner's performance was almost embarrassing. Casey's laugh was soft.

The Admiral rolled on. Economic intelligence: he wanted to make it public. He had two deputies at the intelligence community with its staff of more than two hundred. Two deputies were a good idea—one for the budget, one to set priorities (collection and tasking) he said.

Casey had had enough. Okay, who do you think should be my deputy? He had a list of three names. Fred Ikle, a think-tank and arms control specialist.

Don't know him, Turner said.

Hank Knoche?

Not capable of doing the job, Turner replied. Knoche, who had been Turner's deputy for a short time, had once told the agency people that Turner was well-meaning and that they would bring him around to their way of thinking.

Inman?

A capable man, Turner said. "There are two distinct disadvantages. One: Inman has steadfastly resisted a strong DCI, and if you're going to be a strong DCI that will be a problem. Two: given the NSA–CIA rivalry, the CIA will be suspicious of him."

Casey thanked Turner and left.

Turner revised his opinion of Casey; he was a good listener.

• • •

Casey was still unsure about the deputy slot. Turner's arguments had focused on Inman as the resistant director of the NSA. If Inman came to the CIA, those supposed disadvantages could easily become advantages. A star player for the rival club could become a champ for your club, especially if he were traded under circumstances he found favorable. Casey decided to spend some time with Turner's deputy, Frank C. Carlucci III, a no-nonsense veteran bureaucratic hand. Carlucci was a state-of-the-art survivor: Foreign Service officer; Deputy Secretary of Health, Education and Welfare; deputy director of the Office of Management and Budget; ambassador to Portugal.

Who should be deputy? Casey inquired, knowing that Carlucci was out of the running since he was going to Defense to be Cap Weinberger's deputy.

There's only one person, Carlucci said: Bobby Inman. If you don't pick him, Cap Weinberger and I are going to reorganize all defense-related intelligence—DIA, NSA and the service intelligence agencies—around him, and put him in charge. The implication was that Casey as DCI would want Inman in his control as deputy, not outside in the Defense Department.

Just before Christmas, Casey went out to Langley to see Turner again.

Turner handed Casey a copy of the CIA's report on its mistreatment of Soviet KGB defector Yuri Nosenko in the 1960s. As far as Turner was concerned this was one of the great CIA crimes. Nosenko had been suspected by some agency paranoids of being a double agent sent to provide the CIA with information that would prove that the KGB had no connection with John F. Kennedy's assassin, Lee Harvey Oswald. Nosenko had been kept in an eight-by-eight-foot cell for 1,277 days, more than three years, as part of some smarmy chess game played inside by agency counterintelligence experts over which Soviet defector was a plant. It's important that you read the report, Turner said, important that you understand what can happen, what can go wrong. Turner wasn't sure it couldn't happen again.

Casey accepted the report, but thought it weird that Turner would dwell on events nearly two decades old.

Turner had something else for Casey, he said, producing a notebook. It listed the top twenty or twenty-five jobs in the CIA, who held each job then, how long they had been in it, and his recommendations—the number-one, -two and -three candidates to take over the particular job. Especially the DO.

Casey took this too, though he saw that Turner didn't understand that he had just hurt seventy-five careers; the blessing of the Ancien Régime was certainly a mixed endorsement.

Turner said he was taking his last trip abroad as DCI, to China to close a top-secret deal for two Soviet-missile-monitoring stations to replace those lost in Iran. He would be traveling under an alias, wearing a CIA-supplied disguise that included a mustache.

Casey continued his meetings with the CIA transition team. Papers were flying. Despite his proclivity for new ideas and for risk-taking, he had learned from previous government jobs that the new man in charge had to move slowly, that he had to count to ten before acting. That had been drummed into his head by one of his closest friends, his longtime law partner Leonard W. Hall, who had been the Republican National Committee chairman during the Eisenhower years and had managed Ike's post–heart attack reelection campaign in 1956. Hall had died the previous year, but for fifteen years Casey and he had had a regular Saturday lunch at the same Italian restaurant, Caminari's in Locust Valley, Long Island. The amiable Hall had taught Casey to reach out and connect to people—the workers and secretaries, everyone if possible. But the real lesson had been "Prudence," Casey would say.

Casey could be his own Wild Bill Donovan. But with Hall gone, who would counsel prudence? Casey latched onto John Bross, and Bross was arguing that the transition team's suggestions stank. Nonofficial cover for covert operators abroad would reduce them to a bunch of traveling airplane-parts salesmen. They would have no credibility with foreign officials. Spying and operations had to be conducted from a position of strength. The prestige of the United States government had to be on the line, and that would happen only if the spies had diplomatic standing. Without an undercover role in the embassies, how would a person have secure communications to Washington? How would classified files be stored? In a room in the downtown Hilton? Bross argued that the crazies on the transition team were trying to sell Casey a bill of goods from some spy novel, some romantic notion of a golden espionage past. Well, it never existed and probably never will. Dr. No from some James Bond novel is not our opposition. It's not a matter of destroying Dr. No's headquarters. The Russians are all over the place and will remain so. It's a more subtle, permanent game.

Casey pushed back. He saw the merit of Bross's arguments, but his gut told him to shake things up.

''Ah, come on, Bill,'' Bross said, ''surely a solution can be found that won't be so disruptive.''

Casey heard ''Prudence.''

The final transition report was finished on December 22. On Christmas Day Casey told Bross that the transition team had folded. It had become a debating society. ''They're trying to get me in trouble out there,'' he said. The time had come to draw up his own agenda.

Bross was relieved. Some of the bad witches were dead. For the moment.

After the New Year, Casey and Bross met for lunch in the members' grill at the Metropolitan Club, the most exclusive downtown Washington club.

My top priority, Casey said, is going to be the analytical estimates, the written assessments of the future. Not only do they need improving, but everything, all the intelligence feeds to the estimates. They will help identify weaknesses about our sources and weaknesses in people. The estimates are also the link to the White House and the President, the policy-making.

Bross agreed.

I was once paid six hundred thousand dollars a year to write tax summaries and manuals, Casey said (exaggerating his annual income). Taking lots of complicated information and boiling and distilling it to the essential is what I do well, he said.

Ah, Bross thought. He was struck that Casey felt the need to brag, but he thought the estimates were the right first priority.

Casey said the focus on the estimates would allow him to establish relations personally with each of the intelligence chiefs at State, the military, the NSA, the FBI, elsewhere. ''Stan had a feud with each,'' he added derisively.

His second priority was going to be a new presidential executive order that would loosen the restrictions on intelligence-gathering. Third, he wanted more money and manpower for intelligence. The immediate problem, he said, is people. What were Bross's views on the key jobs?

Inman, Bross said, should be deputy. ''Bill, you'll need someone who has real stature and access, someone who will hold his own in debates with the Defense Department. He'll have that cold. The State Department—he'll have standing there as a respected moderate military man. He has Goldwater in his hip pocket, and reigns as favorite son on the Hill.''

Casey nodded. But clearly he still was hesitating.

Why not? Bross asked.

For one reason, he doesn't want the job.

Bobby is a military man and will do what he is told, Bross said. Maybe a fourth star would sweeten it.

Casey mumbled. The conversation turned to other jobs. How about an executive assistant for me? he asked.

Perhaps the most important choice you'll make, Bross said. You'll need someone who knows the way things work, who knows the National Security Council, the staff, the precise power centers, the paper flow, someone who knows Defense and State intimately.

Casey asked Bross to find the right fellow. Keep your eye out, he said. I've been going through stacks of personnel files, looking for candidates for all the jobs. This was really important, Casey stressed. No mumble, but his arm was thwacking the air in the sedate members' grill.

Bross was now getting the impression that Casey was afflicted with the disease Bross called "I'll-freshen-this-place-up-by-bringing-in-my-people." This was pure Donovan. He had promoted some funny people, characters who were not mainline. In a big organization with eccentric functions, Bross knew, some eccentric personalities were likely to surface, oddballs who would get the job done. Most of the lock-pickers did not come from the best boarding schools.

We need some people with broad business experience, Casey said, we need to bring in some outsiders.

Sure, Bross said.

"One of the things I want to do is get a job for Who-gul," Casey said, destroying the name of Max Hugel.

"Who-gul?" Bross asked. "Who's that?"

"Who-gul," Casey said.

Bross still didn't catch the name.

Casey was determined to find a place in the CIA for Hugel, a most successful businessman who had worked closely with him on the Reagan campaign. Hugel had recruited a cadre of workers from minorities and special-voter-interest groups.

"There are lots of jobs," Bross said finally.

They agreed that Bross would move into a desk outside Casey's office after the inaugural. There he could watch the world go by and help locate the ideal executive assistant for Casey.

Casey went back to Langley and on his new authority had several of Turner's key deputies brief him.

What about covert action? Casey inquired. What had been going on during the Carter years? Was the Directorate of Operations so rusty it creaked? He wanted details.

There were three phases of covert action in the four years, the briefers said. The first and least intrusive form of covert action was propaganda, and it constituted what had become the first phase of limited clandestine activism during the Carter-Turner era. Brzezinski, in particular, had shown great interest in shipping books into Communist countries. The so-called book program involved smuggling thousands of books and other written material behind the Iron Curtain. This, Casey was told, could not change, let alone nudge the course of history, but there had been a feeling that the gospel of democracy should be made available. Turner, they explained, had called the book program a "covert action toy," a "Brzezinski throwaway," a "fly-by-night operation."

Casey was appalled at Turner's cynicism. He made a mental note to make sure he expanded these propaganda programs dramatically. Words, he believed, could make a difference. They were ideas, and ideas mattered.

What else? Casey asked impatiently.

The second phase involved covert undertakings designed primarily to cement relations with friendly nations, particularly the British and the Saudis. These joint operations were supposed to demonstrate Carter's new toughness late in his administration. The main operation was a limited paramilitary support program to undermine the Soviet-supported Marxist state of South Yemen. The operation was under way, and several small teams of Yemenis were being trained to blow up bridges and so forth. Turner had pronounced it "harebrained," and left it to his deputy, Frank Carlucci, to supervise the covert plan.

Why? Casey asked.

Turner had felt the White House was always too anxious to please the British, who were behind the South Yemen operation, and he had worried that the CIA was sharing too much sensitive intelligence with the leaky MI-6, the British foreign-intelligence service. The British had a virtual intelligence stranglehold on the United States, Turner felt, and were receiving too much.

Casey said he liked the British. What else?

Faced with the December 1979 Soviet invasion of Afghanistan, the briefers told him, the Carter Administration had entered into the third phase of its covert program, launching its only serious, large-scale paramilitary support operation. Again it was Brzezinski who had pushed the hardest, believing that the Soviets had overextended themselves. Afghanistan was their Vietnam, and Brzezinski wanted it boldly and ruthlessly exploited. Bleed them, he had said.

Turner's attitude?

The Director, the briefers explained, had wondered long and hard whether it was permissible to use other people's lives for the geopolitical interests of the United States. For the first time, CIA-supplied weapons would be killing regular Soviet Army troops. In Afghanistan the Soviets had about ninety thousand. Turner had worried that U.S. policy was to fight to the last dead Afghan, but he had supported the operation in the end. Saudi Arabia, Egypt, Pakistan and China also were helping the Afghan resistance. The total cost was about $100 million.

Casey's confirmation hearing before the Senate Intelligence Committee was scheduled for Tuesday, January 13, 1981, a week before the Reagan inaugural. He set to work. It would be his fifth confirmation hearing, and he had learned not to use the forum to parade his opinions or dip into a barrel of self-serving recollections, nor to go unarmed and unprepared. Ten years earlier, during the confirmation hearing on his appointment as SEC chairman, he had winged it and almost scuttled his nomination after he had to retract his testimony about a plagiarism suit against him. The 1971 memory was an unpleasant one.*

* Questioned that year by the Senate Banking Committee about an old plagiarism suit against him, Casey, testifying under oath, had waved away the issue, claiming he had not used someone else's material in one of his tax manuals. Without qualification, but with great confidence, he had taken himself to the edge of the cliff, asserting that the judge in the case had felt that a jury verdict against Casey of $40,425 had not been supported by the evidence, and adding that the trial record had been sealed at the judge's initiative.

The trial record and the judge in the plagiarism case were brought in. The confirmation hearing was reopened and Casey was forced to reappear and eat crow. "I would like to clear up testimony . . . ," he said. "My recollection was not the same as that of the trial judge and is not entirely supported by the record." He conceded that two and a half pages of manuscript by the plaintiff in the case had ended up in Casey's tax manual almost verabatim, that the judge thought the verdict against Casey was "amply" supported by the evidence, and that it was Casey himself who had asked that the record be sealed. (The certified court record quoted Casey as saying, "I would like to have the record sealed entirely.")

A pretrial sworn deposition of Casey's was unearthed by the committee considering his nomination as SEC chairman. Casey had told the lawyer for the plaintiff, "God damn, if you're not a gentleman, I will kick your ass out of here. . . . Don't try that again or there will be more violence in this goddamn office." The lawyer said, "I want the record to show that Mr. Casey struck me

So this time Casey prepared carefully. DCI was a major post, sure to have high visibility, and he personally crafted his forty-paragraph opening statement, designing it to avoid trouble. That meant minimizing commitments, pleading ignorance and uncertainty, and assuring the senators that things were not yet decided. It would be easy to say little, since senators love to hear themselves talk, Casey thought.

Casey arrived promptly that morning, wearing an expensive dark, wide-pinstriped banker's suit. Goldwater called the hearing to order at 10 A.M. He asked the committee vice-chairman, Senator Daniel Patrick Moynihan, the New York Democrat who had served in the Nixon Administration, to introduce Casey. Moynihan, an academic by temperament, instinct and speech, rolled out his mellifluous, high-Eastern cadence. For the moment it would be some of Moynihan's be-true-to-your-state, son-of-New-York, local-boy-makes-good parochialism.

"It is the distinguished quality of this man," Moynihan said, "that he has, in one form or another, served every American President since Franklin Roosevelt, when he joined the U.S. Navy in the Second World War. His career is too well known to require any recitation from me, save to make the somewhat sad observation, what the French call *fin de ligne* [end of the line], Bill Casey will surely be the last member of the OSS to direct the CIA."

Casey sat uneasily at the witness table. He blinked passively, his hands moving about, searching for some activity.

Goldwater spoke. Something was wrong, he said. There was not enough intelligence, it was not good enough. "Congressional investigations, mood of Congress, and so forth, has inhibited intelligence operatives around the world from exploiting targets of opportunity. . . . A number of operatives are spending an inordinate amount of time in developing defensive memos in anticipation of investigations or criticisms of their actions."

After opening proclamations from three more senators, Casey darted his head toward the microphone. His goals would be "rebuilding, performance, security."

"The CIA, in particular, suffers institutional self-doubt," he said.

---

in the face." Before the Senate committee Casey was asked whether he had struck the attorney in the face. "I don't recall," Casey said. "I don't believe . . . I haven't struck anyone since high school."

The grilling lasted until 7 P.M. on March 9, 1971, when, irked and humiliated, Casey left. Mercifully, this was before the various Watergate-related confrontations between Nixon's Administration and the Congress, and the senators displayed forbearance. The committee, and finally the full Senate, approved his nomination.

"Many of its most competent officers have retired or are about to retire. The morale of much of the agency is said to be low. Too many have worked to reduce the feeling of self-worth of intelligence officers."

In the preceding weeks Casey had seen it too often, he said—a hesitation and an indirection of expression, a defensiveness. He spoke of the remedies—confidence, trust, honor.

"This is not the time for another bureaucratic shakeup of the CIA," he stated forcefully. He thought the so-called intelligence failures in recent years had been cases in which the facts were available but there had been faulty analysis or misguided policy. He promised to present all relevant information and all views to the President. Twice he pledged to work closely with Congress.

Casey had something for everyone—"rebuilding" for the right, "civil liberties" for the left. The Reagan landslide was trouble for the Democrats, Moynihan, among others, knew all too well. The Democrats would have to walk a fine line. There could be no more attempts to disembowel the CIA, no more Frank Church charges about the CIA as "a rogue elephant on a rampage." Moynihan didn't believe in that approach in the first place. An effective CIA was a prerequisite to national security. Moynihan felt he had no illusions about the Soviets; they could play very dirty.

Moynihan also had few illusions about the capacity of the CIA to deliver useful intelligence. When he was ambassador to India, from 1973 to 1975, his CIA station chief had often rushed in with Indian government secrets in special folders denoting importance, but then the Indian leadership would do something that was not mentioned in the folders; it was clear to him that the CIA was missing a great deal.

When it was his turn to question Casey, Moynihan referred to the recently enacted law that required the DCI to keep the committee "fully and currently informed of all intelligence activities . . . including any significant anticipated intelligence activity." Moynihan noted that in some cases the President could direct that only the chairman and the vice-chairman of the Senate and House intelligence committees be informed. This was reserved for "extraordinary circumstances affecting the vital interests of the United States . . . to preserve the secrecy necessary for very sensitive cases . . .

"Now, there is, however, a gray area," Moynihan said, leaning forward, his voice rising to a familiar singsong he reverted to when he knew he was on top of the central issue. He noted that the law, in a preamble, said that all this had to be "consistent with the President's duties under the Constitution" and consistent with executive-branch responsibilities to protect against unauthorized disclosure of classified information, intelligence sources and methods.

"So since we say it must be done 'consistent with,' we concede the point that there may be occasions when it's inconsistent," Moynihan said. With that concession, the law nonetheless said that some notification would have to take place at some point even after the event. "Therefore there is no exception to our being informed." What was Casey's judgment on "that measure of ambiguity? . . . Because, as you know, there has been an occasion in a long and distinguished career in which it has been charged that you have not been forthcoming to the Congress with materials requested by the Congress."

That was the ITT files, Moynihan noted. "Now, as you expect us to have done, we looked into this matter prior to this hearing, and I took the liberty of getting in touch with Mr. Stanley Sporkin, . . . a distinguished public servant by anyone's standards." Moynihan produced a letter from Sporkin, the legendary chief of enforcement of the SEC, who had for years been a self-appointed special business prosecution force.

Moynihan had been looking for dirt from Sporkin, a hero to antibusiness Democrats, but instead he had received a standing ovation for Casey based on their work together at the SEC. Sporkin had spoken of Casey's "perceptive and thoughtful analysis" and "imaginative and wise decision" in one case in question.

Casey was off the hook; Moynihan didn't even have a question about the past. He turned to the future. "How do you feel about telling this committee things we need to know and you would just as soon not more than two people in the world know?"

"Well, Senator," Casey replied, "I intend to comply fully with the spirit and the letter . . . I cannot conceive now of any circumstances under which they would result in my not being able to provide this committee with the information it requires."

"Well, I thank you, sir," Moynihan said, believing he had obtained a full pledge. "I heard you say that you could not conceive any circumstances in which you could not share information with this committee."

Gently Casey repeated himself: "I said I cannot now conceive."

Moynihan smiled. "You said not now conceive, and not for nothing did you go to the Fordham Law School."

It was Casey's turn to smile. He had gone to Fordham as an undergraduate. His law school had been St. John's; but he didn't correct the Senator.

Casey stepped lightly through the rest of the questioning. He tried to keep his replies to one word or a sentence. To a question about the phrase then in vogue "It's time to unleash the CIA": "I have not used that phrase." About a possible new executive order: "I haven't made up my mind." About what he had done since the election: "I spent most of my time catching up with my law practice and assessing the financial damage that I sustained during the campaign." About the CIA transition team: "an amoebalike creature." On management issues Casey said, "My general style in this has been to set objectives and give people authority to go after those objectives, hold them to their performance, and not get into detailed management. If they don't perform, then you get somebody else."

When Senator Joseph R. Biden, Jr., a Delaware Democrat, hinted that they were having a problem understanding, and that Casey should pull the microphone close, Casey did so, adding, "I have it in my lap now."

Goldwater had some questions. "Are you giving any thought to an assistant?"

"A lot of thought, yes," Casey replied dryly, realizing that the drumbeat was about to begin.

"I think I would be correct in informing you that Admiral Robert Inman is held in very high regard by this committee . . . " Goldwater said, deadpan. "And we, I think, again speaking for the committee, do not want to see just some political person sent over here to be your assistant. . . . I think Admiral Inman would be a great addition."

"I hope he can see his way to come," Casey said, conceding that the job was Inman's if he wanted it.

"I raise the point because I read in the paper that there were quite a few others being considered for your assistant, and I never heard a word of any of them," Goldwater said, and repeated, "And we know Bobby Inman."

"I didn't see that list," Casey said, throwing the bait back at Goldwater. "I will have to get that list." He added tauntingly, "Maybe some of them might be good."

"Well, I won't even tell you where I saw it," Goldwater replied.

Biden pressed on accountability. Casey was not hesitant to push back to this young senator. "I think there is a point at which rigid accountability, detailed accountability, can impair performance, and I think that that should be recognized." Biden's questions ran to paragraphs, and Casey batted them away: "I do not have a considered personal view and I do not want to express an unconsidered personal view." "No." "None." "I will look into that."

Then Biden jumped on the Inman bandwagon: "the absolute best, unquestionably the absolute best person in every respect that has ever testified before this committee.'' Dangling the carrot, Biden said that if Inman got the deputy's post, then, ''When you get a problem . . . you send him up. He knows a way around us.''

The message was not lost on Casey. He had better get Inman, if only as the front man to the committee. Inman had not just done his job before the committee. He had gone to some determined length to perfect and cultivate his image.*

In the days remaining before Reagan took office, Casey followed the intelligence data, particularly on the Iran hostage crisis. He saw the importance of the National Security Agency, which was intercepting communications and breaking important coded messages between Iran and Algeria; the latter country had entered the negotiations as a mediator. It was very important that there be no misunderstanding, that Iran and the Algerians receive precise and accurate information on the U.S. positions. The intercepts were a double check to be sure the Algerians and the Iranians heard and knew what the United States was saying. Several times the intercepts revealed that the positions had been garbled by the mediators, and the U.S. negotiators were able quickly to make corrections. Casey was impressed; this was the kind of intelligence support the White House needed. He noted that NSA Director Inman was directly in touch with the President and others in the White House much of the time.

* The Senate committee sent over some disclosure forms to Casey, including a confidential financial statement. Taking a recent computer printout from his investment adviser, he listed:

- 68,600 shares of Capital Cities Communications stock which he had acquired in the 1950s when he helped found the company; the effective acquisition price was only 13 cents a share. Over the years it had gone up in value nearly 500 times—certainly the best investment he had ever made. The market value was now more than $4.2 million, or precisely $4,253,200.
- 24,800 shares of stock in various oil companies and oil service stocks, valued at more than $2 million ($2,169,037).
- Stock in IBM and various chemical, mining, mineral and other companies, valued at another $1.3 million.
- Government municipal bonds worth $208,000.
- Real estate totaling $1.2 million, including a $500,000 estimated value for his Long Island home, Mayknoll, another $500,000 for the Palm Beach residence, and $200,000 for an apartment in Capitol Towers, Washington, D.C.
- Cash, life insurance and other partnerships valued at just over $700,000.

He listed income for the previous five years, 1976 to 1980, of $183,439; $221,470; $353,995; $252,775; $317,000.

With outstanding debt of only $5,000, his net worth was $9,647,089.

Addressing how to resolve a conflict of interest, he wrote: ''by disposing of assets or establishing a blind trust if necessary.'' *Only* if necessary; he had gone that costly route as SEC chairman.

Casey, like the rest of the intelligence community, was also watching Poland. The forecasted Soviet invasion didn't materialize. As is often the case, the answer was provided in a fragment of information. The CIA had details on the Soviet mobilization plans, including the tedious lists of which troops were supposed to go where. Some of this came from the BIGOT-list colonel on the Polish General Staff. An invasion required precise timing and coordination of vast resources. Mobilization required the harvest trucks from western Russia for transportation. But the satellite photography showed that the trucks had not even been brought to the Polish border. Perhaps the massing of troops on the border had been a bluff, designed to stiffen the Polish government's policy toward Solidarity? Or perhaps Brzezinski's public railing and warnings through diplomatic channels had scared the Soviets off? With the satellite photos, with the Polish General Staff colonel, with other intelligence, Casey was struck that so much remained a mystery still.

Casey also watched with some consternation as Admiral Turner coped with the final serious intelligence business remaining in his term. It was the top-secret estimate on the Soviet–U.S. strategic balance, NIE 11-3-8, which addressed both the capabilities and the intentions of the USSR. After some last-minute back-and-forth, Turner finished it and sent the final printed version to all the key national-security and intelligence officials, including the President. Such estimates are DCI documents and he can say whatever he wishes, knowing that other intelligence agencies can and will tack on their dissents. Because the DCI is also the CIA director, the CIA's position is traditionally his. The CIA had never dissented from the DCI. But this time there was such substantial disagreement within the CIA over Turner's view that for the first time he allowed the CIA representative to dissent in the published estimate. Casey found Turner's view on this no more persuasive in writing than in the Admiral's earlier oral presentation to the President. He also found a fallacy in Turner's argument: even though the United States might have enough nuclear weapons to retaliate after a Soviet first strike, even though this deterrence seemed potent, the Soviets might not react logically. After all, war was not logical.

Casey felt that Turner was analyzing away the American disadvantage. Paper and "rational thought" were no substitutes for military superiority. The influence of any such estimate in policymaking would rest in its unanimity—one document with the collective voice of the intelligence agencies and the DCI.

Casey would have to endure one last encounter with the outgoing DCI. On Thursday, January 15, with five days to go before the inaugural,

Turner was presenting the final secrets to Reagan, Bush and Casey. It was not Reagan who had requested the meeting; Turner had more or less insisted.

It was a cold morning. Bush and Casey joined Reagan in a private room at Blair House for the briefing. The men of the new Administration were uneasy and expectant.

The most important covert action, Turner told them, was the secret support to the resistance in Afghanistan. The CIA also had limited assets in place and some plans for Iran if Ayatollah Khomeini was ousted or if the fifty-two U.S. hostages in Tehran started getting killed.

But, Turner explained, the really dicey operations were not the covert actions. The real secrets were sensitive intelligence-collection efforts, some so secret and important that each day that went by without their exposure made the day a success.

First, there were human sources who if exposed would be not just lost but killed. He revealed some, including a senior official in the Indian government who was a CIA asset. This man sent out information on weapons which the Soviets supplied to India; his specialty was air defense.

A key human source in the Soviet Union worked at the Moscow Aeronautical Institute. A. G. Tolkachev provided "hard copy documentation" —the plans, specifications and test data on both operational Soviet weapons systems and other new systems being developed. His intelligence was the jewel of all jewels. He provided a look at the world of Soviet weapons that was unobtainable elsewhere—reams on their fighter planes, bombers and missiles. The intelligence take included reports on the capabilities and, most important, the vulnerabilities of some key parts of the Soviet arsenal. But he also opened a window into the future—the research, development and new generations of weapons, particularly on new radar-defeating "stealth" technology. Estimates were that his intelligence was worth billions of dollars.

Turner said that Reagan would want to decide who, beyond his Vice-President and the DCI, should know of even the existence of such a source. That obviously was up to the President, he added.

A second category of sensitive collection operations involved spying on our friends and allies, one of the all-time thorny problems. His philosophy, one he hoped the new Administration would adopt, was that such operations were necessary and, if anything, should be expanded. Much was done with passive technical means—satellite photos, interception of communications, a well-placed microphone. Risk of exposure could most likely come from a leak or a spy inside one of the U.S. intelligence agencies. Special Collection Elements—teams of two to three CIA and NSA personnel—in several dozens of our embassies provided some amazing material. The world expected the United States to spy on the Soviets; an eavesdropping device or electronic interception capability discovered there would be followed by a routine expulsion or diplomatic note. That game was known and defined. But serious public-relations and diplomatic problems would erupt if the extent or, God help us, the exact targets of U.S. spying on friends leaked or were exposed. Turner provided some examples. Casey had already done some research and was surprised that there were so few of these sensitive collection operations with microphones or human sources—some three dozen by his count.

Offering another example, Turner explained how the CIA and the NSA had the Egyptian government wired electronically and had agents from top to bottom. For all practical purposes, Egyptian President Anwar Sadat was a full known quantity to the CIA and the U.S. government. Intelligence-sharing operations with several friendly governments also provided some important intelligence-gathering opportunities.

A third category were special operations involving sources and methods that would gravely weaken national security if lost. Turner explained in detail the submarine cable-tapping operations under the Special Navy Control Program. When Bush was DCI, the submarines had had to stay directly over the cable, increasing the risk and tying up a submarine for weeks at a time. Now Navy Special had high-technology pods that could be placed over the underwater cables, left to record the communications for weeks or months, and then retrieved. This was done with a wraparound, breakaway pod which did not have to make physical contact with the transmission wires that ran inside the large cable. If the cable was lifted from the ocean floor by the Soviets for inspection or maintenance, there was no indication it had been tapped. Each operation, especially inside Soviet territorial waters, had to be approved by the President.

No intelligence mission placed so many lives at risk. There had been collisions, one at least with a Soviet submarine, and there had been other incidents. Should a submarine be captured the repercussions could be a U-2 spy plane and a *Pueblo* spy ship incident all wrapped into one. Or worse.

The CIA and the NSA had found some important nonmaritime uses for the devices by tapping into communication lines on land, either on wires running between telephone poles or on buried cables.

There were intelligence-gathering capabilities and equipment in place that had not been activated but were held in reserve in case of an emergency or war. These included backup to existing methods, but also some capabilities and sources that were there just in case. But the intelligence agencies didn't have enough war reserve, because it was hard to get money from the budget for expensive items that were not being used. No one wanted to pay for the future.

NSA code-breaking was also a sensitive area. Of the twenty principal target countries, well, in summary it was possible to break some of the codes some of the time, but not all of them all of the time, Turner said. There were dozens of other countries that were not primary targets and the NSA could break their codes. A key here was tapping into signals and communications links that various countries, especially the Soviets, did not expect the United States to be able to reach, such as the undersea cables or those within their countries. They often didn't use the highest-grade encryption on these circuits, sometimes none at all. In some cases, simply by noting the increase in communications traffic or the activation of new circuits, even without breaking the code, the NSA could get a "tip-off," say, that a missile test was about to commence, enabling U.S. collection assets, such as the RC-135 reconnaissance airborne listening post, to be put into place to gather more data.

There were automated remote relays that could be installed or dropped in various countries to send back intercepted communications. In some instances, the NSA had found "leakage" in microwave communications links that could be intercepted.

In summary, Turner said, there were countless opportunities—many exploited, many not yet imagined.

Casey left with the feeling that there just wasn't enough. Why? What had kept this great intelligence machine in standby?

4

JANUARY 20 WAS the 444th day of the Iran hostage crisis, and Inman was still on watch relaying information on the final Iranian delay directly to President Carter, who was en route to the inaugural. Finally, just after 12:30 P.M., a half hour after Reagan assumed the presidency, the two planes with the hostages aboard left Mehrabad Airport in Tehran.

The next day Casey arranged for the President to call Admiral Inman. When the call came, Inman figured there was a script. Reagan's tone was light, almost playful, as he explained that Casey and everyone else in the intelligence community wanted Inman as the deputy DCI. Then came the killer line: "I need you," the Commander in Chief said with practiced sincerity.

Government service had its rewards, military service its expectations and protocols; but presidential service at the President's personal request had a singular mystique. Inman found himself saying, "I would be honored." He added that he hoped eighteen months to two years would be enough. Please.

That same day, January 21, 1981, the first full day of the Reagan Administration, Casey singled out one other important piece of personnel business. If Inman was all intelligence insider, Casey wanted someone who was equally an outsider. Organization-building demanded variety. Casey had identified the person who was the polar opposite to Inman. He was the "Who-gul" Casey had mentioned several weeks earlier to John Bross.

Max C. Hugel, a fifty-six-year-old Brooklyn-born businessman, was more than a half foot shorter than Casey but bubbled with the same can-do, street-wise energy. Casey felt special affection for this man who was the epitome of the fast-talking, self-made entrepreneur. Like Casey he mashed his words or used improper grammar, mispronouncing big and small words. Nothing had come easily to Hugel, but he had made several million dollars by outworking others. Casey named Hugel his personal special assistant at the CIA.

During the 1980 campaign the two had shared a two-bedroom apartment in Marina Del Rey, a haven for singles and yachting enthusiasts. Rising at about 5 A.M. to be available for early phone calls from the East Coast where it was 8 A.M., Casey and Hugel worked late into the night. Almost from scratch, Hugel built a virtually cost-free organization of pro-Reagan supporters around the thirty major special-interest groups—religious, professional, ethnic, even senior citizens.

Casey and Hugel were an odd couple. At first neither could figure out how to get their stove to work. Casey found a constancy and devotion in Hugel that was touching, even sweet. Hugel learned that Casey loved bananas. When he shopped, he brought back bunches of them. Once when a gust of wind blew Casey's hat from his head, Hugel went chasing after it and a second gust caught Hugel's toupee and sent it flying—providing some of Hugel's critics on the campaign a cherished memory.

Hugel had worked in U.S. military intelligence after World War II. He spoke Japanese and had had twenty years of international business operations with a Japanese firm, Brother Industries, that made sewing machines and typewriters.

Hugel soon was filling out stacks of forms for the highest top-secret and code-word background and security investigation. He was opening every aspect of his past and his life to inspection. The clearance required a lie detector test.

Several days later, Hugel sat down before the polygraph machine, sensors strapped on. The questioner began a series of carefully ordered inquiries.

Have you ever stolen any money? the man administering the test asked.

No, Hugel said, knowing he had to limit his answers to yes or no.

Ever engaged in any homosexual activity?

No.

Have you ever used any illegal narcotics such as marijuana or cocaine?

No, Hugel said. He hadn't, but he figured that if he were lying, the little needle tracing his destiny would blow right off the chart.

Ever been blackmailed?

No.

There were more questions and it seemed to Hugel that the ordeal lasted for hours. The questions reached far back. They were sweeping but demanded absolute answers—yes or no. The validity of the test was open to question, Hugel knew, and courts would not accept it as evidence of any sort. Yet everything was riding on it. How could you remember if something had never happened or been said or done?

The examiner finally told him that he had passed—with flying colors, he added.

With Inman accepting—acquiescing, perhaps, was the better word—Casey could begin his reign over the entire intelligence empire of the United States. Some important things were shaking out in the new Administration that made his position look even more attractive. The national-security adviser, Richard Allen, was going to have to report to Reagan through Ed Meese, the new White House counselor. This was an unprecedented reduction in the security adviser's authority and access, but it enhanced Casey's role. As further good news, James A. Baker III, a smooth Texas attorney who had been a Casey deputy in the campaign, was appointed White House chief of staff, with Casey's firm backing.

Baker, who had managed George Bush's presidential campaign, was a strong, efficient manager, the opposite of Meese. Anything could disappear in the bottom of Meese's briefcase or in-box. Casey also knew Mike Deaver well enough from the campaign; Meese, Baker and Deaver were the troika who would run the White House. Casey was confident he had good lines to all three and that they would want to have a channel to him. On top of that, Casey felt he could pick up the phone or make an appointment to see the President directly.

Relations with Haig and Weinberger seemed good. Casey struck a noncompetitive posture with both senior Cabinet officers. Haig had "diplomacy," Weinberger "war." If it turned out there was a scarcity of both, the foreign-policy goal of the Administration, aggressive anti-Communism, might be carried out through "intelligence."

He arranged a meeting with Inman to outline his plans. There was nothing to be gained by being less than frank.

I want to take direct control of the CIA's analytical directorate to improve the reports and the estimates, Casey said. I also want the Operations Directorate; both covert action and the sensitive collection operations need and will receive beefing up.

Inman was surprised. These directorates were the two main parts of the CIA.

Technology and the scientific end of the CIA were Inman's if he wanted them, Casey said. In addition, the administrative and personnel operations, matters which didn't interest him, would be Inman's.

Normally, the DCI looked outside the CIA, using his authority as the intelligence coordinator for the entire U.S. government, as Mr. Outside. Casey was describing his role as Mr. Inside; he intended to keep his hands on all reports, all operations. Inman detected an overbearing quality that had not been visible before. Casey's convictions were strong, and his large, awkward body shook, his arms getting into the action. The listening mode was over. Things were about to change.

He would work and rule his own institution—the CIA. Other interagency, interdepartmental matters were Inman's, except for the White House. Casey would handle the White House. He referred to himself as the President's intelligence officer, the one who would provide the latest and the hottest and make sure the President knew.

Inman was somewhat disappointed.

On January 26, 1981, the first Monday of the new Administration, the Cabinet was summoned to the White House. Though neither Casey nor Inman had yet been confirmed by the Senate, they were included, Casey as the DCI designate and Inman still representing the NSA. The subject was terrorism.

Secretary of State Haig, the high-strung former Kissinger protégé, NATO general and self-proclaimed "vicar" of a new hard-line foreign policy, was worked up, declaiming about what a band of terrorists or fanatics could do. Iran was proof. Haig was certain that they were entering a period of uncertainty in which the new Administration would be tested. Resolve and will had to be demonstrated. He had the State Department's terrorism expert, Anthony Quainton, there to address the terrorist issues.

It's possible for a terrorist group to strike directly at the United States in the United States, Quainton said. The United States is vulnerable.

It was an electrifying moment. The members of the new government were being put on notice that while Iran was astern, with the hostages back, the problem of terrorism was not.

Meese unfurled some of the still-fresh campaign rhetoric: Carter and Turner had made the intelligence problems worse by putting too much restraint on the intelligence agencies to conduct effective investigations of either terrorists or foreign spies.

FBI Director William H. Webster said he disagreed. An all-American, boyish-looking former federal judge with a pleasant, nonconfrontational style, Webster emphasized that it was important to be careful about what was done within the United States to catch spies or stop terrorists. He spoke softly. His bureau, which was in charge of the counterintelligence and counterterrorist efforts within the United States, basically had the tools it needed. It could function within the existing rules and law, he said, dousing Meese's campaign fire.

Inman supported Webster, saying it was more a problem of resources. There simply were not enough people to do the work. The task was to get the intelligence into the hands of those who needed it in time.

Casey didn't have much to say. Webster and Inman were certainly no parlor pinks. He would have to examine terrorism, certainly a major intelligence issue.

At the end of the meeting, it was agreed that Casey would examine the Carter executive order on intelligence, the basic directive that had the force of law. If changes were needed, and the sentiment was high that they were, Reagan would issue a modified order.

The next day the Senate, without debate, confirmed Casey as DCI by a vote of 95 to 0, and he was sworn in the following day. But it was Haig who made the news that day. He stepped unhesitatingly before the State Department press corps for his first press conference as Secretary and tagged the Soviet Union with "the training, funding and equipping" of international terrorists. Digging sarcastically at the Carter Administration, he added, "International terrorism will take the place of human rights . . . The greatest problem to me in the human-rights area today is the area of rampant international terrorism."

The Soviets, he said without qualification, "today are involved in conscious policies, in programs, if you will, which foster, support and expand this activity."

This salvo was big news and left some of Haig's senior aides sputtering in disbelief. Ronald I. Spiers, the head of the State Department's intelligence branch, told the new Secretary privately that his statements would not hold up against the latest intelligence reports.

Wait, Haig said, he had read about the Soviet role in the advance galley proofs of a book about to be published called *The Terror Network,* by Claire Sterling, an American correspondent based in Italy. Sterling had fingered the Russians conclusively.

It was possible there was something new, Spiers conceded, and certainly the matter was of sufficient importance to merit immediate attention. Spiers sent a formal request to Casey for a Special National Intelligence Estimate, SNIE (pronounced snee), designed to give the best collective assessment of what all the U.S. intelligence agencies knew and what the policy-makers should expect.

Casey welcomed the request. These estimates were the meat and potatoes, a chief focus of his revitalization efforts. The finished estimate would go to the President, the National Security Council, the key Cabinet officers. These forecasts were the early-warning system in the intelligence community. He was going to make them very good. He was going to take personal direction of the process; terrorism would be an appropriate first topic.

On his third day in office, Casey received a copy of a twelve-page SECRET SNIE, completed just before he was sworn in. Headed "Libya: Aims and Vulnerabilities," it was a brief course on what to expect from Qaddafi in the coming months. Qaddafi was no longer an abstract problem; he was Casey's problem. The document bore the legend "WARNING NOTICE: Intelligence Sources and Methods Involved."

"This estimate is issued by the DCI," Casey read. "The National Foreign Intelligence Board concurs, except as noted in the text." The NFIB was the board of directors of all U.S. intelligence agencies that Casey now chaired.

"Key Judgments" summarized the conclusions:

First, "Qaddafi's recent success in Chad ensures that his aggressive policies will pose a growing challenge to U.S. and Western interests." Several months earlier Qaddafi had dispatched thousands of troops into neighboring Chad, directly to the south of Libya. Chad, a French colony until 1960, was one of the many new African states whose leadership and loyalties were continually up for grabs. The estimate said the Qaddafi problem was not going to go away; the prospect was "more adventurism."

Second, "the domestic and exile opposition to his regime is poorly organized and ineffective." That meant that a covert action would require more than just passing along money or arms; problems of organization and morale would have to be tackled.

Third, "Soviet objectives are served by Qaddafi's anti-Western policies . . . the Soviets gain substantial hard currency earnings from massive arms sales to Libya." The estimate put this at $1 billion a year. Though he was not a Soviet pawn, Qaddafi's relationship with the Soviets was far too intimate.

Recently, the estimate continued, Qaddafi had "employed political intrigue, diplomatic activism, terrorism, assassination and now, in Chad, military occupation."

The agency employed psychologists and psychiatrists who took the raw intelligence data collected on the ground and turned it into psychological profiles, a kind of Freudian spycraft. In analyzing Qaddafi's personality, the estimate said: "Because of special circumstances in his childhood, Qaddafi absorbed, in exaggerated form, the Bedouin characteristics of naive idealism, religious fanaticism, intense pride, austerity, xenophobia, and sensitivity to slight."

Qaddafi was the son of a nomadic shepherd. "As a result of the discriminatory treatment he encountered as a Bedouin during his early schooling in Libya's cities—at the hands of urbanized Libyans as well as foreigners—Qaddafi developed an intense disdain for established elites, a rigid adherence to his Bedouin ways and a strong identification with the downtrodden."

One result, the estimate said, was "his own rebellion against authority" and "his indiscriminate support of rebel causes throughout the world."

Sinking into armchair psychoanalysis, the estimate said: ". . . to defend himself psychologically, Qaddafi has developed an exalted, even grandiose sense of self-importance. Qaddafi's vision for Libya seeks to restore the purity and simplicity that he supposes existed in earlier Arab history."

The estimate touched on other countries where Qaddafi was working underground. "Libya has engaged in covert activities through black Africa," including "bribing leaders." In Tunisia, which shares a 200-mile border with Libya, the estimate said, "recent clandestine reporting"—a term for information from sources, either human or technical—"suggests accelerated training and recruiting of Tunisian dissidents."

Qaddafi had for years claimed territorial waters beyond the internationally recognized 12-mile limit, holding that the Gulf of Sidra, the massive 275-mile-wide indentation opening directly on Libya's 800-mile Mediterranean coast to the north, was all his. "While there is some question whether Qaddafi would actually risk U.S. retaliation," the estimate continued, "his military has standing orders to attack U.S. ships or aircraft penetrating this line." And the intelligence agencies concluded: "Chances for an incident off Libya involving the U.S. are relatively high."

About 10 percent of imported U.S. oil, the estimate noted, came from Libya, "a major supplier of hard-to-replace light-density, low-sulfur oil." A cutoff or ban on that Libyan oil could result in what the estimate called "a serious gasoline shortage on the U.S. East Coast."

Overall, Qaddafi's hold on power was not that certain, the estimate said, adding, "We have evidence of one near coup attempt last May, and of another, more serious one in August." To protect himself, Qaddafi has "a system of informers," but the organized exiles got support from abroad, "notably Egypt, Morocco, Saudi Arabia and Iraq." And some of these exiles had "support within Libya." Nonetheless, the estimate said, "barring an assassination, he could continue in power for many years."

In paragraph 51, former Chad Defense Minister Habré was mentioned. Habré, the quintessential desert warrior, had been battling the Qaddafi forces in Chad. (CIA files showed that Sudan's leader Jaafar Nimeri had several months before secretly urged the CIA to assist Habré. Nimeri feared that Sudan, the largest country in Africa, was next on Qaddafi's menu.) The estimate said that "Morocco, Egypt, Sudan and France are providing increased covert support to Habre's rebellion."

Though it was not simple, Casey saw equivocation: Qaddafi could be out, there was "evidence" of coups, or he could be around. The document was laced with "coulds," "mights," "possibles." For Casey's taste it was written by equivocators for equivocators. But he was interested in how it spelled out the hazards of fighting Qaddafi:

"Indeed an open Western challenge could rebound to Qaddafi's advantage, transforming him from outcast to Muslim martyr. Arab regimes that did not then oppose any anti-Libyan actions by the U.S., especially military action, could be threatened by their own people—a possibility they greatly feared when the U.S. threatened military action in Iran."

The last paragraph, number 71, stated that the Arab states' "actions could turn against them at home and in the Arab world."

It was a quibble. Qaddafi spelled trouble for everyone—for the West, the United States, the Arab states, friend and foe, and even for himself. The document put the intelligence agencies in the bureaucratically secure position of being able, no matter what happened, to dust off the estimate and say, "See, we told you. We said that *could* happen." To say everything was to say almost nothing, Casey thought.

Yet the last sentence of the last paragraph offered some redemption. Referring to the Arab states, it said: "*A measure of their subtlety is the discretion with which some of Qaddafi's regional foes, including President Sadat, are focusing their resources on quietly bleeding Qaddafi at his most vulnerable point—his overextension in Chad and the danger this poses for him at home*."

The last sentence rang a bell. If you focused only on it, the estimate could be seen as an artful document, building its argument to a rather cunning call to action, suggesting, pointing the way to the minimum risk, the "subtlety" and "discretion" of "quietly bleeding" the Libyan colonel. The message was that the Chad adventure was the Achilles' heel for Qaddafi, and the implied course to thwart Qaddafi in Chad appealed to

Casey's strategic sense. Casey wasn't going to have the CIA sit on its hands with such an opportunity available.

Soon, within Haig's new State Department and Casey's new CIA, a proposal for covert support to Habré was drawn up. It was called the "second track" as distinguished from the normal or "first track" of standard open diplomacy and aid. Haig's stated purpose was to "bloody Qaddafi's nose" and to "increase the flow of pine boxes back to Libya." Casey pushed the policy. Chad, Sudan and Egypt were on Libya's east and south; they formed an important wall of resistance that needed reinforcement.

There were interdepartmental meetings and finally one at the White House with the President, solidifying the basic philosophical agreement among the major players. The consensus was not just on the pledge to reactivate covert action, but also on the need to rehabilitate the international reputation of the United States. Soon the President signed a formal intelligence order, called a "finding," releasing several million dollars of covert support to Habré. Casey's first covert action was under way.

In the first weeks he had found some of what he expected—an institution withdrawn into its shell. He had to coax it out. These were people who weren't going to come out unless there was a reason. They certainly hadn't come out for Carter and Stan Turner. But the seeds of boldness were there. The Libya estimate was an example. To bring his people out, Casey would have to alter the point of reference. If Turner's approach had been to minimize risk, Casey would demonstrate a willingness to take risks. To break the logjam, he might have to prove that the Administration, the President and he were willing to take the heat.

Air Force Lieutenant General Eugene Tighe made sure he was on time for the 11 A.M. meeting with the new DCI on Monday, February 2, 1981. He had met Casey only once before, and that had been at a party. Tighe (pronounced "tie") had learned in thirty-six years of intelligence work that politics and intelligence are roommates. A genial, grandfatherly-looking man with glasses, Tighe had a disarming, intense smile that he often held long after the laughter had passed. He had seen administrations, Secretaries of Defense and DCIs come and go, and the shape and tone of intelligence work change. But he had found that the real squabbles arose when they didn't have enough information. When U.S. intelligence had a lot of good data, there was rarely a fight.

Tighe had been head of the Defense Intelligence Agency for nearly four years under Carter, and he wanted to stay on. The DIA coordinated the intelligence gathered by the Army, the Navy, the Air Force and the Marine Corps. Tighe had access to the intercepted communications intelligence of the NSA, the satellite photography of the National Reconnaissance Office—the supersecret agency that wasn't even in the Pentagon phone directory—and the CIA. His first responsibility was to provide early warning of Soviet military moves. The CIA did revolutions, political upheaval and change. That meant that its product was on the White House table every day, since there was always a hot spot or a crisis somewhere. Tighe did war. That meant the DIA product was tested less frequently; in the case of the Soviets it might never be. He hoped it wouldn't be. There were war games and debates within intelligence circles, the White House, State, Defense, think tanks, the press, but they were abstract. That worried him, and he was determined to keep the DIA on its toes.

Tighe was not one of the shooters. His philosophy was simple: the more you know, the less chance of war. The task was to get the intelligence that made it possible for the United States to act peaceably. Tighe knew that among the intelligence agencies the DIA was thought of as back-bench, a no-account organization that had meager intellectual sophistication. Yet he was conscious of the burden carried by the DIA and the 4,500 people who worked for him. About 95 percent of the U.S. military intelligence was done by the DIA, not only the analysis of the hardware, the threats and the military intentions, but the targeting plans within the Soviet Union that provided the crucial information for SIOP, the Single Integrated Operation Plan, the big war plan for nuclear war with the Soviet Union.

He believed that the DIA was the chief line of intelligence defense. President John F. Kennedy and Secretary of Defense Robert McNamara had discovered, upon taking office, that there was no missile gap with the Soviets as Kennedy had loudly proclaimed in his 1960 presidential campaign. So they had created the DIA to make sure that military information was shared, properly vetted, and not ignored. They wanted an overall Pentagon intelligence authority that would provide answers independent of interservice rivalries.

The message had to be simple: the Arabs are going to attack or not attack; the Russians are coming or not coming; or the Chinese, or whoever.

The meeting this Monday morning was the first of the National Foreign Intelligence Board that Casey chaired and included the heads of the NSA, the DIA, the service intelligence agencies, the State Department intelligence branch, INR, and the intelligence branches of the FBI and Treasury. In all, about a dozen agency chiefs or representatives were in the room awaiting the new Director.

Tighe had always felt that the DCI should be a professional like himself, but after the Helms and Colby experiences he had come to the conclusion that there might never again be a DCI up from the ranks.

Casey lumbered in and took his seat, looking terribly old. His walk was not straight, and there was a grayness about him. It was in striking contrast to Turner's youthfulness and military bearing.

Casey began with a little upbeat speech. Every voice would be heard; the intelligence board would spend as much time as necessary to carry on their business; there could be no shortcuts in intelligence work; he understood intelligence, he realized its importance; he would do whatever he needed to keep informed.

Good signs, Tighe felt. Casey had done enough homework to know the objections to the way Turner had chaired the board. Turner had allocated an hour or so for the meetings, and he had made sure they ended on schedule. Every voice might be heard, but few got their whole message across. Sometimes they'd get to the meat and Turner would have to go. Since Turner was No. 1, he could just go ahead and make decisions. Turner was rigid and often distracted.

As Casey continued, Tighe was mildly surprised to find him so well versed in the special language of intelligence. The new DCI was congenial, he said he wanted to come see each agency head personally.

Casey also mentioned that there were a lot of people in the room, perhaps too many, and on some sensitive matters they would have to find a way to eliminate those without a need to know. He would make sure of that. He repeated that security was one of his main priorities.

A few days later Casey called Tighe. How about lunch at your place? Casey asked. When Tighe said he did not have a private dining room, Casey said they could eat in Tighe's office. Several days later Casey appeared at Tighe's Pentagon office, Room 3E258.

Both ordered shrimp salads, and Casey began at once to extract details about each of Tighe's previous intelligence assignments. But he had two real questions: What do you do? What do you know about what is going on in the world? Tighe was soon launched on a *tour d'horizon*.

Beginning in the South Pacific, Tighe said, the intelligence assets are too thin. The Soviets are buying wool from the New Zealanders, a classic Soviet stunt, exploiting economic trouble to get a foot in the door. In the North Pacific, the situation in Korea is bad, with intelligence resources cut in recent years as the North Koreans add more troops. The Soviets are trying to increase their influence wherever the U.S. has abdicated, particularly in Southeast Asia, Vietnam.

Casey took some note cards from his pocket and began writing, encouraging Tighe to keep going. Korea, Vietnam—old problems, old wars—might not be over.

The Nixon-Kissinger opening has not solved the China problem, Tighe said. Chinese policy could change 180 degrees overnight. The Chinese strategic nuclear force, their submarines, their orbited satellites, their ICBMs make them a world power. There is a serious error in the way we've looked at the Chinese, viewing them only as some kind of giant Third World country, focusing on them as a massive regional threat. The new listening posts the Chinese are allowing the United States to set up on Chinese territory are a sign though not a guarantee of friendship.

Mexico, Tighe said, is a big concern. There is insurgency in the countryside; local police, not the central government in Mexico City, control certain areas. In the capital, poverty is so extreme that another Khomeini-type leader could appear. Central America is a sea of instability, Tighe said, a breeding ground for leftists. Cuba is getting more and better planes that would allow it to project its power over more territory.

Things will get worse in the Middle East before they get better, Tighe said. Iran under Khomeini hasn't had its civil war yet, but it's inevitable. U.S. mediation in the Middle East seems always to get us into trouble.

India is key, he went on, but power is divided between the Gandhi government and a Defense Ministry that is almost wholly under Soviet domination. This two-tiered government will make things difficult for the U.S., he explained, because it is often unclear who has the real say.

There is also a wake-up factor, Tighe said. Often the White House wouldn't listen. Frankly, it had been almost impossible to get President Carter to see the intelligence that showed conclusively that the Soviets were preparing to invade Afghanistan. Six months before the invasion, a Soviet general who specialized in extending military influence and had previously been active in North Vietnam was tracked to Afghanistan. Tighe had tried calling the Carter White House personally to warn them. It was as if no one were home; certainly no one was listening. Satellite photos and signals intelligence made the Soviet intention clear. But the White House had been obsessed with Iran and seemed not to want another problem. Now, after more than a year, Tighe said, the Soviets are still very serious in Afghanistan.

Look, Casey said, glancing up from his cards, if you ever have a message to pass, you come to me directly. "We'll get through." He was emphatic.

In the Soviet Union, Tighe said, the military is dominant to a degree that few recognize. The intelligence analyses, particularly from CIA, have not been willing to give it credit for having that authority. The Soviet generals have been calling many of the shots for a decade. Their instrument is reform. By becoming more modern, the military has become more powerful. The intelligence reports show that a significant segment of the Soviet military was against the Strategic Arms Limitations Treaty, SALT II. Given this opposition, Tighe said, he believed the Soviets would cheat.

Casey agreed. The Soviets are cheaters and cannot be trusted.

Worse, Tighe said, it was his opinion that the Soviet leadership was becoming more and more entrenched. Russia is becoming a class society. About three thousand families had formed an elite. They wanted to remain elite. Their dachas and their possessions were being passed on to their children, a sign that they would not release their hold.

The Soviets did not trust the Eastern European military one hoot, Tighe said. With the possible exception of Bulgaria, the Soviets were resented throughout Eastern Europe where the leaders were fed up with having to buy the old military junk that the Soviets made them purchase. But the Soviet military presence was growing in Eastern Europe, and it was very threatening.

Tighe said that he had just recently been to Turkey where trouble was brewing.

In December 1978, about six weeks before the revolution drove the Shah out of Iran, Tighe had visited Tehran, he recalled. The CIA station chief there was pleading for more Farsi-speaking agents. He didn't get them; almost no one was able to find out what was going on. To get a firsthand view, Tighe dodged his security protection by changing into civilian clothes and climbing out an embassy window. He had walked around for three hours. At 11 A.M. the shops were all open. At noon they all closed and one million demonstrators poured into the streets, whipped into an anti-American frenzy. It was a stunning display, showing true emotion or precision organization, or both. It was clear that dramatic forces were at work, that a hurricane was about to hit.

Later, at the American Embassy, the head of SAVAK, the Iranian secret service, Lieutenant General Nasser Moghadam, had taken Tighe to a private room for three hours and pleaded for crowd- and riot-control equipment. What were the lines of communications from the Iranian government to the United States government? Apparently the lines were screwed up and there was paralysis in both countries. Iran was a ghastly intelligence failure. It deserved more searching analysis, even now.

Casey once again nodded assent. He left shortly afterward, heading down the corridor of the E-ring, out of the building and to his waiting car.

God damn, there was a lot to do. Korea, Vietnam, China, Mexico, the rest of Central America, the Middle East, India, the Soviet Union of course, Iran still.

The image of the DIA chief crawling out the window of the U.S. Embassy in Tehran for a firsthand look around was appealing, even admirable. Casey decided there was only one way to do his job: he would draw up a list of major countries and make an inspection tour, visit the CIA stations, see for himself what they did and what they knew.

Casey and John Bross had sifted through some personnel files in search of a chief doorkeeper, paper-sorter, facilitator and executive assistant for Casey. They finally selected Robert M. Gates, who had just taken over the job as the national-intelligence officer for the Soviet Union, reporting directly to the DCI. NIO for the Soviets was the senior analytic position in the number-one area of concern. But more valuable to Casey was Gates's White House experience. From the spring of 1974 to December 1979, Gates had been assigned to the National Security Council staff and had seen the uses and abuses of intelligence under Presidents Nixon, Ford and Carter. At thirty-seven, with fourteen years of experience in the CIA, Gates, a short man with gray hair and a bright, open smile, had what Casey wanted.

During the Carter years, Gates had worked for Brzezinski's deputy at that NSC, David Aaron. Gates called Aaron "the Strasbourg goose" because his feet almost had to be nailed to the floor to get him to focus on issues. The afternoon sessions at which Gates force-fed Aaron the latest intelligence and extracted the necessary decisions to make it through the day were called "the Strasbourg hour." If others weren't organized or methodical, Gates was willing to assist.

Casey had done some checking. When Gates joined the career training program at the CIA in 1966, he had lamented that the CIA was so filled with good World War II and OSS vets that there was no way around them to the top, unless you were plugged in with political connections. He had found a way. After complaining to a fellow CIA officer, John T. Smith, whose father was Gerard Smith, Nixon's chief arms control negotiator, Gates was introduced to the elder Smith. Within a short time he was assigned as a CIA analyst to the arms control delegation.

More important, Gates had some unorthodox notions that Casey found attractive. Though he had a doctorate in Russian history, he argued that the CIA was too academic, that it shied away from controversy. "If no one gave a shit about what the intelligence analysis was saying, there would be no controversy, no pressure," he said. Controversy and pressure brought intelligence analysts closer to the policy-makers. Intelligence people had to understand the worries of the policy-maker, not so that estimates could be tailored to suit the White House, but so that obstacles could be identified early and warnings issued. Gates argued that the main intelligence failure had been not educating policy-makers on the limits of intelligence. Given the billions spent on it, a President might think there should not be unknowns. There were.

Though he was an analyst, Gates had one operational experience that demonstrated a willingness to bend the rules, in a way Casey liked. Carter's White House had wanted to open relations with Cuba, and David Aaron had been sent to a secret meeting in New York with two of Fidel Castro's top intelligence officers. Believing that blatancy was the best cover, Aaron, accompanied by Gates, met the Cubans at a fancy old-line French restaurant in midtown, off Fifth Avenue. Gates had agreed to wear a "wire" recorder which came in a vest provided by the FBI. As Aaron and the Cubans argued about Cuban troops in Angola and Ethiopia, Gates sat stiff and erect in the FBI vest, the human microphone.

Casey sat down for some discussions with Turner's Deputy Director for Operations, John N. McMahon. DDO was key. The Operations Directorate would be the instrument of change. McMahon, a husky outgoing Irishman (Holy Cross '51) with 1960s-style long sideburns, was not a covert operator by training, though he had been in the CIA nearly thirty years. Turner had named McMahon DDO to gain control of the directorate, which he didn't trust. Casey found the agency personnel files very informative as he reviewed McMahon's. After joining the CIA in 1951 as a GS-5 code clerk, McMahon had worked his way through the administrative and paper-handling hierarchy. He had been a case officer for U-2 pilots. He had navigated his way around the problems of the seventies. As the agency's reputation foundered, McMahon had been promoted. He had been director of the office of ELINT, electronics intelligence, an obscure but important form of intelligence from radar and other noncommunications emissions. Before he was made DDO, McMahon had been running the intelligence community staff for Turner and pondering retirement.

McMahon had a reputation as a man of caution. Several years earlier, when the CIA put together what was known publicly on who supported and funded several dozen anti-CIA groups and publications such as the

Covert Action Information Bulletin, which tried to expose CIA operations and operatives, McMahon had blown up. "Stupid sons of bitches," he had yelled at a senior-staff meeting, "spying on Americans. If anyone got hold of this . . . Don't you see? The perception."

Casey nonetheless liked McMahon personally. He was open and cooperative and he seemed willing to follow orders.

How about more nonofficial cover? Casey asked him. Sending some of the boys out as businessmen, consultants, et cetera—getting them out of the embassies?

McMahon raised all the objections: security, control, the need for CIA officers to have the stature of diplomats.

What about the Afghanistan operation?

It's a massive cooperative venture, transshipping weapons primarily through Egypt, McMahon explained. Pakistan is the funnel to the Afghanistan resistance. Saudi Arabia is providing more funding than the CIA.

Casey said he thought it was an important operation, probably the most important one inherited from Carter. President Reagan would want to continue it, probably even expand the support. This was a major point of engagement with the Soviets.

Yes, McMahon said dryly, the Soviet invasion was wrong, a serious mistake for them. Yet he wondered about the purpose of the United States policy. Is it in need of reassessment? It is unlikely that the Soviet army would allow itself to be defeated. Each U.S. move would be met with a Soviet countermove, an escalation. Could U.S. policy designed to "bleed" the Soviets work? Could it be sustained? Are we putting enough diplomatic pressure on the Soviets to leave Afghanistan?

Casey turned his campaign buddy Max Hugel loose in the agency on a fact-finding mission, to get briefed and learn as much as possible. After about three weeks Casey asked him, "All right, what do you want to do?"

"I'll leave it up to you," Hugel replied.

"Well, here's what I want you to do," Casey said. Deputy director for administration has opened up, he said—one of the top three deputy slots, equivalent in rank to DDO and deputy for intelligence analysis.

On February 13 Hugel's new job was announced. He soon realized that it was a business job, handling all the support functions including worldwide security, communication and logistics for headquarters and the CIA stations abroad. It was important, but it was removed from real intelligence work, from the secrets he had associated with the CIA.

• • •

In late February, Casey attended a memorial service for an old friend, Raymond R. Dickey, a longtime Republican stalwart and Washington lawyer. After the service, he returned to his CIA car and sent his security guard to ask one of the mourners, Stanley Sporkin, to join him.

Sporkin, a rumpled man who looked like an overweight Vegas pit boss, strolled over and opened the Director's car door.

Stan, Casey said, thanks for the letter of endorsement to the Senate Intelligence Committee. Why don't you ride back with me?

Sporkin got in and they drove off.

"Look, you turned me down twice before," Casey said, referring to two previous job offers at the Export-Import Bank when Casey was there in 1974 and 1975. "I want you to come work at the CIA." As general counsel, Casey said. There were going to be many tough legal calls.

Sporkin said he was interested. He was bored after nineteen years at the SEC, and there was no real enforcement action there.

Intelligence operations are different, Casey said. They're ruthless and cutthroat.

Why are you doing this? Sporkin asked.

"This is what I want to do," Casey said. "I don't want to make another million dollars." He added that if Sporkin was interested, he had better be fully briefed on what the agency did. If you find anything objectionable and can't operate and can't live by your principles, then don't do it. We've got to turn the water back on out there, and we'll have to do it slowly, carefully.

The car pulled into CIA headquarters, dropped Casey off and took Sporkin back to the church.

Casey loved Sporkin. He was one of the few government people who wouldn't stop. As SEC chairman, Casey had asked Sporkin a simple question, "Stan, what do you need to do your job?" Sporkin had been waiting years to be asked. He wanted the power to continue or close SEC investigations, and Casey had given it to him. With that leverage, Sporkin had forced disclosures of questionable business practices and overseas bribery.

Sedate on the surface, Sporkin could reduce a team of well-heeled Park Avenue lawyers to soup. Casey admired the way he conducted himself in long negotiation sessions. He would lean back in his chair, even close his eyes, only to tip forward, open his eyes, pop up from his chair, strut around the room, jab the air and yell about the intolerable behavior that had been uncovered. Or he would cluster his fingers at his temples and shout, "Unbelievable!" Or slink into a dark, penetrating gaze, or break into a smile of approval. Then he would return to his Columbo detective mode—the asker of simple questions, seemingly confused. It was pure theater, Casey knew, but it had often caught the corporate opposition off guard.

Casey's first weeks were a delight. He was treated as the old OSS hand come back as the leader. It had not leaked that he had wanted State, and the widely held view in the agency was that as the Reagan campaign manager, he could have chosen any job, and he had picked them. Perhaps no head of an agency or department was treated with such deference as the DCI. Nearly everyone used the appellations "the Director" or "Director Casey" or "the DCI" or "sir." That was the culture. Every message leaving Langley was headed "Cite Director," followed by a sequential number giving the cables, requests and orders the stamp of ultimate authority, though Casey saw only several dozen of the hundreds that went out each day. Every message from the stations to headquarters was addressed to the Director. People noticed him in the corridors, moved out of his way, very nearly saluted.

Each day there was a pile of new material on his plate. The morning messages from the Langley operations center highlighting occurrences overnight came in a separate folder. Another folder contained the embassy and station reports routed for his attention. He received a nice crisp copy of the beautifully printed President's Daily Brief (PDB), ten pages of the best intelligence that went each morning to Reagan, Haig and Weinberger. The National Intelligence Daily (NID), a less sensitive but nonetheless top-secret code-word document, was circulated to hundreds in the government—and Casey. Occasional blue-border human-source reports were hand-carried to him throughout the day. Big red folders marked TOP SECRET TALENT KEYHOLE—the code word for overhead surveillance—arrived, containing reports of satellite and other reconnaissance photography. Most of the intelligence reports were all-source, meaning that someone had taken the intercepts, satellite, human and other reports and digested them into a summary. At times, Casey called for or was automatically routed the full intercept. Whenever he wanted more, all he had to do was indicate so and the file or a summary or a briefing would be provided. At certain times he had to restrain his instincts as a reader and an amateur historian. The records were often good, and they told many stories.

Yet in all this paper there was a strange disconnect. Casey found himself wondering more and more, What was going on out there? "Out there" meant the stations abroad. Reports showed that several of the stations provided great intelligence on the host government and the Soviet Embassy in that country, but many stations sent in little of significance, often drivel. He was eager to start on his station visits.

In early March, Casey flew off to the Far East. The CIA stations he visited there had set up systems and operations to provide a systematic monitor on the growing Soviet presence in their countries. Using the local police, the host intelligence, immigration and customs services, the stations pretty well tracked all arrivals and departures of Soviet citizens. They generally received a copy of the passport photo; a surveillance team with a photo and audio van could follow and monitor selected targets; observation and photo posts provided good data on the comings and goings of key Soviets; the Special Collection Element could conduct telephone tapping and room eavesdropping. Postal interception was possible in selected cases. The stations had "access agents" who knew Soviet targets and provided personality data. Several stations had high-level sources in the host government, but really useful political intelligence was scanty.

The operations officers ranged from excellent to adequate, Casey found. But no one seemed to be going for the big play. The atmosphere was not creative. No one spent enough time brainstorming, listing the real targets and then maximizing the effort to recruit human agents or place the key eavesdropping device. The stations waited for opportunities, rather than going out and finding them. There was hesitancy and doubt.

Everywhere he went, he was well attended by his own team—the chief of station, his own security officers, his own communications channels. Casey wanted to set an example, and his former status as the President's campaign manager carried the implication that he was Reagan's representative on a range of foreign and defense policies.

Casey came home with an overriding impression: America's allies and friends were looking for the United States to take the lead, and his stations were looking to him.

5

SINCE CARTER AND TURNER had hit an iceberg in Iran, Casey read everything he could find in the agency on the subject. Like many he was still wondering, What had the CIA been doing? Could American intelligence have failed as badly as DIA chief Tighe said? How had the CIA missed the precariousness of the Shah's position, his physical condition, his utter weakness? One of Casey's jobs was to make sure it never happened again—in Iran or anywhere else.

The CIA had probed the failed hostage rescue mission in the spring of 1980, when malfunctioning helicopters forced cancellation; the pictures of the wreckage in the Iranian desert had become a symbol of Carter's impotence. The mission supposedly had been DDO John McMahon's finest hour, because he had infiltrated some half-dozen agents inside Iran to assist. Casey thought that was way too low. Six months after the hostages were taken, the CIA should have had many more agents inside. Casey forwarded to President Reagan a top-secret after-action report on the rescue mission. It underscored the inadequacy of these human sources.

Another top-secret study that had been prepared for Turner, "Iran Postmortem," went a long way toward describing the CIA role in the overall Iran catastrophe. Stamped "NODIS"—no distribution to others than Turner and a few top deputies and aides—it was a one-hundred-page analysis on why and how the CIA had missed the Iranian revolution.

The study had been done by Robert Jervis, a Columbia University political scientist brought in as a CIA scholar-in-residence. Expert in studying misperceptions in decision-making, Jervis had been granted access to everything the CIA analysts had at the time—human-source reports, all the State Department cable traffic, the "eyes only" messages, NSA intercepts. He had spent two months going through two file drawers of this data and had interviewed the four main CIA analysts who had done nearly all the work on the intelligence distributed to the White House, State and elsewhere.

"Iran Postmortem" began with a soft point: Iran was a hard case to get right, and a good person could easily get it wrong; there was almost no other instance in which a leader like the Shah, with vast military and security forces, had been overthrown by unarmed rebels. Then the study proceeded to tear apart the CIA's handling of Iran.

The intelligence problems:

- The CIA was not set up to jump ahead on a fast-moving situation, and the analysts had become enmeshed in the daily production line—cable summarizing or "cable-gisting," feeding the National Intelligence Daily or the President's Daily Brief.
- The senior Iran analyst at the CIA, Ernest Oney, said he got four or five kind notes from people up the line who liked the reports, but he was never really questioned; there was no effort to sit down and puzzle it out; there was no indication that there was even a problem to puzzle out. Intelligence had been reduced to unintelligence—getting a lot of facts and throwing them at people; if intelligence was going to answer the "tomorrow" question, it would be necessary to make assumptions, but assumptions were speculation, and that was bad.
- The CIA and State Department cables had little more factual content than the daily newspaper and television reports. But publications like *Le Monde,* the center-left French daily newspaper, and the British center-right *Economist,* which tended to be more speculative and critical, came to the CIA analysts by regular mail, a week late; they were considered old news and were not read. There were few outside catalysts to jar the thinking of the analysts; little to suggest that they might be on the wrong track; no intellectual badminton.
- The CIA station in Tehran was split over what was going on in Iran, but the disagreements among the members did not show up in the cables and reports.
- The formal priorities for the Tehran station listed the Soviets first, and Iran's efforts to obtain nuclear weapons second. Near the bottom was the internal political situation. Several months before the upheaval in Iran, the CIA station started to change the priorities, but there was only a tentative sense that a political struggle was under way.
- There was no electronic eavesdropping device in the Shah's office or on his telephones; there was no intelligence from high-technology equipment of any importance from within Iran. An NSA proposal to set up the most advanced electronic listening post in the U.S. Embassy,

with one third of the coverage on the Iranian government, had been rejected by the American ambassador, William H. Sullivan, who felt he had an abundance of good intelligence through his direct access to the Shah and because "SAVAK is in our palm." The CIA had no paid agent near the Shah. Such measures were apparently considered too risky. The CIA had picked the wrong political opposition groups on which to gather intelligence. It had agents in the moderate middle-class opposition national front, but had failed to understand how little strength the moderates had. The question that should have been asked —How strong are the moderates?—might have led the station to the clergy, the truly powerful opposition.

- There was lots of internal communication within the CIA or within the NSA or within the military intelligence agencies, but, for instance, little between the CIA and the NSA.
- No method existed to ponder alternative explanations of the data. Analysts were not forced to marshal evidence that supported alternatives; there was no peer review of any significance; there was no system for challenging the assumptions.
- The station personnel seemed to assume that in modern times a religious opposition could not mobilize into a political opposition. The CIA and the embassy did not realize or consider the possibility that Iranian nationalism could be directed against the United States, though that conclusion could have been easily learned from the clerics, who thought the Shah was a 100 percent made-in-the-U.S.A. tool directed by Washington and the CIA.
- Circularity was the most common feature of the analysis; it started with the fact that the Shah had the security and military forces, and went on to assume that he would use them if necessary. Because the Shah was not using force, the analysis continued, the opposition then was obviously no threat. This was a circle that couldn't be broken into. The Shah's failure to act was taken as proof that things were okay. The unasked question was, What inhibitions on the Shah keep him from using force to stay in power? Part of the problem was that the CIA had failed to learn that the Shah had cancer and was taking medication which probably contributed to his indecisiveness.
- Words and phrases were used in the reports that meant different things to different people. The phrase "the Shah will take decisive action" meant to many that he would use force to put down any popular uprising, but to others that he would reform and moderate his despotic rule.
- A CIA paper of August 1978 said, "Iran is not in a revolutionary or even a prerevolutionary situation." And a November 22, 1978, paper

concluded specifically that the Shah was "not paralyzed with indecision" and was generally "in accurate touch with reality." A National Intelligence Estimate that year was never completed as the situation in Iran fell apart, but on an early draft Turner's only comment was: "What would happen if Russia invaded Iran?"

Iran proved one of Casey's long-held views: intelligence could not sit idle; every effort had to be made to get the policy-makers to act.

National-security adviser Brzezinski had wanted the Shah to use force to quell the street rebellions; Secretary of State Vance opposed force. The President couldn't decide. And the crux was that the Shah would not act unless he was told by the President of the United States what to do. Carter's hesitation, the Shah's hesitation, was all the revolutionaries had needed to flourish and eventually win.

The analytic side of the CIA needed a shake-up, Casey determined. Some heads needed to be thumped and perhaps even to roll. Casey also had to replace DDO John McMahon. His cautious approach in Operations was not going over at the White House.

In a meeting McMahon had had with Allen and his deputy Bud Nance, a retired Navy rear admiral, Nance had proposed that the CIA launch a covert operation to sabotage a floating drydock off the coast of Ethiopia. Satellite photography showed that the Soviets almost always had one of their destroyers or frigates in the drydock.

"No way," McMahon had said. "We're not going to get involved in that." It would be an act of war.

After the meeting, Allen told Nance, "The rogue elephant is now a chicken."

Casey decided to move McMahon to head the analytic directorate.

Khomeini was a frequent topic of conversation in White House meetings. There was sentiment to remove him if possible. After some discussion with the President, who seemed more than usually attentive, Casey was asked to see if some covert plan might be undertaken to oust Khomeini and replace him with Reza Pahlavi, the young son of the late Shah. When Casey presented this idea at Langley, all the faces turned ashen. Iran was a tar baby. The Pahlavi family was even worse. No one in the DO wanted anything to do with this. The State Department also resisted. But Casey, reading his President, felt that the Administration had to act. The best he could come up with was a covert-action finding that authorized the CIA to conduct exploratory discussions with the various anti-Khomeini exile groups to see which, if any, might be able to mount an opposition. Casey presented the finding to the White House as a necessary first step, and the President signed it.

As Casey perused the flow of current intelligence and the old files—he liked to read old files—his attention kept being drawn to the tiny impoverished agricultural country of El Salvador.

El Salvador—"The Savior," so named by the Spanish conquistadors—had a population of about 4.5 million and the smallest land mass of the Central American republics, just the size and almost the shape of Massachusetts. Nestled on the Pacific coast, seemingly hidden and tucked up on the belly of Central America, it offered no direct ocean access to Cuba, except through the Panama Canal. But there was a growing Communist insurgency in El Salvador. To lose in that backyard—or, as Reagan called it, the "frontyard"—of the U.S. would be unforgivable.

Casey wanted answers. Who was supporting the leftist El Salvadoran insurgency? Where was the military support? The political support? What were the lines of communication? How was all this possible right under the nose of the United States? How might it be stopped?

Reagan was ordering a gradual increase of the number of U.S. military advisers from twenty to just over fifty to assist the Salvadoran government. Press attention was focused on the number, as if it were a thermometer that measured the bellicose temperature of the new Administration. The numbers were the media's trip wire that would sound the alert if the United States was heading for another Vietnam.

For Casey that was not the issue. CIA reports showed that planeloads of weapons had been delivered to the Salvadoran rebels from neighboring Nicaragua. He could see from reports going back to Carter that the evidence was overwhelming. Two days before Carter left office, there had been a draft memo for his signature stating that U.S. aid to Nicaragua should be denied because there was "compelling and conclusive" evidence that Nicaragua was supporting the rebels in El Salvador. The evidence was an intelligence windfall in the diaries and papers of the secretary general of the small El Salvadoran Communist Party, Shafik Handal. They recounted trips to the Soviet Union, Eastern Europe, other Soviet Bloc countries and Cuba; agreements had been reached on ammunition and medical supplies to be shipped through Cuba and Nicaragua. American-made M-16 rifles had been seized from rebels in El Salvador; the serial numbers showed conclusively that the weapons had been lost to the North Vietnamese during the Vietnam War. It was a near-perfect case, painting a paper picture of Communist global conspiracy that conformed with Casey's predisposition. The hands of the Soviet Union, Cuba, North Vietnam, Eastern Europe and Nicaragua were all involved in directing a supply route aimed at El Salvador. The case was almost as tight as a drum.

Carter had not signed the memo, and the issue had been left for Reagan. In its last year, the Carter Administration had fought hard and won congressional approval for $75 million in aid to Nicaragua; but Congress had required that before the aid could be forwarded the President must certify that Nicaragua was not supporting insurgencies anywhere in Central America, and Carter had been on the brink of pulling the plug on the U.S. assistance.

The real issue in Central America turned on Nicaragua and its eighteen-month-old Marxist government. The Nicaraguan leaders were members of the Sandinista party, named for a martyred guerrilla leader, Augusto Sandino, killed in 1934 by the first Somoza family ruler. Nicaragua, with seven times the land of El Salvador, was strategically located and had large coastlines on both the Caribbean to the east and the Pacific to the west.

Casey was intrigued to find that within six months of the Sandinista takeover, President Carter had signed a top-secret finding authorizing the CIA to provide political support to opponents of the Sandinistas—money and backing to encourage and embolden the political opposition, newsprint and funds to keep the newspaper *La Prensa* alive. Designed to work against one-party rule, the operation was a standard political-action program to boost the democratic alternative to the Sandinistas—to develop alternatives to parties and people thought to be close to the Soviet Union and its line.

This covert action was intended to build ties for the agency to the political center, to keep an opposition alive and insure that the agency would have contacts and friends among new leaders or a new government. Several hundred thousand dollars had been spent covertly, but for Casey its importance was more symbolic, demonstrating that the previous administration had at least seen the danger from the Sandinistas. A stand had been quietly taken against them, and the nonleftists knew that the United States was on their side.

Casey was discovering that the CIA had virtually no good intelligence penetrations or human sources among the Sandinistas. Right-wing dictator Anastasio Somoza's intelligence service had had such penetrations, but when he fled the country the intelligence files had been left behind and had fallen into the Sandinistas' hands. The Sandinistas then eliminated the Somoza "collaborators," who were the CIA's main sources.

The situation reminded Casey of the CIA's reliance on SAVAK in Iran. Indeed, he was discovering that throughout the Third World the CIA was feeding too much off in-country intelligence services or people identified with ruling interests. He wanted "unilateral" human assets—sources paid and controlled exclusively by the CIA, people less subject to the whims and fortunes of those in power, especially in unstable regions of Latin America and Africa.

The intelligence showed that Cuba had deeply penetrated the Nicaraguan government. About five hundred Cubans were well entrenched in the Nicaraguan military, intelligence service and key communications facilities. The Palestine Liberation Organization was active in the country, and its chairman, Yasir Arafat, had visited Nicaragua. In addition, Casey found that the whole Communist world had an active presence there—the Soviets, the North Koreans and the Eastern Bloc countries.

Nicaragua had become a safety zone for the El Salvador rebels—a place to do all the things that cannot normally be done in the middle of a guerrilla conflict: rest troops, find sanctuary, move in and out of the fighting.

Two months after their victory, the Sandinista leadership had met in secret for a three-day marathon session to outline their goals. An internal report, seventeen pages in translation, became known as "the 72-Hour Document." It was filled with references to "class struggle," "vanguard party," "traitorous bourgeoisie" and "revolutionary internationalism." The Sandinista fight was against "American imperialism, the rabid enemy of all peoples who are struggling to achieve their definitive liberation."

It contained a ringing declaration that the Sandinistas meant to assist "national liberation" movements in Central America.

Casey believed they had the means, the philosophy and the faith to try.

In Managua, the capital of Nicaragua, U.S. Ambassador Lawrence Pezzullo saw the Sandinista problem as at least controllable, perhaps even solvable through diplomacy. Pezzullo, a fifty-five-year-old career diplomat, considered the Sandinistas a bunch of kids not qualified to run the corner grocery store. And in fact most of the Sandinista leaders had been teenagers when they joined the fight against Somoza. Gutsy and tough, they had been handed a victory they did not expect against Somoza, and thrown into power without a blueprint to govern. Pezzullo, a Latin America specialist, recognized that much of the Latin America intelligentsia leaned toward Marxism. But these people could generally be dealt with; it was important for a diplomat not to take their intellectual pretensions too seriously. At times, he knew, the United States had to be forgiven its rhetoric, especially what was flowing from the mouth of the new Secretary of State. Pezzullo saw the Sandinistas as a practical problem, which in diplomatic terms, Pezzullo's terms, meant carrot and stick. He had pushed hard for the $75 million in U.S. aid in 1980. It had given him the carrot. He kept a close watch on the CIA reporting. There was no doubt the Sandinistas were, as he put it, ''pollinating''—helping other rebellions, such as the one in El Salvador. He had raised this directly with the Sandinista leadership in 1980. Jaime Wheelock, the Nicaraguan Minister of Agricultural Development and a member of the ruling group, had told Pezzullo, ''It's none of your business.''

''Look, to be perfectly frank,'' Pezzullo had responded, unsheathing the stick, ''I've spent ten months fighting for this goddamn money [the $75 million], and if that's your attitude I'll tell you to fuck off.''

Wheelock had argued that Nicaragua had a right to its own foreign policy, and that American aid should not be used as blackmail.

Pezzullo considered Wheelock the best-educated and wisest leader in the Sandinista leadership, though he had less power than the others. Still he would carry back Pezzullo's message. In Pezzullo's view, he was the most housebroken.

''You have a sovereign right to do what you want,'' Pezzullo said, ''and we have a sovereign right to do what we want, which is to do nothing and give you no money.''

Pezzullo felt that the CIA station was arguing, both to him and back to Langley, that if something looks like a duck and walks like a duck it is a duck. Therefore if a Sandinista is a Communist he or she must be controlled by Cuba and Moscow. The initial intelligence in 1980 on the Sandinista revolutionary exploits over the border had been spotty—third-hand sources not clearly identified, no pictures, no documents. After Reagan's election victory, when the telltale papers of the Salvadoran Communist leader Handal came into CIA hands, Pezzullo had gone straight to Tomás Borge, the powerful Minister of the Interior, and asked who was helping the Salvadoran rebels.

''You know, Pezzullo,'' Borge replied, ''you're making too much of nothing. Those are friends.''

''Friends my ass!'' Pezzullo had shouted. And thus began ten grueling conversations and meetings in which Pezzullo tried first to get the Sandinistas to acknowledge that they were involved as a government in supporting the Salvadoran insurgency, and then to get them to see the consequences of that action. To the new Reagan Administration their involvement would be a mortal sin, an alignment that would put the Sandinistas irrevocably in the Russian-Cuban camp.

In mid-February, Secretary of State Haig called Pezzullo to Washington for consultation. The remaining $15 million in aid to Nicaragua had been suspended but not terminated. Pezzullo felt that it should be kept that way. It was their only financial leverage, and he believed that his ranting and raving at least had the Sandinistas' attention.

When he arrived in Washington, Pezzullo read a secret option paper that had been prepared for Haig. There were three options, and all called for permanently terminating the assistance. Pezzullo told Haig that the options were for all practical purposes the same. There had to be another one. Pezzullo called it "a zero option," meaning there would be no change. This was to maximize the diplomatic pressure, to keep it ferocious. There were already some reliable signs that the arms flow was drying up. After a long discussion, Haig said, "I'll buy the zero option."

The Secretary took the ambassador to the White House, where Pezzullo argued to Reagan that it was still possible to deal with the Sandinistas, that diplomacy was working. He was encouraged when the President suggested that overinvolvement by the United States could compound the problem. Reagan quoted an unidentified Mexican friend: "Don't make the mistake of Americanizing the Central American problem."

Later, Pezzullo told Haig that they shouldn't kid themselves about some fundamental facts: The Sandinistas felt very close to the Salvadoran rebels and that was not going to change. The Sandinista revolutionary kinship was not going to be sold out for $15 million. But the United States might alter some behavior, work against the arms support to the rebels. Haig said he understood.

"Or you're going to have to spend a helluva lot of energy to get rid of these guys," Pezzullo added, alluding to the unspoken alternative—a covert paramilitary operation to attempt an overthrow. "And to do that you're going to have to mount something big. They're tough kids—you'd have to mount one hell of an operation to get them out of there, and you know I don't see it happening and I don't think we can do it." Pezzullo added that the new Administration, with its conservative, anti-Communist credentials, could have an effect if the Sandinistas could be convinced that the United States was serious and not going to bend.

"Oh no, we can handle that," Haig replied.

• • •

Haig, trained by Kissinger and Nixon, knew how to play for keeps. As a young Army officer he had watched America fumble in Korea and then in Vietnam, failures of resolve in his view. The advice or the intelligence may have been bad, but the real problem had been a collapse of will. Now he was the briefing officer for a new President unschooled in foreign affairs. The issues had to be forced on the President.

Haig was looking beyond Nicaragua. He was arguing passionately that something should be done to choke off the export of arms from Cuba. He wanted a blockade. "Go to the source," he pleaded in White House meetings. Lay down a "marker."

"This is one you can win," he told the President.

Casey was opposed, as was everyone else at the top of the Administration. Meese, Baker and Deaver were concerned that Haig would generate war fever and scare the public into believing Reagan was going to get the United States involved militarily in Central America. They wanted to keep the President's eye on the domestic ball—economic reform and the promised tax reform. A foreign crisis or a military confrontation, especially with Cuba, with all the overtones of the Cuban Missile Crisis blockade of 1962, would upset the domestic agenda.

It was time for a middle course. Casey favored something between doing nothing and a military action like a naval blockade of Cuba. Covert action was designed for just this purpose—slow, steady, purposeful, secret. He had a finding drafted. It was not targeted on the source of the trouble, Cuba, or the intermediary, Nicaragua, but on the country that was threatened, El Salvador. The finding called for propaganda and political support—legitimacy and financial backing to moderate Christian Democrats and military officers in El Salvador.

On March 4, the President signed the top-secret finding.

One beneficiary of the CIA assistance was a fifty-five-year-old civil engineer who had been educated in the United States, at Notre Dame University—José Napoleón Duarte. He was listed in the files as a CIA asset with a coded cryptonym. CIA assets run from "casual informants," who might not know they are giving information to the CIA, to the full-blown "controlled assets," who are paid and directed by the CIA. There is a broad gap in between, which was where Duarte fit. He had been a good source of intelligence over many years, but he was a man of independence who was in no sense controlled and may not have known he was giving information to the CIA. Casey preferred it that way. A strong leader was not going to be moved about the chessboard by the CIA. It was not realistic. Currently, Duarte headed the American-backed civilian-military junta that governed El Salvador.

• • •

Back at Langley, Admiral Bobby Inman was installed in the deputy's large seventh-floor office adjoining the DCI's. Both offices overlook the lush Virginia countryside. All that is visible is treetops, giving the impression that the CIA is secluded in the middle of a giant forest.

Tuesday morning, March 10, Inman's overriding concern was a *New York Times* front-page headline: "Intelligence Groups Seek Power to Gain Data on U.S. Citizens."

The story reported a proposed new executive order that would lift some of the restrictions on CIA spying and counterespionage in the United States. Someone had got his hands on a sixteen-page proposed executive-order revision that had been drafted at the CIA and that Inman had seen just the day before. He had regarded the draft as a disaster, conceived in the fear that somehow the CIA didn't have enough power.

During the first days of the new Administration, Casey had put the CIA legal staff to work on a new executive order. It was this first draft that had proposed repealing the restrictions on the CIA which had been put in place by Ford and Carter. The draft cut the Justice Department out of its role in reviewing covert operations; it also, by implication, would have given the CIA the authority to conduct covert operations in the United States; and the ban on CIA electronic surveillance and surreptitious entries within the U.S. would have been lifted. Inman knew immediately that it was not going to be easy to put this back into the bottle. Civil-liberties activists were gearing for an assault, and that would give the Administration hard-liners more reasons to hold their ground.

Inman had seen stacks and stacks of paper pile up on Casey's desk in the adjoining office. Now, to his distress, he found that Casey had initialed the draft executive order, meaning that he had seen it and approved. Inman suspected that Casey had not read it or at least not thought it through. The Director had voiced concern that the old executive orders used disparaging adjectives such as "clandestine" and "covert" to describe agency activity. He had wanted positive words. Inman decided to act as if the draft had gone too far the other way. He knew that if anything like this was ever approved, he would have to resign.

Only a dramatic, public position from the CIA could strangle the draft proposal in its crib. Casey was in the Far East, and Inman was acting DCI, and so, without consulting anyone he invited the press to Langley headquarters for a rare on-the-record press conference.

Appearing in uniform, Inman labeled the document a "first draft" that had no real standing other than some ideas and a first-blush attempt. "To the best of my knowledge," he said, "there is no intent to proceed anywhere down that line."

At the White House, national-security adviser Allen was furious. But Meese, to whom Allen reported, more or less agreed with Inman. He said the Administration was not going to put the CIA into the business of domestic spying. Inman concluded that Meese was the more important ally.

When Casey returned, he chided Inman for not calling him about the press conference. He thought Inman was grandstanding to press-generated worries that the CIA was going to spy on Americans. But, he added, he had no desire to do any such thing. There was not enough spying on foreigners.

On March 17 Casey delivered a St. Patrick's Day speech in New York on Irishmen, God, passion and patriotism. In it he declared, "Some things are right and some things are wrong, eternally right and eternally wrong."

John Bross, who was still helping Casey, realized that he meant it. There is a moment when a man speaks his mind, and a moment when he speaks his heart, and a rarer moment when he speaks both. Bross sensed that this was Casey's. The tough, cold, even hard Irishman was sure he knew right from wrong.

Several days later, Casey invited Pezzullo, who was again in Washington, to his office to talk about the Sandinistas. Pezzullo had just been told that the U.S. aid to the Sandinistas was going to be cut off entirely, and he was unhappy. He had argued unsuccessfully, in this round at the State Department, that the United States was giving away its cards and that closing the negotiating door could be disastrous. But Casey wanted his assessment. No one knew the Sandinistas or Latin America better.

When Pezzullo arrived at CIA headquarters, he was greeted by John McMahon, still the DDO, Nestor D. Sanchez, a senior Latin America expert and a diplomat in the U.S. Embassy in Managua who was the CIA station chief under Pezzullo.

Look, Sanchez warned Pezzullo, Director Casey rarely spends more than fifteen minutes in these briefings, so state your case simply. He gets impatient, restless. If you go longer, he's likely to nod off.

Can you do business with the Sandinistas? Casey asked. What are they like?

Yes, they respond to our pressure, Pezzullo said, but they are slippery.

The Sandinista leadership is unstable; lots of internal intrigue can be exploited.

If you were Castro, whom would you support in the ruling group?

The Ortega brothers, Pezzullo replied, referring to Daniel Ortega and his brother, Humberto Ortega, the Defense Minister. The Cubans were probably banking on Borge, a corrupt and unstable man, in Pezzullo's view. Castro is wired in, and whatever he has going won't come unstuck, Pezzullo added. Cubans are all over the place and they are pains in the ass, but they are clumsy. Borge had recently complained to Pezzullo about the Cubans and had made jokes about them. Some member of the Soviet Politburo had come through Managua, and Borge had protested angrily to him about being ordered about like some party hack.

What do the Sandinistas want? Casey asked.

For one, they wanted a relationship with the United States. Proof was what had happened to the arms flow into El Salvador.

"That thing was cut off, wasn't it?" Casey asked.

Precisely, Pezzullo said. Nothing had come down the Nicaraguan pipeline since the major airfield they used was closed. The planes had been decommissioned, the ambassador explained, and the main network of Costa Rican pilots disbanded.

McMahon, Sanchez and the station chief agreed. There were several defectors who supported this, and a Costa Rican pilot who had crashed had confirmed a great deal about the supply network. The Cuban coordinator of the Salvadoran network had left. The only qualification was that one of the radio networks seemed still to be operating, and there was always the possibility that some avenue created elsewhere had gone undetected.

That caveat annoyed Pezzullo. He argued that they could deal only with what they knew. And the CIA, in fact all the reporting, showed nothing moving by land, air or sea.

Everyone, including Casey, agreed with that.

Yet, Pezzullo said, I don't want to kid you. The Sandinistas will always have their hearts and sympathies with the Salvadoran rebels. They will consort with them, provide safe haven, take care of the sick, allow them to transit Nicaragua to Cuba and back the other way. But on the arms flow, if we continue to show the cost, we may stay their hand.

But, Casey said, the country is becoming a nest of Soviets, Cubans, et cetera. That was his worry.

We should keep cool, Pezzullo argued, make our case and not be driven by rhetoric, either ours or theirs.

How strong is the Sandinistas' control? Casey inquired.

It is eroding, Pezzullo said, adding carefully that the erosion was *not* in the revolution's control, but rather with some of the leaders, their respectability, their popularity. "You'd be terribly mistaken if you think that the revolution is unpopular—the revolution is very popular and these fellows are cloaking themselves in the revolution. And the more you attack the revolution, the more you strengthen them." The Somoza era was one of humiliation, and criticism of the revolution—particularly by the United States—is interpreted as support for the past, for Somoza. So the Sandinistas want to defend against any counterrevolution. They are paranoid. They are soldiers; they have been outgunned for years, so they like tanks and artillery. It makes them feel secure. They want to concentrate power. The Cubans have convinced them that that is the way to go, the way to preserve the revolution.

"Should we knock these guys over?" Casey asked. Would Pezzullo advocate covert action to overthrow the Sandinistas?

If you go that route, Pezzullo said, repeating what he had told Haig, you'll have to put in more than you might think. The Sandinistas are the best fighters in Central America.

After nearly an hour, Casey indicated that he had heard enough.

Pezzullo left with the operations people. McMahon expressed his pleasure; he was glad that Casey had been so interested. McMahon had no heart for any kind of a covert operation. Some of Pezzullo's arguments were among those he had been making.

Pezzullo thought Casey had been a terrific listener, quite reasonable. But he knew that raw intelligence information could build a false case, weighty as it might seem on paper. Casey was obviously concerned about the Cubans in Nicaragua, and this naturally meant that the CIA, the NSA and the military intelligence services had been formally instructed, or "tasked," to gather as much intelligence on the matter as possible. Intelligence tasking often led analysts to paint the worst case. The 500 Cubans looked huge. After Iran, no one wanted to miss the next disaster. Yet the numbers didn't address the question of effectiveness. In Pezzullo's opinion, the Cuban presence was deeply undercut by the attitude of the Nicaraguan leaders; Borge had even laughed. But laughter was not an intelligence topic of normal interest, though Pezzullo felt at times that it should be.

Pezzullo returned to Managua, and the suspension of the U.S. aid was announced by the State Department in Washington. Though State applauded the cut in the arms flow to El Salvador and said there was "no hard evidence of arms movements through Nicaragua during the past few weeks," the suspension of aid triggered a barrage of anti-U.S. hostility.

The Sandinistas' newspaper called the decision "Yankee economic aggression" and their television said, "The final objective of the warmongers is to finish off popular power in our nation."

Pezzullo was sure the Administration had taken away all its usable influence, almost nullifying his reason for being. The ambassador had no hand now.

Two months and ten days into his presidency, Reagan was shot by John W. Hinckley, Jr. The bullet, lodged about an inch away from his heart, was removed during surgery. "Honey, I forgot to duck," he told Nancy, and to his doctors he quipped, "Please tell me you're Republicans." His display of courage and optimism won universal praise. When Reagan left the hospital on April 11, after a two-week stay, the cameras were allowed in close to record the almost miraculous recovery of this seventy-year-old President. Though slightly thinner in the face, he emerged cheerful, wearing a red cardigan sweater. He and Nancy had an arm around each other, their other arms high in the air, just as on that night nine months earlier, on a raised platform, when Reagan had accepted the Republican presidential nomination. The famous smile was intact, as was the presidency.

Reagan's closest advisers soon learned it was an act. The next morning the President limped from his bedroom to an adjoining room in the upstairs residence. He emerged slowly, walking with the hesitant steps of an old man. He was pale and disoriented. Those who observed were frightened. Reagan hobbled to a seat in the Yellow Oval Room, started to sit down and fell the rest of the way, collapsing into his chair.

He spoke a few words in a raspy whisper and then had to stop to catch his breath. He looked lost. The pause wasn't enough, and his hands reached for an inhalator, a large masklike breathing device sitting next to his chair. As he sucked in oxygen, the room was filled with a wheezing sound.

Reagan could concentrate for only a few minutes at a time, then he faded mentally and physically, his wounded lung dependent on the inhalator. During the following days, he was able to work or remain attentive only an hour or so a day.

Meese, Baker, Deaver and the few others who were granted access to the President were gravely concerned. This was supposed to be the beginning of the Reagan presidency, but at moments it seemed the end of Reagan, the Reagan they knew. At times he was overcome with pain, he seemed in constant discomfort. His hearty, reassuring voice sounded permanently injured, his words gravelly and uncertain. His aides began to consider the possibility that his was going to be a crippled presidency. That it would, at its very beginning, devolve into something similar to Woodrow Wilson's at the end, a caretaker presidency, and they reduced —or elevated—to a team of Mrs. Wilsons.

All the senior aides were intent on protecting this terrible secret and their own uncertainty, at least until the prognosis was clearer. Those, like Casey, with intelligence or law enforcement responsibility were reminded of the vulnerability of the presidency, the necessity to take every extra measure of security to protect the country and its institutions. The precariousness of the world situation seemed clear enough. These men sensed that more than the President had been wounded.

On the day of the shooting, March 30, 1981, many things had gone haywire, exposing weaknesses in both people and systems. Asked on live television, "Who's running the government right now?," spokesman Larry Speakes had flubbed, "I cannot answer that question at this time." Haig, watching this shaky performance in the Situation Room, had marched before the cameras and misread the Constitution, placing himself after the Vice-President, who was not in Washington, in the chain of presidential succession: "As of now, I am in control here, in the White House."

At the hospital, the President's military aide, the emergency-war-orders officer, who carried the codes and orders that might be used by a President to launch nuclear weapons, had entered into a losing battle with the FBI. Seizing Reagan's possessions and clothes as possible evidence, the FBI had carried off the President's secret personal code card, which he kept in his wallet. The card provides a code that can be used to authenticate nuclear-strike orders in an emergency, should the President have to use unsecure voice communication to the military. Officials insisted there was no loss of control over U.S. nuclear forces, but the confusion pointed to a weakness in fail-safe management of nuclear weapons.

Now the President's condition heightened a feeling of executive disorientation. Slowly Reagan's voice returned, and he had periods that suggested he was on the road back. Ten days of rest in the White House residence were helping, and on April 21 he spoke on a radio talk show to lobby for his spending- and tax-cut plans. The next day he granted an interview to the senior wire-service reporters and seemed fine. But he had no endurance, and his aides still worried.

On Saturday, April 25, the Reagans went for a weekend to Camp David in Maryland. The spring days at the mountain retreat seemed to perform a miracle. When the President returned to Washington, he had snapped back and the crisis abated. But everyone who had seen or knew was on edge.

The Reagan presidency, from the inside, would never be the same. That sense of peril, that anyone or anything might strike—terrorists, a quick move from the Soviets, other adversaries—became a permanent, ingrained maxim of Administration policy.

Nowhere was this more true, or more deeply felt, than in the office of the DCI.

Casey immediately realized that an unanticipated part of his job was protecting the President. Whenever an intelligence report was received about some plot against Reagan—however bizarre or improbable—Casey followed up. The operations people and the analysts often responded that such reports were not to be taken seriously and generally amounted to nothing more than two guys in a bar in Tanzania saying they would like to shoot Reagan.

"I want a team on it," Casey ordered after each report.

Casey had a complete check done in CIA files on John Hinckley. Aware that, nearly twenty years after the Kennedy assassination, questions lingered about the connections between Lee Harvey Oswald and the KGB, Casey wanted to make sure this time. But there was nothing. He rechecked, he did everything except go down to records himself. But the assassination attempt made Casey more concerned with the work being done on the special estimate on the Soviets and terrorism. He wanted to insure that the CIA inquiry into that left no stone unturned.

Casey had been impressed by a cover story in *The New York Times Magazine* on March 1, "Terrorism: Tracing the International Network," by Claire Sterling. Adapted from *The Terror Network,* the book that had so impressed Haig, it began with a quote from Haig's headline-making assertion of Soviet involvement in international terrorism.

Sterling noted ruefully that even CIA experts were telling journalists that Haig's charge was "nothing more than an old cold warrior's refrain" and that there was no hard evidence. Casey was struck by Sterling's conclusion: "There is massive proof that the Soviet Union and its surrogates, over the last decade, have provided the weapons, training and sanctuary for a worldwide terror network aimed at the destabilization of Western democratic society." She posited a "Guerrilla International" as Cubans, KGB instructors, Palestinians and Red Brigades intertwined in their conspiracies, holding conventions and meetings at various terrorist training camps.

Casey had marked up his copy of the article and carried it to the office. He asked John Bross to get on the subject. He said it looked as though Sterling sure had the names, the dates and the locations of those who planned and carried out murders and bombings. Her three case studies were Turkish terrorists, the IRA in Northern Ireland and the Italian Red Brigade. Direct KGB connections were cited in each.

Her article suggests that the press is out ahead of the CIA, Casey said. He wanted the experts in the building to provide an explanation. The main analysts and operations people were brought together.

Papers flew around the room as Langley's experts underlined portions of the nine-page piece, trying to correlate what was in the CIA files and penetrate the Sterling method. Sterling had written that "a kind of post-graduate school in international terrorism emerged" in South Yemen. Foreign guests to the campus supposedly included members of various terrorist groups including the Red Brigades. Because South Yemen was "a Soviet satellite state tightly controlled by the KGB," the implication was obvious: Red Brigades were Soviet surrogates.

In all the CIA files, the staff could find only one instance, in one report, of a member of the Red Brigades having visited a camp in South Yemen. But the tone and sweep of Sterling's article asserted that somehow the Red Brigades had "links" to the KGB. When? Where? How? In itself, the visit of one Red Brigade member was suggestive, but there was nothing more. The result, for the purposes of serious intelligence conclusions, was zero, no more significant than two gangsters passing each other on the street or being at the same bar. The questions remained: What did they do? Say? Or, more importantly, plan?

The covert operators argued that Sterling's method was preposterous. Her verdict followed from flawed reasoning—a kind of McCarthyist "linkmanship." In her three case studies, Turkey, Northern Ireland and Italy became, by some leap of logic, "target nations" of the Soviets. In each section, the KGB was mentioned once.

Meanwhile, the national-intelligence officer for the Soviet Union—the senior Soviet analytic post in the U.S. intelligence agencies—had finished sifting the available intelligence for the special estimate on the Soviet involvement in terrorism. His draft took a strong anti-Sterling line. Casey was appalled. It pretty much cleared the Soviets of involvement in terrorism, saying there was little evidence that they encouraged it.

"Read Claire Sterling's book," Casey said, "and forget this mush."

He added tartly, "I paid $13.95 for this and it told me more than you bastards whom I pay $50,000 a year." The Soviet hand, he said, was not going to show directly with the kind of evidence they could take to a court of law. Based on Soviet statements of intent, a willingness to work with terrorists and a realization that terrorism befuddled the West, it would be logical for the Soviets to promote it, Casey felt. It is "bullshit," he said, to think that proof would be marched in on a platter. "You have to form a judgment."

Inman concurred. He thought the agency's draft was way out of line. "This reads like a brief for the defense," he said.

Casey also got a hot letter from DIA chief General Tighe complaining about the draft. Tighe believed, almost as an article of faith, that the Soviets were involved in terrorism even if it couldn't be proved. The Soviets loudly claimed they were not. To Tighe that was reason enough to conclude the opposite. Second, Tighe said, there is a serious counterintelligence problem: why believe the sources who said the Soviets were not involved? Didn't these sources have reason to distance themselves from the Soviets?

Casey liked Tighe's hard edge. This was not a court of law, and there was no reason to presume the Soviets innocent. Casey asked the General to have the DIA prepare its own draft. Tighe, pleased with the opportunity, put a hard-line DIA analyst on the case. Predictably, a draft that went to the other extreme soon emerged from the DIA.

Casey had a standoff, two drafts that contradicted each other—the CIA draft that found the Soviets largely uninvolved, the DIA that found them guilty.

Several weeks later, Casey received a memo from Lincoln Gordon, a former president of Johns Hopkins University, who was one of three members of a senior review panel at the CIA charged with bringing non-intelligence professional and academic review to the formal estimates.

The CIA draft, Gordon wrote, had a startlingly narrow definition of terrorism, dealing only with the "pure" terrorists like the Baader-Meinhof Gang in Germany, the Red Brigade in Italy, the Red Army faction in Japan. These groups were interested in violence for the sake of violence; they were nihilists. An attempt to define terrorism by its motivation was not enough, he said. In a practical sense, terrorism had to be defined by acts. A bomb going off in a Paris bistro was an intelligence problem whether it was carried out by nihilists or was part of some internal struggle among factions of the Palestine Liberation Organization, whether it was carried out for propaganda purposes or for political objectives. On the other hand, Gordon said, the DIA draft held that any violent action against constituted authority was a form of terrorism. That would make George Washington and Robert E. Lee terrorists.

Casey told Gordon to undertake his own draft of the Soviet-terrorism estimate. Gordon gathered all the raw intelligence and sifted through it. The bulk came from the NSA, including intercepts of communications on open, nonsecure radio links or telephone lines, and some that came from broken codes. Information from coded messages was designated code word UMBRA and was among the most sensitive. Technical intelligence, including satellite photographs, was not very much help. Moreover, Gordon found that the human intelligence was poor and it was difficult to assess the reliability of informants, many of whom had been paid. He developed a rule: unless a second source, and preferably a third, confirmed something, it was not given any credence. There were many cases where one informant or source said something that had no backup.

On May 13, Pope John Paul II was shot and wounded in St. Peter's Square, Rome. Casey, a Catholic, was revolted that anyone would try to take the Holy Father's life. Since 1978, when Cardinal Karol Wojtyla of Poland had been elected Pope, no one had emerged more as a symbol of righteous anti-Communism than this Pontiff from behind the Iron Curtain. John Paul's spirit, by many accounts, had planted the seed that had led to the formation of the Solidarity trade union in August 1980.

The next morning, May 14, Casey gathered the National Foreign Intelligence Board at its headquarters on F Street in downtown Washington, near the White House. The topic was the pending estimate on the Soviets and terrorism. He wanted an answer. The attempted assassinations of the President and the Pope within six weeks of each other had heightened the awareness of terrorism and the vulnerability of leaders. What was going on? There was no evidence to suggest that the two events were related. Or that the Soviets had a role in either. But something was fishy and he wanted to make sure intelligence was all over the possibilities. Every lead or possible connection was to be followed up, and he was to be informed at once.

Casey wanted to know whether the Soviets were up to something. If so, the policy-makers at a different table, the one in the White House where Casey also sat, would have a bigger problem.

Copies of Lincoln Gordon's new draft, about twenty pages, had been circulated, and Gordon had been invited to give a brief presentation to the board.

Gordon said his draft SNIE, "Soviet Support for International Terrorism," had arrived at something between the CIA and DIA extremes. Part of the problem was the confusion over what constituted terrorism. Clearly, the Soviets supported Third World wars of liberation against entrenched autocratic regimes or others sympathetic to the West. Soviet willingness to provide money for arms, training and other assistance—in other words, to encourage liberation—meant there would be violence and terrorism. Certainly, there would be less terrorism if the Soviet superpower did not export revolution abroad. But, he said, the intelligence provided no evidence that the Soviets were playing a mighty Wurlitzer organ of terrorism. There were some cases in which they had actually discouraged terrorism. The U. S. ambassador to Nepal had been warned by the Russians of a kidnap plot by four Arabs. The Bulgarians had let the West German police arrest a member of the Baader-Meinhof Gang in 1978. At times, the Soviets seemed to have determined that thwarting terrorism furthered their objectives, and at other times that terrorism promoted them. Their assistance, particularly through their satellites East Germany and Bulgaria, also clearly contributed, at least indirectly, to more terrorism because these countries aided some extreme groups such as the PLO.

Overall, however, Gordon said, the Soviets were not using terrorism as a primary tool to destabilize the Third World and the Western nations. The clear implication, Gordon felt, was a strong refutation of Haig's public charge and Sterling's thesis. There was just no evidence.

Tighe was not satisfied. He had come armed with a stack of cables which, he said, implicated the Soviets in ten to twelve instances of terrorism that had eluded Gordon, some of them fairly recent.

Gordon felt he was being accused of overlooking evidence. A heated discussion followed as the group tried to sort out the meaning of various scraps of intelligence.

"I don't know if this affects the conclusions," Casey finally said, "but let's send it back." The Gordon draft estimate was not approved, it would not be published, it would go back for rewrite.

Four days later, on May 18, Gordon convened the working group from each agency and painstakingly they went through the references the DIA had dug out. All but two or three had been reviewed earlier and rejected because there had been no second source. After some haggling, some words but no conclusions were altered.

On May 27, the secret estimate was issued to the departments and the White House. It stated that the Soviets were not the hidden hand behind international terrorism. At the end it addressed the implications for intelligence needs in the future—as estimates are intended to do. The conclusion: human intelligence must be strengthened and some way must be found to penetrate the terrorist organizations for timely intelligence on planned operations.

Gordon felt that Casey had been open-minded on the matter and had not let his ideology drive the conclusions. At the same time it was clear that Casey would not have been upset if they had found more Soviet tracks on the terrorist landscape.

But Gordon discovered a final irony. It turned out that a small part of Claire Sterling's information had come from an Italian press story on the Red Brigade. The story was part of an old, small-scale CIA covert propaganda operation. Sterling apparently had picked up some of it in her research. Domestic fallout, or replay of information *in* the United States, called "blowback," is one of the nightmares both for the CIA and for journalists, particularly when it receives wide attention or is disputed.

Gordon found the sequence particularly telling: from CIA propaganda to Sterling's book galleys, to Haig's reading of the galleys, to Haig's press conference, then Haig's comments picked up in the *New York Times* article by Sterling, then finally in Sterling's book. Even though Gordon felt that the CIA had finally sorted through all this to an essentially thoughtful position, that estimate was classified secret. Neither it nor its conclusions was made public. As far as the American public was concerned, the Soviets still stood publicly branded by the Secretary of State as active supporters of terrorism. And the record was never corrected.

Gordon wondered what the Soviets thought of all this. What additional erosion was there in the relationship? What attitude would they have toward other public declarations by the United States? Did the war of words between the two superpowers have much meaning? What price in credibility, if any, had been paid?

6

CASEY LEFT WASHINGTON for a tour of the Middle East CIA stations. He had asked the station chief in Saudi Arabia to arrange for him to attend Catholic mass there on Easter Sunday, and the Saudi intelligence service provided guards. Here was an intelligence service willing to do just about anything, to spread around vast sums of money for intelligence and operations. In Israel, Casey was extremely impressed with the Mossad, which had good human-source intelligence penetrations. Throughout the region he saw a great reliance on human sources. A solid human source was a great advantage, a twenty-four-hour-a-day watch who would provide early warnings. Intelligence services with such sources didn't have to tune in to precisely the right frequency or communications channel at the right moment, or count on the overhead satellite being in the exact spot. A human source could also provide an evaluation of the information.

When he returned to Washington, Casey decided to concentrate on selecting his DDO, the man who would run the human spies. He found something a little too smooth about the people already in the Operations Directorate. Too much HYP—Harvard, Yale, Princeton. The clothes were too fine, perhaps, the manners too refined, the talk, on the other hand, not sufficiently defined. Not enough street. They were certainly good and devoted people, but they were too often elliptical. Not enough fire in the belly.

None seemed to have the broad, worldly experience of Casey's own generation, an understanding of the post–World War II era and business.

Casey had not yet put a name to this description. But Max Hugel, meanwhile, had told him that he wanted more of the action than a Deputy Director for Administration could claim. He had gone so far as to say that someone, whom he did not identify to Casey, had suggested him for DDO. Hugel said he thought he could be of great assistance.

Casey said he would decide soon. He also mentioned the possibility of Hugel to John Bross.

Bross was adamantly opposed. He had been part of the Operations Directorate. Believe me, he told Casey, it's subterranean. No outsider could fully understand the directorate, let alone lead it.

Bross wanted Casey to have Dick Helms's views. Helms agreed to come up. He wanted to provide his opinion personally to Casey. Casey told Helms he just knew that Hugel would be good at this. Hugel had learned Japanese and had run a big business in Japan, penetrating the culture and bringing Japanese typewriters and sewing machines here.

Let him punch his ticket as part of the team first, Helms argued. Deputy Director for Administration was important. Why not leave him there for two years and then promote him to DDO? What was the hurry? Helms reminded Casey that in the past the DDOs either had come from the directorate or, in the case of McMahon, had had thirty years at the CIA. Casey ought to be worried about security, Helms said. Not that Hugel was untrustworthy, but he had no background. Security, silence, was second nature to an operations veteran, ingrained, a first commandment. All those secrets in the hands of a neophyte?

Casey thanked Helms, who left thinking that the Director had seen his overwhelming logic.

On the morning of May 11, Casey told John Bross that he was still seriously considering Hugel for the job. Bross continued to oppose it, but he sensed that this was the one matter on which Casey was not going to listen. To push more would be to challenge Casey's authority. Casey was laying claim to his prerogative.

Later that day, at the meeting with his senior deputies and staff, Casey without prelude, snapping his fingers, waving the issue away, said that Max Hugel was being appointed the new DDO.

There were about fourteen people jammed into the conference room. Normally, there was no way whatsoever to read anyone at one of these open meetings. But this time the silence was stunning; a growling stomach would have been heard. The CIA people had just barely accommodated themselves to Hugel as the DDA.

There was not a word uttered. What was there to say? And Casey had not invited comment. One beat and he moved on to the next subject.

A joke already in circulation was, "What does Hugel say each morning to Casey? '*Boss, Boss—the plane, the plane!*' " Just like the doting, white-suited midget Tatoo in the television show *Fantasy Island* announcing a new batch of visitors to Ricardo Montalban.

After the meeting, word spread throughout Langley: Casey has made a typewriter-and-sewing-machine salesman the DDO.

In his second day on the job, Hugel called together his senior assistants in the DDO. He had written out his main points. He pledged to work for the directorate, to build it, to support it. He told them that they were underpaid and that things should be done to rectify that, reminding them that many of their colleagues had left because they couldn't afford to send their children to expensive colleges.

The experienced hands knew that this was an idle promise. Government pay is set in stone by Congress and little can be done about it, especially by an agency deputy.

Hugel said that people should advance only on merit, and that the younger people should be given a chance. They needed more language training, better human intelligence, more effective counterintelligence.

When he finished, there was no reaction—nothing. Hugel looked around the room. All these people had been trained to conceal their purposes, their feelings. There wasn't a single clue on a single face. Hey, Hugel wondered to himself, have I said something wrong? But these people considered inexpressiveness an art.

Hugel met the challenge with more work. He was given a code name, a secure phone, a car, a driver, and a home safe in which to store secret documents. As he scanned the secret-agent reports and the outlines of some of the operations, it was clear that much of the secret information came from people who were betraying their countries. He was uneasy. Why were these people selling out? Was their information reliable?

Hugel paid a courtesy call on Senator Goldwater. The Senate Intelligence Committee chairman was a key base that needed covering. When Hugel came in, it was obvious that Goldwater didn't know him from beans. Goldwater sat, asked no questions, said almost nothing.

Hugel left feeling ice. There had been no advance preparation by the CIA liaison with the Congress. Hugel's way had not been greased.

On May 15, four days after his appointment, Hugel picked up *The Washington Star,* which carried a regular column by Cord Meyer, who had been with the CIA for twenty-six years. Passionately anti-Communist, pro-CIA, and a friend of John Bross, Meyer, a Yale graduate who had lost an eye in combat during World War II, was the embodiment of the Ivy League Cold Warrior. Class. Tweed. Connections. He had risen to be the No. 2 in the Operations Directorate before leaving the agency in 1977. As a columnist for the *Star* he reflected old-boy thinking and had instant access to its latticework, fed daily by phone calls and lunches of retirees who seemed never to leave town.

Hugel read the headline of Meyer's column in astonishment: "Casey Picks Amateur for Most Sensitive CIA Job."

". . . Casey has rejected the unanimous advice of old intelligence hands," Hugel read of his own appointment as DDO. "This government job was once described by columnist Stewart Alsop with only slight exaggeration as 'the most difficult and dangerous after the president's.'

"Allen Dulles, Richard Helms and William Colby all held this job before subsequently becoming CIA directors but they earned their promotion by many years in intelligence assignments.

"The KGB chiefs in Moscow will find it incredible. . . ."

Meyer noted that the only other case where a CIA director had reached outside for his DDO had been the appointment of Richard Bissell, a brilliant economist who as DDO "became the unfortunate architect of the Bay of Pigs." The Hugel appointment, he wrote, was "a breathtaking gamble for which the country will have to pay heavily if Casey has guessed wrong."

Hugel was deeply hurt. Meyer had not called to hear his side.

The next day Hugel glanced at *The Washington Post*. "Daggers Drawn for New CIA 'Spymaster,' " said the front-page headline. The old boys were coming out into the open. George A. Carver, another CIA veteran from Yale, was quoted: "This is like putting a guy who has never been to sea in as Chief of Naval Operations. . . . It's like putting a guy who is not an M.D. in charge of the cardiovascular unit of a major hospital."

Casey was quoted defending Hugel, saying that the criticism was coming from "a bunch of guys who think you can only understand this business if you've been here 25 years."

The New York Times editorialized against Hugel's appointment, under the sly headline "The Company Mr. Casey Keeps."

Casey and Hugel discussed the matter and agreed that things were going well, not badly. They were challenging the status quo, and the status quo didn't like it. Casey dashed off a letter to the *Times* that was published May 24, praising Hugel's "drive, clarity of mind and executive ability . . . abilities and experience."

Reading the articles at home, where he was beginning a new career as a writer, Stan Turner understood the old-boy attack. It brought back a rush of disagreeable memories. Turner felt kinship with Casey, who was obviously getting the full treatment. As a gesture of support, he wrote a letter to the *Post*, published on May 25:

"Mr. Casey is ultimately responsible for how well the directorate performs. He is entitled to select his own team and should be judged on the results, not the appointment.

"I received similar criticism in 1977 when I made changes and reductions in the Directorate of Operations. These proved to be eminently successful. Let's give Director Casey his chance without the burden of premature criticism."

At the White House, Meese, Baker and Deaver were uneasy about all the attention that was focused on Casey's man Hugel. Sensitive intelligence work was under way, and if Hugel was a fuck-up there could be problems for Reagan. Their protective instincts were running high. They had always been skeptical about the value of Casey's and Hugel's operational work during the presidential campaign. Were clowns running the CIA?

Casey wrote a private letter to the President arguing that Hugel possessed valuable business skills, hinting that Hugel's efforts in organizing special-interest groups, especially ethnic voter groups, were not all that different from covert work.

The Reagan aides decided there was no way, and no good reason, to intervene.

Casey first noticed the cool eyes, though the man was six foot eight.

"Mr. President, we have been on the defensive ideologically," the man said in a booming, confident voice. He continued with a well-crafted paragraph about El Salvador. The junta, backed by the United States, was hard to defend; the human-rights violations were too frequent, too visible, though Duarte was doing his best. The Administration must return to the offensive, and not just with a military program and a diplomatic program. The Reagan Administration must work for free elections in El Salvador, he said. Even though the Special National Intelligence Estimate just issued that month, June, by Director Casey had concluded that there was a military stalemate between the Salvadoran junta and the rebels, and that it would be two years before the junta could gain a clear upper hand, democracy must be the goal.

Casey saw President Reagan perk up, stir in his chair. A real nerve had been struck. It was a simple idea, and certainly far in the future.

"Let's go with that," the President said.

Casey had been impressed with the presentation made by Thomas O. Enders, the Assistant Secretary of State for Latin America. In several months, Enders had taken charge of Administration diplomacy and policy for his region with flair and drive. He had a seasoned understanding of interagency infighting as State, Defense, Casey's CIA and the National Security Council fought for control. By tradition, he chaired the meetings of the normally contentious representatives, which he called the "core group." Some weeks they met daily, even twice a day. Enders knew he needed consensus, and intellectually he was attempting to develop a coherent plan. Casey knew Enders from his own SEC and State Department days. There was no more perfect product of the Eastern seaboard than Enders: parents, Ostrom Enders and Alice Dudley Talcott, of Connecticut; Yale '53, graduating first in his class. When he was appointed assistant secretary, Enders didn't know Spanish, but he was a brilliant linguist and learned it in several months. He had an affected manner and was intellectually impatient, try as he might to conceal it. He was suspect by both left and right; by the left for his role during the Vietnam War in the U.S. Embassy in Cambodia, carrying out the "request-validate-execute procedure" for the heavy bomber attacks; by the right because he had been a Kissinger protégé.

Casey made sure he sat down with Enders later to pick his mind.

"There is no structure for decision-making in the White House," Enders lamented. His boss, Haig, had tried preemptively to take full control and had lost. "But no one won."

Casey took note.

"But I can make the interagency core group work," Enders said.

Casey pledged that the CIA would cooperate—no turf battles from him. But he wondered whether the thinking was large enough. The set of concepts—free elections and democracy—for El Salvador was just a start. The Administration needed a plan for all of Latin America; in fact, one was needed for the whole world.

Enders agreed. The splintering of foreign-policy authority was going to make things difficult. "Al came in with a cry of alarm but no plan."

Casey dipped into the CIA institutional memory some more—the files, briefings. He probed the key CIA people, frequently jotting on small index cards. World history in the last six years had been dominated by one conspicuous trend: the Soviets had won new influence, sometimes predominant influence, in nine countries:

South Vietnam, Cambodia and Laos in Southeast Asia.

Angola, Mozambique and Ethiopia in Africa.

South Yemen and Afghanistan in the Middle East and South Asia.

Nicaragua.

How had this been done? It was clear to Casey that the Soviets, exploiting the aftermath of the U.S. withdrawal from Vietnam, had used surrogates and proxies to stage revolutions and takeovers. Was there a way to do it to the Communists? Not just a piecemeal approach, such as seizing on the Afghanistan invasion to support the rebels there; or acceding to the requests of Saudi Arabia to help covertly in South Yemen, or promoting democracy in El Salvador and creating a firewall against the leftist rebels.

In the same six-year period the Soviets had lost considerable influence in six countries—Bangladesh, Guinea, India, Somalia, Iraq and the Congo. But this was ambiguous as far as Casey was concerned. He was interested in taking one back from the Soviets—a visible, clean victory.

"Where can we get a rollback?" Haig had asked.

"I want to win one," the President had said.

Casey realized that this meant guerrilla warfare. He had reinforced his education in the importance of guerrilla movements five years earlier while researching his book on the American Revolutionary War. Published in 1976, for the Bicentennial, the 344-page book, *Where and How the War Was Fought,* was the result of the Casey method—extensive reading and on-scene inspection. He had immersed himself in the main books on the Revolutionary War. He had sailed through the key volumes of Douglas Southall Freeman's seven-volume *George Washington;* Casey would say that Volumes 3 and 6 were indispensable. A speed reader, he raced through many pages a minute, grasping concepts and point of view, lingering where he wanted, skimming where he lost interest. Friends considered him a book thief who would borrow and rarely remember to return. The books became precarious stacks at Mayknoll. The literature on Revolutionary intelligence operations, deception and political warfare sparked particular attention, including Pennypacker's *General Washington's Spies,* Ford's *A Peculiar Service* and Carl Van Doren's *The Secret History of the American Revolution.*

The real joy in his research had been a string of weekend field trips with Sophia and Bernadette. Casey loved traveling with his wife and daughter. It was a comfortable trio. One Thursday they all took a night flight to Maine and for four days they followed the route of Benedict Arnold along the rivers to Quebec, then along the St. Lawrence to Montreal, and the Richelieu to Lake Champlain. A three-day weekend was spent following General Washington's trail from Valley Forge across the Delaware into New Jersey battle sites. They did Boston, Philadelphia, New York, the Carolinas, Georgia. On a cruise they retraced the route from Annapolis to Yorktown down Chesapeake Bay. Casey had his notes, his books, photocopies of the relevant maps, Boatner's *Landmarks of the American Revolution.* He went to the hilltops, walked the trails, carefully eyed the relics. Sophia and Bernadette followed each step.

"I found the most vivid and immediate sense of being there, actually seeing the tactical and strategic significance along the Arnold trail . . ." he wrote. Each time he wanted to go to the exact spot and unravel the Revolutionary geography as it was then, often hidden under modern cities and pavement.

On the excursions, or as he waded through the books, Casey asked the central question: How and why did the Americans win? How had such a ragtag group been able to defeat the foremost world power, the British? The Revolutionaries, he finally wrote, were victorious because they used "irregular, partisan guerrilla warfare." They were the Vietcong, the rebels in Afghanistan. The spirit, the techniques, the tactics were with the irregulars. You really had to appreciate a native resistance, he said. It was the side to be on. This was, Casey felt, a point of continuity between the eighteenth and twentieth centuries. Now he could apply it. If the native resistance did not come banging on the door of the CIA, as the Afghans had done, then maybe the CIA had to go out and discover it.

To further avoid surprises, Casey began looking for another outsider. He wanted someone to act as an intellectual tripwire to alert him to looming foreign disasters, perhaps someone on the analytic side to mix it up with the CIA insiders. There was just too much wooly thinking. He invited up to his office Dr. Constantine C. Menges, a tall, bespectacled, scholarly-looking forty-one-year-old Hudson Institute conservative who had worked on the Reagan campaign. Menges had a radio announcer's voice and spoke with eternal self-confidence. When Casey questioned him about major foreign-policy problems, Menges presented to him copies of several short op-ed pieces he had written for *The New York Times.* In a 1980 article, Menges stated that events in Iran, Afghanistan and Nicaragua marked "a turning point in the invisible war between radical and moderate forces" for control of oil, the Middle East and Central America. In another, "Democracy for Latins," he called for a strategy to defeat the Soviets in Latin America by promoting democracy and the center; ties and support to right-wing dictatorships alone would not work, he said. In still another, "Mexico: The Iran Next Door," Menges forecast trouble to the south.

Casey glanced at the articles, which seemed to show strategic thinking, relating events taking place in different parts of the world, and as well a willingness to give weight to ideas. Menges had developed a rational calculus about Communist expansion. He brought a two-page paper in which he described how the Communists joined in partnership with others in what he called the "Destabilization Coalition."

Included was a chart for three strategic areas:

POLITICAL-PARAMILITARY WAR AGAINST U.S. INTERESTS IN THREE STRATEGIC ARENAS

Target Countries	*Destabilization Coalition*
LATIN AMERICA	
Colombia	*Cuba*
Venezuela	Regional Communist/guerrilla groups
Central America	USSR
Panama	Palestinian terrorists/Libya
Belize	
*Mexico**	
MIDDLE EAST	
Israel	USSR
Egypt	Pro-Soviet regimes (South Yemen, Syria)
Iran (post-Khomeini)	*Cuba*
Oman	Palestinian guerrillas
North Yemen	Libya
Persian Gulf regimes	
*Saudi Arabia**	
AFRICA	
Zaire	USSR
Morocco	*Cuba*
Sudan	Libya
Namibia	Pro-Soviet regimes (Ethiopia, Angola, Mozambique)
*South Africa**	Regional guerrillas/Communist groups (SWAPO)

*Designates the main strategic target.

These were overall strategic objectives and techniques, but Menges said the Communists had no timetable. They were patient.

Casey later read the articles and asked Menges back for a second meeting, during which he invited him to be candid. Menges said he was worried about the competence of the whole CIA, which, like any bureaucracy, avoided accountability and responsibility. Back in the 1970s he had been a deputy assistant secretary for education and had worked for Frank Carlucci, then the deputy at Health, Education and Welfare. When Carlucci had moved to become deputy CIA director in 1978, Menges had warned him about trouble in Iran. No one had listened. In 1979, before the Sandinista revolution, he had forecast leftist trouble in Nicaragua. Again he had gone to Carlucci and the CIA, where his views were ignored. This was not hindsight. He produced more of his published articles, including one, "Echoes of Cuba in Nicaragua," in June 1979, before the Sandinistas overthrew Somoza. It forecast that the Sandinistas would pose as moderates and use "coalition government" before revealing their true Marxist-Leninist colors.

"Success," the article said, "would create the political base and momentum for beginning revolutionary warfare against Mexico during the early 1980s." Menges told Casey that what disturbed him was not so much the way his ideas had been treated as it was the smug failure of the CIA to anticipate and prevent crisis.

Casey offered Menges the job as his national intelligence officer for Latin America. For that region he would represent the DCI in the interagency meetings, oversee the writing of the National Intelligence Estimates, head a monthly "warning" meeting on potential threats, and recommend the U.S. response.

Menges was reluctant to join the CIA. He said it might taint his academic work.

"Look," Casey said, "you're so concerned about this, and here you were warning the Carter Administration for three years about Iran and Nicaragua, and now I'm asking you to come and serve. . . . What are you waiting for?"

Menges accepted.

Casey was surprised that the agency provided regular background press briefings to reporters heading overseas on assignment. He told Herb Hetu, Turner's public-affairs man who was still at the CIA, to discontinue all such briefings at once. Hetu thought the briefings provided important media contacts and began to protest, "But—"

"I didn't ask for discussion or debate," Casey said. "Do it."

• • •

One evening in early July, CIA general counsel Sporkin received a strange, muffled call at home. The caller finally identified himself as "Max," and requested an urgent meeting "at the place." Sporkin realized it was Hugel, who wanted to talk at headquarters. When the two met within the hour, Hugel said that he needed help. Two former business associates from New York, securities dealers Thomas R. McNell and his brother Samuel F. McNell, were making some accusations that they had secretly taped Hugel giving out insider information on his company Brother International six or seven years before.

On Friday, July 10, Sporkin called the *Post*. Another reporter, Patrick Tyler, and I had received copies of sixteen Hugel tapes the previous month, and we were pursuing a possible story. Sporkin said he wanted to hear the tapes. We said it was premature. Sporkin offered to help, adding that if anyone in the CIA had done anything wrong, he and Casey had to know. Finally, we agreed that Sporkin could come and listen to the tapes if he brought along Hugel, whom we wanted to interview. Sporkin insisted on coming that afternoon. Casey wanted to know now.

Several hours later, more than a dozen people assembled around the table in the board room on the eighth floor of *The Washington Post:* Sporkin; Hugel, with several of his personal attorneys, including Judah Best, a Washington lawyer who had represented Vice-President Spiro Agnew; Benjamin C. Bradlee, executive editor of the *Post;* Tyler; myself; two attorneys for the *Post* who were securities experts; and four other *Post* editors.

Hugel, five foot five, wore a conservative chocolate-brown pinstriped suit, a plain tie and a shirt with small light, subdued dots. His smile was warm.

"I'm here to find out what the hell's going on," Sporkin said, adding that he represented only the CIA and not Hugel personally. He then slouched back in his chair and looked bored.

We tried some general questions. Had Hugel ever provided inside information to the McNells? Had he ever threatened to kill one of the McNells' lawyers? Did he know that money he had loaned one of the McNells had been intended to go into their securities firm, which had been pushing the stock in Hugel's company?

Though his lawyers intermittently protested, they let Hugel answer before any tapes were played. "Untrue, completely one hundred percent untrue" that he knew the loan was going to the securities firm. He denied everything. "The answer is absolutely, unequivocally no—absolutely not. Never." He nervously rubbed his large, chubby hands together. His voice had a sweet quality as he made a plea and began to refer to those in the room by their first names. Yes, he wanted his stock to go up, of course he wanted his stock to go up. "If a guy's taping you on the other side of the phone," he said, looking for understanding across the table, "I don't know how he's wording the question or what he's saying. If you don't know you're being taped"—and he looked up—"you can set everybody up.

"That's an unfair thing," Hugel added.

Sporkin interrupted. "I don't care if I stay here all night, but if you've got the stuff on the tape I must have it. I'm just telling you I'm going to be here until hell freezes over and I want to hear that. I've got to make recommendations.

"Those are very serious charges," Sporkin said. "I mean some of them are. Some of them, I think from my [SEC] background, are just bullshit, quite frankly. But some of them when you're talking about market manipulation, it's a very"—and he thumped the table loudly—"serious charge. And if you've got the proof on that, I've obviously got to see it."

Tyler played a December 13, 1974, tape of a conversation that had taken place after the McNells' lawyer threatened Hugel with a lawsuit. Hugel's voice came through loud and clear: "And then he had the audacity, the nerve, to threaten me with some goddamn cockamamie lawsuit, that I—it's so distasteful to me that I'm ready to throw up. . . . What the fuck kind of shit is that? . . . Let the fuck sue me . . . That's bullshit, Sam, I've been at that cocksucker, I'll put that bastard in jail. . . . I'll kill that bastard."

Tyler clicked off the recorder.

"What's there to comment on?" Hugel said sheepishly. "It is what it is."

"That's your voice? Do you recall the conversation?"

"Yes," he said.

"But you indicated earlier that . . ."

"Obviously my memory failed me," Hugel said stiffly, bravely facing the contradiction. In pain, he said again, "The tape is what it is." And he asked to hear the next tape.

We played a tape in which Hugel told Tom McNell, "Get some pencil and paper, will you? What I'm giving you is strictly confidential stuff, okay?"

It was a long tape, again clear and precise, in which Hugel provided the dollar figures on sales forecasts.

Is that insider information?

"I can't answer that question. I will not answer . . ."

Hugel hesitated. More tapes were played. What about the insider information?

"You know, you take me back into '74, and the only reason I could possibly do it is like any aggressive businessman that's complimenting his company and saying things are happening, but, you know, and you're proud of what you're doing, that's the only possible reason. I'm a very enthusiastic guy, I could . . ."

But if you're proud of what you're doing, you wouldn't want to keep it confidential?

"Well, I said 'confidential,' you know, that's what the tape says. . . . Ah hell, it's a way of . . . Jesus it's . . . Why would the man tape my conversation?" Hugel was almost inconsolable on this point. "Why?" he asked, looking around the room. "What does it, what's the purpose?"

Sporkin, still wearing his hat as the foremost securities enforcement expert in the country, said that the missing element in all this was evidence that Hugel had profited from his disclosures of the information. That was the necessary element to make it a crime, he said.

"I guarantee you," Sporkin said, "that there's none of us sitting at this table that hasn't said something on a phone that if it had been taped we would not be very happy with it." There were nods all around.

Sporkin asked Hugel and his personal attorneys to leave the room. After they left, Sporkin said in almost a whisper, "This is going to be a very difficult decision on my part. . . . You know, I can make an easy decision. There's an easy decision I can make."

"Cut," Bradlee said.

"Yeah," Sporkin said. "Whether it's a correct one I don't know." He wanted to listen to all the tapes in full and make an assessment for Casey.

"It's not our job to help you make your decision, that's the short of it," Bradlee said, but Hugel, of course, would be provided a chance to respond to anything before it went into the paper.

"I don't know whether you have a smoking gun there or not," Sporkin said.

Hugel returned to the room, saying he was postponing a trip abroad as DDO on an important operation.

"This is a very serious matter, my friends," he said. "My personal reputation's at stake. I intend to see this thing through to its very end."

Midafternoon Sunday, July 12, Casey returned from a three-day trip abroad and convened a 4 P.M. meeting at Langley attended by Inman, Sporkin and Bob Gates. The information was still fragmentary, Sporkin told the others, saying that it was not clear whether there were possible violations or stock manipulation.

Inman told Casey that when a problem like this arose there were two overriding considerations. First, there could be no cover-up or appearance of a cover-up. Second, the potential problem had to be isolated. That meant Hugel should go on administrative leave. If there wasn't anything to it, he could then come back. If there was something, he was effectively out the door.

Sporkin said he was opposed to administrative leave. What event in the future would change the situation? Who would decide there was nothing to it? These things could hang fire for months or more.

Casey, too, was reluctant to agree to administrative leave. It might be terribly unfair. These things often came to nothing—headline charges that are investigated and lead nowhere. And in the meantime someone's career and name were muddied. Casey wanted to know what was the worst aspect of the whole matter.

Sporkin said it was the tapes—the language and the calls with advance information.

Casey felt that chief executive officers call their stockbrokers, call them all the time.

It is going to be a problem, Sporkin said, having the DDO quoted on tape saying some pretty rough things. On one tape, for instance, Hugel told his stockbroker, "I'll cut your balls off. . . . I'll get my Korean gang after you and you don't look so good when you're hanging by the balls anyway."

Sporkin decided he had an obligation to be frank with Hugel—in private. "Look, Max," Sporkin said later when the two were alone, "the statute of limitations has run. So no one can prosecute you. But you have to go."

Why? Hugel asked.

"Quit," Sporkin said. "You go to the Hill to testify and they'll eat you alive." The problem, Sporkin explained, was perjury, certainly unintentional. You could go pitch out your categorical denials, but you can't argue with those tape recordings. Congress is not some newspaper where you can say anything, deny anything. "You want only one story to come out after the one on those tapes," Sporkin said. "That's the one on your resignation—then the Hill will leave you alone. You'll be history. That's my advice. You asked for my advice as a lawyer, as a friend. That's it. It's in the interest of the agency and in your interest, so I can say it to both you and the Director."

That evening Hugel invited both Casey and Sporkin over to his house for dinner. Hugel felt a strong personal obligation to Casey for the DDO job in the face of all the internal opposition. He was deeply aware of the trouble his appointment had already caused. Among the three CIA newcomers who were gathered around Hugel's table there was less than a year of CIA experience. Hugel said that the charges were a bloody lie.

In the presence of Casey, Sporkin hovered in a neutral position.

Casey mentioned that Inman had suggested administrative leave for Hugel, an indefinite leave until the matter was cleared up.

"Bill," Hugel said, "there is no way that I came to Washington to get myself clobbered in the face every day." In an office as visible as the DDO, he didn't see how he could win a battle to clear his name and do his job. His hands would be tied. "I can't win that battle as a public servant. The only way I can win it is as a private citizen."

Sporkin said he was sure that the newspaper story would be published soon.

Hugel told Casey, "If the article is detrimental to the agency, to myself, to you, I'm going to resign."

Casey wasn't sure. Administrative leave was not a great solution, but it was looking better than resignation.

"If they come up with an article that's damaging," Hugel said, "I'm not going to hurt the agency. I'm not going to hurt you. And I'm certainly not going to hurt the President. I'll resign."

"Look, Max," Casey said, "it's your shot to call."

The next morning Hugel's lawyer, Judah Best, called the *Post* and said they wanted a second meeting. Best brought sixteen documents from Hugel's business files and a letter saying that they needed additional time to gather more information. A story now would be "reckless," he said.

That afternoon the same group gathered in the fifth-floor news conference room. Hugel seemed subdued and even more nervous. We said we wanted to avoid a repeat of Friday's meeting when he had issued blanket denials about certain actions and then was faced with the contradictions on tape.

Hugel began to protest.

Sporkin said to him, "Listen to his question and if you don't know, why don't you just say you don't know. That's what's not helping you. If you don't know, say you don't know."

We said we planned to run a story the next day and it would include any statement from Hugel.

"I want to make my request," Sporkin said impatiently. "Fairness or whatever it is, I still want to hear those tapes."

More were played. Twice Hugel excused himself to go to the bathroom. He finally asked for the floor.

"I want to apologize for my very quick answers on Friday to your questions," he said, "without having the chance to think through. . . . My responses could have been much better. I had no intention to give deceiving or misleading statements." He was wringing his hands and leaning forward. He said he had never profited from those stock transactions. He might have been a novice; he might have been naive. But he had started a company from almost nothing and left it when it was doing $100 million a year in business. His net worth was $7 million.

Hugel paused. He said that in a 1957 book called *Operation Success* there was a chapter devoted entirely to his success in business with Brother International.* "I was on the front cover of *Coronet* magazine, and we're trying to get a copy and will send it to you . . . So I was proud of what I did and I'm proud of it now."

He listed his qualifications, his fluency in Japanese, his international experience, his ability to deal with foreigners.

"I took this job because I wanted to serve my country. I did it at great financial sacrifice. My whole life and reputation is at stake here," he said. Tears were welling in his eyes. "That it would be most damaging to me and my family . . . Who are perfectly innocent. And should not be treated that way. And it's a *shame,*" he said, raising his voice dramatically, the Hugel of the tapes, "that an individual willing to give up all kinds of potential monetary gain just to come and serve this country, just to try to do that, should be condemned by people of this type on information that goes back well over seven or eight years . . ."

Hugel said it would be "most difficult in the future to get people to come to Washington to accept jobs.

"I'm just giving you gut, heart."

At CIA headquarters, Casey was growing increasingly anxious that he had not heard from Sporkin. He figured he had better advise the chairmen of the congressional intelligence committees. Casey reached Edward P. Boland of the House committee, but was unable to get through to Goldwater.

Later Hugel's attorney issued a three-paragraph statement emphatically denying any wrongdoing, and saying he was "deeply disappointed" that the story was going to be published. Hugel added, "I shall continue

* "Occidentally on Purpose" chapter, pp. 131–42.

to serve my country as long as it requires my services, and long after these rantings from the past have ceased."

Hugel thought it must be about 3 A.M. when he was awakened by Sporkin's call. The story was out, Sporkin said, reading the headline, "CIA Spymaster Is Accused of Improper Stock Practices," and continuing: " 'Max Hugel, who holds one of the most sensitive jobs in the Reagan Administration as chief of the CIA's clandestine service, engaged in a pattern of improper or illegal stock market practices . . .' "

"That's disgusting," Hugel said.

Sporkin read on, outlining the allegations, saying that there were extensive quotes from the tapes.

"Okay," Hugel said. "That's it. Don't read me any more. I'm resigning."

Soon after sunrise, Hugel called Casey. "I'm done," he said emotionally. "I'm doing it. I'm resigning."

Casey said it was unfair—totally unfair.

Hugel, choking up, agreed.

Casey didn't try to change Hugel's mind.

It wasn't until 9:40 A.M. that Casey reached Goldwater to tell him what the Senator already had read in the newspaper. Goldwater was angry. Why was the DCI so late with the news? He had heard a reliable rumor several days earlier that the story was coming.

In the White House, chief of staff James Baker and counsel Fred Fielding were worried. They wanted the damage limited at once. Fielding was pushing hard for an immediate resignation and had made the point directly to Casey. Baker called Casey.

"Max is going to step aside," Casey said.

Baker was surprised and relieved that it had moved so fast. When Baker told the President later that morning, Reagan too was quite surprised, remarking that he was not sure what Hugel had done wrong.

At his home, Hugel read the article for himself. There was his picture on the front page. Jesus, Hugel thought, it was a lousy picture. He had so many better ones.

There were columns of transcripts from the tapes with all his bare language concealed as if it was not fit for the *Post*. Fuck was "f---." Shit was "s---." Cocksucker was "c---sucker." Piss was "p---." But nothing was left out. All very clever, dirty and crude, Hugel felt.

He dressed, and his driver took him to CIA headquarters. It was painful in the corridors as he walked to his office. All eyes were on him. Some people seemed to be crying. Some came up to him and said how unfortunate, how unfair. Some couldn't say what was on their minds. Hugel was sure that many were elated: the outsider was out. And there was a coldness in others, the professional chill.

He wrote a "Dear Bill" letter which he walked down to Casey's office. Both Hugel and Casey were very emotional. It was a most difficult parting.

Casey's letter accepted the resignation "with deepest regret."

Hugel went back to his office, picked up his briefcase and walked out.*

For the moment Casey had had enough of bucking the system in the Operations Directorate, and he immediately named John H. Stein, forty-eight, the new DDO. A Yale graduate with a twenty-year career in the agency, including assignments as CIA station chief in Cambodia and Libya in the seventies, Stein was low-key, hard-working, and not a wave-maker.

It was time, Casey concluded, to settle down the Operations Directorate. In practical terms, he would just have to be his own DDO.

Casey decided he would have to set an example. For some time, one of his Middle East stations had been talking about placing an eavesdropping device in the office of one of the senior officials in that country, a main figure whose conversations would provide vital hard intelligence. At the station it was back and forth about the risk assessment; there was hesitancy and floundering as the DO officers debated how to make an entry into the office. They had raised irresolution to an art form. "I'll do it myself, goddamm it," Casey said. Though it was totally against tradecraft practice to risk using even a DO officer for such a mission, the DCI, insisting, placed the bug during a courtesy visit to the official—another violation of tradecraft. By one account, he inserted a thin, miniaturized, long-stemmed microphone and transmitting device shaped like a large needle in a sofa cushion during his visit. By another account the listening device was built, Trojan-horse style, into the binding of a book that Casey brought as a gift for the official. One senior agency officer insisted that the story was apocryphal, but others said it was true. Among several DO officers it was accepted as gospel. Casey only smiled when I asked about this incident several years later. But he glowered dramatically when I mentioned the name of the country and the official, and said that that should never, never be repeated or published.

* The McNells fled, allegedly with about $3 million from two small oil and gas firms they controlled, and stayed in hiding, apparently abroad. Later Hugel won a default judgment against them for $931,000 because the McNells failed to appear to answer Hugel's charges of libel against them.

7

UNDER THE FRONT-PAGE *New York Times* story of Hugel's resignation was a smaller headline: "Judge Asserts Casey, CIA Chief, Misled Stock Buyers in '68." Two months earlier, the story said, a federal judge had ruled that Casey had knowingly misled investors in a New Orleans farming and agribusiness firm called Multiponics Inc. that he had helped found in 1968. The judge had ruled that Multiponics and its directors—Casey was on the board—had failed to disclose to potential investors that the firm had assumed a mortgage debt of the founders, including Casey. Casey's share was $301,000, and his declared tax losses were about $145,000. There were other alleged misrepresentations in the offering, and the judge pinned responsibility on the board and Casey, who, the judge said, "omitted and misrepresented facts."

Barry Goldwater was disenchanted after the first six months of Bill Casey's directorship. He felt cut out. He had never understood the Hugel appointment. "You know," Goldwater told his friend Quinn, "if Casey is of a mind to hire someone like that, the President ought to fire his ass." The heralded CIA security and background check on Hugel was obviously not worth piss, Goldwater said. Either Casey knew and was covering up for Hugel or the security review was so flimsy that Casey ought to be removed for incompetence.

And the Senator was growing more infuriated by Casey's incoherence; the DCI just wouldn't speak up and speak clearly, leaving Goldwater with the impression that things were being hidden. "Did you understand what the shit he was talking about?" Goldwater would ask another senator or a staff member. He called Casey "flappy" or "flapper lips." He thought Casey was not making an effort. Casey, goddammit, had not even had the courtesy or the political IQ to warn the committee before the Hugel story broke. Word of that had come from the *Post*'s editor, Bradlee, the weekend before the story ran. Why did Goldwater have to learn these things from newspaper people?

Quinn called Casey. "Bill, don't ever surprise him again. Call him. It's very important to call him. Number two, I suggest you go to the heart of things, clear things up with him. He'll understand."

On Friday, July 17, three days after Hugel's resignation, Goldwater convened the Senate Intelligence Committee and it was agreed, during a two-hour closed-door session, to conduct a routine review—not an investigation—of the Hugel matter and any questions that might lurk about Casey's own business matters. It seemed inconsistent to some committee members that Hugel had been strapped up over seven-year-old business dealings while Casey was not being held accountable for his. Senator Biden said that if there was no good explanation on the Multiponics case, "Mr. Casey should be asked to do what is best for the agency and the country and step aside." But Goldwater told reporters that unless there was more he saw no reason for Casey to resign.

The next Tuesday, July 21, the Senate committee held a routine public hearing on the CIA's appeal that it be exempted from the Freedom of Information Act. Moynihan, who had been closely monitoring the staff inquiry on Casey, seized the opportunity. He had had enough.

"For the past two days we have been urgently trying to find out whether the Director of the CIA has been involved in illegal activities that would make him unfit to hold his office," Moynihan said, his high-pitched voice rising indignantly. "We called the White House and we called the White House. I've called the Attorney General and he doesn't answer. Maybe he doesn't know who I am, or maybe he doesn't know what goes on up here or think that it matters.

"Well, it damn well does matter. . . . They had better help us establish whether or not the Director of the CIA should resign. If they are going to cover up, they are going to lose themselves their Director of the CIA damn fast."

Less than an hour later Moynihan left, clutching two urgent telephone messages—one from Attorney General William French Smith and the other from White House counsel Fred Fielding.

Goldwater agreed that the committee wasn't getting proper attention. Casey was out of town again. His disdain for Congress was apparent, and Inman was left again to take the heat. Goldwater grumbled in private that it would be better for all concerned if Casey just resigned.

On Thursday night, CBS Television reported that Goldwater had told this to Casey. It was a goddamn lie, Goldwater said. He was furious. His back was giving him problems and he had had his evening drink. At first he told himself not to say anything. But he couldn't control his anger, and he called a press conference in the Senate Radio-TV Gallery to get his denial on the record before the story took on a life of its own.

He was asked his personal feelings about Casey. Goldwater was uncomfortable telling a lie or even a half-truth because half-truths had to be reserved for important matters. This wasn't one. Maybe a public tongue-lashing would send a message to Casey.

Stiffening, Goldwater let fly. "That he appointed an inexperienced man to be, in effect, the nation's top spy was bad enough. I must say that as a person with a long involvement with intelligence matters that it was a very bad mistake and I might even say dangerous because he is the man in charge of clandestine activities. That in itself constitutes the worst thing Casey has done. . . . The damage done by Mr. Hugel's appointment to the morale of the CIA, in my opinion, is a sufficient position for either Mr. Casey to decide to retire or for the President to decide to ask him to retire."

Now CBS and every other news organization had a new and more dramatic story. The message that had not been delivered privately was now a headline. The conscience of the President's own party had just said that Hugel had been "dangerous" and that Casey ought to go.

There was more. Goldwater had said also that there were some suspicions of missing records on some of Casey's business dealings, and other "inconsistencies," including a report that Casey had made over $750,000 on the Multiponics transactions, not lost $145,000 as he had claimed.

Goldwater went over to the Quinns' apartment on Connecticut Avenue for dinner.

"Barry," Quinn said, "you shouldn't have said that."

Bette Quinn agreed. "You shouldn't go blowing off half at the seam like that."

Well, I did, Goldwater said. Time would have to wear it out. It had been a long, terrible week full of conflicts between party loyalty and common sense.

Casey was at home sleeping when the late news shows carried the Goldwater statement. The phone rang. It was Sporkin.

"Bill," Sporkin said, "did you hear what that son of a bitch Goldwater just said?"

No, Casey said, so Sporkin explained.

"Don't worry about it," Casey said.

"What do you mean, 'Don't worry about it'?" Sporkin screamed.

"I'm going back to bed," Casey said, hanging up.

About 3:30 A.M. Casey woke up, put on his bathrobe and went downstairs. He got up in the middle of the night like this about two or three times a week. It was a time of total peace. Often he just read in bed, but he knew that the reading light bothered Sophia. She appreciated it if he went to another room.

This morning Casey didn't read. He called and woke Sporkin. Stan, what the hell did Goldwater say?

Sporkin repeated. Yes, he had seen it on the late television news, Goldwater standing there before the reporters—it was a press conference, intentional—effectively calling for Casey's head. "I'm sure Goldwater didn't mean it," Sporkin said. "Don't worry."

"I'm calling to boost *you,*" Casey replied. He had Goldwater's home phone number, and he dialed it.

"I can't believe you said that," Casey said, waking the chairman. His voice resonated the message of betrayal. There was no mumble.

"Well, Bill," Goldwater shot back, half-asleep and grouchy, "you better believe it, because that's what I said."

Casey stayed up for several hours, trying to read but brooding. About 6 A.M. he finally went back to bed—that was the best hour of sleep, just before breakfast, even that day.

Within several hours—it was a Friday—Casey began a round of one-on-one meetings with key senators. In a twenty-minute meeting with Senator Howard H. Baker, Jr., of Tennessee, the Senate Republican Majority Leader, Casey pleaded for a fair hearing. He was showing the signs of strain. He had never made $750,000 on Multiponics; he could prove it and he would. This was a witch hunt.

Baker said he agreed in principle, but he had to back his committee chairman. Casey and the White House had better come up with something in twenty-four hours, Baker said.

But there was no way to stop other Republicans, who took their cue from Goldwater. If Barry was bailing out, the situation had to be critical. While lunching with reporters, the assistant Republican leader, Senator Ted Stevens of Alaska, who rarely strayed from the Republican reservation, said he had sampled opinion on the intelligence committee. "Mr. Casey would be wise to accept Mr. Goldwater's advice," Stevens said. "It's my judgment that Barry doesn't make these recommendations lightly. He has the interests of the agency at heart." Senator William V. Roth, Jr., of Delaware, one of eight Republicans on the Intelligence Committee, went further: "These charges have so damaged Mr. Casey's credibility with the Intelligence Committee that I believe it is impossible for Mr. Casey to effectively discharge his duties. He should go—*now.*"

Startled by the attack from Casey's natural allies, the White House released a statement in the President's name—"I have not changed my mind about Bill Casey"—that seemed tepid. Casey told reporters who were trailing him from office to office in the Senate, "I feel when all the facts are out it will be clear I am qualified and ready to lead the central intelligence community." The statement seemed unintentionally to concede that he had not yet begun to lead the CIA, though he had been in office six months.

By Friday night, Howard Baker had Goldwater's agreement to bring in a special counsel to handle the Casey inquiry. They selected Fred Thompson, who had been Baker's chief staffer when he was the vice-chairman of the Senate Watergate Committee in 1973–74.

Baker told Thompson that he was trying to calm everyone, but, he said, it was obvious that there was little love for Casey, and that unless Casey could turn it around quickly he was gone; everyone wanted the inquiry completed quickly. Thompson went to the records, documents and financial disclosure statements. It was soon clear that Casey had a financial situation just slightly less complex than that of Aristotle Onassis. "I like Bill Casey," said Thompson in his slow Tennessee drawl, "but I like my ass better." So there could be only one way: a complete investigation.

In New York, on the twenty-second floor of 90 Park Avenue, John Shaheen, a wealthy oilman, an OSS veteran and a Casey friend for thirty-five years, read the news accounts with disbelief. The Republican Party was a kind of religion for Shaheen, as it was for Casey. It made no sense that Goldwater, Mr. Republican, was calling for Casey's head. It was almost as if the line of leadership in U.S. intelligence from their beloved General Donovan to Casey was in jeopardy. In the 1950s, Shaheen and Casey had been among a group of old hands who, like extra sons, had stayed close to Donovan. He would call them if they were out of touch for too long. Then Donovan had a stroke and was hospitalized in Washington at Walter Reed.

On February 8, 1959, when Donovan died, Shaheen and Casey had flown down to Washington. The weather was gray and awful. Even though it was not an open casket, Casey had wanted to be there early. That whole day Casey had moved slowly and said little. He was numb, replaying the memories, walking around with little shakes of his head, wet eyes, gazing off. At the funeral at Arlington, it was as if he were putting part of himself away. Almost as if he had lost his father. Shaheen said, "Donovan was part of his heart."

Casey's appointment and service as DCI had been greeted with jubilation among Donovan's boys. It was continuity with those wartime experiences that none of them had found anywhere else in their lives. Casey at the CIA kept so many important things alive; it meant that their work was not over.

Shaheen called Casey in Washington.

Casey said it was a cheap shot, the whole matter was unfair. Yes, he resented it. Everyone had tried to get something on him. No one had succeeded. This was just politics.

But Casey and Goldwater were on the same side, Shaheen said. From New York it looked bad.

"A tempest in a teapot," Casey said.

"Listen," Shaheen said, this was a friend speaking, "if you don't get busy and make some peace gesture to the Senate Intelligence Committee you may have to walk the plank."

Shaheen called Geoffrey M. T. Jones, president of the OSS veterans. Jones (Princeton '42) was out of OSS central casting—tall, dapper, affable, back-slapping, perfect suit, starched shirt, and a British air about him. He had turned the El Morocco nightclub into a private club and run it for five years. The OSS vets were no mere hobby for Jones. He put out a regular thick newsletter that practically reported the meeting of two OSSers as a reunion, kept up on address changes, maintained the old club ties and pro-intelligence faith.

Shaheen and Jones agreed that Casey needed help. A comrade was down in enemy territory, the Congress of the United States.

The first step was a visible demonstration of public support. About four hundred telegrams were fired off requesting contributions for the OSS vet. Large "Support Bill Casey" lunches were quickly organized in New York and Washington, with speakers George Shultz and William E. Simon, two former Republican Secretaries of the Treasury—a nice touch amidst the financial allegations.

In Sporkin's first months, it seemed that the ghosts of Senator Frank Church and his investigators still stalked the halls of CIA headquarters. Everyone was afraid and looking for reasons not to do things. Sporkin labeled this the "no syndrome." He would give a legal clearance for some sensitive covert action or sensitive intelligence-gathering operation, and it would be vetoed up the line, before it arrived on Casey's desk. So Sporkin worked out a system to alert Casey. They agreed that the elephant was not rogue. It was asleep. If Casey was booted now, Sporkin calculated, no one would ever get the intelligence agencies moving again. And if Casey wouldn't act, Sporkin would. All the old Casey business skeletons were rattling and coming out for a public reckoning. The next day, Saturday, July 25, Sporkin and two prominent Casey friends held a press conference at the Mayflower Hotel in downtown Washington.

Sporkin not only was willing to defend Casey's legal position, but, in an unusual step for an attorney, went so far as to vouch for his character. "It would be a tragedy for this country to lose this man's talents. I know a securities fraud when I see it, and I do not see it in this case," Sporkin said, speaking as a former SEC official.

Senator Paul Laxalt, the Nevada Republican who was a very close friend of both the President and Nancy Reagan, also spoke out. He credited Casey with saving Reagan's faltering 1980 presidential campaign. In a raw political appeal, Laxalt said, "I believe that were it not for Bill Casey, Ronald Reagan would not now be President."

Jones concluded it was time to move to the scene. He flew to Washington, set up headquarters at the Madison Hotel, and assembled a two-man team of OSS veterans for one more mission: Dr. James Kellis, a genuine World War II hero who had risked his life in operations that were part of OSS lore, and former Congressman John Blatnik, a liberal Democrat who had been in the House for twenty-eight years and had chaired the House Public Works Committee from 1970 to 1974.

One of their first stops was Senator Daniel K. Inouye, one of the seven Democrats on the Intelligence Committee. He had been on the Senate Watergate Committee and had been the first chairman of the Senate Intelligence Committee (1976–77), right after the Church investigation. He had lost his right arm in World War II combat. Kellis explained how impressed he had been with Casey's performance in OSS, with his loyalty, with his sincere efforts to improve the agency. Yes, Casey had not scored well with Congress, but they all had to understand Casey's Irish stubbornness.

Inouye listened intently and finally said, "If John Blatnik trusts Casey, then I'll trust him, too."

The Kellis-Blatnik team hit twelve senators on the committee and many more staff members, not always doing as well. But they were able to convey an impression that they were only a faint reflection of the affection and support that was out there for Casey.

About two o'clock on Sunday afternoon Casey sent ten volumes, two feet of documents, to the Senate committee to illustrate his desire to respond to the four pages of questions. There were twenty copies in each of twenty boxes—one for each senator on the committee. A letter to Goldwater said Casey would be happy to appear before the committee. On Monday, Casey delivered an upbeat status report and pep talk to hundreds of CIA employees. He said he was surprised that so many allegations could surface in only one week, but asked them to bear with him because he was confident he had done nothing wrong and would remain as director.

Their standing ovation was reported to the press.

Casey went to see Inman and said he had a personal favor to ask. Would Inman speak out publicly in his favor?

Inman could see that this was a most difficult request for Casey, and he agreed at once. He accepted an invitation to appear that night on ABC Television's *Nightline* with Ted Koppel.

Privately, Inman thought that the Casey–Goldwater feud might be traced back to 1966, when Casey had run for the Republican nomination for Congress against Goldwater supporter Derounian. Inman had the impression that these men did not easily forget such alignments, even if fifteen years old.

Casey then made another round among the senators. He knew more about his many business and investment affairs than anyone else. He could and would answer questions about each one, down to each dime if they desired. There was no embarrassment in being a venture capitalist, he said, and that meant taking risks. Risks often led to failure, unhappiness, lawsuits. But he had been charged with nothing illegal. As far as Multiponics was concerned, yes, he had been on the board, but he had been on many boards and he had had nothing to do with the drafting or the legal review of the stock offering. Jesus, directors got sued all the time but he could not be held responsible for every action of the management. The corporation might be liable for money damages if something had been done wrong, but the entire matter had been wrapped by the press in an aura of moral or criminal wrongdoing. It was nonsense and anyone who had business interests should understand.

Senator Lloyd M. Bentsen, a wealthy Texas Democrat on the committee, understood completely. Bentsen knew about the hard rocks in the road in the business world. After meeting with Casey, Bentsen said, "They haven't laid a glove on him. . . . I have yet to hear or see any credible evidence that would lead me to believe Mr. Casey should resign."

Casey had an increasing air of confidence as he swept from one private meeting to another in the Senate. "The bottom of the barrel has been scraped," he told a group of reporters tagging along outside one office. "There's nothing there . . . You know, fellas, I'm not concerned about anything. My life is an open book. I'm ready to discuss any phase of it."

Inman watched all this with some dismay. That Monday, *Newsweek* said that the White House had a short list of possible replacements for Casey if necessary. Conspicuously absent from that list was Inman. White House aides were making it clear that if Goldwater got Casey dumped, he would not get his favorite.

On *Nightline* Inman said, "Bill Casey is the right man to continue as the Director."

The OSS vets helped to get former CIA Director Colby on Public Broadcasting's *MacNeil-Lehrer Report* to defend Casey. Colby said, "I think the worst thing that would happen right now is for Mr. Casey to resign, because it would indicate that all you have to do is get a few little outrageous stories, and then the head of the agency quits or has to leave." In sum, the Casey issue was "a lot of kangaroos jumping to conclusions."

On Wednesday, July 29, fifteen days after the Hugel resignation, Casey arrived for a closed session before the Senate committee in the secure hearing room on the fourth floor of the Capitol. Jaunty and waving a long arm before he got on the elevator, he said, "It's going to be a cakewalk. . . . I've been through this before." Casey felt increasingly confident; Democrats on the committee were siding with him, Hugel was gone, and all the financial matters dealt with pre-1971 venture-capital investments.

Testifying under oath, Casey answered questions all over the lot: about allegedly poor intelligence in the Middle East, about "political" overtones in some recent analytic reports. He acknowledged that Hugel had turned out to be the wrong choice. Under the grilling, he finally said uncle —yes, Hugel's appointment was a "mistake."

Tiptoeing delicately, Casey said he was like Inman, he wanted nonpolitical intelligence, and, yes, the CIA did not need to get into domestic spying, and he would help the committee perform its oversight function. His appearance had its degrading moments. Senator after senator picked on favorite topics, imagined or real grievances, or press reports. Senator Biden wouldn't let Casey up, flicking at one scab in his financial past after another.

Finally Casey lashed back, saying that he was a businessman and, in the American tradition, he had taken business risks. In venture capital, some things didn't turn out, leading to business fights, nothing illegal, only civil suits, private disputes. And if the senators didn't like it, that was their problem, not his.

Democrats Henry M. Jackson and Bentsen, near the end, proposed that the committee express its "full confidence" and undo the damage that had been done in the last days. But they couldn't get a majority to support a sweeping endorsement.

After some wrangling, the senators agreed unanimously on a public statement: "No basis has been found for concluding that Mr. Casey is unfit to serve as DCI."

The backhanded seal of approval, dripping with innuendo, burned Casey, and when he walked out of the five-hour inquisition he declined to answer any questions.

Over at the White House, President Reagan was rehearsing a victory statement on his tax reduction bill, a major part of which had just passed the Democratic-controlled House. It was Reagan's biggest victory since his election. It had been the focus of White House attention for months, and the major demonstration that he would control the political agenda of the nation. An aide offered congratulations.

"Oh, yeah, I know," Reagan said, beaming, doing a little skip and thrusting his arm forward in affirmation, finding the silver lining. "But did you see that report on Bill Casey? Unanimous."

Out at Langley, Casey watched the Chad covert operation get off to a slow start. Designed to support former Chad Defense Minister Habré's effort to take power from the Transitional Government of National Unity (known by the unfortunate French acronym GUNT) and to rid Chad of Qaddafi's influence, it involved across-the-board support—money, arms, political support and technical assistance. This should have been easy. It meant tapping into the money pipeline used by France, which had spent close to $100 million over the years to stabilize its former colony. Casey could see that the machinery at Langley was not well oiled. The Directorate of Operations displayed insufficient knowledge about the international arms market—the best rifles, the best prices, certain transportation routes, banking protocol to launder funds. Hesitant, the agency had concentrated on the negative, insisting that Habré pledge that the lethal aid would not be used against his political opposition. This human-rights nicety was a big issue in the congressional oversight committees.

God damn, Casey wondered, did they want a note from Habré's mother? Habré was a brutal, calculating survivor. Didn't they read their own reports? Where was the realism?

The operation also had triggered a sequence of press reports, some that made the CIA look foolish.

The finding on the Chad operation had been presented to the House

Intelligence Committee by DDO Hugel before his resignation. A number of committee members had worried aloud that the wording of the finding was sufficiently ambiguous that it could be used as justification for going after Qaddafi directly.

Some of the congressmen wondered whether Habré was the ideal choice to receive covert aid. From the left there were questions about his past involvement in massacres. From the right, some recalled his statements that he admired Mao, Castro and Ho Chi Minh. He had once called for "revolutionary ferment in all of Africa." In addition to these problems, Habré, years earlier, had had close ties to Qaddafi and had received arms from him. Did the CIA have the best anti-Qaddafi alternative?

Casey had provided the committee with a copy of the detailed "scope paper" that outlined the specific types of weapons that would be supplied, the contacts, the estimated cost and the duration. The House committee members, nonetheless, sent a top-secret letter to President Reagan, protesting the operation. News of this letter leaked, and news reports appeared saying that the House had objected to some operation in an unnamed country in Africa.

Representative Clement J. Zablocki, the chairman of the House Foreign Affairs Committee and a member of the House Intelligence Committee, had reviewed the Chad finding and the letter to Reagan. The sixty-nine-year-old lawmaker leaked to *Newsweek* that the letter to Reagan about the yet unnamed operation in Africa was a plan to topple Qaddafi. *Newsweek*'s brief but sensational story, headlined "A Plan to Overthrow Qaddafi," claimed that the CIA was about to launch "a large scale multiphase and costly scheme to overthrow the Libyan regime. . . . To members of the House Intelligence Committee who reviewed the plan, that . . . seemed to imply Qaddafi's assassination."

Casey was furious at the report. The CIA had undertaken a subtle support operation where there was a real chance of success, where U.S. allies France and Egypt were already heavily committed. Now Qaddafi's paranoia would be fed by fears of a fictitious frontal assault plan when the agency was going in the back door. This had to be denied publicly. So the White House issued a rare public denial to the *Newsweek* story, though it confirmed that there had been a letter of protest on some operation from the House committee.

A search for the unnamed country was begun. Several White House officials decided that it would be better to help set the record straight, leak the real target country, and make their Libyan denial credible.

President Reagan had signed off on another top-secret covert finding at about the same time. This one, requested by the State Department, was to provide political-support money to the pro-Western leader of Mauritius, a small island in the Indian Ocean off the coast of Madagascar, near oil routes vital to the United States. The leader, Prime Minister Ramgoolam, an eighty-year-old medical doctor who had been in power thirteen years, was facing a tough battle against a Marxist-based militant movement and was certain to lose without help. Given its strategic location, the island could become a possible Soviet naval base if it was lost. This kind of covert operation, benign political support and money, could keep a friendly leader in power. The risk and the cost were low and the potential gain high. And no one on the Hill had any real objections to that low-level political support. It was a standard State Department plan, shovel some money to a friendly foreign leader of a small country where a few dollars could win, or buy, the election.

But White House aides unfamiliar with the world got confused, and leaked that the target nation was one whose name has the same first five letters, Mauritania.

Mauritania, a large country in Northwest Africa, was in the press the next day as the CIA target country in Africa. The implication was that the United States wanted to overthrow the government.

Casey suspected White House shenanigans as well as ignorance. It was absurd on its face; a little research would have shown that the United States had friendly relations with the Muslim military-ruled government in Mauritania. To cap the total ridiculousness of it, CIA reports showed that Libya was involved in an abortive coup attempt in Mauritania in early January.

But there it was. The Mauritanians were upset and lodged protests. Having caused more trouble by trying to straighten out the inaccurate *Newsweek* Libya report, officials at first told the Mauritanians that they could not discuss news accounts of supposedly secret operations. If it was false, why didn't the White House spokesmen say so as they had done with Libya? The official public silence only tended to confirm the report. Finally the State Department tried to convince the Mauritanians that the press reports were wrong, but this again required the naming of the real target if the denial was to be believed.

In the end a Mauritania operation was denied and reports of the true target, the island of Mauritius, were quietly leaked, but with the all-important point that the operation was one of support to the current leadership, not one to overthrow it.

Casey was disdainful. Reporters rushed with whatever latest version was leaked. Wasn't anyone thinking? But, more important, the White House political operators needed to be educated about covert foreign policy; it couldn't be run like a political campaign with speeches, leaks and clarifications. It was nuts—Congress, the White House, the State Department, the press were all over his operations. At a later White House meeting with the President, Casey protested the leaks, saying that if he was to run operations all details had to be ruthlessly restricted. The recent news stories created the impression that heavy-payload covert operations had been carelessly launched throughout Africa—Mauritius, Mauritania, Libya. Did anyone realize what a press story about a covert operation in a country did to the CIA station there? He did. Intelligence-gathering, relations with the local intelligence service could be wiped out.

Newsweek reporters went back to House Foreign Affairs Chairman Zablocki after the Libya plan was denied. Zablocki went to House staff members, tipping them that he had been a source for *Newsweek*. He was set straight, but the House Intelligence Committee chairman, Edward Boland, decided to take no action against Zablocki, since leaks were epidemic.*

On Sunday June 7, 1981, Inman received word that Israel, using U.S.-supplied warplanes, had just bombed and destroyed Iraq's nuclear reactor about ten miles outside Baghdad. He checked and found that, under the intelligence-sharing arrangement set up with Casey's approval, Israel had almost unlimited access to U.S. satellite photography and had used it in planning their raid. Casey was giving away too much. The Administration was walking a tightrope in the Arab–Israeli dispute, but Inman didn't see how the United States could maintain any balanced policy if Israel was permitted to drop bombs all over the Middle East using American intelligence. He quickly created new rules by which Israel could get photos and other sensitive intelligence only for defense. Israeli access

* The next week *Newsweek* stepped back only slightly from its anti-Qaddafi plot story—"White House officials also tried to help Casey by denying that there had ever been a CIA plot against Libya." But the newsmagazine said that various anti-Qaddafi schemes had been discussed with House Intelligence Committee members. Rival *Time* magazine reported that "misinformation was leaked to *Newsweek*" from CIA sources. *Time* said it too had learned of the alleged plot but had concluded that it was untrue, and added that "the White House last week flatly denied *Newsweek*'s story." The mysterious covert plan, *Time* said, was a much broader operation designed "to shore up U.S. interests in the Middle East and North Africa."

would be restricted to photos of those countries that posed an immediate threat or were on Israel's border. Baghdad was five hundred miles away and off the list.

Casey went along. But he was pleased that the Israelis had disposed of the problem, and he admired their audacity. When the White House expressed shock and imposed sanctions on Israel, withholding delivery of several F-16s, Casey felt it might be a necessary diplomatic and political gesture, but privately he called it "bullshit." Going back to the Carter Administration, the Israelis had urged the U.S. to pressure the Iraqis to curtail their nuclear-development program and had threatened that if nothing was done, they would do it. The Mossad had even explored the possibility of a sabotage operation, but the air strike was, correctly, determined to involve less risk for both Israelis and Iraqis. Only one person, a technician at the Iraqi plant, had died in the raid.

Casey saw that Israeli intelligence had a special hurdle of skepticism to overcome within the agency. Before 1974, the celebrated CIA chief of counterintelligence James Jesus Angleton had run the Israeli desk at the agency, keeping vital information from the Middle East operations people and analysts. Even after Angleton was fired, all Israeli intelligence was for years viewed as little more than a Mossad press release, designed to serve Israel's political goals.

Mossad, in fact, had some good human sources in three places of vital significance—Lebanon, Syria and the Soviet Union. Casey had to work to make Mossad credible.

In some important respects, Israel was more sinned against in intelligence matters. The CIA had secret PLO sources that at times provided operational details about PLO attacks in Israel. The DO had convinced Casey that such information could not be passed to the Israelis, because the sources would dry up. It was a tough game, and Casey admired the way Israel accepted the rules: sources had to be protected at all costs. They were very sophisticated about this; they realized that an ally could not give everything.

Weren't there some relationships so vital that no one could know? Casey said yes. Preserving the source, protecting identity, had some relationship to the value of the information. If the information spoke for itself, who needed to know? The bombing of the reactor had so much more to do with preserving the long-term relations with the Israeli services. The month after the bombing, Major General Yehoshua Saguy (spelled "Sagi" in the agency computers), the head of Israeli military intelligence, visited Casey. Saguy understood the West, Casey felt Saguy could be trusted, and they agreed that if there ever was a need for something special they would deal directly with each other.

The Director usually devoted some part of his day to the Soviets. He wanted the most precise hold on the number-one enemy. One of his early conclusions was that the scope and the sophistication of Soviet propaganda efforts were not understood. Casey urged the Directorate of Operations to make that case and get a wide hearing for it.

The first salvo was a TOP SECRET code-word study called "Soviet Active Measures." It was issued in July. A SECRET version of the report, with less information on sources, had a press run of about three thousand copies—perhaps the largest distribution of any CIA report. The report described "active measures"—*aktivniye meropriyatiya*—as just about anything done "to insinuate Soviet policy views" throughout the world, not only in covert action or clandestine propaganda, but "active measures" that ranged from manipulation, disinformation, military operations, the overt use of "disarmament" and "peace" issues, even "objectivity" and "reasonableness" in various presentations. These active measures, which seemed to include everything the Soviets did, were, according to the report, "one of the major instruments of Soviet foreign policy.

"We know from a reliable source that specific directives concerning individual active measures have been personally signed by party leader Leonid Brezhnev . . . ," the SECRET version said.

Some specifics cited in the thirty-page study were: substantial control over the two major daily newspapers in Ghana by two KGB officers who made cash payments to editors; the KGB's 1976 forging of the last will and testament of the late Chinese Premier Zhou Enlai, which claimed that the Cultural Revolution was a mistake (a KGB defector later said KGB headquarters evaluated this active measure as "the most successful ever carried out"); contributing $85,000 to a leftist candidate in Nigeria; a campaign in support of the ratification of the SALT II Treaty that included a KGB agent who edited a newsletter favoring the arms limitation treaty.

Disinformation campaigns included Soviet support of the leftist insurgency in El Salvador, working through political front groups, solidarity committees (seventy demonstrations in the first six months of 1981), and manipulation of international organizations, including the United Nations.

Other case studies focused on Pakistan, the efforts to disrupt U.S.–

Egyptian relations, and the efforts in Mauritius to establish a pro-Moscow regime (the CIA was providing covert support to the pro-Washington government of this Indian Ocean island).

Inman concluded that Casey was in overdrive, using the active-measures study for some ideological grinding, mixing apples and oranges. Transparently false accusations about U.S. policies in El Salvador that had appeared in *Pravda, Izvestia* and Tass and on Radio Moscow were given prominence as active measures. Soviet foreign policy itself was, practically speaking, being treated as an active measure. But Inman judged most of the elements of the CIA study essentially accurate, based on good human sources. The Soviet campaign was not a figment of Casey's imagination but it was necessary to distinguish between, on the one hand, forging a will and invading Afghanistan and, on the other, *Pravda* editorials.

The study's wide circulation was designed to raise consciousness and to suggest CIA action to counter the Soviets. But, to Casey's disappointment, the CIA had been unable to calculate what these measures cost the Soviets. It analyzed Soviet efforts aimed at mobilizing opposition to the U.S. plan to build a neutron bomb—the ERW, or enhanced radiation weapon, that destroyed people but not buildings. The CIA study said merely: "The scale of the Soviet effort can be gauged by analogy. We calculate that, if the U.S. government were to undertake a campaign of the magnitude of the Soviet 'neutron bomb campaign,' it would cost over $100 million." Casey called such numbers "flaky."

Nonetheless, on August 13, about a month after the CIA study was distributed, President Reagan remarked to reporters, "We have information that the Soviet Union spent about one hundred million dollars in Western Europe alone a few years ago when the announcement was first made of the invention of the neutron warhead, and I don't know how much they're spending now, but they're starting the same kind of propaganda drive."

The record was never corrected. Inman felt that it served no purpose for the President of the United States to spread misinformation, but Casey wasn't particularly bothered. The Soviets lied all the time, and the CIA estimate was probably about right.

8

By August, Pezzullo had decided to quit his ambassador's post in Nicaragua. For at least three months—March, April and May—he had stopped the arms flow to the Salvadoran rebels. But the Administration's decision to cancel aid to Nicaragua had left him with no leverage, and the arms were now starting to run again. As a final effort, however, he convinced Assistant Secretary of State Enders to come to Nicaragua to meet with the Sandinistas. Pezzullo thought Enders was a stuffed shirt, but a smart, powerful stuffed shirt who had control of Administration policy.

In Managua, Enders leveled with Pezzullo. Both knew that the new CIA reports of the arms flow were heightening concern in Washington. The NSA was intercepting 60 to 70 percent of the radio traffic from Managua into the rebel positions in El Salvador, showing that Managua was heavily involved. The Sandinistas' arms buildup in their own country was worrying Nicaragua's neighbors, particularly Honduras to the north. Policy from Washington, Enders said, was starting to run in directions that would bring about a collision.

Pezzullo presumed that meant covert action.

"I want to prevent that," Enders said. Maybe diplomacy could still work.

So Enders and Pezzullo held a round of meetings with the Sandinista leadership. The Sandinistas were always willing to meet and confer, but they made it clear that they were not going to be pushed around, and that they would defend themselves to the last person.

Enders complained that they were harassing the church, the press and the labor unions. He complained that non-Marxists were being expelled from the government, and promised that the new Administration in Washington wanted democracy in Central America.

Internal matters, the Sandinistas replied.

Several times Enders blew his stack, telling them that their country was a goddamn flea that could be knocked off by the United States with its hands tied behind its back. Don't get silly, Enders said. We're talking about survival—your survival. Here I am offering you a deal with the United States. Think about it seriously.

Pezzullo could see that Enders did not mean it as a threat, but as an honest statement, a realistic warning. Yet he had gone a step further with diplomatic bombast. It was heavy-handed.

The Sandinistas wanted specifics.

You must commit yourselves to limiting your military buildup, Enders said, and pledge not to get involved in the external or internal matters of neighboring countries—in sum, agree not to export revolution. In return, the United States would promise not to support any of the various elements and former Somoza National Guards working against the Sandinistas. There had been reports that these so-called contras—from the Spanish *contrarevolucionarios*—were training on U.S. soil. In addition, Enders said, the U.S. would sign a mutual-defense and nonaggression treaty with Nicaragua. "We don't like your regime," Enders said, "but there is not much we can do about it. But you have to get out of El Salvador."

Ortega said no. "The Salvadoran revolution is our shield—it makes our revolution safer."

Back in Washington, Enders examined international law, which favors the existing regime in any country. The only way for the United States to do something was through covert action. Overall, Enders determined that the Administration had to shift public attention from El Salvador, off the question of how many human-rights violations took place there last week. Enders sent Haig a secret memo summarizing his trip, with his conclusion that despite the harsh exchanges the signs were hopeful that an accord of some kind might be reached with the Sandinistas.

Haig returned the memo with a scribbled note in the margin: "I'll believe it when I see it, and meanwhile let's not hold up on the other plans."

Enders went through the exercise of proposing treaty language to the Sandinistas. It was pugnacious and insulting, almost asking the Sandinistas to renounce their revolution and its ideals. They rejected it out of hand.

Casey remained worried about Qaddafi. Because of the inaccurate *Newsweek* report that the CIA was planning to overthrow or assassinate him, tensions were high. Casey wanted more intelligence assets directed at Libya. Libyan diplomatic and intelligence codes had been broken, and

Qaddafi often spoke on unsecure telephone lines, providing the United States with an increasingly clear picture of his expanding subversion.

One of Qaddafi's instruments was United African Airlines (UAA), ostensibly a nonscheduled passenger and cargo air carrier. In fact the CIA's information showed it was the air transport service of the Libyan armed forces and, more important, the Libyan Intelligence Service (LIS). The airline's management and flight personnel were riddled with Qaddafi intelligence operatives.*

A report in late August 1981 noted that Qaddafi had ordered the airline to open eighteen new offices in Africa, at a cost of $30 million. These offices provided a ready-made intelligence network of communications, shipping, courier and passenger transportation service. According to the CIA's information, known Libyan intelligence agents were listed on manifests as "students"; the airline pursers offered lavish bribes; the airline was used to ship mines, artillery, ammunition, jeeps and weapons into Chad; Libyan-trained Zimbabwian troops had been flown to Salisbury; arms had been transported to the Libyan Embassy in Burundi; and UAA had been used to ship Soviet-made surface-to-air missiles to Syria.

Qaddafi was also stepping up his plans to get a nuclear weapon. In December 1980, the Soviets had delivered 11 kilograms of highly enriched uranium (HEU) to the research center outside the Libyan capital of Tripoli, at Tajura. Though it was not enough to fabricate a bomb (they wouldn't have enough until 1990 at the present rate, the CIA estimated), the 11 kilograms exceeded what the CIA expected the Soviets to deliver at one time.

Other reports showed that uranium yellowcake was coming in from Niger, the other Central African country to the south of Libya, on the UAA flights. A July 5, 1981, SECRET intelligence memo from the State Department had been titled "Niger: Libya's next target," and made that point convincingly about Qaddafi's aspirations there.

A West German firm had tested a rocket in Libya, according to another report.

A major Administration policy review was under way, and Casey knew that intelligence-reporting fueled the policy fires. The more the CIA threw at the White House, the more natural impulses for action were stirred—particularly in Reagan and Haig. Casey concurred fully in a decision to challenge Qaddafi's declared sovereignty over the Gulf of Sidra with a U.S. naval exercise. It was a limited, nonprovocative move, and the

* A secret memo dated August 17, 1981, headed "Libya: Covert Airline Operation," said that United African Airlines was "in fact funded by the Libyan intelligence service."

international community joined the United States in deriding Qaddafi's claim that Sidra was a Libyan sea.

About 7 A.M. on Wednesday, August 19, two U.S. Navy F-14 fighters on dawn patrol more than thirty miles inside the territorial waters claimed by Qaddafi were attacked by Libyan Air Force jets. Under instructions to defend themselves, the American planes retaliated and shot down two of Qaddafi's jets.

That morning the President greeted his top aides by acting out a Western-movie version of the incident, drawing two imaginary six-shooters and blasting away.

Rhetoric flew, but there was no more shooting. Three days later, August 22, Qaddafi was in Ethiopia's ancient capital, Addis Ababa, meeting with the country's leader Lieutenant Colonel Mengistu Haile Mariam, a young, fiery Marxist.

In the room at the time was a senior Ethiopian official, a secret CIA source of such sensitivity that his reports went only to the BIGOT list. The Directorate of Operations evaluated him as "generally reliable" to "excellent." At that meeting, Qaddafi declared he was going to have President Reagan killed. When the report reached Washington, it carried this evaluation: "Mengistu was convinced Qaddafi is very serious in his intention and that the threat should be taken seriously."

Shortly afterward, the NSA intercepted one of Qaddafi's conversations in which he said essentially the same thing: Reagan was the target. Both reports received prominent mention in the President's Daily Brief.

Casey realized that this was about as good as the intelligence ever got —an intercept and a human-source report that his own Operations Directorate said should be taken "seriously." Other than a military attack, the warning was perhaps the most serious matter he might ever address, a threat to the life of the President. Casey discussed the matter with everyone, with anyone who would listen. Something had to be done. But what? They couldn't go shoot Qaddafi. After a week passed without an attempt on the President's life, everyone seemed to cool off. Not Casey. He ordered all the intelligence agencies to report any whisper to him directly. But the White House still wouldn't take direct action.

By late summer 1981, Casey was certain that the CIA was going to have a large, perhaps even spectacular role in Central America. That meant having the right people. Casey didn't care for the Directorate of Operations' division chief for Latin America, Nestor Sanchez, a thirty-year veteran who had maybe spent too much time in the region and was too prone to see the Latin side and too uneasy about covert operations.

Sanchez retired in August, and Casey helped him get an appointment as a deputy assistant secretary at Defense, where he would be involved in the military side of Latin American policy. Casey had an idea for his replacement.

Division chiefs, with their feudal regions, were the "barons." They had hands-on control, ran the day-to-day operations of the CIA. The DCI himself, the DDCI, even the DDO had too much on their plate. A "baron," given a free hand, and operating with the confidence of the top, could achieve things.

When Casey had gone to Paris for a meeting of the Western European station chiefs several months earlier, one man had stood out: Duane R. Clarridge, known as "Dewey," the Rome station chief. He had arranged a lavish dinner for Casey in Paris, attending to each detail, even to the special sauces that Casey liked. "Can do" and "no problem" seemed to be Clarridge's middle names. It was a style Casey appreciated. A flashy dresser (occasionally white shoes, a white suit with a colored handkerchief in his jacket pocket), Clarridge, forty-nine, had had undercover experience only in Asia and Europe. But Casey appointed him Latin America division chief. Clarridge was the right mixture of old agency and new blood.

Clarridge immediately had a "privacy channel" to the DCI. He didn't have to report through DDO Stein or Inman. Casey was available for a meeting or a phone call anytime. If Casey was away from Langley, the operations center answered his phone, day and night, seven days a week. Messages were regularly relayed, including Dewey's, and Casey would be on the phone shortly, asking, "What have you got?"

On October 6, Casey received a flash report that Egyptian President Sadat had been shot while reviewing a parade. Reports from the Cairo station parroted for three hours the official Egyptian government line that Sadat was not seriously injured, even though American television news reports were saying that the Egyptian leader was dead.

Helping to keep Sadat in power had been a monumental task for the Administration and the CIA, which had provided covert security assistance and intelligence to his government. Since the Camp David Accord of 1978 and the peace treaty with Israel in 1979, Sadat had been isolated in the Middle East. He had been, in some respects, a creation of the American people and his American press clippings. He had no comparable standing in his own country. And his wife Jehan Sadat's Western dress, customs and ideas of female independence were anathema to many of the fundamentalist Muslims.

The CIA's intelligence feed to Sadat had contained data about his vulnerability and the forces arrayed against him. The previous month, in a personal briefing, he had been given detailed information on the threats to him from Libya, Ethiopia, Syria and Iran.

About three hours after the initial report on October 6, the Cairo station confirmed that Sadat was dead. He had died instantly of multiple shots.

Casey was mortified. Reagan had spent the morning in the Oval Office being assured that the television report was wrong. Casey and Inman worried that the new Egyptian government of Sadat's protégé Vice-President Hosni Mubarak would lodge a strenuous, perhaps emotional protest because the CIA, which had trained Sadat's bodyguards, had failed to warn them. But there was nothing, not even a mild complaint.

It turned out that the assassins were part of a domestic fundamentalist group within Egypt. The CIA had paid so much attention to wiring and penetrating the Sadat government, and warning Sadat about external threats, that it had ignored the forces inside Egypt. It was dangerously close to a replay of the Iran debacle, and Casey had a fit. The CIA needed more and broader independent channels of information in Egypt. There just could not be any boundaries in the area of clandestine collection, especially in the volatile Middle East, especially now in Egypt. He wanted more—both human sources and electronic collection, even at the highest level of the new government. "And get some people out in the fucking street to see if someone's going to shoot Mubarak," Casey ordered.

Casey didn't like large White House meetings. He said little at them. When he spoke up, he knew that he was not articulate and that someone at the table would attempt to translate him for the President, saying, "As Director Casey was saying . . ." or "As Bill said . . ." Several times, Casey noticed, Jim Baker had cracked up at this.

His direct channel to the President was more useful. When Casey had something really important, he called the Oval Office. One Friday he had an important Saudi Arabian prince who wanted to see the President, and he took him over to see Reagan. When Haig found out he was livid, but Casey believed that certain sensitive relations had to be kept away from State, where they could be leaked or sabotaged.

The CIA had some special relations elsewhere in the Arab world, among them King Hassan II of Morocco. After Libyan-backed guerrillas routed a Moroccan garrison on October 13, 1981, in the former Spanish Sahara, Casey carried the King's request for U.S. support directly to the President. "We want to back him," Casey told Reagan. Soon a team of twenty-three Pentagon, State and CIA officials was dispatched to Morocco. Again Haig and State were left out.

Meanwhile, Goldwater was still waiting, that fall of '81, for an end to the probe into the labyrinth of Casey's finances. The inquiry was sputtering to a conclusion with an exhaust velocity approaching zero. He had to find a graceful retreat or the committee staff had to find a smoking gun. Nearly 38,000 pages of documents had been reviewed, and 110 persons interviewed. The inquiry had turned up omissions galore in Casey's sworn disclosure statements. He had failed to list nine investments valued at more than $250,000; personal debts and other potential liabilities of nearly $500,000; four additional civil suits in which he had been involved; and more than seventy law clients he had represented during the previous five years, including two foreign governments, the Republic of Korea and Indonesia.

A new special committee counsel, Irvin Nathan, a former senior Justice Department official, took a sinister view of Casey's financial habits. Though Nathan could not subpoena documents, did not get Casey's tax returns and was never allowed to interview him, he drafted a confidential report of some ninety pages outlining the unanswered questions and pointing out Casey's pattern of cutting corners. Casey had chalk all over his feet from playing close to the foul line most of his life. But Nathan had no smoking gun.

Goldwater had selected a tall, wiry thirty-eight-year-old former CIA covert operator who had ten years in the DO, Rob Simmons, to be the new staff director for the Senate committee. Simmons had worked undercover in Taiwan for the CIA from 1975 to 1978 and had run an operation that had prevented the Taiwanese from obtaining material to build a nuclear weapon; the Taiwan government's bomb plans and files had been stolen and its attempts to purchase sensitive parts choked off. His first assignment for the Senate committee was to wrap up the Casey investigation.

"I want nothing longer than one page," Goldwater said, asking for a final report.

Simmons came up with a five-page report that reaffirmed the committee's earlier judgment that "no basis has been found for concluding that

Mr. Casey is unfit to hold office as Director of Central Intelligence." Given the repeated failure to make full disclosure, Simmons applied terminology from his service in the Army: Casey was "at minimum inattentive to detail."

Simmons went out to Langley in late November with a copy. In Casey's seventh-floor office, now decorated with French Empire furniture, the committee staff director felt somewhat like a junior officer delivering headquarters' reprimand to the general. But Simmons explained that the five-page report was an accomplishment. It would fly with all or nearly all the committee members and would bury the issue for good. "There are people who want to publish an eighty-to-one-hundred-page report."

Casey protested that he was clean.

A fight over this compromise, Simmons told him, might lead to a protracted battle with the committee, where there were lots of unhappy members. Simmons hinted that the battle could be bloody, resulting in permanent unhappiness, perhaps the DCI's departure.

"No one takes my job away," Casey said briskly, his back stiffening. "I work for the President."

This is the final compromise, Simmons said.

"Well," Casey said at the end, "I'm going to fight it."

The report, unchanged, was released in December, when it was old news. There was little comment, and no fight from Casey, who told friends and Sophia, "All that stuff that comes out in the press, it only hurts for a day."

Simmons realized that Casey was not going to be pushed any further. For people who served in war, Simmons thought, that was the primary experience, real danger. Everything else paled by comparison. They had sent people to certain death. So to hustle some bucks was nothing. It was easy. To be criticized was nothing. So some judge or senator or reporter or cartoonist was beating on you. So what? You have served in war and survived.

Casey still wanted a comprehensive plan of action for Central America, but there was no consensus within the Administration. The President craved agreement among his top advisers, and when he didn't get it he wouldn't decide. Haig was obsessed with Cuba; Weinberger raised Vietnam with its twin specters of overcommitment and escalation; he wouldn't have American boys trapped in another unpopular jungle war. Baker and others inside the White House wanted Reagan to stay on his domestic agenda and were determined that the Administration not be diverted by a foreign adventure, particularly one promoted by Haig, whom they viewed with increasing skepticism, even alarm. Haig had not adapted to the President's informality. One moment he fawned over Reagan, the next he was overbearing, lecturing him that the Reagan foreign policy hinged on a particular course of action as urged by Haig. Often he wound up discrediting his own recommendations.

Casey was probably the only senior Administration official who got along with Haig. They had a regular Tuesday breakfast, often accompanied by their deputies, alternating one week at the CIA, the next at State. Haig understood foreign policy, Casey thought, and had some familiarity with the world, and he shared Casey's hard-line views.

If Casey was going to get anything substantial going to save El Salvador, he would have to juggle the interests and demands of Haig, Weinberger and the White House political apparatus. The effort to promote democracy was well and good, but it was not enough.

Haig and Enders had agreed they had to expand covert action. Ideally, the United States should buy into someone else's operation, much as it had piggybacked on the French operation in Chad.

Dewey Clarridge found a route through Buenos Aires, where the CIA station had extremely close relations with the Argentine generals who ruled the country. The Argentine military intelligence, G-2, had elevated anti-Communism to an ethos and ran a counter-Marxist indoctrination program. The generals were worried about the Montoneros, guerrillas opposed to their dictatorship, who operated out of Nicaragua. Argentina was supporting resistance efforts aimed at the Sandinistas and was training about a thousand men north of the Nicaraguan border in Honduras.

Clarridge presented this to Enders and the core group. The only alternative was to work through Chile, and that dictatorship was worse and even more visible.

Would the Israelis do it? Enders wondered.

Not viable, Clarridge answered. The Argentines were in place.

Enders outlined a possible covert action to Haig.

Not enough, Haig said. He wanted to locate a place of vulnerability. Since the White House wouldn't back a strike directly at Cuba, how about a strike on a Cuban military camp in Ethiopia without warning? But Haig couldn't even get support for his proposal from his own State Department. He feared that a Nicaragua operation would turn out to be a serious diversion; it would appear tough but not be much; and if it didn't work the United States would walk away. But he saw that it was the only proposal that had support at the White House, Defense and the CIA.

On Monday, November 16, at 4 P.M., Reagan convened his National Security Council in the Cabinet Room. Enders, who had won agreement among the core group, made the presentation.

The political program for El Salvador must continue to be democracy, he said. Democratic institutions must be put in place there and in the rest of Central America. "It is the only way to gain legitimacy for them and for us."

Economic and military assistance must be increased, perhaps more than $300 million for the region and the Caribbean, he said. "We must find a way to return to negotiations with Nicaragua or we will have to send troops." Going to the source, Cuba, was "an empty box," because we are not ready and it probably would be too large an undertaking. The war must be taken to Nicaragua through covert action. Enders said that the operation, supporting the resistance, would not overthrow the Sandinistas. "It will harass the government, waste it."

Haig was the only one to voice objections, expressing doubts but not outright opposition. In principle, the President agreed and adopted a wide range of actions, but held off on approving a CIA covert plan to assist the Argentines.

Haig was to make a last stab at diplomacy, and six days later he flew secretly to Mexico City to meet with Cuban Vice-President Carlos Rafael Rodríguez. But he could find no grounds for agreement with the Cubans.

On Tuesday, December 1, Haig and Casey had their regular breakfast, and that afternoon they met with Reagan for forty minutes with the National Security Planning Group in the White House Situation Room. The NSPG was the informal high-level gathering for the important foreign-policy issues; included were the President, the Vice-President, Meese, Baker, Deaver, Haig, Weinberger and Casey. An occasional aide also attended. National-security adviser Richard Allen had just taken a leave of absence, pending the outcome of an investigation into charges that he had accepted $1,000 from Japanese journalists and kept it in a White House safe.

Casey outlined his covert plan. He wanted $19 million to help Argentina develop a five-hundred-man force that would be the nucleus of an anti-Sandinista resistance. It would operate from camps in Honduras. More money would probably be needed, he said, and the five-hundred-man force would certainly grow.

The White House troika was on board. Haig still felt it was a half-measure, but he went along. Weinberger was happy that the plan kept the Pentagon out. Bush was content to see a modest revival of the agency's paramilitary capability. There was little further discussion.

That day Reagan signed a broad top-secret finding authorizing political and paramilitary operations designed to curtail the Sandinistas' support to the various rebel movements in Central America, including El Salvador.

General David C. Jones, Chairman of the Joint Chiefs of Staff, the senior military person and the only holdover from the Carter Administration on the National Security Council, looked on the approval of a Nicaragua operation with some dismay. From his reading of the intelligence, it was not clear that all the trouble in Central America was Cuban- or Soviet-inspired. Casey was seeing it in terms of the East–West conflict, as if the problems would go away if Communists would go away. To Jones, the social and economic problems loomed larger, making the countries fertile ground for the Marxist insurgencies. He saw senior Reagan Administration officials grabbing at pieces of intelligence to justify a course of action. Jones knew enough about intelligence to realize that it could be gathered and used to emphasize the Communist role.

But the worst of all this was the selection of the Argentines. Jones knew the Argentines—good anti-Communists, but they weren't going to do much. Nicaragua was more than 2,500 miles from Argentina (Buenos Aires to Managua was 3,707 miles by air). Why were they so worried that a band of Montonero guerrillas could organize a revolution against the Argentine regime from a continent away? It didn't make sense except that the Argentines could be influenced and would do anything the United States asked.

The assessment at the White House had been that the Administration wouldn't be able to get public and congressional support if the U.S. role were out in the open to be debated.

And everyone at the table at those meetings seemed haunted by Vietnam analogies. Jones and the other chiefs wanted more than the fifty-five advisers in El Salvador—a ceiling placed by the White House. But Jones saw that everyone else was worried sick that any increase in the number of U.S. advisers would have to be done publicly and that the rhetoric would begin: "That's how we got into Vietnam," "It's the foot in the door," "That's the first part of escalation."

Inman too watched the development and approval of the Nicaragua covert action with skepticism. It was true that the undercover support to the Argentine paramilitary operation was a middle course, more moderate than some of Haig's ideas. But it was painfully obvious that the Administration did not want to expend any of its goodwill or political capital in Congress to get approval for such a policy. An open request to Congress for funding would spark a public debate. As far as Inman was concerned it was domestic political concerns that were once again driving covert action. But there was little he could do. Casey had made it clear that he would handle these operations himself, that the line of authority would run directly from Casey to the DO, and in this case it was to his new Latin America division chief, Dewey Clarridge.

Inman found another part of the operation troubling. Covert operations seemed to get started when the White House and the State Department were frustrated with diplomacy. That was clearly the case here. The diplomatic route had not been successful, and the process of diplomacy—the painstaking steps of negotiation and endless meetings, proposals and counterproposals—was tiring. The secret covert action provided a shortcut. It provided an administration, particularly a new one, with the comfort of action, the feeling that there was a secret way to get things done, that there was an undercover foreign policy quietly moving U.S. interests forward.

Inman also wondered about these non-Americans we were going to support with millions of dollars. Who were they? What were their goals? Were they the same as those of the United States? Could they be controlled?

If the real goal was to halt the arms flow from Nicaragua to El Salvador that had already been substantially stopped, something was wrong. Interdiction of arms is not something that is normally done covertly. There were no joint borders between the two countries. The only overland route was through Honduras. And the United States would have every legitimate right to give overt assistance to Honduras and El Salvador to prevent an arms flow. That would be more effective as an overt, public undertaking, with open border surveillance. But obviously no one wanted to make the effort to sell that to Congress.

The easiest water route for an arms flow from Nicaragua to El Salvador was via the Gulf of Fonseca—a short twenty-mile run. The U.S. naval attaché in El Salvador and others were watching the gulf like hawks. Nothing was getting across.

Inman tried to find ways to share his skepticism gently around the agency. He asked Casey if DDO John Stein was backstopping him on the operation to make sure there was an experienced professional fully informed of each step, someone who could raise questions and objections.

But Casey was impatient and left Inman with the clear impression that his views were neither needed nor welcomed. The Director mumbled, "Yeah, yeah."

As required, the new covert finding had to be reported to the Senate and House intelligence committees. Senate committee chairman Goldwater was recovering from a hip operation, so Moynihan chaired the meeting. When the finding and the backup scope paper were outlined, Moynihan couldn't believe it. If they wanted to put pressure on the Sandinistas, he thought, that was an understandable goal, but for God's sake don't use the Argentine generals. The Argentines were a symbol of right-wing dictatorial rule. To link up with them was to suggest that the United States was endorsing counterrevolution. In some respects, Somoza had been little more than an Argentine general in a Nicaraguan setting. It was idiocy, it showed no political deftness. Moynihan could ask questions, and he did. But there was not much more he could do.

The law required simply that the committee be informed of major anticipated intelligence activities. The conduct of foreign affairs, defense and intelligence policy was constitutionally reserved for the President. Any President, especially this one, would guard those powers jealously. Moynihan didn't disagree, so the committee could do little else unless it wanted to attempt to deny funds for the operation. But the President had a $50 million contingency reserve fund for intelligence operations. It would be difficult to tackle.

There was another problem. The committee members were sworn to secrecy. It was an oath that Moynihan took seriously. So the committee's hands were tied; it had been told the latest secret. Their silence outside the committee room amounted to implied acquiescence. A single member could take it upon himself to blow the whistle publicly or leak privately, but that member would have to be morally certain that that was the right thing. How could anyone pit what had been learned in a one-hour briefing against the hundreds of hours of calculation and debate that he hoped had gone into the issue by the National Security Council and the CIA? Moynihan had a sense the committee was being co-opted, but it was only a glimmer, an uneasiness, that he felt. At least it was better to know. Now he and the committee could ask follow-up questions as the operation got under way.

Over on the House side, Casey himself made the top-secret presentation to the Intelligence Committee. He said that the operation had already begun; the Argentines had started it and the United States was buying in.

The camps were already set up in Honduras, and the Hondurans were allowing the Argentines to use their territory as a base.

To do what?

Hit targets inside "Nic-a-wha-wha," Casey said. He could not pronounce "Nicaragua" properly. When he came to it, he would pause each time, trying to get it right, but out it came—"Nic-a-wha-wha." Anyway, Casey said, the resistance group of contras were going to hit specific and identifiable targets in that country—the parts of the Cuban support structure involved in supporting insurgency.

How? When?

Crack commando teams in cross-border operations, hitting targets in the dead of night and getting back to their bases in Honduras.

Many of the House members seemed to jump. They had not expected a paramilitary operation, particularly one of this scale. There were a lot of questions. What happens if you get caught training in Honduras? What if the Sandinistas go into Honduras as a response? Could this trigger hostilities between the two countries? What if the Sandinistas' response is to ask for more help from the Cubans?

Casey replied that those speculative questions could not be answered precisely.

Representative Lee H. Hamilton, a respected and careful Indiana Democrat, wondered whether the operation was legal under international law and various regional treaties. The United States was putting itself in the posture of joining aggression against a country with which it had diplomatic relations. How could this be done?

The Cubans and the Nicaraguans were the aggressors, Casey replied. They were supporting insurgency. But he was vague about dates and amounts. He spoke of it as a given.

His approach was not going down well, not even with the committee Republicans. Representative J. Kenneth Robinson, a conservative Virginian and Administration friend, glanced at Casey and said sternly, "You haven't thought through the repercussions."

Casey was watching the flow of intelligence from Polish Colonel Wladyslaw Kuklinski, the agency's source in the Polish General Staff. This information came right from the inner circle, and a remarkable system of signals, dead drops and communications had been worked out to insure that the data was timely. The colonel had handed over an operational plan for a martial-law crackdown on the independent Solidarity trade union by the Polish government. Casey made sure it was forwarded directly to the President. It was a big accomplishment for the CIA; all that was missing from the plan was the date of implementation, and they all held their breath.

In early November, Langley received an urgent request from its Warsaw station. Colonel Kuklinski had given a prearranged emergency signal that meant he was sure he was about to be exposed. The Soviets had asserted at a meeting that day that their secret plans were leaking to the United States. To maintain his cover, Kuklinski had to join in voicing outrage. He wanted out.

Those were the terms: the CIA had promised him asylum whenever he found it necessary. Casey approved an "exfiltration" order, allowing the Warsaw station secretly and hurriedly to withdraw the colonel, his wife and one of their sons. It was an elaborate, expensive and risky undertaking creating an underground railroad for three people. By November 6, the three were safely out of Poland and on their way to new identities in the United States.

The colonel's information was sorely missed. When special police units began mass arrests of 5,000 Solidarity activists in the early-morning hours of December 13, the CIA was caught by surprise. The first independent trade union movement in a Communist country was effectively ended.

Inman was growing increasingly uncomfortable. The covert actions were straying far afield from what he felt was the real mission of the intelligence agencies. Intelligence was collection, what Inman called "positive intelligence," information about other countries that was useful to the U.S. policy-makers.

Inman focused on the "indications and warnings" about the activities of governments. That meant beefing up human intelligence, as well as making the investment in satellite and signals intelligence to insure multiple sources and a timely flow of information. It also called for a long-range plan, one that looked ahead five to seven years. But he knew that no administration would likely care much about that far in the future. Immediate problems received 99 percent of the available attention. Inman had launched a Casey-style campaign on the future, ordering a study, setting up meetings, focusing attention. In March 1981 he had convinced national-security adviser Richard Allen to ask each department and agency to study and list all world problems they expected to deal with in the period 1985 to 1990. Included were all Soviet activities, political uprisings, the world economy, terrorism, nuclear proliferation.

Using his Navy contacts, Inman had helped launch a similar request for a study to the Joint Chiefs of Staff.

The White House asked Casey to coordinate the effort, but, as Inman expected, Casey quickly passed the task to him. Inman asked for a statement of intelligence needs from each department and found little resistance, since it was bureaucratically nonthreatening. Within several months Inman had a catalogue, or wish list, that all could agree on, since no item was given priority. Next, the hard part, he asked each department and agency to state what they thought they could and should do in each area. He also asked each to say what they expected other departments or agencies to do.

When Inman had finished, the gaps were obvious. Communications for clandestine agents needed upgrading. For some time the CIA had employed the so-called "burst transmitter" which sent a long message at high speed in a burst of several seconds or less, reducing the chances of detection. Technological advances were astounding but expensive. Miniaturization was another problem. Electronic devices, including the ones for satellites, had to be small enough to fit on space platforms or be hidden in Iron Curtain countries. They had to work for years and be maintenance free.

Inman was certain that intelligence-gathering had to be geared to the hard cases—crisis or war. That required an ability to communicate and transfer large blocks of information securely to and from places that were not necessarily on the list of hot spots. U.S. intelligence also needed more backup systems, alternative sources, an increase in frequency of coverage for satellite photos and signals intelligence, and more timely processing of information. By the fall of 1981, Inman had a first draft of a plan, entitled "Intelligence Capabilities 1985–90." Casey went through it, asked a lot of questions and requested changes, but he liked the overall scheme. It set a consensus on the requirements and specified how they might be achieved. The basic question was whether this multibillion-dollar increase in the budgets was going to be done as part of the Reagan defense buildup or separately. Inman was pretty sure he could sell the program in the Defense Department. Deputy Secretary of Defense Carlucci felt that intelligence-gathering was the first line of defense and that improvements would be cost effective, saving billions in the Defense budget in the long run.

Casey won agreement among all the departments and agencies, and only then did he call the inch-thick top-secret plan to the President's attention. There were few documents more sensitive in the U.S. government. It was the map of the intelligence future.

President Reagan met with the National Security Planning Group on the five-year intelligence plan. The NSPG was becoming the basic foreign-policy forum that hashed out the issues. Inman's plan envisioned an intelligence budget which had been $6 billion in 1980 but which would go beyond $20 billion during the plan's first year, 1985. In the psychology of peace through strength, crack intelligence-gathering was a main pillar. The exploitation of the American edge in technology, space and electronics appealed to Reagan.

After the review and discussion, the President said, "I don't see how we can afford not to do this."

9

CONCERN AGAIN MOUNTED at the White House as intelligence reports continued to lend plausibility to Qaddafi's threat to kill Reagan or launch a terrorist spectacular against the United States. To Casey it was the classic "mosaic," the small bits that formed a pretty clear picture.

The file had started to build in late August, when a CIA European source reported that a key Palestinian had conferred with a member of the Libyan General Staff and had agreed to a joint action against Reagan; a report from another high-level Palestinian said that the shadowy group Black September had been reactivated to move against U.S. and Israeli targets. And there had been the Ethiopian source who had reported Qaddafi's threatening remarks in Addis Ababa.

In early September, a relative of a Libyan diplomat in New Delhi wrote an anonymous letter to the U.S. Embassy in New Delhi saying that Libya planned to assassinate Reagan. It was a fragment, untested and unexpected. Was it a cry of conscience that should be taken seriously? Casey thought even unlikely sources had to be paid attention until their information was discounted.

Next "a casual informant with excellent access to senior Libyan military officers" delivered two reports: one, that Libya was preparing to attack American interests in the Mediterranean area; the other, that Libyans in Rome were preparing to kidnap or murder the American ambassador to Italy, Maxwell Rabb.

On September 9, a European intelligence service reported that the Italians had arrested and expelled a number of Libyans believed to be involved in the plan against Rabb. A week later this same intelligence service confirmed that a Palestinian group had agreed to assist Libya in attacking Reagan and other American targets.

On September 19, a report stated that Libya would launch a suicide attack against the aircraft carrier U.S.S. *Nimitz,* which was off the coast of Libya in the Mediterranean.

On October 9, another report from a European intelligence service said that during Qaddafi's trip to Syria two months earlier he had met with four terrorist groups to enlist their support in attacking U.S. targets in Europe.

On October 17, "an informant with demonstrated access to senior Libyan intelligence personnel" reported that Libyans had left for Europe to engage in attacks on U.S. embassies in Paris and Rome. Six days later the same source listed embassies in Athens, Beirut, Tunis, London and Madrid as possible targets. Within a week, there was a report from a CIA source with access to Libyan intelligence officers that five Libyans, possibly members of a hit team, had arrived in Rome. While on a trip to Milan on October 21, Ambassador Rabb was called back to the United States for his own safety, flown out without even a change of clothes.

On October 30, the Italian intelligence service, SISMI, told the CIA that the hit team had transited Rome and gone on to an unknown destination.

On November 12, a gunman in Paris fired six shots at the U.S. chargé d'affaires, Christian A. Chapman. He narrowly escaped. Libya was believed to be responsible.

On November 16, an informant walked into a CIA station at a U.S. embassy abroad, claiming he had left one of Qaddafi's training camps. He gave detailed descriptions of their training exercises—how, for example, to hit an American limousine caravan. The informant passed polygraph tests.

This informant added that if President Reagan proved too difficult a target, the Libyans were to go after Vice-President Bush, Secretary of State Haig or Defense Secretary Weinberger as "potential alternate targets."

Casey had been assembling more secret intelligence that indicated that Qaddafi was on the move. Back on August 19, during the Gulf of Sidra incident when Qaddafi lost two planes, Libya had signed a cooperation treaty with Ethiopia and South Yemen. It was a grouping of three of the most radical states in Africa, and it isolated U.S. allies Egypt and Sudan between Libya on the west and Ethiopia on the east. South Yemen, at the toe of the Arabian Peninsula, was a severe irritant to the Saudis. Casey's CIA was continuing the covert paramilitary support begun under Carter. Qaddafi had promised his alliance exactly $855.1 million and made the first $150 million transfer, a gesture of seriousness that worried Casey and his analysts.

The CIA had found out about several secret military annexes to this cooperation treaty among Libya, Ethiopia and South Yemen. The three countries had agreed to maintain—at Libyan expense—a force of 5,000 Libyans, 5,000 South Yemeni and 50,000 Ethiopian reserves. And 20,000 Ethiopians were to go to Libya.

CIA reports also said that the three countries had agreed to coordinate the insurgency in Somalia, to the southeast of Ethiopia. Intelligence showed that Cuba was maintaining 11,000 to 13,000 military personnel in Ethiopia; and there were approximately 500 Cuban advisers in South Yemen.

Qaddafi had promised $3.3 billion from 1975 to 1980 in foreign military and economic assistance around the world. Though he had made good on less than half, or $1.4 billion, he had met about 70 percent of his military-assistance commitments.

A special National Intelligence Estimate had been ordered on the pact. Completed November 4, the secret study said that the motive of the three countries was "to defeat U.S. policy in the region."

Against this backdrop, Casey felt, Qaddafi's enterprises, assertions and promises had to be countered. Any adventure within the borders of the United States had to be thwarted at almost any cost, at once. First priority was protecting the President. The White House was inundated with this information—in the NID, the PDB and in special papers. Casey wasn't going to be caught napping. Better too much than too little.

Reagan's White House aides ordered a stepped-up security effort, including the dispatching of decoy limousine caravans about Washington while Reagan traveled in an unmarked caravan. Ground-to-air missiles were stationed next to the White House.

This high-level White House attention to security and threats, especially by Deaver, sent ripples throughout the government. No measure was considered an overreaction. Casey reminded his colleagues in the Administration of the earlier, nearly successful Reagan assassination attempt, the shooting of the Pope, the killing of Sadat.

On December 4, *The New York Times* reported that a five-man Libyan hit team had entered the United States. Within three days there were reports that it was a ten-man squad. The Immigration and Naturalization Service sent a seven-page memo stamped "EXTREMELY SENSITIVE" to its major border-crossing and airport offices. Composite sketches of five of the alleged hit men were on television.

In the flurry, Reagan's top aides, Meese, Baker and Deaver, decided that they too might be targets. Security guards were assigned to them. A Secret Service car followed the bus that carried Deaver's daughter each day to and from her private school, Holton Arms.

• • •

Haig had given Robert C. "Bud" McFarlane, a former Marine lieutenant colonel who was State Department counselor, the task of coordinating Libyan policy. After five weeks of interagency meetings, McFarlane sent a ten-page ACTION/TOP SECRET/SENSITIVE memo to Haig. On page nine, Haig initialed approval of this option: "Work with the Defense Department and CIA to develop responses to Libyan provocations that involve U.S. and Egyptian forces in covert, tactical air and commando operations. Discourage planning for major ground force operation." The U.S. was not going to invade Libya, but Haig wanted to explore the options short of that.

It was recommended that collection from SR-71 and U-2 surveillance flights be stepped up, at the cost of $200,000 for each five-hour mission.

At a top-secret November 30 NSPG meeting, the President asked that plans be developed for "a military response against Libya in the event of a further Libyan attempt to assassinate American officials or attack U.S. facilities." A long TOP SECRET memo on "counter-terrorist planning toward Libya" was drafted for Reagan on December 5 by Haig, Carlucci (standing in for Weinberger) and Casey. It included everything from a plan for dealing with Congress and the media to contingency economic sanctions against Libya. Most important was the part on contingency military action. State, Defense and the CIA were unanimous in recommending to the President that he "should immediately direct the Joint Chiefs of Staff to ready assets to carry out military action against Libya in self-defense, following a further Libyan provocation."

A TOP SECRET chart listed five "graduated responses." First a direct attack on terrorist training sites in Libya. Satellites and other intelligence had identified sixteen possible targets, thirteen of them on the coast. This could be done by the Navy from aircraft-carrier bombers, which were given a "moderate" chance of success; the response time after a presidential order to strike was put at from four to forty-eight hours. B-52 bombers were another alternative, but were given a "low" chance of success because a good radar signature was necessary and not likely to be obtained; the bombers had a response time of twenty-eight to forty hours. The third were AC-130 aircraft and had only a "moderate" chance of success. The Pentagon was not encouraging such an operation and did not want to paint an overly optimistic picture of the chance of success.

The second contingency was a strike at Qaddafi's airfields; the third, a strike on his naval facilities; the fourth, on his military-equipment stockpiles; and the fifth, an attack on the naval vessels in port, using special Navy Seal teams. This last was given a "moderate to high chance" of success, but the response time for a Seal squad was listed as forty-eight to seventy-two hours after a one-to-two-week mission preparation time. Such an attack could conceivably be done covertly, and it was the only alternative that was given a better than 50 percent chance of success.

On Sunday, December 6, 1981, Qaddafi appeared in a live interview on ABC Television's *This Week with David Brinkley*. Speaking from his private office in Tripoli, Qaddafi heatedly denied that he had sent any hit teams or assassination squads.

"We refuse to assassinate any person," the Libyan leader said, placing his hand under his chin and looking up in the air dreamily at one point. "It is the behavior of America, preparing to assassinate me, to poison my food. They tried many things to do this." He challenged the Administration to produce the evidence. Americans, Qaddafi said, "How you are silly people. . . . This is silly, this Administration, and this President. America must get rid of this Administration and fell it down as they did with Nixon."

Under questioning, speaking through an interpreter, Qaddafi said, "And you will see, Reagan is liar" and his Administration practicing terrorism against Libya militarily, economically, psychologically. "We are ready to make judgment of an investigation, to see this evidence, because we are sure we didn't send any people to kill Reagan or any other people in the world. And we want to see this big lies."

Senate Intelligence Committee Vice-Chairman Moynihan responded that it was Qaddafi who was a liar, and a mad dictator. "We have concrete evidence that there have been officials of the United States government targeted." When pressed, Moynihan hedged; there was about an 80 percent chance the evidence was true.

The next day, Reagan said publicly, "I wouldn't believe a word [Qaddafi] says if I were you. . . . We have the evidence and he knows it."

But eyeball-to-eyeball in the media was judged insufficient by the Administration. A direct threat was sent off to Qaddafi. Since the United States and Libya had no diplomatic relations, a TOP SECRET EYES ONLY message from President Reagan to Colonel Qaddafi was dispatched through Belgium:

"I have detailed and verified information about several Libyan-sponsored plans and attempts to assassinate U.S. government officials and attack U.S. facilities both in the U.S. and abroad. Any acts of violence directed by Libya or its agents against officials of the U.S., at home or abroad, will be regarded by the U.S. government as an armed attack upon the U.S. and will be met by every means necessary to defend this nation in accordance with Article 51 of the United Nations Charter."

Article 51 allowed member countries of the United Nations to take action in self-defense. Information about the general warning was provided to the American press, but the actual invocation of Article 51 was not mentioned. Rather, officials told reporters about "the most serious consequences." On December 10, President Reagan appealed to the 1,500 Americans living in Libya to leave and suspended American passports for future travel to Libya. But nothing was done to cut off the $10 billion in oil that Libya sold to the United States.

The warning seemed to work. Within the next week, a senior Libyan intelligence official came to the United States as an envoy and said that Qaddafi was "desperate" to open a channel to the United States and pledged there would be no terrorist or assassination operations.

On December 18, the CIA Intelligence Directorate issued a SECRET report on alleged plans to assassinate top U.S. leaders. It noted that the first report on the threat to Reagan—issued during Qaddafi's meeting with the Ethiopian President in the third week of August—was from an "excellent source." The report then proceeded to pour some cold water. "Subsequent reports on actual plans to carry out attacks against senior U.S. government officials, however, have come from sources with only indirect access, whose credibility is open to question. It is possible that some of the reporting may have been generated because informants are aware we are seeking this information."

A later SECRET State Department analysis from the department's intelligence division stated: "CIA records indicate, however, that the source of one of the reports that Libya intends to attack the Sixth Fleet has in the past had sustained contact with a Soviet diplomat." The other reports of plans to attack U.S. principals were "most later discounted." The analysis also noted "the obvious probability that reporting breeds reporting where the U.S. is perceived to have an interest." In all, the memo suggested that all the hit-squad reports may have been misinformation feeding off itself.

Much of this latter information was traced to a shadowy figure with ties to Iranian and Israeli intelligence services—Manucher Ghorbanifar, a wealthy Iranian arms salesman who had been a secret CIA source. He saw the initial hit-squad reports as an opportunity to make trouble for the Libyans, and he single-handedly kept the issue alive for several months. Soon the CIA officially and secretly declared Ghorbanifar a "fabricator."

In a television interview, CBS anchorman Dan Rather asked President Reagan if the reports of hit squads were untrue.

"No," Reagan responded. "We had too much information from too many sources, and we had our facts straight. We tried to sit on them. We tried to keep that all quiet . . . but our information was valid.''

Congressman Michael Barnes, a studious-looking thirty-eight-year-old Maryland Democrat, had heard the rumors, that winter of 1981–82, that covert plans were being drawn up for Central America. Barnes was chairman of the House foreign-affairs subcommittee on the Western Hemisphere that had responsibility for Central America, but because he was not a member of the House Intelligence Committee he couldn't find out what was going on. Barnes had leverage with the State Department, particularly with the regional assistant secretary, Tom Enders. He was convinced that no one could expect him to do his job of chairing the subcommittee if he didn't know about major CIA operations.

''There's something I want to talk to you about,'' Barnes said in a phone call to Enders, ''and I don't want to talk about it on the phone.'' They agreed to have breakfast at the Hay-Adams, a plush downtown hotel where the tables are far enough apart to permit private conversation.

As breakfast was served, Barnes said, ''I have a report that the CIA is hiring mercenaries to blow up bridges in Nicaragua.''

''You'll need to go to the Intelligence Committee,'' Enders replied blankly. They both recognized the rules. The absence of a denial from Enders convinced Barnes that his information was near target.

Barnes sought out the House Intelligence Committee chairman, Edward Boland, the seventy-year-old Massachusetts Congressman, a friend and former roommate of House Speaker Thomas P. ''Tip'' O'Neill. Boland did not share the younger generation's distrust of intelligence operations, but he felt that Barnes should know what was going on in his region. So Boland explained to Barnes the CIA plan to use Argentina to train 500 contras to interdict the arms flow from Nicaragua to El Salvador.

Barnes was stunned. He knew the Latin American players: no one, including the CIA, would be able to control the Argentines, who were known for their ruthlessness. The agency might as well have picked Chilean strongman Augusto Pinochet.

Boland said that there were to be no terrorist actions, no burning of farms and so forth. The CIA effort was to be limited, it did not seem a particularly big deal.

Barnes asked Enders for another meeting, this time lunch at the Metropolitan Club. When they met, he came on strong: It sounded like a stupid plan. People were going to get killed.

Enders knew how to press the right buttons on Barnes's console to reassure him. He was merely acceding to certain necessary covert action. So should Barnes. There would be no assassinations. The operation would be tightly controlled. There would be no human-rights violations.

Barnes resisted. The CIA operation would give the Sandinistas a precise rationale to tighten the clamps on the press, the labor movement and the political opposition. It would give them reason to bring in more Cubans.

Enders' answer was, "Trust me." As the assistant secretary, he was involved directly. This would be done right.

Barnes felt that his hands were tied. The Senate had the real power in foreign affairs, with the authority to ratify treaties and approve executive-branch appointments. The House Foreign Affairs Committee was a debating society at best. Without knowledge of secret operations, the House committee was to be denied even that role.

At a public hearing of the committee, Haig refused to rule out an anti-Nicaragua covert action, adding, "But that must not be interpreted by mischievous inquisitors as articulation of our policy one way or the other." Barnes replied, "Based on your responses, if I were a Nicaraguan I'd be building my bomb shelter."

Senator Christopher J. Dodd of Connecticut also felt locked out of the Central America debate, even as a member of the Senate Foreign Relations Committee. Dodd, a thirty-seven-year-old liberal Democrat, had spent two years as a Peace Corps volunteer in small mountain villages in the Dominican Republic and spoke fluent Spanish. He had heard the CIA rumors, but he could not find out what was going on.

This CIA was acting out the Big-Stick, meddling-Yankee imperialism of other eras, Dodd felt. The United States was in bed with the slave owners. With some work, Dodd figured, he could learn the general outline of the CIA plan. But then he would be caught in the snare of "official" silence, unable to speak out in public. It was a Catch-22. Either he had to remain ignorant about the secret operations and sound like a paranoid or, if he learned of them, he was muzzled.

Dodd had attended a closed December 10 Senate Foreign Relations Committee briefing by the CIA's intelligence officer for Latin America, Constantine Menges. He knew that Menges was Casey's man, and that he would provide a clue, if not about operations, at least about attitudes.

The briefing had turned into a political harangue against Havana. It sounded like Ronald Reagan's stump speech—denouncing Communists and attributing the woes of Central America to Moscow and Marxism. With two colleagues, Dodd wrote a letter to Casey, protesting Menges' behavior. It was obvious where events were heading even if Dodd couldn't prove it. But even if he could, he wouldn't have the freedom to express his views.

When Casey saw a February 14 *Washington Post* front-page story on the CIA's $19 million Nicaragua plan, he was relieved to read: "It could not be learned whether the CIA proposal has been approved and implemented."

The next afternoon, from 2:30 to 3:45, Casey gave a special top-secret briefing to President Reagan in the Situation Room. He reported that Dewey Clarridge had been successful in organizing some anti-Sandinista resistance fighters in Honduras, and that cross-border operations into Nicaragua would soon begin. The action was expected to lessen the Nicaraguan predisposition for exporting trouble and revolution.

In late February, an official who knew the intelligence the Administration was receiving and what operations they had launched, agreed to talk during a long walk in a Washington suburb. The current concern was reports that the Soviets were training Nicaraguans on advanced MiG aircraft, he said. This was viewed as "very alarming," because the planes could foreshadow a dramatic Sandinista military move to spread the war of liberation to other Central American countries, particularly El Salvador. There was a lot of broad strategic thinking going on by Haig, Casey and others. According to their calculations, the MiGs could give the Nicaraguans potential influence over the sea lanes in the Caribbean and near the Panama Canal—a condition the United States could not permit.

The official said, "Nicaragua is now a Soviet-managed government the way we managed the South Vietnam government during the war." He added, "The key to the area is Nicaragua and not El Salvador—there is too much focus on El Salvador." He posited a line of crashing dominoes racing into Mexico.

If the new MiGs went to Nicaragua, the official said, Reagan would take them out with some kind of covert action. The President would not send troops to Central America, he explained, but Reagan did not want to say that publicly. Also, he said, Reagan would not send thousands of advisers.

How about covert action now? If the stakes were half as great as he said, certainly a modest covert undertaking would be logical, especially given the pro-CIA, pro-covert-action pronouncements during the presidential campaign.

He declined to answer.

On March 4, 1982, Jaime Wheelock of the Sandinista ruling directorate delivered a speech in Washington in which he claimed that a CIA operation was under way.

"There are too many things happening at once to be a coincidence," he said. "All these elements lead to one conclusion. The CIA is the only force with the power to do these things at once. It's difficult to prove it specifically, but the tracks are there."

On Monday, March 8, Bradlee asked me to a 9 A.M. breakfast. We now had it solid from three sources that the Nicaragua operation had presidential approval. He said he wanted to go slowly, reminding me gently that the political climate was very different from the 1970s. This is Reagan's government now, he said, and the presumption is no longer that the airing of CIA secrets is automatically good. It could be bad. What's the justification for running the story? Bradlee asked. "I want to hear the reason, tell me the precise reason."

Could such an operation or such an act of war work? I asked. Could it stay secret? Should it stay secret?

"I don't know the answers to any of those questions," Bradlee said. "Is the CIA out of control?"

I said I didn't think so, Reagan had signed off.

There has to be a reason to publish, then, Bradlee said. The Reagan Administration had made it clear it would take steps to protect its national-security secrets. That meant possible court action or God knows what. Do the sources want it out? he asked. "What's their motive?"

They were unsure it was the right step.

Why don't they step forward and say this on the record, with their names? Bradlee asked. That would sure make it easier.

They're not so certain that they're willing to do that, I answered. They're willing to let Bradlee make the publication decision.

"Shit," Bradlee said.

Later he contacted Goldwater, who under the new congressional-oversight laws would have to know. Goldwater said he had never heard about this alleged operation, not a single word. Bradlee said he was morally certain that Goldwater would not lie to him.

Within minutes Bradlee received another call.

"Goldwater just called again," he said, "and apparently made some inquiry, and now guess what? He said that this moment 'Casey is waiting in my outer office.' Something is up, for fucking sure."

Bradlee was to talk with Casey himself, and Goldwater couldn't answer any questions. The implication was that Goldwater now knew something or soon would know something.

Casey had hotfooted it over to Goldwater's office to explain what was going on. But why? Goldwater had been out with hip operations for several months. Maybe he had missed the key briefing.

The next day, Tuesday, March 9, Casey and Bradlee lunched together at the CIA. Bradlee came back about 2:30 P.M., just before the *Post*'s daily news conference. The story was ready to go, but Bradlee had not given the go-ahead. He was wagging his head. There was such lack of clarity in everything about Casey, Bradlee said. His speech was unclear; as he chewed his lunch, there was more distortion. Vagueness and side-stepping.

Did he confirm or deny the story? the *Post* editors asked.

Neither, when you get down to it, Bradlee said. Yet Casey talked about a five-hundred-man force as if it existed or would soon exist. At one point he indicated it would grow. But it was unclear whether this force was Argentine or CIA. Casey said that anything by the CIA would be to stop the weapons flow from Nicaragua to El Salvador. Casey said that this force was not going to blow up things like power plants and bridges, as our sources had said. Casey had also suggested that whatever the CIA might do had been authorized three or four months earlier, back in November.

Was that some kind of confirmation?

It was and it wasn't, Bradlee said. He was uncomfortable, looking out his office window, replaying the luncheon conversation in his mind. There is something missing or they are trying to discourage us, not scare us, Bradlee said. Yet, he added, "Casey did not say, 'Don't run the story.' That would have scared me—I'm glad I do not have to go through that red light."

Had Casey made a national-security argument?

No, Bradlee said.

The story draft was ready. Was he going to run it?

"I don't know," Bradlee said.

Meanwhile that same day, March 9, in the State Department auditorium, Inman had assembled the press for an unusual show-and-tell.

"I'm Bob Inman," he began grimly. "I'm here this afternoon because I'm concerned and because I'm angry." His worry was the Nicaraguan military buildup. "I'm angry because I've watched, over the past couple of weeks, public servants trying to grapple with the difficulty of conveying information while protecting critical intelligence sources and methods and finding that they're standardly greeted with 'How can we believe you unless you show us all the detailed evidence?' " Skepticism had gone too far, he said, and he hoped for greater neutrality, more trust.

John T. Hughes, a deputy director of the DIA, who had presented the photo evidence in the Cuban Missile Crisis twenty years earlier, stepped forward and jabbed a six-foot-long pointer over wall-size blowups of aerial photographs of Nicaragua (taken by U-2 and SR-71 spy planes; there were none of the top-secret satellite photos). They showed that the Sandinistas had built thirty-six new military bases in the last two years. In 1979, at the time of the revolution, the Sandinistas were a band of 5,000 guerrillas, and they now have 70,000 men under arms, Hughes said. Whipping through the eerie, grainy photos, Hughes identified Soviet equipment, including tanks and small field cannons, called howitzers. This is not a defense force, he said—the fingerprints are Cuban, and the garrison areas have Soviet-style layouts down to the obstacle courses.

After the display, Inman took questions. He was asked about the earlier report (the one that had run in the *Post* in February) about the CIA's $19 million covert plan. Inman virtually knocked down any idea that it had been approved. "I would suggest to you," he said with all his sincerity, "that $19 million or $29 million isn't going to buy you much of any kind these days, and certainly not against that kind of a military force."

The briefing was big news; Casey hoped for a Cuban Missile Crisis–scale blast of publicity. It was widely interpreted that Inman was carefully but emphatically denying that any $19 million covert plan had been approved.

That was troubling. It would not be like Inman to take a public potshot at a program that had been approved by the President. Inman's tone at the briefing was supportive of Reagan, Casey and the efforts of these "public servants" to explain the peril in Central America. Yet we were sure of the story. It seemed inconceivable that Inman was unaware.

The *Post*'s national editor, Bill Greider, had changed the phrase "limited covert warfare" in the lead of our story to "covert operations." Pat Tyler argued that this was a dilution of the article's central point. Paramilitary action of any type, Tyler argued, was war, and he had gingerly coined the euphemism "limited covert warfare."

William J. Casey at CIA headquarters. Behind him is an aerial photo of the Agency's Langley, Virginia, headquarters. [Dennis Brack/Black Star]

◀ Richard M. Helms, Director of Central Intelligence, 1966–1973. [Gerald Martineau/*The Washington Post*]

William E. Colby, DCI, 1973–1976. [Lucian Perkins/*The Washington Post*] ▼

Stansfield Turner, DCI, 1977–1981. [Jimmy Carter Library]

In the Oval Office, President Richard Nixon at Casey's swearing-in as Securities Exchange Commission chairman on April 14, 1971. Nixon hailed Casey as the "best man" for the job. Sophia Casey and U.S. District Court Judge John J. Sirica look on. [UPI/Bettmann Newsphotos]

Presidential candidate Ronald Reagan and campaign manager Casey chat aboard plane during the 1980 campaign. [AP/Wide World Photos]

Bill and Sophia Casey outside their Long Island compound, Mayknoll. [Wally McNamee/Woodfin Camp & Assoc.]

The Director, a double bogey golfer, demonstrates his swing. [Wally McNamee/Woodfin Camp & Assoc.]

◀ Admiral Bobby R. Inman, Deputy Director of Central Intelligence, arriving to testify before the Senate Intelligence Committee in July 1981. [AP/Wide World Photos]

Max C. Hugel, appointed by Casey as Deputy Director for Operations, resigned in July 1981 after accusations of questionable stock dealings. [Fred Sweets/*The Washington Post*] ▼

"SIR, ABOUT YOUR CHOICE OF MR. HUGEL AS CHIEF OF SECRET OPERATIONS—"

CIA Director Casey

©1981 HERBLOCK

[From *Herblock Through the Looking Glass*, W. W. Norton, 1984]

.. John N. McMahon testifying during his nomination hearings as Deputy Director of Central ntelligence in May 1982. *R.* Robert M. Gates during his confirmation hearings as Deputy)irector of Central Intelligence in April 1986. [Both James K. W. Atherton/*The Washington Post*]

L. John R. Horton, national intelligence officer for Latin America, quit because he said Casey pressured him in 1984 on an intelligence estimate on Mexico. *R.* Stanley Sporkin, who served at the SEC during Casey's tenure, was CIA counsel 1981–1986. [Both AP/Wide World Photos]

L. William Buckley, CIA station chief in Beirut, was kidnapped in 1984, tortured, and eventually died in captivity. The CIA was unable to obtain a 400-page transcript of his confessions to his captors. [UPI/Bettmann Newsphotos] *R.* George Lauder, veteran CIA operations officer and head of CIA Public Affairs, sits by as Casey is interviewed, October 1985. [Dennis Brack/ Black Star]

Representative Michael D. Barnes, Maryland Democrat, and Thomas O. Enders, Assistant Secretary of State for Inter-American Affairs, at a House Foreign Affairs Subcommittee hearing in 1982. [James K. W. Atherton/*The Washington Post*]

Jeane Kirkpatrick, U.S. Ambassador to the United Nations 1981–1985. ▼

Air Force Lieutenant General Eugene Tighe, Defense Intelligence Agency chief 1977–1981. ▼

L. Anthony "Tony" Motley, Assistant Secretary of State for Inter-American Affairs 1983–1985. [Dennis Brack/Black Star] ▼

Lawrence A. Pezzullo, U.S. Ambassador to Nicaragua 1979–1981. [UPI/Bettmann Newsphotos] ▼

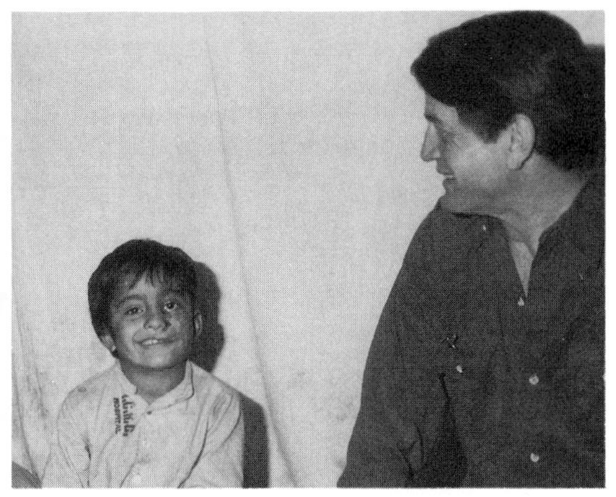

Congressman Charles Wilson, Texas Democrat, with Afghan child, who Wilson says was injured by a Soviet booby-trapped toy.

Ronald and Nancy Reagan as they depart for a Camp David weekend. Reagan displayed a T-shirt "Stop Communism in Central America." [John McDonnell/ *The Washington Post*]

Angolan guerrilla leader Jonas Savimbi at UNITA headquarters in July 1986. [Patrick Tyler/*The Washington Post*]

Reagan at a reception on March 21, 1986, holding up a button "If You Like Cuba, You'll Love Nicaragua." [Rich Lipski/*The Washington Post*]

Egyptian President Anwar Sadat. He was assassinated by Moslem fundamentalists on October 6, 1981. [UPI/Bettmann Newsphotos] ▶

Prince Bandar, the Saudi Arabian Ambassador, and President Reagan at the White House in 1983. [Lucian Perkins/*The Washington Post*] ▼

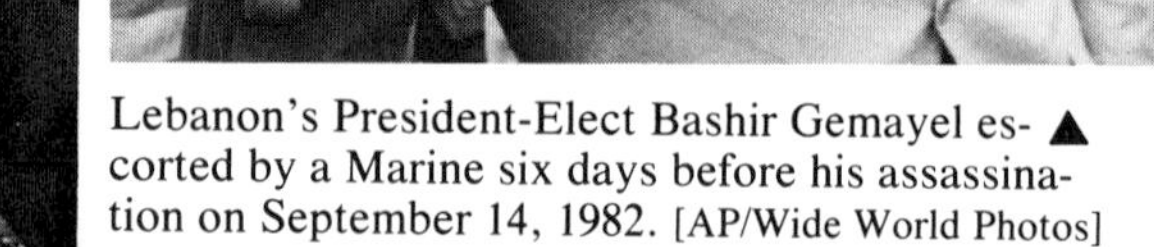

Lebanon's President-Elect Bashir Gemayel escorted by a Marine six days before his assassination on September 14, 1982. [AP/Wide World Photos] ▲

Chad President Hissen Habré [Reuters/Bettmann Newsphotos]

HOME DELIVERY

This cartoon by Gary Brookins appeared after a November 3, 1985, *Washington Post* story revealed a covert operation authorized by President Reagan to undermine the regime of Libyan leader Muammar Qaddafi.

Libyan leader Qaddafi in January 1986 [Peter Turnley/Black Star]

Iranian leader Ayatollah Khomeini in 1985 [Manoocher/Black Star]

Cuban President Fidel Castro and Nicaraguan President Daniel Ortega confer in 1985 in Nicaragua. [Reuters/Bettmann Newsphotos]

Casey and Reagan in the Oval Office on ▲ October 22, 1985, a month after the first secret arms sale to Iran. [Bill Fitzpatrick/ White House Photo]

"IT'S A WHOLE DIFFERENT SET-UP — CASEY, HERE NOW HAS TO HAVE HIS LIMO DRIVE HIM HERE TO THE NSC TO PLAN MILITARY CAMPAIGNS"

NICARAGUA
WAR ROOM
$640
Wm Casey
CIA
National Security Council
CONGRESS
©1985 HERBLOCK

Reagan with his National Security advisers in the White House Situation Room on June 16, 1985, during the TWA 847 hijacking crisis. *(L–R)*Secretary of Defense Caspar W. Weinberger; Vice President George Bush; the President; Secretary of State George P. Shultz; DCI Casey; and White House Chief of Staff Donald Regan. [Terry Arthur/White House Photo] ▼

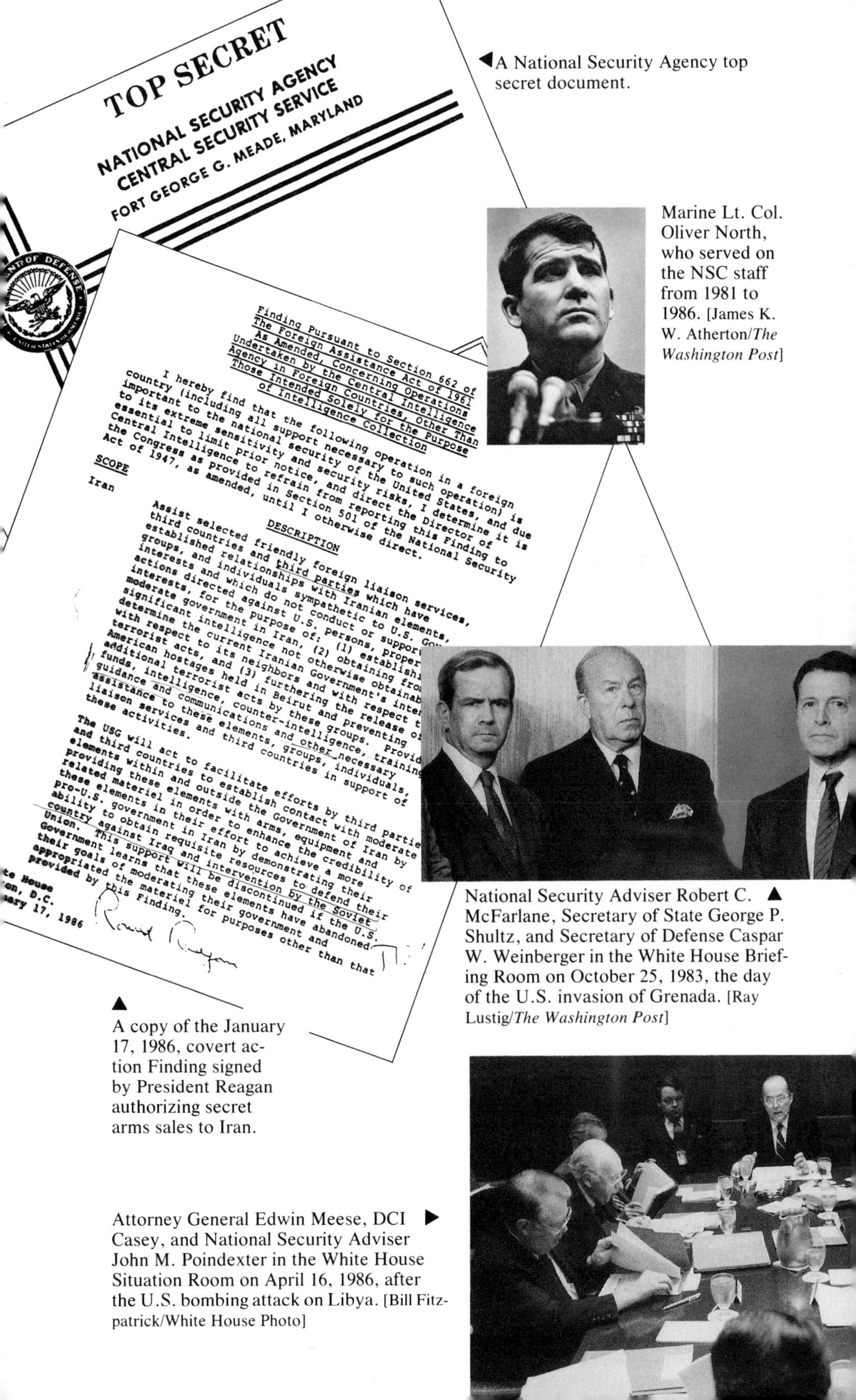

TOP SECRET

NATIONAL SECURITY AGENCY
CENTRAL SECURITY SERVICE
FORT GEORGE G. MEADE, MARYLAND

Finding Pursuant to Section 662 of
The Foreign Assistance Act of 1961
As Amended, Concerning Operations
Undertaken by the Central Intelligence
Agency in Foreign Countries, Other Than
Those Intended Solely for the Purpose
of Intelligence Collection

I hereby find that the following operation in a foreign country (including all support necessary to such operation) is important to the national security of the United States, and due to its extreme sensitivity and security risks, I determine it is essential to limit prior notice, and direct the Director of Central Intelligence to refrain from reporting this Finding to the Congress as provided in Section 501 of the National Security Act of 1947, as amended, until I otherwise direct.

SCOPE

Iran

DESCRIPTION

Assist selected friendly foreign liaison services, third countries and third parties which have established relationships with Iranian elements, groups, and individuals sympathetic to U.S. Gov interests and which do not conduct or suppor actions directed against U.S. persons, proper interests, for the purpose of: (1) establishi moderate government in Iran, (2) obtaining fro significant intelligence not otherwise obtainab determine the current Iranian Government's inte with respect to its neighbors and with respect t terrorist acts, and (3) furthering the release o American hostages held in Beirut and preventing additional terrorist acts by these groups. Provid funds, intelligence, counter-intelligence, training guidance and communications and other necessary assistance to these elements, groups, individuals, liaison services and third countries in support of these activities.

The USG will act to facilitate efforts by third partie and third countries to establish contact with moderate elements within and outside the Government of Iran by providing these elements with arms, equipment and related materiel in order to enhance the credibility of these elements in their effort to achieve a more pro-U.S. government in Iran by demonstrating their ability to obtain requisite resources to defend their country against Iraq and intervention by the Soviet Union. This support will be discontinued if the U.S. Government learns that these elements have abandoned their goals of moderating their government and appropriated the materiel for purposes other than that provided by this Finding.

te House
on, D.C.
ary 17, 1986

◀ A National Security Agency top secret document.

Marine Lt. Col. Oliver North, who served on the NSC staff from 1981 to 1986. [James K. W. Atherton/*The Washington Post*]

National Security Adviser Robert C. McFarlane, Secretary of State George P. Shultz, and Secretary of Defense Caspar W. Weinberger in the White House Briefing Room on October 25, 1983, the day of the U.S. invasion of Grenada. [Ray Lustig/*The Washington Post*] ▲

▲ A copy of the January 17, 1986, covert action Finding signed by President Reagan authorizing secret arms sales to Iran.

Attorney General Edwin Meese, DCI Casey, and National Security Adviser John M. Poindexter in the White House Situation Room on April 16, 1986, after the U.S. bombing attack on Libya. [Bill Fitzpatrick/White House Photo] ▶

◀Casey arriving on Capitol Hill, December 5, 1984, to testify about the CIA-distributed manual which advised Nicaraguan contras on the "selective use of violence" to "neutralize" Nicaraguan officials. [AP/Wide World Photos]

"SOMEBODY MINED THE I.R.S. OFFICES!"

Casey's complicated personal finances ▲ were a source of congressional concern sporadically throughout his tenure as DCI. [From *Herblock Through the Looking Glass*, W. W. Norton, 1984]

◀Casey stands behind Senate Intelligence Committee leaders, Senator Daniel P. Moynihan, New York Democrat, the committee vice chairman, and Senator Barry Goldwater, Arizona Republican, the committee chairman, prior to Casey's confirmation hearings on January 13, 1981. [AP/Wide World Photos]

Senator Gary Hart, Colorado Democrat, and Senator William Cohen, Maine Republican, who might have been killed if their plane had landed on schedule at the Managua airport in the fall of 1983. [Martha Hartnett/© 1985 *Los Angeles Times*]

Congressman Edward ▶ P. Boland, Massachusetts Democrat and author of the famous Boland Amendment, which first restricted and later prohibited United States assistance to the contras, with longtime colleague House Speaker Thomas P. "Tip" O'Neill.

◀ Senate Intelligence Committee chairman Senator David Durenberger, Minnesota Republican; Robert M. Gates, nominee for Deputy CIA Director; and committee vice chairman Senator Patrick Leahy, Vermont Democrat, in 1986. [AP/Wide World Photos]

Jonathan Jay Pollard and his wife at Reagan's ▶ second Inaugural Ball. He was later convicted as an Israeli spy. [AP/Wide World Photos]

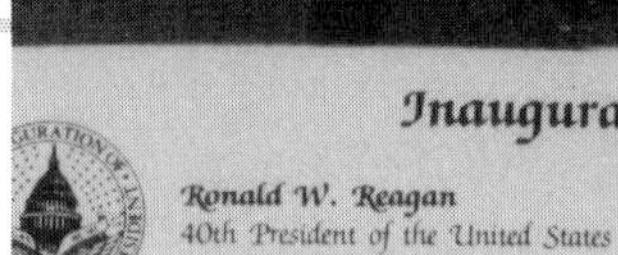

ESPIONAGE; INTERSTATE FLIGHT - PROBATION VI

WANTED BY F

EDWARD LEE HOWARD

ck Brian, Patrick M. Brian, Patrick M. Bryan, Edward L. Houston, Ed Howard, James Rogers,
son, Roger K. Shannon

NCIC: D05407191911081O

Photograph taken 1983

DESCRIPTION

DATE OF BIRTH: October 27, 1951
PLACE OF BIRTH: Alamogordo, New Mexico
HEIGHT: 5' 11"
WEIGHT: 165 to 180 pounds
BUILD: medium
HAIR: brown
EYES: brown
COMPLEXION: medium
RACE: white
NATIONALITY: American
SCARS AND MARKS: 2-inch scar over right eye; scar on upper lip
OCCUPATIONS: economic analyst; former U.S. Government employee
REMARKS: Knowledgeable in the use of firearms. Reportedly speaks and understands Russian and Spanish fluently. Trained in disguise and surveillanc techniques.
SOCIAL SECURITY NUMBER USED: 457-92-0226

CRIMINAL RECORD

Howard has been convicted of assault with a deadly weapon.

CAUTION

HOWARD SHOULD BE CONSIDERED AR
BE APPROACHED WITH CAUTION INAS
ASSAULT WITH A DEADLY WEAPON
PROBATION.

rant was issued on September 23, 1985, at Albuquerque, New Mexico, charging Howard with
le 18, U.S. Code, Section 794 (c)). A Federal warrant was also issued on September 27, 1985,
e, New Mexico, charging Howard with Unlawful Interstate Flight to Avoid Confinement-
ation (Title 18, U.S. Code, Section 1073).

E INFORMATION CONCERNING THIS PERSON, PLEASE CONTACT YOUR LOCAL
TELEPHONE NUMBERS AND ADDRESSES OF ALL FBI OFFICES LISTED ON BACK.

rder 4998
35

The FBI's "wanted" poster for Edward Lee ▲ Howard, a CIA operations officer who was being trained for undercover operations in the Soviet Union. After being fired, he sold secrets to the Soviets and then defected.

Ronald W. Pelton during his spy trial in June ▶ 1986. Pelton, a former NSA employee, sold information on multimillion-dollar espionage technology to the Soviets for $35,000. [UPI/Bettmann Newsphotos]

Casey chats at a Washington party in 1985 with Arkady Shevchenko, former Under-Secretary General of the UN for the Soviet Union, who defected to the United States in 1978. [Fred Sweets/*The Washington Post*] ▶

KGB officer Vitaly Yurchenko defected ▲ to the United States in the summer of 1985, but returned to the Soviet Union three months later. The CIA was never certain he was genuine, but he did provide clues to uncovering spies Edward Lee Howard and Ronald W. Pelton. He is seen here waving goodbye before boarding a plane in the U.S. bound for the Soviet Union. [AP/Wide World Photos]

During his CIA debriefing Yurchenko met ▶ Casey for dinner one evening at Langley headquarters. [Copyright © 1985 by Herblock in *The Washington Post*]

Casey testifying in Congress. [James K. W. Atherton/*The Washington Post*] ▼

CENTRAL INTELLIGENCE AGENCY CREDO

We are the Central Intelligence Agency.

We produce timely and high quality intelligence fo
Government of the United States.

We provide objective and unbiased evaluations anc
perceptions and ready to challenge conventional

We perform special intelligence tasks at the requ

We conduct our activities and ourselves accor
integrity, morality and honor and accordi
law and Constitution.

We measure our success by our contribution
enhancement of American values, security and national in

We believe our people are the Agency's most important resource. We seek
best and work to make them better. We subordinate our desire for public recognition to the need for confidentiality. We strive for continuing professional improvement. We give unfailing loyalty to each other and to our common purpose.

We seek through our leaders to stimulate initiative, a commitment to excellence and a propensity for action; to protect and reward Agency personnel for their special responsibilities, contributions, and sacrifices; to promote a sense of mutual trust and shared responsibility.

We get our inspiration and commitment to excellence from the inscription in our foyer: "And Ye shall know the truth and the truth shall make you free."

▲
After reading the best-seller *In Search of Excellence: Lessons from America's Best-Run Companies,* Casey directed that this "CIA Credo" be drafted and distributed.

The Reagans accompanied by Father Daniel Fagan on May 9, 1987, at Casey's funeral on Long Island, New York. ▶
[UPI/Bettmann Newsphotos]

It was not clear that Bradlee was going to okay the story in any form. He was jingling a lot of pocket change as he treaded about his glass-walled office.

Bradlee paraded editors and others through his office, seeking advice. Greider, probably the most passionate in his beliefs, was the coolest. He would not accept *secret* government, *secret* plans, *secret* wars. If we find out about them, we publish what we know. In this case, he said, there are no surprises here. Anti-Communist covert action is the implied promise of the Reagan election victory and his Administration. That's what people voted for, and no one knows that better than Ronald Reagan himself. Greider said that possibly the White House would be happy the story was out. He argued that we were too focused on the CIA aspect, the secrecy, the grand strategic dimension. We were overlooking the politics of declaring secret war on the Sandinistas. In the political forum, which was the chief concern of Reagan himself, an anti-Sandinista campaign would go over. Reagan's constituency would love it. But, he added, there was no assurance. The only assurance was that this was the newspaper's task and we ought to deliver.

Greider reminded everyone that the 1980 Republican presidential platform had said, "We deplore the Marxist-Sandinista takeover of Nicaragua. . . . we will support the efforts of the Nicaraguan people to establish a free and independent government." The platform had also promised an aggressive CIA. This was the logical marrying of the two. In one sense, he said, we were just reporting that Reagan was delivering on a campaign promise. Casey had not asked that the story be withheld. "Hell," Greider said, "he probably wants it out and will make sure it's leaked if we don't go."

There was a subtext. More than a year into the Reagan Administration, the relationship between the Administration and the news media was not clear. Overall, reporting had not been that aggressive. Reagan was still, nearly a year after the attempt on his life, enjoying an extended honeymoon. At the same time, the Administration was not gunning for the news media in any concerted way. There was the usual criticism of the media, but nothing approaching the scale or the hostility of previous administrations, such as Nixon's. It was evident that no one, including Bradlee, wanted to fire a first shot that might unleash a round of press-bashing.

About 6 P.M., Greider said that Bradlee had decided to run the story the next day. He said it was a straight call. There had been no single concern that anyone had raised which gave him more hesitation than any other. But totaled up, he had hesitated.

"It's as close as I've ever seen you come to not running something," I told Bradlee.

Yeah, he said, that might be true.

Why did you decide to go?

"The moderation of Casey's objection."

The story was placed on the front page under a small one-column headline, "U.S. Approves Covert Plan in Nicaragua" at the top of the right-hand side under the lead story about Inman's intelligence briefing showing the Nicaraguan military buildup. Anyone interested would see the covert story, but it was not one of those displays that suggested that the *Post* thought it had discovered the key to the creation of the universe, or to some "dirty" covert operation like assassination.

The next day, the 7 A.M. network news had the covert-plan story as its lead. There had been, as yet, no blast from the Administration. During the day, the Administration was tight-lipped. Haig said merely that it was "inappropriate to comment on covert activities—whether or not such exist." Weinberger said, "I'm just not going to comment—I never have. They are all highly classified, the whole subject is." Casey said nothing.

That evening all three major television networks had a lead story confirming the report. It was clear that the White House was taking the position that Reagan was being tough with the Nicaraguans and that he wanted it well known, that he judged it a political plus. Greider had been right.

On March 15 *Time* quoted Goldwater as saying, "Everything in the *Post* story was true. They didn't have everything, but everything they had is true."

That Saturday, Casey spoke at the Center for the Study of the Presidency in Washington. Casey believed in public speaking. He worked hard on his speeches, often writing them entirely himself. They mirrored, almost perfectly, what was occupying his work day, and the tasks, as he saw them, before the Administration and the CIA. To a degree few realized then, these speeches were a look inside.

Casey began by quoting General George Washington endorsing secrecy in intelligence operations: "For upon secrecy, success depends in most enterprises of the kind, and for the want of it, they are generally defeated, however well planned and promising. . . ." Casey then stepped to the world stage. The world was, he said, "plagued and beleaguered by subversion and a witch's brew of destabilization, terrorism and insurgency . . ." It was primarily "fueled by Soviet arms, Cuban manpower and Libyan money . . ."

He provided this history. In the aftermath of Vietnam, "beginning in 1974 and 1975, the Soviet Union undertook a new, much more aggressive strategy in the Third World . . . fully aware of the political climate in this country." By using proxies such as the Cubans in "relatively risk-free" operations, the Soviets went about stirring up trouble. In the seventies the Soviets' proxy successes, Casey said, had been in "Angola, Ethiopia, Cambodia, Nicaragua. . . .

"It is much easier and much less expensive to support an insurgency than it is for us and our friends to resist one. It takes relatively few people and little support to disrupt the internal peace and economic stability of a small country."

10

SENATOR PATRICK J. LEAHY, a lanky Vermont Democrat on the Intelligence Committee, watched a few skimpy secrets fly in committee briefings, but he was often uncomfortable. As with a magician's deck of cards, there was no telling if hearing or seeing should be believing. Members received the overview summary; or a system name and description from a spycraft catalogue; or a line-item budget entry; sometimes a bit of insider information about a head of state.

Leahy was a Watergate baby, elected to the Senate at thirty-four after Nixon's resignation, the only Democratic senator in the history of Vermont. He was used to the outside. Skeptical of secret concentrations of power—particularly in the Reagan government—Leahy wondered what he would see if all the intelligence cards were revealed. In eight years as the Chittenden County prosecutor, he had tried all the important cases personally. Getting your hands and eyes on the evidence was the only way to find out what was going on.

Each senator had a staff member assigned him—a so-called ''designatee''—to guide him through the complicated, jargon-laden maze of intelligence. Leahy had inherited Ted Ralston from a former member, and Ralston had told him that if he wanted to understand intelligence he would have to learn about the National Security Agency and intercepts. A satellite called VORTEX targeted special areas of the world and provided listening capabilities equivalent to a U.S. embassy listening post in the various countries. The NSA was the source of the most and the best information. Interpretation of intercepts took painstaking hours of listening, detecting patterns, frequencies, new methods and communications links, determining routing, deciphering meaning.

That's where the action is, Ralston said. Intelligence-gathering had become frightfully technical: you had to learn what could be done and how, and get a grasp on what was coming in future years. Ralston suggested that Leahy visit NSA facilities abroad, and a European trip was planned.

Ralston had had a close relationship with Inman during the Admiral's era as head of the NSA, 1977 to 1981. He was in charge of arms control monitoring by the Senate committee and was one of three staffers intimately familiar with the NSA. Ralston had bought Inman a set of four stars when Inman was promoted to full admiral as Casey's deputy. New stars were normally bestowed by the newly promoted flag officer's family.

Over the years Inman had guided Ralston through the labyrinth of technical-intelligence-gathering, and Ralston had kept Inman informed about goings-on at the Senate committee, so that when Inman made his rounds with the senators, or came up for a briefing, he knew what each senator cared about.

Like two veteran case officers they worked each other well. Each had both a reason and a need to know. If Inman was, on many or even all occasions, able to be solicitous with the senators, at times uncannily so, that made both their jobs easier. If Inman made a strong, positive impression on the senators, both Republicans and Democrats, it was to the benefit of the committee and the process of oversight. No one complained, though several staff members thought their professional association had evolved into personal fealty. After all, Inman was supposed to be working for Casey, and Ralston for Leahy.

Senator Leahy and Ralston visited the NSA facility at Harrogate, some two hundred miles north of London in the Yorkshire moors.

Leahy had practical questions about the capabilities for communications intercepts. The Russians were massing tanks at the Polish border, and Leahy wanted to know whether the Harrogate station could pick up communications from individual tanks.

What about the megawatts (millions of watts) of this exotic subsystem? Ralston asked before anyone at Harrogate could answer Leahy. As he rubbernecked through the VIP tour, Ralston asked technical questions that revealed his dazzling knowledge. Leahy wanted his own questions answered over his staffer's, but Ralston seemed unable to control himself in the spy candy store. He wondered aloud about the overhead systems, and, yes, what about the connection with the NSA facility on the opposite side of the world at Pine Gap in Australia?

"Shut up," Leahy said caustically. "Let me ask the questions."

As they went on to Germany, Leahy daydreamed about tossing Ralston out of the plane. In Turkey, Ralston grabbed a handful of the U.S. Ambassador's cigars from the embassy humidor, and Leahy told his administrative assistant later, "I don't know what to do with that son of a bitch."

Upon his return to the States, Leahy figured out what to do. He fired Ralston.

Ralston applied for a job on the intelligence community staff downtown on F Street. It was one of the areas Casey had left to Inman. As a Senate staffer, Ralston had not had to take lie detector tests, but part of the application procedure at the intelligence community included a polygraph. So he was given a routine examination. Several of the basic questions concerned Ralston's handling of classified material. Had he ever taken classified documents home?

It was not unusual for busy government employees to take classified documents home. That's why the question was there. The practice was so common that it was a perfect test of whether someone was being straightforward. The purpose was not to uncover innocuous infractions but to find serious security breaches, leakers or, in rare cases, a spy. But the question presented a real predicament, and it was one of the reasons so many people had such distaste for the polygraph. Answers had to be yes or no. Major and minor matters got lumped together. The choice was to acknowledge or gut it out and risk flunking.

Ralston did not pass. He had taken home a copy of a secret report he had written on what the U.S. intelligence agencies had been doing in Iran since World War II. Ralston's polygraph trouble was devastating both to him and to Inman. There would be no job on the intelligence community staff. Worse, the new staff director of the Senate Intelligence Committee, Rob Simmons, launched an investigation of Ralston. There was more. Ralston had taken home about five hundred pages of classified documents. Some of them were top secret. He had returned some of the papers to the committee security director and some directly to the CIA. In the Iran study a couple of sensitive human sources could have been identified; they were not named, but someone might have deduced their identity from the document.

Simmons drew up a list of the documents Ralston had taken and sent it to the CIA, asking them for a routine damage assessment.

Shortly afterward, Simmons received a memo from the CIA. It said there was no evidence that the documents had actually been compromised. Though they had been improperly stored in Ralston's home, there was no indication that anyone else ever saw or handled them, so no compromise, no damage.

Simmons couldn't believe the reasoning. Damage assessments normally considered the worst possible case. Storage of such documents in a nonsecure area automatically meant possible compromise. But there was something more troubling. Simmons traced the memo and its conclusion from the CIA to Ralston's friend and godfather, Bobby Inman. Simmons thought that Inman might be protecting Ralston, so he began a full-scale internal investigation.

It was tedious work, but, by checking back into the files, Simmons found that Ralston had either signed out or signed disclosure forms on nearly every important or sensitive document and report that came to or through the committee, going back years. If he had read it all, Ralston could be an encyclopedist of the U.S. intelligence capabilities and operations.

Simmons determined that for practical purposes Ralston had been Inman's spy on the Senate Intelligence Committee about committee activities and plans. It was a most informal spying relationship, Simmons realized, and perhaps spying was too harsh a word. There was nothing illegal about it, nothing improper, merely unseemly. For both the committee and the CIA, for both Ralston and Inman. From his ten years as a CIA operations officer, Simmons knew that some of the best spies did not realize what they were doing. They got caught in a web, convinced that they were gathering information for their side. The best spying was subtle, embedded in normal intercourse, so that everyone could say, "Just doing my job." In the daily, unconscious, unthinking acts of communication—reading, talking, questioning—reams of information would be disseminated to the wrong places. The Ralston affair was perhaps nothing more than a careless leeching by two men.

Simmons outlined the problem for Goldwater. The chairman elected finally not to refer the matter to the Justice Department for prosecution. There were several reasons: Ralston apparently intended no harm; no damage to the national security and no compromise could be proven; and if it became public it would be an ugly mess, severely damaging the oversight process and the credibility of the committee; and, finally, there was the Inman angle, which Goldwater could not stand to see aired and subject to misinterpretation. Simmons had Ralston's security clearance pulled.

"Good," said Goldwater, apparently concluding that that was about the right punishment. Ralston was unable to obtain a new clearance when he tried to get a job with a major defense contractor.

Some of the committee staff members were still having lunch with

Ralston, so Simmons convened the entire staff and explained that Ralston was persona non grata; they would be better off without Ted Ralston in their lives.

Senator Leahy was dumbfounded when Ralston asked him for a reference.

In his final report, Simmons concluded that it was possibly the biggest compromise of classified material from Congress, and certainly the biggest from the Senate committee. He ordered a security review of everything at the committee, thousands of documents. After a search that sent security officers into every file cabinet and corner of the committee spaces, it was determined that forty documents were unaccounted for. Most of these were years old (and many had been signed out to a former senior committee staffer), and Simmons decided that there wasn't much that could be done about it. A number of important lessons had been learned.

Later, when Casey complained about alleged leaks from the committee, Simmons defended their security record. "What about the guy who took all the documents?" Casey asked. But he said no more, and did nothing.*

For Inman, the suggestion that Ralston was his spy was absurd. By definition a spy and his spymaster—presumably Inman himself in this concocted scenario—operated against the interests they were supposed to be serving. Well, Inman served no other interest than United States intelligence. Nor had Ralston. Yes, Ralston had made mistakes, but no harm had come from them. That anyone could see this as espionage showed deep bureaucratic sickness. It reflected a prevalent view, both within the CIA and within the congressional oversight committees, that the other was an enemy to be treated as a hostile intelligence service.

Casey's view of the oversight committees was simple. When it came to big secrets, his instructions were, "Limit access. Don't go brief."

With Ralston gone and Goldwater in the hospital for nearly three months, Inman felt cut off. To top it off, William Safire, the *New York Times* columnist, had been taking a number of informed jabs at Inman, calling him a "detentnik" who controlled Goldwater and opposed covert action. Most recently Safire had charged in a column that Inman was "planting a phony story with reporters that Israel was publicizing the Libyan assassination teams (the hit teams) in order to set up an air strike at the Libyan nuclear reactor . . ."

* Ralston declined comment on these matters.

Inman felt this attack personally. He had not planted anything; it was obviously a leak to Safire from a pro-Israel source who was smarting over Inman's insistence that Israel not get any satellite photos that could be used in an offensive raid, as had been the case in the bombing of the Iraqi nuclear reactor. Inman felt that the Israelis would do almost anything against Qaddafi and Libya. In fact, he believed that the Israelis would assassinate Qaddafi if they felt it would earn enough points with the United States.

But Inman had a darker suspicion about Safire's attacks. Perhaps the criticism had been directly or indirectly provided by Casey. Inman knew there was a back-channel relationship between Casey and Safire, going back some fifteen years. Safire had managed Casey's unsuccessful 1966 run for Congress, even sending Casey to a speech coach, who had failed to cure his mumbling. Circumstantial evidence of more recent contact between Casey and Safire had fallen recently into Inman's lap. It was one of those bits of information an intelligence officer places in data storage. An editor at *The New York Times* had called Inman with an urgent request. Arthur Ochs Sulzberger, his publisher, was trying to call Casey, using Casey's unlisted, personal home number, but getting no answer. Was the number correct? the editor asked, reading it off. It was a number that Casey had given to a few people, including Inman, and Inman was surprised that the *Times* had it.

So, the *Times* editor said, Bill Safire had the right number.

Yes, Inman said.

Inman could not be sure that Casey had had a role in Safire's blasts, but he could not shake his hunch or the wariness he felt toward Casey.

At 3 P.M. the day after New Year's, President Reagan met with Deaver and Bill Clark at the Walter Annenberg estate, Sunnylands, in Rancho Mirage, California. For two and a half hours the three discussed the National Security Council. Allen was resigning. The President decided that Clark would move over from the State Department as the new national-security adviser. Clark would be granted "direct" access to the President and would be the sole White House spokesman on foreign affairs, according to a memo of the conversation prepared by Clark.

Casey was glad to hear about this. Clark, who had served as his chief of staff when Reagan was governor of California, was an intimate of the President and a staunch anti-Communist.

After his appointment was announced, Clark sought Inman's advice on what to do with his National Security Council staff. Inman told him to clean it out, especially the NSC staffer on intelligence, Kenneth de Graffenreid. Clark listened carefully and avoided committing himself, and Inman realized that he had announced a declaration of war on de Graffenreid.

De Graffenreid's agenda was counterintelligence, and he had turned his attention to a new-fad hypothesis called "Camouflage, Concealment and Deception" (CCD), which emphasized Soviet efforts to deceive. De Graffenreid wanted to examine the possibility that some of the intelligence gathered by the United States could be part of a vast Soviet hoax —particularly satellite photos and communications intercepts. It was logical, he argued, that the Soviets conducted deception operations. Since the U.S. had never really uncovered one, it was important to examine the possibility that some larger, successful deception was under way and had been missed.

Inman believed in the basic NSA position on these matters: what was heard and seen came in relatively pure. Skepticism was necessary, and occasionally there might be deception, but the far side of skepticism was paranoia. If the Soviets erected electronic and photographic Potemkin Villages, they would have neither time nor money for much else. The vastness of the intelligence "take" from the Soviet Union and the pattern and continuity going back years, even decades, made de Graffenreid's axiom impossible, Inman concluded.

Inman was unhappy that de Graffenreid, a forty-one-year-old former Navy pilot who had spent only a year on the Hill as an investigator and another year at the DIA, could have so much influence. But Inman realized that in many ways the intelligence community, which had been set up to serve the President, in practical terms worked for the NSC. A powerful, well-placed and highly opinionated staff member could drive intelligence priorities as well as resources—even policy.

De Graffenreid adopted one of Inman's methods of control. He promoted a comprehensive counterintelligence study much along the lines of the "Intelligence Capabilities 1985–90" study that Inman had pushed successfully. Bureaucratic barriers needed to be broken down among the FBI, the CIA and the military intelligence agencies, de Graffenreid said. If necessary a centralized counterintelligence authority with centralized records should be created. The split of counterintelligence functions at the U.S. borders (CIA abroad, FBI at home) was artificial. It was a civil-liberties bugaboo to worry whether they were joined. It was not a distinction the KGB observed.

Clark's arrival at the NSC was an opportunity for de Graffenreid. De Graffenreid carried to Clark for the President's signature a proposed

National Security Decision Directive (NSDD) calling for a broad counterintelligence study. Clark was enthusiastic about it.

Word came back to Inman that de Graffenreid would stay on the NSC staff. It was delivered by Clark's new deputy, Bud McFarlane, who had moved from State with him. He told Inman that de Graffenreid had important support.

Soon Inman received the NSDD signed by Reagan, setting up two potentially powerful Senior Interagency Groups (SIG) for intelligence—one chaired by FBI Director Webster, the other by Deputy Secretary of Defense Carlucci.

Inman had been beaten in a major bureaucratic battle. It was clear that de Graffenreid not only was staying but had found a place of influence.

Casey was not comfortable with the new NSDD on counterintelligence which gave policy control to the FBI and Defense, but he did not think it was a big deal. Certainly it was not turf to worry about. He marveled at the ability of longtime government servants to take such battles seriously. Perhaps, Inman concluded, Casey had a point. He tried to cool down.

After a year, Inman had come to regard Casey as a "piece of work," a term that Casey often applied to the oddballs in their midst. Casey was a combination of hard and soft. Just recently there had been a National Intelligence Estimate on the Middle East, and four strong views had been expressed: one by CIA experts, another by the DIA, one by Inman and one by Casey personally. Had Casey exercised his authority as DCI to overrule everyone and put forward his own view as the main conclusion? No. He had simply, and rather courageously, Inman felt, taken all four views to the President.

But on the operations and covert-action side, Inman was growing increasingly troubled. Casey was aligning the CIA with some of the major unsavory characters in the world.

Casey had received a visit from Israeli Defense Minister Ariel Sharon, a burly, truculent former general with extreme hawkish ideas. Israel was giving covert paramilitary support to the main Christian militia in Lebanon—the rightist Phalangist party, headed by Bashir Gemayel, a baby-faced ruthless warlord. At thirty-four, Gemayel had developed into one of Lebanon's most important and charismatic leaders, forging a unique and powerful future role for himself. The Israeli game plan was working, and Sharon wanted $10 million in secret CIA paramilitary support to go to Gemayel.

Inman was opposed. In 1978, Bashir's forces had made a lightning attack on the summer-resort home of Tony Frangieh, the political heir to the rival Christian faction, slaughtering him, his wife, their two-year-old daughter, the bodyguards and even the domestic staff. In 1980, Bashir's militia had come close to wiping out the rival Christian militia of Lebanon's ex-president Camille Chamoun.

Bashir was a savage murderer.

But there was more—something hidden in the intelligence files.

Back in the 1970s, after studying political science and law in Lebanon, Bashir had come to the United States to work for a Washington law firm and had been recruited by the CIA. As the youngest of the six children of Pierre Gemayel, he was no doubt destined to relative obscurity in the powerful family. The older son would inherit leadership in the Phalangist party, founded in 1936 as a sports and military youth movement. Bashir was not an agent who was controlled, though he was paid CIA money regularly and given a crypt—a special coded designator—so that his reports could circulate widely with very few people knowing the source's identity. The payments were initially token amounts of several thousand dollars—a straight exchange of cash for information.

But in 1976, after Bashir defied Lebanese custom and took charge of the militia in place of his older brother, both the payments and his importance to the CIA grew. The CIA maintained a large presence in Beirut, the crossroads of the Middle East, the most Westernized of the Arab capitals, teeming with intrigue, as powerful and wealthy Lebanese traveled the region, providing good intelligence about less accessible Arab countries. Bashir's role, and the quality and scope of his information, expanded. The CIA soon considered him a "regional influential," a major asset. At the same time, within Lebanon, he was evolving into a leader with wide appeal, a patriotic visionary who spoke of a "new Lebanon."

Inman thought that Bashir was still a murderer, and that the CIA should not dance with this devil anymore and should not provide the $10 million in covert assistance to his militia. The Israelis and Sharon were cooking up something; they had too much influence in Lebanon, and were seeking more. Sharon, who was close to his fellow former general Al Haig, turned up the heat all through the top reaches of the Reagan Administration. Soon his pressure was being transmitted through Haig.

Casey considered the reports from the stations. Oddly, his station in Beirut was anti-Bashir. It agreed with Inman that he was a barbarian and a cynical manipulator who played off the Israelis and the Americans, crying on any available shoulder to obtain support and equipment. The Tel Aviv station, reflecting the Israeli-Sharon view, maintained that Bashir was moving up fast, a likely leader who would stabilize Lebanon.

It expressed no admiration but advised an accommodation to reality. Casey appreciated a sense of inevitability. At times the CIA had to work with some undesirables. Bashir also was deeply antagonistic to the PLO, which Casey knew was a real threat to Israel.

Inman lost that argument too. President Reagan signed a top-secret finding authorizing the $10 million covert aid to Bashir's militia.

By mid-March 1982, Inman had made another personal assessment. In two weeks he would turn fifty. He had risen as high in the Navy as possible. The only higher post he might seek was DCI, and that was unavailable. He was approaching a point of no return in his life. If he was going to begin a second career, he had to start now. He couldn't stand the prospect of some washout job as consultant, or as arms salesman, or hustling real estate on the Maryland Eastern Shore, a depository for retired senior military officers. His teenage sons, Thomas and William, would be going to college soon. The bare fact was that Inman could not afford to send them to expensive private colleges. After nearly thirty years in the Navy, he had three assets—his mortgaged (8 percent, 22-years at Arlington Trust Company) four-bedroom house in Arlington, Virginia, a few thousand dollars in the Navy Federal Credit Union and a couple of thousand in U.S. Savings Bonds. (Casey would have laughed that someone would put money in such a low-yield investment; Casey had zero in savings bonds.)

Inman also realized that his interest in intelligence was waning. He had been fascinated for years with how to get intelligence, and for years after that with what the intelligence meant. But all those breakfasts Casey had taken him to with Haig or Weinberger had kindled his interest in how to *use* intelligence. That was policy, and policy was what counted, he now knew. He was in the wrong job.

That March, public disclosure of the Nicaragua operation had brought several problems into focus. Casey and Dewey Clarridge were running the project. DDO John Stein had complained to Inman that he was being cut out. Though the general operation was not kept from Inman, it was going on around him. He had to crowbar in just to find out details, and he did not like what he found. Covert assistance was about to be given to Eden Pastora, a former Sandinista, the notorious Commander Zero who had broken with the Sandinistas after the revolution. Pastora was a "barracuda," Inman said, the Central American equivalent of Lebanon's Bashir Gemayel. Pastora operated out of Costa Rica, which was to the south of Nicaragua. El Salvador was north of Nicaragua. All someone had to do was look at a map and see that Pastora was operating more than three hundred miles from any possible supply routes for arms into El Salvador. That simple fact put the lie to assertions that the Nicaragua operation was for the purpose of interdicting arms. Inman knew that assistance to Pastora was intended to demolish and oust the Sandinistas. The uncompromising, even snarling comments from Casey about the Nicaraguan regime told Inman all he needed to know.

As Inman looked further, his distrust grew. He asked questions, he looked at more files, he began to question the underlying reasons for making the Nicaragua program covert. He concluded that the Administration did not want it out in the open where they would have to pay the domestic political price. It was covert in order to avoid a public debate, Inman was now absolutely convinced. With the operation public, no one seemed to care. The clear message was that Reagan and Casey could get away with covert operations even if they became public. The State Department, the White House, Casey would all want more. Diplomacy was a long, drawn-out process, very frustrating. Covert action was, at first blush, cheaper and certainly less frustrating. That was naive. The quick, covert fix was a fantasy.

Inman never liked the Operations Directorate people, going back to 1965 when he had been the assistant naval attaché in Stockholm. He had had a terrific source who provided significant military information on other countries. The CIA station, small and arrogant, had tried to steal his source, and failing that tried to burn the source, dropping hints to Swedish authorities that they had a "blabbermouth." Inman never forgot.

When had one of the directorate's paramilitary covert plans worked? Not ever, in Inman's view. And even if it were to, a new, U.S.-backed government could easily turn out to be worse than the one it had replaced, or it might not be able to govern or to hold power.

It had probably been sound to mount covert action in Afghanistan after the Soviets invaded. Or when the Soviets used Cuban proxy troops. This could raise the cost for Russia. Covert action could effectively counter a Soviet propaganda campaign. But that was generally it.

Inman was concerned about the clandestine mindset that was dominating the business of intelligence-gathering. The sensitive collection operations—phone taps, room bugs and other equipment placements abroad—were being expanded. Such clandestine technical collection had its appeal and could yield intelligence coups that went down well at the White House—the verbatim conversations of a prime minister, for example. Inman had been surprised at the amount of amorous activities that was picked up. But in four years as director of the NSA, he had learned the downside of such efforts. There was the danger of exposure, though that was not seriously considered. In addition, such efforts had limited life spans, eighteen months to two years. The bug would be found, the batteries would wear out, or there might be some malfunction; a key target would be transferred to a different job; or some countermeasure would be developed intentionally, or by accident.

The nonclandestine operations—satellite photography, collecting radio and other signals, the decoding of messages—that did not require the secret placement of a bug or a phone tap were more reliable and less vulnerable. This methodical, workmanlike approach did not conform with the new clandestine mindset or with Casey's impatience. Casey liked to make a splash at the White House.

The previous Christmas, Inman's older son, referring to his father's grueling hours and the tension, had put a question to him that was still resonating: "Where's the quality of life in all this?"

Inman left for what was supposed to be a two-week getaway in Hawaii. After ten days, he returned to Langley and intentionally barged in on Casey and Clarridge. They were busy building an army, and Inman had some questions: Where are the contras going? Where is the CIA heading? The Administration? Is there a plan? Won't the Pastora connection make it clear that this is not an arms interdiction program? Do we know who these people are? They are not fighting to save El Salvador. They want power, don't they? This is an operation to overthrow a government, isn't it? That raises problems with the finding that authorized the program. The agency is on the verge, in the midst, of exceeding that authority, isn't it?

Casey and Clarridge didn't have answers, and they didn't like the questions. This was Administration policy, approved all the way up the line to the President—perhaps not in the finding, but it was what Ronald Reagan wanted. Casey was sure he was on solid ground.

After half an hour, Inman stiffened, uncomfortably aware of his proximity to raw anger. Bonfires were burning inside. He marveled momentarily at his absolute consternation. Casey and Clarridge, uncaring, intoxicated with their certitudes, were not listening. Inman was an outsider. An obstacle.

Finally he rose and stormed out. There was nothing to say.

Inman had never done that before. His advancement through the officer ranks of naval intelligence had been based on an ability to convey soothing impressions, avoid confrontations. He had crossed a threshold with Casey, and with himself.

• • •

Casey found Inman brilliant but brittle—a golden boy worried about his own image, unwilling to risk it, or the agency's, to get a tough job done, too concerned about how covert action went down with his liberal, Democrat and media friends. Inman's departure would be trouble with the Congress, but that could be handled. Inman's bipartisan popularity was a cushion up there, doubtless. But he now understood all the parts of the DCI's job, and a deputy less concerned with his press clippings could be more useful.

Inman believed there remained only the formality of resignation. On March 22 he composed a three-paragraph letter to President Reagan, reminding the President, "I reluctantly accepted your request last year that I serve as the deputy Director of Central Intelligence. . . . Accordingly, I would be grateful if you would accept my resignation."

Praising Reagan for commencing the "rebuilding" of the intelligence agencies, Inman said, "You and Director Casey have my best wishes for continued success." Before handing the letter to Casey, he sent copies to Bush, Weinberger and Clark, insuring that it was final. Casey was peeved and worried that it would leak, but the resignation was kept quiet as Casey began the search for a replacement.

On Wednesday, April 21, 1982—about six weeks after the *Post* ran the story on the Nicaragua covert operation—I went to see Goldwater, hoping to find out whether the CIA had informed him fully about the operation. Senate offices are attended to as racing cars are by pit crews. There are mementos and awards crowding walls and tables, all the signs of status and party. In Goldwater's office, not a pencil was out of place. The only singular feature was the stack of ham radio equipment on a table behind his desk.

"When Ben," Goldwater said, referring to Bradlee, "called me on the Central America thing, there weren't ten words out of his mouth and I knew he knew about the whole thing. So what I did was say, 'Ah, uh, uh, I don't recall anything about that. Why don't you call Bill Casey.' I played dumb with Ben."

He had misled us but not lied. It seemed a too subtle distinction.

"I thought the American people should know about that," Goldwater added. "In fact, I'm tickled to death it was made public." He had confirmed the operation on the record to *Time* for that reason.

He explained his theory of the CIA's "overt covert" operation—secret but public: that was good, no one would be caught by surprise, no justifiable public outcry down the road. A covert operation was the lesser of two evils because it avoided sending U.S. troops, he said. "A lot of this stuff should be made public. The American people should know what is being done—seventy-five percent of what we hear [in intelligence briefings] should come out.

"We are out of the business of overthrowing governments. We may cause a little economic trouble, a little publicity [propaganda] and other aid, but we don't overthrow governments." He was stern and emphatic. It was not a moral position, rather a statement of the political and practical reality.

Was intelligence on the Soviet Union any good?

"We don't have many eyeballs in there now," Goldwater said. "I knew about twelve years ago we had only five sets of eyeballs there working for us.

"We have the best electronic intelligence now of anyone," he said confidently, "but maybe not for long."

What about the satellites?

"I've been trying to get them to put out these [satellite photos], but they say, 'No, no, no!' because they would look so good in magazines but they say the Russians can tell." The Russians would be able to calculate our exact capabilities and it's beyond their expectation, he indicated.

"Well," Goldwater said, leaning back and lowering his voice again, "pictures are not that important anymore. We have a new—" he began and then broke off. "I can't talk about it at all, but it's spooky. I wish some night we could go on a trip, and it's amazing, you'd see." Through some infrared or electromagnetic or even advance radar technology, the United States apparently had something that was better than a picture.

Goldwater moved the discussion away.

What about Casey?

"A fine man," Goldwater said. "Honest. A real spy when he was with the OSS, a real guy with a"—and Goldwater raised his hand as if to stick an imaginary knife in his desk—"dagger." He smiled.

"But," he continued, shaking his head, "we do it differently now, and he is not a pro.

"I call him Flappy." The Senator puckered out his lips in pantomime and suddenly blew hard, causing his lips to spit a fine spray into the air.

Casey's lack of forthrightness was also a problem. "So when I want to know what's going on I call Inman," Goldwater said. "As soon as I pick up the phone I can tell from the first word whether he [Inman] is going to tell me anything." Pause. "You know we are going to lose Admiral Inman?"

There was not even a rumor going around about this. Is it final, Inman is going?

"Yes, it is," Goldwater replied, indicating that he had tried to prevent it, "and we're going to have trouble finding his replacement."

A Goldwater aide passed word to the White House that Goldwater had spilled the Inman story. Later that day the White House announced Inman's resignation and released a pro-forma letter just out of the typewriter.

Two days later, Senator Richard G. Lugar, a conservative Indiana Republican on the Intelligence Committee, announced that he intended to "send some signals" publicly to the White House about Inman's replacement. Lugar, a friend of Inman's since they had served together as junior intelligence officers in the late fifties, said that as far as the Senate committee was concerned Inman was "our man." Without a professional replacement, the committee would be cut off. "Bill Casey is a very able American who has made some pretty good decisions," Lugar said, and then took a square shot at him. "But there are complexities that would take more years to understand than Casey will be alive.

"We voted for Casey and Inman as a package—Casey because he has access to the President, Inman because he knows what's going on."

Casey was well aware that the DCI was a public whipping boy, and he expected to get cuffed around by the Democrats and the intelligence-suspicious liberals. But Lugar was a fellow Republican, and generally soft-spoken. Casey suspected Inman's hand.

In his interviews, Inman skirted the issues that had divided him from Casey and the Administration. He felt he was right, but these were policy decisions to be made by the President and the DCI. There would be no public denunciations, no sour grapes, no disloyalty. He said simply that he had lost his zest for bureaucratic battle, that his relations with Casey were good, but not close.

In farewell, Casey asked him why they had not been close. And why had Inman said that to the press?

Inman pointed out how complimentary he had been of Casey in his public statements.

But Casey was offended. "Cold," he finally snapped.

For Inman, it was the simple truth. They had not been close. They disagreed about too much, intelligence, the world.

Inman took a job as head of a research consortium, Microelectronics and Computer Technology Corporation (MCC) set up in Texas by ten large high-tech firms to develop a supercomputer that might come close to thinking, integrating and merging data, breaking any code.

Among the several hundred employees of MCC was former Senate Intelligence Committee staffer Ted Ralston. Casey and Inman never spoke again.

Casey was given forty-eight hours by the White House to come up with a deputy acceptable to the Senate committee. The only choice was John McMahon, the former DDO under Turner, former head of the analytic side, and now the executive director of the CIA, technically the No. 3 man. Not hard driving or single-minded enough to be a good DDO, an effective DDO, McMahon had found the line between independence and loyalty. He could put up a fuss but he knew how to take orders. He did so without resentment. He was not a lackey like Hugel, nor an outsider like Inman. He was skeptical of but not a detractor of covert action.

As he advanced, McMahon had become persuaded that besides the exotic technical intelligence and the inside human sources, the agency had to get what he called "the ground truth." That meant not just servicing the dead drops but getting out into the churches and the bread lines behind the Iron Curtain.

One of the agency's former undercover men, turned spy novelist, had written that the CIA perhaps had once had the most brilliant people ever brought together in one organization, people who understood every country in the world—except their own. McMahon knew it was so easy to lose touch.

There was no better way to receive a dose of ground truth than to make the rounds in the Congress. Since a DDCI had to be confirmed by the Senate, McMahon called on a number of senators on the Intelligence Committee, and he found that the main topic was always Casey. There was distrust everywhere. It ranged from senators who wanted to make sure McMahon would be available to answer questions, to those like Pat Leahy who wanted a pledge etched in stone that McMahon would be their early-warning system.

As McMahon made the correct promises, he was surprised that so many of the senators were spring-loaded against Casey. McMahon thought Casey was too smart to bullshit the senators, but clearly they felt that he did. Afterward, as he sat down with Casey, he thought the DCI was entitled to an honest appraisal. Of the fifteen senators, McMahon reported, more than half had their pistols cocked.

"Bill," McMahon said, "you've got some stroking to do on the Hill."

Yeah, okay, Casey agreed.

• • •

That spring, Casey had another hot spot to watch as Argentina invaded and seized the British crown colony the Falkland Islands. The Reagan Administration, after initially trying to remain neutral, eventually sided with its old ally. There were press reports that the British had benefited from U.S. satellite photos. Casey did not correct this misinformation. Actually, the region of the remote South Atlantic was not covered by satellite. Later, the U.S. put up a satellite to cover the region, and the Soviets followed with two of their own.

The real intelligence breakthroughs had come from good human sources that were tied to the ruling junta in Buenos Aires. Argentina, taking seriously the declarations of American UN Ambassador Kirkpatrick, had deluded itself that the United States might remain neutral. So Argentine officers and officials provided a steady flow of intelligence to the CIA station and the U.S. military attachés in Buenos Aires, who forwarded it to Langley and on to the State Department and the White House. It was then only a matter of who could beat a path more quickly to the British.

Casey thought the North Atlantic Treaty Organization was a leaky "sieve," but, as a certified Anglophile, he made sure the channel between the CIA and MI-6 was open. Intelligence was gathered to be used. And the President had defined the policy tilt toward the British. So delivering a batch of secrets to an ally struggling through war, not to mention a period of political stress—Prime Minister Thatcher's continuation in office hinged on the outcome—was what it was all about. This was one intelligence success that could not be publicized.

The tilt toward Britain in the Falklands would eventually drive Argentina out of the Nicaragua operation, ending its "fig leaf" cover for what was becoming a CIA project, but that too was all to the good. It would give Clarridge a freer hand to build his contra army, Casey concluded. Casey's admiration for Clarridge only increased as he went about his task. No detail was too small; no obstacle too great.

On Wednesday, May 26, 1982, at 10:30 A.M., McMahon appeared before a closed session of the Senate committee to begin his confirmation hearing.

He said in testimony that it was a pleasure to have the congressional committees looking over the agency's shoulders; their review imposed a discipline on the CIA. He did not want intelligence to be some dark enterprise removed from the political process. In an unusually candid assessment, he said the committees protected him: "I for one, as an individual who has had to testify before the oversight committees, drew a great deal of comfort knowing that I was sharing with them, with the representatives of the American people, our programs and what we were up to . . . It was a protection to me as an individual and it was a protection to the institutions to know that Congress was a joint partner in these programs.''

Moynihan wanted to make it clear that the committee too needed protection. ''We have to be able to believe that everything that we need to know you will tell us. We have no independent sources of information. We have to trust—'' He paused. ''If you ever learned that wrong information is being given to this committee—that the committee is being misinformed or misled—would you consider it a matter of personal honor and professional responsibility to tell this committee that that was happening?''

''Yes, sir,'' McMahon replied. ''I cannot imagine anyone in the intelligence community in a position of responsibility ever attempting to mislead or misconstrue facts or events to Congress.''

''I just want to make one final thought,'' Moynihan said, staring over at McMahon, ''. . . it is not your job and ought never to be your job *not* to imagine something bad happening.''

''I stand corrected, Senator,'' McMahon replied.

Other senators questioned Casey's honesty more directly. They were asking McMahon to rat on his boss, to admit that Casey might mislead them. ''I can't imagine anyone over me doing that,'' McMahon said.

Moynihan pounced: there was that lack of imagination again. He interrupted, insisting that McMahon had to deal with the possibilities of bad things happening.

''I would correct the record, Senator,'' McMahon answered.

The next day McMahon appeared in public before the committee.

Moynihan said, ''If anyone would like to know what it means to be a professional career intelligence officer in this country, they would do well to read the financial-disclosure statement of Mr. McMahon, which consists of thirty blank pages.''

The room erupted in laughter.

''There's a tin cup at the end of that,'' McMahon said, pointing at the table.

More laughter.

McMahon's net worth was meager. His 1981 salary was $52,749; all other income amounted to $658 in interest from about $10,000 in the CIA credit union; his home in the suburbs was valued at about $170,000, less a $30,000 mortgage to his in-laws.

Senator Malcolm Wallop, the ultraconservative Republican from Wyoming, was convinced that agency professionals like McMahon were concerned primarily with protecting the reputation of the agency, rather than implementing the Reagan mandate. Men like that were siphoning off the energy and political will of even strong conservatives like Casey, he thought. Wallop believed that Casey was letting the agency run him. Even in covert action, Casey's speciality, once again there had not been enough gain. There was an unwillingness to put the country's money, men and prestige on the line for things that might make a real difference. Agents abroad were not given the electronic capabilities and the authority they needed. Cheap, relatively risk-free little electronic taps and bugs could be placed all over, but the CIA station chiefs had to get approval from headquarters before going ahead. The result was too much caution. Intelligence conducted operations to dazzle themselves—"technological navel-gazing," Wallop termed it—often devoting millions of dollars to gather worthless juicy gossip about the private lives or the health or the movements of world leaders, or high-resolution photographs of faces and cars.

The CIA, Wallop said, did not cope well with new ideas or with anyone who questioned its assumptions. With a chance to express his frustration, he lashed out at McMahon, hurling such invectives as "professionalism," "petty bureaucratic treason" and "no-fault intelligence policy."

McMahon sat and took it, but it was clear to all that he was a candidate of neither the left nor the right.

Goldwater was tired of surprises, so he had had four senior staff members read all of McMahon's personnel and security files. The six-inch file showed that McMahon was clean; he had never been near the assassination plots, the drug tests, the domestic spying exposed in the 1970s. There was a single security violation: an unlocked safe had once been found in his office. But that violation told volumes about McMahon. It had been a secretary's fault, and with one more security violation she would not have gotten a scheduled raise in pay. McMahon, the loyalty-down manager, had taken the rap.

So Goldwater threw a few softballs to McMahon, and then Biden praised Inman and turned to Casey. "With some of us at least, the utterances of Mr. Casey are not always as—well, we do not always leap at them to embrace them as being the whole story when he makes them." Biden then gave a speech about the need for McMahon to act as a monitor for the committee.

Goldwater said that Inman used to signal them when Casey strayed. "I think if the new Deputy Director will develop the habit that the Admiral had of pulling up his socks when there was something being said . . ."

A roar of laughter went up.

"Or else," Biden added, "slide your chair back. He used to just slide it back like this."

"If I may comment," McMahon said, "Mr. Chairman, and also to Senator Biden, I think when the Director hears or reads of the perceptions that you have, he will certainly move to allay your fears and correct that, and I think he will do that personally in any future testimony."

The committee approved McMahon's nomination unanimously, and the Senate followed.

That the Operations arm was indeed rusty came home vividly to Casey in late March 1982. A thirteen-man team of Yemenis sponsored by the CIA that had been sent into the Soviet-dominated state of South Yemen on the Arabian Peninsula for sabotage work was captured. The operation, carried out in conjunction with Saudi intelligence, had been one of the few paramilitary support operations authorized by the Carter Administration and had been in preparation ever since. The Yemenis were tortured and confessed that they had been trained by the CIA. Where was the deniability for the CIA? Casey wondered. Where was the operational security? In the paperwork setting out the covert plan, the Yemenis were supposed only to deal with intermediaries or cutouts, so that they would not know the CIA was involved. But the only way to make the operation credible to the Yemeni recruits had been to reveal the CIA role.

A second team of Yemenis, already inserted into South Yemen, had to be withdrawn and the operation ended. Several weeks later, prosecutors in South Yemen announced that all thirteen men of the first team had pleaded guilty to smuggling explosives to blow up oil installations and other key targets. They also had confessed their CIA sponsorship. Three members of the team were given fifteen-year prison terms. The others were executed.

In contrast, Casey's first covert paramilitary operation, the support to Habré in Chad, paid off. On June 7, 1982, about two thousand of Habré's men took control of Ndjamena, the capital of Chad, and set up a provisional government. For the moment, Qaddafi's influence in Chad was reduced and his nose "bloodied," as Haig and Casey wanted. The Libyan leader now had a hostile French- and U.S.-supported government along the six-hundred-mile border to his south.

The atmosphere was right, finally, to win White House support for a limited covert support operation to the active anti-Communist resistance in Cambodia. Assistance to the Angola resistance was banned by law; and the operations in Nicaragua and Afghanistan were under way.

The mere mention of covert activity in Southeast Asia stood hair on end throughout the agency. The region was the supreme tar baby. But Casey insisted that they look beyond the past. Administration policy had to be consistent: the effort to aid anyone fighting Communists had to be universal. The Soviets supported subversion worldwide; the United States could do no less. The problem was that the primary opposition to the Communist regime in Cambodia, which was a puppet of Vietnam, was the Khmer Rouge. Also Communist, the KR, as it was known, was a notoriously savage group. The KR had killed one million, possibly as many as three million, Cambodians during the time it ruled the country, 1975 to 1979.

But there were two other non-Communist Cambodian resistance groups, and Casey argued that funds could be funneled to them. The agency had unilateral assets in the Thailand military, through which the money could be channeled to make sure it did not aid the Khmer Rouge.

A number of State Department officials disagreed, arguing that the Khmer Rouge was joined in a loose coalition with the two non-Communist groups and was dominant. To help the non-Communists was to help the KR.

Casey had to settle for nonlethal assistance, and in the fall of 1982 President Reagan signed a finding authorizing up to $5 million in aid to the non-Communists. Though the money could not go for weapons, it would free up other money to buy military equipment.

That spring, Casey met with Israeli Defense Minister Sharon, who was in Washington making the rounds. Lebanon and the PLO strongholds there were on Sharon's mind. He spoke of countermoves—if Lebanon does this, then Israel will do that; if the PLO strikes here, Israel will strike there. "Lebanon," Sharon said, his tone dripping sarcasm, as if the country were a geographic fiction. "Don't be surprised. Let's get the cards on the table. If you don't do something, we will. We won't tolerate it."

Casey understood that Lebanon was the one Arab state where Israel could extend its influence, and he concluded that Sharon wanted to create circumstances that would justify an Israeli military move. Things will happen in Lebanon and there will be no choice, Sharon said. It was also clear that Sharon had Israeli Prime Minister Menachem Begin mesmerized. Sharon was calling the shots.

Casey appreciated Sharon's style, seeing him as both an activist and a thinker, a man who had a sense both of his country's vulnerability and its destiny.

On June 6, 1982, Israel invaded Lebanon, declaring its intention to drive the PLO terrorists out of southern Lebanon. It cited as justification the attempted assassination of its ambassador to London three days earlier and called its invasion "Operation Peace for Galilee."

Israeli intelligence, the CIA and soon the British knew that this stated reason was bogus. The Israeli ambassador's assailants were part of the Abu Nidal faction that had split off from the PLO and was at war with the mainline PLO, harbored in Lebanon. The Israelis were striking the wrong Palestinians, but in Sharon's view that made little difference. Within days, his Israeli Defense Force (IDF) was on the outskirts of Beirut.

The CIA analysis painted a picture of great opportunity and great risk.

Casey convened a meeting in his office. One question was whether Israel was using U.S.-supplied weapons, and many at the meeting voiced concern that the U.S. would be seen as an accomplice and Congress would raise questions.

"I don't give a fuck about that," Casey said. "The situation is fluid. Anything can happen. How do we turn this to our national interest? That's the question I want answered."

The CIA man, Phalangist militia leader Bashir Gemayel, was playing an increasingly important role in Lebanon, and over the years Bashir had developed close relations with Sharon and the Israeli Mossad. The CIA had played matchmaker, putting the Christians and the Israelis in touch with each other, making Bashir a shared CIA-Mossad intelligence asset.

There was an inclination in the CIA to side with the Christians over the Muslims in Lebanon. But old CIA hands who had served in Lebanon knew that the Christians, particularly Bashir and his Phalangists, were as brutal as anyone. The relationship was hazardous.

"What worthwhile relationship isn't?" Casey asked, trying to calm the agency's hand-wringers.

There were indications that Bashir was headed for the presidency. He had eliminated his competition among the Christian factions. His good relations with the invading Israelis gave him a lever. The pro-Israeli elements within Lebanon looked on Bashir as the new light. The anti-Israeli elements (Muslims and leftist Druze led by Walid Jumblatt) considered Bashir the only person who might be able to get the Israelis to withdraw. Bashir had become the rallying point.

Casey approved a plan for the CIA to sever its formal relationship with

Bashir, who clearly now had more important things to do than work for the CIA. Since the 1977 public disclosure that King Hussein of Jordan had been a CIA paid agent for twenty years, the agency had been reluctant to keep heads of state on the payroll. As Bashir was thrust more into the limelight, an exposure could end his career, if not his life. The relationship was one of the most guarded secrets. Everything was being done to protect it, but there was never any absolute guarantee.

On August 23, two and a half months after the Israeli invasion, Bashir was elected president of Lebanon, slated to take office the next month. The few who knew about the recently severed CIA relationship could feel only a mixture of joy and horror. Lebanon was a country of no permanent friends, no permanent enemies. The very things that made Bashir the likely leader left him with numerous enemies. The Muslims were fortified by the rise of Ayatollah Khomeini in Iran; the well-financed PLO still had a presence in Lebanon, though the evacuation from Beirut of eleven thousand PLO fighters, including Chairman Arafat, had begun.

Strategically allied with Israel and the United States, a Lebanon under Bashir would upset the regional balance of power. Powerful Syria to the north and the west had occupied the Bekaa Valley in Lebanon since 1976 and, in fact, considered all of Lebanon part of greater Syria. Syria's Soviet allies were also unhappy.

Faced with this array of internal and external enemies, Bashir passed a message to the CIA requesting that he be provided with covert security and intelligence assistance.

Casey felt the CIA had an obligation to help Bashir. It could not be done in the open. A large-scale covert operation was necessary. To be effective, the CIA would have to become more closely involved with the Lebanese intelligence service. It would have to share sophisticated weapons as well as equipment for electronic surveillance and communications. President Reagan approved a finding for the support operation that called for an initial expenditure of about $600,000. It was projected to grow quickly to more than $2 million a year, perhaps $4 million.

On the afternoon of September 14, 1982, nine days before he was to take office, Bashir Gemayel was speaking at the local office of his Phalangist Party in East Beirut. He was scheduled to meet at five with a group of Israeli intelligence officers touring Beirut. But at 4:10 a bomb detonated, bringing the building down and killing him.

The CIA had not had time to get its covert-assistance program into play. There was no evidence that the CIA relationship had leaked. Still, it was a major disaster for the CIA to have a former asset assassinated.

The several million dollars allocated for the security operation was put on hold and kept in the presidential contingency fund.

The assassination was the first in a chain of calamitous events. Within two days, Israeli forces allowed Phalangist units to enter Palestinian refugee camps in Beirut on a mission of revenge. The names of two of those camps, Sabra and Shatilla, would become a part of the history of massacre. Israeli intelligence calculated that there were 700 to 800 Palestinian victims, many of them women and children. The accounts of the slaughter stunned the civilized world—bodies of diapered babies, the elderly, corpses in stacks. Even horses, dogs and cats were butchered. Breasts and penises had been cut off; a Christian cross was carved into the flesh of some victims. Pregnant women had their wombs torn open.

Within two weeks, the U.S. Marines had taken up a strategic location in barracks near the airport. As a peacekeeping mission, they had no specific goal other than to assist Lebanon and oversee the eventual withdrawal of foreign forces.

Both the Mossad and Israeli military intelligence began inquiries to determine who had killed Bashir. The bomb was traced to Habib Chartouny, twenty-six, whose family were members of the Syrian People's Party, rivals of the Phalangists. Pooling intelligence with the Lebanese, the Israelis established that Chartouny had installed a long-range electronic detonator for the bomb.

Chartouny's "operator," or case officer, was a captain in the Syrian intelligence service named Nassif. He had convinced the young Chartouny that the bomb was designed to scare Bashir, not to kill him. After sifting the intelligence, including all the Mossad's best Syrian agents, surveillance reports and electronic intercepts, the Israelis established that Nassif reported directly to Lieutenant Colonel Mohammed G'anen, who was in charge of Syrian intelligence operations in Lebanon. Both Syrian Army and Air Force intelligence had some knowledge of the planned bombing, as did the brother of Syrian President Hafez Assad, Rifaat Assad, who headed the country's security forces.

The Israelis believed that President Assad had such an iron grip on his country that he had to have known that such a plan was under way. But there was no proof, and the intelligence reports showing the complicity of the Syrian intelligence officers were highly classified.

Casey saw these reports, provided by Israeli intelligence. They were convincing enough. But, just as important, it was necessary to consider who had benefited most from Bashir's death. Who wanted a weak Lebanon? Who most feared a strong tie between Israel and Lebanon? The answer was obviously Syria. Still, in the end, Casey had to accept the unwillingness of the White House and the State Department to publicize a Syrian role.

The head of Israeli military intelligence, Major General Saguy, knew that any attempt by the U.S. to exploit this information about Syrian involvement would be counterproductive. Saguy had long been skeptical about his country's relations with the Gemayel Phalangists, and he realized that the United States now had the Lebanese monkey on its back, that the Administration would have to deal with Syria to achieve anything resembling a settlement in Lebanon. Accusation might be satisfying propaganda, but would prevent Syrian cooperation.

Casey had an intelligence failure on his hands. The CIA relationship with Bashir, the decision to break it off, Bashir's request for protection, the Administration's decision to grant it, and the subsequent assassination were a mess. But it was a highly classified mess. It stayed secret.

11

IN EIGHTEEN MONTHS AS DCI, Casey had received a technical education, particularly in the supersecret overhead systems, the satellites used for photography and gathering signals intelligence. He became knowledgeable about state-of-the-art technology, and he pushed for the best even when it was the most expensive. Though not sold on the idea that technical intelligence was all-important, he had come to see that it provided key pieces in the mosaic.

With satellite photography, his people could count Soviet tanks. Through imagery enhancement—the second- or third-phase exploitation or refinement of the basic photography—they could determine whether a tank was in working order. The early-warning system could normally detect any movement of Soviet forces, or a major new weapons program. Satellites might miss tightly held research and development projects in the Soviet Union, where a few people were working secretly, away from the population centers or military bases, but that was about all they missed.

Casey was facing a huge decision on one of the U.S. intelligence community's most top-secret and important research and development projects in overhead systems. It was being billed as the biggest technological spy development of the 1980s.

First code-named "Indigo" and now "Lacrosse," the new overhead satellite system would use the most advanced radar to provide all-weather and day-night capability. Using radar imaging—the enhancement of radar signals—computers could create the equivalent of photographs. Clouds and darkness would cease to be barriers. There was the possibility that sometime a future system might see through buildings.

But Lacrosse would eventually cost more than $1 billion, a staggering sum even if it worked. There were vast cost overruns and numerous problems already in the development stage. The Martin Marietta Corporation was the principal contractor, and General Electric was doing the ground processing—the handling of the signal after it arrived at the ground stations.

Funding of about $200 million was needed to keep Lacrosse alive for 1983. Martin Marietta needed the money now; the "drop-dead date" was approaching. Hundreds of millions of dollars had to be provided or the project would die. Casey called some of these expensive projects "onesies," because often only one would be built.

Those of his critics who thought Casey was all covert action were mistaken. The $200 million needed now equaled his entire covert-action budget, and here was the Director anteing up that amount for a *preliminary* expenditure on a satellite system that he hoped would never be discussed in public. Because of the secrecy, the public debates lacked this sense of proportion, he felt.

Though the Soviets had radar imaging, the intelligence reports showed they did not have the computer power or the processing sophistication to create good-quality, high-resolution pictures. So Lacrosse could give the U.S. a significant edge.

Casey had been briefed on the history of the U.S. satellite systems. It had been a remarkable twelve years since 1971, when the first Big Bird was launched. The giant flying spy satellite—some fifty-five feet across—took extraordinary photographs. But the film had to be ejected from the satellite, retrieved, and developed on the ground. Appropriately, gold canisters or buckets were used to protect the Big Bird's exposed film from various rays in space. The gold canisters, stacked to the ceiling in one storage facility, were a metaphor for the expensive satellite program.

In December 1976, just before Carter came to office, the first KH-11 satellite had been launched. This was the big breakthrough of the 1970s, because KH-11 provided the first real-time photographic capability sending back to earth high-quality telephoto television signals. The pictures of the Soviet Union or the tanks were nearly instantaneous, giving the CIA and the Pentagon details of what was going on that moment.

The real-time KH-11 satellite, of course, did not eject film, but transmitted its pictures back to earth in radio waves. The Soviets monitored the ejection of film to identify a photo satellite. Since KH-11 was also a signals intelligence platform, the Soviets did not suspect that the passing satellite was taking pictures. Thus they failed to conceal or camouflage various military installations and equipment, including the missile silo doors, when the satellite passed over. Soviet ignorance had created an enormous U.S. advantage.

The great secret of the KH-11 capability lasted only about a year. William Kampiles, a disgruntled low-level CIA watch center employee, sold a copy of the top-secret KH-11 manual to the Soviets for three thousand dollars. The CIA knew something had happened when the Soviets began closing silo doors as the KH-11 passed over. Kampiles was caught, convicted of espionage and sentenced to forty years in jail, but the damage was done.

There was one negative for Casey in Lacrosse. That system and its successor systems would be the means to verify the next arms control agreement, if there ever was one. Casey wasn't opposed to arms control entirely, but he felt that the importance of reducing the number of nuclear weapons was merely symbolic. Suppose there were a third fewer nuclear weapons, or a half fewer? The world could still be destroyed. The Soviets were a world power because of their vast military machine, not because of their economy, culture or business acumen. Their military alone bestowed superpower status upon them. Casey was sure that the Soviets would never really want to give up much of what gave them their place in the sun.

But that was no reason to stop Lacrosse. Casey decided to go ahead with the $200 million for Lacrosse in the budget submitted to Congress.

Boland, the chairman of the House Intelligence Committee, opposed Lacrosse. The overruns and problems seemed insurmountable, and the National Reconnaissance Office (NRO), which managed the satellite systems, had lied about the cost. It became a moral issue for Boland.

These satellites, and the so-called "black" CIA, NSA and other intelligence projects, were buried in the Defense budget, which Democrat Boland felt needed cutting. The Defense Department was also concerned that Lacrosse was taking money away from the military. So the House cut the funding from the secret portion of the Pentagon's 1983 budget.

Goldwater's Senate committee retained Casey's $200 million Lacrosse request, so Boland and his vice-chairman, Ken Robinson, had a sit-down with Goldwater and Moynihan.

Goldwater felt intensely about Lacrosse. He made a speech. The spy planes—the famous U-2 and the less famous SR-71 (SR for Strategic Reconnaissance)—had cost overruns and all kinds of problems, but look how they had added a whole new dimension to intelligence-gathering. How could anyone calculate cost in the vital secret intelligence war in the sky? The issues went right to the core of congressional responsibility. The risk was not doing enough. The risk was in falling behind. The President and Casey wanted this. Radar imaging was working at the 26th Tactical Wing in Germany for the border between East and West, where the real-time read-out from the planes was relayed to ground stations. Lacrosse wasn't perfect, but there was more than promise.

Determined, Goldwater offered his opinion: "We'll take it at any cost." He paused, and finally added the words "And it could work to prevent war."

Boland still held out, but he had been softened.

Okay, Goldwater said, since they could not resolve the difference he would let the armed-services committees take care of it. In the Senate, Goldwater's committee shared responsibility for intelligence matters, including the budget, with the Senate Armed Services Committee. In the House, Boland's committee was more nearly autonomous. Goldwater remarked that the Senate Armed Services Committee, chaired by John Tower, a Texas Republican, was meeting just down the hall. He was sure that Tower would go along with Lacrosse. At that, Goldwater pushed his chair back, stood up and limped down the hall, apparently determined to deliver the issue—and, by implication, some of the power over it—into Tower's hands.

Boland knew he could not face down the entire Senate. The armed-services committees wielded great power because they were handling a military budget of more than $200 billion, and if the chairman wanted a $200 million project he would get it. That was one one-thousandth of the total—peanuts.

Boland was flustered as Goldwater began his slow, unsteady amble down the corridor. He scooted over to his fellow Democrat, Moynihan.

"Well," Boland said, "what do we do?" He did not relish a disagreement among Democrats on this issue. It was clearly a long walk down the hall, and Goldwater's hip hurt. It also was obvious it would be better if the two intelligence committees could settle the matter themselves.

"I recede," Boland said abruptly, agreeing to one year's funding. "Stop Goldwater!"

An aide was dispatched to run down the hall with the news: "They just caved." The tactical maneuver had worked. Goldwater was convinced that one of the most consequential intelligence programs was safely under way. He turned, smiled and trudged back. He agreed that if there were future cost overruns the plug would be pulled.

When word was passed to Martin Marietta, there was a big celebration. Once the ground processing problems were licked, Lacrosse was set to be launched in space from the National Aeronautical and Space Agency's latest achievement—a future space shuttle mission.

• • •

There was, however, a matter on which Boland would not recede: the covert Nicaragua operation. He didn't like it, and his friend House Speaker O'Neill hated it, too, and was a missionary in his opposition.

O'Neill's aunt Eunice Tolan, who had died the previous year at ninety-one, had been a Maryknoll nun. The Maryknoll missionary order exerted a profound and almost mystical influence on O'Neill. With his aunt gone, another Maryknoller, Peggy Healy, who was based in Nicaragua, corresponded with O'Neill. She painted a picture of Nicaragua torn by civil war—a war encouraged, supported and masterminded by the CIA. Politics was a world of shifting sands, loyalties and values, but nuns and priests spoke the truth, O'Neill believed.

"I believe every word," he told an aide after one two-hour meeting with Sister Healy. He spoke with absolute fervor. The covert war conjured up all the negative feelings of the Ugly American and CIA manipulation. O'Neill recalled the United Fruit Company, the American entity that had given rise to the appellation "banana republic." Covert support for the contras cast the United States in that older role of neo-colonialist exploiter.

Boland could accept the Administration's goal of trying to stop Nicaragua from exporting its fight to El Salvador, but it was clear that the CIA was supporting camps in Honduras from which the contra resistance staged hit-and-run missions into Nicaragua. His select committee of nine Democrats and five Republicans, carefully chosen by O'Neill and Boland, represented the strategic center of the House of Representatives. Any action from that committee would almost certainly be approved by the full House. Boland wanted to cut the funding for the Nicaragua operation completely, and he had the backing of his committee. Goldwater was seeking some middle ground between Boland and full funding. In the House-Senate conference in August 1982 it was agreed to include language that prohibited the CIA and the Defense Department from furnishing military equipment, training or support to anyone "*for the purpose of overthrowing the Government of Nicaragua.*"

The language was kept secret in the authorization bill and was approved by both the Senate and the House.

But on November 1, 1982, Boland read *Newsweek*'s election-week cover story, "America's Secret War, Target: Nicaragua." The article said that the covert operation had expanded into "a larger plan to undermine the Sandinista government." Casey, appearing before Boland's committee, claimed that the chief aim of the operation was still arms interdiction. Great success had been achieved, he said. The contra force had grown to 4,000. That was eight times the initial 500-man force that had been proposed the year before. This growth, Casey argued, was based on the widespread hatred of the Sandinistas. Central America did not want Communism, and this was the clearest measurable manifestation of that sentiment.

Boland was angered. Somewhere, as the authority had passed from the President to Langley, through the ideological prism of Casey with the support of the Administration, to the covert operators and the CIA stations in Central America, and finally into the hands of the contra leaders and their fighters, a massive change had taken place. Boland decided to go public. On December 8, 1982, he read on the House floor his phrase prohibiting the use of funds to overthrow the Nicaraguan government. It was quickly tagged the "Boland Amendment." The least secret covert operation was now officially public. As an amendment to the Intelligence Authorization Act the language passed unanimously, 411 to 0.

Moynihan too was becoming increasingly disturbed, and Dewey Clarridge was more and more part of the problem. He had come to brief the Senate committee in secret, placing a map of Nicaragua before the senators. He had explained a plan to split Nicaragua in half: an east side and a west side, just like New York City, or Beirut, to be more accurate. As Clarridge told it, the CIA-backed contras would take the east side, and the Sandinistas would be left with the capital, Managua, and the west side. Moynihan thought this was mad. The CIA had only fifty people running the operation. The splitting of the country would be a major military feat.

Moynihan could imagine cartoonist Herblock's rendition of the scene, the gung-ho shape of Clarridge laying out his fantasy behind closed doors, perhaps cutting the map with scissors, demonstrating the ease with which the division would take place—all playing to a bunch of beefy, sleepy legislators with long cigars.

Goldwater leaned over to Moynihan and said sarcastically, "Sounds like war to me!"

Moynihan nodded. What could they do? It was all top secret.

In the following weeks, Moynihan heard no more. Apparently the Clarridge plan had gone nowhere, but Moynihan had lost his confidence in them all. Clarridge reflected Casey, and Casey the Administration. The operation was becoming a curse.

On December 9, the day after the Boland proposal passed the House unanimously, Casey came to the Senate committee to argue that arms interdiction remained the primary goal, but that the CIA was hoping to "harass" and pressure the Nicaraguan government to become "more democratic" and perhaps to accept some moderates into the government.

Moynihan felt there was a question of political literacy. "If you say these people, the Sandinistas," he told Casey, "are the people you say they are, and I'm prepared to believe you, then they won't become more democratic. . . . You can overthrow them or leave them alone, but you can't do this in-between thing." And how, Moynihan wondered, can you draw the lines between harassment and an effort to overthrow them? To the Sandinistas it probably all looks the same—most unfriendly activity.

His goals, Casey said, were to stop the spread of Communism and to make the Nicaraguan government pay a high price for its choice. The CIA wanted to keep the Nicaraguan government "off balance," he explained.

The word hung in the air.

Moynihan saw that the Administration was looking for a way to make its enterprise appear just one degree more severe than a harsh diplomatic note. But what about the contras themselves? Moynihan asked. They are fighting to overthrow the government and gain power for themselves. They are not, could not, be fighting just to interdict arms. No one would do that.

His question was not answered. Casey simply repeated that the CIA had to work with what was available: the CIA was supporting the contras, it had not created them.

Moynihan was by now very uncomfortable. The Administration and the Congress were supporting an operation that wouldn't work and was heading for disaster. He wrote to Casey saying that the Senate committee supported the "Boland amendment." Familiar with Casey's lawyerly dodges, Moynihan said he expected the CIA to conform to both the letter and the spirit of its language. Moynihan introduced the Boland measure in the Senate, and it was passed.

Casey's reaction was simple: the new language did not prohibit anything they were already doing. It was a lawyer's game, divining "purpose," it had to do with state of mind, something elusive, an unavoidable, perhaps even useful ambiguity. He told the White House there would be no problems, and on December 21, 1982, Reagan signed the Boland Amendment into law.

Casey's CIA counsel, Stan Sporkin, immediately assembled the best agency lawyers at Langley. Even though it was almost the Christmas holiday season, Sporkin said they had to come up with something at once.

"This thing is going to come back and bite us in the ass like nothing you've ever seen,'' he said. Congress would be watching from the CIA's back pocket on the Boland Amendment. It could be a ''Trojan Horse,'' he said. It was just short of a setup for the agency. ''They'll be watching, looking for a violation,'' Sporkin explained. He wanted ideas on compliance.

The other lawyers resisted, saying the law was an attempt to enforce a negative; the agency just had to make sure nothing was done ''for the purpose'' of overthrowing the Sandinistas. ''Well,'' said one agency lawyer, ''we can do it for all other purposes.''

''We can't be cute,'' Sporkin said. He said they had to have a broader notion of their task. The contra operation, he noted, was important at the White House and for their Director. The lawyers had an obligation. This, he said, is what counseling is all about, preventing problems, not just responding to them. He drafted a tough list of dos and don'ts for Casey to issue to the field. It reminded everyone that the operation was not to ''overthrow,'' and that none of the normal means of executing a coup—particularly assassination—could be supported or employed, directly or indirectly. Assassination was already banned by executive order, but Sporkin felt it did not hurt to restate it.

''Stan, you don't know how to write,'' Casey said, and he reworked the language, making it tougher. They could live with this.

The Director of Operations, John Stein, thought the list of prohibitions and guidelines was a terrific idea to protect them all, and Casey approved sending it in a cable to the Honduras station, which was overseeing the operation and the contra camps. The single-spaced cable of several pages took the Boland Amendment with faithful literalness: nothing should be done—no equipment, training, support, meetings, conversations—specifically ''for the purpose of'' overthrowing the government of Nicaragua. Contra leaders or fighters who talked about using CIA assistance for such purposes had to be cut off.

To emphasize the Administration's seriousness about arms interdiction, President Reagan signed off on a separate top-secret finding for Guatemala, which shares a border of nearly one hundred miles with El Salvador. This finding was to permit the gathering of information and to act on the arms flows along that border. There were reports that weapons were being transferred in trucks supposedly carrying fruit; the trucks were bonded and could not be searched at the border. Sophisticated detection stations were built to sound an alarm when a truck with large concentrations of weapons-grade metal passed. A building was erected and about sixty men trained for the monitoring. A few shipments of arms were stopped, but word about the detection stations leaked out, and little more was discovered. The cost of the detection operation was more than $1 million.

The National Security Agency communications intercepts were not yielding the evidence Casey wanted to demonstrate that Nicaragua was supporting the arms flow to the Salvadoran rebels. These leftist rebels used their radios skillfully, keeping their communications short, using one-time code pads, not using the air except when absolutely necessary, and observing radio silence with professional discipline at all other times, he concluded. Other times the rebels stayed off the airwaves altogether, using land telephone lines that had to be tapped to intercept. Or at times they used couriers and runners. The rebels had better communications security than the Salvadoran military. Cubans, perhaps even Soviet advisers, were behind this, thus depriving Casey of the kind of convincing evidence that could have won congressional and public support for the operation.

"The hardest thing in this world to prove is what is self-evident," he said many times, but he didn't have the goods, and many in his own agency were not sure this proof existed, at least on a scale to justify the Nicaragua covert action.

Senator Leahy decided to visit Central America for a firsthand look. All the world is a fingerbowl for an aggressive senator from the Intelligence Committee, and Leahy was anxious to plunge an ex-parte digit or two into Casey's war. To avoid partisan crossfire Leahy asked Goldwater's staff director, Rob Simmons, to accompany him. Simmons had a special session with DDCI John McMahon to make it clear that the trip was not a junket. They wanted to go into detail with the station chiefs in four key countries: Honduras, where the major contra operation was run; El Salvador, where the leftist rebels were threatening; Guatemala, where the CIA was also trying to stop the arms flow under the separate finding; and Panama, where the CIA had a supersecret training site for the contras.

Leahy, Simmons, three other Senate staffers, a military escort officer and a CIA legislative liaison officer from Langley made up the traveling party. Casey had requested that the CIA have someone on the trip and chose Burton L. Hutchings, an experienced officer who knew the station chief in Panama. The others joked that he was "the eyes and ears of Langley."

Based on the CIA briefings and CIA promises, Leahy had formed an idea of what to expect: the contras were to stay in small units; the contras would not capture and hold territory; they had pledged to work to prevent atrocities; former Somoza-regime war criminals were to be kept out of the leadership. The CIA was to be once, even twice removed from actual operations.

After a routine visit to the interdiction site in Guatemala, the seven men flew to Tegucigalpa, the capital of Honduras, and stayed at the plush residence of the ambassador. Leahy came to like the station chief, who seemed serious and informed.

The CIA had set up a separate base in a Tegucigalpa safe house to manage the contras program. The chief of the base was a former Army Special Forces lieutenant colonel named Ray Doty. He had a direct communications link to CIA headquarters—"a dedicated point-to-point circuit," in communications jargon, with a scrambled top-secret code. Though Doty was subordinate to the station chief in the capital, the base was the operational arm of the covert action. Doty had run paramilitary training in the CIA's war in Laos during the Vietnam War.

Doty, a man in his late forties, said at his briefing that the training camps in Honduras were the best he had ever seen. Of the seven contra combat units, Doty explained, five had been sent across the border into Nicaragua. He brought out a map of Nicaragua showing vast areas of the country progressively shaded, forecasting the combat units' movement south. These combat units were to link up with those coming up from the south through Costa Rica.

"Wait a minute, wait a minute," Leahy interrupted. That was a link-up covering more than 200 miles, a sweep across the eastern half of Nicaragua. This had the look of the old Clarridge plan to split the country. "And this looks like you're planning to overthrow the Sandinistas," Leahy said.

"No," Doty replied, "absolutely not." He knew that Congress had prohibited the expenditure of money "for the purpose" of ousting the government. Casey's cable was there, posted on a bulletin board.

"Well, what the hell do you think your plan is going to do if it succeeds?" Leahy asked.

"It will break the overland route between this eastern side and Managua, which is near the west coast," Doty said. The east coast, on the Caribbean, receives supplies by sea from Cuba and the Soviets. With the overland route severed, the Cubans and the Soviets would have to use the Panama Canal and come up the Pacific, or western side. Thus the arms flow is being interdicted, he said.

"Wait again," Leahy said. How was this going to look to the Sandinistas, to have their country divided in two—split down the middle—and for the United States to be saying we are not trying to overthrow their government?

Doty retorted that since El Salvador did not face the Caribbean, and had just a coast on the Pacific facing southwest, the operation was straight arms interdiction—cutting the flow from Cuba to Nicaragua to El Salvador.

Technically Doty might be correct, Leahy realized, but he was not buying. What control is the CIA able to exercise over the contra combat units? Leahy and the staff members asked.

Since the CIA has given the contras the communications equipment, Doty said, the CIA has the frequencies and listens in secretly to see whether the contras are adhering to the plans and operation that have been outlined.

What if the contras don't say everything on the air?

Well, Doty said, we're recruiting people within the contra force to spy for us and they'll report back.

How many do you have recruited?

"We've got a line on one or two," Doty said, "but we're just getting started."

How will these "spies" report?

Face-to-face meetings, Doty explained.

They'll just walk into your safe house here, risking their lives? So you'll see them, say, twice a year?

"Hey," Doty said, "we'll work it out."

Leahy felt this must have been what it was like in Saigon during the early 1960s, a slush fund of good intentions, big plans and small steps toward war.

In the U.S. Embassy in Tegucigalpa, officials told Leahy and the others that the embassy was staking the outcome on some kind of negotiations. They expressed concern about the small war that was being ginned up around them.

Next Leahy had a private meeting with the Honduran armed-forces chief, General Gustavo Álvarez, who was in charge of the Honduran end of the operation.

"Hell," Álvarez told Leahy, "we'll have our soldiers in Managua by Christmas."

"Hey, wait," Leahy said. U.S. policy is specifically designed *not* to overthrow.

"Oh, yeah," Álvarez said, but wouldn't it be great to do it anyway?

The group flew to Panama. Dewey Clarridge had left just the day before. Using the alias "Dewey Maroni," he was visiting the CIA stations in the region. He would arrive with cigars and brandy, the agency equivalent of pressing the flesh, keeping the station chiefs up much of the night reviewing professional and personal matters and recounting "old war" and "new war" stories.

Leahy's briefing with the station chief was scheduled for the next day, but he went in as a matter of courtesy to say hello and introduce himself. The Senator said he wanted particular information on the Nicaragua program, specifically on its dimensions—time, money and numbers of people involved.

"Division chief has instructed me not to answer," the station chief replied, referring to Clarridge.

Leahy and Simmons were astonished, and tried to get through to McMahon in Washington without luck.

The next day the station chief repeated his instructions.

"I intend to get answers and will stay until I do," Leahy said.

The station wouldn't let Leahy or Simmons get a message out to Casey or McMahon. Leahy threatened to use the regular telephone to call McMahon. That could be a security breach, particularly if Leahy unleashed his temper over an unsecure line.

By 11 P.M. Leahy got a secure message out.

Seven hours later, about 6 A.M., there was a knock on the door of his hotel room.

There was Clarridge, wearing what Leahy thought could only be described as an Italian silk safari suit, custom-made jacket and pants. There were no pleasantries, and the hotel radio was turned on to thwart possible eavesdropping.

"Who do we have here?" Leahy asked sarcastically. "Tinker, tailor, soldier . . ." Pause. ". . . sailor." As in the children's rhyme, not "spy" as in the Le Carré novel.

"You know me," Clarridge said. "You have some questions, Senator?"

"As a member of the Senate Intelligence Committee, my oversight is not limited to Washington, D.C.," Leahy said formally. "When I travel to the stations I expect answers, and in this case I had the assurances of John McMahon." Leahy explained that they had a cover story to give to the news media so that the trip into Panama would not be linked to the contra operation.

Clarridge sat down on the bed. The strongman leader of Panama, General Manuel Antonio Noriega, the former head of Panamanian military intelligence, has for some time been a key provider and facilitator for the CIA, Clarridge explained reluctantly. But Noriega plays both sides and has cozy relations with the Cubans—an advantage and disadvantage to the CIA because sometimes Noriega provides good Cuban intelligence. Of course, there's no telling what he's providing the Cubans. In all, this is a deadly game. Nonetheless, Noriega is going to allow the CIA to set up a contra training facility here. The facility has to be kept secret at almost any cost. If it leaks, Noriega will have grounds to cancel and refuse to allow the training.

Why train contras in Panama, which is three countries south of El Salvador? What does that have to do with arms interdiction?

To prepare contras to hit Nicaragua from the south through Costa Rica, Clarridge replied.

Leahy pictured the map of the region: there was Costa Rica some 300 miles from El Salvador. This was clearly not arms interdiction.

The group's next and final stop was to be El Salvador, but the NSA forwarded a message to Panama about a report that some of the right-wingers in El Salvador were planning to shoot down a U.S. congressional plane. Senator Christopher Dodd, who was also flying into El Salvador at about the same time, was apparently the target. Simmons suggested they put a sign on their plane saying: "Don't Shoot, right-wing senator's assistant on board."

Back in Washington, Leahy and the staffers put together a long top-secret report. It contained memoranda of conversations from each of the meetings. The conclusion was inescapable: the operation was bigger in nearly every respect than it had been described. Not just the numbers of contras—now heading for 5,500—but everything about it was big. The U.S. military had undertaken intelligence-gathering efforts costing millions of dollars; support or training or interdiction efforts were under way throughout Central America. All of Central America—Guatemala, Costa Rica, El Salvador, Honduras, even Panama—was being knit together into an anti-Nicaragua alliance.

On the ground, the plan was to split the country east–west by summer, attack from the north through Honduras and the south through Costa Rica, and be in Managua by Christmas. It was war from all points of the compass. The operation was totally different from what had been presented by the CIA briefers in Washington. It was obvious that covert policy was frequently out ahead of or overriding stated or implied U.S. foreign policy. A regional war was getting off the ground, and much of the planning was unspoken and subtle.

At the next Senate committee meeting, Leahy asked for fifteen minutes to present a summary.

"Oh shit," Goldwater whispered, "that guy talks too much."

Enders was attempting to keep the Nicaragua operation embedded, if not hidden, in the larger Central American strategy. He wanted to keep the covert action from looming too large with the public, with Congress or even within the Administration. In his estimation, Casey was not a crass Cold Warrior and they had been working together with a set of broad concepts—democracy, economic assistance, covert action. Enders had carefully designed the mix so that Vietnam sensibilities would not be shocked. Tailored this way, Administration policy was marketable to Congress. But the perspective had changed in the White House, largely because of the new national-security adviser, Bill Clark.

"Too little, too late," Clark was saying. He had a sense that the Administration policy was going under.

Enders argued that Congress had the hammer. Those in Congress who fully opposed the covert operation constituted a minority; so did those who fully supported it. For Congress to be held, the 10 to 15 percent in the middle had to be convinced. "The only way to do that is to demonstrate that Administration policy is the road to peace and settlement," Enders said. "Negotiations cannot be abandoned." Realism dictated that Administration policy be tailored to the Congress.

Clark said that if the middle-of-the-roaders and the Democrats were confronted in a national debate, they could not remain in opposition. He would relish such a debate. He wanted to discipline Congress, to remind it that the President could go talk directly to the voters. Public opinion could be mobilized.

Smelling trouble, Enders set down his thoughts, urging the maintenance of a regional "two-track" strategy. In Nicaragua, that meant continuing covert support to the contras but attempting to force the Sandinistas to negotiate with the contras. In El Salvador, it meant continuing the support to the government and Duarte, plus forcing negotiations between the government and the leftist guerrillas. The goal would be a broad settlement that would remove the forces of the Soviet Union, Cuba and the United States from the region.

Clark obtained a copy of Enders' memo, and he was boiling. Enders was trying to cap his career with some breakthrough, a professional success at the expense of consistency in Administration policy, Clark felt. No way was the United States going to pull out of Central America and abandon its friends. To Clark, this could be a repeat of Carter's mistake—saying one thing, doing another. He sent Enders' report to the President, arguing that it showed Enders was not adhering to Administration policy.

On February 10, 1983, Enders' memo leaked to the news media, and inside the White House he was accused of incipient defeatism. Clark made it clear that not only did he himself have a distaste for negotiations, but he was not sure the White House wanted the centrist congressional support. A major political battle might best serve the President.

Casey told Enders that he remained skeptical of a negotiating strategy, but that he was not opposed to the attempt and saw that it provided the Administration and the CIA good cover in the intelligence committees. Then in March, Casey called Enders.

"Tom," Casey said, "I know you got your difficulties, but in addition to Bill Clark you got another guy after you. Mike Deaver."

"Thanks for the tip, buddy," Enders replied, realizing that that meant Nancy Reagan.

Casey had heard Deaver referring to Enders as "tea and crumpets" and the "striped-pants set." That was fatal.

Casey was pleased to see the White House preparing to step out front on Central America. In fact, Bill Clark seemed to be nicely reorienting foreign policy.

One of Casey's chief pipelines into the White House was Reagan speechwriter Anthony R. Dolan, winner of the 1978 Pulitzer Prize for investigative reporting. Casey had brought Dolan to the 1980 Reagan campaign. Dolan was a true believer in the conservative cause, a protégé of William F. Buckley, Jr., and had seen the 1980 presidential campaign as the final game of the World Series for Western civilization. He had landed in the President's speechwriting office. Though he was kept leashed by Jim Baker, Dolan filled a role as the Reagan attack dog. A steady stream of notes, ideas and phone calls flowed between the DCI and Dolan.

Dolan admired Casey's cooler version of true conservative commitment. He admired the way Casey took criticism, which Dolan felt was comparable to the criticism of General Grant for taking casualties in pursuing General Robert E. Lee. Shots had to be fired and political hell paid on occasion. Casey did not brood about his press clippings. He was too busy. Happily, he was a man who found the world, its books, its ideas and its challenges more interesting than he found himself.

Casey promoted Dolan's talents to Clark. Dolan was assigned a relatively routine speech that the President was to give to a convention of fundamentalist ministers. In reworking it, Dolan believed that finally he had tapped into the President's subconscious.

On March 8, 1983, at 3:04 P.M., the President addressed the National Association of Evangelicals in the Citrus Crown Ballroom of the Sheraton Twin Towers Hotel in Orlando, Florida. Quoting the Declaration of Independence, C. S. Lewis, Whittaker Chambers and Tom Paine, the President called the Soviet Union "an evil empire."

This created something of a sensation. Later that month, the President unveiled his Strategic Defense Initiative, or "Star Wars" plan, to defend against Soviet missiles by deploying weapons in space. The Soviets branded Reagan a "lunatic."

In this atmosphere of fervent anti-Communism, Casey could survive, even flourish, but not Enders. The battleground was Nicaragua. Reagan, Clark and Casey were playing hardball, and were questioning the patriotism of anyone who wanted to continue a dialogue. Enders viewed the proper policy as one that would get the Soviets and the Cubans out of Nicaragua. But U.S. policy now was clearly to get the Sandinistas out also.

Enders was removed and sent to Spain as U.S. ambassador. He took several months to get out of town, and there were a number of major going-away dinners. Casey attended them all. As if his presence was not statement enough, Casey rose at one to give a toast. He spoke well of Enders' work, emphasizing his distinguished career, projecting a sense of long association with Enders, the things they had been through together. He was not particularly articulate, but he was empathetic and warm, making it clear that he and Enders would always be friends.

By the spring of 1983, John McMahon's own worries about Casey, the CIA and the contras were increasing. The ranking House Intelligence Committee Republican, Ken Robinson, braced McMahon one day about the growing number of contras. Why had 500 grown to 5,500? Robinson, an Administration and CIA loyalist, was almost harsh. McMahon answered that the intelligence committees were being fully briefed. But, he explained, the members were losing track because often months elapsed between hearings. It was easy to imagine that the latest update had been only last week. But in the intervening months the contras might have hit a village and signed up a hundred more, and a hundred more in the next village. They could not turn away new recruits, this expression of popular support. Sensing the skepticism, McMahon acknowledged the agency's active recruiting program to sign up young fighters with the contras. Of course the numbers were growing. But Robinson was not happy, and McMahon figured that his testiness meant the Nicaragua program was headed for further trouble.

McMahon also appeared before a closed session of the Senate Intelligence Committee, where there was sniping from all quarters—suspicion, even hostility, about each number, as well as about the program's broad intentions and goals.

Leahy jumped hard on McMahon: "You guys are setting yourselves up for a fall." The operation was going to get out of hand and it probably wouldn't succeed. "No one is going to blame the White House," Leahy said, "or the State Department or the Pentagon for this." When this all fails, Leahy said, the CIA will be blamed. It's their war, not Reagan's war, or even Casey's war, but the CIA's war. Reagan, Casey, McMahon will be out of office someday, but the agency will have to remain. The Intelligence Committee has some obligation to protect the institutions of American intelligence-gathering, Leahy said. "So do you."

Yes, McMahon said, he agreed. The contra operation is going to get the agency in trouble, deep trouble, he said. It's going to get the Congress in trouble, too. McMahon turned red and began waving his hands for emphasis. He had been there in the 1970s when the agency was driven right down into the pits with public opinion, the press, the Congress. Its entire mission, he said, was endangered every time it was exposed as the implementer of U.S. foreign policy.

Deep emotions began to pour forth. McMahon said this exposure would not just hurt his buddies in the agency, or his particular notion of how they ought to gather intelligence and run operations, but would destroy the value of anything the CIA might do. The reputation of the CIA was on the line. No less. At the same time, they had to go along with what the President and the Director ordered. They ordered and supported this operation each step of the way. So the task was to find a way to work themselves out of this hole—to protect the CIA but obey the orders. And they, the senators on the oversight committee, should realize that he understood those high stakes. He needed their help, he said.

There was silence in the hearing room when McMahon had finished.

With the expansion of the secret war, the CIA was running out of funds for the contras. Casey decided to reprogram some money from the secret contingency fund. This "put and take" fund of about $50 million was always available in an emergency, or when Congress was not in session. After the emergency, or when Congress reconvened, the money would be authorized and the fund replenished. Several million dollars was left over from the failed operation to provide security and intelligence assistance to Bashir Gemayel. Those funds were reprogrammed to the contras. But there was a delay of at least three weeks or perhaps six weeks, depending on how the calculation was made, before the paperwork arrived at the Senate Intelligence Committee, informing it of the transfer.

Given the mounting sensitivities about the operation, the delay in giving the routine notification to the committee renewed feelings that the CIA was not leveling with its overseers. A secret hearing was scheduled, and the CIA comptroller, Daniel Childs, was called to testify. Childs, a former aide on the committee to Senator Inouye, said that the several million was just a small item and he had bigger matters on his mind. Inouye, a moderate Democrat, was angry.

Some of the Democrats saw it as an opportunity to string Casey up.

But Senator Malcolm Wallop found another angle. The record showed that Casey had been out of town at the time of the disbursement. It was McMahon who had not acted promptly. This was almost too good to be true. Wallop was delighted. McMahon, the admin officer par excellence, had not moved the paper on his desk, a bureaucratic crime of the first order. Wallop's colleagues who were hunting for Casey's scalp on this had come up instead with McMahon's. McMahon had to explain his slip to each of the key senators. In the course of this, he realized he was not up to speed on the Nicaragua operation. He had not realized the magnitude of Casey's and Clarridge's undertakings from one end of Central America to the other. He was the deputy director and he had been bypassed, there was no other word for it. The situation was intolerable.

He went to Casey to explain that he could function as deputy only if he was in the loop. There could be no repeat of the Inman experience. Neither of them wanted that. Casey stared and then agreed; new procedures were established, the paperwork would pass through McMahon.

Seeing more only increased McMahon's unease. In his best I-am-loyal-to-you style, he urged that they try to find another way; perhaps now that the operation was out in the open, it belonged in the hands of the Defense Department. It did, after all, have the appearance of war.

Casey didn't like the idea. If the CIA couldn't handle the tough questions, if it had to shuffle them off to the military, the paramilitary capability that he had vowed to restore would be a joke. These operations were the hard calls. In addition, the military didn't have the stomach for such an operation. On top of all that, a superpower could not take on a pipsqueak nation like Nicaragua with a frontal military assault.

McMahon argued passionately, insisting that he was on Casey's side. He had been there in the 1970s, during the investigations, the low morale, the crack-up and the crippling of the agency that Casey had halted.

Casey suggested that they both talk to others on the National Security Council. The idea of passing the operation to the Defense Department was presented to Weinberger, Bill Clark and George Shultz, who had replaced Haig as Secretary of State the previous year.

Weinberger's response was simple: over his dead body would the Defense Department take over. He was determined to keep the military out of anything that did not have the full backing of Congress and the public. And this operation already smelled of no confidence.

The Secretary of State said he found the covert approach manageable on the diplomatic front. That would become impossible if the Pentagon took over.

Clark agreed that the operation was best in the hands of the CIA. He praised Casey's efforts. Clarridge was performing miracles. Clark saw victory on the horizon.

The President was effusive. "Bill and the CIA are doing the right thing," Reagan said.

Goldwater instructed the Senate committee lawyers to see whether the operation could not be funded directly and openly through the Defense Department. The lawyers found about a dozen legal obstacles, and Goldwater concluded that he was stuck. A Defense Department military operation would be war, it would require a congressional declaration. Who wanted to declare war on Nicaragua? Covert action had that one advantage, even if the covert was a fiction, the emperor's latest new clothes. Though it was not recognized under international law and various treaties, nations were going to conduct covert action anyway. So no nation was likely to call the U.S. on it.

Over in the House, Boland wondered whether a fence of some sort might not be built in Honduras to prevent arms flowing from Nicaragua into El Salvador. The cost estimate on Boland's idea—privately dubbed the Boland Line—indicated that it might cost $300 million to $500 million. It was quickly dropped.

Casey reported the President's tribute to the CIA to McMahon, who acquiesced. The Nicaragua operation was with the CIA to stay. Casey, after all, had let him make his pitch. Now, under the rules of loyalty up and loyalty down, the situation required that McMahon support Casey.

• • •

Now, McMahon and covert action bumped heads again. Exiles from the small country of Suriname, a former Dutch colony on the north coast of South America just above Brazil, had come to the agency seeking support. These Dutch exiles wanted nothing less than to overthrow the authoritarian government of Lieutenant Colonel Desi Bouterse, who had pro-Communist leanings and had brutally executed fifteen people, including his chief political opponents and some journalists and union leaders.

Casey was all for the idea; Bouterse was nothing but leftist trouble, and the Dutch exiles seemed credible. But Casey and McMahon agreed that they needed an independent evaluation. The Directorate of Operations drafted an "enabling finding" that authorized a limited covert action to see whether CIA support of the exiles made sense, whether they had a chance to oust Bouterse. An actual operation to attempt the overthrow or to provide direct lethal support to the exiles would require a separate, regular finding. President Reagan signed the "enabling finding," and several hundred thousand dollars was allocated to send a CIA team into Suriname to gather intelligence and do a coup-feasibility study.

McMahon briefed the matter to the Senate Intelligence Committee. He was met by a chorus of "You've got to be kidding." Why, several senators asked, is the Reagan Administration considering a coup in a country that has no significance? The Suriname people were primitive and gentle, much like Tahitians in the South Pacific. The population was about 350,000. That's the size of Tucson, Arizona. Goldwater, particularly, was incensed, declaring, "That's the dumbest fucking idea I ever heard of in my life."

McMahon replied that the Bouterse government was talking with the Cubans and the government of Grenada, a tiny Caribbean island also led by a leftist government. The CIA had a group of Dutch exiles who would do the work.

When had a U.S.-supported coup such as this ever worked?

McMahon had to go back to the CIA-backed 1954 coup in Guatemala to find an answer. He made it clear that the enabling finding meant only that the Administration was looking into the possibility, and that a go-ahead would require another finding and the committee would be notified.

It wasn't enough. After the briefing, the committee agreed to send a letter of protest to President Reagan, telling him of its opposition to covert action in Suriname.

Goldwater sent a personal message to Reagan saying, in effect, "Do you really need this?"

In the House committee also there was overwhelming bipartisan opposition. When the CIA team did return, they had little intelligence and reported that a coup was probably not achievable.

The plan was dropped, but McMahon was shaken up on the play. He rededicated himself to keeping the CIA out of comic-book operations.

12

IF CASEY WAS going to sell the Nicaragua operation in the Democratic House, he would have to hold conservative Democrats from the South and the West. One such person was Dave K. McCurdy, a thirty-three-year-old Democratic congressman from Oklahoma, who had joined the House Intelligence Committee that January. An Administration friend and avidly pro-defense, McCurdy was assumed to buy the whole Reagan foreign-policy and defense-program package. In a private conversation, Casey told McCurdy that the CIA would "do whatever it takes" to influence the Sandinista government. McCurdy had a feeling of slipperiness in his discussions with Casey.

At one hearing, McCurdy asked Casey how much the Sandinistas were spending on schools, roads and hospitals in their country.

"I don't know," Casey snapped. There was a tone of intolerance that reverberated through the secure committee room on the top floor of the Capitol building. It was a small room, and the congressmen were arranged around a built-in horseshoe table. Casey was on edge. He was making it clear that he found the hearing tedious and McCurdy's inquiry silly and irrelevant.

McCurdy asked whether this was because Casey himself didn't know, or whether the CIA didn't have the information.

"What's your point, Mr. Congressman?" Casey asked.

"I grew up in rural Oklahoma," McCurdy said, "and you ought to understand why we are Democrats in rural Oklahoma." McCurdy went on to explain about FDR's New Deal and the Rural Electrification Administration (REA) that had brought the farmers of Oklahoma into the twentieth century. And the question, he said, is whether the Sandinistas are on that road. Are they winning the people?

Casey got the point and became somewhat more approachable. The Catholic Church was opposing the Sandinistas, he said, and if there were truly free elections in Nicaragua the Sandinistas would not win.

How about the U.S.-backed contras? McCurdy wanted to know. What kind of message were they spreading in the countryside in the battle for hearts and minds of the locals? They were blowing up bridges. A granary and a ranch had been hit. A power plant had been attacked; the CIA had said the power plant was a military target, but it turned out that only about 10 percent of the power was for the armed forces; the rest was for civilians. That was the opposite of REA. That was destroying, not building.

On the first day back from Easter recess, April 5, 1983, Moynihan and Leahy went to the Senate floor to voice concern about the Nicaragua operation. Moynihan spoke of a "crisis of confidence" between the Congress and the intelligence agencies. Privately, Moynihan thought this kind of military and, for all practical purposes, terrorist pressure within a country was precisely the kind of action that could not achieve more democracy. How had the Sandinistas reacted? They had suspended civil liberties. The press was heavily censored, and the apparatus of a junior police state had been put into place.

A week later, on Tuesday at 11 A.M., Goldwater had Casey, McMahon and Sporkin before a closed session of the Senate committee. In chorus, they made the case that the operation was legal and authorized; it had the support of the President, the State Department, and the CIA professionals. Afterward, Goldwater took to the Senate floor and gave an impassioned defense of the CIA, saying, "I believe we have been kept fully and currently informed."

In a direct poke at Moynihan, Goldwater said, "This talk of a crisis of confidence is a throwback to the rhetoric of the 1970s when the Church and Pike committees were crawling into the headlines on the backs of the intelligence community." He noted that the Sandinistas had created the largest military force in Central America, at least forty thousand including reserves. "Do any of my colleagues seriously believe that this Marxist military machine is going to be brought to its knees by several thousand freedom fighters?" Covert action is risky, Goldwater said, those called on to implement it get left holding the bag. "This is just damn unfair and this kind of cowardice makes me mad as hell." Outlining the Senate's role and its total knowledge about these operations, Goldwater said, "It is essential that we face up to our own responsibilities in these matters—to our own involvement—and not run out of the kitchen just when it is beginning to get hot." If the Senate didn't like what was going on, it had a remedy—the power of the purse. "If funds are being spent for actions which we do not support, then let us cut the funds."

• • •

That winter Casey puzzled over Lebanon. The agency had diminished influence and intelligence since the assassination of Bashir Gemayel. Bashir's brother Amin had been elected President and had taken office. Amin Gemayel was stepping back from Israel, from the United States, and attempting to forge Lebanon's Arab ties. But Amin sought the protective umbrella of the United States. To maintain influence for the United States, the White House had suggested a candidate to become the new Lebanese national-security adviser. Amin agreed and named Wadi Haddad, a forty-two-year-old Lebanese who had worked for the World Bank. Haddad, a short, neat, precise man with an intellectual bent, was known as "the American" because of his close ties to the United States.

Casey had met with Haddad in early 1983. Both were worried about Syrian influence in Lebanon and over Amin Gemayel himself. Haddad believed firmly that the Syrians would try any tactic, and that if it worked they would call it their policy. "If you feel you have been betrayed by the Syrians, then you don't understand them," he said.

Casey concurred and wanted to know about the personality and strength of Amin, since there were many negative reports on the new President. In the midst of the latest turmoil, he had been in Paris on a shopping spree, buying twenty-four new suits and new formal wear at Christian Dior. He was hated by the Army and considered weak. Did Amin, Casey asked, have the support of the military?

Yes, Haddad said, but added that his answer was based on hope. In other words, no. The tension between the Lebanese national-security adviser and the new Lebanese President was obvious. The relationship could not last, Casey concluded.

For his part, Haddad had determined that if he wanted to get a message to President Reagan, Casey was the route.

Another avenue of influence for Casey in the Administration's Middle East policy was through Robert C. Ames, the region's chief CIA analyst, a legendary CIA officer and one of Casey's most important people. Ames often put on a casual air, wearing lightly tinted aviator glasses and cowboy boots. He was an idea man, full of new, even offbeat approaches. As a DO officer, he had been a brilliant recruiter of agents and sources for the CIA. In an earlier assignment in Beirut, during the Helms era, Ames had been the first to make a real penetration into the PLO for the CIA, developing two key sources.

One Ames recruitment had been Ali Hasan Salameh, the security and intelligence chief to PLO Chairman Arafat. Salameh, code-named "the Red Prince" by the Israeli Mossad, had been killed in a 1979 car-bombing that probably had been carried out by the Israelis. Ames was the master player of the so-called "war of the secret services" in Beirut, where spies and intelligence services crawled all over each other, and where nearly every shot, bomb or diplomatic move had a secondary intelligence implication. In this world, survival at times meant balancing and hedging your double crosses.

Ames felt that Israel was a zero-sum game. For the Israelis, any gain by any other country or individual in its relations with the United States would eventually be at Israel's expense.

Casey was glad to see Ames assume the role of unofficial Middle East adviser to Shultz. The previous year, Deputy Secretary of Defense Frank Carlucci, the former DDCI, had told Shultz there was one way to understand the Middle East. "Listen to Bob Ames," Carlucci had said, "please listen to him. He's good because he's balanced and he has no ego hang-ups." Some months later Shultz had taken Carlucci aside and said, "One of the best pieces of advice you gave me was to listen to Bob Ames."

Ames's celebrated coolness appealed to Shultz. He was soon the reader of intelligence and the virtual handler of the Secretary of State when it came to the Middle East. Ames's message was simple: Things were getting serious in Lebanon with the two occupying powers, Syria and Israel. Something ought to be done. But, like everything else in the Middle East, it would not be simple at all; and, like almost everything in the Middle East, it might not even be possible.

In April 1983 Ames left for a field mission to the Middle East, and on April 18 he was at the U.S. Embassy on the Beirut seafront when a pickup truck filled with explosives entered the grounds and detonated. The midsection of the seven-story salmon-colored structure collapsed, and when the bodies were pulled from the rubble the count was sixty-three dead, including seventeen Americans, among them Ames, the CIA station chief, the deputy station chief and another half-dozen CIA officers.

Casey couldn't bring himself to believe the first reports. It was like a personal wound—nothing quite so devastating had ever happened in an organization he headed. The CIA men had been meeting on terrorism. Had that been known to the terrorists?

The NSA had been reading and breaking the coded message traffic from the Iranian Foreign Ministry in Tehran to the Iranian embassies in Beirut and Damascus, Syria. After the bombing, the analysts reviewed every intercept and scrap available before the bombing. The messages indicated pretty clearly that some kind of operation was being planned against the American community. One cable showed that a $25,000 payment had been approved for an unspecified operation. These decoded cables and other intelligence had been passed to the U.S. ambassador before the bombing. There was, however, no specified day, no specified target and no clear indication that the embassy was a target. There had been some backup human sources, but nothing could be confirmed and one of the sources was untested.

Columnist Jack Anderson and CBS News reported that the Iranian communications were intercepted by U.S. intelligence. Casey was incredulous at these leaks. Though the news stories received little attention in the U.S., they apparently were read in Iran. Soon there were no more messages. This was particularly distressing because Casey had hoped that if the NSA could continue listening in on the Iranian communications, it might learn who had carried out the bombing. Future messages might also have given clues to new plans or actions against the U.S. But now there was nothing. A major source of intelligence had been carelessly lost.

It was a sobering experience for Casey. An investigation was launched to find who had leaked. But the intercepted cables had received comparatively wide circulation within the White House, State and Defense. Two days after the bombing, the National Intelligence Daily contained a summary of the intercepted communications. Hundreds of people, including the members of the congressional intelligence committees, read the NID.

The 150 copies of the "TOP SECRET CODEWORD" intelligence daily were supposed to be returned each day, but only fifty were coming back, meaning that about a hundred copies were being improperly retained throughout the government. Photocopying the NID was prohibited, but handwritten instructions to make copies were often found on the returned copies. In one instance seventy-five photocopies from just one office were found.

Casey had not known that Jack Anderson and CBS were about to report the intercepts. This certainly was a consequence of his decision to shut down media access to the CIA. Perhaps that had been a mistake. Casey felt that he might have been able to talk Anderson and CBS out of zeroing in on the exact source and method used to gain the information. He had no early-warning system for the American news media. He began thinking that maybe, of all things, he needed a press officer.

Over in the Executive Office Building, the large gray building next to the White House that contains the staff offices for the President, down one of the huge, wide black-and-white marbled corridors is Room 351.

There, in the spring of 1983, a heavyset, bearded Oxford graduate sifted through the piles of papers and intelligence flowing into his cluttered office. This office and this man were a nerve center for the Reagan Administration on the Middle East. At the desk, slugging through the detail, Dr. Geoffrey Kemp, the chief NSC staff expert on the Middle East and South Asia, pondered what the Administration now faced.

Certainly there was an Iranian hand in the embassy bombing. But the key question was Syria, and the key part of that question was whether the Syrian connection was "operational." The bombing had the Syrian trademark—sophisticated malevolence. U.S. intelligence didn't have an answer, or at least not the kind of clear answer that could be diplomatically useful. U.S. policy could not be based on circumstantial threads. Certainly Syrian intelligence would have known what was happening, but when, at what point if any did the Syrians, the Syrian leadership, get hands-on control? The inability to answer that question reflected the confusion about what was going on in Syria. There were many separate empires in Syria. President Assad, one of the most enduring, cunning Middle East leaders, knew and controlled most but not necessarily all of those empires.

Syria was as hard a problem as existed in the intelligence morass. And when Kemp faced the facts he found that intelligence was becoming increasingly irrelevant to policy, not just in Syria, but everywhere in the Middle East. Kemp found the raw intelligence overwhelming. There were hundreds of messages, intercepts, source reports, summaries each day. There was no way to make sense of it. The so-called finished intelligence —the NID or the morning intelligence summary from the State Department or the estimates or the watch reports—seemed almost to feed on itself. The graphics or the maps might be great, but, as he examined it all, Kemp was hard pressed to find anything useful. There was no set of organizing principles. If he was working on what to do in Lebanon, the intelligence from Egypt that day might be better or more relevant.

What Kemp needed was a precise, rigorous, exacting understanding of the true intentions, goals and behavior of nations and their leaders. That was acquired only over years. The death of Bob Ames had left a gap. It had cut George Shultz off from in-depth understanding, leaving him out in the cold. Kemp's boss, Bill Clark, was inexperienced and had really ceded the Middle East to Shultz.

Four days after the bombing, President Reagan announced that he was sending the Secretary of State to the Middle East.

On May 17, 1983, Lebanon and Israel signed an agreement on the withdrawal of Israeli troops and guarantees for Israel's northern border. President Amin Gemayel had raised Syria twenty times in the discussions with Shultz and other U.S. diplomats. Shultz was confident that Syria could not exercise a veto power over a settlement, and he believed the U.S. had more influence over Syria than anyone realized.

Gemayel had one theme: if he had to submit to the Syrians, he wanted to do it when he was strong. The agreement with Israel would unite the internal factions in Lebanon against him. He needed an American pledge.

So on the day of the Lebanon-Israel agreement, President Reagan sent President Gemayel a secret letter. It was a kind of guarantee, promising that the U.S. would not allow Lebanon to be attacked or to suffer as a result of signing the agreement with Israel. As Bashir Gemayel had been promised secret CIA support and protection, now his brother was being promised secret U.S. presidential support—the diplomatic and implied military umbrella, the continued presence of the U.S. Marines in Beirut.

At the CIA, a settlement was viewed as a nonstarter. Report after report said that Syria would not go along. The State Department's intelligence branch, INR, agreed. These reports made three essential points. First, the internal problems in Lebanon were so great that the United States could not solve them with diplomacy, even with troops, unless there was a willingness to commit 50,000 U.S. fighting men. Second, Amin Gemayel was an inherently weak leader. Third, U.S. peacekeeping troops in Lebanon were eventually going to start killing Arabs in the name of one faction or another. And that was not going to be accepted by the other factions.

Moreover, the analytic reports concluded that, despite the tendency of some U.S. policy-makers to see Syria as a Soviet pawn, Syria had its own agenda and President Assad was a determined, formidable master strategist compared to Amin Gemayel.

At the NSC, Kemp felt that one of the biggest failings of the intelligence was the inability to produce good psychological, personal and political profiles of the leaders. The personalities of Assad, Gemayel and Begin were what it was all about, but U.S. intelligence wasn't adequately describing them. So the top U.S. leadership simply was not getting the essential. For example, a SECRET psychological profile of Libya's Qaddafi done the previous year by Dr. Jerrold M. Post, the head of the Political Psychological Division at the CIA, relied heavily on clichés. The profile had stated: "Despite popular belief to the contrary, Qaddafi is not psychotic, and for the most part is in contact with reality. . . . Qaddafi is judged to suffer from a severe personality disturbance—a 'borderline personality disorder.' "

This "borderline personality disorder"—a hot topic in psychiatry—was not a major mental disorder but simply meant that the person alternated between crazy and noncrazy behavior. How, Kemp wondered, could this help the policy-makers? The Qaddafi profile added: "Under severe stress, he is subject to episodes of bizarre behavior when his judgment may be faulty." A later CIA profile attributed some of Qaddafi's behavior to an approaching or actual midlife crisis. To Kemp, this was silliness. But it was dangerous silliness. At one point Kemp suggested that the White House bring in a novelist to assist in these profiles.

Since Reagan did not read many novels but watched movies, the CIA began to produce profiles of leaders that could be shown to the President in the White House or at Camp David. One was of the new Egyptian President. "SECRET NOFORN" flashed on the screen as the narrator began, "This is Hosni Mubarak." Music, color and then followed some pictures of the small village in which Mubarak was born—Kafra el-Meselha, located in a northern Nile Delta province.

The more remote a leader was to ordinary intelligence or even to American television interviews, which could be as revealing as anything, the less value the profiles. Where a leader had a well-defined international presence and reputation, the CIA profiles were dramatic and effective. One of the best was of Israeli Prime Minister Begin. The profile opened with footage of bulldozers, their operators masked, pushing stacks of bodies at a Nazi concentration camp, and Begin's voice-over, "Never again, never again." The profile seemed to go into the mind of Begin and was therefore powerful. But Begin's mind was well known.

Reagan was impressed by the video profiles, and Kemp figured they were useful in educating Meese, Baker and Deaver, who knew next to nothing about foreign affairs. Deaver liked them so much that he passed word to the CIA that Reagan was pleased; soon the CIA began providing a classified travelogue, or "advance," of countries and foreign capitals that Reagan planned to visit.

Under the May 17 agreement, Lebanon was not supposed to have contact with the Israelis. But Gemayel allowed his Lebanese intelligence service secretly to keep up relations with the Israeli Mossad and to pass information on the whereabouts of Palestinians. The Israelis had standing orders to allow attacks on the Palestinians in Lebanon without approval from the top; air raids were conducted with increasing frequency.

Shultz, an ex-Marine, urged that the 1,600-Marine peacekeeping unit remain in Lebanon. Casey went along. Weinberger and the Joint Chiefs objected strenuously. But the President did not want to seem to back down, so the Marines stayed.

Kemp was persuaded that the U.S. military presence was achieving nothing. There was no system of policy debate within the Administration that would force a confrontation with basic questions: What if the troops get bogged down? What if they become part of the problem rather than the solution?

In his basement office in his Virginia town house, Stan Turner was writing articles—sixteen published his first year of retirement—and working on a memoir of his CIA days. Sitting at his Radio Shack computer, Turner typed out his thoughts on Nicaragua and refined them.

Like every CIA employee, no exceptions, he had signed the required contract agreeing to submit any writings for review.

The review officials at the CIA had already come down hard on Turner, saying that as a former insider he could not state as fact that the CIA was covertly assisting the contras. The CIA justified this censorship on the grounds that there had been a smaller covert political-support operation when he was DCI. Turner thought their objection was absurd. The Reagan Administration paramilitary support covert operation was entirely different, and besides, there had been a public debate on the Boland Amendment on the floor of the House. The agency would not budge, and Turner interpreted that as a campaign to stop him from speaking publicly against the Nicaragua operation. After much haggling, a compromise was reached: Turner would refer to the press reports and the congressional debate and would make no assertions of his own; all his discussion and criticism would proceed from a qualifying "if."

Turner's final, approved draft began: "If the Central Intelligence Agency is as deeply involved in providing 'covert' aid to guerrilla bands in Nicaragua as reports suggest, it has made a bad mistake."

The Turner piece appeared in *The Washington Post* on Sunday, April 24, 1983, headlined "From an Ex-CIA Chief: Stop the Covert Operation in Nicaragua." Casey was willing to listen to criticism, even from Turner, but he thought that the article was merely warmed-over "Inmanisms," and that Turner had it backward. Public disillusionment would follow if the CIA and the Administration did not do what was necessary. There would always be opposition; it was as natural as the sunrise. But Casey was more determined than ever not to be guided or driven by that opposition. Central America could not be turned over to the Communists. He had taken the measure of Ronald Reagan.

At the White House, Casey explained that the Nicaragua operation was in danger. He needed help. The President agreed to campaign to insure that Congress would not cut off the funding. In Dallas, Shultz charged that Nicaragua had become a base for "a new form of dictatorship" that was targeted on "all of Central America." Reagan had key members of Congress to the White House for private arm-twisting, and he called many others by phone.

The night of April 26, Reagan delivered a thirty-four-minute nationally televised speech to a joint session of Congress during prime time. It was the first time in his presidency that he had appeared before a joint session on a foreign-policy issue. He called on Congress to approve his request for $600 million in overt aid to Central America. He observed the protocol and did not mention covert support to the contras, but no one missed the unspoken point when the President said, "We should not, and we will not, protect the Nicaraguan government from the anger of its own people."

In Senator Dodd's televised response for the Democratic side, he adapted a typical Reagan tactic, one single graphic and vivid image. He chose El Salvador: "I have been to that country and I know about the morticians who travel the streets each morning to collect the bodies of those summarily dispatched the night before by Salvadoran security forces—gangland style—the victim of bended knee, thumbs wired behind the back, a bullet through the brain. We recoil at such an image for our association with criminals . . ."

Within minutes, a major foreign-policy debate erupted—not over the President or his speech, but over Dodd and his. The Democrats began flinging bricks at Dodd—had he gone too far, had he insulted the President, and America?

The National Security Agency had a communications intercept from several months earlier, when Dodd had visited Nicaragua. In the message, the Sandinista government discussed how to handle Dodd and described him as a good guy, understanding if not sympathetic to them. A copy of the intercept was forwarded to the Senate Intelligence Committee, as was the practice when anything about a senator surfaced. Dodd saw this as an intentional smear. He complained privately to the White House. He had copies of the State Department traffic showing that he had been tough in his meetings with the Sandinistas.

Casey could not have been happier with the turn of events. For the moment, the issue was more Senator Dodd, his "wired-thumbs" speech and his "good guy" reception in Managua, not the CIA.

On May 3, the Director appeared before the House Intelligence Committee. The committee voted 9 to 5, along partisan lines, to cut off covert funding.

On May 6, Casey appeared before the Senate committee, his last chance. He allowed the discussion to drift to a technical question of the presidential finding that had been signed in 1981. Clearly, the members agreed, the goal had changed beyond arms interdiction.

Casey was deferential. Yes, the finding should be recrafted.

Goldwater suggested a new finding, one that laid out a new purpose—pressure, democratization, efforts to force the Sandinistas to negotiate.

Casey was conciliatory. The Administration would look at the program and articulate its goals more exactly. This was a substantial concession. Presidential findings are the zealously guarded prerogative of the executive branch—the President decides on covert action, the congressional committees are "informed."

Moynihan, Leahy and some Republicans thought they had a clear majority to cut the funding immediately.

But Goldwater, who had conferred beforehand with Reagan and Casey, proposed a compromise—neither full continuation nor full termination.

Casey knew that compromises appealed to legislators. Call it a compromise, put Goldwater's name on it, and it could not fail. The Goldwater compromise continued funding for the operation for another five months, and authorized another $19 million for the following fiscal year contingent on a new presidential finding that described the purpose of the program. But it also specified that next year's $19 million was "subject to a majority vote of the committee."

Moynihan and Leahy claimed that this was a new and important assertion of congressional authority over covert action, since it gave the committee power to vote it up or down. Moynihan said, "The presidential finding will have to be approved by a majority vote of the committee."

The compromise passed 13 to 2, only Republicans Wallop and John H. Chafee voting against.

Casey was delighted. The committee had been rolled. He was no more going to let the committee approve presidential findings than he was going to let them write them. Congress had temporarily won some words. The CIA had got its money.

The news media were filled with leaks. Casey was certain that his opponents in Congress had begun a rearguard effort to scare the public. Two days later, the *Post* had a banner headline: "U.S.-Backed Nicaraguan Rebel Army Swells to 7,000 Men.'' With dark hints, the story questioned ''the candor of the CIA briefings for the members of the Intelligence committees.'' A *New York Times* story quoted an unnamed Democrat on the House Intelligence Committee, ''The CIA lies to us anyway.'' Then, several days later, the *Times*'s lead story was headlined ''CIA Is Reported to Predict Ouster of the Sandinistas.'' This was untrue, and Casey got the *Times* to run what was effectively a front-page correction the next day.

That evening Casey joined five hundred guests at a black-tie dinner in the Grand Ballroom of the Washington Hilton for the presentation of the Donovan Award to Dick Helms. As far as Casey was concerned, it was the final shovel of dirt on the 1970s, the end of the anti-CIA decade. The dinner had a special flavor for a man on the comeback. Casey spoke and praised Helms. So did Bush. A letter from President Reagan saluted Helms's ''commitment to the call of conscience.''

Helms was greeted with a returning war hero's welcome. He stood at the podium before a ten-foot blowup of an old grainy photograph of Donovan himself, handsome, wise and wearing an open shirt with the general's stars on his collar. ''I am touched and honored,'' Helms said, beaming. ''My reasons can be no mystery to any of you.''

Jeane Kirkpatrick, the U.S. ambassador to the United Nations, sat next to Casey at the top-level NSPG meetings held in the Situation Room. On one level, Kirkpatrick loved those ''PGs,'' as she called them. It was the meat-and-potatoes gathering, the foreign-policy inner circle, hashing out worldwide overt and covert policy. Attendance at the NSPG gave the former political-science professor a rare opportunity to participate in the making of foreign policy. Casey came with his homework done, a typed brief in hand, often heavily reworked with his own pencil. He mumbled through his presentations, and he certainly was not one to turn the tide with articulate argument or passion, but he could answer questions and he had a body of knowledge that went deeper than his summary. In this, Kirkpatrick was saddened to find, Casey stood almost alone.

When a middle-level Administration thinker had suggested that they lay out some long-term national foreign-policy goals and strategy, Kirkpatrick had replied, ''It will be a drill in futility, because most of the people won't understand it—perhaps only Bill.''

Kirkpatrick had come to Reagan's attention and eventually obtained her UN post because of a 1980 article in *Commentary* magazine, ''Dictatorships and Double Standards.'' ''The Shah and Somoza were not only anti-Communist, they were positively friendly to the U.S.,'' she had written, lashing Carter for his failure to see that those right-wing regimes were preferable to the Ayatollah and the Sandinistas.

During the first two years of the Administration, she was repeatedly surprised to find that the conservative views held by Reagan, Casey, Bill Clark and herself had not taken hold fully as policy. The bureaucracy and the pragmatists won too often. The only general exception was in Casey's intelligence operations, from which some coherent strategy had emerged.

Over those two years, she and Casey developed a strong affection and respect for each other. They agreed on what Kirkpatrick referred to privately as the real "scandal" in the Reagan Administration, the ignorance about foreign affairs among the senior policy-makers, including most definitely the President. But the President was so nice about not knowing, that there was a tendency by all, including Kirkpatrick and Casey, not to hold it against him. The result, they agreed, was that foreign policy was not well focused, not competent.

Secretary of Defense Weinberger and Secretary of State Shultz engaged in continuing bureaucratic warfare that set the tone of nearly all debates. Determined to protect the corporate well-being of the Defense Department, Weinberger was fixed on avoiding a military involvement. Shultz was a smart man, but for practical purposes his hands were tied and diplomatic initiatives with the Soviets were minimized because that might mean giving something away in negotiation—the great and primary fear of the right wing. The Shultz-Weinberger standoff left a vacuum. Someone had to fill it. Reagan had neither the knowledge nor the inclination to bump heads and decide who. Vice-President Bush had nothing close to the authority to do so. Bill Clark, as the national-security adviser, had neither the background nor the endurance to get into the substance.

For practical purposes the void was filled by chief of staff James Baker and presidential assistant Richard G. Darman. Along with Deaver, they controlled the President's schedule and the paper flow. They managed what Reagan did, whom he saw, what he read. Before a presidential decision was required, Baker and Darman would conduct an all-sources review, finding an alternative acceptable to Shultz and Weinberger, consulting with congressional leaders and others. A consensus recommendation would be presented to the President for ratification.

The apparatus for making decisions, thus diffused, often strangled the true presidential intentions, Kirkpatrick and Casey believed. They complained privately that the Administration's foreign policy represented the lowest common denominator of like-mindedness.

Kirkpatrick had come to genuinely admire Casey. He led a balanced life—much work, serious play, he always had time for a drink. He had good taste, in her opinion, from music to rugs. He was sophisticated, rich, broadly educated and civilized. From her years in academic life she was used to brilliant people who might chew their food loudly or not know or care how to knot a necktie perfectly. She had learned a long time ago that those things didn't matter. In her view, Casey stood alone among those at the NSPG in his great underlying seriousness and passionate concern about policy. Whenever they met at some party around town, they were soon off in a corner alone, talking policy. But on one important subject the two came to disagree.

Kirkpatrick believed that the Reagan Administration could not conduct covert action effectively without popular support and congressional debate.

Casey said that was McMahon's line. In this Administration, Casey argued, diplomacy and direct military action were not options. The President neither wanted to sit down with the Soviets nor wanted to fight them. Covert action was the mechanism for containing or limiting U.S. involvement abroad while getting the job done. And he wanted to keep as much secret as possible.

Despite this disagreement, Kirkpatrick and Casey remained the closest of friends. She felt it was very much to his credit that he would listen to other points of view. Obviously it was why he kept John McMahon around. Casey was not afraid to have his judgments tested.

In addition, Kirkpatrick was glad Casey was not part of any cabal that sugarcoated what was told to the President. He said the Soviets were on the move. Casey's impact could be felt most strongly when he argued about the extent and persistence of Soviet expansionism. It was a matter on which the key players in the Administration concurred. In the midst of their options, problems and hesitations, the constant was Casey's covert operations. Now that he had won continued funding for the Nicaragua operation, for at least five months, it was time to move further forward.

After Enders had gone, Casey and Kirkpatrick tried to promote Constantine Menges as his replacement. The Assistant Secretary automatically chaired the interagency group that ran the covert operation. But Shultz did not want a right-wing zealot.

A compromise was found in L. Anthony Motley, the U.S. ambassador to Brazil. A profane, happy-go-lucky forty-four-year-old, Motley had been an Alaska real-estate entrepreneur and a Republican fund-raiser.

He had been born in Brazil and spoke Portuguese fluently. Reagan and Deaver had been impressed with his cut-the-red-tape style on an earlier presidential trip to Brazil.

And Casey thought he had guts. That spring the CIA had had a report that several Libyan planes that were scheduled to stop in Brazil on their way to Nicaragua were carrying arms, not medical supplies as the Libyans claimed. Motley had called Casey. "I'll make my move," he said, "go around the Foreign Minister, get the planes searched and stopped, but I've got to be sure this isn't somebody guessing." Casey had come up with a copy of the real manifest from a human source in Libya. The planes were stopped and seventy tons of weapons and explosives were uncovered, creating a double-barreled propaganda victory over both Libya and Nicaragua.

Casey was also impressed with Motley's intelligence-gathering in Brazil. He regularly had steak and beer with the Brazilian President, and he filed brilliant reports that outshone the CIA station's as well as the NSA intercepts.

Most important, Motley was willing to play a little rough and dirty. After the CIA's plan to overthrow the leader of Suriname proved unfeasible, the Brazilian intelligence service had drummed up its first covert operation. Brazil and Suriname shared a border of about 100 miles. With Motley's encouragement and with slight assistance from the CIA, the Brazilian service had sent intelligence agents into Suriname posing as teachers, to wean the Suriname government away from the Cubans. The leader, Lieutenant Colonel Bouterse, later did turn away from the Cubans and Brazilian intelligence informed Motley that all records of the sensitive operation had been destroyed.

Motley was called to Washington, where Shultz told him that he was being promoted to assistant secretary. "Let's not have the contra operation become an election issue," Shultz instructed. "At the same time, we can't let the Sandinistas up."

At a White House meeting, Jim Baker gave Motley the same guidance. The President's policy, Baker said, was to maximize heat on Nicaragua but avoid a public collision.

Casey realized that this represented Deaver's assessment. Deaver was in charge of the President's popularity, which was the driving force in the White House. Nicaragua was considered a negative; the White House had never been able to get ahead of the curve of public opinion on this, despite the President's convictions and repeated public explanations.

Bill Clark, on the other hand, was determined on a pro-contra, anti-

Sandinista policy. He had had Jesuit training and believed in a vertical chain of command from the lord on down, and the President was the lord in foreign policy, and Clark his deputy. But, for the moment, Deaver and public opinion held the upper hand. The result was mounting tension between Clark and Deaver.

Unable to sell Menges to Shultz, Casey still had to get him out of the CIA, where he had become a lightning rod. CIA analysts agreed that there was a Soviet Communist threat out there in the world and that their job was to determine how much and where. Menges assumed total evil, everywhere. His numerous CIA critics called him "the Constant Menace." He was creating friction between Casey and McMahon. It was the one major Casey personnel decision that was eating away at McMahon. He could not tolerate Menges' ideological fervor. And Menges had served his useful purpose, Casey felt, by raising consciousness about the potential subversive thread in ordinary events. "These intelligence bureaucrats don't know what they are talking about," Menges would say, and Casey had loved it. He liked having some key assistants to his right, making his positions seem more reasonable. But Menges' time was up. Bill Clark asked Menges to join the NSC staff. Casey told Menges that he could have more influence there, that Clark was key, that he had Reagan's trust and that he shared Reagan's view of the Soviets.

Many analysts and some who worked under Stein in Operations and did not trust Menges were astounded that a man who was intellectually unsustainable at the CIA would be acceptable to the White House. At State, Motley marveled at Casey's ability to farm out his problems, even to disengage a bit from the hard right wing without creating problems for himself. Casey had already shipped his Nestor Sanchez problem to Defense. He knew not only how to get rid of his problems, but also how to park them where they might stay of use. Motley called Casey "the slave-trader."

Picking Menges' successor was going to be very important. Casey had increased the stature and prominence of the NIOs—his free-floating personal agents who acted as communications links and clearinghouse. First, the NIO had to deal successfully with and have the respect of the other analysts. Second, the best NIOs had to have good relations with the DDO, had to know the operations cold, know where U.S. policy was headed and what the President and Casey wanted accomplished. Third, the NIO was a key connecting link to the other intelligence agencies, particularly the NSA and the Pentagon. Fourth, as the supervisor of the estimates for his assigned region, the NIO would have an impact on policy. A well-reasoned, well-documented estimate could help policy as much as good intelligence information. And no estimates were more important these days than those in Latin America.

Casey wanted a good old boy, someone who had served in his war, World War II. The difficulty was that most of the old boys were gone, retired or dead. A generation had passed. Casey had brought some former DO officers from retirement, and now he decided to do it again.

John Horton seemed perfect, one of those operators with rich experience who had retired from the CIA eight years earlier after twenty-seven years. Horton had a dream resumé: naval officer in World War II, service in CIA Far East stations, station chief in Uruguay 1965–68, then station chief in Mexico in the early seventies, deputy chief of the Latin America division and finally head of the Soviet division in the DO. Horton was no ideologue. He was, in fact, a registered Democrat. More important, Horton's name was mentioned with great respect, even affection, by the old-timers. The joining of his Soviet and Latin American experience would be just right. If anyone would be able to chart Soviet tracks in Latin America, it would be this man.

Horton was sixty-two and living in the nearby Maryland countryside, raising grapes. Flattered by Casey's call, he jumped at the chance to go back. It was clear that Casey was rebuilding the agency, and Latin America was key. After a round of interviews, Horton went to meet Casey.

Casey found him slightly stiff and formal but brainy and articulate. He knew the intelligence tasks and how to formulate answers that went to the heart of the matter. The conversation was amiable and polite, and Casey quickly hired him.

Horton took over at the NIO for Latin America in May 1983 and at once spent some time with his counterpart in the DO—Clarridge. Clarridge made it clear to Horton that he knew who they were working for—the President and Bill Casey. They wanted a contra program, and Clarridge was giving it to them. Anyone else in between didn't matter. As they drove over to State to attend an interagency meeting run by Tony Motley, Clarridge tried to explain what had gone on during the eight years since the Congress and the press had held their public inquisitions on the CIA, and since Horton had retired.

"Things are different now," he said. "Casey's in there and he's got a lot of clout, so at State they now listen to you." Casey represented the real voice of Reagan, the White House, the Administration. "At State they are defensive and don't do what the Administration wants—those bastards," he growled. "If the agency ever gets like that, we don't deserve to exist."

The major stumbling block on Nicaragua, Clarridge said, was that "McMahon is against this. He's never done a thing for this." Tagging McMahon with one of the cardinal sins, Clarridge said that McMahon had friends in Congress and they were feeding one another's hesitation and doubt.

Horton saw immediately that the sun rose and set on the Nicaragua operation. It was getting the only real attention in Latin America.

In early summer, Casey scheduled a secret two-day trip to Central America. He decided to take McMahon along. It was highly unusual for both the No. 1 and the No. 2 to leave the country, but Casey wanted his deputy more closely involved in the Nicaragua operation. The joke around the agency was that Casey was trying to implicate McMahon, to get his fingerprints on the secret war. Of course Clarridge would come. And, making good on a promise to Horton, Casey decided to include his new NIO. The fifth member of the travel party was Robert MaGee, who headed the International Activities Division (IAD), a unit within the DO that handled the outside contract work, the so-called "talent."

The IAD moved from one covert operation to the next, providing logistical support, particularly aircraft, boats, maritime support and back-up for propaganda and psychological-warfare operations. Most of this was contract work to outsiders. Operating out of the first floor of Langley headquarters, the IAD was an efficient way of moving equipment and contract employees from operation to operation. One week the IAD might concentrate on the contras, the next the Afghan resistance, the next a propaganda operation in the Caribbean or an intelligence support operation in the Middle East.

MaGee was a man who could handle the pressure from Casey, who wanted immediate action and no delays.

"Oh, God," MaGee once answered when Casey asked about a postponement in a certain flight operation, "I don't want to answer that." Everyone had laughed, even Casey.

MaGee had a theory about Casey's loyalty to Sporkin. It's a club of sloppy eaters, he said. Sporkin's the only guy who drops more of his lunch on his necktie than Casey.

Casey felt comfortable with all four of his traveling companions; McMahon, Clarridge, Horton and MaGee all had extensive experience in the DO.

McMahon and Horton drove out together to Andrews Air Force Base, where a twelve-seater special-mission aircraft waited. A summer thunderstorm had just blown in. His initial impression, Horton volunteered, was that, overall, CIA work in Central America was suffering. Stations weren't keeping tabs on the Soviets. Penetration of political groups in most of the countries was weak to nonexistent, much less than he had imagined. It should be better, but Nicaragua was receiving all the attention.

McMahon didn't respond.

Nicaragua is eating them up, Horton said.

"I've been up one side of the decision tree and down the other side," McMahon said. He shook his head. He was worried. The contra effort is too public, too much politics, he said. How can it work? He had a very pessimistic feeling about the program. It isn't going to turn out well, not well at all. But it is bedrock with Casey and Reagan.

When they arrived at the plane, one of Casey's security men begged them not to let Casey nap during the flight. "If he does," one said, "he'll be up talking and asking questions all night."

After the plane took off, Casey settled in. He was a seasoned traveler, laughing off any turbulence in the air. "Like bumps in the road," he said. He was off with his boys to plan war.

They landed in Tegucigalpa, Honduras. Casey had his bags dropped at the residence of the U.S. ambassador and was immediately off on a whirlwind. He wanted to see everyone, and he scheduled back-to-back meetings, making sure he chatted at least briefly with each CIA operations officer in the station. The group piled into cars and went to Ray Doty's safe house, where the contra operation was being run.

Clarridge kept trying to direct the discussion to the nuts-and-bolts issues: How many weapons do we have? Are there enough people being recruited to use them? Are there enough weapons? How about ammunition? Let's try this, try that.

Casey and McMahon attempted to focus on the next phase. They were thinking about how the operation was going to be explained to Congress. Senator Leahy's visit to the region earlier in the year had uncovered the larger ambitions of the operation, and regular leaks were showing the ever-increasing numbers of contra fighters. There was also criticism within the CIA that the contras didn't have any political sophistication, that they were just armed bands of malcontents roaming the mountains. Casey said he had a broad goal. The contras had to come down from the hills, enter the cities, spread their message, incorporate the mounting anti-Sandinista feelings, become a political force.

Clarridge didn't like this kind of talk. He was running an army, not a political party. And such notions skimmed precariously close to violating the Boland Amendment, which prohibited efforts or operations "for the purpose of overthrowing'' the Sandinistas. A sophisticated political force could overthrow a government, and that certainly would be their goal; an army of irregulars didn't have quite as visible or identifiable a political purpose.

Casey wanted a political message, he wanted the contras to emerge as a political force inside Nicaragua. He believed that the Nicaraguan people would flock to a new force that espoused both democracy and capitalism. People would respond to image and message.

''Well, look at Savimbi,'' the Director said, suggesting that the leader of the Angolan resistance since the mid-1970s was a model of freedom fighting. Though the CIA was prohibited by law under the 1976 Clark Amendment from aiding him, Savimbi had become a permanent force of armed resistance, pinning down tens of thousands of Cuban soldiers who required a billion dollars of Soviet weapons.

Several of his traveling companions thought that Casey was swallowing uncritically the rosy picture of Savimbi painted by the South African intelligence service. Savimbi was their man and the white minority government in South Africa had funneled him several hundred million dollars over the years.

The band flew 140 miles west to El Salvador for another series of political and intelligence meetings. Casey took the time to have a friendly word with each of the CIA operations officers, the cherished field men and women who did the real work. He had a politician's ease with people —looking them in the eye, offering a brief, informed word of encouragement, or asking a pointed question and stopping dead in his tracks to listen to the answer. The DO officers felt he had shown real interest and concern.

Casey also wanted to issue a stern, personal warning in El Salvador both to the government and to the military, intelligence and security services about the continuing right-wing death squads. The notorious squads that had developed in the late 1970s to combat the armed left had assassinated an archbishop and murdered four American churchwomen. Human-rights groups charged that up to 30,000 had been killed in the last four years. It was probably an exaggeration, but surely it was a serious problem; it was the wired-thumbs image that Senator Dodd had used. El Salvador conjured up images of torture.

Acting president Álvaro Magana had a dinner for them that evening, and Casey went right to the point. ''We have a real problem with [the death squads] and you've got to do something about it,'' he said firmly yet with grace. ''Now, how can we help?''

Horton observed that Casey had strong credibility with the Salvadorans on this issue. They knew that he was a right-winger and that he despised the left as much as they. His argument was not moralistic, but pragmatic. The death squads don't work, Casey said, and they're going to cause trouble for you out of all proportion to what they cause the left —which he called "Communist." In jeopardy was not only the tens of millions of dollars in U.S. aid, but the backing of the Reagan Administration. Casey's urgings were untainted by sentimental appeals about human rights.

Casey had private meetings with all the top people. One was particularly delicate. It took place in a small room. On the other side of the table was Colonel Nicolás Carranza, the head of the Treasury police. Carranza had been the Deputy Defense Minister in 1979–80 and had close ties to the rightist Republican National Alliance (ARENA) party of the controversial right-wing former Army major Roberto d'Aubuisson. The previous year Carranza had been a potential contender for the presidency of El Salvador. That was now impossible. For at least five years Carranza had been a paid informant of the CIA, receiving about $90,000 a year.*

It was the intelligence section of Carranza's Treasury police that probably was most responsible for human-rights abuses. Carranza himself was pretty clean, but, the CIA claimed, the culture of violence was deeply ingrained in the police and the military. Casey could speak with a bit more authority to his well-paid agent. Knock it off, he said, the whole relationship between the United States and El Salvador could founder because of the right's excesses. To make it more personal, Casey also implied that such a rupture would mean the suspension of all agent payments and subsidies.

At the end of the trip, Horton jokingly asked Casey why the trip had been so short. Why were they in such a hurry?

"What the hell else do you want to do?" Casey replied, smiling, as if he had proved he could cover the territory faster and better than anyone.

* Carranza's role as paid CIA informant was first disclosed by Philip Taubman in *The New York Times,* March 22, 1984.

13

AFTER SETTLING INTO HIS NEW OFFICE on the seventh floor of the State Department, Tony Motley called Clarridge. "I'm devoting a whole day to it, and I want to come out there." Motley wanted the full dose.

Clarridge brought out maps, lists, charts, files. He was a walking encyclopedia on the operation, the detailed geography, hills, roads, weather, and every important contra personality. "A real asshole," Clarridge said many times of the various contra leaders. There were, however, many tough fighters, for example "these animals down south." That was Pastora, Commander Zero. On occasion, Clarridge would remark that someone else was a "good guy."

In some respects, the contras were the Hell's Angels of Central America, but, overall, Motley was impressed. Clarridge had created an army and had a personal, hands-on working knowledge that was staggering. "How come you know so much," Motley asked, "for a guy coming out of Europe, the Middle East, dealing with ragheads?"

"These people are Mediterranean Latin," Clarridge replied. "I've dealt with Italians, North Africa. I know the type. They tell you what you want to hear, they figure six ways to say no, they have a love-hate relationship with America."

So, Motley asked, what's next?

"Fucking Casey wants something that makes news," Clarridge said, explaining that they were all under tremendous pressure to get the contras to come out of the hills. Beating bands of Sandinistas in the mountains was no longer enough, he complained. Casey wanted the contras to "do the urban bit." Clarridge quoted Casey as saying, "Get something." This "news" was not just going to be for domestic political consumption in the United States. It was to establish credibility within Nicaragua for the contras.

This sounded reasonable to Motley.

We can't just fucking jump from the hills to the cities, Clarridge said with exasperation. It is much more complicated. The ragtag contras wouldn't do any better than any hill people going into any city. It takes them forty days to get into a city, creating a resupply nightmare.

So what are you going to do?

Clarridge smiled. There was a way, always some way. He'd find some one-time operation, something to make a big splash. War was hell and you had to improvise.

Casey was determined to do everything possible to protect the Nicaragua operation. That meant soothing his ailing relations with two potential saboteurs—Congress and the media.

For the past two and a half years, he realized, he had had the wrong man handling these sensitive relations. He was J. William Doswell, who headed the CIA's Office of External Affairs. A lifelong Democrat who had supported Reagan in 1980, Doswell, fifty-three, had no previous intelligence background. He had been a newspaper publisher and one of the most successful lobbyists in the gentlemanly Virginia legislature. But Doswell had less enthusiasm for the Nicaragua operation than Casey, who no longer could afford to have a salesman who had any doubt about their product. Doswell thought Casey's disdain for Congress and his confrontational style counterproductive.

He was exhausted and left. Casey decided to put the agency's best foot forward with two new separate high-powered offices, one for Congress and another for the media. Both would be headed by covert operators—practitioners of the art they would have to sell.

Casey picked Clair Elroy George, a survivor of twenty-seven years in the DO, as the new head of congressional relations. George had a good, outgoing sense of humor and was strong on CIA tradecraft. Within the agency George was an old-warhorse symbol of the CIA at its best and proudest.

In 1975, in the midst of the Church and Pike investigations, Richard Welch, the CIA station chief in Athens, had been gunned down in an ambush outside his home. Though the residence of the station chief was well known in Athens—it was even pointed out on local bus tours—the killing generated a surge of public sympathy for the CIA. Welch's CIA position had been published by disaffected former agents caught up in the anti-CIA fervor of the times. But Welch, dead, rendered a final service to his CIA. He became a martyr, his body arriving in the United States to live television coverage, his full-military-honors funeral attended by

CIA Director William Colby and President Ford, his caisson the same one that had carried the body of the slain President John F. Kennedy.

Despite the danger of the Athens station, the CIA had sent a man into the breach. It was Clair George, whose presence lobbying the Congress would be a useful reminder of bravery. George accepted the job, went to the committees, and promised them a whole new ball game of cooperation and mutual trust.

About this time, George V. Lauder, the No. 2 in the Inspector General's Office, the in-house watchdog at the CIA, got word that he was wanted in Casey's office.

Lauder was one of the original breed of covert operators, going back to the salad days of the 1950s. He had a law degree and nearly thirty-two years with the CIA. A tall, rumpled man who wore clothes that looked like college remnants, Lauder was a true believer in the CIA's mission and achievements. A clumsy man who often spoke too loudly and with exaggerated cadence and language, he was not the "gray man," but he was nonetheless a seasoned, dedicated spy.

Lauder felt that Casey had been a breath of much-needed fresh air for the CIA, immediately accepting of the undercover, behind-the-scenes role—the very opposite of Turner. When Turner was DCI and Lauder the deputy Latin America division chief, Lauder had been unable to convince him that the CIA was not off on its own, running a secret covert operation in Jamaica without the DCI's knowledge. Lauder had failed to convince Turner to keep a meager $1,500 annual-retainer payment for a foreign newspaper editor who assisted the CIA—all because the congressional oversight committees were nervous. Casey had eliminated the atmosphere of distrust inside.

When Lauder entered Casey's office, he knew it was time for an assignment change but was not sure what Casey had in mind.

"Congratulations," Casey said to Lauder.

"What for?" Lauder asked suspiciously.

"I've selected you to be my new director of public affairs."

"What did I do to deserve that?"

Casey said that the agency needed someone to handle the news media —to stop damaging stories. It might have been a mistake to close things off so entirely, because the news media was getting access to CIA information through the Congress or the White House, State and Defense Departments.

Lauder said he had spent a lifetime avoiding the news media—had even kept his own CIA status secret from a relative who was a newspaper reporter.

You're selected, Casey said firmly.

Lauder effectively clicked his heels.

A DO officer instinctively savored a moment like this: the call from the top. In such obedience there was a comforting, almost exhilarating recognition of being a part. Lauder had risked his life many times out in the field. The press room could be no more dangerous.

Casey knew he would get his assent. That was one of the things he liked about these people in DO. And Lauder was, according to his personnel record, a staunch loyalist. But he also was a realist, and as deputy inspector general he had been involved in checking to see what arms had been interdicted in the Nicaragua covert operation. Lauder had been honest enough to say that though several caches of weapons had been discovered, the operation had not had any impact on the arms flow. "We did not find a mouse," he had once said. But Lauder was still a supporter of the operation.

First he would have to spread the word that Casey now had an active press officer, then he would have to get to know the reporters and learn how they operated. He would make himself available, establish relationships with the reporters, try to determine who could be trusted and at least let Casey know when some story that might be trouble was in the pipeline. He would have to gather information and see if he couldn't—recruit was not exactly the word, but it was close. Maybe handling reporters might not be too different from his previous work.

"Casey Traded Heavily in Stocks," John McMahon read on the front page of *The Washington Post* the morning of June 2, 1983.

"Oh shit," McMahon said. Casey's annual financial disclosure form had once again provided fodder. The form showed that Casey had bought at least $1.5 million in stocks in a single twenty-six-day period. McMahon had laughed the first several times he heard the joke that "CIA" really meant Casey Investing Again. Casey had adamantly refused to put his investments in a blind trust, saying that his investment adviser of twenty years really made the decisions. All except one, when McMahon had forced Casey to sell his IBM stock or recuse himself from a major decision on agency computers. The stock then doubled in value. Casey felt it underscored his integrity.

McMahon had tried several times gently to push a blind trust. Casey refused. A crazy screening process within the agency had been set up in which McMahon and the other top officials were regularly given a list of the dozens of companies in which Casey had interests. But it was impossible to keep track, and hoots of laughter went up at Langley as memos circulated tracking the shifting sands of Casey's portfolio (Add Delta Airlines, delete La Quinta Motor Inns, said one memo). Even Goldwater had tried, writing a sarcastic letter to Casey noting that Casey was rich enough and wouldn't be able to take his assets with him after death. Casey replied that the Intelligence Committee members had similar access to sensitive intelligence and where were their blind trusts?

McMahon realized that the screening arrangement hadn't worked perfectly, and research showed that thirteen companies in the Casey portfolio had done business with the CIA during the previous year, ranging from $12.00 to nearly $4 million.

Does the CIA need this? McMahon wondered. No. McMahon wanted to bring to the surface the cool sphinxlike reserve of the tax attorney in his boss.

He went to Casey. The public impression, he said, was that Casey was up here phoning his stockbroker half a dozen times a day, cavorting with Wall Street, dipping into secret intelligence to get a step up on other investors.

"It's a goddamn lie," Casey said.

Exactly, McMahon said. But the aroma wouldn't go away. Casey was in an untenable position. On the one hand he was insisting that he didn't exercise his opportunity to buy and sell stocks, that his investment adviser did it. On the other, he was insisting on retaining that unexercised option. There was no way he was going to have it both ways. So it gets down to one question: Given your habit of letting your adviser make the decisions, would it make any difference if it was a blind trust?

"Not really," Casey answered.

"Well, goddamn do it."

Casey gazed back stonily.

On Monday, July 18, Casey issued a public statement saying that during his first two and a half years as DCI he had had "a de facto blind trust" that had been both legal and proper. "Nevertheless, to avoid further confusion and misunderstanding, I plan to establish a formal, blind trust."

Late in the summer, Casey left on a secret trip to Africa and the Middle East to visit the stations. He still had an almost physical need to see for himself. Like the plaza in Dallas where JFK had been shot, everything looked different, meant more, when you actually stood there. The station chiefs still needed his personal, hands-on prodding to conduct more intelligence-gathering in the field, to get out of the embassies, to expand relations with locals, to attend political-party meetings undercover.

Accompanied by half a dozen aides on a special VIP Air Force jet, Casey planned to cover eleven countries in eighteen days. After crossing the Atlantic, they stopped first in Senegal and then the Ivory Coast in West Africa. In these countries, as in all he would visit, Casey saw the heads of state or government, the chiefs of intelligence or their deputies, visited with the U.S. ambassadors, and had the station chiefs drive him around as he peppered them with questions. How far from the palace to the army barracks? To the university? Who's the chief opposition leader? What are the KGB men like?

After West Africa, there was the 500-mile flight to Nigeria. The road from the airport into the capital, Lagos, was a sea of cars and street vendors. It took hours to traverse it. The deputy chief of Nigerian intelligence led a team that attempted to clear the way. "Imagine John McMahon trying to clear the George Washington Parkway for them," one of Casey's aides said. Casey's car came to a halt. A native tapped on the window and attempted to sell the DCI a fifty-foot garden hose. "Not exactly an impulse-buy item on the way from the airport," Casey remarked.

In Zaire, formerly the Congo, Casey met with the leader Joseph Mobutu. CIA ties with Mobutu dated back to 1960, the year the CIA had planned the assassination of the Congolese nationalist leader Patrice Lumumba. An August 25, 1960, cable to the CIA station chief from then DCI Allen Dulles stated that Lumumba's "removal must be an urgent and prime objective and that under existing conditions this should be a high priority of our covert action." Before the CIA plot could be effected, Lumumba was murdered by another group of Mobutu supporters. Casey had an important, personal relationship with Mobutu, and now they exchanged intelligence.

The Director wrote out some remarks in French to give at a dinner that night. "After World War Two," he said, "I attended a dinner held by resistance leaders, and I spoke as I do now, in French. The next day's newspaper said that Mr. Casey spoke in his native tongue. I realized that meant they thought my French was so fluent that I was a Frenchman, or perhaps that my French was so bad that they thought I was speaking English."

The room broke up.

The party then flew to Zambia and next headed for South Africa. Casey went to the cockpit and directed the pilot to fly very low up the Zambezi River and pull up only as they passed directly over the spectacular Victoria Falls. One pass was not enough, and he requested another as he stared out the window. In Pretoria, he made the usual rounds within the government, the embassy and the station, and attended a barbecue luncheon in the countryside with a dozen of South Africa's business executives. One of them, who knew nothing about Casey's background, remarked afterward, "This guy is smart. He could make money in business."

Casey admired the South African intelligence service and maintained close ties to it. South Africa appreciated Communism's threat to their region, and had provided probably $200 million in assistance to the rebel movement of Jonas Savimbi, who was fighting the Marxist regime in Angola. Casey still hoped to obtain a repeal of the 1976 Clark Amendment which banned covert CIA assistance to Savimbi. He promised officials that the agency would join the fray as soon as possible.

Casey's laundry had piled up in the hot climate, and he turned over nearly everything he had to the hotel's valet service, which had promised twenty-four-hour service. By the midnight before their scheduled 6 A.M. departure his clothes were not back. His security men had to break into the hotel laundry to retrieve them so that he could stay on schedule. The next stops were Zimbabwe and then Kenya, where they arrived at about 10 P.M. Casey had two meetings that night with business acquaintances, and at breakfast the station chief was almost embarrassed by Casey's familiarity with the country.

After a 2,200-mile flight to Cairo, Casey met with Egyptian President Mubarak and then spent hours with the station chief, who oversaw one of the biggest CIA facilities outside the United States; most of the weapons and support to the Afghan rebels flowed through Egypt. The entourage then proceeded to Turkey, which, with its borders on the Soviet Union, the Black Sea, Syria, Iraq and the Mediterranean, was, in Casey's opinion, one of the most vital but strategically overlooked countries in the world. The final stop was a visit with King Hassan in Morocco. All of these relations were vital, and Casey was not going to let one slip by. Not only did the agency provide security and intelligence to these countries, but its favors to their leaders included providing them with the latest medicine, government airplanes, and contacts that arranged for their nationals to get an education in the United States.

Back at Andrews Air Force Base, Casey's aides were so exhausted they almost had to be carried home. The DCI went directly to Langley.

• • •

Senator William S. Cohen, a Republican from Maine who had been on the Senate Intelligence Committee for only nine months, took an opportunity after one committee hearing to have a few words with Casey. As a Republican, Cohen wanted to support the Administration on Nicaragua. He knew that Goldwater had personally recruited him for the committee. But, Cohen added, he sensed that Casey and Goldwater could easily lose the consensus in the committee. The Goldwater compromise hung by a thread.

If you cut out the money for the Nicaragua operation, Casey said, Congress is going to be responsible for what happens.

Cohen was skittish. Casey might be right. The President had called Cohen personally. "Bill, guess what I'm calling about?" Reagan had said, and, as always, he had been very low-key and solicitous. "We'd like to get your help if we can." Cohen had told the President that he would support the Administration but that he was concerned.

Casey told Cohen that he should visit Central America. See for yourself, go to Nicaragua, talk to the Sandinistas. They'll talk to a United States senator.

To Cohen, a former prosecutor, going to the scene and examining witnesses were appealing. He tried always to be precise, to know the facts. To learn about the arcane world of signals intelligence, he had read through all 532 pages of *The Puzzle Palace,* the 1982 book on the National Security Agency by James Bamford. The answer for the Nicaragua operation wasn't in some book or briefing, but in the field.

Cohen did not fall neatly into any point on the political spectrum, and he was a poet—his own volume, *Of Sons and Seasons,* had been published in 1978. He was also a fact man. In 1974 Cohen had been a key swing vote on the House Judiciary Committee that voted to impeach Nixon. Before the "smoking-gun" tape had been revealed, Cohen had spoken, in a nationally televised debate, about drawing inferences properly: "If you went to sleep on the ground outside here, and woke up with fresh snow on the ground, certainly you would reasonably conclude that snow had fallen during the night even if you did not see it."

One of Cohen's best friends in the Senate was Colorado Democrat Gary Hart. For several years the two had been secretly writing a spy novel, born of a late-night Senate session when they had talked about their suspicions of intelligence agencies and operatives. The novel, *The Double Man,* seemed destined, if not for commercial success, at least as a bipartisan novelty toy. The hero was a senator who headed an investigation into worldwide terrorism; one of the villains was the CIA Director, who kept things from the Senator's committee and planted a woman agent, or "mole," in the committee to report back to the CIA.

In the Senate dining room one afternoon during that summer of 1983, Cohen approached Hart, who had previously served on both the Church Committee and the Intelligence Committee. Hart had begun his run for the Democratic presidential nomination and was still way back in the pack, with only 4 percent of the Democrats favoring him for the 1984 presidential nomination.

"You know, you've got to broaden what you do," Cohen chided. He proposed that Hart attach himself to some issue on which emotions ran deep—like Central America.

From his time on the Church Committee, Hart had concluded that the CIA bungled covert operations like Nicaragua. He had immersed himself in the secret 8,000-page record of the CIA assassination plots in the 1950s and 1960s, especially those against Castro. It was a macabre tale: the Kennedy brothers, Robert and John—Hart's heroes and models—entangled in the ultimate, sordid expediency, "plausible deniability." It was a world without official records of the planning, the approval, the implementation or the ultimate failure. But there were shattering and sickening pieces of data.

For instance, in one of the anti-Castro plots, a CIA agent code-named AM/LASH was given a ballpoint pen rigged with a hypodermic needle so fine that Castro might not notice its insertion. The CIA case officer had recommended the use of Blackleaf-40, a commercially available high-grade poison. The delivery of the assassination device took place on November 22, 1963. A CIA Inspector General's Report of 1967, made available to the committee, noted almost offhandedly, "It is likely that at the very moment President Kennedy was shot."

The Church Committee found no connection between the Cuban plots and the Kennedy assassination, but Hart did not believe it was coincidence. It was almost like Cohen's morning snow on the ground. He had not seen it fall, but he knew something had happened.

Early on the morning of Thursday, September 8, Cohen, Hart and a Marine major escort officer left on an Air Force C-140, due to land in Managua about 9:15 A.M.

About an hour outside the Nicaraguan capital, the pilots were told that the Augusto César Sandino Airport was closed. There had been some kind of air attack. A propeller-driven twin-engine Cessna with a 500-pound bomb strapped under each wing had been shot down, crashing into the control tower and the terminal building.

The senators' Air Force plane circled for about forty-five minutes before it was rerouted to the Honduran capital. Once there, they phoned Washington to try to find out what had happened. Word meanwhile came from Managua that the airport would be opened for them.

After they finally arrived at the Managua terminal, in the early afternoon, Hart was astonished at the destruction. Smoke damage was everywhere and the center of the terminal was wiped out. Broken glass and oil were scattered all about. And the fuselage of the downed plane was cut in half. The pilot and the co-pilot were both dead. Forty people waiting for flights had run for their lives. One worker had been killed. The VIP room where the senators were to have given their press conference had also been hit. Cohen calculated that if they had arrived before schedule that morning, they might be dead.

The Nicaraguan news media was there to ask questions.

One reporter said that the bombing attack was obviously a CIA-supported contra raid.

"The CIA is not that dumb," Cohen said.

The Nicaraguan officials produced a briefcase which had been retrieved from the plane. Cohen and Hart peered inside. There was a manifest instructing the pilot to meet someone in Costa Rica at a certain restaurant, a bill of lading from Miami and the pilot's Florida driver's license, U.S. Social Security card and American credit cards.

And there was more, including some code-word identifications for the operation and the contract. Both Cohen and Hart recognized them as authentic CIA paperwork.

The Sandinista officials explained that the airport normally had only two antiaircraft guns in place. But that morning, they said, they had increased the number to seventeen. The attack had been anticipated. As the senators talked to more officials, it was clear to them that the Sandinistas were obtaining inside intelligence on the contras. They went on to receive a military briefing from the Sandinistas and later met with Nicaraguan junta coordinator Daniel Ortega, who gave them a hard-ass, anti-American lecture in front of the press.

When Cohen tried to turn the tables a bit and ask about the leading Nicaraguan newspaper, *La Prensa,* which had been closed down for anti-government criticism, the reporters shut off the cameras.

That evening, Hart and Cohen had dinner with Nora Astorga, a Nicaraguan society woman turned Sandinista guerrilla fighter. Astorga, thirty-four, was a legend. In 1978 she had lured a top Somoza general, the number-two man in the hated Somoza National Guard, Reynaldo Pérez Vega, who was known as "the Dog," to her bedroom, where his throat was slit by three Sandinista commandos. The senators were also told that in a moment of revolutionary zeal "the Dog's" testicles were cut off. Astorga had several months earlier been proposed as Nicaragua's ambassador to the United States. The Reagan Administration had rejected her. Cohen and Hart enjoyed the joke that had made the rounds in Managua about her: Don't ask Nora Astorga, "Your place or mine?," and if she asks you to stay the night, *don't*. It seemed a fitting close to the day.

After dinner, Cohen and Hart, both exhausted, went for a midnight meeting with the CIA station chief. They reported that information on contra operations was leaking to the Sandinistas. The station chief hesitated, shuffled around, began to justify the bombing raid, an initial effort by Eden Pastora's "new air force."

Hart was tightly wound and popped off. These stupid, fucking operations are what will kill the CIA, thinking you can get away with something like this, he said. The pilot had the name and phone number of a CIA operator from the U.S. Embassy in Costa Rica in his pocket.

A civilian airport, Cohen said, not even a military target. How could they think it would achieve anything? It would be a fundamental mistake to turn the people of Nicaragua against the contras, and that's exactly what will happen. There had been dozens of civilians in that airport. Suppose someone had tried to bomb a civilian airport in the States?

The station chief said that it was intended to show that the contras were serious and could strike at the capital.

What do you think this was, asked Hart, yelling, some kind of first Doolittle raid over Tokyo?

Well, the station chief said, the contras are free agents and the CIA cannot control them. They pick their targets.

What kind of stupid idiot would carry the CIA paperwork in a briefcase on a covert bombing raid? Hart asked. You're fools, incompetents. Raging and red-faced, Hart shouted, "This is bad politics, bad diplomacy and bad operations."

The station chief sent a high-priority cable to CIA headquarters, explaining that two very, very unhappy senators were about to return to Washington.

The same day, Tony Motley, traveling in Honduras, received word of the failed bombing raid. He called Clarridge.

"Dewey," Motley said, "you're fucking crazy! How can you do this when the Assistant Secretary of State for the region is in Honduras? I don't want any more shit like that going on when I'm traveling."

"Look," Clarridge replied, "there isn't any instant command and control on this. You can't pin down an operation—whether it's going to happen this day or that day. You can only get within several days." Casey wanted news, something to get attention, Clarridge added. Well, the contras were out of the mountains as the Director had demanded.

The next day Cohen and Hart went to El Salvador. They visited the village of San Lorenzo, where a Communist rebel attack had cut power, reduced a church to rubble and destroyed the looms used to produce blankets, a major source of income.

Traveling around El Salvador, they flew in an old helicopter without doors that had been used in Vietnam. Cohen had donned a pair of earphones so that he could hear the pilots talk. Once up about 1,200 feet over the capital, San Salvador, the helicopter started suddenly to drop.

"God damn, I'm losing fluid fast," the pilot shouted. "I'm going to park this motherfucker down!"

Cohen thought they would go down over the big city, be killed and not by the Communist-backed rebels. How fitting to go that way—not from a gun, not from shots fired in anger or as part of this great surrogate confrontation between superpowers, but because of a leak in the hydraulic fluid system.

The pilot tore into his maintenance manual, and all of a sudden the helo was shooting up, up and up to ten thousand feet. It was more than frightening, leaving their stomachs at one thousand feet.

"What's going on?" Cohen demanded.

"Have to get out of the range of the fifty-caliber machine fire from the rebels," the military escort answered.

Cohen decided that if they were going down, he wanted it to be from one thousand feet, not ten thousand. One of his own, earlier poems, "Free Fall," came to mind: "I have no fear of flying/No fear of dying. The process,/Yes, the act (if seconds long), Yes."

But the helo did not crash.

When Cohen was back in Washington, Casey came by his Senate office.

The CIA, Casey said emphatically, did not authorize that bombing.

It was dumb, Cohen said, worse than dumb. There wasn't even a sophisticated method for releasing the bombs.

Casey didn't agree or disagree. He could see that Cohen was not happy. A man who has had a brush with death feels differently about everything, Casey realized. In a friendly way he asked for Cohen's impressions.

Cohen said, You have to realize that your operations—the contra operations—are penetrated. The nightmare of any military or intelligence leader has come true. The antiaircraft batteries had been increased at the airport from two to seventeen. Casey promised to check into that.

Cohen later learned that the plane used in the bombing raid had been supplied by the CIA, and one CIA official told him that the raid had been approved pretty much up the line in the agency. The contra leader Pastora had been behind the raid.

He was not told that the raid stemmed from Casey's pressure to make news.

Nonetheless, Cohen felt there was no way for him to try to make an issue of the bombing raid, since it might appear that his concern was only his own safety. He decided he could keep supporting the covert program as long as it was useful in pressuring the Sandinistas to negotiate, but that he could never embrace the operation fully. And he didn't feel right about Casey. He was slippery. Obviously he had not told him the full story.

Casey also asked Hart out to the CIA for coffee.

I just want to assure you that no one wanted to kill you, Casey explained.

Hart said that his problem was that someone, anyone—the CIA or the contras on their own—would undertake such an idiotic mission. An attack like that on civilians could sow an unimaginable amount of hate.

Casey said, I realize how upset Cohen and you must have been.

You miss my point, Hart replied. I really don't care about that. It is the policy, the ideas and the people behind such stupidity. How could it happen?

"Our policy is to support the democratic forces," Casey said. "We want them to retake the country if we can't force the Sandinistas to moderate."

Hart saw no distinction between that "retake" and the "overthrow" that was prohibited by law.

"We've got Commander Zero down there," Casey said, referring proudly to Pastora. "They have to be allowed to do their own thing." The goal in the bombing was to show that the contra operation is not just a border skirmish but a national effort against the Sandinista government, Casey said.

Hart tried again to engage the Director in a discussion of the counterproductive nature of such operations.

Casey replied that he thought Hart had some good ideas on defense and he would like to get together with Hart and Senator Sam Nunn of Georgia, another defense expert, and talk about various defense issues.

Hart left, certain that the CIA was veering out of control and would blow up someday. Casey did not call him again, about defense issues or anything else.

Two weeks later, on September 20, Casey and Shultz appeared before the Senate Intelligence Committee to make the case for the Nicaragua operation. Acting on the Senate committee's four-month-old request, Reagan had finally signed a new finding designed to chart a semantic course between simple arms interdiction and overthrowing the Sandinistas. The top-secret document was two pages long, consisting of five paragraphs—the longest finding that Reagan had ever signed. It authorized "material support and guidance to the Nicaraguan resistance groups."

The goals were:

- "inducing the Sandinista Government in Nicaragua to enter into negotiations with its neighbors; and
- "putting pressure on the Sandinistas and their allies to cease provision of arms, training, command and control facilities and sanctuary to leftist guerrillas in El Salvador."

An implied goal was democratization within Nicaragua, to create pressures for human rights, civil liberties, a free press and the opening of the political process to the opposition. This would appeal to the Democrats and the moderates of both parties, Casey felt. He was not unaware that this was precisely the accommodation for which Enders had been criticized and eventually fired. But the center was his only hope, since the House had voted to cut off the $80 million for the covert program that he had requested. The House vote of 228 to 195 had followed three days of extraordinary public debate on the Nicaragua operation. Casey thought it an unseemly outpouring of liberal guilt.

Casey liked having Shultz along. Shultz was thought to be the Administration moderate. As they outlined the finding, all seemed to go well.

Moynihan was thinking that this must have been how the Vietnam War began. Yes, certainly it was different, but the underlying currents were the same—seemingly rational step followed by rational step, denying the real-world meaning of certain actions, portraying them as benign when they weren't. He felt that Casey and Shultz had to be fooling themselves or the committee. Anyone who read the finding, as he had, had to see the consequences, though they were hidden and unstated. The finding said the CIA wanted to stop the Sandinista chief foreign-policy aim of spreading revolution, and wanted to alter its internal policies relating to elections, civil rights and ultimately the makeup of its government. It was like saying you wanted to blow someone's brains out but had no intent to kill. Moynihan could be still no longer. He jumped in and tried quietly to raise this point. Even though the CIA says the finding is not designed to overthrow the regime, he said, the net cumulative effect of these actions and goals makes it obvious what the Administration wants.

On the Republican right, Wallop agreed essentially with Moynihan's analysis, but his solution was different. "Why don't we say what we believe?"

"Sounds okay to me," Goldwater said.

"We ought to overthrow 'em," interjected Senator Jake Garn, a conservative Republican from Utah.

No, said Casey and Shultz. They would adhere to the prohibition of the Boland Amendment—nothing "for the purpose of" overthrowing. Moynihan's point was soon lost in the discussion. Casey believed that a substantial bone had been thrown to the Democrats, giving a human-rights wrapping to the fundamental anti-Communism of the Reagan Administration. The senators were realistic politicians. This finding was the best they were going to get. The committee had requested the restatement in a new finding. The members had been party to the covert operation for nearly two years, and the finding simply described what was happening. To reject it would be to disavow their own participation. That, Casey calculated, was unlikely.

Two days later, the committee voted 13 to 2 to accept, with only Senators Leahy and Biden opposed.

That summer the first serious public fissure appeared among Reagan's inner circle when White House chief of staff Baker said it was Casey who had provided him with briefing papers that President Carter had used to prepare himself for the nationally televised debate in the 1980 presidential campaign. Investigations by Congress and the FBI were launched.

"I have no recollection that I ever received, heard of or learned in any other way," Casey said of the briefing book. He and Baker had a Sunday sit-down together to see if they could get their stories straight, put the controversy to rest and even find some grounds for resolving the disagreement. "Say you saw it," Baker urged, pleading that it wouldn't get Casey into trouble. Casey hardened his position. No, he had not seen it, and he had not given the briefing book or papers to Baker, not to anyone.

Old campaign memos began to surface. One was from Hugel, who had been a campaign aide to Casey. It claimed the Reagan campaign had a "mole" in the Carter camp. This tantalizing bit of information suggested that Hugel's first espionage work for Casey might have been before they both went to the CIA.

Attempting to determine whether there had been an organized campaign espionage operation, I went to interview Casey on September 28 at his EOB suite next to the White House. I had never met or talked with him. Casey's corner office was very large, an ornate Victorian room well suited for ceremony. His welcome was warm, hearty, though he did not look me in the eye. He was much larger than I had expected, and there was a rickety swagger as he stepped forward, as if he might tip over. His face and head seemed not just old, but haggard.

The Director wore a well-tailored conservative blue suit. His shirt was perfectly pressed, the collar stiff and the tie clearly expensive. My eyes darted to the desk. There were stacks of folders and paper, almost a foot high. The covers had large TOP SECRET markings in red denoting communications intercepts. He came around from the desk and sat down. He seemed mildly impatient, as if to say, Get to your point.

I quickly summarized some things I had heard.

"Hearsay," Casey said, almost hissing the word.

When I tried to take notes, he snapped, "This is off the record." He said that I could come back the next day for quotes, but this session was for my understanding, and he wanted me to see how preposterous Baker's accusation was. Casey's tone and demeanor announced that I'd be out in the hall if I didn't go along. Each time I raised an issue, he produced a document to support his specific position: in one case a six-page memo; in another a five-inch-thick blue binder that Hugel had done for the campaign. He handed it to me, and I began to thumb through. The volume was standard boilerplate, press releases and long lists of groups and individuals who had supported Reagan. Padding.

Casey came over and almost snatched the Hugel binder out of my hands. Nothing secret there, see, he said as it disappeared from my lap.

I indicated that I wanted to look more, or perhaps study the binder.

No, Casey said.

So while we're on the subject of Hugel, I said, what about the memo he supposedly sent?

Casey said the FBI had obtained the Hugel memo out of the file storage from the 1980 campaign.

What did it say?

Casey shrugged his shoulders. He didn't know, or care, or wasn't going to say.

But there was such a memo?

He nodded yes, but added nothing, allowing me to have the silence. His churning body language almost commanded that we move on, but he sat there bearish and in control.

What about memos from Tony Dolan, the newspaperman whom Casey had brought to the Reagan campaign and who was now a White House speechwriter?

Another cosmic shrug. Casey was at the files again and showed me a memo about the purported misuse of federal employees by the Carter White House, and referring to Dolan's "source" in a department.

May I have a copy?

Casey took it politely but forcefully out of my hands. It was just this side of a snatch. No, he said.

Casey was dealing out memos fast now. He flashed a few more, adding that it was all nonsense, standard campaign information. "There was one memo from Dolan and one from Hugel about having sources, but there was no intelligence operation and it doesn't mean a damn thing."

Would you testify under oath?

Sure, gladly, he said, dabbing reflectively at the spot halfway between his chin and his lower lip, his head cocked up, as if wondering why I was wasting his time on this. "This is a goddamn dry hole." He had a very effective way of waiting out a question he saw no point in answering. He just sat. These questions were the small ones where the answer, any answer, might lead him down a path he did not want to take, or down one that could only lead to trouble, contradiction. He avoided engaging in any speculative banter, the kind of acceptance or dismissal of theories that can be useful.

I tried to go over something we had already covered once.

Casey stood up. "Look, I got to go to a meeting." He then took his stack of top-secret papers and prepared to place them in his briefcase. The stack was so high that he momentarily lost control and they sprayed out on his desk. In a few seconds he had the briefcase stuffed and closed. We walked out together, and he handed the briefcase to his security man. Casey was obviously late for an appointment. I followed him out, and we kept talking. He was almost running down the hall as I left him. He and the CIA security man entered an elevator, the door shut quietly and they were gone.

There was never any real investigation of the matter by the FBI or the Congress, and "Debategate" disappeared. Up in the Senate, Goldwater's and Casey's old friend, General William Quinn, watched the unfolding story with relish and several good chuckles. It was no riddle for him. The former G-2 intelligence officer in Quinn sensed that Casey had done it. Quinn couldn't prove it. Casey played by the rules, like any good intelligence officer. One of the first rules of espionage was the protection of good sources. Elaborate diversions and false trails were often constructed to protect such sources. To lie was nothing, even to lie in public or under oath was perhaps insignificant compared to the risks the source had taken. And nothing probably instilled more confidence or a sense of mutual danger than for the source to see the case officer out there on a limb, even publicly. The secret source, if there was one, probably slept well at night knowing that exposure could bring down his case officer, who in this instance may well have been the DCI himself.

14

TONY MOTLEY RODE UP TO CAPITOL HILL one morning with Casey. They were to testify on the Nicaragua operation. ''These fuckers,'' Casey called the senators. Their ideas and statements were ''bullshit.'' Motley was thunderstruck by Casey's manner before the committee, as he assumed a defiant, buccaneering air. Every shield was up. Motley saw the senators' reaction as they walked away grumbling that they didn't trust the son of a bitch.

Fortunately, there had been no more about the Managua airport attack, and Casey, Motley and Clarridge felt free to proceed with the war. With the new presidential finding, Casey felt it was time to step up economic warfare. ''Let's make them sweat,'' Casey told Motley and Clarridge at one meeting, ''let's make the bastards sweat.''

What will have an economic impact? What's important? Clarridge asked.

Oil. Clarridge drew up a plan to attack the Nicaraguan coastal fuel depots, but not with half-assed amateur contras in operational roles. The CIA would run and coordinate it. Clarridge had hired so-called ''unilateral controlled Latino assets''—UCLAs. These were full-time agency Latinos who might give it more of a ''contra'' feel.

Casey knew how to handle the White House. He presented the plan to the President and to national-security adviser Clark as the next logical step under the finding that had been sold to the Congress.

On October 11, CIA-trained speedboat teams with their own force of CIA Latino assets conducted a pre-dawn raid against the Nicaraguan fuel storage depot at the port of Corinto on the Pacific side. Five storage tanks that supposedly had most of the Nicaraguan oil reserves were blown up. About twenty thousand residents of Corinto had to be evacuated because of fires.

Casey was elated. This was big time, not some trivial cross-border op. He carried reconnaissance photos to Reagan immediately, and the

White House aides found him like a schoolboy with a good report card.

Questions were raised at the CIA about the scope and intensity of the operation. There were some that noted that it was an act of war. Clarridge replied to them all, "That's what the President wants. He knows and that's what he likes."

Three days later the raiders struck Puerto Sandino, another major Nicaraguan port.

Motley asked the American oil companies for an evaluation of the damage. He wanted to determine whether the impact was short or long term. The American companies reported back that they had asked the Nicaraguans for up-front money before repairs would be commenced.

Casey and Clarridge were quite pleased. The Nicaraguans were notoriously slow payers. Repairs would be prolonged.

Surprisingly, one oil company at once received a $100,000 cashier's check from the Nicaraguans requesting immediate repairs.

Casey and the others were even more pleased. The attacks had hurt.

A pipeline inside Nicaragua was sabotaged as part of the CIA operation, and an Exxon Corporation group informed Nicaragua that it could not continue to supply tankers for oil transportation.

Casey was not yet satisfied. The NIO for Latin America, John Horton, was in his office one day, and Casey asked him, "What [more] can we do about the economy to make these bastards sweat?"

"Not much," Horton replied.

"Well, we've got to do something, goddammit, we've got to do something." Look what the CIA had been able to get away with: full-scale economic warfare. A next step could put the Sandinistas in a corner; he wanted them out.

Horton mentioned the Boland Amendment.

That's just Congressional sniping, Casey said.

He turned up the pressure on Motley's working group, demanding some new ideas, directing them to think big. Motley had changed its name several times and limited the group to as few persons as possible in an effort to keep the meetings secret. Most recently, it was called the RIG —Restricted Interagency Group. Motley, Clarridge and Lieutenant Colonel Oliver North of the NSC staff were the core. North said that the White House would go along, and if it looked as though Shultz or someone would resist, North said, "fuck the Secretary of State." But it was Clarridge, not North, who had the operational know-how. Motley rejected two out of three of Clarridge's ideas, but Clarridge was endlessly creative, difficult to deal with, not always precise, but always putting new things together.

At one meeting in the Situation Room at the White House, Clarridge proposed mining the Nicaraguan harbors. From his study of the Russo–Japanese War of 1904–5 at Columbia University's Russian Institute, he knew the effectiveness of mines. The Russian naval commander had been killed when a mine struck and sank his flagship in that war. Clarridge proposed a less ambitious mining program. Since the Mexicans and others were supplying oil to Nicaragua by ship, the goal would be to scare them off. There was no need to sink a single ship. Lloyd's of London would pull insurance on ships going into mined harbors or increase insurance rates sufficiently to discourage entrance into those harbors.

All they needed, Motley said, was a mine that would create the impression of danger—"a loud fart."

The working group approved a plan employing mines with low explosive power, designed to be all noise and splash. Motley dragged Clarridge up to his sixth-floor State Department office for a session of Twenty Questions. "Okay, Dewey, just tell us one more time how this works." Clarridge had the answers.

Again Casey was able to present the plan to the President and Clark as a routine, logical extension of the latest intelligence finding. Reagan approved.

Shultz was not at the meeting, so Motley informed him later. The Secretary of State said, Fine.

They soon learned that all the mines in the U.S. arsenal were powerful monsters designed to sink ships. So the CIA located a former Martin Marietta plant in the Carolinas where homemade "firecracker" mines could be made, though some were to have as much as 300 pounds of explosives. A large vessel like a towing ship with a large flat stern for two helicopters was kept in charter by the CIA, to act as a mother ship from which speedboats and helicopters could be used for laying the mines. The ship would be an operational island in international waters, giving them several months to get everything in place.

Casey saw one of his vital alliances in the White House collapsing. Bill Clark was a beaten man, fed up with the bitter staff infighting at the White House that often sent him home late at night with painful headaches. He was barely on speaking terms with Deaver, and he knew that Baker and Darman provided an unending stream of vicious criticism, either to his face or, more often, behind his back.

Casey tried to persuade Clark to stick it out: the struggle was right there in the White House. But on October 13 the President stunned Washington by naming Clark the new Secretary of the Interior, replacing James G. Watt, who had resigned under fire. Casey said of Clark, "Bill always liked a ranch. The President gave him the biggest in the country." Casey also thought lots of these California people were not serious. "They smell California on the weekends. They will walk over you to get to the helicopters." Now Casey's only pipeline to the White House staff was through Meese, who was too disorganized, and Dolan, who was too removed from the center of events. He began lobbying for UN Ambassador Kirkpatrick as Clark's replacement. He needed a conservative national-security adviser. If the Baker-Deaver-Darman faction planted one of their own in that job, the CIA would be less able to get its way.

Several days later, Casey was at an NSPG meeting on the Middle East when Clark began passing a note around. This was highly unusual, and Casey watched it as though it were a hand grenade with the pin removed. When it reached him, he opened it and read in bewilderment. The President had decided to use Clark's departure, it said, to reorganize the White House staff. Baker was going to be the new national-security adviser, Darman the NSC deputy, and Deaver the new White House chief of staff. A press release was being prepared.

After the NSPG, Casey joined Clark, Meese and Weinberger, who had requested a meeting with the President. Clark and Meese spoke longest and most forcefully. Weinberger and Casey took supporting roles, but all told the President that these appointments would send the wrong signals to the Soviets. Baker was a moderate, not a true conservative. Darman was a liberal, a clone of Elliott Richardson, Nixon's Secretary of Everything. They would not be able to work with these people in these positions.

Casey was particularly horrified at the prospect of Baker as national-security adviser. It would be "intolerable," he told the President, his voice almost trembling. The security adviser was in some respects the DCI's reporting channel to the White House. All the efforts to force the Reagan line on foreign policy through the bureaucracy and to the world over the last two and a half years could be nullified with such an appointment. He suggested Kirkpatrick again.

The President, faced with four of his heavyweights on the verge of threatening resignation, indicated he would wait to make a final decision.

Baker saw the right wing allied against him. He might beat them, but they would not go away. In a more visible policy role as the security adviser, he would have to pass the true-believer "conservative" litmus test on each issue. Baker went to the Oval Office later and suggested that Reagan forget the idea.

The President, in effect, said thanks. It might be better after all that Baker stay on as chief of staff during the upcoming presidential campaign.

Casey continued to campaign for Kirkpatrick, visiting her at her Bethesda home, where she was down with a severe cold. The UN ambassador had wrapped herself in blankets and was popping cold pills and reading Alexis de Tocqueville. It looked as though she wasn't going to get the job. If she didn't, Casey urged her to take some job in the White House, perhaps as a senior counselor like Meese. The conservatives needed her there. Pragmatists were going to outnumber true conservatives if they were not careful.

Kirkpatrick complained of shabby treatment. She had had no direct communication with the President. Leaks were flowing from everywhere, one suggesting that she was going to be ousted as UN ambassador.

Casey told her to ignore the leaks. He led the league as victim of White House leaks.

Meanwhile, the two chief players and faction leaders, Clark and Baker, agreed on a compromise candidate—Bud McFarlane, Clark's No. 2 at the NSC. The President ratified the compromise.

Casey felt that an opportunity to place an articulate spokeswoman at the forefront of Reagan's foreign policy had been lost. McFarlane was slow and a make-no-waves type. His credentials suggested that he was a staff man—a former lieutenant colonel who had not advanced further in the Marines, a Kissinger military assistant for two years, another two years as a staffer on the Senate Armed Services Committee. His appointment would strengthen Baker's hand, and Baker liked to craft foreign policy to suit the Congress.

On October 17, Reagan announced the McFarlane appointment and spent the following hour stroking Kirkpatrick, who subsequently announced that she would stay at the UN.

A sixth Marine had been shot and killed in Lebanon the day before, and Reagan was asked by a reporter why the 1,200-man Marine contingent remained in Beirut.

"Because I think it is vitally important to the security of the United States and the Western world," Reagan replied in a strong voice.

Six days later, on October 23, a Sunday, at 6:22 A.M. Beirut time, a large yellow Mercedes truck drove into the Marine compound in Lebanon, detonated the equivalent of 12,000 pounds of TNT and killed 241 American servicemen.

More than a year earlier, a July 23, 1982, estimate had warned that peacekeeping forces in Lebanon would have "intractable" political and military problems. Casey found that the intelligence agencies had provided some one hundred warnings of car bombings in the six months since the previous bombing of the U.S. Embassy. But worse, after the embassy bombing Casey had sent some CIA officers to Beirut to conduct an investigation, and they had traced it right to Syrian intelligence. One CIA officer had used an electric-shock device on the suspects to assist in expediting the confessions, and one suspect died. The CIA man had to be fired, rendering the "investigation" useless.

The death of so many American servicemen was a major domestic political and emotional trauma for the Administration. Casey asked the Mossad and Israeli military intelligence to investigate. Israel's secret Branch 40, the coordinator of terrorism intelligence, focused on the case.

Israeli intelligence had over the years given great attention to developing human intelligence sources inside Syria. These were some of the most intricate and risky undertakings, manipulating and tricking people by using false flags—Mossad agents who posed as businessmen from Lebanon, other Arab countries and Europe, not just Western Europe but the Eastern Bloc. In some cases, the Israeli agents posed as Soviets. These agents would put out lots of money, seeking information. By the use of several agents—say a European, an Arab and even a Soviet—so-called "interlocking false flags," an entire illusion could be created. Since the stakes, Israel's survival, were so high, the effort and the expense were worth it. The intelligence product could be remarkable.

Soon Israel passed intelligence to the CIA tracing the mysterious Beirut death warriors to Iran and Syria. Among the intelligence:

- The payment of $50,000 to a shadowy Lebanese financial emissary named Hassan Hamiz; payment was made from the Iranian Embassy in Damascus, Syria, often called "Iran's foreign brain center."
- A Syrian intelligence lieutenant colonel was believed to have been involved in planning the attack several days before, and a grandfatherly man with a black turban and brown robes was traced to the Soviet-Palestinian friendship house in Damascus where the attacks were discussed three days before the bombing. He was a key figure in the militant Shiite movement, Sheikh Mohammed Hussein Fadlallah.

In all, the Israelis connected thirteen individuals to the bombings of the Marines, and to the bombing that same day of the French military headquarters in Beirut that had killed fifty-eight soldiers.

Casey was impressed with the evidence. But the operations experts in the DO were less so, including the head of the Near East division, Charles Cogan, and Dick Holm, a respected senior DO officer. The human sources were probably good, they said, but there was no way of knowing for sure. While the broad descriptions—Syrian intelligence, the Iranians in Damascus, Fadlallah—had the ring of truth, the case fell short. "There is no smoking gun," Holm declared. He noted that the key Syrian and Iranian officials allegedly involved had operational cover—using couriers and the protected diplomatic pouch for communications.

At the White House, Reagan okayed a retaliatory bombing raid into the Bekaa Valley in Lebanon, the staging ground for the terrorists. At the last minute he pulled back, leaving it to the Israelis and the French, who tried to bomb several suspected terrorist training facilities, including what was called the Hospital of Khomeini. The Israelis were convinced that a mosque was being used to assemble car bombs; but it was deemed off limits, and the holy place was not bombed.

Motley supervised relations with more than thirty countries in Latin America—any place with a stamp and a flag—and he had spent much of the past ten days dealing with the tiny Caribbean island of Grenada, only 133 square miles in area, population 110,000, producer of about a third of the world's annual consumption of nutmeg. The island had become a minor obsession for the President. Its leader, Maurice Bishop, a young, charismatic Marxist, was building a 9,000-foot jet runway; Cuba was assisting, and the Soviets had been granted permission to use it.

Reagan had complained publicly of "the Soviet-Cuban militarization of Grenada" and had released a classified reconnaissance photograph showing a Cuban barracks and the airstrip construction. His Administration feared the formation of a red triangle in the hemisphere, with Cuba to the north, Nicaragua to the west, and Grenada to the east ninety miles from the South American mainland.

Motley had gone on alert when a group of extremists, which the CIA identified as even more closely affiliated with the Cubans, had staged a coup. On October 19, Bishop was executed. The new leftists imposed a twenty-four-hour-a-day curfew and placed the country under virtual house arrest. Motley called in the State Department crisis group. Its immediate concern was the 1,000 United States citizens, mostly students, who lived on Grenada. The State Department had contact with no one who said they represented a government; no one seemed to want to say he was part of the government, and with no government there could be no diplomacy. Motley initiated contact with the British and the Canadians to discuss possible joint evacuation of all their citizens. Continuing efforts to make diplomatic contact on the island were rebuffed. The CIA had no real sources. With the U.S. government blind, officials began imagining the worst.

It had taken Constantine Menges several months to disengage from the CIA, and he had just arrived at the NSC two weeks earlier to head the Latin America section. He was deeply disappointed. He had taken his post under Clark, whom he considered a judicious implementer of the President's will, and was now going to serve under McFarlane, whom he considered a surrogate for the State Department compromisers.

McFarlane was no Reaganite and lacked the moral courage to be a real national-security adviser, Menges felt. In his first days, Menges had seized on the Grenada crisis, and had drafted a short plan for the protection of U.S. citizens there. McFarlane had looked upon this with some wonder but had agreed to consider it.

Menges shared his plan with some hard-line friends in the Defense Department. One official told him to be careful, that McFarlane would use it as a pretext to remove him. Menges showed it to Lieutenant Colonel North. North was skeptical: there had been repeated hesitation; the State Department would favor negotiations. Menges also mentioned his plan to Casey. The DCI said merely that it sounded interesting.

Menges was convinced that the Soviets were intent on using Grenada, with its deep-water port and its new runway, as a staging island for Soviet nuclear missiles on submarines or aircraft.

McFarlane agreed to have one of the Administration's most secret meetings for crisis management, the so-called CPPG, Crisis Preplanning Group, meet on Grenada. That evening, at about 6:30, Menges spoke with Casey on the secure phone. The DCI was leaving soon for another trip abroad, and Menges was about to explain that McFarlane had been presented with the plan and had agreed to the CPPG meeting. Upon reflection, the probability of McFarlane's acting, let alone taking the plan to the President, seemed so low to Menges that he did not mention it to Casey.

The next morning, October 20, Vice-Admiral John Poindexter, McFarlane's deputy, convened the CPPG. Poindexter included Motley, Menges, North, and Clarridge and the key people from Defense. To minimize attention, the group gathered in Room 208 of the EOB, the latest high-tech operations center, which included the most advanced computer, audio-visual and secure communications systems.

Intelligence showed that a Cuban transport, *Heroic Vietnam,* was in port on the small island. Menges argued that Castro had forces of nearly 300,000 and could airlift thousands to Grenada on short notice. He proposed an "in-out rescue." Given this opportunity, he argued that Communism should be eliminated permanently, and democracy restored, also permanently. He offered his argument that to do less would be to leave the Communists with a base for nuclear weapons.

At 6 P.M., Vice-President Bush convened the Special Situations Group, the highest-level crisis management group in the Reagan Administration.

Fear of a new leftist government taking Americans hostage raised the ghost of Iran. "Forceful extraction" and "surgical strike" were both discussed.

McFarlane wanted to keep a twenty-one-ship Navy flotilla, including the aircraft carrier U.S.S. *Independence,* bound for Lebanon on a track that would take it to the Caribbean—just in case it was needed. The Joint Chiefs refused to do so without a presidential order. McFarlane said it was crazy that he had to have a presidential order to keep one aircraft-carrier group going in a certain direction. The Chairman of the JCS, General John W. Vessey, dug in.

McFarlane drafted an order, which the President signed. The Navy flotilla was kept on course for the Caribbean.

General Vessey at first opposed military action, but when it became clear that Americans might have to be rescued from several locations on the island, the JCS said it would be necessary to secure the entire island. Menges sought out Darman and made the argument for the full-fledged restoration of democracy. He hoped to soften up Jim Baker. From his two years in the CIA, Menges had the arguments down pat: Cuban aggression had gone unchecked in the 1970s when Castro dispatched thousands of troops to Africa—Angola, Mozambique and Ethiopia. Since the Nicaraguan revolution in 1979, this hemisphere was clearly the new target, with thousands of Cuban advisers being used to prop up the Sandinistas. This was a once-in-a-lifetime chance, the island small, a manageable operation.

Casey and Shultz saw an opportunity. The absence of a government on Grenada provided a rare chance to invoke mutual-security agreements the United States had with other small Caribbean islands.

"Hey," Casey said at one point, "fuck it, let's dump these bastards."

Shultz was at first inclined to a less ambitious scheme, but he favored readiness for possible military action. Reagan's other normally fractious and divided senior advisers and Cabinet officers agreed.

The Administration needed a firmer grounding, more legitimacy. The 9,000-foot runway, the fear for the 1,000 Americans, the absence of a government did not quite justify a full-scale invasion. The President's advisers did not want to have to say that the Administration had just decided to violate international law.

The solution surfaced the next day, Friday, October 21. Prime Minister Eugenia Charles of Dominica, another small Caribbean island, headed a group called the Organization of Eastern Caribbean States. They were meeting that day in Barbados, and word was sent to them that the likelihood of U.S. military action would be substantially increased if they requested it. The OECS decided to do so, phrasing their request for U.S. assistance to restore order and democracy on Grenada. The oral request was passed to the White House, which, in turn, asked that the OECS issue a formal written request for intervention.

Charles was a sixty-four-year-old passionately pro-American leader who Motley felt made British Prime Minister Margaret Thatcher seem like a kitten. Menges considered her a Caribbean Jeane Kirkpatrick. In 1982, the United States had begun supplying funds to build a thirty-mile, $10 million road on Dominica.

CIA records show that at one point $100,000 had been passed to her government for a secret support operation. For the CIA, the $100,000 provided supplemental leverage, and a key senator on the Intelligence Committee considered it a "payoff." Charles firmly denied any knowledge of any direct payment to her, her party or her government. She said that her decision to request U.S. intervention was based solely on her assessment and that of the leaders of the other islands in the group, Antigua, St. Lucia and St. Vincent.

That evening Menges and North spent three hours drafting a National Security Decision Directive for the President to order an invasion. It was sent to Reagan, Shultz and McFarlane, who were now in Augusta, Georgia, for a weekend of golf. Reagan did not sign it.

Menges urged that the NSC prepare for Soviet countermoves. He said they might encourage the Libyans to launch a terrorist attack; or they might move in Berlin or Korea. He called Motley on the secure phone and said this invasion might deter Suriname from moving closer to Cuba.

At 9 A.M. Saturday, October 22, the National Security Council met. In Washington, Bush, Poindexter, McMahon, Motley, Menges and North gathered in Room 208. Using secure speaker hookups from Georgia, the

President, Shultz and McFarlane joined in. By 11:30 there was full consensus.

The next day, October 23, the day of the Marine bombing in Beirut, Charles's group transmitted an eight-point written request for intervention. The deaths of the servicemen were a personal blow to Reagan, who was keenly aware of his role as Commander in Chief. That many servicemen had not been lost since Vietnam. He voiced a feeling that sinister forces were at work—terrorists in Lebanon, Communists in Grenada. That day he signed the formal order for the Grenada invasion.

Casey had a case officer, one of the few women in the DO, who had been to Grenada for observation under deep cover several weeks earlier. She was dispatched a second time to gather intelligence before the invasion. This would be the first large-scale military intervention in the hemisphere since the 1965 invasion of the Dominican Republic. All four U.S. military services wanted, and received, a piece of the action.

The next day Charles was flown to Washington secretly in a U.S. government plane.

North worried that the Beirut bombing would absorb all the attention and become grounds for canceling the invasion. He slept that night in his office.

The morning of October 25, the U.S. force, plus several hundred token soldiers from the other Caribbean nations requesting the intervention, began operations and landings. They encountered stiff resistance, and had little better than gas station maps to use on the island. Intelligence had not warned of antiaircraft weapons. Three U.S. helicopters were shot down. In all, nineteen U.S. servicemen were killed and another 115 wounded.

At 7:30 that morning an unusually early fire was burning in the Oval Office fireplace. Reagan, Shultz, McFarlane and Menges met there with Prime Minister Charles for about a half hour over juice and coffee. The President asked her to join him for a press briefing later that morning. She agreed. Menges took her to the White House dining room, where he explained that the American news media would be hostile, negative and difficult. He assisted her in working out answers to meet the skepticism.

At the last minute, the State Department deleted from the President's statement the phrase "restore democracy" as a reason for the invasion. Menges argued, however, that its absence would make it appear that the Administration wanted a right-wing government on the island. The phrase was reinserted.

At 9:07 A.M. the President appeared in the press room to announce the invasion.

"Early this morning, forces from six Caribbean democracies and the United States began a landing," the President said. The first reason he gave for the action was "an urgent, formal request from the five member nations of the OECS," chaired by Charles. Reagan introduced her, and she, appearing by Reagan's side, said, "It is not a matter of an invasion. It is a matter of preventing this thing [Marxism] from spreading to all the islands."

Her forceful presentation at the White House and during a round of other interviews and speeches was a public-relations coup for the White House. Reagan was later shown a videotape of his joint press appearance with Mrs. Charles.

"Wow," the President said, "she was great!"

Menges discovered that North not only was key to Grenada but was the primary officer on all armed resistance support operations, including the contras. The compartments in the NSC were so restricted that virtually no one other than McFarlane and Poindexter was involved. The memos and messages on the subjects had the narrowest distribution. As the head of the Latin American section, Menges had little idea what was happening.

North was working an incredible eighty-five to ninety hours a week, more than the usual sixty to seventy-five put in by the other NSC staffers. "Ollie," Menges said one day, "you have four wonderful children. We're not at war now. Why don't you spend some time with these wonderful children?"

"You're right," North replied. "Next week."

Thursday night, October 27—just four days after the Beirut bombing and two days after Grenada—Casey agreed to have dinner with me. I had invited him to my house, but he said he'd prefer that I come to his home. His office at the CIA had told me to show up at 6:30 P.M., and I was given his address in a posh new development carved out of the old Nelson Rockefeller estate off Foxhall Road in northwest Washington. Reagan was going on television that night to address the nation on Lebanon and Grenada.

A youthful, dark-suited, expressionless CIA security man answered the door at Casey's new tan brick house, about sunset. The Director appeared almost at once in the small foyer. He offered a greeting, motioned down another half level and said we would go down to have a drink before dinner. We proceeded through three beautifully furnished sitting rooms. The wealth and the taste were evident but not overdone—fine fabrics on chairs and sofas, rich Oriental rugs and Oriental art all about. We stopped in the third or fourth room, a kind of den. He fixed two scotch and sodas. We sat down in a pair of chairs off to the side of the room. Casey sat quietly, his hands carefully still as he held the glass.

"Back in the 1960s or sometime when Allen Dulles was director," he said, "and Dick Helms was deputy or in one of those jobs, DDO or something, there was concern that people were leaving the CIA because of low pay. I was invited out to the CIA by Helms." The CIA was setting up some private fund to assist employees or agents with loans for college and other matters, Casey said, adding that he contributed something to the fund. "There were a lot of people leaving then," he explained, "and I asked Helms why he didn't leave. Helms said, 'When you sit here each day and you see all of this, and see all the Russians are doing you feel' "—he paused—" 'you feel beleaguered and you just can't leave.' " He rattled the ice in his crystal glass. He would not necessarily use the word "beleaguered," but the sentiment was correct. He nodded.

What of George Kennan's view that we just don't understand the Soviets, that there is some great stupid rush to war and it will turn out that we've misread each other?

Oh, yes, he said, he was sure about the Russians. They had taken seven or eight countries before Reagan. "Grenada," he said emphatically, "is the only setback for them since World War II," with the exception of Chile when Allende was thrown out in 1973. He failed to mention Egypt.

Look, Casey said, Grenada is the first time we've got a look inside a Communist regime, first time one has been ejected. Even at this early stage it shows that it was worse than we thought. Much more sophisticated equipment than expected. Secret documents were booby-trapped; to get at them we had to defuse them. There was the glint of the document archivist in his eye. They were getting lots of documents, he said, and that would tell the story.

We thought initially that there were about 600 Cubans on the island, Casey went on. The Cubans say about 700, but we now have reports from the invading force that there might be 1,000. The Cubans on Grenada are construction crews, but, like the U.S. Seabees, they are also fighters, he said. The Cuban workers had a special hook by their bunks to hang their AK-47 automatic weapons on. We found "terrorist communications equipment," Casey said.

You've got to see the context, he said. The 1,000 Cubans represent one percent of the 100,000 population of Grenada. The equivalent one percent of the population in the United States would be 2 million plus. Would we tolerate a foreign militia or even a construction battalion that size here?

There was a Cuban training facility on the island. Three Russian diplomats, Casey said, came out of their embassy on Grenada with a white flag and said the total with dependents was forty-nine Russians. Also, there were about twenty North Korean diplomats, including one high-ranking official. Also some East Germans. They were now all in the Soviet Embassy. These high numbers were standard where the Soviets had or wanted to set up a proxy or client state. There were also several KGB agents on the island.

The Soviets were doing what they had done in Afghanistan in 1979 when they were unhappy with their puppet, and had him killed and replaced. The Soviets had sent in "assassination teams" and had had Maurice Bishop killed. He added this matter-of-factly, paused, nodded as if to confirm it, stood abruptly and suggested we go upstairs for dinner.

In the dining room three places were set. A well-dressed woman in her midthirties came in.

"This is my daughter, Bernadette," Casey said. Bernadette was rather striking. She was an actress for commercials in New York City, and very cosmopolitan, her hair and makeup perfect.

Casey explained that his wife, Sophia, was at their Florida home supervising a cleanup because some kids had broken into the garage and started a fire.

Bernadette had cooked lamb chops. It was a simple, good meal, nothing fancy.

Casey was an avid eater, preoccupied with his food at first, particularly his lamb chops. Glancing at Bernadette, I thought several times I detected some smiling recognition of this. But she waved me off with her large eyes as if I had trespassed.

Grenada, he continued, was something that happened over a weekend —an "opportunity" to finally turn things our way. The new leaders were all young and did not represent anyone other than themselves.

The archives were not a real find, Casey said, back-pedaling a bit, but they were an important byproduct of the invasion. The CIA has sent in five interrogators to Grenada to talk to the Cubans, he said. We've already learned that the Cubans will fight more than we expected. They had generals, colonels and lieutenant colonels in Grenada. It might take six months for a democracy to be established, but it will be, Casey said.

Bernadette stayed out of the conversation. Grenada has to be seen in the context of the whole Caribbean, Casey said. The Soviets are spending

$4 billion a year in the region—$3 billion to Cuba and $1 billion elsewhere. For the Soviets that's lots of money. They have 6,000 to 7,000 troops in Cuba. So the Cubans can and do send about the same number to Nicaragua. Now we've learned that there were more Cubans on Grenada than we thought. So the extent, he said, of Soviet-Cuban involvement in—Casey paused and raced over the word—Nicawawa may be underestimated. For example, the Cubans sent to Nicaragua are told to shave their Castro beards and burn their Cuban uniforms and are integrated into the regular Nicaraguan military. We believe that the Cubans are in every Nicaraguan unit now. So the Soviets and the Cubans have about 12,000 men dispersed around Latin America. By contrast, the United States spends about $400 million and has about 100 advisers in El Salvador. That imbalance must be corrected.

Where did that $4 billion figure come from?

"It's flaky," Casey said. He would not vouch for it. He added that $4 billion was the number used and believed in Administration circles.

He had just read LBJ's memoirs, *The Vantage Point,* on the invasion of the Dominican Republic in 1965, and had found the reasons for intervention somewhat the same as for Grenada—to thwart Communists and protect Americans. The Grenada invasion is important, he said, because it is a step in correcting that regional imbalance, and it will send the Soviets and the Cubans a message.

"That we might strike in Nicaragua," he stated. The word "strike" was given strong emphasis.

At the same time, the Soviets will be cautious, are cautious. Their overall goal in the hemisphere is to divert our attention from the real battleground, the Middle East. He said it as if it were obvious. The strategic stakes and the oil fields made it the major concern.

Dinner and dessert were over. Casey played with silverware. Bernadette cleared the table and brought in coffee.

Casey rose and suggested we go watch the President's speech, which was to begin shortly.

So the Caribbean was a playing field and the Middle East was the real contest. That seemed to be Casey's genuine assessment.

We went back down to the den and set up two chairs in front of the television set. We had a few minutes to wait. What about Afghanistan, how was the war going? I did not refer to the CIA's covert support.

Casey frowned. The Soviets will overpower and wear down the rebels, he said.

How about the Korean jetliner, KAL Flight 007, that had been shot down two months earlier by the Soviets? All 269 aboard had been killed, and the President had declared moral warfare on the Soviets, labeling the act "barbarism."

Casey's answer was free of bombast. Well, ah, it turns out that it was really a mistake by the Soviets and they just didn't go look at what kind of plane had intruded over their territory. He seemed unperturbed at contradicting the President.

"Foul-up," he said, his eyes nearly twinkling. He shrugged and seemed confident.

The President, seated behind his desk in the Oval Office, came on the screen, and Casey turned up the sound.

Reagan began with a reference to the downing of the Korean airliner—"brutal massacre," he called it.

Casey did not flinch. His gaze was respectful as Reagan threaded his way through an account of the Marine bombing and the Grenada invasion.

The Director winced slightly when the President said that the morning before the invasion the U.S. military "had little intelligence information about conditions on the island."

No worry, Reagan said, the military planned and carried out "a brilliant campaign." There were some casualties, "few in number" but he didn't give a count. The Cubans and the weapons show that Grenada "was a Soviet-Cuban colony being readied as a major military bastion to export terror and undermine democracy. We got there just in time."

Casey did not react, though Reagan's statement was much stronger, more apocalyptic, than what I had just heard. Casey had in no way implied that the United States had arrived there just in time.

"The events in Lebanon and Grenada, though oceans apart, are closely related," Reagan said. "Not only has Moscow assisted and encouraged the violence in both countries, but it provides direct support through a network of surrogates and terrorists."

Now, the President asked in his most sincere voice, "may I share something with you I think you'd like to know? It is something that happened to the commandant of our Marine Corps General Kelley, while he was visiting our critically injured Marines." There was a Marine, Reagan quoted Kelley as saying, " 'with more tubes going in and out of his body . . . He could not see very well. He reached up and grabbed my four stars, just to make sure I was who I said I was. He held my hand with a firm grip. . . . We put a pad of paper in his hand, and he wrote, "Semper Fi." ' "

Reagan explained that it was short for "Semper Fidelis"—Always Faithful—the Marine motto.

"General Kelley has a reputation for being a very sophisticated general and a very tough Marine. But he cried when he saw those words, and who can blame him?"

Casey was rapt.

Reagan closed, invoking honor, ideals, country, sacrifice, God, prayer and freedom. The twenty-seven-minute speech was quite moving, even stirring.

"You know who wrote that?" Casey asked.

"You?" I asked.

"Ronald Reagan," Casey corrected. "His greatest skill is as a writer. I think that is perhaps the best speech he has ever given," Casey said unequivocally, the unabashed fan. "Do you know the energy it takes to do that?"

Undoubtedly it was a powerful and clever speech. It would take some time for anyone who heard it to erase the image of the Marine feeling the four stars of the Marine commandant or forget the meaning of "Semper Fi." But what about the facts? Soviets, Cubans, terrorists had all been thrown together into a single stew. Marine presence and invasions, the President seemed to be saying, were the only answer.

"I've never seen anyone talk quite so fast," Casey said, "say so much without stumbling."

He escorted me to the door, saying he was testifying before the Senate Intelligence Committee the next day.

What else is going on?

He said he was giving a speech in two days at Westminster College in Fulton, Missouri, where Winston Churchill had given his famous Iron Curtain speech thirty-seven years earlier, just after World War II. He handed me a copy of the eighteen-page text, containing a few of his pencil edits.

Is there anything else happening?

He looked at me stone-faced, as if to say it was time for me to go.

Bernadette came up and said good night. One night several years later Casey told me proudly that Art Buchwald had mentioned Bernadette in print before his column had become exclusively a humorous spoof. It was 1956, when Casey had taken her to the rubber-stamp "Ike and Dick" Republican Convention in San Francisco. She had been thirteen and head of the Children for Eisenhower. "Well," Buchwald quoted Bernadette as saying, "we just go around and try to talk people into being Republicans. . . . We say it's the best party."

What if they inquire how you know this? Buchwald had asked.

"Because my father said so. That's why."

• • •

Later that night as I typed a detailed memo of the dinner and the discussion, it seemed in general that Casey fell somewhere between the President's the-Russians-are-coming rhetoric and a reporter's skepticism. Clearly, he approved of the President's speech, its world view and the performance, but he didn't seem to be cheering.

Casey's own speech contained some clues. "How much more alarmed would Churchill be if he looked around the world today and saw how the Soviets have grown in strength and how far they have extended their power," Casey had written. He listed five areas: Vietnam, Afghanistan, the Horn of Africa (Somalia, Ethiopia), Southern Africa (Angola, where the Clark Amendment still prohibited U.S. covert assistance), and the Caribbean and Central America.

Turning to Lebanon and Grenada, the speech said, "For reasons which you will understand, I am not in a position to go into any detail beyond what you have learned from the media, and like any good reporter I'm prepared to go to jail to protect my sources."

Churchill "would have been gratified" with Grenada. Casey likened it to the threat of fascism of the 1930s. "He would rejoice that for the first time the West has restored to a colony of the Soviet Empire the freedom which had been stolen from it."

"Soviet Empire"—not the "evil empire," the controversial term used by the President eight months earlier in Florida.

"Grenada provides a vivid illustration of how the Soviets practice creeping imperialism by proxy. . . . It is a microcosm of Nicaragua."

To challenge this Soviet proxy strategy, he said, "The U.S. needs a realistic counterstrategy." That strategy, he said, had to include a realization that these Third World countries "will be the principal U.S.–Soviet battleground for many years to come."

He knew precisely what he wanted to say and was in the habit of writing or heavily editing his own speeches. His colleagues often kidded him, one saying, "The only thing worse than being the president of Lebanon is being your speechwriter."

Before the weekend, the Pentagon announced publicly that about 1,100 Cubans were on Grenada. Only about 600 had been captured, and hundreds were in the hills. Casey wanted a quick but thorough assessment. How many Cubans were in the hills? Was Grenada, as the President had asserted, "being readied as a major military bastion to export terror"?

Early Sunday morning, October 30, analysts from the various agencies gathered at the Pentagon. By evening they had finished a classified assessment of about ten pages that was immediately printed and circulated.

Casey received his copy on Monday. It flatly contradicted the President, Casey himself and the Pentagon's public pronouncements. According to the assessment, there were no Cubans in the hills—all had been killed or captured by the 6,000 U.S. troops. The early overestimate resulted from interviews with the first Cuban prisoners, and from exaggerations of the opposition forces by inexperienced U.S. troops. Second, the assessment said that the caches of arms and weapons on Grenada were for the army and the militia and were not sufficient or intended to be used in overthrowing the governments in the neighboring islands. Third, the Cuban construction workers were not combat troops in disguise, though they had some weapons training and did fight.

Casey pronounced the assessment "unimaginative." But it was classified, and was never released publicly.

A number of Administration conservatives were furious over the assessment. Herb Meyer, a Casey assistant, said, "I think it stinks." Constantine Menges, at the NSC, proposed that the Administration try to get Castro to urge in a radio broadcast that his troops on Grenada surrender, but now it turned out there were no more Cuban troops. As an alternative, Menges suggested that the captured Cuban prisoners not be released. He urged that the Cubans be made to suffer.

"We have won," Tony Motley replied, rejecting the idea out of hand. The Cubans were released.

Grenada grew as a positive symbol in Administration lore. It was routinely invoked as a sign of a new toughness, reaffirming the Monroe Doctrine, big-stick and gunboat diplomacy—anti-Communism—burying once and for all the specter of Iran. The images were those of American students returning from Grenada, kissing U.S. soil as they disembarked from airplanes, or a defiant Prime Minister Charles at Reagan's side proclaiming the United States the savior of Caribbean democracy.

Several days after the invasion, the U.S. ambassador to Nicaragua was called in by Minister of the Interior Borge. Anytime you feel a need or want to evacuate Americans from Nicaragua, Borge said, here's how you can do it. We'll help. There will be no problem, he promised.

At Langley, Casey received this report with glee. The Sandinistas were obviously worried.

Later, when Tony Motley was in Nicaragua meeting with Daniel Ortega, he raised the fate of Maurice Bishop in Grenada. Leftist leaders are not safe from other leftists, Motley said. You don't want to be the Maurice Bishop of Nicaragua. Dead, in a box.

Whenever Motley received a phone call from Dominica Prime Minister Eugenia Charles, he took it, stating that he had his pencil in hand ready to deal with her requests. He felt like a cross between the local mayor and the public-works manager as he micromanaged the thirty-mile, $10 million road. Eventually, U.S. assistance included $2 million more for Dominica schools and another $150,000 in self-help aid for river crossings on the island.

Convinced of the need for more propaganda efforts in the Caribbean, Casey proposed a top-secret finding that would allocate about $7 million for radio transmitters, loudspeakers—a traditional Latin political tool—and other CIA propaganda work in the Caribbean. Reagan was enthusiastic and signed the finding immediately.

Grenada's political future was uncertain. The only political organization on the island was the remnant of Bishop's leftist New Jewel movement. Casey and other senior Administration members were determined that what had been won by force not be lost at the ballot box. Eventually, under another presidential finding, $675,000 was allocated from CIA political-action funds. The money was for education and get-out-the-vote work for the coming Grenada election. The CIA even had a pollster conduct surveys and analyze the data to make sure that a strong pro-U.S. leader emerged. Thirteen months after the invasion, a U.S.-backed coalition headed by Grenadian political veteran Herbert Blaize won a landslide victory. One of his first acts as Prime Minister was to ask President Reagan to maintain the 250 U.S. troops on the island.

15

THE SOVIET ATTACK on Korean airliner Flight 007 (269 dead), the Beirut Marine bombing (241 American dead) and the Grenada invasion (19 U.S. servicemen dead) had helped create an atmosphere that assisted Casey in his final push to win the $24 million for the Nicaragua operation. The world was dangerous; it was difficult for anyone to contend that it was time to back away. Casey was able to argue that American spine needed to be stiffened. And there were a few sweeteners for those opposed. A new National Intelligence Estimate was circulated, concluding that there was no way that the contras could overthrow the Sandinistas; neither military nor political victory was possible. This suggested that the Nicaragua operation was less ambitious than critics had maintained. The final draft of a top-secret White House summary stated for the first time that President Reagan was seeking a general amnesty for the contras. This had the overtones of an eventual political settlement.

In the conference between the Senate, which had approved the $24 million, and the House, which had voted to terminate the program, the Senate had the ammunition. The new finding, the Senate representatives argued, also made it unnecessary to renew the Boland Amendment to insure that no money was spent for the purpose of overthrowing the Sandinistas, because the new finding made clear that the purpose was not to oust the Sandinistas.

Boland won only one major concession: an agreement that the $24 million would be an absolute ceiling; the money would have to last all the next year or the Administration would have to come back for additional funds.

On December 9, 1983, President Reagan signed the authorization into law. Casey had won. He now turned his attention to the plan to mine the Nicaraguan harbors. He demanded regular reports from Clarridge. Did they have the right people? Had the mines been tested? Secrecy, the DCI ordered.

• • •

As the third calendar year of Casey's tenure as DCI was nearing an end that month, it was clear that the endless congressional and media debate about the Nicaragua operation had turned out to be a plus in several ways. Like golf, Casey's favorite sport, running intelligence was a game of recovery. After a bad shot or a bounce, it was necessary to turn position to maximum advantage. First, Casey thought, the operation established the resolve within the Administration. Second, it was a broad political statement about determined anti-Communism. Third, it drew the attention and fire of the Congress and the media. The result had been a kind of cover and diversion, surely unintended at the time, for some of the other important intelligence-collection efforts.

From the beginning of his tenure, Casey had pushed human intelligence —urging the DO to get penetrations. He wanted human sources, then more human sources, and still more human sources. When a report came in about a promising young political leader or a smart minister, Casey would write in the margin, "Can we recruit?" or just "Recruit?" and sign the note "C." Recruiting was going to be expensive, risky and time-consuming. McMahon and the DO warned him about "unrealistic time lines"—the Soviets allegedly had spent decades nurturing and planting their human sources. But Casey's prodding and patience were paying off.

In early December, about the same time Casey was obtaining the $24 million for Nicaragua, Sudanese President Nimeri visited Washington and held a very secret meeting with the leader of the Libyan opposition. The Libyan leader, Dr. Mohammed Youssef Magarieff, had been auditor general for Qaddafi and in 1979 had exiled himself to Egypt, where he had denounced Qaddafi as a corrupt tyrant squandering Libya's oil revenue. Magarieff had set up the National Front for the Salvation of Libya, which was dedicated to assassinating Qaddafi and overthrowing his regime.

A SECRET source report from the DO of December 5, 1983, gave a full account of the Nimeri-Magarieff meeting and showed that Qaddafi was in for more trouble in the future. The source of the information was listed—under what the DO called a "byline"—as "a high level Sudanese official who was aware the information would reach the U.S. Government." In other words, a human agency asset—either a paid or witting voluntary informant. It was possible the informant was passing on this information either with or without the knowledge of Nimeri himself. Casey accepted the shorthand to protect sources on the widely circulated reports, but he would frequently ask, "Who's this guy?" The DDO would tell him or provide a file.

Nimeri's contempt for Qaddafi was well known, and his support of the anti-Qaddafi exile opposition was widely suspected. But in the meeting, according to the SECRET source report, Nimeri promised that he "would increase assistance in the form of training facilities, weapons, ammunition and travel facilitation in the form of Sudanese passports and other documents." This was the crucial kind of operational cover that the anti-Qaddafi forces would need to work inside Libya.

"Nimeri told Dr. Magarieff that he had carte blanche to conduct any type of activity against Libya including military action." Short of a formal declaration of war, this was as far as any country could go—allowing its territory to become a staging area for a military strike. Nimeri also said that the exile movement should continue to work through his own intelligence service, the Sudanese Security Organization (SSO), and that if there were problems he should be contacted directly.

Dr. Magarieff, according to the report, said that "he believed that Sudan and the U.S. were his only friends. . . . he said that following another period of training he hoped to mount a campaign against Libya that would give his organization more credibility."

The report included a comment from the source that Magarieff "did not state what types of campaign he had in mind but the implication was that it would be some form of military activity, possibly inside Libya."

In a matter of great concern, Magarieff said, the Libyans "have penetrated the Moroccan security service and . . . it is no longer safe for him to visit there or for his organization to operate from Morocco."

The possibility of some dramatic anti-Qaddafi military demonstration inside Libya appealed to Casey. It would show that Magarieff and his front had some strength. Until this happened Casey would not be able to get a presidential finding supporting the anti-Qaddafi movement. Qaddafi was too entrenched—billions in military equipment from the Soviets, a ruthless pursuit of opposition elements both in Libya and abroad.

Meanwhile, Casey continued to focus intelligence-gathering assets on Qaddafi and Libya—in Casey's view a threat to the stability of the entire region of North Africa and the Middle East. More finished intelligence reports—estimates, assessments and formal papers—were being issued on Qaddafi and Libya than on almost anywhere else. The number of meetings at the CIA and the amount of attention to Qaddafi exceeded Libya's importance. At times, Libya got more attention than the Soviet Union. Numerous intelligence collection assets were allocated to Qaddafi, trying to keep up with him, follow him around, photograph him and his compound, his various forays into the desert, to decrypt his diplomatic traffic and listen to his phone calls and other conversations. The absence of a U.S. embassy in Tripoli made it all the more difficult, but Casey insisted, frequently asking, "What's damn Qaddafi up to this week?"

The project of paramount importance to Director Casey was the recruitment and development of human sources within the Soviet Union. Bill Colby had urged it three years earlier just before Casey had taken over as DCI; others had stated the need repeatedly. Casey's own instincts pushed in that direction. That would be the trophy. China and the Soviet Union were the "hard targets," and Russia was the harder, the less penetrable. Soviet society made the simplest exercises of privacy that might allow intelligence operatives to work and make contact nearly impossible. There was almost nothing immune from the pervading suspicion—presumably no untapped phone call, no innocent meeting, no unmonitored travel, no real safe house or place even inside the U.S. Embassy.

Casey understood the limits. It was possible to get more information and still not have answers to the big questions, such as the true Soviet intentions. The answer was not just a collection problem. Gates, who now headed the analytic side of the CIA, and some of the others convinced Casey that it was also hard for the Soviets to understand the intentions of the United States. There was probably a KGB analyst in Siberia now because he had failed to predict that a peanut farmer would oust an incumbent President in 1976, and another for failing to predict that the farmer would be ousted by a Hollywood actor and that this would lead to the biggest peacetime military buildup in United States history.

The groundwork for an improved human-source program had been laid years earlier, in the 1970s, when a program of what was called "management by objective" had specified requirements for promotion. One was that a DO officer must make a human-source recruitment, commonly called "a skin on the wall" by DO officers. The "skin" was controversial since recruiting abroad often depended on luck. A DO officer undercover in an embassy somewhere might cultivate an official or a military officer in the host country for years before making a pitch. Tradecraft generally dictated that in such a case the DO officer not make the eventual pitch himself, in order to preserve his own cover. So he would introduce the prospective recruit to a "friend" who was a CIA officer. If the person declined recruitment, the first DO officer could deny it all and share shock and dismay. If the recruitment was accepted, it was the second CIA officer—the one who had done the least work—who got the "skin."

Casey felt that recruitment had received too little attention under

Turner. Though there had been some definite successes, there seemed to be a general feeling in the DO that Turner had accepted the barriers to recruitment in the Soviet Union. Casey forced more emphasis on ways to get around the problems. Soviets, for instance, were traveling more and could be contacted outside the Soviet Union. Casey was sure these Soviets detested their government and its system. In his opinion, an offer to work for the United States was doing someone a favor.

One top-secret source right inside the Soviet Union was A. G. Tolkachev, who had been recruited before the Reagan Administration. An employee of a Moscow aeronautical institute, Tolkachev worked through a very sophisticated system with a DO officer in Moscow to allow the regular delivery of important secrets.

There were also walk-ins. Casey found too much suspicion about walk-ins. The CIA had to be careful that they were not plants or double agents, but he felt it was important to let it be known that the door in every station or facility was open. A walk-in had advantages: you could get down to business in a short period of time; years of nurturing and foreplay, which itself could be indirect and very ambiguous, were not necessary. Though lots of walk-ins might be useless or potential doubles, Casey felt it the most natural thing in the world for a Soviet or Eastern Bloc official to want to assist the West.

Casey pushed hard, raising the question of human-source recruitments time and time again with the elite Soviet division in the DO. He made it clear that he was willing to take chances. Yes, he said, there would be mistakes. He *expected* mistakes. He *expected* that some Soviets might be offended. "So what?" he said. "Proves we're active." If there were no mistakes, there was not enough effort. Every lead had to be followed up. No hint, clue, tip or intuition was to go unexamined as they shifted Soviets' names and files for possible recruitment. This was the long, deep game with the major adversary. Casey wanted it played well, aggressively.

Coordination with the FBI, which handled counterintelligence in the United States, was increased. The CIA stations developed a list of possible recruits suggested by the behavior of Soviets abroad; if these Soviets—KGB or diplomatic or whatever—were later assigned to the United States in a trade mission or even the embassy, their names and copies of their files were forwarded to the FBI. In turn, the FBI provided names of those Soviets who had served in the United States and then had gone to another post abroad, where a CIA station could pick up the trail. The CIA felt that the FBI got the best of this exchange, because the physical and psychological factors in the United States were most favorable to recruitment. The FBI made a few potentially important recruitments from leads provided by the CIA.

In the first years of the Reagan Administration, Casey had been able to exploit the crack in the Iron Curtain, particularly in Eastern Europe. Much attention was on Poland, but in the other countries officials traveled more. The movement between East and West was increasing, permitting comparatively easy and cost-free exploratory operations to see who might be bought or won over.

After three years, Casey had more than twenty-five regularly reporting human sources within the Soviet Union or the Eastern Bloc. Nearly all had been developed during his time. The sources were in the military, KGB or Eastern Bloc intelligence services, the scientific fields or other walks of life.

Casey was particularly proud of one of these sources. When the handful of U.S. officials who were on the BIGOT access list learned of the source's status, they were very impressed.

Casey acknowledged that no single CIA source was as good as Soviet Colonel Oleg Penkovsky had been. A legend from the early 1960s, Penkovsky had been a Soviet military-intelligence officer who had passed thousands of pages of documents to the CIA for sixteen months before he was arrested and executed. He had provided material crucial in identifying Soviet weapons in Cuba during the 1962 Missile Crisis.

Casey's successful Soviet penetrations were not viewed as terribly significant in the White House, where there was much grumbling, particularly by the national-security advisers, Allen, Clark and now McFarlane, because there was no intelligence flow directly from the Politburo. The White House wanted political intelligence that would be useful to the President, and on that front Casey wasn't delivering much. This White House obsession was first for data that would help the President outmaneuver the Soviets. A President's leadership would be judged, in part, by his skill at handling the Russians. Inside Politburo information would be priceless, and Casey didn't have it. Second, the White House wanted information for the President in his role as the chief architect of U.S. foreign policy. Again, inside tips that might provide an occasion for a deft diplomatic or other move against the Soviets could pay immense dividends. Even something that would allow the President to outflank the Soviets in international public relations through a well-timed speech, a scientific advance or a trade matter might help.

Casey felt, nonetheless, that the CIA was providing its best information in a third, perhaps more important area of presidential responsibility. That information served the President in his role as Commander in Chief.

This was the early-warning and military intelligence. It was not perfect, Casey realized, but it was often comprehensive and Casey felt that it gave President Reagan what he would need in case of some major Soviet military move. Granted, much of this information came from technical sources—the measuring of the movement of troops along a border by satellites, or intercepts from NSA. Casey touted his success at the White House and noted proudly that, so far in the Reagan Administration, the Soviets had not handed them a major surprise, perhaps other than the shooting down of Korean Flight 007; and that had been an error, not a plan the CIA could have been expected to anticipate.

The Director was as determined to expand and maintain human sources within governments friendly to the United States. It was risky but essential if he was going to give the White House a full, true picture of the world.

A good, reliable, well-tested human source who sat at all the Cabinet meetings of a government was often more useful than a pile of verbatim transcripts from electronic eavesdropping on every single Cabinet meeting. Such a source might participate in or be near the corridor conversations or decisions, would participate in the life of the community, its parties, its gossip. He might know that words of leaders, even those delivered in the most intimate of forums, meetings or phone conversations, might not tell the real story. A good human source could sift through facts, penetrate smokescreens, sort out the conventional wisdom. He was the truly coveted asset, a twenty-four-hour-a-day on-duty warning system.

In the most politically unstable regions of the world—Asia, Africa, the Middle East and Latin America—the fears of the leaders provided a means for developing human sources. A main concern was destabilization efforts from both internal and external forces—coups, terrorism, even assassination. The regimes almost universally wanted protection. That meant training, expertise, the most modern equipment. And no country was more equipped to provide that protection than the United States. And no arm of the U.S. government was more experienced in aiding leaders secretly than the CIA.

Any effort by the CIA abroad to influence events in a foreign country was defined as covert action and required a formal presidential finding. Technically, a CIA station chief giving advice to a foreign head of state, a chief of intelligence or, for that matter, anyone, was going beyond simple intelligence-gathering. It was "covert action."

A special category of covert action had evolved over the years to provide security-assistance and intelligence-training programs abroad.

These programs were not designed to change a regime; quite the opposite, they were to preserve the regime.

At a cost of anywhere from $300,000 to a gold-plated version of more than $1 million, the CIA sent in a team, often of only three to four agents. Run by the CIA's special International Activities division, with assistance from the Office of Technical Service and the DO, the team would set up the training and the delivery of equipment. Training was given to the personal security force or palace guard; often also to the country's intelligence service or the local police. Equipment included the best automatic weapons and handguns; high-tech night vision equipment; walkie-talkies, the most advanced communications equipment, often with encryption capability; even a helicopter (many of these countries loved getting an advanced helicopter); security alarms, locks; some equipment used to protect the President of the United States such as the light but effective bulletproof vests. Advanced techniques in perimeter defense of a building or palace, in monitoring terrorists and in insuring liaison with the intelligence service and the police were passed on.

One such covert assistance program was in place in Morocco, where for years the CIA had provided technical assistance, training and liaison to King Hassan II. (During World War II, a young U.S. military officer, Vernon Walters, had met the young Crown Prince Hassan, who then was age thirteen. That began a friendship that extended to the period 1972–76, when Walters was DDCI, and was almost considered the King's case officer.) The CIA assistance program over the years had helped keep Hassan in power since 1961, his twenty-two-year rule one of the longest of any African state. In return, Hassan allowed the CIA and the NSA virtually free run of his country. Extensive, sensitive U.S. intelligence operations with sophisticated advanced technologies were set up in Morocco. This was particularly important given Morocco's strategic location at the Straits of Gibraltar, controlling the western entrance to the Mediterranean Sea.

In effect the United States and the CIA station in Morocco—and dozens of other countries—were saying, "We are your friend and we want to take care of you." In highly volatile domestic political environments, this CIA assistance could mean survival.

But there was another side to intelligence- and security-assistance operations. It was based on opportunity and suspicion—two requirements of good intelligence work. Friends could turn overnight. Or, as happened more often, the friendships were all a matter of degree. Definitions of national interest changed. King Hassan might be with the United States on most matters, but there would be the inevitable areas of disagreement.

In the Mafia, the Godfather's credo was to hold friends close, but to hold enemies even closer. In the intelligence agencies, with shifting friends and enemies, the credo was to hold all countries close.

Invited into the presence, office, palace and life of the leader, the CIA team learned a great deal—schedules, routines, the identity of those with real influence and real information, the quirks and peccadillos of the friendly leader, his family, his advisers. There were also opportunities to plant eavesdropping devices, access to telephone lines, offices and living quarters. The communications gear issued to the security and intelligence forces was known to the CIA and the NSA, as were its precise uses, its frequencies and, if applicable, the codes.

But perhaps most important, there was a chance to recruit those human sources. In weeks or months, the visiting CIA team or the station personnel were living in the back pockets of the key security and intelligence officials. The CIA team had access to the working level, the guards and the radio operators. Training sessions, discussions, meetings, long lunches, longer dinners were all part of protecting the leader, honing the skills, learning the equipment, sharing the risk, the purpose. Foreign-intelligence information and assets increased, ranging from the recruitment of a well-paid agent to informal "let's-keep-in-touch" acquaintances who could be contacted for specific needs.

Particularly promising were people who could be put on the payroll as agents of influence or as sleepers—people who could be pulled out for specific information or a specific task. Often these people would not feel they were recruited agents, since the CIA had come in at the request of the leader, giving the relationship a feeling of "official" sanction. Others helped unwittingly.

The result was effective and multiple penetrations, human "moles" or electronic devices in many key friendly countries. Some CIA people considered this extremely dangerous—little more than intelligence "sting" operations designed less to help the leader than to gather intelligence. On one level some of the operations gave the CIA a sophisticated "Trojan horse" inside the host country, parlaying security assistance into intelligence. Casey felt it would be criminal not to use the advantage that had been handed to them. At various times he called these operations "a duty" and "business." The United States was vulnerable, he said. There were no standards, no rules, no laws, on spying abroad. Only one rule, he added: "Don't get caught. If you do, don't admit it."

It was Casey who determined that each operation had to be handled differently, even moderating the degree of intelligence-gathering in some cases where exposure could jeopardize relations with the friendly host country. A CIA source in India had been compromised and rolled up; Indian Prime Minister Indira Gandhi had been furious that the United States had a spy in her midst. But both countries had decided it was best to play down the matter.

If Casey was in the business of anticipating and preventing international surprises, he had to accept the risk of spying on friends. Some critics within the agency, perhaps, had a point when they said that too little attention was given to the cost of failure or a blown operation. But that was the mentality that Casey was fighting: defense, not offense; caution, not boldness.

Enhancing the power of his chiefs of station abroad was another of Casey's goals. Nothing increased a COS's power and status within the country and at Langley as much as the security- and intelligence-assistance operations. The station chiefs were even given a laminated plastic card that listed the available services, including head-of-state protection. The card was handed to heads of state so that they could select from the menu. There were so many two- or three-man teams from Operations or the Office of Technical Service running around that no one, including Casey, could count them all. Some foreign leaders became dependent, begging for the latest equipment as the means of retaining power. Successful operations gave the station chiefs fantastic power within the American embassy, particularly if the security operation yielded good political intelligence from within the presidential palace.

These operations provided the kind of information sought by the political apparatus of the Administration, the Secretary of State, the national-security adviser, the White House.

The security- and intelligence-assistance operations were producing. In all, Casey had twelve, including aid to:

- President Hissen Habré of Chad, the former French colony to the south of Libya. Habré had come to power the previous year after receiving covert CIA paramilitary assistance as part of one of the early Reagan Administration findings designed to bloody Qaddafi's nose. Friendly leadership in Chad was key to keeping Qaddafi boxed in.
- Pakistani President Mohammed Zia. No leader ruled a country in a more precarious geographic situation, surrounded by unfriendly nations —Iran on the west, Soviet-dominated Afghanistan to the north, a small portion of the Soviet Union itself, an equally small shared border with

China, and bitter foe India to the east and the south. Most crucial was President Zia's willingness to allow the CIA to funnel growing amounts of paramilitary support to the Afghanistan rebels through Pakistan. Casey, the CIA and the Reagan Administration all wanted Zia to stay in power and needed to know what was going on in his government. The CIA station in Islamabad was one of the biggest in the world.

- Liberia's leader Samuel K. Doe. The deputy chief of Doe's personal guard, Lieutenant Colonel Moses Flanzamaton, became a CIA agent and eventually attempted to seize power by leading a machine gun ambush on Doe's jeep. Doe was not injured, but Flanzamaton was captured, confessed to his CIA ties and not unnaturally embroidered his tale to include CIA sponsorship of the assassination. It was white knuckles at Langley for days, fearing that the agency would be accused unfairly of an assassination attempt. Liberia had been founded by freed American slaves and had been Africa's first republic. Apparently, Flanzamaton had signed on with the CIA with a view to enhancing his own political ambitions. But he was executed a week after the coup attempt, and the accusations died with him.
- Philippine President Marcos, a key U.S. friend, who permitted the United States to maintain air and naval bases. Marcos was also dealing with a Communist insurgency.
- Sudan President Nimeri, who maintained close relations with the United States and was another barrier to Qaddafi in Africa.
- Lebanese President Amin Gemayel. The CIA was anxious to insure that he was not overthrown or killed like his brother, the late Bashir Gemayel.
- President Duarte of El Salvador. Given the vast effort to interdict arms shipments to the leftist rebels in El Salvador and to prevent a leftist takeover, it was essential to keep Duarte alive and in power.

There were more—some obvious, some not so obvious. But in Casey's bag of intelligence operations, the security-assistance operations were among the best.

Casey realized that he had to be the unremitting advocate for these covert actions and relationships, even if they counted only for marginal gain, or if there were no apparent gain at all. It was a way of getting the agency's foot in the door, and as far as Casey was concerned the CIA needed its foot in every door in the world. Could these arrangements go too far? Yes, he realized, at least theoretically. So how were they to be controlled? Casey's answer was simple. He would assert personal control. After the overseas bribery scandals of the 1970s, which Sporkin, then at the SEC, had been instrumental in exposing, the Congress had made it illegal for American business to make payments or bribes abroad to obtain business. The payments and favors to foreign leaders or intelligence sources were exceptions—legal bribes, Casey realized. For example, he made certain to visit Pakistan's Zia once or twice a year. Soon he had the closest relationship with Zia of any member of the Reagan Administration. So when Zia wanted assistance from the United States or just needed someone to listen, his avenue was Casey.

In addition, the U.S. military presence or exercises in certain parts of the world were, for practical purposes, virtually covert operations. For example, in the last several years the Defense Department had conducted an extensive series of exercises in Honduras. It was a heavy dose of gunboat diplomacy to scare neighboring Nicaragua; and in the course of the exercises, equipment and temporary bases and airstrips were left behind in Honduras. These operations were treated as covert, and the congressional intelligence committees were formally briefed since the net effect was equivalent to a covert assistance program in support of the sitting government.

The security- and intelligence-support operation for the late Egyptian President Anwar Sadat illustrated the advantages and disadvantages of these kinds of covert operations. Sadat had come to power in 1970, and two years later he had thrown the Russians out of Egypt. The CIA soon had one of its premier bodyguard and intelligence-assistance programs under way. First, the United States wanted Sadat alive, but second it wanted a flow of inside intimate information about Sadat and about palace politics and maneuverings. Much of it was useless, but there was exhilaration within the CIA at having the close-in sources, cataloguing the vagaries, ambitions and policies of dozens of ministers and deputy ministers.

At points there was not sufficient evaluation of the intelligence "take." Quantity overwhelmed quality as a great flood of data poured in to the analysts. Secret intelligence became an addiction. At times it became impossible to evaluate, hard to sort out. The more the CIA knew, the less the CIA had. Leaders like Sadat used the operations as a kind of wedge, as if the operations gave them a back door to the United States government, a way of skirting normal diplomatic channels and calling upon the CIA, seeking special information, favors, even money.

Sadat treated the DCI himself like a case officer at times. William Colby opened his memoir *Honorable Men* with a description of a trip he made to Florida in 1975 "for a protocol meeting with visiting Egyptian President Anwar Sadat . . . to pay my respects." He had cooled his heels that afternoon, had spent the night sitting in a car outside Sadat's temporary residence and had never seen him. Sadat, instead, had given an interview to Barbara Walters. Colby mentioned the incident because it was the weekend he was fired by President Ford. He was not traveling from Washington just for "protocol" or to "pay respects." Even the gentle and unassuming Colby would not have spent his Saturday night in a car unless the relationship was important. Broadly speaking, Sadat was an intelligence asset, not directly in the pay of the CIA, not in any sense under its control, but he had opened himself and his country, in his definition of their mutual self-interest, to the CIA. It was very much a two-way street. But it was dangerous, for both sides.

Some very experienced CIA officials were skeptical of the relationship with Sadat, concluding that it was Sadat's method of operation: make everyone think they owned him. In some respects, he sold 110 percent of himself to the major players. The United States and the CIA thought they owned him; so did the Egyptian Army; so did the other Arab states; and at times after Camp David the Israelis thought so too. This was how Sadat held things together. Perhaps this tactic fostered his isolation from his own people. The day of reckoning came in the midst of complacency: the bodyguards and the security that had worked so long failed. His assassination at a public parade October 6, 1981, ended one of the CIA's most important intelligence relationships.

There was another key area in sensitive intelligence collection that Casey thought was turning out a lot of good material, often in the area of political intelligence. He had been the beneficiary of a dispute that had arisen and been settled during the Carter Administration, in 1978. At that time, the CIA and the NSA had run relatively independent and often overlapping signals intelligence surveillance operations abroad. The CIA's effort was an elite group called "Division D," which consisted of fewer than 100 CIA personnel. Generally speaking, the NSA did the intercepting of communications out of the air, and the CIA Division D people planted telephone or room eavesdropping devices. Hopping from country to country, U.S. embassy to U.S. embassy, Division D did some of the risky breaking and entering in foreign-government offices abroad to plant eavesdropping equipment.

By 1978, the overlap and the competition between the CIA and the NSA for signals intelligence was getting out of hand. In response, the congressional oversight committees cut off the funding for the CIA signals intelligence-gathering. This forced a joining of CIA and NSA efforts in the embassies.

By the end of 1983, joint CIA-NSA groups were working in about a third of the U.S. embassies abroad. Often manned by just two or three people, the teams were highly secret, highly compartmented, pooling the technical expertise of the NSA personnel and the more daring skills of the CIA. Called Special Collection Elements or Special Collection Sites, the teams produced excellent intelligence, especially when the U.S. embassy had a good, high location or was placed near foreign or defense ministries or other key offices or residences in the host country. The site chief was selected from either the CIA or the NSA, depending on the mission and the targets. These Special Collection Sites were particularly effective in Eastern European capitals.

But the key to success was advanced technology. The CIA and the NSA had developed techniques barely imagined by the host countries. Electronic eavesdropping of one sort or another was far ahead of the movies and the spy novels; phone lines and rooms could be tapped or bugged without physical intrusion or connection. Room conversations could sometimes be picked up from windows by electronically measuring the vibrations of the window glass with a small, invisible beam. Sent from a transmitter hundreds of feet from the window, the beam glanced off the window at an acute angle and was received and amplified at a receiving site several hundred feet away. In the late 1970s, the U.S. intelligence agencies had discovered that a standard microphone from a "hung-up" telephone in its cradle transmitted small impulses through the telephone wires that could be isolated and converted to sound. With access to the telephone lines and highly sophisticated equipment, the microphone in the telephone in every room or office became a potential room bug.

The special CIA-NSA sites in dozens of U.S. embassies were providing better and better intelligence, not only as technology and miniaturization improved, but as Casey pestered for more.

"Why don't we have coverage on this guy?" he would ask. He wanted an answer and generally didn't forget that he had asked the question. Over the years it was clear that the only acceptable answer was to get the coverage.

Casey realized that part of his problem was managing the giant bureaucracy. He had speedread the popular book *In Search of Excellence: Lessons from America's Best-Run Companies*. He was very impressed with the message endorsing action, entrepreneurship and simplicity, and wanted to do all those things to improve the CIA. He convened meetings, insisted that each branch submit ideas on how to make things better, the workers happier. In all about eight hundred ideas were submitted. During a period when he was sick at home he read every one of them and dictated his conclusions. In February 1984 a one-page CIA "Credo" was published and distributed, with nine points, each beginning, "We . . . ," making it clear that the CIA worked and produced for the President.

The objectives, according to Casey's "Credo" are ". . . timely and high quality . . . objective and unbiased . . . ready to challenge conventional wisdom . . . integrity, morality and honor and according to the spirit and letter of our law and Constitution . . . American values, security and national interest . . . confidentiality . . . unfailing loyalty to each other and to our common purpose . . . initiative, a commitment to excellence and a propensity for action."

The "Credo" generated a good deal of smirks and jokes throughout the agency.

By early 1984, Clarridge was reminding Casey they would need more than the $24 million that had been provided by Congress. Yeah, Casey knew. They were fighting with one hand tied behind their back, and that was the way Congress wanted it. It was absurd: $24 million was less than the cost of a modern jet. Casey thought Clarridge had done a magnificent job, keeping a contra army of 10,000 plus in the field, launching the mining—all on a shoestring. Casey might now have to go beg for a supplemental, mid-fiscal-year appropriation, something on the order of another $21 million. That would be humiliating and also difficult, especially with the approaching presidential campaign. Polls showed that a majority of Americans were fearful of a Central American war, and political calculation in the White House was simple: Keep Nicaragua and the CIA out of the headlines. Jim Baker was watching.

Casey needed a shortcut around Congress. Was there some way to skirt the meet-and-confer, debate-and-leak cycle of the past? He wanted some new ideas. Was there a way to beat Congress? With its own rules?

Nearly fifty years earlier, Casey had learned that rules could be mindlessly obeyed or imaginatively interpreted. That was 1937, when he was a twenty-four-year-old law school graduate. It was mid-Depression, and jobs were hard to come by. Casey found employment with the Tax Research Institute of America in New York. For twenty-five dollars a week, his task was to read the New Deal legislation closely and issue reports explaining and summarizing it. Businessmen, the leaders of American industry, neither understood nor welcomed FDR's efforts. Dictating his summaries into a primitive machine that used wax recording cylinders, Casey quickly established that the businessmen wanted neither comment nor praise nor criticism. Instead, they wanted to know what to do to achieve minimum compliance with the law: How do we get by FDR and Congress's new programs? Casey had done well at this.

Casey claimed he now wanted something imaginative. "I ain't going to violate the law," he asserted. Instead he would get around it. He wanted the minimum compliance that would protect him and the agency and lead to more money for the contras. Over the past several months he had watched with some amazement the Congress being manipulated from within by one of its own members. It was an object lesson.

At the time of the CIA's hard-won $24 million for the contras, the CIA had requested about $30 million for the covert assistance program for the resistance movement in Afghanistan. Then along had come a congressman, not even on the House Intelligence Committee, who virtually by himself had another $40 million added to the Afghan program, more than doubling the expenditure.

The congressman, Charles Wilson, was a tall, dapper, back-slapping Texas Democrat, an outspoken hawk whose congressional district exemplified the Texas wildcat spirit. Within the last year, Wilson had made three trips to Pakistan, where the Afghan covert program was being run. He had crossed the border into Soviet-controlled Afghanistan with the rebels. For Wilson, it was the right war at the right time. The $30 million, he concluded, was "peanuts." He wanted more dead Russians. "There were 58,000 dead in Vietnam and we owe the Russians one." On his most recent trip to Pakistan, Wilson learned that the problem for the rebels was the Soviet helicopters that dominated the air.

Wilson began lobbying to get some advanced antiaircraft weapons to the rebels. Claiming it was Pakistani President Zia's idea, Wilson proposed the high-tech, rapid-fire Swiss-made Oerlikon gun. Normally, Casey would have blown the whistle on some congressman who was attempting to micromanage agency business. But Wilson had made it a crusade, and he had found the means in the rules of Congress. The House Intelligence Committee was the so-called "authorizing" committee, but, in the complex, arcane divisions of congressional power, "authorization" of funds was only the first step. There was a two-tiered system: the actual money that had been authorized had to be formally appropriated by powerful appropriations committees. For that there was the House Appropriations Committee, where Charlie Wilson had a seat. When that committee met to deal with the Defense Department budget, Wilson said he wanted only one thing—more money for the Afghan rebels, the brave freedom fighters. Even though the Intelligence Committee had not authorized it, he wanted the money appropriated. He told how on one of his trips to the region an eleven-year-old Afghan boy had come to him and said don't kill all the Russians, because he wanted one left for him to kill when he grew up. Wilson's colleagues were moved not so much by his rhetoric as by his steadfastness.

How much more did he want?

Wilson said $40 million, pulling the number right out of the sky.

Since the committee was dealing with a Defense budget of close to $280 billion, that $40 million was an unnoticeable fraction. It was as if the committee was considering spending $7,000 and one member had only one obsession, the additional appropriation of $1. Wilson said that he would be willing to vote favorably on other matters to support those who would go along with the $40 million. He won.

Wilson was next assigned to the conference committee between the Senate and the House on the entire federal budget. His leverage was even greater. He won again.

Suddenly, Casey had an extra $40 million for the Afghan operation. The money was to come from the Pentagon budget, and Defense officials raised a storm within the Administration. The Pentagon circulated a secret study saying the antiaircraft Oerlikon gun was the wrong weapon for a guerrilla war. The special, expensive sophisticated ammunition that could pierce armor was state-of-the-art; the gun would require careful maintenance and would not last on the rough road to the Khyber Pass. But Wilson, a Naval Academy graduate, was a Pentagon friend, and the Pentagon gave in.

The Administration, through Budget Director David Stockman, sent a top-secret letter to the two intelligence committees, requesting "authorization" for the $40 million. Goldwater was enraged at the attempt to circumvent his committee and reverse the normal authorize-appropriate congressional process. It was a matter of power. If the Intelligence Committee didn't control covert operations by okaying the funding, the committee might as well not exist.

Wilson continued his campaign. He camped out at the offices of the House Intelligence Committee and lobbied hard. He found a way to use the controversial Nicaragua operation to his advantage. Many of his House colleagues who opposed the Nicaragua operation wanted to show they were not soft on Soviet expansionism. As Wilson presented it, the Afghan operation was the perfect vehicle to prove this. Among some Democrats, Nicaragua was the "bad" war, beleaguered Afghanistan the "good" war.

DDCI John McMahon weighed in with a top-secret letter supporting the $40 million increase and the Oerlikon gun. He had been the DDO during the Carter Administration when the operation was started (Casey called McMahon the "father" of the Afghan operation). Usually, McMahon was the resident skeptic about covert operations, but the nearly unanimous congressional support for Afghanistan had convinced him. His attitude helped turn the tide, and both the Senate and House committees approved.

Wilson told the CIA officials in the DO that they were too shy; they should have asked for more money themselves.

For Casey, it was a windfall. Not only was the $40 million an important boost to the Afghan program, but it showed that Congress could support and even get out ahead of the Administration on covert action. Casey felt it was a strong statement of purposefulness, which, for the moment at least, was as important as money or new weapons. The CIA was not familiar with the Oerlikon; one was obtained for testing and purchase of nine anticipated. It would take months, perhaps more than a year, to get them into the field in Afghanistan. But the psychological momentum was with the CIA. Casey wondered whether it might be redirected to Nicaragua, although it seemed that as support for Afghanistan grew, support for Nicaragua diminished. The real lesson, however, was in Wilson's method. He had wheeled the entire system—the DO, McMahon, Casey himself, the Administration, the House and the Senate.

16

ASSISTANT SECRETARY OF STATE TONY MOTLEY wanted to do his part for the Nicaragua operation, which was running out of money. Alaska Senator Ted Stevens—Motley's mentor—headed the Senate appropriations subcommittee for defense. Instead of dealing with Goldwater's Intelligence Committee (the authorizing committee), Motley suggested that the Administration try an end run as Charlie Wilson had done. Who gives a shit about the Intelligence Committee, Motley argued, when the Administration could deal directly in the real world—the appropriations committee that handled the money. So Motley carried a request for $21 million more for Nicaragua to Stevens, and explained that there was probably only a one-in-five chance of sneaking it through this way.

Stevens agreed to give it a try.

Before the first step could be taken, Goldwater found out. The goddamn Administration, he said, was its own worst enemy. It was a mindless, insensitive act, contrary to long-standing Senate rules and customs. He was their friend, on their side, in the same party. The CIA congressional-relations man, Clair George, said that it was Tony Motley's doing and that the White House did not know.

Nonetheless, on March 12, 1984, Goldwater and Moynihan wrote a secret letter directly to President Reagan strongly protesting the violation of Senate protocol. A copy of the letter was sent to Casey. Secretary of State George Shultz offered an apology to Goldwater.

This brought Goldwater back to the Administration's side, and late Thursday night, April 5, he was on the Senate floor attempting to win the $21 million for Casey. It was after the cocktail hour, and Goldwater, still suffering from various hip ailments and operations, was well medicated. At seventy-five, he was two years older than President Reagan, but as willing as ever to slug it out. Serving up the standard pro-Administration line, Goldwater chastised his colleagues for "congressional meddling with the efforts by the President to defend the national security."

As Goldwater spoke, Senator Biden, one of the more outspoken Casey critics on the Intelligence Committee, was at his small desk reading a classified memo prepared by a committee staff member. The memo stated that the CIA had played a direct role in placing underwater mines in three Nicaraguan harbors. This, according to the memo, all had been done by "unilaterally controlled Latino assets"—the UCLAs. Biden was surprised. He hadn't known about this, but it was possible that he had missed a hearing or a briefing. So he stood up and carried the memo over to his fellow Intelligence Committee member, Republican Bill Cohen.

Cohen read carefully. The memo made it clear that the CIA had planned, ordered and carried out harbor-mining. This was not a matter of support or supply. This was direct CIA action. Mining was not a borderline covert activity. It was one step further along the road than that memorable day when the Managua airport was attacked. Mining was an act of war. The squalor of the entire operation became clearer than ever, Cohen thought.

He walked over to Goldwater and handed the memo to him.

"Barry, what the fuck is this?" Cohen asked sharply. "Is this true? Why haven't I been told?"

Goldwater, angry and caught off balance, asked for permission to speak on the floor, and began reading the classified memo to his colleagues. Goldwater's staff director, Rob Simmons, raced over to Cohen, demanding, "Get him off, get him down, stop him from reading that."

It was one of Simmons' nightmares that Goldwater or some other senator might take to the floor with sensitive, classified information, giving Casey and the CIA ammunition to further cut back on the information flow and brand the committee untrustworthy.

Cohen didn't move fast enough on Goldwater, and Simmons shot across the floor himself and almost pulled the memo from Goldwater's hands.

Goldwater and Simmons looked at each other. Mining? Why hadn't they been told? They, if anybody, were supposed to know. Was this something that Casey had passed on to Goldwater personally? Goldwater said it was not. Simmons said he hadn't a clue, either. They had saved the covert program several times in the last couple of years. Why were they kept in the dark?

"You get hold of Bill Casey," Goldwater said, "and find out what the fuck's going on."

Simmons had Goldwater's reading excised from *The Congressional Record*. Nonetheless, David Rogers, a reporter for *The Wall Street Journal,* had it in the next morning's paper, though the account was somewhat understated—"U.S. Role in Mining Nicaraguan Harbors Reportedly Is Larger Than First Thought."

Simmons spent the next day trying to get John McMahon on the phone.

"I've been busy," McMahon said when Simmons finally reached him.

"Did you know about this?" Simmons asked coldly.

McMahon was evasive, but he said that Casey had told the committee members at a breakfast at the CIA.

Simmons checked. Goldwater had never been to one of Casey's breakfasts at the CIA.

The information came in slowly to the Senate committee. About seventy-five so-called "firecracker" mines had been laid on the bottom in three Nicaraguan harbors. But many of the homemade mines had up to 300 pounds of C-4 explosive. Simmons had worked with C-4, and 300 pounds was enough for a giant explosion. A number of merchant seamen or fishermen had been wounded and there was a report that one had been killed. Before the mining, Nicaragua had received much of its oil from Mexico and Europe. Now the Soviets had become the chief supplier of oil, providing up to 80 percent. So, Simmons calculated, the first immediate result of the mining had been to drive the Nicaraguans further into the arms of the Soviet Union.

Simmons could remember, from his time as a DO officer, the expression the real cowboys used for this kind of harassment: "Let's bring a little pee on them." The mining was like the CIA operations run out of Miami against Cuba in the 1960s. The CIA had become the bogeyman, and that helped Castro secure total control over the population.

"You know," Goldwater told Simmons, "I feel like a boob. I misled my colleagues." The committee existed to prevent such surprises, and Goldwater felt that he had failed. The mining, Goldwater said, endangered neutral shipping. A British ship had been hit. Imagine what would happen if an American ship hit a British mine secretly laid in some port. Goldwater shook his head. "You tell Casey that he's on his own. I've pulled his nuts out of the fire often enough."

Goldwater went off for the weekend to the Quinns' farm on the Eastern Shore of Maryland. It had become Goldwater's regular weekend retreat, where he did various electronic chores—fixing the TV antenna or wiring up stereo speakers. It was a beautiful spring weekend, but Goldwater could not shake the feeling of betrayal. It just struck him dumb. Obviously, the Administration and Casey had no confidence in him.

Goldwater carried a little cassette dictating machine which he regularly filled with notes, ideas and letters. Pushing the record button, he began a "Dear Bill" letter to Casey:

"... I've been trying to figure out how I can most easily tell you my feelings about the discovery of the President having approved mining some of the harbors of Central America.

"It gets down to one, little, simple phrase: I am pissed off!"

Goldwater ordered it sent to Casey.

Casey called Quinn. "I don't understand the degree of his concern," Casey said. "He's so exercised."

Quinn reminded Casey that Goldwater cooled as rapidly as he got hot. Casey acknowledged that and hung up. He too was pissed off. He too felt caught in the middle, this time between the White House/State Department, which wanted more in Nicaragua, and the Congress, which wanted less.

Casey had been asked by the White House whether there was not some way to divert money from other CIA operations or "slush funds" to the Nicaraguan operation. Couldn't the CIA just dip into the $50 million contingency? Wasn't that its purpose?

The contingency fund was for emergency operations, or to be used when Congress was not in session. Casey knew he would be tarred and feathered if he took an extra penny for Nicaragua. And further, McMahon, general counsel Sporkin and the others in the DO were vehemently opposed to any effort that might make it appear that congressional will was being thwarted. A legal opinion was drawn up that warned sternly against any attempt to skirt the letter or the spirit of the congressional authority.

Casey had thought the mining was a dream operation: results without real bloodshed. Now it looked as though the only blood might be his own. Reports showed that the mines were doing the job. Just recently seven ships had been hit by mines in Corinto, the largest Nicaraguan port. Other ships were turning back. Cotton was stacked two stories high there awaiting ships willing to brave the harbor. Coffee beans and sugarcane, Nicaragua's two other major exports, were also piling up. There was talk inside Nicaragua of economic devastation.

Newspapers had widely reported the mining and its impact. Statements by the Sandinista leadership charging the United States with responsibility had been published. So why was the Senate surprised? Casey and his aides went to the transcripts of his previous top-secret presentations to the Senate committee. There in clear prose was all he needed—a rare, graphic vindication.

• • •

A month earlier, on March 8, Casey had said to the full committee, "Magnetic mines have been placed in the Pacific harbor of Corinto and the Atlantic harbor of El Bluff, as well as the oil terminal at Puerto Sandino." Then five days later, on March 13, Casey repeated the same sentence, omitting only the word "magnetic" because some of the mines were activated by the sound of a ship passing overhead.

This was no offhand disclosure. He had said it, and the committee members had had no questions. If no one had understood, that was their problem. Casey went to see Bud McFarlane at the White House, where the mining was now perceived as a blunder, especially by Jim Baker. In principle, no one had been opposed to the mining when it was approved. The question was, why couldn't it have been kept covert.

McFarlane thought Casey was one of the strong, independent forces he had to attempt to coordinate. Casey had a separate, well-defined agenda and a mandate given to him by the President. But at times, especially in various maneuverings or compromises with Congress, Casey could be a problem. McFarlane, who had worked several years on the Hill, found it pigheaded and self-defeating that Casey would not get along with the intelligence committees—the obvious source of the latest flap.

But this time Casey cited the record of his March 8 and March 13 testimony, plunking down copies of his testimony before the national-security adviser. What more was he supposed to do? Goldwater's tirade had been because the Senator was tired or overmedicated or both.

McFarlane seemed convinced.

On Tuesday, April 10, Casey made a detailed presentation to a group of senators not on the Intelligence Committee, explaining how and when he had told the committee. He had spent a hundred hours up on the Hill testifying. As always, he said, we answered any question the committee or an individual senator asked at any time. Overall, the mining was not that important or integral a part of the covert operation. All the fuss was unnecessary.

Some senators criticized the indiscriminate nature of a mining operation. On the mine that had gone off under a British ship, one senator asked, What were we doing trying to harass our closest ally? Another mine had been detonated by a Soviet vessel. Did Casey want to start World War III? How would the United States react if a U.S. merchant ship had run into a mine field laid by the KGB?

Casey went to the Intelligence Committee. It was apparent from the reaction, particularly among Republicans, that there had been a monumental lapse in communication. Though Casey had said it, no one had heard or comprehended.

Senator David Durenberger, a Minnesota Republican, was incredulous. It seemed to him that the DCI was saying that the United States had committed an act of war for the hell of it. Cohen was still stewing. There was a hole in the logic. Casey was saying that the mines were designed to do little damage, and yet mining was a general act of belligerency. Why take such a risk if there was no military or strategic value? The mining was being perceived as an escalation of an ambiguous and unclear policy. When do you call the secret war off? Cohen wondered. When does covert action become simple (or complicated) war? The committee was there to be a top-secret sounding board; if a new operation passed by them without heavy opposition, it would likely be tolerated by the public. The committee could have warned Casey about the mining.

Wallop was one of the few senators on Casey's side. Criticizing the mining as a half-measure, he said they might as well blow up everyone and everything in Nicaragua. Several liberal Democrats suggested that the only way out was to make the entire contra program overt, suggesting that they would support such a move. Wallop laughed. He figured they would say that only in a closed and classified hearing. Some Democrats began saying in public that the next step was sending U.S. combat troops, and several press reports suggested that such plans were afoot. So Casey, Shultz, Weinberger and McFarlane issued an extraordinary three-page public statement under all four names, saying in part: "We state emphatically that we have not considered, nor have we developed plans to use U.S. military forces to invade Nicaragua or any other Central American country."

It was too late. The Senate, seized with antiwar fever, delivered the coup de théâtre the night the statement was released. In a tone that suggested that Casey shoots his friends too, Goldwater said on the Senate floor that the previous week he had had his remarks struck from *The Congressional Record*—the first time in almost thirty years of Senate service.

"I am forced to apologize to the members of my committee because I did not know the facts on this case," Goldwater said. "And I apologize to all members of the Senate for the same reason."

It was clear that a moral boundary had been crossed and some loathsome fragment of sin excavated. There was a crucial division that separated the acceptable from the unacceptable. Mining was unacceptable. The debate asked the question: Have we, as a nation, no decency? It was almost as though the mining was a "national" act, a statement of national character. Mining was sneaky, a shadowy endeavor, akin to planting a bomb in a restaurant, a trap for the unsuspecting and innocent. Goldwater's disapproval magnified the issue. He loomed as an arbiter of toughness and common sense. Privately he called the mining "the dumbest fucking idea I ever heard of."

Senator Edward Kennedy introduced a nonbinding, sense-of-the-Congress resolution condemning the mining and proclaiming that no money could be spent for the "planning, directing, or supporting the mining of the ports or territorial water of Nicaragua."

It passed 84 to 12.

Casey could not believe that the Republican-controlled Senate would do this. The senators might disagree, but this was national policy—approved by the President and carried out by the CIA, after proper notification of Congress. The vote was not a rejection. It was self-mortification.

At a state dinner for the President of the Dominican Republic, President Reagan said publicly of the Senate vote, "If it is not binding, I can live with it. I think there is a great hysteria raised about this whole thing. We are not going to war."

Goldwater's letter to Casey leaked from the Senate and was broadcast and printed with no expletives deleted.

The next day, April 11, 1984, Senator Leahy had drinks with two of his aides in his hideaway office in the Senate. It was a small, cavelike room that had once been used by Daniel Webster. Leahy was pleased. As far as he was concerned the mining exposed the bankruptcy of the entire covert operation. Furthermore, he said he knew for sure that Casey was not trying to deceive the senators or keep them, particularly Goldwater, from knowing about the mining.

Why?

Because Leahy had known about it for weeks. His father had died and he had been out for several weeks. Upon his return to the Senate, he had asked for a CIA briefing to update him on the Nicaragua operation. The CIA had laid out the mining in detail. No way would they tell him and consciously keep it from Goldwater.

Why had he not said or done something?

Because, Leahy said, the mining was a logical extension of an undeclared, secret war. Once you accepted the assumption that there was a need for such a covert operation, the mining made sense. Of course, he accepted none of those assumptions. He didn't think covert action was a substitute for a long-term, reasoned foreign policy. There was an unstable, makeshift, on-again, off-again quality to any covert operation. In fact, Leahy said, Casey was justified in being stunned by the outcry. The Congress had gone along with everything else in the secret war. Why not this?

It's an act of war, one of the aides said.

Leahy almost laughed. What did they think organizing and supplying the contra army of thousands was? Peace?

"This thing is a watershed," Leahy said, because it will split the intelligence committee and destroy the bipartisanship. "There have been many unanimous votes—we have been a sounding board for many cockamamie ideas." He promised that in the future that would not work as well. Casey and the Administration, he said, need a united committee to tell them when the ideas and plans are crazy. The committee acts as a final screening, and if there is general consensus or agreement, then something can be turned off or stopped.

"I've never seen Casey so on the defensive," Leahy said. "They are like a bunch of kids sitting down there. It's like playing cowboys and Indians, playing games, a Saturday-afternoon matinée." It's not going to work, he said. "We've put people in motion whom we have no control over." The end result, he said, would likely be some kind of combat in Central America.

Clair George could see his twenty-seven-year CIA career ending in flames. He alternated between defensiveness and contrition. "We busted our ass to keep them informed," he shouted into the phone to one caller. "We brief them, brief them, brief them! I don't know what the fuck to do." And, he said, the senators now think, "Those evil bastards" out at the CIA. It was all politics, and each legislator was positioning himself according to the latest winds. "The only thing more we could have done is install a teletype down there and let them see the daily cables!" He felt that some of the senators might have legitimate gripes. Others didn't. And others were just lying and posturing. "If some had been shown movies, they would not be satisfied."

George had been in tighter spots, and when he cooled off he realized that the covert war, the mining, was of course a sensitive issue. "It is as emotional an issue as we can have in our time, and we are perceived to have hidden it. This is so fucking demoralizing!"

He felt that Goldwater was a good man, a dedicated supporter. When Goldwater said he was not satisfied, that carried a lot of weight. When Goldwater said he was pissed off, he carried the whole Senate.

How was Casey handling the criticism? George was asked. Casey was attending a family funeral that day.

"With strength," George said, adding admiringly, "He has balls of magnesium!"

In his nine months as head of congressional relations, George had had a regular monthly lunch at a downtown restaurant with Goldwater's staff director Rob Simmons to insure that there was regular communication.

Simmons realized he had been had. George was treating Congress like the host government in a foreign country where he was sent to spy. Simmons told George, "I don't consider you my case officer and I hope you don't think of yourself as my case officer."

"No, no, no," George said. Simmons said technical compliance by burying the mining in two long statements was insufficient. The committee needed and expected a tip-off to what was important. George had no answer, and their relationship was over.

The next day, I went to the CIA to be briefed for a trip I was making to Libya. The Libyan Foreign Minister had said that I should be able to interview Qaddafi. I was surprised that one of the briefers was a very senior officer in the DO, a cool, perfectly dressed man with no smile. His message was: Qaddafi feels increasingly threatened and has turned up the heat and the assassination squads on any external anti-Qaddafi group. Qaddafi is a man of big, big dreams, a leader without a true base or center, a man in search of a country, the DO officer said. He moves all the time, sleeping in different places, fearing and thinking that the CIA is trying to kill him.

I didn't ask whether the CIA was trying. The DO officer's manner seemed to turn aside the question as I contemplated asking it.

Qaddafi is trying to break out of a psychological vise, he said. He is like Castro, implacable, but also in Arab fashion trying to approach his enemies, sending signals to the United States that he would like to talk. The officer alternated between labeling Qaddafi treacherous and calling him weak. For example, Qaddafi, he said, has female bodyguards, knowing that an Arab assassin would have trouble shooting a woman. Clever, the officer said. Qaddafi's reinterpretation of Islam has caused problems, "his irregular fundamentalism" placing a cloud over his relationship with Iran and the Shiite world. And Khomeini refused to accept an invitation to meet with Qaddafi, "an extraordinary snub."

Qaddafi's relationship with the Soviets is cynical and practical, he said. There is no formal or secret agreement. It is a mercenary relationship. Qaddafi buys so much from them, a billion a year, but that is also to insure redundancy so that he won't have to go begging for spare parts, the officer explained.

What about the reports that Qaddafi is supplying arms to Nicaragua?

It's the "Third World Club," the officer said. More solidarity than anything. The arms to Nicaragua are not substantial, only small arms.

He noted that the Libyan economy is primitive and so it is hard to hurt. Economic sanctions mean little.

What should I ask Qaddafi?

Poker-faced, the officer suggested that I ought to ask, "I understand you are full of sleeping pills—you look drugged. Do you have trouble sleeping?"

There was a kind of social and intellectual disdain for Qaddafi, a tendency almost to twit him. But there was also the combatant's esteem. The officer said that Qaddafi had had a respiratory problem when he was in his twenties, and was not in great health. Qaddafi, he said, is overwrought, high-strung, capable of doing much and of doing little, and has recently been making morbid references in his speeches.

I had received valid information, I thought, a rather carefully calibrated introduction, but I also had a lingering feeling that this master covert operator had been planting a seed. He had overdone it slightly, painting the Libyan leader a little too much a loon. As I reviewed the conversation and my notes, I realized I couldn't tell whether I was being "fed." As facts or analysis, it seemed honest, straight, certainly helpful. But I couldn't get rid of the notion that the suggested question to Qaddafi had other purposes.

As I was leaving late that afternoon, one of Casey's senior deputies who was familiar with the Nicaragua operation took me aside and suggested we talk. We went into his seventh-floor office, and the door was closed. This was "background," he said, plopping himself down in a chair. He knew that meant I could use the information as long as I didn't identify him or the agency by name.

It was virtually the end of the Nicaragua operation, he said flatly. The DO had just been informed that the money would run out next week, perhaps as early as Sunday. Three days from now. The accounts showed that two weeks ago $22 million of the allocated $24 million had already been spent, leaving $2 million. Clearly the requested $21 million more was not going to be forthcoming from an enraged Congress. He laughed hard, recalled the Senate anti-mining vote, 84 to 12, and noted the likelihood that the House was about to do the same (it did so, by a vote of 281 to 111, several hours later). So steps were going to be taken to begin the painful process of disengagement, he said, get the agency out.

Casey, the official continued, is considering a request to another friendly country to take up the slack and send money to the contras until the funding problem is solved.

You said you were on the verge of disengagement.

Oh, the official said, Casey thinks we'll eventually get the new money, that the mining storm will blow over. But "the Director," he said for emphasis, is the only one here at the agency who thinks that.

What country is he going to ask?

Saudi Arabia, but no final decision has been made.

I wrote it down in my notes. It had to be clear to him that I would publish this, but it was not clear to me whether what I was being told was a trial balloon or whether I had been told in the hope that publication would sabotage the possibility of asking the Saudis for help.

This official described to me how Casey had been the moving force behind the secret war and the controversial mining. "Casey cooked this whole thing up," he said categorically.

I scribbled the word "distancing" in my notes; evidently this was an attempt to separate the mainline CIA from Casey and Casey's war, "cooked up" or whatever.

There was much opposition in the building to the whole thing, the official volunteered. John McMahon believed from the beginning that it was folly, ill-conceived.

There had been whispers of this before, but I was surprised to have it put to me so directly, and I asked a few questions. The official looked at me as if I were asking him which side Abraham Lincoln had been on in the Civil War.

"John just knew it would come to this, where there would not be enough public and congressional support and we'd withdraw," he said flatly. He turned to the State Department, which had recently issued a legal opinion saying the mining was "self-defense." The State Department opinion "unfortunately is bullshit," the official said scornfully. The real issue was that it proved once again that the left and right hands of the Administration did not know what the other was doing. Nothing like that would have come out of the CIA legal department, he said.

The whole operation, he continued glumly, was pretty much a bust. While the effort was hurting the Nicaraguan economy, it had not slowed the flow of arms into El Salvador. "It went down after Grenada, but now it's going up and may even be higher."

But, I said, we all know the real reason is to overthrow the Sandinistas.

He laughed, and laughed again. Ha, ha, ha. Oh, that was funny, no fucking chance of that either.

Simple arithmetic, he said. Outnumbered four to one. The Sandinistas had a military and police force of about 75,000. And the National Security Council had pegged the ceiling on the number of CIA-supported contras at 18,000. At maximum the contras had 15,000 operating and the till was nearly dry. End of operation.

I made a number of phone calls to see whether the broad outline was correct. It at least represented the position of the agency professional core. I had talked with George Lauder, the CIA spokesman, about McMahon's position on the Nicaragua operation. The McMahon position opposing the operation was known all over the agency and all over the Hill, he said. Lauder added only that whatever personal opinions and conclusions McMahon may have voiced, he was not opposed to any current CIA operations. The story ran as the lead on the next morning's front page under a large, three-column headline, "CIA Funds Run Short for Covert Operation."

When I got to the office the next morning, there was a call from Lauder. I was pretty sure that Casey would be upset with his portrayal as chief architect of the operation. A deputy, identified as an "informed source" in the story, was quoted as saying, "Casey cooked this whole thing up." Lauder was icy and said he had a statement that John McMahon had told him to issue, shotgun style, to all main news organizations.

McMahon? I asked.

Lauder began reciting: "I am anxious to refute the reference to my views on our Nicaraguan activities which appeared in *The Washington Post* in its April 13 edition. While Director Casey encourages debate on all our intelligence proposals, he and I are of one mind when it comes to agency activities and that includes those involving the Sandinistas in Nicaragua. This position is also shared by other senior agency officials."

What the hell am I supposed to do with that? I asked.

I don't know, Lauder said, up to you, and he said he had to run.

McMahon's statement was thrown into the bottom of one of the next day's mining stories—there were three or four each day now.

There were sophisticated forces in the CIA itself now that were arrayed against Casey. The CIA official who had cornered me the day before knew the art of propaganda: scatter the seeds of doubt, water them, let them spring up, and cut them down if necessary. The groundwork was being laid for the postmortem of the Nicaragua operation. McMahon, the repository of good sense, had been opposed all along, had seen the inevitable bailout from Casey's "cooked-up" war. At the same time, he was on record with a loyal-to-the-Director declaration. McMahon was squarely on both sides of the issue. If the operation turned out to be the disaster it seemed to be becoming, he and his allies could point to the original account, and to his track record of doubt. Should the operation flourish, they could point to his rare public pronouncement in which he declared himself to Casey.

Over at the State Department, Tony Motley read McMahon's public statement with amusement. In nearly a year as the working-level point man for the Administration on the covert Nicaragua operation, Motley had come to a deeply cynical view of internal maneuverings at the CIA. McMahon was the most accomplished bureaucratic infighter. Unparalleled. Anyone who knew him knew that McMahon was fighting more than Nicaragua. He was after the paramilitary capability Casey was trying to recreate. The commando days of the CIA were over, McMahon had decided, with rare exceptions like Afghanistan. He had said it a hundred times: the CIA was supposed to steal secrets and to analyze. Period.

In Motley's opinion, McMahon was disloyal. It was he who followed up after Casey, often within a few hours, carefully edging the Director's policy the other way, always with well-crafted indirectness. It was hard to find a single phrase or sentence from McMahon that contradicted the boss. He knew how to present the opposite side as if it were an abstraction: "Critics will say . . ." But often the weight of McMahon's statements and position went the other way. "John, I'm confused," Motley once said to McMahon. "The Director said the exact opposite." It was a highwire act, and Motley was often convinced that McMahon had gone off the end and would be fired. But it never happened. Motley finally concluded that McMahon had figured out Casey better than anyone else, understood that Casey felt it necessary to have someone pushing him hard. But that was not a sufficient explanation, and Motley wondered whether McMahon maybe had something on Casey. Motley had once said jokingly, "McMahon had somehow caught Casey sucking cock!"

When McMahon heard that, he burst into uncontrollable laughter and his flabby face turned beet red. He seemed as if he might explode, fly out over the orange chairs in his seventh-floor office, break through the large picture windows and plunge over the balcony onto the Virginia countryside. The very excessiveness of his reaction was a perfect diversion, because he didn't have to comment. He let the laughter die and he had said nothing.

At his alma mater, Holy Cross, he had been called "Smiling Jack" and a "Mother Hen," according to his yearbook, "most welcome in any bull session. His hearty laugh is a sure thing after every anecdote," even distinguishable in a crowded, dark movie theater—"a deep-throated roar." His senior thesis: "The Emotional Conflict of Four of Shakespeare's Tragic Heroines." A man of mystery, conflict and mordant wit, he had learned to play Casey perfectly.

Casey just didn't believe that McMahon had been disloyal. "I don't believe it," Casey said firmly when asked about possible disloyalty or discrepancy.

Motley finally figured out the answer: the CIA was going through an identity crisis, wrestling with its role in the world. Were its people dirty-tricksters? Yes, when asked to be. They served the Director and the President. Did they fight the Soviets at every turn, at all costs? Yes. Did they watch the entire world? They tried. Were they the intellectual, high-camp analysts, turning a phrase, doing brilliant "papers" that dazzled the few who had the security clearances to read them? Did they do Casey's bidding? Or the bidding of the institution, with McMahon as their spokesman? There weren't complete answers to these questions, Motley concluded, and the answers seemed to change daily. So the agency was run in an atmosphere of total contradiction.

A daily environment of changing answers can lead to more than an identity crisis, Motley realized. If it is not stabilized, the result can be, even for an institution, a nervous breakdown. It had happened in the 1970s. It could happen again. Half the agency men seemed to be following Casey around panting, bowing to his every wish—Dewey Clarridge for one. The other half seemed to pause—John McMahon for one—pondering this question: What after the storm of this man?

On Friday afternoon, April 13, Goldwater left for a trip to the Far East. Moynihan became acting chairman of the Senate Intelligence Committee, which placed the mining fiasco in his lap. Moynihan had been mortified to learn of the mining first from *The Wall Street Journal* because he had not been on the Senate floor that night. He had called Clair George.

"Clair, what have you done?" Moynihan asked. "What are you doing to us?"

"The ship that did the mining," George responded, "is now, as we talk, passing through the Panama Canal." No more mines would be laid, he promised.

That wasn't enough. Moynihan had watched with relish as Goldwater dished out his "I-am-pissed-off" letter and as the Congress came down firmly against mining. Casey and McMahon were going to come by later in the day to go over the entire matter with Moynihan. Maybe that would straighten things out.

When Casey and McMahon arrived at Moynihan's office, Moynihan came out smiling and threw his arms around Casey. Casey had a question: Was Goldwater losing his marbles?

Moynihan seemed willing to forgive because Casey seemed to half apologize. But later Moynihan saw a front-page story in *The Washington Times* reporting on NSC adviser McFarlane's statements at a Naval Academy conference about the mining: "Every important detail . . . shared in full . . . as provided by law . . . faithfully" with the oversight committees. Moynihan had helped draft the Intelligence Oversight Act of 1980 that required the committees to be "fully and currently informed of all intelligence activities."

It just hadn't happened. The mining reference was twenty-seven words, about ten seconds in a two-hour-and-eighteen-minute presentation; one sentence in eighty-four pages of transcript. Moynihan decided that the CIA posture amounted to a flat rejection of Goldwater's letter. In an interview with ABC Television's David Brinkley show that afternoon, which was to be broadcast Sunday, April 15, Moynihan said, "Senator Goldwater made his judgment as clear as words could do, and four or five days after that they still reject his judgment, so they now have my judgment in the only way I can make it, which is to say, I resign." He was quitting as vice-chairman.

Senator Durenberger lashed out at Casey, saying that "on a 0 to 10 scale, Casey rates a 2 on the trust factor." For *Time* he went further: "There is no use in our meeting with Bill Casey. None of us believe him. The cavalier, almost arrogant fashion in which he has treated us as individuals has turned the whole committee against him."

President Reagan stayed above the fray. Over the weekend he appeared at the downtown Washington Hilton Hotel for the White House Correspondents Association annual black-tie dinner.

"What's all that talk about a breakdown of White House communications? How come nobody told me?" Laughter. "Well, I know this: I've laid down the law, though, to everyone there from now on about anything that happens, that no matter what time it is, wake me, even if it's in the middle of a Cabinet meeting." Laughter. The official presidential documents recorded that the President received twenty-six more laughs.

He did not refer to the mining.

Casey gave a long interview to *U.S. News & World Report* in which he declared, "I think that people in the long run are less concerned about reports of mining Nicaraguan harbors than they are about the danger of creating a wave of immigration into this country if Central America or any part of it should fall under Soviet-Cuban domination." Over the weekend, in a salvage operation, the CIA released agency figures on the hemispheric threat offered by the Soviets and the Cubans: up to 10,000 Soviets in Cuba, but only 100 in Nicaragua; and possibly 10,000 Cubans in Nicaragua. The CIA and the DIA had had several six-hour meetings to come up with a reliable estimate and had failed to do so. The numbers were flaky. But numbers couldn't cloak the problem. Nor did a CIA statement that claimed, "The subject of mining of Nicaraguan ports has been discussed with members or staffers of the committees and other members of Congress 11 times."

Simmons publicly laid into Clair George, saying the congressional liaison man had "the same mindset as Casey. . . . That match is a prescription for disaster."

At the CIA, John McMahon saw the matter spinning out of control, putting Casey and the agency back in the soup. With Goldwater in the Far East and Moynihan on the warpath, McMahon phoned Simmons. McMahon, an administrative officer, knew what it was like to be cut out. Simmons was probably furious because he felt like a fool. Yes, he was supposed to be informed by the CIA, but it was also his job to find out. Simmons had to know from his previous work at the CIA that good intelligence—even intelligence to which he was entitled—did not come on a silver platter. Simmons needed a little bucking up.

"Hi, Rob," McMahon said.

"Hello, John," Simmons replied.

"Look," McMahon said, "we've got to cut down the noise level. This is hurting everyone. Why don't you work your side and I'll work mine." They were all about to self-immolate. McMahon's pitch was they had crazy bosses and it was up to them to keep the ship afloat—good staff men to the end.

Simmons replied that Goldwater was being attacked, and that false and very misleading statements were being given to the press, and that he had in these circumstances an obligation to set the record straight. Casey and Clair George had not kept them informed. Goldwater's work on the committee for five years had been undercut. The work had been supposed to help create a new image for the CIA, insure protections for all, money, rebuilding the bridges. Five years of honest effort had been destroyed by this idiotic lapse in communication. Barry and I feel we're in the dustbin and our whole philosophical approach—trust, confidence—has been shattered, Simmons said.

McMahon said he understood. The pieces had to be picked up. He was encouraging.

"Having got that off my chest," Simmons finally relented. "Okay, let's tone down the rhetoric."

Within the White House and the National Security Council there was concern that Casey had poisoned the well in Congress, making further intelligence or foreign-policy maneuvers by the Administration more difficult. Still committed to an aggressive Central America policy, the White House wanted to reframe the debate, get it away from a discussion of Casey's forthrightness, the CIA and covert action.

Casey, on the other hand, saw the covert war in Nicaragua partly as a war of nerves. It was crucial that the CIA not let the Sandinistas up. Pressure. Harassment. Diversion. Hit them from all sides. All fronts.

Casey's fear was that the current flap would lead to White House hesitation. Downtown was the real constituency. He never wanted to lose sight of that. This led Casey to the eternal problem of reading the White House. It spoke with too many voices. It wasn't hard to figure what the President wanted—no U.S. combat troops and virtually all the covert support possible. But in the tug and pull among the staff, things sometimes came out differently. On one hand, Jim Baker had ordained election-year caution. On the other, someone on Bud McFarlane's National Security Council staff was always coming up with a new action plan. One called for a blockade of Nicaragua. In its extreme version, the plan seemed to call for almost half the U.S. fleet to control all the sea lanes going into Nicaragua. Casey never took too much of that seriously. But neither could he discard it. There was no telling when the President would act. It had happened unexpectedly in Grenada.

The passive Reagan approach to decision-making compounded the problem. Casey knew, clear as a bell, where Ronald Reagan stood, what he believed, but there was no telling what Reagan would do. "Yes," the President would say. Then "Well . . ." Then "No." "Yes . . . well . . . no" became a metaphor. There were many other variations—starting with a "no" and skidding through a "yes" to eventual irresolution. Jim Baker had buttoned up Reagan's decision-making completely. Casey could get his say, he could even get a private meeting with Reagan in the White House residence. Casey played this card about twice a year. The President was always so friendly, all ears and nods. But at the end of the meeting or later, through Baker or McFarlane, came the inevitable questions. What does George or Cap think? That brought Shultz and Weinberger into the issue. Properly so, but then the wobbly seesawing would begin. "Yes . . . well . . . no."

Reagan didn't chair, formally or informally, the National Security Council meetings or the more important NSPGs. McFarlane usually did so. Reagan would be given a one-sheet agenda, indicating what each person was going to talk about and for how many minutes. Most of the time was spent on status reports. Often the decisions went out later over McFarlane's signature for the President.

Baker and Darman got the daily phone log of every call in to Reagan and every one that he placed. Separate logs were kept for the regular phone lines and the secure line, which Reagan didn't like because of his hearing problem. The Secret Service kept a log of all his movements and meetings; even the White House ushers kept logs. There was a weekend log, even of Nancy's social calls, lunches and dinners. Some of Nancy's activities often drifted into the President's orbit. A talk with the President after a simple greeting or a quick hello could become, in the mind of the visitor, a firm expression or even a decision. So Baker or Darman followed up everything, making sure nothing escaped their net. The President was obviously comfortable with the system, and no one broke through.

But the mining disclosure now required some White House decisions. Casey had intelligence reports showing tons of material flowing into El Salvador, some from Nicaragua. He pressed the White House with intelligence information about a possible major autumn offensive by the leftist rebels in El Salvador. He compared such an eventuality to the famous Tet offensive of 1968 in Vietnam. It was strong language, but in the election year it commanded attention.

Motley believed the intelligence, but it was fragmented, not simple. "All you need is that thirty-second news clip that proves it to put this debate to bed," he told Casey. But the news clip never came.

After a series of meetings and discussions at the White House, Casey obtained as clear a decision from the President as he was going to get. Reagan agreed: Until the November election, the CIA would conduct a "holding action" in the covert program. When he was reelected, as he expected, the Administration would go all out, obtain more money for the contras some way, gain the upper hand and win.

For Casey, a holding action meant he was going to have to mend some fences in Congress. That included a personal, door-to-door grovel. One of his first visits was with Senator Richard Lugar, the Indiana Republican on the Intelligence Committee who was also chairman of the Republican senatorial-campaign committee. Lugar said they had a bad situation, and Casey said he had tried to keep everyone informed, but acknowledged that the brief references to the mining were not satisfactory.

Casey wanted to undo the Moynihan resignation. Moynihan was basically a hard-liner on foreign policy and had been useful to the CIA. A more liberal, anti-CIA Democrat such as Leahy as the Intelligence Committee vice-chairman would be disaster.

Casey went to see Moynihan in his Senate office. Sitting in the leather chair by Moynihan's office fireplace, the Director was contrite.

He made it clear that it had been his job to keep the committee informed at a level the senators found satisfactory. If they were not satisfied, no matter how sincere or conscientious his efforts, he had failed them. He stopped just short of saying that his failure broke the legal requirement for congressional notification. "I profoundly apologize," Casey said. Adding a personal appeal, he requested that Moynihan stay on as the vice-chairman.

Moynihan was touched. Casey seemed quite sincere—what a complicated man, so many different personalities. There was no way to reject such an apology. Moynihan agreed to withdraw his resignation.

The final act of contrition for Casey, on hands and knees, was a handwritten letter of apology to Goldwater.

On Thursday, April 26, Casey faced the music and met with the full committee. The atmosphere was tense, because some members felt that up to this point Casey was saying only that what hadn't happened in the first place would never happen again.

But Casey quickly shifted ground and acknowledged that the briefings had not been adequate. He wished he had done more. There was no intention to hide anything, some of the senators had been told, the House had been told.

A question about the mining itself: Wasn't it illegal?

No, Casey said.

This unleashed the pent-up resentment, and nearly everyone pounced hard on Casey, raising questions about law, good sense, judgment, practicality, competence. Hadn't ships of our friends, the British and the French, been hit by the mines? Why had the Administration declared in advance that it would not abide by a decision on the mining by the World Court, flouting the law in the face of the rest of the world? Wasn't mining state-supported terrorism? Hadn't all this added up to the United States being convicted before the eyes of the international community?

Casey said, "I apologize profoundly."

Jake Garn, the Utah Republican, was enraged. He felt that the two sentences had been clear and amounted to satisfactory notification. The CIA had always answered his questions, even if he had to go out to their headquarters to get the answers.

"You're all assholes," Garn screamed, "you're all assholes—the whole Congress is full of assholes, all five hundred thirty-five members are assholes."

Members stood up, including Moynihan, who wanted to prevent a further confrontation. "Smile," Moynihan said, "when you call me an asshole."

Garn later wrote to Goldwater and apologized for disrupting the committee.

After the meeting, the committee issued a public statement saying that Casey concurred in the assessment that the committee "was not adequately informed in a timely manner" about the mining and the speedboat attacks on the Nicaraguan harbors. The committee and Casey agreed to develop new procedures to guarantee there was no repeat of this lapse.

At a meeting with the President's Foreign Intelligence Advisory Board, Casey suggested that it appoint a subcommittee to investigate the mining. The chief question to be answered: How did it leak?

"You are a master of diversion," said board member Edward Bennett Williams. "You are caught with a smoking gun in your hand, and you yell robbery."

Casey laughed. There was no leak investigation.

Later, when McFarlane was up in the Senate, Moynihan disputed his public claim that the committee had been fully and adequately informed about the mining.

"Then what I was told was either disingenuous or someone was lying," McFarlane replied.

In a closed-door session with the committee, McFarlane summarized the mining incident: "In addition, you have to look to the future and, learning from the past, make sure that you don't make the same mistake again, *if indeed you have*."

17

CASEY HAD ANOTHER Central American agony that spring. Mexico, with its 77 million people, was a time bomb.

Though Constantine Menges was gone from the CIA, tucked away in the National Security Council, his ghost and some of his simmering worries about Mexico remained. He had swayed Casey to the view that Mexico might be a potential Iran on the U.S. border. No analogy resonated more strongly than Iran—the premier intelligence failure for the Carter Administration.

Menges argued that Mexico was ripe for revolution; the government was dangerously anti-American and anticapitalist and had a debt crisis that could lead to expropriation of foreign investments. Its social conditions were a breeding ground for the radical left.

Casey knew that Mexican President Miguel de la Madrid was a big pain in the ass for the Administration. The Harvard-educated de la Madrid was obsessed with his internal anticorruption campaign, dubbed "moral renewal." A worthy cause, Casey felt, but de la Madrid's real problems were economic and the chain around Mexico's neck was its $80 billion foreign debt. De la Madrid's other obsession was trying to get the United States and Nicaragua to negotiate a settlement of their differences. That would mean abandonment of the contras. Casey was opposed, and he resented the intrusion. Negotiations with Communists were essentially futile. De la Madrid could sound like a professor at a left-wing think tank, preaching nonintervention and claiming that U.S. actions radicalized the Sandinistas. This, Casey felt, was standard left-leaning crap that was always hard to take, but even harder from a close neighbor and supposed ally. Casey ordered stepped-up intelligence-gathering on Mexico and de la Madrid that produced a flood of data.

Casey had argued that the Nicaragua operation was in part about protecting Mexico. If Nicaragua was allowed to exist as a model leftist state, the revolutionary fires could sweep north. The leftist push currently was in El Salvador, but after that there were only Honduras and Guatemala. Immigration would get out of hand—hordes always fled Communism, "feet people," Casey called them.

A sensitive top-secret report from the President's Foreign Intelligence Advisory Board had been sent to him. The five-page report charged that the CIA had its analytical head buried in the sand and didn't know what was going on in Mexico. Among those behind the report was Anne Armstrong, the chairman of the PFIAB, former ambassador to Great Britain, who lived on a sprawling cattle ranch in Armstrong, Texas, in the southern tip of the state near the Mexican border. Other board members were pushing the view that it was an unfriendly act for the Mexicans to let the Soviets run so much anti-U.S. espionage out of the Soviet Embassy in Mexico. The board had hired a former CIA Mexico expert from the late 1970s as a consultant, and he had recommended that the CIA station in Mexico City be strengthened.

The report forecast leftist activity, particularly around Acapulco. It attacked de la Madrid, calling him a technocrat. Damaging anecdotes and rumors provided by businessmen were reported as fact. The report reflected some rather primitive attitudes about Mexico and its people.

Casey asked the DO to see whether any of it was true. Even though the report was not "intelligence," Casey had to take it seriously. The facts and the method were off the wall, but the conclusion could be right.

Menges had, a year earlier, started working on an intelligence estimate on Mexico, but it had bogged down in the press of more urgent Central American issues. No Mexico estimate had been done for several years. Casey had told Menges' replacement, John Horton, who was a former Mexico City station chief, that one of his first tasks would be the Mexico estimate but over the months the Director had seen little progress, and he began the sniping to get the damn thing written.

"I don't see why it takes you so long," Casey snapped at Horton one day. "I could dash this off in an hour."

Horton assigned analyst Brian Latell to write the first draft. Latell, a Ph.D. in history, was the kind of high diver that Casey liked. He had done an intelligence paper on Fidel Castro that had knocked Casey's socks off. He had described Castro as a man on the ropes going through a delayed midlife crisis, unable to handle his unrealized revolution, insecure about his place in history. The Cuban experts had dismissed Latell's paper, charging that he had produced psychofiction, a parody of intelligence work.

Latell went to Mexico for about a week to obtain a firsthand look—a new perk for the analysts, affordable because of the Casey budget increases.

When the draft, "Mexico Under De La Madrid," was completed, Latell carried it in to Horton.

"Casey thinks this is okay," he said.

Horton went into a slow burn. Casey was supposed to get the estimate drafts at the same time as the heads of the other intelligence agencies, not before, but Latell had broken the chain of command. Casey's influence could be out of proportion to his knowledge. He could distort the process with a casual remark. Nor was he reluctant to do so. Casey's prejudices could drive the estimate.

Casey got so worked up at times that he would thump a finger into someone's chest and yell, "False! False!" if he didn't agree. Horton wanted the hard information—and nothing more—steering the course.

Horton read the god-awful thick estimate. It described Mexico as perilously close to revolution. There was urban unrest, peasant unrest, alarming potential for capital flight—investors and businesses were leaving in a panic, there was little business-community confidence in the government, there was widespread corruption. A senior executive of a major defense contractor who had been raised in Mexico had expressed his views and they were reported as "intelligence."

Anyone who read Latell's draft, the President or the Secretary of State, could not help but get a strong impression that there was dangerous instability to the south. The draft hinted that there could be rioting and that the Mexican Army might have to be called in to suppress it. Echoes of Iran.

Not only had Horton been sidestepped, he knew that the intelligence information in the files did not support the draft's intimations. Horton agreed there was corruption, unrest and unemployment. The report seemed to assume that Americans in the same spot as the Mexicans would become revolutionary or radical. An amateur's mistake, Horton felt. There was no evidence that the Mexicans would behave like Americans.

The most alarming implication in the draft was that the Soviets and the Cubans were quietly organizing in Mexico. Or soon would be.

Horton knew that Casey wanted a frightening document that would get the White House and the PFIAB off his back. He wanted to show that Mexico was weak. Casey and his followers did not understand Mexico's historic belief in noninterference in the affairs of other countries. No Mexican President was likely to support the United States on the contras.

"You are interested in conventional wisdom," Casey argued after Horton voiced his concerns. "You're giving the conventional-wisdom argument."

These conclusions—in general and in their parts—are not substantiated by intelligence, Horton replied; they should come out of the estimate. The estimate was a contortion.

Wait, Casey said, some of the views should be included.

Rumors and anecdotes, Horton said; the thoughts of some businessman who had passed through Mexico City or had vacationed in Acapulco were not informed intelligence, not even "soft" intelligence.

Casey said that Horton wanted to suppress evidence.

Horton stiffened. That was a most serious accusation and he resented it.

"Mexico could be the next Iran," Casey said defiantly.

Thus began a series of almost daily discussions and rows between Casey and Horton as they transacted normal business. Horton was determined to remove anything from the draft that was not well sourced. Maybe the Reagan Administration chose to make policy on the basis of subjective "feel" and "talk," stray conversations from Republican clubs and fund-raisers, but Horton was not going to let such elements work their way into intelligence estimates.

Horton got a long, single-spaced memo from Casey trying to feed some material back into the evolving estimate. Then there was a second Casey memo, which Horton was sure had been authored by Menges. It was a standard Casey tactic to show the draft of a paper or report he didn't like to an informal panel of conservative advisers and ask for a memo. If he liked the memo, he forwarded it over his own name.

The memos cited information on rural dissatisfaction, unrest in the slum sections of Mexico, a Cuban-sponsored group in a remote area. Much of it was unsourced, and Horton was not convinced that there was any reason to change his mind.

The intelligence deputy Bob Gates tried to point to a middle ground, but Horton didn't think a middle ground was sufficient. It was a matter of how one dealt with hard-won intelligence information. Either it had weight or it was distorted by gossip and surmise. And Horton saw a further complication. Casey was interpreting Horton's defiance as if he were recommending another policy. The overriding policy concern for Casey was the Nicaragua operation. Trouble in Mexico fit neatly. A forecast that did not promise trouble did not fit Casey's scenario. It implied that de la Madrid would be around for a long time. If a wave of Communism and consequent immigration was only a remote concern, it gave less urgency to the contra cause.

With each mention of the estimate, Casey grew more annoyed. The estimates came out in his name; the other intelligence agencies could voice objections. That was enough. One analyst, even a respected senior NIO like Horton, could block the road only so long.

For the moment Horton had control of the draft and he wouldn't go with anything that was not backed up. To get something on the table before the NFIB meeting of the intelligence chiefs, Casey agreed finally to circulate a draft that Horton had reworked.

Herb Meyer, one of Casey's aides and vice-chairman of the National Intelligence Council that was now supervising the estimates, called all the intelligence agency chiefs to tell them a draft was coming. Having heard from their representatives that Horton and Casey were about to murder each other, they were extremely interested.

The meeting was held in early April (at about the same time as trouble was blowing up in the Senate over the mining of Nicaraguan ports) at the F Street intelligence community headquarters, a stark, unattached building a block from the Old Executive Office Building. Horton presented an oral summary: there was crisis but no real sign of collapse.

Casey said that the draft took a complacent view. And I'm annoyed, he added, that the draft doesn't contain the probabilities. I want our best estimate of the chances that Mexico will collapse. He made it clear that he thought Mexico was on the verge.

The State Department representative was concerned that they ought to be looking at other Latin American nations, such as Argentina and Brazil, which had heavy foreign debts. They were as much a cause for concern.

The FBI assistant director focused on the active operations of the Soviets in Mexico. The KGB residency in Mexico was the major launching pad of espionage operations into the United States; Mexico was virtually an espionage free-fire zone from which the KGB operated easily. There was new information that the CIA had identified some Soviet agents working in the Mexican Foreign Office, and the Mexicans had not shown proper concern.

One of the NFIB members remarked that this had nothing to do with Mexico's instability, the topic of the estimate.

Someone pointed out that it showed that Soviet influence was increasing.

The representative from the Commerce Department, a CIA analyst on temporary duty there, seemed ready to fall at Casey's feet. Horton found it an oily performance.

Treasury also had a bleak view, due largely to concern about the debt crisis. American banks were on the hook to Mexico for billions.

The military intelligence agencies—the NSA, the DIA, the Army, the Air Force and the Marine Corps—voiced only moderate concern about Mexico. With armed forces totaling about 120,000, the Mexican military was not of much strategic interest.

Except for the FBI, Commerce and Treasury—the least-important intelligence agencies—Casey was almost alone. He decided to force the issue.

"I want to have a vote on the chances of complete chaos," he said, striking the table. He personally thought that there was a 50-50 chance of collapse. Circling the table again, Casey got support only from the same three agencies.

"I take it you feel that it's about a one-in-five chance," Casey said, plunging for middle ground.

No one replied.

I want this redone, Casey ordered, and those numbers—a 20 percent chance of collapse—in the estimate. There was no way he was submitting an estimate to the President that did not raise the possibility.

Horton was sure that the professional opinion was on his side. It was going 20 percent Casey's way because he sat at the head of the table.

After the meeting, Casey uttered an obscenity to Horton and directed Herb Meyer to rewrite the key judgments.

Horton complained to Gates. Gates promised to watch for the Meyer draft. But Horton himself was soon dipping into Meyer's version, correcting historical mistakes, toning down the more drastic statements. The estimate was not going to become the "Doomsday Scenario" that Casey wanted. The final draft ended up more or less a gurgle. Several of the military intelligence services noted their disagreement in a prominent footnote on the front page. It stated that the intelligence would not support the judgment that Mexico ran a 20 percent chance of a revolution.

The final version, classified secret, went to several hundred officials and was likely read by only a handful, and Horton was left to wonder what it all meant. One concrete result was that more CIA operations officers would be assigned to Mexico City to deal with the Soviets, a matter that the estimate had not really been designed to address. But at the least, Horton felt, the process had been kept honest. Still, the more he thought about it, the more he was troubled. It had all been done at a great personal price. Casey had apologized after the NFIB meeting, but their relationship was finished. Casey suspected him. He suspected Casey.

Shellshocked from Iran, the agency thought it could protect itself by predicting revolution, collapse and disaster. That way it would never be "wrong." But it would also never be "right" with estimates that cried wolf.

Iran had left a terrible scar, worse than Horton at first thought. He had heard Casey warn the Latin American station chiefs, "Look for the Ayatollah—a man coming up who could lead the angry masses." This thinking still infested the agency too much.

Horton had other grievances against Casey. General Paul F. Gorman, the U.S. southern commander in Panama, had reported that events in El Salvador were looking up, as President Duarte was giving commands to honest officers with honorable human-rights records.

"Why isn't our intelligence showing that?" Casey asked Horton, who was ordered to check. He returned to tell Casey that the information was in the National Intelligence Daily that circulated to top officials.

"No one reads that garbage," Casey snapped. He meant that the President, the Secretaries of State and Defense, and the national-security adviser—those who really counted—didn't pay much attention to the NID. It was a careless remark, as if the top-secret NID intelligence was merely an aside in the flow of intelligence. Certainly it was possible that Casey hadn't meant what he said. He was the one who was always trying to restrict access to the NID, to prevent photocopying, and complaining when bits from the NID appeared in the news. But the remark reflected his insensitivity and a tendency to vent his daily pique. Casey's people worked hard on the NID. If the Director had offhandedly called it "garbage," more than likely he had said it other times. And this view would have got back to those who broke their backs each day on the NID.

Horton had felt uncomfortable about some of the other intelligence efforts in the year he had been the Latin America NIO. Casey wanted an assessment of the opposition to Castro inside Cuba. Horton wasn't able to come up with much hard intelligence, because it didn't exist. CIA sources in Cuba were meager, it was true, but Horton concluded that it was also possible that Castro didn't have much internal opposition. That didn't sit well with Casey and he responded suspiciously, as if his contempt for Communists was universal and of course Castro must have opponents. But Casey's hardheaded, self-confident intuitions were no substitute for real information.

It was an intellectual trap. Casey showed joy and relish only when someone brought him intelligence that supported his preconceptions or Administration policy.

Just before the election in Argentina the year before, Horton had undertaken a Special National Intelligence Estimate to forecast the election. Looks like this guy Raúl Alfonsín, a center-left lawyer who heads a party called the Radical Civic Union, is going to win, Horton told Casey. Casey grumbled a question, and Horton said that it looked as though Alfonsín's victory was going to be good for Argentina after eight years of military dictatorship, but that, given his left-of-center position, it probably wasn't going to be so good for the United States.

Casey gazed at Horton and asked, "Is he a Marxist-Leninist?"

Horton wondered why that was the only question from the DCI.

Alfonsín won.

Several days after the Mexico estimate was circulated, Horton went to Gates and said he was going to quit and would stay only until they found a replacement. But nothing happened, no replacement appeared. So Horton went back to Gates and said, "Look, my contract date is the end of May—why don't I just plan to leave then." Gates said okay.

Horton felt sour. Perhaps it was unfair, but he found a metaphor that he thought apt: Casey was like the new chief executive officer of a large corporation who came in to milk the corporation for what he could get out of it before throwing it to one side. Sure, Casey saw himself as an old OSS operator and had a sentimental feeling about intelligence work, but if any cans were going to get hung around any neck for Central America, it wouldn't be Reagan's or Casey's. Those cans would go around the CIA. The seeds for a gigantic backlash, a repeat of the Church and Pike investigations, were being planted.

Horton knew that Casey had to be credited with keeping in touch with many people, but almost all shared his world view, as Mexico demonstrated. Horton had spent hours sitting in Casey's office, before his desk, dragged in for one matter or another. Casey was too rough on people, on Horton.

He thought that Casey was not attached enough to the CIA and its need for independence. The CIA had become once again a tool of an Administration bent on forcing its view on the world. The distortions and ploys were many. Some were subtle. Horton felt he could stand stubbornly at the gate only for so long. He didn't want to be a martyr. It was personal. Somebody else could have handled Casey much more smoothly. Gates did it. For him, a few or even many compromises on paper maybe didn't add up to much.

There was another factor in Horton's decision to leave. It was hard for him to evaluate the significance of this, but it wasn't that he just didn't get along with Casey. The DCI was a bully.

• • •

Ten days after the briefing which had left me wondering whether I had been "fed" by the CIA on Qaddafi, I flew to Tripoli. Like most visitors, I waited days for my appointment with the Libyan leader. Finally, one of his translators moved into a room next to mine on the twelfth floor of the Bab el-Bahar Hotel on the Mediterranean. We stayed up most of the night chatting, reading, waiting. Fatigue loosened everyone up. When we took a wake-up walk outside in the cool air by the sea, the translator, a tall, powerful man, said he was particularly distraught about a crackdown on internal dissent. He said a total of twenty-three students and dissidents had been publicly hanged that month. He added that there were thousands of political prisoners who had spoken out against the revolution or Qaddafi.

Come on, I said, how could there be thousands?

"Thousands," he said emphatically, "I tell you thousands. The country is in turmoil. We expect something."

I told him that I had sent in a story about the hanging of two Libyan students at Tripoli University. Gallows had been erected in a university courtyard, and thousands of students had been commanded to watch, many vomiting and running off shrieking.

About 5 A.M. I was told there would be no interview that night. We waited most of the next day. My patience held only because Qaddafi's translator was being kept with me virtually incommunicado.

In the room next door, the translator seemed as upset as I. He took me down the hall.

"I wish you would see him," the translator shouted, raging about Qaddafi. "You'd see how small, out of it, he is—how crazy!" He pointed his index finger to his temple to indicate that Qaddafi was deranged.

Crazy, I said.

"Insane," he said, and then took his index finger and thumb, bringing them an eighth of an inch apart. "A pinhead!" he said, as if to parade his grasp of slang.

He said that Qaddafi took sleeping pills and other drugs. He described Qaddafi's unpredictable life, hermit and demigod.

It was a carbon of the picture that had been painted for me by the CIA operations officer. It was not only the words, the reference to sleeping pills, all the rest of the description, but the attitude of derision and scorn on one hand, and wonder and grudging respect on the other. It was as if the translator, who had spent hundreds of hours with Qaddafi, and the CIA official, who had spent hours studying him, had had the identical experience.

I considered the possibilities that the translator was a CIA asset, that this was a setup, or that both the CIA and the translator had it right.

But a copy of my story about the public hangings arrived at the Foreign Ministry, and I was whisked to the airport and sent back to the States so fast that it bordered on an expulsion.

Back in Washington, we published a long story about Libya. The translator's information about the sleeping pills and that of the CIA were tied together. The story ran that Sunday under the headline "Qaddafi's Authority Said to Be Weakening."

On May 8, two weeks after I had left Libya, I was at the *Post* when urgent wire service reports started coming out of Libya, reporting a coup attempt against Qaddafi, including an attack on his "Splendid Gate" barracks. Reports said a pitched battle in the downtown area had lasted for hours. One said, inaccurately, that Qaddafi had been killed.

After the reports were sorted out at Langley, it was clear that it had been the largest coup attempt inside Libya in the fifteen years Qaddafi had been in power. And, for the first time, anti-Qaddafi forces outside Libya and inside apparently had linked up. The attempt was foiled when three plotters were caught at the Tunisian border. They had been tortured and had led Qaddafi's forces to about fifteen rebels holed up in Tripoli preparing to attack Qaddafi.

The support provided to the plotters by Sudan's Nimeri had at least helped get something off the ground, even though it was thwarted.

Casey concluded, "It proves for the first time Libyans are willing to die to get rid of this bastard." He ordered an immediate assessment on Qaddafi's vulnerabilities. It was time to do more.

Casey was concerned that he was about to suffer another public inquisition on his personal finances. The Internal Revenue Service was after him in its unfriendly and bureaucratic way with a slow drumbeat of letters and notices. The IRS was claiming back taxes on some business deductions that Casey had taken in the late 1970s before coming to the CIA. Normally, such disputes were confidential between the taxpayer and the IRS. But some of Casey's partners were challenging the IRS claims in tax court, dragging his name into the open.

This was the area of public criticism that most infuriated Casey. Most people just didn't understand the capitalist system. Like many things, this understanding went back to the OSS and World War II. Then OSS had set up an important but simple intelligence-gathering operation. U.S.

citizens had been asked to send in their vacation photos taken in Europe, especially at ports and beaches. One OSSer had reduced the photos to microfilm and had them pasted on computer cards. It was all done by hand with paste and scissors, but the files had provided a ready reference to any beach or port, so the Allied troops at least had something to go on before an agent drop, a commando raid, a landing or a bombing. During the war a businessman had planted the seed with Casey that there would be endless commercial applications for this microfilm organization system.

After the war, the businessman came back to Casey and put up the money. Casey hired an engineering firm in Boston to make a machine that would do the cut-and-paste work. A company called Film Sort was formed, and Casey began selling the machine and the technique to land title companies around the country. In 1949 the company was sold. Casey's share was several hundred thousand dollars, an extraordinary fortune in those postwar days. It was the first real money he had made. He took $50,000 and bought Mayknoll.

Since then Casey had placed great premium on seeing the future, finding applications and connections that others did not. He could have dumped his money with the big stock exchange corporations and been safe, free of any management role, disputes or lawsuits. Instead he had placed money in a minisubmarine venture to hunt for sunken treasure off Key West, a firm importing Yugoslavian and Belgian rugs, a computerized tax return program, an estate-planning firm and a racquetball partnership.

One of his investment groups was set up to develop a pen that transferred handwriting directly into a computer. Casey had put up $95 for a 1 percent share. The group, called PenVerter Partners, had bought confidential technology from another firm for $4 million, but only $100,000 of that had been laid out in cash. The other $3.9 million was in notes that would be paid only if the pen was developed and marketed. Using such techniques, PenVerter had losses of $6 million over four years. As a 1 percent partner, for his $95 Casey had taken $60,000 in tax deductions—all of which the IRS was disallowing.

The incident was potentially explosive—the CIA Director getting 600 times his investment in tax deductions. The Attorney General, William French Smith, had just been publicly raked over the coals for taking a deduction only four times his investment.

On May 10, Casey phoned me about an inquiry that Chuck Babcock, one of the reporters assigned to my staff at the *Post,* was conducting into his IRS troubles. Yes, Casey conceded, he might owe $100,000 in back taxes. That was nothing, he said, and he'd be happy to pay, and could afford it.

Babcock wrote a long story about Casey's tax and investment troubles, headlined "CIA Director Disputes IRS Claim to $100,000 in Back Taxes."

At a later tax court hearing in New York, Casey testified, taking the offensive and disputing the IRS attorney's claim that he had signed up with those in the business of "selling tax deductions."

"I would like to take exception to any notion that I purchased a tax deduction," he said, "I purchased their future. . . . But to say I purchased tax deductions is an outrageous distortion." He noted that he had written the first book on tax shelters, the 1952 *Tax Sheltered Investments*. "I started the whole thing," he said, smiling, adding in terms of Catholic atonement, "When I became chairman of the SEC, I redeemed my sins."

No one in Congress or anyone else in the media had the stomach for another look into the thicket of Casey's personal finances. Casey was surprised. A little openness and candor had gone a long way.

Though Congress was balking at the Administration's request for $21 million more for the contras, Casey felt that no elected official, particularly a Democrat in the age of popular Republican Reagan, wanted what Casey called the "black eye" that would accompany abandoning the resistance movement. He pressed this theme whenever he could, and urged the President and McFarlane to play that political card. Yet he knew that Congress could do anything, and that delay was likely. The Administration needed a backup plan. He wrote an "Eyes Only" memo to McFarlane on March 27, 1984: "In view of possible difficulties in obtaining supplemental appropriations to carry out the Nicaraguan covert action project through the remainder of this year, I am in full agreement that you should explore funding alternative with the Saudis, Israelis and others.

"Finally, after examining legalities, you might consider finding an appropriate private US citizen to establish a foundation" that would receive nongovernment funds.

He signed the memo with a large "C," hand-carried it to McFarlane at the White House, and asked the national-security adviser to return his copy when he was finished. There should be no copies, no distribution to others.

Casey knew that McFarlane was no great believer in the contra covert operation; he pursued it to the extent the President insisted. McFarlane was just another player, no umpire, no leader. Casey would pursue his own avenues.

On the way back to Langley, he called the office and said he wanted the key Nicaragua people in his office when he arrived. After hanging up his coat and hat, he sat down quietly in his blue swivel chair, grabbed a paper clip and began untwisting it.

"You know, boys," he finally began, "the White House is going to be making some decisions about the contras. What have we got going on this?"

A few operational details from the field were offered, some analytic points about Sandinista activity.

"What the hell are we," he said, "some kind of goddamn think tank? I tell you that the contras will be at the top of the agenda. . . . Now, let's figure out what the President's going to need, and then figure out how to do it."

Chuck Cogan, the operations division chief for the Near East, was called "Mr. Hathaway Shirt." Tall, thin, with a perfectly trimmed mustache, he sported everything but the eye patch.

At fifty-six, Cogan had previous CIA service as an operations officer in India, the Congo, Sudan, and Morocco, where he had been station chief. A 1949 graduate of Harvard, he had come to the agency in the second wave in the 1950s Cold War period. He had a chilly, all-business handshake, and eyes like a detective. A modest, barely noticeable scar down one side of his face heightened the effect.

For a division chief, duty at Langley headquarters was not all cable reading and dispatching orders to stations. It included important liaison work with the embassies in Washington—pipelines of good intelligence and political data. These bonds could be as important as any that were developed in the field.

One of Cogan's back-channel relationships was with the Saudi ambassador to the United States, Prince Bandar. A flashy, handsome man-about-town Bandar, the thirty-five-year-old son of the powerful Saudi Defense Minister, exemplified the new breed of ambassador—activist, charming, profane. The former air force pilot was a kind of Arab Gatsby who waved Cuban cigars around, laughed boisterously, and served his favorite McDonald's Big Mac hamburgers to guests on sterling-silver trays in his private office.

During the Carter Administration, before he had been appointed ambassador, Bandar had developed and nurtured connections with the White House through presidential assistant Hamilton Jordan. He could always get a hearing for Saudi Arabia through Jordan. Now under Reagan it was different. Bandar perceived that authority was diffused throughout the departments and among various White House factions. Given the pro-Israeli tilt of the Reagan Administration policy, especially from Secretary of State Shultz, the unofficial connection through Cogan was important.

As ambassador, Bandar had unusual maneuvering room. He had access to vast wealth. Under the Saudi monarchy, there were no legislatures, courts or oversight committees with power to second-guess. The State Department, well aware of this, could go to the Saudis for military or economic help when it wanted something that the Congress might resist. If the operations were in line with Saudi foreign policy, they often got that help. The Saudis got credit with the country they might be helping and with the United States. Their dollars did double duty.

The opportunities in the intelligence field for such arrangements were tantalizing. For example, the Saudis were helping the resistance to the Marxist government in Ethiopia. This was a natural for the Saudis, who didn't like extreme leftists or Communists, especially those just across the Red Sea. Casey and the CIA were grateful.

Relations between the CIA and the Saudi intelligence service were generally good, going back to the days when the legendary and enormously wealthy Kamal Adham had been its head. In 1970, the Saudis had provided then Egyptian Vice-President Sadat with a regular income. It was impossible to determine where Saudi interests in these arrangements ended and American CIA interests began.

Now, in the spring of 1984, Cogan was leaving the Near East division. In a farewell conversation with Bandar, he almost offhandedly raised the matter of the difficulty Casey was having getting money for the contras. Cogan recalled an article in the *Post* the previous month in which it was suggested that Saudi Arabia might send some money to the contras. Did you place that story, Cogan asked Bandar, was the Saudi Embassy the source?

No, Bandar said.

It might be a trial balloon, Cogan said. Someone over here or elsewhere was hinting an interest. It sure would be helpful. The contras just need $20 million to $30 million. "Peanuts," Cogan added. He mentioned that the goodwill-to-dollars ratio would be the highest possible.

Bandar said he had heard of no suggestion beyond the *Post* article, which certainly sounded as if it had come out of the agency or the Administration. In fact, the article had said that Casey was considering whether to ask another country such as Saudi Arabia, hadn't it?

Cogan said that the CIA was not asking.

Bandar got the drift. He said he would check at the top in Riyadh to see whether there was any interest. "Let's get an official response," he said.

Within days, Ambassador Bandar received a negative reply from Riyadh. These reasons were given:

- The CIA could not or would not offer anything in return, or at least nothing had been suggested.
- Saudi foreign policy in Central America was at odds with the U.S. The Sandinista government in Nicaragua was basically pro-Arab, while the two U.S.-backed regimes, Costa Rica and El Salvador, had recently engaged in unmistakable anti-Arab diplomacy and moved their embassies in Israel from Tel Aviv to Jerusalem.
- The Saudis had no confidence that secrets could be kept in the Reagan Administration; any covert Saudi aid to the contras would leak and embarrass them all.

Bandar passed the word to the CIA that it couldn't be done. But the CIA and Bandar agreed that, since all this was exploratory and unofficial, the CIA had never asked and the Saudis hadn't said no.

Bandar received other emissaries on the contras. Two chief executive officers of major American corporations asked him to contribute. Bandar said no. An assistant to retired Air Force Major General Richard V. Secord came and asked whether the Saudis could help. Secord, a veteran of the covert war in Laos, ran a private network for transporting arms. Bandar said, "Can you pass a message directly to him?" He thought Secord an arrogant man. The assistant assured the ambassador that he could. "Tell him to go fuck himself."

The groundwork for a denial was carefully laid. Bandar spent lots of time with McFarlane. Earlier they had traveled together on secret missions to the Middle East, and every several months they met to review areas of mutual interest. McFarlane clearly had an inferiority complex as national-security adviser, operating in the shadow of Kissinger and suffering the endless unfavorable comparisons, Bandar concluded. But with the intense loyalty of a former Marine, McFarlane was the President's man, a protector of Reagan, and the closest thing to a real channel to the President.

One night the two met alone over drinks in the greenhouse room in the back of Bandar's vast residence in McLean, Virginia. McFarlane said that the contras were in trouble, running out of funds. The result was going to be an immense political loss for the President. U.S. friends in the region, Honduras, Costa Rica, El Salvador, would be let down. Latin America could unravel.

Bandar agreed. He wondered at the inconstancy of American foreign policy. Why were commitments like the one to the contras made when they could not be sustained?

As they talked, McFarlane felt that Bandar was volunteering to help. Bandar was sure he was being solicited. Nonetheless, it was an opportunity neither could pass up. They almost fell into each other's arms, and they quickly agreed that the Saudis would contribute $8–$10 million to the contras at the rate of $1 million a month. But it would have to be done in the greatest secrecy and be one of those things between nations and its leaders that would remain hidden forever, no matter what the circumstances.

Bandar was aware of the capabilities of the NSA to intercept his diplomatic traffic, and he sent a message to King Fahd by courier.

That month Iran was increasingly threatening oil shipping in the Persian Gulf, and Bandar went to see Shultz. Soon President Reagan dispatched a letter to King Fahd affirming support for the Saudis in any confrontation with Iran. Fahd and Bandar also wanted several hundred advanced antiaircraft Stinger missiles, but in the course of negotiations the United States placed some restrictions on the sale. Fahd forwarded a secret seven-page letter to Bandar with strict instructions for his ambassador to take it directly to the President. At the White House, Reagan read it, then looked up and said, "We don't put conditions on friends."

The President then invoked emergency procedures to bypass the Congress on a weapons sale, and over the Memorial Day weekend four hundred Stingers were flown secretly to Saudi Arabia.

Bandar then traveled to Saudi Arabia and, with the King's approval, obtained a Saudi government check for $8 million for the covert aid to the contras. McFarlane obtained a contra bank account number for his NSC staff assistant Lieutenant Colonel North. It was account number 541-48 at the BAC International Bank in the Cayman Islands. On Friday, June 22, McFarlane and Bandar met at the White House and McFarlane handed the ambassador a typed card with the account number. To insure secrecy, Bandar said he was going personally to Geneva, Switzerland, where he had a house, to set up the transfer through a Swiss bank. They agreed that as soon as the money was on its way, Bandar would send word. If they had to mention the operation on the telephone, they also agreed on a code word and would refer to the delivery of "cigarettes."

Bandar arrived in Geneva on June 27 and requested that an official from the Swiss Bank Corporation come to his home, where he handed over the $8 million Saudi check and the Cayman account number into which he said he wanted $1 million a month disbursed. He directed that the $8 million be deposited in the Swiss Bank Corporation's general account and sent from there, so its origin could not be traced.

Meanwhile, McFarlane was concerned about the delay. He reached Bandar by phone. "My friend did not get his cigarettes," he said, "and he's a heavy smoker."

It took the Swiss Bank Corporation more than a week to clear the Saudi check, and the first $1 million was transferred on July 6.

McFarlane sent a card to the President informing him that the Saudis were now secretly funding the contras. The President expressed his deep appreciation. Over the next eight months, the Saudis funneled the $8 million to the contras. It was the difference between their life and death.

After discussions with Casey and Clarridge about the immediate operational and logistic needs of the contras, North sent a SECRET memo to McFarlane asking for permission to go to Central America. McFarlane initialed "RCM" under approve and wrote in: "Exercise absolute 'stealth.' No visible meeting. No press awareness of your presence in area."

Casey had leverage with Israel. He had given the Israelis broader access to U.S. satellite reconnaissance photos than they had previously enjoyed. Israel was suitably grateful. Its intelligence agencies were always on the lookout for cost-effective favors that might be returned to Casey and the U.S. Its embassy in Washington, tuned in to public and political opinion, noted that there was often more coverage of Nicaragua in the news media than of the Soviet Union.

Officially, Israel had already denied it was helping the contras. But reports persisted. No country buries its intelligence and other secrets better than Israel. It was clear that Israel was getting credit within the Congress and the Administration for finding ways to slip several million dollars in arms or money to the contras—perhaps through a South American intermediary. But getting credit was short of proof that they were actually doing something.

As I made the rounds, I finally found a very well placed Israeli source who said yes, it was happening, "Yes, of course" it was happening. It was too fine an opportunity—golden, clean and cheap. And, the source added, the United States would find some way to repay Israel in the current $2.5 billion annual military- and economic-aid package. If the repayment was not in money, given the "technical" problem that Congress might have, it could come in one of many other forms. The source referred only to what he said some called "Casey's gift." This was not merely the satellite photos but an array of intelligence. Israel was still not receiving real-time transmissions from the advanced KH-11 satellite, nor was any block of time allocated to Israel on the U.S. satellites as had been requested.

The U.S. did not have a sense of the real meaning of timely tactical intelligence, the source noted. Israel, which was surrounded by enemies, did. To Israel, intelligence-sharing was as or more important than the normal diplomatic, foreign-ministry-to-State Department corridor.

Any help to the contras would be concealed, he said. Too much success, or visible success, was failure. The CIA and Casey might not see the peril of exposure. Like the private matters that can take place between two individuals, there are things, shadowy, unreadable, that can and do take place between two nations that remain out of view. It defies interpretation and will not stand illumination. But it was true, though there could be no details. He did not know the details himself.

How could he say it was true?

There are truths that need no details, he said. For example, Israel sells arms to Honduras, the country from which the contras operate. The answer could be there.

Was it?

I doubt it, he said. The answer would be more roundabout, circumventing the obvious. Cutouts, he said, people in between who may not know whom they work for, or for whom they are picking up arms or money, or to whom they are making deliveries.

I placed a call to Casey. He called back shortly, and I said I had been reliably told about the approach the CIA had made to the Saudis for contra money.

"Totally unauthorized."

How about the Israelis?

"Lots of conversations," Casey said, "But nothing of that character that was official."

What about Israeli General Saguy, the former head of military intelligence, and those satellite photos?

"A good guy," Casey said, "knew him well."

The photos?

"Those relationships . . . I'm not going to talk about."

Where were the contras getting money? Last month there had been desperation, now there was all this confidence.

"Not our desperation," he said. The contras "don't want to quit."

That's no substitute for money.

"Lots of scrounging around."

How? Where?

"We aren't supposed to know." He didn't have any more to say.

Will they get by? Will you? Everyone was desperate last month.

"It's an exaggeration to say 'desperate,' " Casey said.

How could Casey say that? The CIA had identified the Sunday when the money would be gone.

"Human nature," he replied, and provided his crisis theory. When there is a problem or bad news, people overreact, often do too much. After some time, they focus on solutions. "They calm down, deal with the problem—it's a psychological change, nothing external." He seemed to be applying this both to himself and to the contras.

Will you get the money from the Congress, the $21 million?

He said he was confident, hopeful. "The Democrats don't want to take responsibility," he said. It was "the unspoken factor on the chessboard."

One such factor, Casey said, is political fear. Only yesterday, the Democrats had tried a compromise route—"a bailout fund," a kind of severance pay of several million for an orderly and humanitarian withdrawal, and for the resettlement of the contras. The Administration and the CIA were not going along. He reintroduced his line about the coming "fall offensive" in El Salvador; indications were that it would be "very strong" and "early."

There was a story the next morning, May 19, on the front page of the *Post* ("CIA Sought Third-Country Contra Aid") that pedaled softly but raised the possibility that the Saudis and Israelis were giving contra assistance. A strong denial from a senior Israeli official was included in the third paragraph: "We have not supplied any money to the contras, either directly or indirectly. We are not consciously or with knowledge passing anything to the contras. . . . We are not a surrogate for the United States."

The official who had spoken to me phoned. He was delighted, almost elated. The story was fair. Obviously I had accurately reported some things that people were saying. He seemed to be winking over the phone. The story was perfect for the Israelis. They got both credit and denial—emphasizing one or the other to their pro-contra and anti-contra allies in Congress and the Administration.

The CIA spokesman George Lauder called. He was all happiness, too, but just wanted, in the friendliest of ways, of course, to pass on something about the story. It was wrong. "We didn't do it," he said. The CIA had done nothing of the kind, they weren't out approaching Saudis and Israelis, or anyone else, either officially or unofficially. "It just didn't happen." The CIA wasn't issuing a statement and didn't want anything printed. He just wanted to pass this "fact" along.

I was not surprised that Lauder might not know what Cogan and Casey were doing. I did not want to mention that I had talked with Casey. I told Lauder that I was sure of my sources.

He said it just couldn't be. He had checked thoroughly, talked to everyone, gone way up, including "the man." The big guy, Lauder said.

Who?

John McMahon, Lauder said reluctantly, suggesting that he had top authority.

Had Lauder spoken with anyone else?

Why would he have to check further?

Quickly, I tried to steer it away from Casey, too late.

Oh, okay, Lauder said, catching himself. By his silence, he seemed to be saying that he realized he had a runaway DCI.

So Casey was not only running the contra operation out of his office, as well as some of the fund-raising efforts, he was running his own public-affairs office. He wasn't even telling McMahon what he was up to.

A few days later, May 24, Casey met President Reagan's helicopter at the Langley headquarters. It was a bright spring day, and a beaming Casey escorted Reagan to a crowd of some 2,000 agency workers who sat on a sunny hillside, Casey's 219-acre "campus."

The President had arrived for the ground-breaking ceremony for a new $190 million addition to the headquarters, often called the "Casey Memorial Wing." Growth, especially the need for more computers and data storage, required a seven-story addition. Wielding shovels, Reagan, Bush and Casey turned the symbolic earth.

At the ground-breaking, Reagan told the crowd, "Your work, the work of your Director, the other top officials, have been an inspiration to your fellow Americans and to people everywhere."

Casey was irritated by the continuing pressure from the Senate committee for a formal written surrender on the Nicaragua mining operation, which was still being treated as a major felony. The committee was pressing for an agreement by which the DCI would inform it in advance of any activity in an ongoing major or sensitive covert operation or of anything approved by the President. With Moynihan as the driving force, the agreement said that the CIA would:

- Provide extensive material in writing whenever a new presidential finding had been signed, including the backup details in the scope paper outlining the exact nature, goals and risks of the covert operation.
- Notify the committee of new activities within an ongoing covert operation when the activity might be politically sensitive, had new potential adverse consequences if it became public, changed the scope of the operation, involved new U.S. personnel or had been approved by the National Security Council or the President.
- Give regular updates on all ongoing covert action and a yearly comprehensive briefing on all covert action.
- Report on any subject of CIA activity about which the committee expressed special interest or reservation.

Goldwater and Moynihan signed the agreement on June 6, and they wanted Casey's signature at once. Both senators wanted to be informed if Casey's signature was not obtained that day. Committee counsel Gary Chase, who had previously served as an associate general counsel at the CIA, was dispatched to Langley about 4 P.M. to obtain the signature. The task was certain to be unpleasant. It was suggested to Chase that he get the signature and go on home and have a drink.

At Langley, Chase went to the lobby and called Casey, who wouldn't let him come up. "I've got a good mind to tell you to get the hell out of my building," the DCI said.

"You don't want me to call the Chairman and Vice-Chairman back with that," Chase replied. He explained that the document had been negotiated out fully at the staff level, and that a signature would be routine.

Casey said he would check with his staff, but meanwhile Chase could wait—in the lobby. Chase called the Senate committee and was told to wait it out.

Upstairs, Casey was sore. The agreement effectively gave the committee a peephole into his office; they might as well tap his phone and assign someone to sit in his office and travel around with him, taking notes, rummaging through his desk drawers and files. It was a kind of straw-boss monitoring that went far beyond what the White House did, or anything that was done anywhere else in the executive branch. The committee was usurping. He checked and found that his staff had agreed. Those were the terms of continuing business. If Casey didn't see Chase, the senatorial demons might be unleashed again.

After an hour, the Director called down and told Chase to come up.

"What's this?" Casey asked, glancing at the agreement.

Chase explained that nothing in it went beyond the current oversight legislation or detracted from the constitutional role of the President. It did not give away any of the President's powers.

Since Casey's staff had agreed orally, they discussed whether Casey's signature would make any difference. Chase said that the Chairman and Vice-Chairman would like it signed, just to make it clear. After more than twenty minutes, Casey finally took the document, scrawled his name and handed it over.

Instead of returning home for a drink, Chase went back to the committee offices. Several staff members cheered him, and he raised the document in the air. One staffer was reminded of Neville Chamberlain—peace in our time. Chase had everything but the umbrella.

18

CASEY REALIZED THAT after the President, Secretary of State George Shultz was the most substantial presence in the Administration, the man of apparent moderation, the reasonable voice—thoughtful and articulate. That spring, Casey watched him go through a much-needed transformation. At White House meetings, his hands folded as if in prayer, Shultz crossed a threshold on the use of American force—covert or overt—in response to terrorism. After the failure of diplomacy in Lebanon, it was time to act. The United States had been driven out of Lebanon by terrorism. The problem could not be solved by diplomats. As the discussions went on, Shultz became excitable on the subject of terrorism and pushed for an active response. Retaliation or preemption was all that the terrorists, and the terror states, would understand.

Casey tolerated Shultz. The economist and businessman had a tough side, getting tougher. When Shultz turned to Reagan at the NSPG meetings and said in his deep voice, "Mr. President . . ." everyone listened. American credibility and foreign policy hinge on demonstrating that we can adapt and act against the new butchers, Shultz said. Our authority in the Middle East rests on it.

Under NSDD 30, which Reagan had signed in 1982, the State Department was in charge of anti-terrorist policy. Shultz was indicating that he wanted the Pentagon and the CIA drawn in more. Someone would have to do the dirty work.

This initiative by the Secretary triggered a series of working groups and meetings coordinated by the White House and the NSC staff. Lieutenant Colonel North drafted a decision document for the President. In North's language, it was time to kill the "cocksucker" terrorists. His draft NSDD called for CIA-backed and -trained teams of foreign nationals to "neutralize" terrorists known to have struck Americans or known to be planning such attacks.

McMahon received a copy of North's draft at his office, but it was not until after midnight that he reached North at home.

"Motherfucker!" McMahon shouted. Did North have his head in the sand during the 1970s? Was he oblivious to the Reagan executive order banning any involvement in assassination? What was he trying to do to the CIA? What were the chances that they would ever have solid enough intelligence to allow a preemptive attack?

North said yes sir, and hung up. Every time they got something going, McMahon would step on it. "McMahon has lost his nerve," North told a friend. "Maybe he used to be good, but he's worthless to Casey now."

Casey wanted strong action, and so he took the matter to his general counsel, Sporkin. As usual, he wanted an immediate answer.

Sporkin's conclusion was that actions against terrorists would not constitute assassination—the prohibition referred to political assassination, to the old Castro plots. If the CIA had its facts right, and minimized any hazard to civilians, and if the President signed a formal finding, and if the proper congressional committees were notified, there would be no problem. If there was hard intelligence that terrorists were about to strike, Sporkin said, the right of self-defense would put them in the clear.

Casey was not as successful with the Pentagon. Weinberger was uncomfortable using battleships to fight terrorists as they had done in Lebanon, and the Pentagon was ambivalent about plans for the CIA to preempt terrorists' attacks. Defense's attitude was partly relief that the dirty work would be in CIA hands, as would responsibility for any failure. But its attitude was also proprietary and bureaucratic. Paramilitary action, any such training by the CIA, was in competition with the Pentagon.

McFarlane knew that when the President's advisers were not unanimous, little would happen. He proposed a comprehensive study, and on April 3, when President Reagan signed the secret NSDD 138 on counterterrorism, it was little more than a planning document that called on twenty-six federal departments and agencies to propose how to stop terrorists. It endorsed in principle the notion of preemptive strikes and retaliatory raids.

That night, in a dinner speech in Washington, Shultz called for an "active defense" and suggested the need for "preemptive" moves. He spoke at length with somber conviction. And the Secretary spent the better part of the next month on the hustings with his message.

Casey was looking at the problem from a different angle. The brand of terrorism practiced in Lebanon by the Iranians and the Syrians was shadowy, hard to pin down. Though he was convinced that Iran and Syria were behind much of it, he did not have the kind of proof required by American law, or even by common sense.

Partly because of the emphasis that Casey had placed on Libya, regular intelligence showed Qaddafi's brazen tactics. In March, communications intercepts, satellite photos and some human sources demonstrated conclusively that Libya was intervening in Sudan. Libya had sent a Soviet-built Tu-22 fighter to bomb a Sudanese radio station outside the capital, Khartoum. The intelligence had been so good that Shultz was able to declare publicly, without qualification, with his stern professorial, unsmiling gaze, "It is a fact" that Libya conducted the raid. What Shultz did not disclose was that the Libyan pilot had been captured and had admitted that it had been a practice run for future raids on Cairo.

The intelligence also showed that Libya had signed an agreement with Greece for an exchange on naval matters. Since Greece was still a member of NATO, this could threaten secrets in the West's most important alliance. Within the United States, the FBI had concrete evidence that a Libyan students' committee in a Washington suburb was involved in intelligence and terrorist work. There were suggestions that the People's Committee of Libyan Students be expelled from the United States, but the FBI argued that the group provided a window on Libyan activities in the country. There was particular concern because of the upcoming Republican and Democratic national conventions and the summer Olympics in Los Angeles. The conventions and the Olympics would be an opportunity for a spectacular terrorist act.

Qaddafi was so unpopular with his neighbors that Sudan, Egypt and Iraq were providing secret support to the opposition, the National Front for the Salvation of Libya (NFSL).

Casey kept pushing this sort of intelligence through the system; the NID, one day for example, said: "Satellite photography shows normal activity on Friday around Qaddafi's compound." The May 8 attack on the compound heightened a sense of opportunity. The NSC's Terrorist Incident Working Group, middle-level officials from key departments and agencies, was on Qaddafi alert. Casey encouraged Shultz to take the lead; without State's support, the Administration would not do much. Shultz's deputy and old friend, Kenneth W. Dam, initiated a review of policy toward Libya.

On May 18, Dam received from the State Department's intelligence branch a SECRET/SENSITIVE ten-page paper called "Countering Libyan Terrorism." It brought together the several strands within the Administration—desire for counterterrorist action, anti-Qaddafi sentiment, good intelligence, and an opportunity.

The options were laid out on pages six and seven. They ranged from "do nothing" to the more positive option 8: "Establish a pattern of directly reacting to Libyan terrorism by going after carefully selected Libyan targets . . ." and then on to option 9: "Mount a program of covert actions to preempt, disrupt and frustrate Libya's plans," and finally option 10: "Seek a regime change."

The next day, a Saturday, Dam held a meeting in his office with a handful of top officials. There were four options; number four was to "forcefully expand existing policy . . . For example, re-examine the feasibility of other military or covert options."

On June 13, Bob Gates received a SECRET/SENSITIVE request from Hugh Montgomery, head of State's intelligence branch: "In connection with the very sensitive policy review which he is now conducting, Ken Dam has asked for an interagency assessment of the threat which Libya poses to U.S. interests." It set forth a tentative list of the subjects to be addressed, formally "the terms of reference." Gates was to come up with a judgment on the exact threat posed worldwide by Qaddafi. Was he the archterrorist requiring a U.S. response? Was he merely a nuisance who had to be tolerated, as the Europeans generally believed? State asked for a reply within three weeks. "We have also been asked to emphasize the sensitivity of this subject and the need to restrict knowledge . . ."

The national intelligence officer for the region, the Near East and South Asia, had already undertaken a delicate top-secret review, addressing Qaddafi's vulnerabilities. Where was Qaddafi weak? How and where might U.S. policy have an impact? Representatives from the CIA, the DIA, State and the NSA went to work.

In contrast to the pressure for action from the policy-makers at State, the intelligence representatives from State were intensely skeptical of the bits of information that suggested substantial unrest in Libya. Libya was something of a diplomatic black hole, and the State Department was more skeptical than the CIA of communications intercepts and source reports.

All agreed that the current U.S. policy of trade restrictions was laughably ineffective, though an abrupt withdrawal of U.S. and British oil workers might force a drop in Libyan oil production by 25 to 50 percent in the short run. There were some intelligence reports showing that a Qaddafi five-year campaign to instill a new revolutionary spirit in Libya had backfired, creating a climate conducive to his overthrow. Members of Qaddafi's own Bedouin tribe had urged him to abandon his totalitarian policies, warning him that his tribe and his family faced isolation and disgrace unless he moderated his policies.

Qaddafi's suspiciousness was a psychological vulnerability, the NIO's group concluded, though it was also a form of protection. Intelligence suggested that Qaddafi wore a bulletproof vest, and that an elite, specially equipped military unit, a countercoup force, protected his Tripoli headquarters, where the main communications networks and the city's radio station were located.

Clandestine reports, code-breaking and intelligence liaison reports showed that the anti-Qaddafi exile movement was getting support from six countries:

- Egypt, Qaddafi's obsession.
- Iraq, partially in response to Qaddafi's support of Iran in the Iran–Iraq war.
- Morocco, though relations were improving.
- Saudi Arabia, whose support was highly secret.
- Sudan, which Qaddafi was always trying to buy or take over.
- Tunisia, despite Qaddafi's close relationship with a senior minister who was virtually on his payroll.

The list included three of the six countries on Qaddafi's borders. He was at war with a fourth, Chad.

But Egypt and, to a lesser extent, Algeria were the keys to bringing military and other pressure on Qaddafi. The intelligence representatives agreed on language for an assessment of Egypt and Algeria: "Both also would have serious reservations about cooperating with the United States in covert activity aimed at overthrowing Qaddafi. These reservations are based in part upon a perception of U.S. unwillingness and an inability to participate effectively and meaningfully, and upon U.S. inability to prevent such actions from becoming public."

The CIA, DIA and NSA representatives concluded that there was substantial discontent within the Libyan military. Over State Department objections, they wrote: "Successful internal operations, on a relatively spectacular level and with some frequency, combined with other external pressures and setbacks, could serve to spark action against Qaddafi by some disaffected elements in the military." Qaddafi's deputy, Major Salaam Jalloud, and the chief of the armed forces and his deputy "probably have the strongest motives."

The assessment was taking shape, with the State Department, ironically, on the outside objecting to conclusions that would support a covert operation to undermine or overthrow Qaddafi. But the others continued and on page five went several steps further, for all practical purposes arguing for strong action by the United States:

> We believe the exile groups, if supported to a substantial degree, could soon begin an intermittent campaign of sabotage and violence which could prompt further challenges to Qaddafi's authority. If exile activity were coupled with other factors—increased propaganda, visibly deteriorating relations with foreign countries and broad economic pressure—disaffected elements in the military could be spurred to assassination attempts or to cooperate with the exiles against Qaddafi. However, widespread military rebellion is unlikely.

It was nearly an invitation to assist in an assassination of Qaddafi, despite the President's executive order banning any involvement, direct or indirect, in the support or planning of assassination. The 1981 Reagan Executive Order 12333 said: "Prohibition on assassination. No person employed by or acting on behalf of the United States government shall engage in, or conspire to engage in, assassination." The assessment was, at minimum, an unusually provocative document, virtually urging coordinated action, warning against halfhearted efforts:

> This paper concludes that no course of action short of stimulating Qaddafi's fall will bring any significant and enduring change in Libyan policies. A fundamental conclusion of this paper is that Libya has significant vulnerabilities, but that these can only be exploited successfully through a broad program in cooperation with key countries combining political, economic and paramilitary actions. Isolated paramilitary, economic or political actions are likely to have little or no effect.

It was a call for a major covert action, and the State Department intelligence branch disputed the very foundation of the conclusion—the underlying intelligence. In a footnote on the first page, State filed a stinging dissent, saying, "The paper rests too heavily on fragmentary, unsubstantiated reporting and fails to give sufficient weight to Qaddafi's enduring popularity. Qaddafi's security grip is so tight that no coup is likely to get off the ground."

When it was finished the assessment was twenty-nine pages long and was classified as follows: TOP SECRET, with the code words UMBRA (containing information from decoded communications), NOFORN (could not be seen by foreigners), NOCONTRACT (contract, part-time employees could not see it), PROPIN (containing proprietary information from businesses), ORCON (the originator controlled dissemination, and all copies were numbered).

The document was issued on June 18. It was a source of controversy among the handful of government officials who were cleared to read it. The reference to and the virtual call for "paramilitary operations" and the suggestion that the United States spur the Libyan military to assassination attempts leaped from the pages.

On the Fourth of July, the CIA issued another TOP SECRET paper on Libya. This was the threat assessment; it stated that Qaddafi was continually acting against U.S. interests but that the only immediate concern was what Qaddafi might do in Sudan.

It continued: "An act of Libyan terror in the United States is possible, but we believe Libya would be hard-pressed to mount a successful operation. Libya almost certainly has a few agents among the approximately 1,500 Libyan students in the United States," including "approximately 200 fanatic pro-Qaddafi students here."

Dealing with fears that Qaddafi might obtain a nuclear weapon, the assessment noted on page 13: "We believe Libya will not achieve a nuclear explosive capability within the next 10 years."

An interagency group at the White House began outlining plans for covert support to the Libyan exiles and an array of covert nonlethal and covert lethal alternatives. The rhetorical exchanges between the United States and Libya were at such a high pitch that the officials decided to consider an unusual question: "What is the impression when we don't do something?" The pressure for action was immense. There was lots of tough talk. No one wanted to sound weak. Options were drafted and circulated.

Casey was out of town when they arrived at the CIA. McMahon received the paperwork and lost his aplomb. This was madness.

McMahon knew some of the CIA's history concerning Libya. In the years immediately after 1969, when Qaddafi had come to power, there had been discussions about trying to overthrow him, but the State Department had opposed an attempt and had won. Director Helms had agreed with State that there was then no way to accomplish this. During the Carter Administration, Turner had asked once what might be done about Qaddafi. McMahon, then the DDO, had answered, Not much.

McMahon felt that the group that had drafted the option had no handle on the exile groups. They were little more than Boy Scouts in his book. The intelligence suggested that they couldn't land a rubber raft on the Libyan coast, let alone overthrow a government, let alone take Libya over and run it. Qaddafi had penetrated the movement and followed every step its members made. Qaddafi would have had a potentially strong leader in that movement bumped off.

McMahon knew how to kill a covert operation with questions, demanding details he knew no one had. Did the CIA have penetrations? How many security guards did Qaddafi have? Were they loyal? What were the chances for success? The answers, as expected, were vague. McMahon said that even if there were a half-assed chance they could not go forward, but they weren't even that close. If you don't have the tools and the people, don't screw around, he argued. And what about the prohibition on assassination? he asked. This would not be an operation against a regime. It would be against an individual. There was no conceivable, credible way to set something like this in motion and then tell the exiles not to kill Qaddafi.

When Casey returned, he backed McMahon on a number of grounds. First, America's allies, especially in Europe, would not agree. It infuriated Casey that Qaddafi was gaining, rather than losing, respectability in Europe—the secret Libyan-Greek agreement was only an example. Without the coordinated support of the Western Alliance, there was no way for covert pressure or operations to work. If the CIA went ahead anyhow, the United States would end up isolated. Second, there was insufficient political backing for such an operation within the Administration. The May 8 coup attempt had only shown that there was an opportunity to unseat Qaddafi, but he had done nothing immediately threatening to warrant such a move.

With the Nicaragua operation in trouble with Congress, Casey was in no mood for another fight. The 1984 presidential election was several months off. There was no way Casey wanted to step off a cliff, though he was sure that an operation against Qaddafi would be very popular with his two most important constituencies—the public and Ronald Reagan.

On June 22 Casey found a highly classified letter from Attorney General William French Smith in his in-box. It was trouble. The letter contained a summary of a very sensitive FBI leak investigation that was nearly two years old. On July 13, 1982, the NSA had intercepted commercial communications from the Mitsubishi office in Washington to Japan. To the great alarm of the United States, Mitsubishi had detailed, verbatim information from the top-secret National Intelligence Daily of July 7 and 9. Mitsubishi's communiqué reported on Iran and Iraq troop movements, including the massing of 120,000 Iranian troops to oppose 80,000 Iraqis at a particular border location. There was sensitive intelligence that the Iraqi leader would have to fall before there would be peace talks. Mitsubishi sourced its information to an unidentified member of a U.S. government intelligence agency who had told it to a Washington consulting firm that Mitsubishi had hired. A second NSA intercept of the Japanese company's traffic out of Washington on July 29, 1982, had contained extensive quotes from the NID of three days earlier. NSA Director Lincoln Fauer had been anxious to find the leak and had asked for an investigation.

The FBI had zeroed in on one of Casey's senior analysts, Charles Waterman, vice-chairman of the National Intelligence Council. Waterman, a thin, balding, nervous former operations officer with twenty years' experience, had been authorized to deal with the Washington consulting firm that published a bimonthly newsletter which often contained terrific material on the Middle East. In fact, Waterman had gathered good intelligence from the consulting group.

Waterman had not made it through a barrage of FBI and CIA polygraph examinations in 1983, and Casey remembered the episode as a glorious mess. The CIA security office had recommended that Waterman resign. Waterman was a good man who denied leaking, and Casey was of the opinion that everyone the agency sent out to gather information and maintain contacts around town talked more than he should. Some goddamn numbers about Iran and Iraq troop strength were nothing—typical garbage from the NID. A firing would send the wrong message internally at Langley. So Casey, with McMahon's agreement, overruled the CIA's own security office recommendation. Waterman would receive a slap on the wrist—two weeks' leave without pay.

But the FBI hadn't dropped its investigation and had opened a criminal espionage case. Waterman had been placed on leave with pay in December 1983 as the FBI continued working.

Now, seven months later, Attorney General Smith was saying that the Justice Department might not be able to prosecute Waterman because sensitive sources and methods would have to be disclosed at a trial. But, he said, the investigation had reached a stage where it would be appropriate for the CIA to take some action; dismissal and a public statement about the reasons would serve as a substantial deterrent to others; finally, the Attorney General would like to know what final action is taken.

"God damn Bill Smith," Casey yelled. The letter obviously had been written by the Justice Department or by the FBI bureaucracy, both bent on protecting their ass. They hadn't been able to find the leak, so they would try to get Casey to shove Waterman out the door as if they had. Smith had signed the letter blindly. Copies of the letter had been spread all over town to the departments and the agencies.

"This goddamn thing isn't going to leak," Casey said. But he knew that the Smith letter making Casey appear soft on a senior leaker was likely to get out.

Casey summoned Sporkin and showed him the letter and a Justice Department report on the investigation. Sporkin believed Waterman was innocent. Under oath, Waterman had denied leaking, and his calendars had not shown any meetings with the newsletter people at the time of the leaks. The newsletter people had also denied that Waterman was the source. Sporkin felt sorry for Waterman. When he had been put on administrative leave, Sporkin had helped him find a lawyer. Three months before that, when Sporkin had gone down to the FBI's Washington Field Office to try to straighten the matter out, FBI agents had suggested that Sporkin might be obstructing their investigation.

He disagreed with Casey on the efficacy of lie detectors. They turned the presumption of innocence on end: if the operator says the machine shows deception, that's it; there is no way to disprove it. The result was a stalemate. The Attorney General's letter was proof of that. They weren't going to prosecute because they didn't have a case, not because a trial would possibly disclose sources and methods, Sporkin said. Justice wanted Casey to kick some ass. The polygraph was no better than a medieval rack or thumbscrew; it was a mind-basher rather than a body-basher, that was the only difference, Sporkin felt.

In an atmosphere of leaks and spies, Casey felt that every tool, even the polygraph, had to be used. It had come up with some impressive results: it scared people, it led to confessions, it warned the agency off hiring unreliable people. Casey phoned Waterman and asked him to come by the next day.

Waterman, as he drove to Langley for the meeting, was glad that something was at last about to happen. It had been a terrible seven months waiting, the worst of his life. He had been in some awful holes for the CIA, bumping around the stations in the Middle East, beginning in 1964. He had served in Beirut, Cairo, Jordan, back to Beirut, and was finally station chief in Saudi Arabia. He had used and taken polygraph tests before. He had no faith in them. There had been four miserable half days strapped to the box over the Mitsubishi incident. The FBI polygraph operator had said to him, "You're in big trouble," but the results of the polygraph, Waterman felt, had been a measure of his inner turmoil. He had talked with one of the newsletter people about the Iran–Iraq war; he may have used the internal CIA figures about the troop strength, but they were virtually the same as those in news accounts. He had not leaked. The idea that he would provide something verbatim was absurd. Waterman suspected that John McMahon believed he had leaked something, but he felt he had a chance with Casey.

When Waterman arrived at Casey's seventh-floor office, he was happy to see that the DCI was alone.

Casey explained the letter from the Attorney General and handed Waterman the Justice Department report.

It's untrue, Waterman said as forcefully as he could. He had big, innocent eyes.

So what can we do? Casey asked.

The leadership in the analytic, open side won't continue an aggressive interchange with the outside world if you terminate me, Waterman said.

My hands are tied, Casey replied.

"I didn't do it," Waterman said, staring directly into the eyes of the DCI.

Casey said he believed him. But there are three reasons, he said. "Your usefulness around town is ruined. You are in a box because of the FBI conclusion that you did it. And if it leaks I'll be charged with coddling a leaker."

Everything that the FBI had done in the investigation had been designed to prove that the polygraph was accurate, Waterman said. There was no real investigation. Someone else had leaked and had gone undiscovered.

I'll think about it, Casey said finally, postponing the decision. Waterman left.

Casey was in agony. He didn't want to violate his own principle about risk-taking. If his people were going to be out there gathering information, they were going to have to exchange information—give some to get some. It was the way the world worked; no way would some newsletter people meet with Waterman if it was a one-way street. A pro like Waterman knew the limits, knew what was truly sensitive. Casey had to back his people if they made mistakes. If he didn't, they would stop, retreat back into the shell as in the previous Administration. In 1977, in the first months of Stan Turner's directorship, Turner had fired two CIA men because of contact they had had with renegade former CIA operative Edwin Wilson. Turner had paid a horrible price in morale, Casey knew.

Casey felt that CIA people shouldn't get fired except for gross, deliberate, incompetent performance. This didn't fit. That night Casey debated with himself. It was one of the hardest decisions he had faced in nearly four years. Waterman was the kind of dedicated man who had done his job; he was the embodiment of the determination Casey needed.

Next day Casey called Waterman and set up a meeting in the EOB office. Waterman arrived. He looked so vulnerable.

I've searched and searched, Casey said, and we can't come up with anything. Sorry, nothing we can do about it.

Waterman choked a bit, and paused. Yes, sir, he said. He saluted and left. On the way out Waterman reminded himself that they all served at the pleasure of the DCI. It had to be that way. That meant that twenty years as a CIA man were over. He could remember his first clandestine meeting—in 1964 in Kuwait. They had sent him out in the awful heat and uncertainty. His instructions had been to locate, at a particular time and place, "an Arab who looks like he just jerked off." What did that mean? He hadn't known. But he had found his contact.

Casey wouldn't have let Waterman go in his first year as DCI. Working on his fourth year, Casey felt he had no choice. Leaks were a bigger problem than morale.

The visibility and controversy surrounding the Nicaragua operation had put a crimp in the Directorate of Operations. There were fears that Congress, the media and the public might once again turn on the CIA. Casey decided it was time to air the directorate, replace DDO John Stein. The post of inspector general was better suited to his temperament. Stein was a good, solid officer but a little too cautious, and Clair George needed to be rescued from the Hill. George, like Casey, had been burned badly in the mining flap. But George had stood his ground. Casey liked the way he had handled it—seasoned, loyal, direct, willing to take and give heat, recognizing the absurdity of congressional meddling.

The difference between a Stein, who had joined the agency in the 1960s, and a George, who had joined in the 1950s, was the margin of difference for Casey. George was a survivor, prudent enough but with instincts born of the Cold War. Daring intelligence work—bribery, betrayal, electronic penetrations—were natural for him. He possessed the covert sensibility. He knew that the work was dirty and that they all had to live with contradictions.

Casey announced the changes at the end of June. The ongoing operations were a mixed bag—the application of money and manpower was progressing easily in some places but was stalled in others.

In July, Congressman Charlie Wilson obtained another $50 million for the Afghan covert operation. With the money he had gotten earlier plus the CIA's request, that meant $120 million, and there was talk of doubling that next year. With the Saudis matching dollar for dollar, soon a half billion would be going to the Afghan rebels. That was fine with Casey, but as he surveyed the globe he concluded that it was not rational to put virtually all the covert eggs into a single basket.

There were two other covert support operations that were important, not because of the amount of money, but because of the principle. Casey had still managed to keep them secret. One was the $5 million in the budget for the Cambodian-resistance support operation, and his plan was to add another $12 million at the end of the year, even though this helped the Khmer Rouge indirectly. The second was a limited nonlethal support operation of about $500,000 a year for the Ethiopian Marxist regime's opposition, which was also supported covertly by the Saudis. This group had a leftist orientation. In both cases, Casey was willing to dance cautiously with the devil. He saw the anti-Communist resistance movements as a unit—Nicaragua, Afghanistan, Angola, Ethiopia and Cambodia were the battleground. This was the "Reagan Doctrine."

Casey had greatly increased the covert budget for propaganda operations. There were now about two dozen, providing money abroad for newspapers, think tanks and institutes. As with the covert paramilitary operations, he had to contend with congressional micromanaging.

In the 1950s and 1960s, the CIA had run pro-NATO propaganda very successfully. Now the Reagan Administration was trying to gain backing for placing the Pershing II missile in Europe. In 1983, Casey had budgeted several million dollars to promote the missile in the European press. Predictably, the intelligence committees had cut the funds. In 1984, Casey tried again to persuade the committees to give him several million dollars for this purpose. The Democrats argued in secret sessions that such efforts could be construed as interfering in the internal affairs of NATO allies. The Pershing II missiles were the subject of hot debate in Britain, West Germany and Italy. If it should leak that the CIA was propagandizing our allies, the impact could be devastating both to relations generally and to the efforts to deploy the missile. There was also concern that the propaganda might "blow back" into the U.S. news media.

Casey argued that the several million was just enough to keep the propaganda network of writers and others active. The committees pushed hard with what Casey thought standard arguments: several million was not enough to get the job done, so why start it? The money was removed from the budget, and the CIA was told to use maintenance funds to keep a few European writers in readiness. Once again, Casey thought, the CIA was being told, Be ready but don't do anything. The committees were combing through the line items in the three-foot-thick stack of highly classified budget volumes, and others in the Congress, especially Senator William Proxmire of Wisconsin, who was always looking for waste, were picking on intelligence operations.

At an overseas U.S. Army facility regularly made available to a Soviet inspection team, there were hot tubs for off-duty relaxation. Army intelligence had installed sophisticated eavesdropping devices and was in the process of upgrading the monitoring equipment. The high cost had been buried in the military budget, the line-item entry listed as improvement of hot tubs. This was an open invitation for Proxmire's monthly Golden Fleece Award for wasted taxpayer money. Army Intelligence chief Lieutenant General William Odom had to intervene and explain that an intelligence-gathering operation of some delicacy was about to be jeopardized.

The U.S. intelligence agencies had space in a high-rent district in New York City that was also targeted for Proxmire's Golden Fleece Award. Someone suggested that the award could provide a perfect cover because the government would never allow a sensitive operation to receive so much publicity. In the end, however, the intelligence agency set up a phony proprietary company out of the reach of Proxmire's investigators.

There was something else that summer that worried Casey. The Catholic Church in Nicaragua had emerged as the most powerful force opposing the Sandinistas. Archbishop Miguel Obando Bravo, who oversaw its nine bishops and all Catholics, was organizing the church to warn the people about Marxism-Leninism. *La Barricada,* the official Sandinista newspaper, had charged that he was involved "in political activity aimed at overthrowing the Nicaraguan government." He was described as a drinking buddy of Somoza. A cartoon showed a bishop twisting a cross into a Nazi swastika.

Under the general finding for Central America propaganda, the CIA was flush with extra money, and at a lower level in the DO some officer had decided to allocate $25,000 to be funneled through a private U.S. foundation to help the Catholic Church in Nicaragua. It was an explosive connection.

Senator Moynihan thought at first that it had to be a joke. When he found out it was not, he summoned a senior official from CIA and plunked him down by the fireplace in his private office. "Don't do it. That man, the Archbishop, is a moral force down there, and under no conditions can he be compromised." Casey agreed with Moynihan, and the $25,000 was cancelled.

Trying to get rid of its propaganda funds required many avenues. When funds went to private organizations, the CIA lost control, but Moynihan was pondering not just control but the basic judgment. That $25,000 could have been a drop of poison. Where was the care? Who was conducting a risk assessment? Where was the moral dimension? It was precisely the sort of thing that fostered the image of the Ugly American. Was it just a matter of shoveling money out the door? Had Congress increased the intelligence budget too much? Didn't someone ask these questions?

Casey replied that the Archbishop would never have known the source, because the money would have been buried in with other funds. But his main effort was to make sure the story did not get out. It would inevitably be misunderstood. In its worst version, it might look as if the CIA, having failed to get its contra funding, was trying to funnel money to the rebels through the Church. Not true, but Casey didn't trust anyone to get it right.

The story, though, began to circulate, and in due course Casey called the *Post*. He said that if the story was printed, the Archbishop was "dead." The story did not run.

An examination of other propaganda funds was launched, and a minor secret channel through a Catholic Church organization in Poland to funnel CIA funds of $20,000 to $30,000 to benefit the Solidarity trade union was closed down because of political risk.

As the 1984 campaign started, Casey was sidelined. The Director of Central Intelligence could not possibly attend campaign strategy sessions. On his frequent trips to the White House, Casey was left to nibble at the edges of the campaign. He would stop by to see Edward J. Rollins, a blunt right-wing Californian who was the master strategist of Reagan's reelection campaign. It looked like a win, for sure, both agreed.

The three briefcases Casey usually took home at night contained stacks of newspapers, clippings and magazines. He followed the media with an intelligence analyst's eye. Public information, or "open sources," could provide some of the best clues about the continuing maneuvering within the Administration. On August 30, a story in *The Washington Times* merited attention: "Five Being Considered for Casey's CIA Job."

What the shit, he thought. *The Washington Times*, started by the Reverend Sun Myung Moon of the Unification Church, was plugged into Reagan's conservative Washington. Several of its staff writers had worked at the NSC. The *Times* was must reading for keeping on top of the plots at 1600 Pennsylvania Avenue.

Casey read with alarm and anger that he "had made known his intention to leave government service" after the election, no matter whether Reagan won or lost.

At one time, Casey had seriously considered asking the President not to reappoint him, but John McMahon and others in the building had gone to work on him, persuading him that he was the only one who could keep the momentum, insure continuing support from the President and continue the flow of money and good relations with other foreign-intelligence services. Their appeal had touched Casey deeply. They had convinced him that even if the CIA or he himself took a whacking in the press, his directorship demonstrated that the CIA had not lost its authority in government, or with the President himself. That authority and credibility were vital if the agency was to continue on the road back. He had agreed to stay.

The article was attributed to "well-placed administration officials" and "White House insiders," and one of the authors was a former NSC staffer, Jeremiah O'Leary. The story stated that the White House had begun to assemble a list of possible successors. At the top of the list was "White House Chief of Staff James A. Baker III."

At such moments, Casey's lower jaw would sink. He went deep into thought. A single newspaper story was like an untested source, it needed backup. Five days later he noticed the "Inside Washington" column in the *New York Post:* "CIA Boss Casey Turning In His Cloak & Dagger." The article portrayed Casey as the initiator, having allegedly "informed" the White House that he wanted to return to private life. Again, Jim Baker was at the top of the list of possible successors.

This was delicate. The polls put Reagan's lead over Democratic nominee Walter F. Mondale at about ten points and growing. A second administration was almost inevitable. What was the play? Any departure of a major Cabinet officer or a White House staffer would set off a chain reaction. George Shultz was the key. Weinberger, Jeane Kirkpatrick, Jim Baker, Casey himself would like State. But it seemed pretty clear that Shultz was planning to stay. That meant that Weinberger would probably remain at Defense. State and Defense were still the only other jobs that interested Casey.

And he liked the CIA, now more than ever. In a second term, White House politics would play a lesser role in decisions, Casey believed—especially decisions about foreign policy and CIA operations. Reagan would feel more inclined to follow his instincts.

The *Washington Times* and *New York Post* articles were being taken seriously in Administration circles. Casey was getting some questions and some ribbing.

Over drinks one evening, Tony Motley prompted him. "So Jim Baker's going to get your job."

"He's the last fucker that will get that job," Casey replied harshly.

It was Casey, together with Weinberger, Clark and Kirkpatrick, who had stopped Baker from moving to NSC adviser the previous year, but it wasn't clear what could be done to keep Baker from becoming DCI. If he were asked to leave, Casey would have a say about his successor, but not a veto. Baker had won Reagan's trust and might have elicited a promise from the President. Nonetheless, it didn't sound right. Casey knew that Baker wanted to get foreign-policy experience. His ambitions were probably limitless—Secretary of State in a future George Bush administration, or elected office. The CIA didn't seem to fit his agenda.

Casey's rule was that leaks can often be traced by answering the questions: Who benefits? Who wants the story out? The answer in this case had to be someone who wanted his job or just wanted him out. His efforts to find the leak were unsuccessful, so Casey decided to ask his benefactor directly. Casey called this "Irish" and "tough." He wrote a letter to Reagan, voicing concern about the stories allegedly coming out of the White House. As the President knew, he had not requested to return to private life and had no plan to, unless, of course, the President so desired. Casey explained that he would gladly serve for the duration of the Reagan presidency. There was, he added, as again the President knew, important, vital work still to be done in the intelligence agencies. He enclosed clips of the two newspaper stories, saying that such reports hurt morale at the CIA, created an air of uncertainty, undermined the stability they had achieved. Nearly four years of work could be set back. These false reports should be stopped.

Casey had crafted his letter to strike Reagan's anti-press, anti-leak, pro-CIA bells. Almost immediately, Reagan phoned. He expressed total, unwavering support. Of course, Bill, I want you to stay if there is a second term. "You're my man at the CIA as long as I'm President."

Casey was satisfied. It was all but a guarantee, a signed contract. Casey felt almost like running down to Pennsylvania Avenue and kissing the President. Damn, he admired this man. It was a good lesson in management: pick and stick. Select your people and hang with them.

19

In September, Casey was spending lots of time at Langley raising consciousness about a possible terrorist attack in the closing weeks of the campaign. He summoned operations officers and analysts to his office, called others, poked around the building, pounding down the corridors, popping into offices and the operations center. He made it clear that the entire U.S. intelligence community was on terrorist alert. He dreaded that a strike again by mad bombers would show the impotence of the United States. The political repercussions could be substantial. Reagan's presidency stood for strength. Nothing in the last years had demonstrated weakness more than an inability to stop these attacks.

For seventeen months Casey had been throwing assets at the problem—training, information exchange, the development of a network involving some one hundred countries. There had been significant upgrading in forty countries of CIA capabilities in paramilitary training, hostage rescue and VIP protection. The CIA had just trained sixty Lebanese. Nearly fifty people at CIA headquarters worked exclusively on terrorism, as well as dozens more at the NSA and in the military intelligence services. Casey demanded results, and there had been some success. Intelligence had determined that Spain's ambassador to Lebanon was being tracked, and the CIA had suggested he leave Lebanon. He did not and was later kidnapped.

The attention to terrorism generated more reports, and finally a flood of information, much of it of dubious value. Operationally, the CIA was still having almost no luck in penetrating Middle East terrorists groups. The reason was simple, Casey concluded. Terrorists knew that CIA agents couldn't kill because they could not target people for assassination. An applicant to a terrorist group was given an immediate test—go kill someone.

Some of the most concrete information was coming in classified reports showing that explosives and timed fuse bombs were being moved by

Iranians operating out of their embassy in Damascus under the protection of diplomatic immunity. In August, reports had shown that explosives had been moved into Lebanon, where the trail was lost. With the Marines gone, the U.S. ambassador's residence and the American Embassy annex in the relative security of Christian East Beirut were the remaining major targets. The CIA and other intelligence agencies cranked out reports. There was a here-we-go-again flavor but not much exactness to the warnings.

At 11:40 A.M. Thursday, September 20, a van with diplomatic license plates pulled into the U.S. Embassy annex in East Beirut, zigzagging and threading its way around the staggered row of concrete dragon's teeth designed to slow all vehicles. One guard's M16 jammed. The security guard for the British ambassador, who was visiting the embassy, opened fire, pumping five shots into the van, which headed into a parked vehicle some thirty feet short of the ramp leading to the garage underneath the embassy. The van detonated, leaving a crater twenty-six feet in diameter. At least twenty-four people were killed, including two American servicemen. Another ninety were wounded, including U.S. Ambassador Reginald Bartholomew, who was buried in the rubble but emerged with only minor injuries.

Casey was sick. Top-secret overhead photography later showed that the van, or one just like it, had been practicing outside a mock-up of the embassy annex in the Bekaa Valley. American intelligence concluded that Hizbollah—the Party of God—and Sheikh Fadlallah were behind this attack, just as they had been behind the 1983 bombings at the embassy and the Marine barracks. In the preelection period, Casey quickly saw, no one in the White House was in the mood to retaliate, having held fire for many months, and after more serious attacks. After all, this could have been much worse.

One of the most intriguing after-action reports came from a Lebanese intelligence service lieutenant colonel. It showed the tight planning that had gone into the operation. The van had left Muslim West Beirut that morning. Two accomplices wearing uniforms of the Lebanese police force followed in an orange BMW. On the way to the embassy annex, the van accidentally hit a small Opel. The driver of the Opel got out and tried to talk to the van driver. The driver was subdued and seemed catatonic. He looked neither to the left nor the right. The Opel driver could not get his attention. At that point the two accomplices walked up and offered the Opel driver 2,000 Lebanese pounds—about $300—many times the cost of fixing his Opel. The driver took the money and left. A Lebanese who witnessed this heard the explosion at the U.S. Embassy annex about ten minutes later and went to Lebanese intelligence. They were never able to find the driver of the Opel, but they believed the witness's story. The CIA could not be certain, but the report suggested that the van driver had been drugged before his suicide mission.

The Lebanese intelligence service wanted more than the $2 million it received each year to pay agents, and Casey had promised to see whether he could get it. The Lebanese were doing what they could to provide intelligence on terrorist attacks and the relationship between the CIA and the Lebanese service was drawing closer.

Casey was not as confident about the Israelis. He knew that they had penetrated Lebanon and Syria with first-class agents, but there was a strong feeling that the Israelis were holding out and that it might be endangering American lives. Relations between the CIA and the Mossad had deteriorated after Israel invaded Lebanon, and the U.S. withdrew the Marines. Lebanon had been a disaster for both countries, and nothing sours relations like shared failure. The agencies worked together without liking each other. Mossad officials disparaged the CIA, one calling its agents ''players who can't play.'' Peter Mandy, the No. 2 in the Mossad, controlled all liaison with the CIA. In Lebanon, CIA and Mossad agents were not permitted to deal directly with one another. There was a feeling in the CIA that Mandy was miserly, dispensing bits of the Mossad's precious human-source reports only when it served Israeli interests.

The assessment at Langley was that the CIA-Israeli intelligence-sharing was a one-way street. Casey had to pressure the Israelis, let them know there was trouble. He could do it himself, but that might be too much pressure.

He decided finally to send McMahon to Israel. McMahon carried sufficient weight to read the Mossad the riot act: henceforth, the CIA would expect all information that might relate to a terrorist attack against U.S. installations. Please, and God damn it, McMahon argued. He felt that he had made only superficial progress; the Mossad was, in the end, like the CIA: it trusted no one.

The September 20 bombing dramatized intelligence problems, if not a breakdown, and Casey had some explaining to do at the White House. His response was simple. He went back ten years to the Church investigation, as well as the Carter Administration—both had crushed the spirit of the CIA, he said. An intelligence penetration or the cultivation of a source was feared more for the trouble it could cause than for its potential benefit. He couldn't rebuild a human-source network in four years.

For instance, President Carter had stopped the secret payments to King Hussein of Jordan in 1977 when the press found out about them. Carter somehow had felt that it was unsavory. Under Casey, the CIA had begun a new covert operation with Jordan to gather and share intelligence on terrorists and the PLO. But, having been burned in public by Carter, the King was wary and distrustful. Memories were long in the Middle East, Casey pointed out.

One person bought Casey's argument—Reagan. Six days after this latest Beirut bombing, the President was on the campaign trail in Bowling Green, Ohio. A student asked him about the security at U.S. embassies. He said, "We're feeling the effects today of the near-destruction of our intelligence capability in recent years before we came here." He added that previously the attitude had been that "spying is somehow dishonest and let's get rid of our intelligence agents. . . . And we did that to a large extent."

If there was any doubt about the target of this grenade, White House aides later explained to reporters that it was intended for Carter and Turner. The next day Carter blasted back, saying that Reagan's charge was "personally insulting and too gross in its implications to ignore." Calling the charge "completely false," Carter went on to say that the calamities in the Middle East were a result of "the President's own deeply flawed policy and inadequate security precautions in the face of proven danger."

Turner responded publicly, his voice almost quivering as he read a statement: "Mr. Reagan's comments are undignified and unworthy of a President. It is Reagan who has damaged the CIA by putting in people of questionable character . . . he has politicized the CIA with Casey." He asked, "What do you read about CIA today? You read about a director who has shady financial dealings and is involved in questionable legality and propriety in the secret war in Nicaragua. . . . No wonder they are not collecting intelligence in Beirut, because they're trying to undermine the government of Nicaragua."

Casey read the back-and-forth carefully, but he was not about to be drawn into partisan crossfire. He declined public comment. But he knew what Reagan meant. The issue was not numbers, money or personnel, though they were all part of it. The real problem was the climate of distrust that Turner had fostered. The spirit of the agency had to be can-do, and Turner had made it don't-you-dare, Casey thought.

The flap died, but Casey was satisfied that the voters understood what it was all about.

• • •

After spending the summer stewing about resigning as the NIO for Latin America, John Horton gave a long on-the-record interview to a reporter for a Portland, Maine, newspaper. Without mentioning Mexico by name, Horton said that there had been an important intelligence estimate and that Casey had "kept constant pressure on me to redo it."

"I refused to redo it, so he finally had the thing rewritten over my dead body, so to speak," Horton said. "As an intelligence officer, I don't work for an administration, I work for the government."

It took three weeks for the news of Horton's public complaint to reach the Washington news media in full. On September 28, *The New York Times* had a front-page story, "Analyst Reported to Leave CIA in a Clash with Casey on Mexico."

Bob Gates, the deputy for intelligence, felt mildly betrayed. Horton hadn't hinted he would go public. It was Horton's one experience in the analytic world, and he obviously didn't understand it. Pressure was the name of the game. There was always pressure from the State Department or the Pentagon or the Navy, the Army, the White House. It was when the CIA struck a nerve or hit upon an important issue, or when its conclusions might have a real impact on policy, that people began screaming.

State was always hostile to the South Africa work the CIA was doing, and the hard-line Assistant Secretary of Defense, Richard Perle, always disagreed with CIA analysis on the Soviet strategic capability. Gates himself had, the previous year, reopened the issue of Soviet defense spending and concluded that it was lower than the DIA had been saying. This was like trying to revise one of the Ten Commandments, but Gates had plunged into the thicket. That was pressure. Horton didn't understand real pressure. Yes, the debate could get pretty rough. Casey could hand it out. These things needed to be tested, and the discussion often became adversarial, hot. In Gates's view, Horton had mistaken legitimate intellectual pressure for political pressure.

Just six weeks before the presidential election, Casey now had to contend with Horton. He felt that Horton had tried to keep out of the estimate information that corroborated the possibility of Mexico's collapse. Casey was determined that there be no estimate on his watch that said something like "The Shah of Iran will have five years in power" and then he's out in months.

The Director was also irritated at Horton's claim that he worked for the "government" and not some particular administration. It was as if Horton thought there was an additional branch of government, a permanent corps of keepers. In Casey's opinion, this was just the bureaucracy. And it was the trouble with government, not the solution.

Casey wrote Horton a personal letter. When Horton read it, he felt as if Casey were accusing him of growing long hair and taking drugs. For all his contention that he wanted a full range of opinion, Casey obviously hadn't wanted an alternative view of his process of doing the estimates. Casey had become part of the Reagan Administration policy-making cabal, and his primary concern was his desire to overthrow the government of Nicaragua. Mexico wasn't going along, it was too uppity in foreign affairs, it was charting an independent course of nonintervention and negotiation. At least unconsciously, Horton thought, Casey had intended the estimate to be a dagger aimed at the heart of Mexico.

Democrats on the Senate Intelligence Committee saw an opportunity. Moynihan read the estimate. A 1-in-5 chance of instability seemed well founded. Since Mexico had for all practical purposes been bankrupt, for Jesus Christ's sakes—*bankrupt!*—Moynihan judged that it was not unreasonable to predict some problem. He rather liked the idea of giving it a numerical probability. At least when someone waded through all the marvelously crafted concerns there was a forecast that might be of some use. After all, when people started saying there was an 80 or 90 percent chance of rain, one took one's umbrella.

And the House Intelligence Committee, no friend of Casey's, came to his defense, saying in a public report that it had "examined the earlier drafts and the final version of that particular NIE and found that dissenting views were printed at the very beginning of the study, a practice the committee applauds."

On Friday, October 12, Casey held a reception for the staff members of both the Senate and House intelligence committees in the executive dining room of the seventh-floor headquarters at Langley. It was an act of conciliation. He also wanted to thank them, to celebrate the final passage of a new law that exempted key DO, scientific and technical, and security files from the despised Freedom of Information Act.* The Pres-

* The bureaucratic problem posed by the Freedom of Information Act had been almost insurmountable for the CIA. Skilled officers had to review the files, making sure that each deletion was justified, and that no little bit of information that was released could, when assembled with other information, provide clues to a source or an operation. It was a dizzying task.

Most important, the search itself caused the breakdown of one of the cardinal rules of intelligence—compartmentation of information. All data related to a request were lumped together, removed from the compartmented sections of the operational files. Copies were made. More than one person became involved in the review. In some cases up to 21 separate CIA records systems had to be searched. Professional requesters flooded the CIA with queries for files and data. A New York law firm representing Iran leader Ayatollah Khomeini had made

ident was going to sign it into law on Monday. Passage symbolized a new, off-our-back attitude toward the CIA.

At the reception, Casey pressed flesh as he made the rounds. He hadn't testified before the Senate committee for nearly five months and had no plans to do so in the near future.

Rob Simmons approached him and mentioned that the main points in the 1980 Republican platform relating to intelligence had already been accomplished. In addition to the Freedom of Information Act revisions, the PFIAB had been reconstituted; an identities-of-agents bill had been passed in 1982 making it illegal to wantonly publish the names of agents; counterintelligence was being rebuilt and reemphasized; and the intelligence budget had been increased 50 percent in the last four years.

Casey jotted these down on a piece of paper. It was a good record.

The next day, Saturday, Casey rose early. It was one of those perfect football-weekend days, or a time to play golf. But he would be going to the office. He had been out of the country paying visits to stations, and he wanted to keep the momentum going at Langley. The Director's presence at headquarters on Saturday sent a subliminal message to all, those who were there and those who were not. On Monday there would be notes, calls, scribbled inquiries. Casey left a trail. He didn't want to get rusty. Though he had put on a blue blazer, a shirt and a tie, he had chosen his green plaid pants—"Republican fund-raisers"—to mark the informality of a Saturday.

One of his senior assistants at the agency came by his house for an 8:30 breakfast. It was a chance to review the first term, though Casey already had his mind on the second. It was twenty-four days to the election, and then almost certainly another four years for both Reagan and himself. Sophia, still in her bathrobe, set out apple cider, fried eggs, bacon and stacks of toast. Casey was relaxed and in a good mood as he sat at the dining-room table.

Sophia gave him total support. To Casey, she was the polar opposite of the wife of John le Carré's fictional British master spy George Smiley. Ann Smiley was self-centered and a drifter. Sophia was a woman of total devotion, her short white hair combed forward, no expensive hairstyle, perhaps a touch of hair spray. Since the day they married, on George Washington's Birthday during the war, she had stuck by him. Their mar-

---

four requests for information on the late Shah. McMahon estimated that it had cost $300,000 to process requests from one of the CIA's public enemies, Philip Agee, the renegade agent who had published lists of CIA agents.

riage was like the church. Sophia was one immeasurable advantage Casey had over Smiley.

The DCI felt that he had done the job at the CIA of conveying the explicit message of the Reagan Administration: America and strength. The world was not safer, because the Soviets were still bent on expansion, but the United States was in a better position to cope.

He shook his head at the mention of the alleged and much acclaimed passion he supposedly had for covert action. "That's bullshit," Casey said. "I am the chief analyst." His real job was as Bill Colby had described, running down to the White House with informed analysis, new information. Each day there was a different problem in a different part of the world.

One big turnaround in the Reagan years so far, Casey felt, was the Soviet Union. The Soviets were hurting; their economy was a mess and corruption was rampant, according to the best, latest CIA information. The Soviets had halted their "We're-the-future" talk by and large. Because they weren't. As Casey surveyed the world, it was clear that some good things were happening through covert action assistance to insurgencies. In spite of his boast that he was the chief analyst, Casey kept coming back to covert action.

- There was good news for the Afghanistan operation in particular. On the ground, in those mountains and in some of the most god-awful terrain in the world, the Russians were getting the tar beaten out of them, Casey thought, and CIA support was increasing.
- In Angola, even though U.S. covert assistance had been banned, there was an insurgency movement of 250,000 headed by Jonas Savimbi.
- In Cambodia, about fifty thousand were fighting the Vietnamese Army, the fourth-largest army in the world, to what he claimed was a virtual standstill, and CIA assistance was still only about $5 million a year.
- In Ethiopia, the resistance to the Marxist government was also in good shape, though most meaningful assistance was coming covertly from Saudi Arabia; the CIA role was nonlethal aid.
- The contras were active in Nicaragua despite the withdrawal of U.S. support. Overall, this controversial operation had been a great success. Casey felt strongly that if honest elections were held, the Sandinistas would lose. Their support was dissolving under the opposition from the Catholic Church and the pressure from the contras.
- In El Salvador, the U.S.-backed army had become more aggressive against the four rebel units. Intelligence indicated that the Soviets and

the Cubans were thinking that they would not win this one, and were willing to pull out in order to solidify their position in Nicaragua. He thought that the U.S. might have lost El Salvador if the pressure had not been kept on.

Casey conceded that some of these operations could be messy, risky, dangerous. But the alternative was to let things drift as they had done under Carter. Together with a full program of diplomatic, propaganda and economic pressures, covert action was effective. There was a time, he acknowledged, when the covert action had been too big a part of the Nicaragua effort.

He felt that in the last three and a half years he had won one point with his critics. The CIA could not be obsessively concerned with its reputation. It worked for the President. If the President's policies took a beating, so would the CIA. But so would the State Department or the Army. Those institutions—CIA, State, Army—were not so fragile that they couldn't withstand setbacks and criticism.

He had been pushy, had insisted on enterprise. As Casey looked down the scorecard, he checked off some other important successes:

- For the first time, real attention had been paid to technological transfers by the hundreds of Soviet-inspired or Soviet-backed trading companies set up to circumvent the law and buy high-technology equipment and plans.
- The intelligence exchange with China was very fruitful, not only listening posts but other intelligence, human and technical. The Soviets, in particular, would find it a nasty shock if they knew details.
- Overall surveillance of the Soviet Union was improved. There were better techniques to monitor its ballistic-missile submarines.
- There was penetration of the international banking system, allowing a steady flow of data from the real, secret sets of books kept by many foreign banks that showed some hidden investing by the Soviet Union.
- Improved CIA counterintelligence had achieved new penetrations. There had also been several high-level defections from the KGB that could not be publicized. The CIA doubted they were double agents.
- The CIA was closer to worldwide coverage for the first time; there were efforts to have some assets or collection resources devoted to each country in the world, no matter how remote, no matter how small. Recruitment of agents in the Third World was up, doubled in Central America.

- Attention was being focused on some long-range problems. The CIA was the only agency looking systematically at potential problems that might arise in five or ten years, or more. It was studying the trends in the Third World to the year 2000—food resources, water, economic development. Questions such as what happens when the population of Mexico City hits 40 million; the impact of the drug supply in Latin America into the distant future. With automobiles made more and more out of plastic and less out of aluminum, what was going to happen to countries that produced bauxite? One such country was Suriname; nearly two thirds of its gross national product came from bauxite. In some cases, problems might be addressed earlier and cheaper. At the least Casey wanted them identified.
- On arms control, Casey was not prepared to say whether a future agreement could be verified or not. He didn't believe in arms control.
- A special quarterly watch list of potentially unstable countries was circulated. At the top of the list was the Philippines, beset by insurgency and by political uncertainty.

Casey had molded and organized the CIA to assist its six true clients —the President, the Vice-President, the White House chief of staff, the Secretaries of State and Defense and the national-security adviser. The CIA was not set up to service Congress, it was not there for the news media or for the public. Though he occasionally courted others, Casey's essential message to any but his major clients was "Fuck you."

In many respects Casey realized that his directorship was a high-wire act, conducted in an atmosphere of no real restraints other than those he himself imposed. Since self-denial was not his style, and the intelligence account his free and clear, he demanded everything. The NSA's intercept program, for example, was now so comprehensive that senior officials had access to more material reporting back some of their own comments or alleged comments. An innocent social visit to an embassy reception could turn into an embarrassment for a Cabinet officer. The next morning's intercept packet would contain the ambassador's intercepted report back to his capital, quoting an unnamed U.S. official; under the NSA rules the names of U.S. citizens, even Cabinet officers, were deleted. Yet at times the social pages of the newspapers reported who attended the embassy parties and it took minimum detective work to determine the U.S. citizen.

The intercepts also revealed the frequency with which the foreign ambassadors in Washington distorted their reports and overstated their intimacy with senior U.S. officials, who in some cases seriously curtailed their dealings with embassy people and avoided the embassy cocktail circuit.

In one example, intercepts showed that the Japanese had developed a good source in the State Department on important trade negotiations. American officials read in some wonder the point-by-point U.S. positions even before they had been presented to other U.S. departments concerned with the negotiations.

Casey only smiled at this. He was reversing a trend, putting the United States back in a winning position on all fronts.

In his own way—private, personal, idiosyncratic—Casey found the roots of espionage idealistic. There was something, in this case the United States, for which it was worth fighting, even fighting hard and dirty. Casey was pleased with his agency but on a scale of 1 to 10 he would give it only a 7. Probably 7 was par, good, but not the best. It was possible to do better. That was why he was going to work that Saturday morning. To keep the ideas moving. That was what interested him. He had little patience for show-and-tell briefings and administering. He kept the notes and the queries flowing. Winston Churchill had a notepad headed "Action Today." That was what Casey wanted.

The next day, Sunday, Casey was alerted to an Associated Press wire report that disclosed a CIA guerrilla-warfare training manual advising the Nicaraguan contras on "selective use of violence" to "neutralize carefully selected and planned targets such as court judges, police and state security officials, etc." By Wednesday, *The New York Times* had the story on the front page: "CIA Primer Tells Nicaraguan Rebels How to Kill." It was difficult to avoid the logic that "neutralize" meant assassination. The ninety-page manual also urged the contras to "kidnap all officials or agents of the Sandinista government . . . "

Casey hadn't seen the manual, but he realized that it was a bombshell and that he had had an important if indirect role in the decision to prepare it. "Psychological Operations in Guerrilla Warfare" had been drawn up and given limited distribution to the contras a year earlier, after Casey's trip to Central America. He had pushed hard to give the contras some political context, arguing that armed bands roaming the mountains on hit-and-run missions weren't going to make a real difference. The contras had to get into the villages and the cities, spread their message, develop political organization, build political backing. The manual had been devised as an educational tool.

Now Casey took a pencil to the manual, scribbled and underlined. The manual was a muddle, a grab bag of ideas, often contradictory, and filled with revolutionary and psychological jargon—"self-criticism," "group discussions."

There was information on how to set up a guerrilla camp, and detailed instructions on how to avoid hostile feeling among the local residents. "Construct a latrine and a hole where wastes and garbage will be buried," Casey read. He laughed. The madness of it would be funny under other circumstances. The manual called for "implicit terror" and denounced "explicit terror."

Under "Shock Troops" he read: "These men should be equipped with weapons (knives, razors, chains, clubs, bludgeons) and should march slightly behind the innocent and gullible participants."

The word "neutralize" appeared under the heading "Selective Use of Violence for Propagandistic Effects." After a Sandinista official had been selected, the manual said, "it is absolutely necessary to gather together the population affected, so that they will be present, take part in the act, and formulate accusations against the oppressor." One sentence had been edited out of some editions of the manual, but unfortunately not all. It said, "If possible, professional criminals will be hired to carry out selective 'jobs.' " This was embarrassingly reminiscent of the CIA's hiring of John Roselli, a member of the Mafia, to assassinate Castro in the early sixties.

Assassination was like no other subject in the American psyche, Casey knew. No subject so challenged the national self-image and moral credibility. Assassination was the Scarlet A of American politics. The use of the word "neutralize" was probably worse than the use of the word "assassination" because it suggested the shadowy, plausible deniability that was supposed to be the bread and butter of CIA operations. In that concealed world, the agency never said what it meant anyway.

Casey was deeply concerned that no one in the chain of command at the CIA had seen the peril of trying to reduce warfare to words. It wasn't logical to go off in two directions, warning against and advocating violence.

The nature of guerrilla warfare revealed itself in the manual. The goal was to crush the constituted government. The take-no-prisoners style could not be denied. To imagine it otherwise would be truly naive. But to reduce it to writing?

A political firestorm erupted. House Intelligence Committee Chairman Boland said that the manual espoused "the doctrine of Lenin, not Jefferson. It embraces the Communist revolutionary tactics the United States is pledged to defeat throughout the world." Goldwater demanded a full briefing for the Senate committee. There were calls for a special prosecutor, and for Casey's head. There were accusations, principally from Democrats, that the United States was sponsoring terrorism. By the end of the day Casey was bananas.

The next day, he decided that he would release a statement pledging an investigation, but the issue of the manual and all it implied so dominated the news that he had to go down to the White House, which now stepped in to take control. The President's name was substituted for Casey's on a statement which said: "The Administration has not advocated or condoned political assassination or any other attacks on civilians, nor will we." Casey was told to have the CIA inspector general investigate, and the President's intelligence oversight board was directed to launch a separate probe. Both the House and the Senate committees started their own inquiries.

Part of Casey wanted to emerge from the shadows and shout back, What the hell do you expect? It's a war, not a picnic. It's messy and violent. People are getting killed down there. It's like that. The world is like that.

On Sunday, October 21, the second televised debate between Reagan and Mondale took place. Like tens of millions, Casey tuned in. The first question put to Reagan was a sharp one about the assassination manual, as it was now being called.

"Is this not, in effect, our own state-sponsored terrorism?" he was asked by syndicated columnist Georgie Anne Geyer.

"No," Reagan said. "But I'm glad you asked that question, because I know it's on many people's minds." He proceeded haltingly to claim that only twelve copies of the manual had got out with the offending language, and that it was the head of the CIA in Nicaragua who had supervised the manual's publication and printing.

"Mr. President, you are implying that the CIA in Nicaragua is directing the contras there?" Geyer asked.

"I'm afraid I misspoke when I said a CIA head in Nicaragua," Reagan said. "There is not someone there directing all of this activity." He then said it was CIA men stationed elsewhere in Central America.

"What is the President charged with doing when he takes his oath of office?" Mondale asked in rebuttal, challenging Reagan with a lecture about political terror and assassinations.

Reagan stumbled badly in the debate. Many asked whether the President was senile. *The Wall Street Journal* had already asked the question directly, publicly, in its lead front-page story: "New Question in Race: Is Oldest President Now Showing His Age?"

Casey was worried. This affair contained all the ingredients of calamity. Though Congress was not in session, the Senate Intelligence Committee demanded a briefing for those members still in town, and for the staff. Two relatively junior DO officers who had been involved in the Nicaragua operation for only about a month were sent up to the Hill.

Casey could make sure the investigations were not completed or released until after the election. Meanwhile, he needed someone out front defending the CIA publicly, someone independent, someone with credibility. Since his relations with Goldwater had been somewhat repaired after the mining fiasco, Casey decided to see whether he could enlist the Senator. But the Intelligence Committee chairman was back home in Arizona. Casey decided to dispatch a hand-carried explanation. He sent a draft press release for Goldwater to issue saying that there was nothing to the manual.

But Goldwater passed word back from Arizona that he could not, and would not, comment until the investigations were completed, adding again, as he had often on the mining incident, "I'm tired of pulling Casey's nuts out of the fire." He said don't send anyone out here, he was resting.

Casey needed a big play. In spite of Goldwater's snub, he decided to send the DDO himself, Clair George, and another senior operations officer, Vincent M. Cannistraro, to Arizona. The Senator would be impressed with such senior men flying almost clear across the country, Casey hoped.

George and Cannistraro boarded an afternoon flight, using assumed cover names, arrived in Arizona about 4 P.M. and took a taxi to Goldwater's house. Goldwater was in no mood. No, he didn't want to listen, no, he wasn't ready to make a statement.

But look here, George tried to explain gently—

No, Goldwater said flatly. They had better leave. The DDO and his assistant were soon on a plane back to Washington.

Senator Moynihan recognized the manual for what it was. At Harvard he had read a paper on Mao Tse-tung's technique of insurgency: identify the landowner, single him out and have a public trial. Focus the hate on one person, make the people in the village vote and then witness the execution. It was an effective bonding technique. He had seen it in a Green Beret manual during the Vietnam War. It brought the populace into the rebellion, gave them a stake, a feeling of satisfaction, a feeling that things were going to be better, that justice would be served.

When the CIA had made certain that none of its top officials, including Casey, McMahon, Stein and Clarridge (who couldn't read it because he didn't know Spanish), had reviewed or approved the manual, that conclusion was passed to the White House. That much of the investigation could be released. It took Casey out of the direct line of fire.

The next day, Casey wrote a personal letter to each member of the House and Senate intelligence committees, trying to explain it away. Taken as a whole, in context, addressing its thrust and purpose, the manual was intended to moderate behavior, he said.

But the Director was exhausted. As far as he was concerned, the real story was how the press and the congressional Democrats operated hand in hand. An Associated Press reporter had obtained a copy of the manual and had passed it to the House Intelligence Committee. The committee had authenticated it as a CIA product, the reporter had his story, and the committee had jumped up and down. Casey's public-affairs man, George Lauder, threatened that someday he would write a story on the leaks out of the Hill committees. Lauder joked that he was going to entitle his book "How Everyone Leaked and Pissed on America."

Shultz had come up with a Nicaragua peace plan and he wanted to deliver it to the President, who was in Des Moines campaigning. Casey conferred with Weinberger and Kirkpatrick. Shultz had to be stopped, they agreed. Casey nearly had to throw himself under the wheels of Air Force One and make it clear there would be plenty of resignations if the Secretary of State went forward. Shultz backed off.

On November 6, Reagan won reelection with 59 percent of the vote, carrying forty-nine states, all but Mondale's Minnesota and the District of Columbia.

20

THE FLAMES WERE flickering in the Oval Office fireplace, suggesting intimacy, even home, for the meeting that fall afternoon just after the election victory. Casey strode in with his papers and a summary of talking points on a single sheet of paper. He was certain he had reduced the issue to its basics. Now, with the second term, it was time. He had in mind a presidential finding that would direct the CIA to train and support small units of foreign nationals in the Middle East which would conduct preemptive strikes against terrorists. When intelligence showed that someone was about to hit a U.S. facility, such as an embassy or a military base, the units would be able to move to disable or kill the terrorists. The President was aware that the fanatics and suicide bombers were a visible demonstration of his Administration's impotence, and he had agreed to do something.

Weinberger had refused to involve the military; the shelling from the battleship *New Jersey* into Lebanon had not worked—it was too much, too indiscriminate, there was no pinpoint accuracy. Air strikes killed the innocent along with the terrorists. No, thanks, not us, was the message from the Pentagon. Cap had folded his arms and said no.

Casey's own CIA had to be dragged in kicking and screaming; McMahon had also issued a no-thank-you; the CIA did intelligence, not killing. But Casey had been stubborn, and Shultz had backed him up.

Casey explained to the President that the finding was simply to train and put the units in place; another finding would be required to take action in a specific case. The Israelis were experienced at this kind of covert preemptive work, but it was essential that the Administration not get into bed with them on this. Any U.S. action had to be seen as antiterrorist, not anti-Arab.

With luck, no one would ever know even about the existence of these new units. At first, three five-man units would be trained and set up in Lebanon. Any preemptive hit would be carried out undercover; it would not be traceable to the CIA or the United States; all would have deniability.

The President told Casey to inform the congressional intelligence committees but to invoke the provision in the law that allowed him to inform only eight people—the chairmen and vice-chairmen of the Senate and House committees, and the Republican and Democratic leaders of both the Senate and the House.

Casey said he would see to it personally. That would emphasize the sensitivity. No loudmouth staffers would know. He saw a chance to show that the CIA could conduct truly secret operations.

Reagan signed the formal finding and an accompanying National Security Decision Directive. The immediate cost for the Lebanese units would be about $1 million. When the program was expanded to other countries, the cost would be $5.3 million.

Rear Admiral John M. Poindexter, McFarlane's deputy, who was at the meeting, later described the afternoon session to a colleague: "Casey mumbled, and Ronald Reagan nodded off."

Casey was determined to see this through. McMahon had fought him every step of the way, littering the bureaucratic landscape with doubts. Could they trust the foreign nationals, particularly the Lebanese? Could the CIA control them? As McMahon saw it, either answer to the second question spelled trouble. If the CIA had control, would it not involve the agency in assassinations? Wasn't participation in preemptive strikes assassination-planning that was banned by the Reagan executive order, no matter how it might be dressed up? If the CIA did not have control, were they not launching unguided missiles? And, McMahon wondered further, would they ever have intelligence of the quality, certainty and timeliness to justify a preemptive attack? They had never had it so far.

Sporkin had helped develop Casey's rationale. He had written a legal opinion asserting that preemptive action would be no more an assassination than would a case in which a policeman gets off the first shot at the man who is pointing a gun at him. "Preemptive self-defense," he termed it.

Casey was focusing on Beirut. The past eight months had posed an emotional crisis for the agency. William Buckley, who had been kidnapped in Beirut on March 16, was described publicly as a political officer in the U.S. Embassy, but he was in fact Casey's station chief. Casey was sure that the Muslim extremists who had kidnapped him knew whom they had. He had pushed the DO nearly every day to come up with a way to locate and rescue Buckley. He had directed that extraordinary measures be taken: he would authorize money to pay informants; he ordered communications interception stepped up; he had satellite photos enhanced to search for clues; he established a special hostage-rescue task force. He was aware that neither he nor the agency could bargain for Buckley without violating Administration policy, which prohibited negotiations to ransom hostages. The ordeal was humiliating. The station in Beirut had had to be cut back to a new station chief and security people. Many of its intelligence functions had been turned over to the Lebanese intelligence service, a tough, lethal group that was in effect the last vestige of governmental authority in the capital. Money, equipment and technical support were being provided them by the CIA.

A group calling itself Islamic Jihad (Islamic Holy War) had claimed responsibility for kidnapping Buckley. Casey was sure the name was simply a slogan or a war cry for extremists. They had also been implicated in the bombings of U.S. facilities in Beirut.

For DDO Clair George, who had been the Beirut station chief from 1975 to 1976, the Buckley kidnapping revived bad dreams. During his time in Beirut, two U.S. government officials had been abducted and held hostage for four months before being released. He had lived that agony. George had turned the DO inside out trying to save Buckley. It was not only that he wanted Buckley back; the effort was a signal to thousands of DO officers abroad that the CIA would do just about anything to rescue one of its own. An expert FBI team trained in locating kidnap victims was sent to Beirut. It came up with nothing after a month.

It was time to hit back. But training the Lebanese was proving to be trouble. They couldn't be controlled; they were willing to commit murder, very willing. Casey's own CIA people began slowing down. No one inside the agency wanted to step out front. Casey saw the shellshocked faces, frightened of a real encounter with danger. He had brought them a long way in four years, but many of them, McMahon, the bean-counters in the budget office, the DO, didn't understand his reading of their obligation.

All the bold planning was going to be a wasted effort. Casey decided to turn to the Saudi intelligence service and King Fahd. They promised help in the form of $3 million.

One day in early 1985, Saudi Ambassador Prince Bandar received a courier directly from the King. A message contained secret instructions to cooperate with Casey. Bandar immediately made an appointment to visit Casey at Langley. Casey saw him, but proposed a second meeting elsewhere, saying, "Let's have a bite." It was as if he didn't want to talk at the CIA's own headquarters. They agreed to have lunch over the weekend at Bandar's residence, a palatial estate just a mile down Chain

Bridge Road. Casey said he would bring Sophia. She realized that she and Bill had once looked at the house and considered buying it. Bill liked the large library. Sophia found the ambassador's wife very friendly and nice. The lunch, she felt, was just another one of the Washington social obligations. "For no purpose at all that I could see," she said later.

After lunch, Casey and Bandar walked alone out to the garden. When they were about as far away as possible from the house and the security guards, Casey withdrew a small card from his pocket and handed it to the ambassador. It contained the handwritten number of a bank account in Geneva. The $3 million was to go there.

"As soon as I transfer this," Bandar said, "I'll close out the account and burn the paper." He would make sure there were no tracks on the Saudi end.

"Don't worry," Casey said. His end would be clean, too. "We'll close the account at once."

Bandar had often found Americans naive about the world, but here was a man with no inhibitions. He considered Casey the J. Edgar Hoover of the CIA.

Bandar knew how to have a conversation that never took place. He was funneling millions to the contras; this was widely suspected and he just denied it routinely with a confident laugh and a long lecture about the implausibility. Their relationship was the kind that both Bandar and Casey valued—one in which men of authority could have frank, deniable talks and emerge with an agreement only they understood. Bandar and Casey agreed that a dramatic blow against the terrorists would serve the interests of both the United States and Saudi Arabia. They knew that the chief supporter and symbol of terrorism was the fundamentalist Muslim leader Sheikh Fadlallah, the leader of the Party of God, Hizbollah, in Beirut. Fadlallah had been connected to all three bombings of American facilities in Beirut. He had to go. The two men were in agreement.

Later it was decided to give effective operational control to the Saudis, particularly as the CIA bureaucracy grew more and more resistant to active anti-terrorist measures. The Saudis came up with an Englishman who had served in the British Special Air Services, the elite commando special operations forces. This man traveled extensively around the Middle East, and went in and out of Lebanon from another Arab state. He would be an ideal leader of a sophisticated operation. The CIA, of course, could have nothing to do with "elimination." The Saudis, if asked, would back a CIA denial concerning involvement or knowledge. Liaison with foreign intelligence services was one CIA activity out of the reach of congressional oversight; Casey had flatly refused to tell the committees about this sensitive work. And in this case, the CIA *as an institution* did not know. Nothing was written down, there were no records. The Saudi $3 million deposited in the Geneva account was "laundered" through transfers among other bank accounts, making certain it could not be traced.

The Englishman established operational compartments to carry out separate parts of the assassination plan; none had any communication with any other except through him. Several men were hired to procure a large quantity of explosives; another man was hired to find a car; money was paid to informants to make sure they knew where Fadlallah would be at a certain time; another group was hired to design an after-action deception so that the Saudis and the CIA would not be connected; the Lebanese intelligence service hired the men to carry out the operation.

On March 8, 1985, a car packed with explosives was driven into a Beirut suburb about fifty yards from Fadlallah's high-rise residence. The car exploded, killing eighty people and wounding two hundred, leaving devastation, fires and collapsed buildings. Anyone who had happened to be in the immediate neighborhood was killed, hurt or terrorized, but Fadlallah escaped without injury. His followers strung a huge "MADE IN USA" banner in front of a building that had been blown out.

When Bandar saw the news account, he got stomach cramps. Tracks had to be meticulously covered. Information was planted that the Israelis were behind the car-bombing. But the Saudis needed more to prove their noninvolvement. There was only one way. They provided irrefutable intelligence that led Fadlallah to some of the hired operatives. As Bandar explained it, "I take a shot at you. You suspect me and then I turn in my chauffeur and say he did it. You would think I am no longer a suspect."

Still Fadlallah was a problem, now more than ever. The Saudis approached him and asked whether, for money, he would act as their early-warning system for terrorist attacks on Saudi and American facilities. They would pay $2 million cash. Fadlallah accepted but said he wanted the payment in food, medicine and education expenses for some of his people. This would enhance his status among his followers. The Saudis agreed.

There were no more Fadlallah-supported terrorist attacks against Americans.

"It was easier to bribe him than to kill him," Bandar remarked.

Casey was astounded that such a comparatively small amount of money could solve such a giant problem.

Bandar undertook two other secret covert operations at Casey's request. One was to bolster anti-Qaddafi efforts in Chad. It cost the Saudis

$8 million. The second was $2 million to assist in a secret operation to prevent the Communists from coming to power in Italy. The two operations were never traced to the Saudis or exposed.

Even though the mission to kill Fadlallah had failed, the Lebanese intelligence service privately began taking credit despite its comparatively small role. A demonstration of strength was necessary; it had to be shown that blood would be met with blood, terrorism with terrorism. Casey was despondent. The CIA relationship with the Lebanese service, to train units for preemptive actions, put the agency in jeopardy. It was too close to an assassination plot. McMahon, who was not aware of the Saudi role, wanted a disconnect; he said urgently that the agency had to get out of covert antiterrorist training. Casey had no choice, and the preemptive finding was rescinded.

Some continuing relationship with the Lebanese service, nonetheless, had to be maintained, since the CIA depended on it for intelligence, for manning listening posts and for security. Later in March, two colonels and three majors of the Lebanese service were brought to Washington for a three-week senior CIA management-training program. They were put up at the Four Seasons Hotel in Georgetown and were shuttled daily to a safe house in McLean, where they received boilerplate lectures, conferred with senior CIA officials and were served lunch by an Asian cook.

Around the time of the March 8 bombing, Casey received one of the most important intelligence reports of his tenure. It was from an important, sensitive source inside the Soviet Union. The CIA had been monitoring the long illness of Soviet leader Konstantin Chernenko, who had been in office only a little more than a year. The report said that he had died, but that the news was being kept from the Soviet people, and the rest of the world, while the Politburo selected a new leader. Casey sent the report to the White House. Several days passed. There was no confirmation, but Casey had faith in the source. On Sunday, March 10, a senior Soviet official visiting the United States was called home, and the next morning came the unmistakable signal: classical music began on Radio Moscow, including Rachmaninoff. At 6 A.M. the leader's death was announced. Four hours later the Soviets said that the youngest member of the ruling ten-member Politburo, Mikhail S. Gorbachev, fifty-four, had been selected as the new General Secretary. The incredibly quick resolution of succession indicated that the CIA's source had been correct: Chernenko's death had clearly been covered up for several days, Casey suspected. In a certain respect this was an intelligence coup for the CIA; there was no more important intelligence task than the monitoring of the leadership in the Soviet Union. But the absence of confirmation or other details only made the real intelligence gaps that much clearer. How useless such top-secret intelligence could be. What was the White House to do with it? And the scrap from inside also revealed how little the CIA knew about the internal workings of the Soviet system. The agency knew virtually nothing about the succession debate.

Casey was amused by press reports hailing Gorbachev as the new Soviet man, pragmatic and open. He was a product of the system in every way, as far as Casey could tell. The Soviet system had most recently been run by three dying men—Leonid Brezhnev, Yuri Andropov and Chernenko. Gorbachev could be expected to appear different. But Casey was sure that was only superficial; he predicted that Gorbachev would only export subversion and trouble with more zest. Casey admired the way Gorbachev played his patronage card, placing some of his people in key posts and in the Politburo. Casey's reports to the White House were warnings not to be taken in by appearances.

Still the contras needed money. Since October 1984, when Congress had cut U.S. funding entirely, Casey had had to operate under a law with little give. It said that no CIA money could be spent "for the purpose or which would have the effect of supporting, directly or indirectly, military or paramilitary operations in Nicaragua by any nation, group, organization, movement or individual."

Casey had approved a cable that said, "Field stations are to cease and desist with actions which can be construed to be providing any type of support, either direct or indirect, to the various entities with whom we dealt under the program." All contact with the contras was "to be solely, repeat solely, for the purpose of collecting positive intelligence and counterintelligence of interest to the United States."

Even when Saudi Ambassador Bandar had offhandedly raised the issue of the contras with Casey, the DCI had responded (with a note-taker present), "By law, Your Highness, I am forbidden from talking to you about this subject."

When retired Army Major General John K. Singlaub, a former OSSer who was raising private money for the contras, raised the subject with Casey, the DCI replied, "Jack, I'll throw you out of my office."

But in half a dozen meetings with contra leader Adolfo Calero, who referred privately to Casey as "Uncle Bill," the DCI listened attentively to reports on contra progress and apologized because the agency couldn't do anything directly.

Joseph Coors, a wealthy Colorado beer executive and an old friend, visited the Director at his office in the Old Executive Office Building and asked to contribute to the contras. Casey told him point-blank, "Ollie North's the guy to see." Coors, a big contributor to conservative causes, was told to step around the corner to North's office. North convinced him to give $65,000 to purchase a light aircraft that could be used on short runways. Showing Coors a picture of the plane, North called it "your plane." The aircraft, called a Maule, was incorporated into the assets of General Secord's private enterprise that had been set up through the NSC by McFarlane and North.

Early in 1985, Casey ordered up four separate National Intelligence Estimates on Nicaragua: the Sandinista military buildup to 65,000 troops; their efforts to consolidate authority within Nicaragua; the outside support to them from the Soviets and the Cubans; and the Sandinista effort to export revolution into neighboring El Salvador and elsewhere in Central America. Reducing the four documents to a single sentence for the President, Casey said: "The Soviet Union and Cuba have established and consolidated a beachhead, put hundreds of millions of dollars behind . . . aggressive subversion."

After the January 20, 1985, second inaugural, Casey watched with pleasure as Jim Baker and Treasury Secretary Donald T. Regan swapped jobs, Baker moving to Treasury and Regan, a longtime Casey friend from Wall Street, to White House chief of staff. Baker had always had a private agenda and had put great pressure on the President. Under the trio of Baker, Meese and Deaver, the President had a system of competing presidents, all of whom tried to kill one another off. That way no one had been able to get away with much of anything. By contrast, Don Regan, a millionaire and former head of Merrill, Lynch, was more directly interested in implementing the President's desires under a unified staff working directly for him. Casey had found the President more relaxed and liberated under this arrangement. He was more comfortable with himself, his opinions, his instincts. At meetings, Reagan was spared the need to navigate the maze of congressional, media and "inside Washington" interests that reflected Baker's "Beltway" view. Don Regan drew out the President. Reagan talked more; his exact notions were given priority. What do you want? the new chief of staff frequently asked.

Casey saw a chance for a concerted effort to win contra funding. But whenever he went to the congressional committees, they wanted to know when the contras would achieve some results. "There's no fucking crystal ball," he told some of the Republicans privately. "I can't tell you."

• • •

One of the first state visits in the second term was from Saudi King Fahd, who arrived in Washington on February 11, 1985. McFarlane and Prince Bandar had met several days before to insure that the King would be afforded special attention. They had searched for a symbol that would emphasize the King's authority and importance and had agreed on a private meeting with President Reagan.

As McFarlane and Bandar talked, the subject of the contras came up. Again McFarlane felt that Bandar was volunteering. To Bandar it was a clear solicitation. Whatever, the Prince indicated that the Saudis were willing to double their secret contributions to $2 million a month. Overall, they would give at least another $15 million.

On February 12, Reagan and Fahd talked briefly in private. The King made it clear to the President that the Saudi contra donations were going up, and Reagan thanked him. McFarlane also passed the good news to the President. But it was a temporary fix, and McFarlane was worried. He was certain that the contra support policy would be effective only if it was seen to have the visible support of the Congress. New and direct funding from the United States Treasury had to be found.

The President heeded Casey's counsel and went public, saying, the contras are "our brothers," and "We cannot turn from them in their moment of need." He said the goal was to make the Sandinistas "cry uncle," and he added in a later speech, "They are the moral equivalent of the Founding Fathers."

But that spring Casey watched, horrified, as the White House became distracted by a single issue. A public flap erupted over a visit that the President planned to make to the Nazi cemetery at Bitburg, West Germany, where some SS troops were buried. Charges of anti-Semitism and insensitivity were heaped on Reagan, paralyzing the Administration as it alternated between hesitation and defensiveness.

Casey worried that there was no White House legislative strategy on a key upcoming contra vote. But there was little he could do personally. He was a negative symbol and had to keep his profile low. The week of the vote, he went to Pittsburgh to give a speech and visit the newspapers, and at the White House it was as if no one were home. On April 24 the anti-contra Democrats in the House brought the issue to a vote. A watered-down proposal for $14 million in nonmilitary contra aid was defeated 215 to 213. Casey was thunderstruck. It had been so close, the switch of a single vote would have resulted in a tie, two votes a victory.

"If Tip O'Neill didn't have Maryknoll nuns who wrote letters," Casey remarked, "we would have a contra program."

Casey regularly gave speeches around the country. The first I attended was April 17, 1985, in Cambridge, Massachusetts, at a conference run by the Fletcher School of Law and Diplomacy. The subject was terrorism. For forty-five minutes he stood at the podium slurring, hunching, hardly audible or comprehensible, reading a twenty-one-page speech. I underlined two sentences in a copy he had handed to me before he spoke: "We cannot and will not abstain from forcible action to prevent, preempt or respond to terrorist acts where conditions merit the use of force. Many countries, including the United States, have specific forces and capabilities we need to carry out operations against terrorist groups."

Casey had no sense of building his speech to a conclusion or finale. When he was finished, he just stopped abruptly and no one in the audience recognized that he was finally done until he said, "Thank you very much." There was mild applause. He stood and answered questions for twenty minutes, making it clear he was bored.

One person, clearly out of step with an audience made up mostly of conservative academics, asked, "What is the difference between the contras and the PLO?" Casey asked angrily, "What?" After the question was repeated, Casey stumbled around and finally said, "The contras have a country and are trying to get it back, the PLO doesn't have one."

The DCI was aware that I planned to write a book about the CIA, and he came over and asked whether I wanted to fly back to Washington with him on the CIA plane. It was about 10 P.M. and I had checked into the hotel where the conference was being held, but I quickly checked myself out. He came out of the hotel with an expensive new heavy overcoat buttoned up haphazardly, like a kid who does not understand clothes and has been dressed by his mother.

His plane was a propeller-driven Gulfstream that would provide a slow trip. Casey took a seat, loosened his tie and had his security man bring us scotches and a fresh can of mixed peanuts, which he stuffed, handful after handful, into his mouth. The security man drew the heavy curtain, leaving us to a two-hour uninterrupted talk. The Director said he was a little uneasy about not having someone from the agency there to monitor him, and he reminded me that he required others in the CIA to avoid interviews with journalists alone. But he proceeded to answer most questions as we ranged over subjects including General Donovan, the new all-weather satellite Lacrosse, the Nicaragua operation, his kidnapped Beirut station chief Buckley, the Republican conventions he had attended dating back to 1940, Reagan, the Reagan Cabinet, McMahon and the CIA. On his father, Casey would offer only one sentence, "He was a civil servant in the New York City pension system his whole life."

Two weeks later I flew to New York to attend his luncheon speech at the Metropolitan Club.

"When I'm asked to speak I usually say I'll talk about the state of intelligence," he said in his opening, "a subject about which I cannot speak very freely. So I'm going to talk about the state of the world, a subject about which I know less but on which I can speak more freely." He received a good long laugh. He was clearly more comfortable than in Cambridge. The refusal of Congress to provide more contra money during those weeks had obviously angered him and opened him up. He virtually said the United States was at war with the Soviets. "This is not an undeclared war," he said, and he compared the times with the years when Hitler was not taken seriously. Marxism and Leninism, he said, had unleashed the Four Horsemen of the Apocalypse—famine, pestilence, war and death.

He let loose with a public rhetorical volley as never before. "In the occupied countries—Afghanistan, Cambodia, Ethiopia, Angola, Nicaragua—in which Marxist regimes have been either imposed or maintained by external force . . . has occurred a holocaust comparable to that which Nazi Germany inflicted in Europe some forty years ago."

He again offered me a ride back in his plane. We covered Reagan, the contras, Lebanon, terrorism, his friends, his money, his goals. He talked about his childhood in Queens, a universe of simple, permanent affiliations. Walking to and from Public Schools 13 and 89, there were fistfights, he recalled. It was the 1920s, after World War I, when boys just circled up and fought. "Win some, lose some," he said. Did he remember any of the kids who beat him? "Of course, do you think I forget anyone?" He stared hard, his dentures full of peanuts. "Particularly anyone who beat me?"

Soon he was back on the contras and the loss in the congressional vote. "Abysmal handling," he said. "The White House can't do two things at once. . . . The President is uninterested. He still has his instincts, but he will not even focus on the objectives, let alone the way to get there." He shook his head in dismay. "The President is not paying attention to Soviet creeping expansionism."

Casey continued to be struck by the overall passivity of the President —passivity about his job and about his approach to life. He never called the meetings or set the daily agenda. He never once had told Casey, "Let's do this" or "Get me that," unless in response to the actions of others or to events. There was an emotional wall within the man. Perhaps it was a response to his father, who had been an alcoholic and unemployed during the Depression. Casey noted in amazement that this President of the United States worked from nine to five on Mondays, Tuesdays, and Thursdays, and from nine to one on Wednesdays, when he'd take the afternoon off for horseback riding or exercise; and on Fridays he left sometime between one and three for Camp David. During the working hours in the Oval Office, the President often had blocks of free time—two, even three hours. He would call for his fan mail and sit and answer it. Many evenings he spent alone with Nancy in the residence, where they had dinner on TV trays. On Saturday nights at Camp David, where they could have any guests in the world, the two had a double feature of old or new movies, and the staff joined them to watch. Casey seemed to be saying there was unexercised authority and unmet responsibility.

Casey found Reagan strange. Reagan had said he would have stayed in the movies if he had been more successful at it. Always jovial, he probably had no real friend other than Nancy. Lazy and distracted, he nonetheless had a semiphotographic memory and was able to study a page of script or a speech for several minutes and then do it perfectly. Casey was a serious student of Reagan, but he said he had not yet figured him out.

The plane was landing at Andrews Air Force Base, from which Casey was immediately departing for a ten-day swing through the Far East and the Philippines, where there was trouble and where he planned to meet with President Marcos.

"Don't say a word to anybody," he directed. He then asked that I stay behind in the plane to hide until he had embarked on the large jet waiting for him. I could see a group of CIA people waiting for him at the foot of the ramp. A van would take me to a taxi, he said. "They might think I'm indiscreet, bringing you out here."

To this day, I do not know why he agreed to those and other conversations.

Just days after the House rejected contra aid, Nicaraguan President Ortega flew to Moscow to ask for $200 million. It stung many of those who had voted against the aid, and a number of legislators said it was so embarrassing that if they had known in advance they would have voted for it. Casey didn't know whose sense of timing was worse—the Administration's or Ortega's.

Rejection by Congress was not necessarily the end, Casey realized. In the White House, NSC staffer Oliver North had moved into the void with a fall-back plan. He proposed in a memo to McFarlane that the President make a public request for private donations to the contras. McFarlane told him to wait on that but approved the establishment of "The Nicaraguan Freedom Fund, Inc." It could exist as a tax-exempt corporation so that the donors would be able to deduct their contributions. North calculated that with another $15–$20 million they would be able to expand the contra force to perhaps 35,000.

North also made arrangements for South Korea and Taiwan to make contributions to the contras. And he increased his operational role, once proposing a plan to sink a merchant ship, the *Monimbo,* which was carrying arms to the Sandinistas.

For more than a month I had known that President Reagan had signed the finding to create three secret Lebanese units for preemptive attacks on terrorists. Lauder, Casey's press man, had tried to dissuade the *Post* from running the story. We had discovered that the top-secret finding had been rescinded after the Beirut car-bombing had killed eighty people. We knew only about the role of the Lebanese intelligence service at that point, and nothing about the secret role of the Saudis or their $3 million contribution to the operation. We saw no reason to withhold a story, since the operation had failed and the finding was history.

"It's like hitting an old wound with a hammer," Lauder said in exasperation. The story ran on May 12: "Antiterrorist Plan Rescinded After Unauthorized Bombing."

Three days later George Lauder wrote to Casey: "It seemed clear that Woodward was planning to go ahead with this story irrespective of what I told him. I strongly stated that his story was grossly irresponsible and an 'invitation to murder.' I said that if he were Fadlallah and had seen a great number of supporters, including women and children, blown up and then read the *Washington Post* story, he couldn't help but want to take revenge against Americans in Lebanon, official or otherwise. . . . I told Woodward that John McMahon had told me to tell him that if he printed this story he would never again be received in this building.

"I further added that this type of irresponsible story would indicate to us that *The Washington Post* not only had no respect for lives of Americans in Beirut, but was continuing its traditional anti-establishment crusade, this time with Hill oversight members and staffers who had their own agenda to 'do in' covert action and create problems for the Intelligence community.

". . . I added that I found his and the *Post*'s actions contemptible. In the future we would handle his contacts with the Agency in the same manner that we do Jack Anderson, Tass and other journalists of that ilk.''*

Casey called me at the paper. ''Lives are in danger,'' he said. ''I'm not sure it was a story that had to be written, but I can't control that. Maybe I should, though. It's the way it got picked up—as if we had our own hit team out there.'' He said that it would make life more difficult for him and his agency. The matter has lethal consequences, he said, and care has to be exercised in not just the facts but the impression that is created. ''You shouldn't have run it.'' His tone was matter-of-fact, but it turned to ice: ''You'll probably have blood on your hands before it's over.''

* I kept detailed notes of all my conversations with Lauder; I have none to suggest he said these things, nor do I recall he said them.

21

"TOWARD A POLICY ON IRAN," Casey read two days later. He had picked up a five-page memo from Graham Fuller, his national intelligence officer for the Near East and South Asia.

"The U.S. faces a grim situation in developing a new policy toward Iran. . . . In bluntest form, the Khomeini regime is faltering and may be moving toward a moment of truth; we will soon see a struggle for succession. The U.S. has almost no cards to play; the USSR has many."

Fuller referred to the "twin pillars" of U.S. policy—denying arms to Iran and preparing to respond to Iranian-sponsored terrorism. These policies had become entirely negative, he argued, "and may now serve to facilitate Soviet interest more than our own.

"It is imperative, however, that we perhaps think in terms of a bolder—and perhaps riskier—policy which will at least ensure greater U.S. voice in the unfolding situation.

"Nobody has any brilliant ideas about how to get us back into Tehran."

Casey felt it was about time. For months he had been pressing Fuller to come up with some. He had decided that in the second term he could get a couple of things done each month at the CIA. They had to have meaning. He had the freedom, could take the initiative, he could get things going, he could throw out some new ideas. He sent a copy of the Fuller paper to Shultz.

A Special National Intelligence Estimate three days later, entitled "Iran: Prospects for Near-Term Instability," said essentially that the United States would not be a player in Iran. Casey was happy to see that several of McFarlane's staffers at the NSC had come up with a draft National Security Decision Directive for the President to sign that would include the authority for the United States to sell some weapons to Iran. As the draft put it delicately, "This includes provision of selected military equipment as determined on a case-by-case basis."

Casey wrote to McFarlane, "I strongly endorse the thrust of the draft NSDD on U.S. Policy Toward Iran, particularly its emphasis on the need to take concrete and timely steps to enhance U.S. leverage in order to ensure that the USSR is not the primary beneficiary of change and turmoil in this critical country."

Shultz wrote to McFarlane to say that he disagreed, particularly "when groups with ties to Iran are holding U.S. hostages in Lebanon." Weinberger wrote "Absurd" on his copy; he felt it was as ridiculous as inviting Qaddafi over for a cozy lunch.

But Casey knew that rejection by the Secretaries of State and Defense was not necessarily fatal to the idea.

Americans continued to be seized in Beirut. David P. Jacobsen, the director of the American University Hospital there, was kidnapped on May 28. CIA station chief Buckley had been a prisoner for more than a year. Something had to be done. Even the unconventional.

In the White House, North had developed a plan. Two agents of the Drug Enforcement Administration had contacted an informant they had used on Middle East heroin traffic. He said that $200,000 could get two American hostages out, and that one of them would be Buckley. The agency operatives raised every doubt in the book. U.S. policy was not to pay ransom. How could they be sure the informant was legitimate? McFarlane won the President's approval for a plan to raise the money privately. The task fell to North. He contacted Texas billionaire H. Ross Perot, who in 1979 had hired a seven-member commando team to rescue two of his employees who were held captive in Iran. The story had been recounted in Ken Follett's best-selling book *On Wings of Eagles* and in a television movie. Perot, who had served on the PFIAB since 1982, was always willing to help the White House. He sent the money.

In a June 7, 1985, TOP SECRET/EYES ONLY/SENSITIVE/ACTION four-page memo to McFarlane, North said that the $200,000 would be only a down payment. He had met in Washington with the DEA "asset" or "intermediary." "The hostages can be bribed free for $1 million apiece," North wrote. "It is assumed that the price cannot be negotiated down, given the number of people requiring bribes." McFarlane initialed —RCM—in the "approve" box. The $200,000 was dispatched to the informant. Nothing happened.

On June 14, 1985, two Lebanese men hijacked TWA Flight 847 taking off from Athens en route to Rome, and forced it first to land in Beirut and then to fly on to Algiers. Thus began a seventeen-day, televised hostage ordeal, a video-age hijacking. The White House Situation Room, the CIA operations center, indeed the entire world, received their best information as TV correspondents conducted interviews with the pilot and continuously monitored the hijack scene. A U.S. Navy sailor, Robert Dean Stethem, twenty-three, was killed, but all the other passengers, including thirty-nine Americans, were eventually released unharmed.

McFarlane, Casey and the other senior national-security principals realized that the Administration had been fortunate compared to the 444 days of the Carter Iran hostage crisis. But they realized that TWA Flight 847 had further exposed the weaknesses of the Administration's antiterrorist capability and the lack of an effective policy. The images of humiliation and vulnerability invited madmen and fanatics to strike and then call in the TV cameras.

Though Casey wasn't certain who was behind the hijacking, the CIA's best overall intelligence on sponsorship of terrorism was still on Qaddafi and Libya. Qaddafi used less sophisticated cryptographic equipment and codes, so the NSA broke them consistently. The sheer numbers of intercepts made Qaddafi appear the most active and dedicated of terrorists. His operatives were sloppy, they left trails. Syria and Iran, in contrast, were more disciplined, they operated in the shadows.

In policy terms, there seemed an opportunity to join the twin goals of combating Qaddafi and combating terrorism.

Casey had kept up a drumbeat of consciousness-raising about Qaddafi's activities through intelligence reporting and regular, formal estimates. Three months earlier, in March 1985, he had issued a Special National Intelligence Estimate titled "Libya's Qaddafi: The Challenge to the United States and Western Interests." For the next eighteen months, the twenty-three-page SECRET report predicted Qaddafi would be stirring up trouble worldwide; intelligence showed that Libya provided "money, weapons, a base of operations, travel assistance or training to some 30 insurgent, radical or terrorist groups."

The SNIE contained a full-color fold-out map of the world on which Qaddafi's subversive tentacles were shown infiltrating the planet on a scale nearly equivalent to portraits of Soviet expansion in the 1950s done by the John Birch Society that showed the world growing slowly "red." In the SNIE's map, countries were colored red where intelligence showed Qaddafi supporting insurgents or terrorist groups. Included were Guatemala, El Salvador, Colombia, Chile, the Dominican Republic, Spain, Turkey, Iraq, Lebanon, Pakistan, Bangladesh, Thailand, the Philippines, Niger, Chad, Sudan, Namibia and eight other African countries.

Another group of countries was colored yellow on the map, to indicate where intelligence showed Qaddafi meddling by providing financial support to the political opposition or leftist politicians. These included Austria, Britain, Costa Rica, St. Lucia, Dominica, Antigua and Australia.

A second SNIE map depicted a large circle centered in Libya and extending over the northern half of Africa, into the Mediterranean and reaching as far as Moscow. This was the range Qaddafi could project his military power with his Soviet-supplied TU-22 bombers and F-class submarines. The estimate said that Qaddafi had become "a judicious political calculator" with new self-confidence that might "spur him to further and potentially more dangerous adventurism."

In a key section, the estimate added: "We believe Qaddafi would directly target U.S. personnel or installations if he:

- could get away with the attack without U.S. retaliation.
- believed the U.S. was engaging in a direct threat to his person or was actively attempting to overthrow his regime."

Casey was proud of the estimate, which he felt put the finger on the problem. The State Department intelligence division demurred mildly. Qaddafi's primary goal, it said, was to destroy his opponents, and his secondary goal was regional dominance.

At the White House, McFarlane kept Qaddafi at the center of attention. President Reagan signed an April 30 National Security Decision Directive (NSDD), No. 168, "U.S. Policy Toward North Africa." The six-page SECRET directive said, "An NSC-chaired interagency group shall be established to review U.S. strategy toward Libya, and to prepare policy options to contain Qaddafi's subversive activities." There were six orders to the main departments. The most notable was: "The Department of Defense will review Stairstep Exercise program and forward options and recommendations." "Stairstep" was the operation name given to an exercise that would be conducted off the coast of Libya.*

As Casey kept up the drive against Qaddafi, the NSA and the analysts in all the intelligence agencies knew he wanted reports, so they stoked the fires. The May 9, 1985, TOP SECRET National Intelligence Daily

* Qaddafi's so-called "union" with Morocco announced on Aug. 14, 1984, created a problem for the CIA and the NSA. But NSDD 168 said that since the Reagan Administration had "King Hassan's personal assurances that sensitive activities will not be placed at risk," it would "maintain correct and friendly working relations." Reagan accordingly directed: "Keep intelligence cooperation with Morocco under continuing review and circumscribe as necessary to prevent compromise. . . . Intercede directly with King Hassan if military information, intelligence methods/sources or controlled technology is compromised or such compromise is imminent."

included a review of Libya on the first anniversary of the May 8, 1984, coup attempt, when Qaddafi's barracks had been attacked. The NID said that the colonel was still an active terrorist, and that Libya was currently supporting a plot to run a truck bomb into the U.S. Embassy in Cairo. According to the NID, Libyan dissident and exile movements, headed by the National Front for the Salvation of Libya (NFSL), were hoping to blow up a military installation in Libya to demonstrate their presence on Qaddafi's soil.

Libyan activities were followed daily. Libya was discussing the purchase of advanced MiG-29s and T-32 tanks from the Soviets; it was negotiating a $500 million arms agreement with Greece; it was planning a two-month military exercise with Turkey; there was a human-source report on the formation of two naval "special operation units to conduct commando and terrorist" raids, headed by Lieutenant Colonel Hijazi, "a senior aide to Libyan leader Qaddafi"; there were satellite photography reports on the missile loads on Libyan MiG-23 Flogger-B interceptors, and so forth.

One report had concluded that "Qaddafi's opponents in exile still pose no major direct threat to his tenure," but it noted that the exiles were "receiving money, training and even use of territory from Egypt, Algeria, Sudan, Iraq and Arafat's faction of the PLO."

So now, after the TWA Flight 847 crisis in June, the Administration was primed to act. In the middle of July, at an NSPG session in the White House, McFarlane opened the meeting with President Reagan and other top foreign-policy advisers by noting that economic sanctions and diplomatic pressure had not curtailed Qaddafi. Stronger measures were needed. Casey, Shultz, Weinberger and the others agreed. Such broad consensus was rare, and an all-fronts plan was adopted.

"Flower" was the overall top-secret code-name designator given to anti-Qaddafi operations and plans. Only about two dozen officials, including the President and Casey, were given access.

Under Flower, "Tulip" was the code name for a CIA covert operation designed to topple Qaddafi by supporting anti-Qaddafi exile movements, including the National Front for the Salvation of Libya, and the efforts of other countries such as Egypt that wanted Qaddafi out.

"Rose" was another code name, for planning a preemptive military strike on Libya in concert with U.S. allies, especially Egypt. The United States would supply air support, and one target would be Qaddafi's barracks, which would be considered a military or terrorist coordination center.

At one meeting, the main question that arose was the one that had plagued the Administration for years: Would this be assassination? The President said that they should not worry about the assassination prohibition. He would personally take the heat on that if Qaddafi were killed.

No one could ask for more; the question was considered settled.

The covert pressure in Tulip and the military planning in Rose were designed to reinforce each other. But if they failed, together they might force a state of alert and crisis in Libya, so that anti-Qaddafi elements in the Libyan military could overthrow him.

A speech was secretly drafted for the President to announce a preemptive or retaliatory attack.

At Langley, Bob Gates, the deputy for intelligence, headed up a quick summary study for Casey, analyzing the pros and cons for preemptive military action. A TOP SECRET paper of July 15 presented Gates's conclusion: Though there were downsides, it was an opportunity to redraw the map of North Africa.

During the June hijacking crisis of TWA Flight 847, Casey's old friend John Shaheen had told him that a man under indictment for attempting to sell arms to Iran had claimed that the Iranian Foreign Ministry was eager to trade hostages for TOW antitank missiles. And then Iran had assisted in the release of the last of the TWA hostages. Casey took that as a signal.

On August 8, as the Libya plans proceeded, Casey attended an NSPG meeting in the White House residence with the President, Bush, Shultz, Weinberger, Don Regan, McFarlane and Poindexter. McFarlane presented a plan in which Israel would ship TOW antitank missiles to Iran. The United States would replenish Israeli stocks, and as a sign of good faith Iran would obtain the release of the remaining American hostages held in Lebanon.

Shultz and Weinberger were opposed, but Casey liked the proposal, which had been authored by David Kimche, the No. 2 in the Israeli Foreign Ministry and a former No. 2 in the Mossad. McFarlane had come earlier to Casey, outlining the prospects. Kimche had asked McFarlane not to consult with anyone else in the United States government, but McFarlane said he needed Casey's personal evaluation. The CIA would stay out of the operation; it was the kind of deniable undertaking that might get some hostages released. CIA involvement would require a finding and therefore notification to the congressional intelligence committees. This was precisely the type of operation with which Congress could not be trusted.

Even though the CIA had reports that its Beirut station chief Buckley, a hostage now for nearly eighteen months, had been killed, Casey clung to the hope that he might turn up if there were some renewed relations with the Iranians.

Lieutenant Colonel North was to be the operational officer. The State Department issued him a passport in the name of "William P. Goode," and Admiral Poindexter, McFarlane's deputy, set up a private interoffice channel with North on the NSC computer system. It was called "Private Blank Check."

On September 12, North contacted Charles Allen, Casey's national-intelligence officer for counterterrorism, who was one of the most informed people on Iran in the intelligence agencies. North knew that Iran could not be trusted, and he wanted all available information. He requested the NSA to target certain individuals in Iran and Lebanon. One was the Iranian middleman Manucher Ghorbanifar, who was to go on a high-priority watch list so that his phone calls, telexes and bank transfers would be intercepted. Ghorbanifar was the key intermediary between the Iranians and the Israelis in the arms transfer. Distribution of the intercepts, North directed, should be limited to Casey, McFarlane, himself and Weinberger, who would have to be kept informed because Defense would be replenishing the Israeli arms. Shultz and all others at State were to be excluded.

Ghorbanifar was well known to the CIA. He had been a secret source since 1974, one of those dashing men of pretense, half politician, half businessman, who hung around the intelligence stage door. Whenever he appeared with flowers, though, the door was slammed in his face. In 1981 he had added fuel to the fire of rumors about alleged Libyan hit teams dispatched to the United States to kill Reagan or his senior aides. The CIA had determined that Ghorbanifar's information not only was wrong but had been intentionally fabricated. In 1983 the agency had terminated his relationship as a source. In 1984 it had issued a formal "burn notice" warning that Ghorbanifar was a "talented fabricator." He had offered once to provide intelligence on Iran to another country if his associates, in return, were allowed to smuggle drugs from that country. He had failed two CIA polygraphs. Casey was alert to the danger of Ghorbanifar, but the man was the sort of person who often became an intelligence agent: sleaze was no barrier to usefulness.

Execution of the arms sales was complicated by distrust between Iran and Israel. Iran did not want to pay until it received the weapons, and Israel would not provide the TOW missiles until they were paid for. To break the impasse, Ghorbanifar came up with a "bridge loan" from Saudi Arabian businessman Adnan Khashoggi, who put up $5 million for what became a purchase of 508 TOWs. On September 15, the Reverend Benjamin Weir, an American hostage, was released.

Casey could see now that hostages and terrorism were consuming the White House and the President. Weir's release was treated almost as high mass at the White House.

Meanwhile, the National Security Council was pushing the Rose planning for a joint U.S.-Egyptian attack on Libya. As with Iran, there were bitter divisions among Reagan's top advisers. Shultz was opposed and had secretly summoned the U.S. ambassador in Cairo, Nicholas A. Veliotes, back to Washington to rebut the NSC plan. "You won't believe what these madmen in the White House have come up with now," one of Shultz's top deputies told Veliotes when he arrived in Washington. After a weekend of intense work, Shultz and Veliotes believed they had turned the plan into a "contingency" and into "reactive and defensive scenarios."

McFarlane was focusing on the upcoming Reagan-Gorbachev summit, so his deputy, Poindexter, was in charge of the Libyan planning. Poindexter insisted on visiting Cairo himself to meet with Egyptian President Hosni Mubarak to continue Rose. State and Veliotes tried to call it off, but over the Labor Day weekend Poindexter arrived in Cairo carrying President Reagan's promise of direct U.S. combat support. Before Poindexter could present his hard-line version of the plan, the Egyptian President, an impatient man with a preference for talking rather than listening, interrupted.

"Look, Admiral," Mubarak said, "when we decide to attack Libya it will be our decision and on our timetable."

Poindexter had meetings with the senior Egyptians in the Defense Ministry, where his approach was better received. Despite Mubarak's apparent reluctance, Poindexter was convinced he had a read on President Reagan's desires for action, and in the end that would be the important factor.

In October, the Italian cruise ship *Achille Lauro,* with 438 on board, was hijacked by four PLO terrorists, and the White House went on terrorist alert. One American, sixty-nine-year-old Leon Klinghoffer, was murdered in his wheelchair and thrown overboard, providing a needed symbol. The cruise ship, still held hostage by the hijackers, docked in Egypt.

Mubarak hated the secure voice system that had been supplied to him by the United States. It had a push-to-talk handset, so that the person on the other end could not receive while talking. That made it hard to interrupt. So Mubarak used an ordinary phone. Stepped-up U.S. intelligence-gathering in Egypt, particularly by the NSA and satellites, had been ordered. Early on the morning of Thursday, October 10, Mubarak was intercepted, and the information arrived at the White House Situation Room within half an hour in a top-secret code-word message. It was a short transcript of a conversation between Mubarak and his Foreign Minister. Mubarak had been saying publicly that the four PLO hijackers had left Egypt. The intercept told a different story. In the intercepted conversation, Mubarak told his Foreign Minister that the hijackers were still in Egypt. He shouted that George Shultz was "crazy" to think that Egypt could turn over the hijackers to the United States as requested. Egypt was an Arab country and could not turn its back on PLO brothers, after all.

By eleven that morning, another intercept arrived at the Situation Room. In it Mubarak mentioned the number of the plane that would be leaving in several hours with the four hijackers. The Egyptair Boeing 737 jet was on the runway at al-Maza Air Base in Cairo.

North knew that such precise intelligence was a rarity, in this case an opportunity that would not last. He presented a bold plan to Poindexter: intercept the Egyptair plane with U.S. jets and force it to land at a NATO base in Sicily; then capture the hijackers.

The idea was relayed to the President, who was in Chicago. He gave his approval.

Over the rest of the afternoon, the NSA provided ten intercepts of Mubarak discussing the final plan to ship out the hijackers. For Poindexter and North, it was as good as being in the Egyptian President's office. The transcripts showed Mubarak's distress as he maneuvered. At first he had not known of Klinghoffer's murder; then, when he found out, he had grasped its significance and realized that the United States would have to act. He had yelled and screamed at his aides, demanding to know why he had not been informed at once.

The NSA passed to the White House the time of the four hijackers' arrival at the plane, the flight number and the flight plan for the trip to the PLO in Algiers. Later that afternoon, four F-14s from the U.S.S. *Saratoga* intercepted the Egyptair plane and forced it down in Sicily. Italy would put the hijackers on trial.

The next morning Reagan stood when Poindexter entered the room, raised his hand in a military greeting, and said, "I salute the Navy."

The inch-thick packet containing dozens of pages of transcripts of Mubarak's conversations had been the key—giving specific plans, intentions, state of mind, Mubarak's determination to deliver the hijackers to the PLO, the when and the how. Reagan was flooded with praise from the public, Republicans and Democrats. It was his first clear-cut victory over terrorists. Knowing the importance of the intercepts, the next time the President saw Casey the Commander in Chief almost bowed before his DCI. It was a sweet victory for Casey. Many of the skeptics, including Bob Gates, had argued that timely tactical intelligence was not a realistic expectation. When the intelligence agencies did provide it, Gates felt it was just damn good luck. But Casey had made his own luck; this was what he had been working for to prove the value of spying.

About two weeks later, Mubarak discovered a tap on his office phone, but the NSA had more advanced methods and continued to get transcripts, including one later that month showing Mubarak's fury at the Syrians for returning Klinghoffer's body, which had washed ashore, to the United States government.

Casey read with fascination a report that three Soviet diplomats who had been kidnapped in Beirut that fall had been released after a month. A fourth had been murdered soon after the kidnapping, but these three had been freed unharmed. Reliable intelligence soon reached him from the Israelis that this feat had been achieved after the KGB in Lebanon had seized a relative of a leader in the radical Muslim Hizbollah, had castrated him, stuffed his testicles in his mouth, shot him in the head, and sent the body back to Hizbollah. The KGB included a message that other members of the Party of God would die in a similar manner if the three Soviets were not released. Shortly afterward the three—an attaché, a commercial representative and the embassy physician—were let out a few blocks from their embassy. A statement telephoned to news agencies said the release was a gesture of "goodwill."

Casey was persuaded that the Soviets knew the language of Hizbollah.

That fall, the Director invited Bernard McMahon, staff director of the Senate Intelligence Committee for the past nine months, to his office at Langley for a talk. McMahon, a retired Navy captain who was not related to John McMahon, had been Turner's executive assistant for several years at the CIA. Casey had lots of questions about Turner, how Turner had run his office, his attitudes, his people. He interrogated McMahon on individuals, he wanted an evaluation, past and present, total candor. Aren't the people here wonderful? Casey asked.

McMahon agreed, high quality, lots of brains.

"Why do you think they do what they do here?" Casey asked in dead earnest. ''Why do you think they're here? What's it all about, really about?''

The excitement, patriotism.

''No, no, no,'' Casey said. ''We have a chance to establish our own foreign policy. We're on the cutting edge. We are the action agency of the government.''

I had received a tip that fall that the Qaddafi obsession in the White House and the CIA had reached a peak, and that plans were being made for a serious covert operation to undermine him. ''Shultz is confidence-inspiring,'' said one source, who added that the Secretary of State had been the strongest advocate, ''laying it out in this way as if it's the Lord's own idea.'' The source said, ''I wouldn't touch it with a ten-foot pole.'' To which another, more senior source added, ''Why such a short pole? I wouldn't touch it with a twenty-foot pole.''

The CIA covert portion of the plan, Tulip, was presented to the Senate and House intelligence committees. Only the thinnest possible majorities supported the anti-Qaddafi plan—eight to seven in the Senate committee, and nine to seven in the House committee.

Even though the new Senate committee chairman, David Durenberger, and the new Vice-Chairman, Patrick Leahy, were not buying, they had not been able to bring along a majority of their committee. They asked how such a plan for support to exiles and dissidents would avoid the prohibition on assassination, since the exile movement wanted Qaddafi dead.

Casey replied that the CIA would help those who wanted to remove Qaddafi. Those people might try to assassinate him, but that was not the CIA plan.

Durenberger and Leahy argued that support to potential murderers was murder, period.

Casey held his ground. The President had authorized it; the Congress could cut off the funding.

Okay, the two senators said, and then they asked for every single operational detail, who, what, where, when. They pored through every file, looked under every bed. They sent a top-secret letter directly to Reagan, protesting vehemently, asking how this would not be ''assassination.'' The White House responded that there was no plan to assassinate and requested that the senators delete the inflammatory word ''assassination'' from their letter. They refused.

Leahy felt that the Administration was deceiving both the committee and itself. In the name of fighting terrorism—as in the name of fighting Communism in Nicaragua—they would commit the country to another secret war. As in Nicaragua, it would not stay secret. In the end, it would, as in the Nicaragua operation, be uncontrollable.

Casey was livid that the committee would presume to involve itself in the details of operations.

On Saturday, November 2, I called Director Casey. His friend and fellow OSS vet John Shaheen had died the day before, and I offered condolences.

Yes, Casey said wistfully. "A nice man."

I said that we were going to run a story that Reagan had authorized the CIA to undermine Qaddafi covertly. The *Post* was not going to give details other than to say that this would be done through CIA assistance to other unnamed countries or exiles seeking Qaddafi's overthrow.

"Some people wouldn't run it," Casey said. "I can't talk you out of it, can I?"

Given the importance of the debate within the Administration and within the congressional intelligence committees, I said that I didn't see why or how we could withhold it.

He grunted.

I mentioned the assassination issue; it would be prominently featured in the story.

"Well," Casey said, "we don't assassinate." He seemed distracted, declined to say anything more, and said goodbye pleasantly.

Within half an hour, he called back to make one central point: the President, the Secretary of State and he were interested only in stopping terrorism, not in supporting the assassination of Qaddafi. He said that the consideration of operations at the highest level of the government focused on ultimate purposes.

I said that point was being made clearly in the story.

He offered nothing else and hung up.

I was reminded of Bradlee's description, three and a half years earlier, of the mildness of Casey's objection to Bradlee's decision to run the story about the Nicaragua operation. The Director either had accepted the inevitability of disclosure or felt that it might serve his and the CIA's purposes to have the covert action out in the open.

The story ran the next day, Sunday, November 3, 1985. Later that day, returning from a weekend at Camp David, the President waved off all questions about the matter. The White House issued a statement: "While in no way attributing any credence to the specific allegations and conclusions drawn in the *Washington Post* article on reports concerning Libya, the President is ordering an investigation of the disclosure of the U.S. intelligence documents cited in this news report in an effort to determine who is responsible for such disclosure and to take appropriate action."

In fact, there was some relief at the White House. Only Tulip, the covert CIA plan, had leaked, and the story had been written in the most general terms. The top secret military planning had held; Rose could continue.

Casey went to see the President and slapped down a copy of the *Post* story on his desk. "See," the DCI said, "I told you congressional oversight can't work. Those bastards all leak." He explained to Reagan that the assassination question had been precisely what the intelligence committees had raked him over the coals about; it was right out of their hearings. Proof positive.

The President wrote the intelligence committees a two-page letter, stating without qualification that the committees had leaked it, and that it was an unscrupulous way to stop a covert action that a minority in the committees opposed. The leak itself is just about the worst thing that ever happened to national security, and it threatens congressional oversight, the President said. He virtually accused committee members of treason.

Senator Durenberger called Don Regan. "There will be a race to find out who leaked it," the chairman said. Both committees investigated and found that the story contained quotes from a twenty-nine-page top-secret "Vulnerability Assessment" that had concluded that disaffected members of the Libyan military "could be spurred to assassination." Neither committee had seen the assessment. This strongly suggested that the leak had come from within the Administration. After about a week, the committees cleared themselves in return letters to the President.

Reagan did not reply.

In Cairo, U.S. Ambassador Veliotes met with Egyptian Defense Minister Ghazalla, the leader of the Egyptian effort to unseat Qaddafi. Ghazalla was distressed that the CIA portion of the operation had leaked, and asked Veliotes how Egypt could trust the United States. He voiced concerns about the military planning. What about the Bay of Pigs? Would the United States, once again, pull back at the last moment?

Veliotes replied that the President was very upset about the leak, and that action would be taken against those who gave out the information.

At the same time, Veliotes said, the story would fade because there was no political controversy. Everyone in the United States wanted to get rid of Qaddafi.

Casey had an analyst complete a detailed targeting study of Libya. The TOP SECRET gray-covered document pinpointed the best time for air strikes as just before dawn. But the Pentagon undertook its own study of direct U.S. military action, and it painted a bleak chance of success, effectively arguing against such an action. The plan was seen as a surprise attack on Libya in conjunction with Egypt. The Pentagon argued that an American military operation might eventually require six divisions, 90,000 men. Pentagon planners were asking, for practical purposes, "Do we want a war with Libya?"

The answer from Weinberger and the Joint Chiefs was no.

Casey went for a physical exam that fall. Things were not right, he knew. The diagnosis was prostate cancer, and the chances were not very good at his age, seventy-two. He asked for all the available literature on the disease and soon agreed to undergo an intensive regimen of daily radiation and chemotherapy treatments. He shared this awful news with Sophia, but decided that no one at the CIA or within the Administration was to know. But Casey told the President himself.

He knew now that there was no limitless timetable. Things had to get going.

On the evening of November 21, North called Dewey Clarridge. After the Nicaragua mining he had been moved from Latin America division chief to division chief for Europe. North was in a frenzy, and said he needed help obtaining landing rights in Portugal for an Israeli plane on a humanitarian mission.

Clarridge sent the highest priority FLASH message on his privacy channel to Portugal summoning the station chief to the embassy at 3 A.M. In a series of messages Clarridge directed that the station chief should "pull out all stops."

"What follows is a National Security Council initiative and has the highest level of U.S. Government interest," Clarridge said. Portugal was to be told that "support of this endeavor will not go unnoticed or unappreciated. . . . The Ambassador should not be informed." The station chief was to meet with General Secord, who was using the name "Richard Copp" and had flown to Lisbon. But Portugal refused. North then said he wanted the name of a trustworthy charter airline. Fast.

The CIA's air branch suggested a proprietary which did clandestine work for the agency—St. Lucia Airways.

Clair George was unavailable, so Clarridge checked with the acting DDO, Ed Juchniewicz, who told North that, in addition to its proprietary work, St. Lucia operated as a commercial venture. So it was available to anyone for special charter missions.

North arranged for St. Lucia to provide two Boeing 707s. They were able to carry HAWK antiaircraft missiles to Israel, where the HAWKs were transferred to Israeli planes for transit to Iran. North was running the operation through a Swiss bank account, Lake Resources, Inc. (number 386-430-22-1 at Crédit Suisse).

For coming up with an airline on short notice, North told Poindexter on their interoffice computer, "Clarridge deserves a medal." But the Israelis didn't wait and released the planes they had been going to use on their end to send the arms on to Tehran. North said this Israeli move was "to save dollars." He had to come up with something, and he was able to divert one of General Secord's aircraft that was scheduled to send a planeload of ammunition to the contras. "So help me I have never seen anything so screwed up in my life," North advised Poindexter by computer message in his update at 7:20 P.M. He would meet a contra leader that night to advise that the ammunition would be several days late. "Too bad, this was to be our first direct flight to the resistance," North told Poindexter.

North was in the Situation Room on Sunday morning reviewing reports on the hijacking of an Egyptair jetliner to Malta. He asked for a copy of the three-week-old *Post* story on the covert operation aimed at undermining Qaddafi. Then he wanted a translation of intercepts on what Qaddafi had been saying that morning. Maybe, North said, they could show that the *Post* story had triggered the hijacking. The intercepts, however, did not reveal any Libyan connection to the hijacking. Later that day Egyptian military commandos stormed the plane, killing 57 of the 80 people on board.

On Monday, November 25, John McMahon was informed that the agency had asked for flight clearance through Portugal for the Iran arms. McMahon hit the overhead. Given the law embargoing arms to Iran, given the fact that agency people had taken a direct role, this was covert action. Where was the finding?

Juchniewicz said that technically the CIA hadn't done it. North had come to them and had been told that the agency couldn't do it. North already had the name of St. Lucia, and his arrangements with the airline were strictly a commercial deal, not covert action.

Look, McMahon said, nice try. He knew covert action when he saw it. Ollie North was a menace, an accident waiting to happen. Now he had dragged the agency into something bad. Clarridge had sent and received some two dozen messages to Portugal and two other CIA stations.

To make matters worse, since Watergate the agency had instituted a firm rule that before any White House request for operational support could be granted by the agency it had to be approved personally by the DCI or his deputy. It was called the "G. Gordon Liddy rule," because Liddy's Watergate burglary team had been supplied with CIA alias identification, a voice-alteration device and a red wig—forever miring the agency in Watergate. Clearly the rule had been violated. Casey was in China, and McMahon felt he had to move fast. He called Sporkin late that afternoon and told him to prepare a draft finding to "cover retroactively the use of the agency's proprietary" airlines. "I will have some operations people come over and brief you on the matter," McMahon said. They came and summarized the situation in twenty minutes. It was an arms-for-hostage trade.

Sporkin brought in some of his top lawyers. He took his cumbersome three-inch-thick wallet out of his suit pocket and placed it in his desk, an indication that it was going to be a long night. It was time for some real business. He knew it was an important moment. "Let's get the President to authorize it," Sporkin told them. He wanted the President's stamp on it. A finding would be an insurance policy for the agency and for Casey. The President had the authority; he could protect them. That would be prudent.

The issues were as sensitive as any the agency might ever have: arms to Iran, the hostages, their safety, even station chief Buckley, now a hostage for twenty months, perhaps still alive, perhaps dead. This could not leak. The possibility of withholding notification to the congressional oversight committees had been discussed before. Casey was anxious to cut out the committees. The findings were leaking; the one on preemptive strikes against terrorists had been in the newspapers, and so had the one on undermining Qaddafi. This one would be, too, and certainly a leak would scuttle the operation. The law requiring "timely" notification of the committees had a loophole. It clearly anticipated, though without elaboration, that there might be extraordinary circumstances when the committees would not receive advance notice. But this had been done in a backhanded way in the law, demonstrating for Sporkin the artistry of legislative compromise. Though the law did not specifically say the President could withhold notification, it did say that in those cases he "shall provide a statement of the reasons for not giving prior notice."

Sporkin went to work, reducing to a single page a finding for the President to sign: "I direct the Director of Central Intelligence not to brief the Congress of the United States . . . until such time as I may direct otherwise."

Sporkin knew from his SEC days that it was not unusual in the corporate world for some executive to bless an activity retroactively, as long as it was in line with policy. To cover the agency personnel who had already assisted North, Sporkin wrote: "All prior actions taken by U.S. Government officials in furtherance of this effort are hereby ratified." The finding described a straight arms-for-hostages trade.

All along, Casey had refused to accept the burdensome procedures of government, and the President clearly felt that the bureaucracy was musclebound. That was a basis for Sporkin's action. It was well after dinner when he finished. The next day Sporkin took the draft to McMahon, who passed it to Casey. McMahon was not going to do this alone. Casey thought the finding was good lawyering, a heroic act that allowed the President to exercise his authority.

Casey was fed up with the intelligence committees. The backbiting with the Senate committee chairman, Durenberger, had reached new heights. It was time to tell them to go to hell. Grievances had been mounting all fall.

First, a senior KGB defector, Vitaly Yurchenko, who had come to the CIA that summer, had bolted from his handler in a Georgetown restaurant and returned to the Soviets earlier that November. He had given a press conference at the Soviet Embassy in Washington, making a big splash, declaring that the CIA had kidnapped him and telling about a dinner with Casey when the DCI had appeared with his zipper down. This had received a big laugh. Casey conceded that the CIA had mishandled Yurchenko, a twenty-five-year KGB veteran who apparently had caught a case of the defector blues. The agency had failed to provide enough Russian-speaking companionship and had not tuned in fully to the psychology of a man who was betraying his country. But Durenberger and the Senate committee had raised hell with Casey, claiming that the CIA had bungled badly. The senators were in the news, it seemed almost daily, with snide criticisms of Casey and his agency.

To make matters infinitely complex, both better and worse for the CIA, Yurchenko had identified two traitors from the U.S. intelligence agencies. Just before his defection to the U.S., Yurchenko had been promoted to deputy in the First Department of the KGB, responsible for spying in the United States and Canada. When he arrived in CIA hands, he naturally was asked whether the KGB had a penetration agent, or "mole," in any U.S. intelligence agency. Only a former CIA officer, Yurchenko said ominously, someone who had been about to be posted to the CIA station in Moscow but had never made it there. His code name had been "Robert" and he had met the KGB in Austria the previous year and had sold them vital secrets.

Unfortunately, the CIA's Soviet division didn't have to conduct much of a search. They went right to the file of Edward Lee Howard. He had joined the CIA in 1981 at the age of twenty-nine. A 1972 cum laude graduate of the University of Texas who had spent two years with the Peace Corps in Colombia, he also had a master's degree in business administration. Quick, fluent in languages, manipulative and a wheeler-dealer, Howard fit the profile of the ideal undercover operative in Casey's new CIA. He knew guns and was hard-drinking. He told the CIA he had used drugs, but that was common in his generation and he said he was no longer taking anything.

Howard had been selected for the elite Soviet division and for assignment undercover in the Moscow station. He had been given intensive training in surveillance and countersurveillance techniques. In Moscow he would be an agent handler, working the streets as one of the few operatives who maintained contact with the human sources and serviced technical collection devices.

Before 1972, intelligence operations in Moscow had been run from Langley and the operations officers had been on a short string, acting as pickup-and-delivery boys, not knowing the true identities of the sources or the information that was being supplied or intercepted electronically. This enhanced security, but it was no way to run espionage. After 1972, the Moscow station chief was given his operations back. It was a small station. The hostility of the environment in Moscow was matched only by the importance of its tasks. The handful of officers were overworked, and everyone from the most junior up to the station chief had to be able to substitute for everyone else. There was no real rank in the foxhole. That meant there were no compartments. Each officer had the full picture. A new officer, such as Howard, had to hit the ground running, arrive in Moscow and be able to begin work at once, know the sources and methods backward and forward. There would be no time for the other officers to brief him, to take the days or the weeks needed to get him up to speed.

To survive in the Soviet division and the Moscow station, the operations officers needed a counterbalance to the "Russian" atmosphere of distrust; they needed something to bond them together. It was total trust and a group support system.

Before he was slated to be dispatched to Moscow, Howard heard all the briefings and saw all the Langley files. He was instructed to learn everything. In early 1983, on the eve of his departure for Moscow, he was given a polygraph examination. It turned up deception, heavy drinking, continuing drug use, womanizing, even petty theft. Instead of Moscow, he was fired, turned loose. What were they supposed to do, put him on a turkey farm? He had his constitutional rights. Casey wasn't even aware of Howard. He was a personnel matter.

The pieces now fit together. A year earlier, Casey had received a cable from the Moscow station chief saying that something was terribly wrong. Human sources were being rolled up, long-established technical collection projects suddenly had gone silent. The cable was like the opening of a spy novel, but no one knew what to do. There seemed to be no clues at the time. Perhaps it was an accident. No source or collection system lasted forever. Then, that summer, Paul M. Stombaugh, a CIA officer undercover as a "second secretary" at the embassy, was arrested and expelled for spying.

Stombaugh had been the case officer for aviation expert Adolf Tolkachev, who had provided critical intelligence for years on Soviet research on stealth, radar-defeating technology. Soon Tolkachev was arrested in Moscow, and later he was executed. Four other CIA undercover men were subsequently expelled from Moscow, virtually closing down the station and its operations.

Only when defector Yurchenko alerted the CIA was the obvious conclusion drawn. The FBI located Edward Lee Howard in New Mexico and put him under intensive surveillance, but Howard, who had been trained to slip around Moscow undetected and unfollowed, eluded the FBI and escaped. Eventually he showed up in Moscow and was granted political asylum.

The Senate committee had savaged the CIA on this. Some senators inquired whether there were any other Soviet "moles" in the CIA. Casey and the agency were able to blame the screw-up on the Soviet division chief who was now gone, but the intelligence loss and the defection of Howard were major blows, nullifying years of work. The Soviet division's Moscow station was the holy of holies, a place of inviolability. The case demonstrated that someone, or everyone, was asleep, not really serious about Soviet intelligence. The matter was so grave that a number of experts concluded it might outweigh all of Casey's accomplishments.

Casey was alternately abject and defensive. Inside the agency he raged at his people. Outside, he erected a wall, telling one senator on the committee, "You pay your money and you take your chances. We had a bad apple, bad procedures. Don't goddamn breathe down our neck. We'll take care of it. We understand how serious this is. We'll fix it."

Everyone had counterintelligence problems. When Goldwater was chairman of the Senate committee, his office had been swept for bugs twice a week. Once they had found in his desk a microphone with a wire that they were unable to trace. Another time a recording device was discovered, and it could not be determined who had placed it, the KGB or some other foreign service. So secrets could have been lost right from Goldwater's office.*

In another long-simmering controversy, the Congress had finally voted to lift the 1976 Clark Amendment banning covert military aid to the Angola rebels. Casey considered this a personal victory. At a White House meeting of the NSPG that month, the President declared, "We want Savimbi to know the cavalry is coming." He signed a covert finding to provide approximately $13 million in paramilitary assistance. This too leaked quickly. The President's response this time was to confirm. In a meeting with columnists and network anchors November 22, 1985, Reagan said, "We all believe that a covert operation would be more useful to us and have a better chance of success right now than the overt proposal." It was an unusual moment, removing any pretense and cover, but it went largely unnoticed because so much covert action was already public.

Durenberger was on a rampage and had said in interviews that Casey's CIA lacked a sense of direction and did not understand the Soviet Union. Casey planned to send a public letter in response. One of Durenberger's aides reached Casey by phone in his car and urged him to refrain. Durenberger was going through a difficult time, he tended to talk bluntly, and he had a strange sense of humor, the aide said. "Don't do it. You'll shoot yourself, all of us, in the foot."

"Goddammit, I'll say what I want," the Director screamed into his car phone, and he flung the handset into its cradle. The public letter conveyed his feelings of betrayal, saying that Durenberger was conducting intelligence oversight "off-the-cuff through the news media" in a manner that "involves repeated compromise of sensitive intelligence sources and methods."

* Goldwater confirmed the discovery of the two listening devices in an interview with the author on September 8, 1986.

Durenberger was also going through a midlife crisis. He had left his wife and had an affair with a former secretary whom he had recommended for a White House job. He had then moved into a Christian retreat residence, and his Senate colleagues were saying he was a "Jesus freak," "unstable" and "about to crack up." This was the man with whom Casey was required to share the nation's most intimate secrets.

So what followed was, in some respects, an easy call. Casey forwarded to the White House the draft Iran finding that Sporkin had written. It contained the extraordinary presidential order that the DCI withhold congressional notification. In a cover memo to Poindexter, Casey said that it "should go to the President for his signature and should not be passed around in any hands below our level."

Within the week McFarlane, exhausted and on the verge of a nervous breakdown, resigned as national-security adviser. Poindexter seemed like the obvious choice to succeed; he was up to speed on Iran, Libya and the contras. Mike Deaver, who had left the White House earlier in the year to open his own public-relations firm, got wind of this. He phoned Nancy Reagan to express his unease. He thought military men were not good as national-security advisers. "Well, what can we do?" Nancy replied. Deaver, in New York, called George Shultz from a phone booth. "Is Poindexter the right man?" he asked the Secretary of State. The Admiral was too secretive, Reagan had such a side, and Poindexter would appeal to it. Poindexter was a good No. 2, but he was too tight for the top job, Deaver said.

Shultz disagreed. "I think he'll be good," he said. "Anyway, it's too late. The President has signed off, and it's going to be announced in fifteen minutes."

Casey was glad to see the change. Poindexter was hard-line and saw no need to play to Congress or the news media. He would build consensus.

In his first briefing for the President in his new role as national-security adviser, Poindexter on December 5 presented Reagan with the Iran finding as drafted by the CIA. McMahon had been pestering Poindexter relentlessly all week to get it signed and take the agency off the hook. As far as Poindexter was concerned the finding was pure CYA—Cover Your Ass—for the agency. The short, one-page finding mentioned only hostages and arms and nothing about a broader strategic opening to Iran. But

Reagan read and signed it. Poindexter put the only copy in his safe and passed word through North to the CIA that it had been signed.

On December 7, Poindexter called another meeting on Iran at the White House residence. McMahon attended for Casey. Shultz was opposed to arms for hostages. It would signal the Iranians that they could kidnap people for profit. Weinberger said the idea opened the United States to blackmail by Iran and Israel. McMahon questioned the basic premise that there were moderates in Iran with whom the United States could deal. They had all been slaughtered or imprisoned when Khomeini took over, he said. The President said no stone could be left unturned to get the hostages back, and the next step ought to be taken. McFarlane, now a private citizen, and Lieutenant Colonel North were sent to London to meet the Iranian intermediary, Ghorbanifar.

On December 10, McFarlane gave a report to the President, Weinberger and Casey. He expressed the lowest opinion of Ghorbanifar, as a person lacking in integrity and trustworthiness. The President was pensive and argued mildly for continuing to have Israel ship more weapons to Iran. It could later be justified on the grounds that the U.S. was trying to influence the Iranian future, the President said.

Casey pointed out that there was precedent. It was precisely Israel's rationale over the years for its secret arms sales to the Ayatollah, amounting to $500 million. No nation could turn its back on the Iranian future.

Later that day, Casey sent a memo to McMahon: "As the meeting broke up, I had the idea that the President had not entirely given up on encouraging the Israelis to carry on with the Iranians. I suspect he would be willing to run the risk and take the heat in the future if this will lead to springing the hostages. It appears that Bud [McFarlane] has the action."

Nine days later, Casey met with Michael Ledeen, an NSC consultant who was close to North and McFarlane. Ledeen told him that Ghorbanifar was coming to Washington with important intelligence and with proposals for operations. Casey set Ledeen and North up with the chief of the CIA's Iran desk.

In Washington, Ghorbanifar stayed at the Madison Hotel under the alias Nicholas Kralis. In a series of meetings involving the CIA, Ledeen and North, Ghorbanifar proposed a "sting" operation against Qaddafi in which the Libyan leader would pay $10 million for the disappearance of Libyan exile leader Magarieff, who then would resurface to Qaddafi's embarrassment. He said also that he had intelligence about a three-man Iranian hit team working in Europe to assassinate Iranian exiles. Ghorbanifar named his source, who had previously turned out to be unreliable.

The CIA's Iran chief sent Casey a memo saying that Ghorbanifar's "reporting on this team is very reminiscent of his previous terrorist reporting which, after investigation and polygraph, turned out to be fabricated. . . . This has been a persistent problem throughout the four years we have known him. . . . It is hard to find in the file any instance where his reporting in fact resulted in a solid development."

Two days before Christmas, Casey sent the President a top-secret memo about five separate hostage-rescue operations. He said he was going out of town and was sorry he would miss the President over the holidays. The first four operations involved other countries secretly assisting the CIA, and the fifth was about Iran. Concerning Ghorbanifar, Casey said it was a dangerous but potentially useful game. Ghorbanifar's intelligence about a hit team was tantalizing. "We have verified their movement but not their purpose," the Director told the President. "It could be a deception to impress us. It is necessary to be careful in talking with Ghorbanifar. Still, when our man talked to him on Saturday and asked him if he would take another polygraph he said he would. We think this is worth doing for what we might learn."

22

CASEY WAS ALSO exerting efforts to obtain direct U.S. funding for the beleaguered contras. Before resigning, McFarlane had taken the heat on North's efforts in the private funding and resupply, by flatly denying to Congress that North was advising or facilitating private donations. Casey thought he could exploit the squabbling in the Congress to his advantage. Only the extreme left wanted to abandon the contras entirely, he felt. So it had turned out over the summer to be comparatively easy to win approval for $27 million in humanitarian aid—food and medical supplies. Casey had also made a pitch that the CIA had to be sure that the contras were not wiped out by the much stronger Sandinista army. The CIA proposed limited authorization for communications, special communications equipment and intelligence "advice" to the contras. This too had passed. But the legislators could not agree on what this meant, and classified letters flew back and forth between the Senate and House intelligence committees, attempting to define whether advice could be provided on transportation and logistics.

For practical purposes, Casey had won authorization for half a war, and the ambiguity would only give the agency more leeway. He realized that, in a jungle war, communications and intelligence advice could be more important to the guerrilla bands than new weapons or ammunition. A finding was drafted and signed by Reagan, and $13 million was allocated for the task.*

As far as Casey was concerned the new law allowed him to become directly involved in gathering his own intelligence on the contras. North recommended that he talk with General Secord, who was running the private resupply operation. Just before Christmas, Casey called Secord and asked him to come to Langley at once. The weather was bad and Secord was late, but Casey waited for him and saw the General right

* Reagan signed the top-secret finding on January 9, 1986.

away. It was their first meeting, but they knew a lot about each other. When they had settled into their chairs, Casey wanted an assessment.

Secord, erect, self-confident, an expert in supply and logistics, blinked calmly behind his aviator glasses. The contras, he said, had no chance of prevailing, none whatsoever if the airlift operation was not moved into the field. Supplies and weapons could be delivered to the region but not to the troops fighting in the jungle. Even if that was accomplished, he had grave reservations about the ability of the contras to achieve any military victories. There was no effective southern front from Costa Rica. Coupled with the inadequacies of the supply effort, the General said, there was no intelligence capability. And, frankly, he didn't see the leadership among the contras for a decisive military victory.

Casey agreed. He had great admiration for the General's efforts under the most difficult circumstances. What can we do to help? he asked.

Intelligence information.

Casey jotted some notes and promised to look into it.

"Mr. Director," Secord said, "if and when you get your hunting license back, whatever assets we are creating right now are yours. I mean, they can just walk in and it's yours, that I assure you."

"Thank you very much," Casey replied.

Two days after Christmas, terrorists in coordinated attacks struck the Rome and Vienna airports, killing nineteen people, including five Americans, among them Natasha Simpson, age eleven. Television pictures of the holiday slaughter were particularly gruesome, bodies and devastation littering the terminals and resembling a Mafia hit. The President, at his California ranch, was stunned. Both the CIA and the NSC suspected that Libya was responsible. A round of meetings began at the White House. Casey's men at these crisis meetings were Bert Dunn from Operations and Richard Kerr, Gates's deputy. They thought Abu Nidal, who was presently in Libya, was behind the attacks, but they couldn't be sure. The hardest piece of evidence was circumstantial: a report showing that Qaddafi agents had transferred $1 million to an Abu Nidal bank account in Bulgaria, but that had happened several years earlier.

Targets were assembled for a military response, ranging from a terrorist training camp near a former golf course in Tripoli to Qaddafi's intelligence headquarters in downtown Tripoli. On the second day of meetings, the Pentagon raised cautions. The Soviets had 1,500 advisers in Libya, and 600 were involved in air defense. How many Soviets would die in a U.S. air attack? What would that mean? Everything was put on hold until the President returned.

Meanwhile, North asked Sporkin to draft a new, expanded finding on Iran that laid out a covert intelligence operation coordinating with friendly foreign liaison services (i.e., Israel) and individuals (i.e., Ghorbanifar and Secord). It had two purposes: "establishing a more moderate government in Iran and obtaining from them significant intelligence not otherwise obtainable . . ."

Hostages or hostage rescue were not mentioned. Sporkin pulled Casey off a golf course in Florida to take a phone call. The line was not secure, so Sporkin said he had been asked to supply "certain services" to the White House and to attend another meeting. Did Casey know what was going on?

No, Casey said.

"Do you want me to attend this meeting?"

Go ahead, but keep me advised, the DCI said.

That night, January 3, Sporkin met with North, who said he would advise Casey.

Sunday morning, January 5, North called Sporkin at home. The two of them were to meet later with the Director, who was en route from Florida, at the Director's house.

Casey read the new Iran finding later that day and told Sporkin and North it looked fine.

As they were leaving, Sporkin stopped North in the foyer. "Tell me again why we're not putting hostages in the document?" Sporkin asked.

North said the State Department didn't want it because it made it look like arms for hostages.

"Well, you know, it doesn't sound right to me. Let's go back and see the Director."

They went back to Casey, and Sporkin said this was going to be one of the all-time sensitive findings. It had better be honest. So a third purpose was added: "furthering the release of the American hostages held in Beirut."

The next week, Libya and Iran seesawed as the White House's top priorities. On Monday, January 6, at an NSPG meeting on Libya in the Situation Room, the President approved a plan to intensify and expand covert efforts to undermine Qaddafi and to continue secret planning (Operation Rose) for a possible joint U.S.-Egyptian strike against Libya. He postponed a decision on a direct U.S. bombing strike. The next day, the NSPG met again to consider the military option. Shultz brought an opinion from the State Department's legal counsel that said terrorism was "armed aggression" and a military response was justifiable self-defense. Weinberger was opposed. Suppose Qaddafi shot down American planes and captured American pilots? There would be more "hostages." The word's effect on them all was plain.

The President rejected the military option, and Weinberger left the Situation Room smiling.

The President, the Vice-President, Shultz, Weinberger, Casey, Don Regan, Meese and Poindexter adjourned to the Oval Office to discuss Iran.

Poindexter presented a plan to continue the arms sales. Iran wanted a show of good faith, he said coolly. The transaction would take place over a short period of time, 30 to 60 days, and Iran would produce the remaining five American hostages. Because of the sensitivity of the deal and the potential danger to the hostages, the congressional intelligence committees would not be informed until the hostages were freed and were on planes out of Lebanon. This would be well before anything was public. Meanwhile, any U.S. role would be deniable.

Shultz was tense. He said he was opposed. It would undermine the entire United States policy on terrorism, which, he reminded them, was not to deal with terrorists, not to sell them arms, not to ransom hostages.

Weinberger too was opposed. The plan would open the United States to the crudest form of blackmail: anytime the Iranians didn't get what they wanted, they would threaten to reveal the arrangement "in Mideast fashion," he added.

Poindexter said that this was a special situation, not at odds with our overall policy, just an exception.

It won't work, Shultz said. Deniability is a fiction, a theory of government that has been tried, he said somewhat sarcastically, and it was established some time ago that it doesn't work, as recently as the prior decade, in the Nixon Administration.

Casey was very much in favor. The deal would be carried out rapidly, and if the first arms transactions didn't produce results, it would be over. Iran had a special role in the world, a special location on the map, right on the underbelly of Russia. The United States could not turn its back on Iran and allow it to fall under Soviet influence.

What about this Iranian middleman Ghorbanifar? someone asked. The CIA's own 1984 "burn notice" had declared him a talented fabricator. Could they use, let alone rely on, someone like this?

But, Casey replied, Ghorbanifar can deliver and he proved it with Weir's release three months ago. He has incredible contacts in Iran, and though he flunked earlier polygraphs, he'll be tested again.

The group split up with the impression that the President was for going ahead.

• • •

Four days later, January 11, Ghorbanifar came to Washington and was polygraphed by the agency that afternoon and evening at the Four Seasons Hotel. The report arrived on Casey's desk. "Ghorbanifar Polygraph Examination: He showed deception on virtually all of the relevant questions. He has lied/fabricated his information on terrorist activities . . . is clearly a fabricator and wheeler-dealer who has undertaken activities prejudicial to the U.S. interests. Deception indicated to 13 of 15 relevant questions."

The people Ghorbanifar had been asked about and voluntarily mentioned were given identity letters A through L in order to protect possible sources. Ghorbanifar had "new" information about C, for example, who had asked another Iranian for 300 kilograms of plastic explosive to use against U.S. facilities in Saudi Arabia; C had another plan to deliver $6 million worth of terrorist armaments.

Casey directed Charlie Allen to interview Ghorbanifar for five hours on January 13. A nine-page report was soon in Casey's hands. Ghorbanifar, it said, "is a highly energetic, excitable individual who possesses an extraordinarily strong ego that must be carefully fed. Intelligent and clearly an individual who has made a considerable amount of money in procurement of arms and in provision of 'other services,' he is relatively straightforward about what he hopes to get out of any arrangement with the United States."

Concerning the hostages, Allen reported Ghorbanifar would "continue to work with the White House on this issue; this effort would be kept separate.

"We have hard evidence that he is close to the Prime Minister, the Minister of Oil, and other senior officials. . . . There is no question, however, that he exaggerates and inflates.

"The worst approach to Subject would be to attempt to lecture him."

The next night, Casey met with North to explain that Weinberger would continue to create roadblocks until he was told by Poindexter that the President wanted the Iran initiative to move, now. Casey suggested a meeting. It took place on January 16 in Poindexter's office with Casey, Sporkin, Weinberger and Meese. Attorney General Meese said it was his opinion that withholding notification to Congress was legal under the proposed finding. Congress could be told when the hostages were out. At the same time, they agreed the President would have to make a report to Congress to justify what he did, even if that meant his last day in office.

• • •

President Reagan signed the finding the next day, authorizing the arms sales to Iran through the CIA. Poindexter placed the only copy in his safe.

DDO Clair George went to the White House and read the finding in Poindexter's office. The CIA would need 4,508 TOW missiles. Because of past dealings with Ghorbanifar, and the polygraph—the only thing Ghorbanifar got right was his name—George did not want to use him.

Casey soon weighed in. Ghorbanifar was a rascal, and the agency had lots of experience with him that established his unreliability, but there was something to this channel that worked. It's worth a try, Casey said, nothing else works, so let's see where it goes. If he doesn't deliver, we'll turn it off.

McMahon went over to Poindexter's office to read the finding, and discovered from the national-security adviser that he planned to give out intelligence to assist the Iranians in their war with Iraq.

"That could give them a definite offensive edge," McMahon said heatedly, "could have cataclysmic results." Jesus, the agency already had an operation in place providing the Iraqis with intelligence on the front. Was the agency, the United States government, to be in the position of providing intelligence to both sides? It was too cynical.

The intelligence would establish bona fides, Poindexter insisted, and the first 1,000 TOW missiles would test the channel to see whether hostages were released.

McMahon objected.

"We have an opportunity here that we should not miss," Poindexter said, though he did not challenge McMahon's points directly, "and we ought to proceed to explore it, and if it doesn't work, all we've lost is a little intelligence and 1,000 TOW missiles. And if it does work, then maybe we change a lot of things in the Mideast."

McMahon rushed back to Langley and, by cable, chased down Casey, who was abroad. Casey confirmed that he was aware of the operation and approved of it. McMahon persuaded North not to provide Iran with the whole intelligence picture at the front, but only a portion. It would be enough to show good faith without giving Iran the fighting edge. North acceded to that.

About 5 P.M. on January 23, Poindexter, erect, stern and with his winter coat draped over his arm, walked into the newsroom of the *Post* and entered Bradlee's office. We had a story on Libya drafted for the next day's paper. It said that the President was secretly dispatching Lieutenant General Dale Vesser, the head of plans for the JCS, to Cairo the next day to continue the secret military planning for a possible joint attack on Qaddafi—Rose. Poindexter told Bradlee that publication of the story would foreclose the President's options for dealing with Qaddafi and terrorism. In a declared war, which this almost is, he said, no American newspaper would consider publishing such information about secret plans; the Egyptians will cancel the Vesser mission if the *Post* goes ahead. Poindexter said that the plan was larger and more complex but that the *Post* had the basic outlines. Nothing is imminent, the Admiral said. Bradlee said he didn't understand why Poindexter would invoke national security if the President was not planning something serious. Poindexter asked that he be informed about what Bradlee intended to publish, and left.

After some back-and-forth, Bradlee determined that a brief reference about the Vesser mission be inserted down in a story on the movement of two aircraft-carrier battle groups off the coast of Libya for exercises. The fifth paragraph would now say Reagan had ordered that "an envoy be sent to Egypt for further discussions about coordinating possible military options."

Bradlee called Poindexter to tell him. Vesser would not be mentioned by name, nor would his planned departure the next day be included in the story. Poindexter objected vehemently; the story would force the cancellation of Vesser's secret mission because the Egyptians were incredibly sensitive about leaks.

At the White House, Poindexter prepared the NSC for what he expected would be a major reaction the next day.

But every news organization reported the next day on the plan for the aircraft-carrier exercise off the coast of Libya, and the mention about an unnamed envoy in the *Post* was not noticed. There was no press inquiry at the White House. Nor did the Egyptian Embassy call either the State Department or the NSC. Poindexter was amazed. When someone on the NSC asked what to do, Don Fortier, Poindexter's deputy, replied, "Embargo copies of *The Washington Post* in Egypt." Everyone laughed.

Poindexter delayed Vesser's mission for several weeks. After a later White House meeting, Poindexter wrote that the President had approved the continuation of Flower and Rose. In the event of an attack on Libya, the United States would provide "combat support inside Libya," Poindexter wrote in a margin note on a memorandum for the files. Vesser was to discuss four options in Egypt: three were defensive in case Libya attacked; the fourth, added at White House direction, was a preemptive strike on Libya. Vesser reported back to Poindexter that he had had very productive discussions.

• • •

Casey thumbed through his quarterly watch report on political instability. Generally it mentioned about three dozen countries. Under the system he and Gates had established, the report had a grid on a covering sheet. Down one side were three categories: countries of high strategic importance to the U.S., those with middle importance, and those with low importance. Across the top ran three additional categories: high political instability, moderate instability and low instability. This created nine "boxes."

In the key box, high importance, high political instability, was the Philippines. President Ferdinand E. Marcos, after twenty years as the leader, ten under martial law, was in poor health. Casey saw an East Asian version of the demise of the Shah. The key was not to abandon Marcos, Casey felt. The Manila station chief, Robert F. Grealy, had returned to head the East Asia division in Operations and was soon part of Casey's Irish Mafia at Langley. He was insisting that the CIA not limit its contact to Marcos. They needed to be in touch with Marcos' political opposition. Serious consideration had been given in the last several years to a covert political support operation to Marcos opponents. For as little as $100,000, the agency would build some important bridges to these groups or prospective leaders by providing funds for travel and printing. But eventually it was agreed that such a covert action would leak; that would do more damage than the $100,000 could do to improve contacts. Marcos was still a powerful figure and friend. Casey had visited the Philippines, and had maintained regular personal and intelligence contacts with Marcos. Casey saw the man swimming in a giant undertow. Given the strategic value of Clark Air Force Base and the Subic Bay Naval Base, the two largest American military installations outside the United States, chaos in the Philippines could make the Iranian upheaval during the Carter years seem tame.

"What about the Philippines?" was a regular Casey refrain within the agency. The problem was the Communist insurgency, not Marcos, he felt. The State Department and Casey's own CIA analysts did not see it that way, and continued to underscore Marcos' corruption, his unpopularity and his isolation. After two estimates, Casey still clung to Marcos. The alternative, Corazon Aquino, the widow of the late opposition leader Benigno Aquino, Jr.—who had been assassinated in 1983—would be weak and would ultimately turn the country over to the Communists, the DCI felt. She was a housewife and had no political experience; it was laughable to imagine that she could stand up to the Communists, Casey said.

Shultz had been converted finally and saw that Marcos was finished. But the President, Mrs. Reagan (who was close to Imelda Marcos) and Casey would not budge. For Shultz it was the most vivid demonstration that Casey had lost any perspective and could not see what was obvious. Casey could have pushed the President and have made the difference. But the DCI's rigid pro-Marcos stance had kept the Administration's policy firmly in the embattled leader's camp. Confidently Marcos called an early election for February 1986. The election attracted wide attention, and a team of observers from the U.S. Congress concluded eventually that Marcos had attempted to steal it. The news footage showed bodies of murdered Aquino campaign workers. Nonetheless, at a press conference, Reagan referred to "the possibility of fraud, although it could have been that all of that was occurring on both sides . . ." The President's remark flew in the face of the facts and of evidence that in the end neither he nor Casey could ignore. Caving to the inevitable, they sent Marcos into exile and Mrs. Aquino became president.

On February 27, Casey and Clair George met with Poindexter and North on the Iranian deal. Casey was eager to remove both Israel and Ghorbanifar from the continuing negotiations as much as possible. The DCI's talking points said, "We can't afford any more telephone conversations which the Soviets and others can listen in on. . . . We need to continuously plan in case the discussions leak. The fact of discussions between the United States and Iran could change the whole universe. . . . The Arab world could go mad unless the discussions are carefully and adequately explained."

Referring to the next step, which included a meeting between McFarlane and an Iranian representative, Casey said, "We should remember that leaking the fact of this meeting could be viewed as working to the advantage of Israel. Only four men in Israel know . . ."

They now believed that Speaker of the Iranian Parliament Rafsanjani would come to a meeting with McFarlane in Europe. North had just returned from Germany, where he had met with an official from Rafsanjani's office.

From his home, McFarlane sent North a computer message: "Roger, Ollie. Well done—if the world only knew how many times you have kept a semblance of integrity and gumption to US policy, they would make you Secretary of State. But they can't know and would complain if they did—such is the state of democracy in the late 20th century."

That night North responded: "Believe we are indeed headed in the right direction . . . God willing Shultz will buy onto this tomorrow when

JMP [Poindexter] briefs him. With the grace of the good Lord and a little more hard work we will very soon have five AMCITS [American citizen hostages] home and be on our way to a much more positive relationship than one which barters TOWs for lives. . . . [Poindexter] is, as only you can know, under tremendous pressure on this matter and very concerned that it go according to plan. My part in this was easy compared to his. I only had to deal with our enemies. He has to deal with the cabinet."

North added that he was trying to set up a meeting with McFarlane, Poindexter and Secord, who was running the private network for transporting arms to the contras. "Dick returns tomorrow night from Europe where he is setting up an arms delivery for the Nic resistance. A man of many talents ol' Secord is."

Casey's Near East division chief, Tom Twetten, who had been present at North's meeting in Europe, took a dimmer view. The man from Rafsanjani's office was dumb, fearful, and saw the United States as the Great Satan. Ghorbanifar, also in attendance, had, as usual, lied to both sides, promising the United States all the hostages, and the Iranians all sorts of advanced missiles and military equipment. This had been calculated to get everyone to the table, and once they were there Ghorbanifar had sat back and watched the slugging match.

Another 1,000 TOW missiles were shipped to Iran—the first direct U.S. shipment—but no hostage was released. Ghorbanifar acted as if the ball was still in the U.S. court, and said at another meeting that Iran had decided they didn't want TOWs after all, so the TOWs didn't count.

Poindexter was fed up and wanted to cut the whole deal off. Forget it, he said, too much double-dealing and mixed motives. It wasn't going anywhere.

North, instead, kept it alive; he understood the President's emotional involvement, his obsession with the hostages' release. There was dread about the yellow ribbons going back up, a fear that this President, like the one before him, would founder on Iran.

Casey agreed that the initiative must go forward; the risks were small, the weapons involved were not that significant, and the intelligence provided to Iran was not capable of determining the outcome of the Iran–Iraq war.

McMahon was deeply concerned about the agency's elaborate, top-secret intelligence-sharing arrangement with the Iraqis that provided Iran's enemy with data from satellite photos. Doling out tactical data to both sides put the agency in the position of engineering a stalemate. This was no mere abstraction. The war was a bloody one. The Iranians used "human waves" of teenagers and irregular soldiers, and almost a million had been killed, wounded or captured on both sides. This was not a game in an operations center. It was slaughter.

This arms scheme, the deception of Congress, was a time bomb, McMahon was sure. It was the last straw. He went to Casey and said that four years as the deputy and thirty-four with the agency were enough. His marriage was breaking up, a particularly painful experience for a Catholic. He needed a change, he wanted out.

Casey was disappointed. McMahon was a good foil. He bobbed up and down on covert action, but in the final analysis he acquiesced to the authority of both the President and the DCI. McMahon said he planned to become vice-president in charge of "black" intelligence projects for Lockheed's California branch. You're too good to be an airplane salesman, Casey told him. You should go out on your own, start your own business, avail yourself of the opportunities of capitalism.

McMahon smiled, and drafted his resignation letter to the President, declaring "mixed emotions" at departing and noting that Casey was "a unique asset." The departure provided Casey an opportunity to promote Gates to DDCI. Putting an analyst in as No. 2 would demonstrate that he was not just concerned with covert action.

On March 1, Bernadette Casey Smith gave a forty-fifth-wedding-anniversary dinner for her parents at the Watergate Hotel. The black-tie affair was attended by seventy people, including Kissinger, Sporkin, Tony Dolan, Jeane Kirkpatrick, McMahon, Gates, and Meese. No Reagan; Bush was supposed to attend, but didn't make it. After dinner, Bernadette rose. "I wanted this to be at least a semisurprise." She paused. "But you all know how hard it is to keep a secret, from Dad especially." Everyone laughed, and someone knowledgeable from the crowd yelled, "That's what the allies said." There was more laughter. Meese spoke, saying that were it not for Casey's work in the 1980 campaign "most of the people in this room might not be here today." He said Bill and Sophia had a marriage of "remarkable unity." Bernadette said, "I hope we'll all be here in another forty-five years to celebrate Mom and Dad's ninetieth anniversary." From the audience again, someone yelled, "I thought that's what this was."

Though his resignation letter was in, it was not over for McMahon. On March 14 he attended the NSPG on Libya for Casey. All the senior people were there, and the President ordered three carrier battle groups assembled off the Libyan coast for an operation called Prairie Fire. He signed a decision directive on the rules of engagement:

- If Qaddafi attacked a U.S. plane or ship, the response would be in proportion, and directed *only* at the source of the attack—a particular Libyan ship, plane or missile site. Strong consideration had been given to permitting the U.S. force commander to respond disproportionately to make Qaddafi pay beyond what he might do to U.S. forces. This had been rejected largely because Weinberger wanted to keep military action to a minimum.
- If there was a single U.S. casualty and the President gave the go-ahead, five military targets would be bombed; the targets were to be mostly Soviet-supplied Libyan aircraft on the ground.
- If Qaddafi took aggressive action, and again after the President approved, U.S. warplanes would bomb Libya inland, striking oil-pumping facilities and other economic targets.

There was much discussion of Qaddafi's personality. The President took particular interest in the details of Qaddafi's personal life as they had been assembled by the CIA. On a trip to Spain and Majorca, the Libyan leader had worn makeup and high-heel shoes; his aides had brought a toy teddy bear for him; and he apparently did not trust the bedsheets at the hotel where he was staying and sent his aides out to buy new sheets from several stores. Reagan came back several times to the theme of Qaddafi as fay, remarking at one point, "Qaddafi can look in Nancy's closet anytime."

And they talked about being tough themselves, "plastering" Qaddafi, "smashing" him, having enough "spine" to instill it in others, particularly their European allies, and being "forward-leaning." There was more than one reference to Grenada.

At one point Donald Regan asked, "Are nuclear weapons going to be used?" and the others jumped. The answer was no.

The White House chief of staff said that he had merely wanted to make sure they would not.

Before Prairie Fire was to begin, Weinberger went to London to meet with the Sixth Fleet commander, Vice-Admiral Frank B. Kelso II. The Secretary directed that "smart" weapons be used as much as possible if the United States had to respond to an attack or provocation. These pinpoint weapons home in on specific targets and limit the damage more than bombs can. Minimize, shoot out their tires, no unnecessary bombing or engagement, Weinberger ordered.

Poindexter and his deputy Fortier, on the other hand, took the view that if they hit the Libyan military hard, Qaddafi's officers would conclude that their troubles were the result of Qaddafi's terrorist ventures. They then might move to overthrow him.

Casey wasn't at all sure. Military action, the threat of military action, the kind of saber-rattling that was involved in the joint secret U.S.-Egyptian planning for an attack on Libya, was well and good. He supported it all. But the visibility of these actions would make the agency's covert plan against Qaddafi that much more difficult to execute and would strengthen him at home and with fellow Arab states. It would build sympathy for him and lend credence to his claim that the United States was the number-one imperialist.

The Libyan exiles didn't seem to be doing the job. McMahon had been right, they were Boy Scouts, weak, amateurs. The CIA had approached Israeli intelligence for ideas on how to oust Qaddafi, but the Mossad had said no. The French had passed word that the only solution to Qaddafi was to go all the way covertly, and spoke of bold plans. But when pressed for help, the French ducked, saying they feared that U.S. military or covert action would only rouse Qaddafi needlessly, since it would never be designed to finish him off.

Casey thought the only solution was to change the finding to allow the CIA to act directly against Qaddafi and not through or in concert with exiles. But all the White House attention was on Prairie Fire.

It was scheduled to begin Saturday night, March 22, but had to be delayed a day because of gale-force winds in the Gulf of Sidra. The high-seas exercise began Sunday, March 23, with the appearance on the horizon of a stunning U.S. armada: forty-five ships, 200 planes, even advanced nuclear-powered Los Angeles–class 688 attack submarines. Three ships crossed the 32nd parallel—Qaddafi's "line of death" more than 120 miles from his coast, drawn in defiance of the internationally recognized twelve-mile limit. More than 100 U.S. planes were flying in a protective arc covering the fleet. Within two hours, the Libyans fired two SA-5 missiles from a land missile base at U.S. reconnaissance planes. The Soviet-supplied missiles missed. As many as four other missiles were launched at the U.S. planes.

Standing off about forty miles, U.S. A-7 attack planes hit back with precision HARM missiles that homed in on the Libyan radar and destroyed it, at least temporarily, effectively "shooting out their eyes" with 46-pound high-explosive warheads and minimizing Libyan casualties. Over the next two days at least two Libyan patrol boats were sunk by U.S. forces.

As he received regular updates, President Reagan asked whether there had been any U.S. casualties. There were none. U.S. intelligence calculated that seventy-two Libyans had been killed.

By Wednesday, March 26, about 1:30 P.M. Washington time, the Prairie Fire exercise was called off. In a story in that morning's paper, *The Washington Post* outlined some of the planning and reported that Poindexter and Fortier had secretly visited Egypt six months earlier "to coordinate possible joint military operations against Libya."

Later that afternoon, I received a call from a National Security Council staffer who said he was calling on behalf of Poindexter and Fortier.

"You've got to know there is such unhappiness over here," he said. "To mention Poindexter and Fortier's names in the secret mission to Egypt—when we're having a confrontation with Qaddafi, given his proclivity for assassination and terrorism. At the high point of the confrontation, to put a face on the secret mission raises their profile. . . . People are worried about their families—this goes beyond the pale. Poindexter and Fortier are targeted already," he said, indicating that there was intelligence supporting this.

The official said, "I've never seen [Fortier] so upset about anything . . . He wants to call you. . . . You've increased the risk ratio for Poindexter and Fortier. It doesn't go with the job. I don't know what can be done," he said in near-despair.

Two days later on Friday, March 28, about 4 P.M., Bradlee received a call from Poindexter. "I'm calling to protest Bob Woodward's story," the Admiral said. Especially the mention of his and Fortier's names. "When it's in the paper, it focuses their thinking."

You mean, Bradlee asked, by naming you and Fortier, that made you more subject to Qaddafi's hit list?

"Exactly."

Bradlee replied that he thought that was out of proportion. After all, there were people out on the line on those ships, and certainly Qaddafi could easily find out who was involved in national-security decisions.

"I just want to be on record protesting," Poindexter said, suggesting that if his or Fortier's body was found blown apart or riddled with bullets, the *Post* would bear responsibility. Adding a second objection, Poindexter said, "Bob didn't call anyone." He said he had not been alerted that the names would be used.

We talked to many people, as you must know, Bradlee said.

"Well," Poindexter said, "you have your job and I have mine."

Bradlee later sent me a short memo recounting the Poindexter call, labeling it not only "feeble" but "sad."

Several days later I talked with a well-placed Administration source and recounted Poindexter and Fortier's distress. "Oh," the source said, "they were just upset that the war was called off.

"It will happen," he said, adding that the determination to "get" Qaddafi or somehow strike back was running at a fever pitch.

This time the *Post*'s references to secret military planning with Egypt were read in Cairo, and the editor in chief of the semiofficial newspaper *Al-Ahram,* Ibrahim Nafeh, a man close to Egyptian President Mubarak, wrote, "The United States has attempted more than once to join in an action against Libya." He cited three attempts and claimed that Egypt had rejected all overtures. In a secret cable back to Washington, however, U.S. Ambassador Veliotes said that Mubarak had vowed to him privately that Egypt would continue the planning, and that the U.S. press disclosures were of small consequence, mere bumps in the road.

Though the CIA's role had been circumscribed by Prairie Fire and the swat at Qaddafi, Casey was now increasingly aware that the President wanted a regime change in Libya, nothing less. The key ingredient that had been missing in any preemptive attack or retaliatory move was proof, absolute evidence, that tied Libya to a specific terrorist action. Casey ordered all the CIA, NSA and satellite assets into play. He wanted answers. Extraordinary assets and attention were brought to the problem. The capture of the *Achille Lauro* hijackers demonstrated that good intelligence could make the difference.

Several weeks before the Gulf of Sidra exercise, Casey's people had begun regularly intercepting the messages from Qaddafi's intelligence headquarters in downtown Tripoli. It was a spectacular intelligence coup. The exact method was a closely guarded secret, but by one count they had received and decoded 388 messages. Immediately after Prairie Fire, on March 25, one message was sent from Tripoli to eight of the People's Bureaus—the Libyan equivalent of embassies. The three-line message instructed them to stand by or be ready to attack American targets and execute the "plan." It was sent by the controller, or head, of the Libyan Intelligence Service (LIS).

Ten days later, on April 4, a message was intercepted from the Libyan People's Bureau in East Berlin to headquarters in Tripoli that said, "Tripoli will be happy when you see the headlines tomorrow."

Just a few hours later, in the early hours of April 5, another intercepted message from East Berlin to Tripoli reported that an operation was "happening now" and it would not be traceable to the East Berlin Libyans.

Within ten minutes, at 1:49 A.M. Berlin time, a bomb detonated at the La Belle discotheque in West Berlin—a known point of congregation for off-duty American servicemen. One American, Sergeant Kenneth Ford, twenty-one, and a young Turkish woman were killed and 230 people injured, including about fifty U.S. military personnel.

The intercepted message had almost provided an advance warning which could have prevented the disaster. Officials were fifteen minutes too late to evacuate the La Belle.

Casey now had his smoking gun. Though the individual messages might be somewhat ambiguous, taken together they provided the elements his intelligence analysts considered crucial—a motive, an order, the time, the place and an after-action report. There was no message from Tripoli ordering the La Belle bombing, but it was standard procedure that Tripoli not become involved in target selection or timing. That was left to the operatives on the scene. Now even the skeptics were convinced.

Secret planning for an immediate retaliatory military raid began. Over the next ten days, the Administration sent out a confusing barrage of public signals, some virtually guaranteeing a strike and others denying the possibility. This reflected confusion within the Administration and widespread doubt that Reagan would ever pull the trigger. One of the chief doubters was Lieutenant Colonel North. He considered Qaddafi the senior terrorist and himself the senior counterterrorist. But somebody in the chain always found a reason to hold back or talk the President out of action.

The specificity of the intercepted information was so rare that some senior officials could not keep quiet. U.S. Ambassador to West Germany Richard R. Burt said publicly of the La Belle bombing, "There is very clear evidence that there is Libyan involvement." NATO commander General Bernard W. Rogers said in a speech April 9 that there was "indisputable evidence" of Libyan responsibility.

The NSA immediately put out a classified advisory saying that these comments were "severely hampering" its ability to obtain information; a new, more restrictive compartment was created, and circulation of the code-word intercepts and transcripts was further limited.

Monday, April 14, at 7 P.M.—2 A.M. Libyan time—some thirty Air Force and Navy bombers struck Tripoli and Benghazi, a port city 450 miles from Tripoli. Eight, perhaps nine, F-111 bombers, each carrying four 2,000-pound laser-guided bombs, were to attack Qaddafi's own barracks, Splendid Gate. At least thirty-two bombs from the F-111 planes were supposed to strike the compound, but at most four, perhaps as few as two, actually hit. A number of the F-111s had to turn back from the fourteen-hour, 2,800-mile flight from England; France would not permit them to overfly, making the route longer. It was a high-tech failure that was kept secret; even DIA analysts were not given the details. Qaddafi, sleeping in a Bedouin-style tent erected in the courtyard, escaped injury. Two of his sons were wounded, and a fifteen-month-old girl described by Libyans as his adopted daughter was killed.

At 9 P.M., Reagan went on television to announce the strike, which had lasted eleven and a half minutes. He cited the "irrefutable" evidence of Libyan involvement in the Berlin bombing, summarizing three of the intercepted Libyan messages and saying that the action was in "self-defense."

"Today," he said from the Oval Office, "we have done what we had to do. If necessary, we shall do it again."

23

FOR MORE THAN SIX MONTHS Casey had been dealing with another counterintelligence nightmare.

Before going back to the Soviets, KGB defector Yurchenko had helped uncover not only Howard but another spy, this one at the National Security Agency. Yurchenko had told his CIA handlers about an incident when he had served as chief KGB security officer at the Soviet Embassy in Washington from 1975 to 1980. There had been an important espionage catch for the Soviets from the NSA—a walk-in, someone who had just phoned the Soviet Embassy. Yurchenko did not know who it was, but recalled that he had spoken with the person by phone. The CIA passed this to the FBI, which dug back to old tape recordings made from the tapped phone lines into the Soviet Embassy. In a six-year-old tape, they heard an unidentified caller: "I have some information to discuss with you and to give to you. . . ." With this, and Yurchenko's tip that the caller had been from the NSA, the FBI zeroed in on the elite Soviet group of about 1,000 NSA employees. The tape was played for some of them. They recognized a former colleague, Ronald W. Pelton, who had worked for the NSA from 1965 to 1979, when he had resigned his $24,500-a-year post in the heart of the Soviet group. Voice analysis showed it was Pelton.

Although he had been a low-level staff man, Pelton had been positioned to have the broadest possible access to the sensitive compartmented and code-word information concerning the sixty Soviet coded signals or communications links targeted by NSA. He had done budgeting, equipment procurement, program-planning, problem-solving. Pelton, then thirty-eight, had been assertive, a good negotiator, a man with an exceptional memory. In other words, the Soviets had had a walk-in oracle. If they themselves had selected from among the thousands of NSA employees, they could not have done better. Pelton was one of those key low-level people in any bureaucracy who has both technical understanding and a broad overview.

The FBI had located Pelton working as a sailboat salesman in Annapolis, Maryland, in November 1985. Two agents interviewed him at the Annapolis Hilton Hotel, and Pelton acknowledged some of the spying. He had declared personal bankruptcy in 1979 while still at the NSA, but apparently no one there had known of it. After a series of business failures, he had gone to the Soviets in 1980 and later traveled to Vienna for a meeting with the KGB, once even staying in the Soviet ambassador's residence for days. He had been paid $35,000 for information about tens of millions of dollars of espionage technology.

Pelton had been arrested immediately after he met with the two FBI agents, and had been charged with espionage. In court papers, the FBI said that Pelton had provided Soviet agents with information about "a United States intelligence-collection project targeted at the Soviet Union." This generated speculation in the press that one of the NSA's important operations might have been sold out.

At a bail hearing, Pelton's court-appointed attorney mentioned the code name "Ivy Bells." The magistrate cut off questioning and prohibited further exploration of the subject.

Though Ivy Bells dated back to the late 1970s when Turner had been DCI, it had been compromised in 1981. Only now, with Pelton exposed, had the NSA and Casey been able to put the pieces together. Deep in the Sea of Okhotsk to the east of the Soviet coast, on the seabed, a U.S. Navy and NSA team, operating from a submarine, had installed one of the most advanced, sophisticated miniaturized waterproof eavesdropping devices in existence—a large tap pod that fit over a Soviet underwater communications cable which connected key Soviet military and other communications lines. The pod had a wraparound attachment that "tapped" into the cable electronically without direct physical contact with the individual wires in the cable. If the cable had to be raised by the Soviets for inspection or maintenance, there would be no physical evidence of a tap on it; the pod would easily break away from the cable and remain on the ocean floor, undetected. Tapes in the pod recorded messages and signals on various channels or communications links for four to six weeks, and the pod had been installed for only two recording sessions a year.

One of the most hazardous aspects of the Ivy Bells system was retrieving the tapes with the stored communications. A specially equipped U.S. submarine had to return to the Sea of Okhotsk. Navy frogmen, using a minisub or even an underwater robot, had to locate the pod and change the tapes. The tapes were sent to the NSA for transcription and possible decoding. Though the messages that were gathered were months old, the operation had provided important data.

Of particular interest were communications that involved Soviet ballistic-missile tests. Missiles from many such tests landed around the Kamchatka Peninsula near the Sea of Okhotsk, and Soviet communications about these missiles and tests were sent through the cable.

The Soviets thought their undersea communications cables or underground landlines were virtually impregnable to interception by the United States. Accordingly, less than the most advanced and highest-grade coding systems were used on some of the channels on the Sea of Okhotsk cable. On some channels the information was not even coded. The best Soviet coding systems were reserved for the most vulnerable communications links through the airwaves, whether standard radio, microwave or satellite.

The Sea of Okhotsk operation had worked until 1981. Then a U.S. satellite photo showed some dozen Soviet naval vessels assembled over the exact spot where the intercept pod was attached to the cable beneath the sea. One Soviet vessel used in deep-sea salvage had been tracked around the world to participate in the operation. Later when a U.S. submarine went in to collect and change the tapes, the pod was missing. NSA authorities surmised that the pod was in Soviet hands, and that the operation was compromised. The Navy studied all the intelligence, and a report was written which was so classified that only a handful of people were granted access. It ruled out coincidence or luck; clearly the Soviets knew what they were doing and had gone precisely to the location of the tap pod. There had to be a leak, almost certainly espionage. The Soviets had a human source, the report concluded. But no one knew who or how.

The 1981 loss of the pod had been a mystery until Yurchenko provided the clues that had led to Pelton four years later.

Casey hoped that Pelton could be tried without revealing anything about Ivy Bells or other secret projects or their screw-up.

The major shortcoming of Ivy Bells had been the months that elapsed between the transmission of the Soviet messages and the time when they were retrieved by submarine. The head of Naval Intelligence, Admiral John L. Butts, and the head of Casey's intelligence community staff, Vice-Admiral Edward A. Burkhalter, had become advocates for a bold solution to the problem of timeliness after the Ivy Bells operation had been compromised.

An undersea cable could be secretly run from Greenland into several tap pods that would be installed on key undersea cables on the north coast of the Soviet Union. The communications would then be available for instant use by the NSA. The distance from Greenland under the Arctic ice cap to the Soviet north coast was about 1,200 miles. The cable would have to be buried in the ocean floor at a cost of about $1 million a mile. Total cost, well over $1 billion—expensive but perhaps worth it, the two admirals had argued. The atmosphere in the congressional intelligence committees was just right. With all the skepticism and sniping about covert action, the legislators needed something that would demonstrate that they were serious about intelligence operations. Another proposal called for spending $1 billion to wire the world, using the same technology—to tap cables around the globe.

I had learned about the Ivy Bells undersea cable-tapping operation earlier in 1985, but we were not absolutely sure it had been compromised, so Bradlee had decided to hold off on a story. Right after Pelton's arrest, we were able to confirm that one of the major intelligence-gathering projects he had sold out had been Ivy Bells. Since the Soviets had captured the tap pod and clearly could identify it as an eavesdropping device, Bradlee felt it would be legitimate to explain the details to demonstrate what damage could be done by one of thousands of clerks, technicians, translators and information processors who operated the latest spy technologies.

On December 5, Bradlee and Leonard Downie, Jr., the *Post* managing editor, went to see the Director of the NSA, Lieutenant General William Odom. Ten years earlier, as a lieutenant colonel, he had been brought into Carter's National Security Council, and that had been the launching pad for his career. An intense, thin, stony man, Odom was a superhawk on the Soviets and a true believer in technical collection. Any story on Ivy Bells, he said, would tell the Russians something they did not know, but during thirty minutes of discussion he declined to say what. He conveyed a sense of alarm and suggested that great national-security issues were at stake.

Afterward, Downie said he thought Odom would try to learn our sources on Ivy Bells, and Bradlee said we should assume that our phones might be tapped.

Pat Tyler and I started some interviewing, none on the phone. Intelligence officials did not want Pelton's upcoming trial to take place in the glare of publicity. One official remarked that the NSA strategy toward the press was often to delay and buy more time. No penetration or operation lasted forever; they lived day to day and were often thankful for an additional week. Despite Pelton's sellout to the Soviets, this official said, it was possible the Soviets had missed something. U.S. intelligence officials had been amazed at what previous spies had failed to reveal to the Soviets or what the Soviets had failed to comprehend.

In addition to Ivy Bells, it turned out, Pelton had probably compromised another seven code-word operations, among them one that was run out of the U.S. Embassy in Moscow, and another a joint U.S.-British operation. Another involved a new and effective clandestine way to intercept Soviet microwave transmissions, and still another involved equipment that relayed intercepted communications back to computers for instant analysis. Officials were concerned that a story on Ivy Bells would launch a competitive feeding frenzy in the news media for more information. A string of stories could follow, revealing a detail here and another there. There were delicate questions. What had Pelton remembered? Had he held back? What precisely had he told the Soviets? How had it been interpreted? Was it believed? Compromise didn't always mean that a capability, a technique or a source was forever lost. News stories on Pelton could open the floodgates, rendering NSA fair game for reporters, no longer off limits as a house of dark arts.

Old newspaper clippings yielded some surprises. More than ten years earlier, on the front page of *The New York Times,* Seymour M. Hersh had reported controversial U.S. submarine operations close to the Soviet coast: "One source said that the submarines were able to plug into Soviet land communication cables strewn across the ocean bottom and thus were able to intercept high-level military messages and other communications considered too important to be sent by radio or other less secure means."

The 1976 Pike Committee report on U.S. intelligence activities said: "[A] highly technical U.S. Navy submarine reconnaissance program, often operating within unfriendly water, has experienced at least 9 collisions with hostile vessels in the last ten years, over 110 possible detections, and at least three press exposures." The committee said that the Navy's own assessment of the program as "a 'low risk' venture" was inaccurate, and that Navy risk analysis was "ritualistic and pro forma."

Tyler and I showed Bradlee the research. General Odom had implied to him that the cable-tapping capability of U.S. submarines or equipment was an absolute state secret; any mention in print could be disastrous. Bradlee called Odom.

"I hoped you wouldn't find that," the NSA Director said.

Bradlee said his reporters would be back on the case. He felt manipulated and was particularly upset by a recycling of the old *New York Times* cable-tapping reference in an article in a Harvard publication that had just come off the press.* If it could be printed there, why not in the *Post?*

On January 27, Bradlee, national editor Robert G. Kaiser and I went to the intelligence community headquarters to meet with Odom and two of his aides. We had a draft of a story on Ivy Bells that we planned to publish, and we hoped they would point out anything they felt might damage national security. The NSA officials huddled over the story draft, reading the eight pages as we waited. Odom was circumspect; his aides murmured. Bradlee inquired why, since the Soviets knew all about this, shouldn't we publish? They had learned about it from Pelton, had scooped the Ivy Bells tap pod off the ocean floor, had it to take apart and examine. Now, with Pelton going to trial, why couldn't this be told to the public?

Odom said they would take the copy, study it, weigh their options, sleep on it, and get back to Bradlee.

The next day, January 28—hours after the space shuttle Challenger blew up—Odom called Bradlee. Odom, the NSA and the U.S. government did not want to see the article published, he said. He was not going to help edit it or broker a "clean" version even if that were possible. Publication would generate attention, all destructive and unwanted, he said. Even if the Soviets knew, they did not know precisely what the United States knew about what they knew. That was something he was going to protect. So the entire subject was in limbo, and he wanted it kept there.

On February 7, Bradlee, Downie, Kaiser and I had lunch with one of the elders of the CIA, a former senior official long gone but keenly aware of the tensions between national security and the news media. Bradlee outlined what we knew about the Ivy Bells cable-tapping, the Pelton sellout and the upcoming trial. Why the resistance? he asked.

"A mother protecting her chick is nothing," the former CIA man said, "compared to an intelligence officer protecting an operation."

But the Soviets know, Bradlee said.

Ah, he asked, but precisely who? Which Soviets? There was no telling. The discovery of the "tap" may have been a sufficient triumph for the leaders to have been told. But the line had been tapped for some time. That might have been embarrassing to those in charge of the military or KGB. There might have been an internal Soviet cover-up.

"Well, you never know, never know for sure," he said. That was the

* "Nuclear War at Sea," by Desmond Ball, in *International Security,* Winter 1985–86.

dilemma. We were looking at it from the wrong angle. Look at it from the Soviet view: a quiet compromise some four or five years ago in some sea, a very quiet trial in the United States with no details released; end of the matter. But look at the alternative if you publish: a general alarm would go off in the Soviet military or the KGB requiring a full investigative response—the motherland had been the victim of espionage, specific place and time. This could be seen as a blow to Soviet nationhood. A search would begin for more espionage, spasmodic perhaps and clumsy no doubt, but the Soviets would go up on their toes. Precisely where the United States government did not want them. This might lead to the compromise of other U.S. operations, totally unrelated. He said that he didn't know about this cable-tapping operation; what he was saying was hypothetical. The goal of the intelligence officer is to put the other side to sleep, make them feel confident, secure, inattentive. So of course U.S. intelligence didn't want any story. It would alert the other side.

He lectured gently. A story in the *Post* could put the issue on the desk of the new Soviet leader, Gorbachev, in power now for only eleven months. Publication, he said, "would send the issue of U.S. espionage right up his rosy red rectum. He'd be on fire. They [the KGB] probably did not tell him—they conceal fuck-ups in the Soviet system just like ours, and that tap on their cable, even if they later did find it, was also a fuck-up, because it never should have been there in the first place."

We later referred to this as the "Gorbachev impact statement"—the notion that before publishing a story we should assess what Gorbachev knew and when he knew it. In practical terms, there was no way to do this. We were very confident, certain that the information was already in the hands of some Soviets, maybe Gorbachev, maybe not. But the luncheon was sobering and served the purpose of reminding us that this story was not simple. It could have unintended consequences.

Now we found ourselves in the business of shopping the story around town to see whether we could get someone with impeccable authority to tell us it would be all right to publish. With both official and unofficial warnings in hand, Bradlee said he wanted to slow down to see clearly what might be coming. No one had yet told us what in the story might do damage. It was clear that the intelligence establishment didn't want the news media mucking around in this area, perhaps for good reason as yet unspecified, perhaps because they didn't want further examination or discussion of their intelligence-gathering operations or of their Pelton fiasco. We saw only yellow cautionary lights, not yet a red one.

I took the latest draft of the story to the White House, gave it to a well-placed official, and asked that he get some sort of answer for us: if there was still objection, we hoped we could learn what it was. Four minor details in the earlier draft shown to General Odom had already been removed because further reporting by us suggested it was conceivable that the Soviets might not know them. The draft said that Pelton "compromised a long-running U.S. Navy eavesdropping operation that tapped into an undersea Soviet communications cable." It said that the compromise had taken place in 1981, and that the Ivy Bells operation had been on a cable in the Sea of Okhotsk. The White House man promised to make an effort.

On February 20, 1986, President Reagan flew to Grenada to celebrate the 1983 victory. On Air Force One, our draft story about Ivy Bells was raised by the White House official with Shultz, Weinberger, Poindexter and Don Regan. Their conclusion was unanimous: the latest version was most unacceptable. They concluded also, with some glee, that they had the *Post* on the ropes. The unusual act of presenting multiple drafts of the story to the NSA and the White House had revealed our hesitation and uncertainty. The officials determined that the story could harm the national security, not so much by revealing a secret as by harming the political relationship between the United States and the Soviet Union. The story, if taken by the Soviets as authoritative, could allow the Soviets to glean what General Odom feared—the Soviets would learn what the U.S. knew about what the Soviets knew. In addition, in NSA operations there were a series of interlocking secrets; it was difficult to rip out a single operation and discuss it in public without potential damage. But the chief concern was about the dynamics of U.S.-Soviet relations. The story might harm those relations, and this rightfully belonged in the category of national security if anything did.

The White House official reported back to us. "It's as high a review as I can get you at my salary level," he said. Bradlee should talk to Admiral Poindexter.

Downie was not convinced that we would not be telling the Russians something new, and we had to be certain we weren't.

Bradlee said that there have been half a dozen drafts of the story, each succeeding one with fewer details. The first drafts could have caused trouble, he said. "We shouldn't publish what others are prosecuted for treason for." Remind me again, he asked, what social purpose is there in this story?

Pelton was one of the biggest spies the Russians ever had. He had given away crown-jewel intelligence-gathering operations, not just Ivy Bells. His job in the NSA placed him at the crossroads of information on all communications intelligence operations aimed at the Soviets. Pelton had been debriefed by the Soviets in Vienna for days on several trips over a period of several years. We were trying to find out, and tell our readers, what he had sold. The story would also show how easy it was to walk into the Soviet Embassy here and sell American secrets.

The editors remained uncertain. Bradlee said he would call Poindexter.*

In mid-March, a senior FBI official told us that the Justice Department had almost lost the battle to prosecute Pelton, because of fears that a trial would expose secrets.

Why should we not print what the Soviets already know?

It has to do with the atmospherics of intelligence operations, the official said. Any reporting on the nuts and bolts of how information is obtained raises consciousness all around the world. The best intelligence coups often occur because someone on the other side makes a mistake, overlooks something, fails to check. The biggest leaks may be staring them in the face. To push their nose into the issues of intelligence might uncork counterintelligence forces we want bottled up. "I'll talk to the Attorney General if you like," he said.

No need, though Meese was the only senior official who had not been consulted.

On Friday, March 21, I saw Casey at a large reception given by the *New York Times* publisher, Arthur Ochs Sulzberger. The party was almost over, and the crowd at the downtown International Club of Washington was thinning. Casey was talking with a reporter from the *Times*. Hunched over, he was stirring a drink with his finger. I walked over and asked whether I could shake his hand.

"I've just talked to you," he said, throwing his arm around me and pulling me close. "This is a great party you're giving."

A number of people in the room seemed as astonished as I was. Casey continued to refer to "your people here."

Embarrassed—clearly he thought I was Punch Sulzberger—I said that I was from *The Washington Post*.

For a split second he seemed to think, That's a fine joke, and he

* Two days later, both Casey and FBI Director Webster came to Bradlee's office to state their concern about a story White House correspondent Lou Cannon and I planned to run the next day on a Sandinista document Casey had obtained outlining their lobbying plans. Casey was trying to win $100 million for the contras from Congress, and the Sandinistas were trying to defeat it. A news story would likely jeopardize the source of the document, Casey and Webster said. But the version of the document we had did not reveal the intelligence source, so the story ran.

laughed. But then he reeled back and began looking around for and found Sulzberger. Apparently to let me know that he realized his mistake, Casey asked about my book on him and the CIA. He had known for more than a year that I was working on it, we had talked many times. He asked whether it could be given a security review to make sure I didn't disclose something that should stay under wraps. I said that I'd listen to any ideas about how that might be done but that I doubted it would work.

"You go ahead and criticize me if you want," he said. "It's your book."

Soon we were in a corner alone, and I asked why General Odom and others were giving us such a fit on the Pelton story and the Ivy Bells operation Pelton had sold to the Soviets.

"If you run that," he said, holding his drink glass in both hands, "go with that, public opinion will build, could build, so we can't do it. I'm letting Bill Odom handle it. He knows more about it."

Public opinion?

Casey didn't answer, leaving it unclear whether "it" was cable-tapping or submarine operations close to the Soviet coast. Or perhaps he meant both.

After the weekend, I told Bradlee about Casey's assertion that the issue was "public opinion." Bradlee made it clear that, for the moment, he was unhappy we were still pursuing the story. I wrote him a memo that evening saying that I thought it was a serious mistake to stop the inquiry, that somehow we had to untangle this.

Bradlee took me to lunch. A number of times over the last several years he had said about the CIA, "It's really out of control, isn't it?" I didn't know, I said. Many intelligence people and others who use it are uneasy, I said, especially about Casey. They pose the possibility that the United States is pressing too much, not just through covert action but through covert intelligence-gathering. Some said the result was a declaration of a kind of intelligence war against the Soviets. The total of all this "passive" intelligence-gathering—a bug here, satellites there, eavesdropping all around, a submarine in some sea—could add up to more than the sum of its parts. The U.S. is way ahead of the Soviets in technology; the Soviets are scared of American technology. Add all this to the covert actions, and the total picture could be an intelligence war.

What is the social purpose of reporting this? Bradlee wanted to know. We can't just publish any fact, any secret, Bradlee said.

I agreed. At some earlier point in the submarine operations conducted against the Soviets, the U.S. had plans to send a U.S. nuclear submarine not only into their territorial waters, but up one of their rivers.

Jesus, Bradlee said.

We had contradictory information on whether it had happened. Maybe it never happened, I said. Maybe it did. Imagine one of our submarines being caught up a Soviet river or in a Soviet harbor. It could make the 1968 *Pueblo* incident seem insignificant. The U.S. spy ship *Pueblo* had been thirteen miles off the coast of North Korea when it was seized.

Odom's argument, I said, amounted to "Trust me." Or, perhaps, "How dare you." They were getting close to making the argument "Which side are you on?"

Was it under control? Bradlee asked again.

The NSA apparently was getting into non-Soviet undersea cables worldwide because the United States was involved in most of the large cable networks—Atlantic and Pacific. Again maybe it made sense, maybe not. In another, more public example, serious people were concerned that the U.S. allowed the Soviets to sweep up or vacuum up telephone conversations from microwave towers all over Washington. It was a massive invasion of the privacy of U.S. citizens. As well as I could piece it together there was a tacit understanding that, in return, the U.S. could operate electronic intelligence-gathering from the U.S. Embassy in Moscow.

Bradlee wasn't buying. Neither of us was qualified to really say, say for sure, absolutely, that we weren't going to cross legitimate national security.

We agreed that Bradlee should talk directly with one of the sources of information on the story, a former senior intelligence official who knew as much about this as anyone currently in government. This was someone who could say confidently that the Ivy Bells story would not tell the Russians anything they did not know.

Most of April was consumed with the Libya bombing, and Bradlee did not get around to meeting with the former intelligence official on Ivy Bells until late in the month. The official convinced him that the story as now drafted would not tell the Soviets anything they did not already know. On Friday afternoon, April 25, about 3 P.M., Bradlee instructed me to call the White House and inform them that the story would be running in two days.

"We must object," said the White House national-security spokesman, arguing once more that the story "in totality" would tell the Soviets things they didn't know. And Bradlee owes General Odom a call before publication, the spokesman said. "Odom feels he has a commitment and it hasn't happened."

The next morning Odom called Bradlee, who had gone to Long Island for the weekend, to say he was unalterably opposed to publication.

"I have talked to people equal to you in rank and loyalty to the United States," Bradlee said. "And they don't see one thing in the story that the Soviets don't know."

Odom conceded that the story would not tell the Soviets anything new. He was really worried about other countries that didn't know about the capability.

Bradlee said it seemed rather late in the game to abandon the Soviet argument and raise a new one.

Odom urged Bradlee to hold off his decision until they could talk.

Bradlee felt he had no choice, he didn't want to go through the red light at long distance.

Meanwhile, some others in the various U.S. intelligence organizations tried to persuade Odom to tell Bradlee exactly what bothered him. Odom refused. He wasn't going to start peeling the onion; it was dealing with the devil.

On May 1, Bradlee and Odom had breakfast. Odom, calmer, insisted it was these other countries, but he wouldn't give an example. Bradlee pleaded. If there was some concrete reason, he needed to know.

Odom said he felt harassed, too much sensitive intelligence material was coming out. He and others were looking into the possibility of using a 1950 law that provides criminal penalties for anyone who "publishes" anything classified about communication intelligence.

Bradlee said he was going to publish.

Does that lance the boil? Odom asked. Would that be the final story on Ivy Bells?

Bradlee said he couldn't be sure, but added that he was not going to devote his life to this, and the *Post* would not dribble out a detail here and another there. Bradlee left with the impression that Odom had folded his hand right there at the breakfast table.

Later in the day Bradlee said there was no stopping now. "I've crossed the bridge." We took the draft and fine-tuned it again to run the coming Sunday.

If the argument that we should worry about its potential impact on Gorbachev had merit, it seemed like a good time, because the Soviet leader had more important things on his mind. The nuclear accident at Chernobyl had just occurred.

The next day, Friday, May 2, Casey visited D. Lowell Jensen, the head of the Justice Department Criminal Division, and proposed that the department consider bringing criminal charges under the 1950 law. He had a list of five news organizations that had published information from communications intercepts recently: the *Post, The New York Times, The Washington Times, Time* and *Newsweek.* The story he cited the *Post* for was one I had written on the intercepted Libyan cables showing Qaddafi's responsibility for the West Berlin disco-bombing.

Jensen was cool to the idea of prosecuting reporters. He wanted to avoid a First Amendment confrontation.

"You have to play tough with these bastards," Casey said. He wanted Jensen to consider going to court to get an order to stop the *Post* from publishing the Ivy Bells story. Jensen didn't think that would work, either. The government had lost the prior-restraint argument in the Supreme Court with the Pentagon Papers case.

Later that afternoon, Casey phoned Bradlee from his car. Let's talk, he said, and proposed the bar at the University Club, right behind the *Post* and next to the Soviet Embassy.

Bradlee and Downie went over at 4 P.M. and handed Casey a copy of the story draft. He read slowly. Finally he looked up and tossed it to the side.

"There's no way you run that story without endangering the national security," Casey said. He sipped a scotch and water. "I'm not threatening you, but you've got to know that if you publish this, I would recommend that you be prosecuted." This, of course, was not the only problem for the *Post*. "We've already got five absolutely cold violations."

He explained that he was referring to the *Post* and the four other publications. He added matter-of-factly that he had just come from the Justice Department, where all five cases were pending upon his recommendation. He implied that the train had already left the station.

Bradlee asked if it was the 1950 law.

"Yeah, yeah," Casey said. "I don't practice law anymore. You know what I'm talking about."

Bradlee and Downie attempted to get some specifics. What was the problem? First it was the Soviets, then other countries, and now what?

"Look," Casey said, "hold the story for a week." He was going to call the President, who was in Japan for an economic summit meeting. The President would talk to Bradlee.

"That important?" Bradlee asked.

Yes, Casey said, pulling out the final argument: lives could conceivably be in danger if that is published. He did not elaborate. On the way out, Casey said to Downie, "How you and Ollie getting along?" Downie had okayed a public identification of North by name as the active NSC officer who was aiding the contras, and North had objected in a letter to Downie. Casey knew all about it.

With this sudden escalation, Bradlee and Downie agreed not to publish on Sunday. Back at the office, the two editors huddled with lawyers. No one had ever really focused on the 1950 law, but it clearly specified that anyone who "publishes" communication intelligence information was subject to prosecution. The lawyers felt the law was of dubious constitutionality, but no one was certain. They urged caution.

Tyler and I were convinced that the story could not possibly cause damage. It had been laundered down to a mere rag. Quite likely Casey was bluffing. He wanted to stop the news media from writing about these matters. "The story creates an atmosphere ripe for deduction," Tyler summarized, "and that's what they want to avoid."

Bradlee decided to get the issues out into the open. On Tuesday, May 6, he gave his notes of the Casey meeting to *Post* reporter George Lardner. If the dog that didn't bark could tell you something, so could the story that didn't run.

At 5:45, Bradlee received a phone call from Casey. The DCI said he had just had a call from Henry Grunwald, the editor in chief of *Time,* about a report that *Time* was about to be prosecuted. Did Bradlee know about it?

Sure did, Bradlee replied. He had assigned a reporter to write the story for the next day's paper.

"I thought we were having a private conversation?"

You requested the meeting, Bradlee said, and no ground rules were set. Casey had made a statement of vital importance to the *Post* and, Bradlee presumed, to the other publications. The *Post* had to report that. It was news.

That ended the conversation, but a few minutes later Casey called back to ask what the next step was going to be. Am I going to be reading about that?

Yes, Bradlee said.

"I thought we were going to have more talks?" Casey said.

What more is there to say? Bradlee asked.

"When am I going to read about it?" Casey asked.

Tomorrow morning, Bradlee said.

"My name in there?"

Sure is.

Casey said that no reporter had called him.

A reporter called your people, starting early this morning, Bradlee said.

"First I've heard of it," Casey said. "That ever happen to you?"

Not when you call, Bradlee said. Do you want to talk to our guy?

No.

The front-page story, "U.S. Weighs Prosecuting Press Leaks," ran the next day, named the five news organizations on Casey's list, and said that under threat of another prosecution the *Post* was holding back on "another story it has prepared concerning U.S. intelligence capabilities."

The day after, Casey had breakfast with the *Post*'s lawyer, Edward Bennett Williams. Later Williams laid it out to us. The government could prosecute, but Williams said he doubted they would. "I have lots of experience with their cowardice." But now the *Post* and Casey were in two corners, fully painted in. Williams said to wait.

On Friday, *The New York Times* ran a story stating: "The CIA, according to officials, has argued within the Administration that publication of a story by The Washington Post would be damaging because it would authenticate and explain what the Soviet Union has already obtained from Mr. Pelton. They argued that the Soviet authorities at this point were not entirely certain of what they had learned from Mr. Pelton . . ."

To us that seemed to give the KGB all they would need to review everything Pelton had told them in his marathon debriefing sessions in Vienna.

The next day, Saturday, May 10, Katharine Graham, chairman of the board of the Washington Post Company, received a call from the President.

She congratulated him on the summit.

Reagan said that he had talked with Casey and that the story on Pelton would be damaging. This one is important, the President said, suggesting that priceless secrets were at stake. He said that good intelligence had prevented 125 terrorist incidents over the last year. It was a number Reagan had used at a recent press conference, but he left the impression that it was somehow tied up with Ivy Bells.

Graham told the President that Bradlee had been careful. She as the owner could say don't publish, as could her son, Donald Graham, the *Post* publisher. Neither had said it. It would be better for all if Bradlee made this decision, she said.

Reagan seemed to understand. He said goodbye.

Graham told Bradlee that she was impressed with the President's argument. She wondered why we had to write this story. If intelligence agencies were trying to overthrow governments, we probably should publish, but how could the United States gather too much intelligence? Listen too much? The Soviets did it to us. Even if we were ahead in the various technologies, should we wait for the Soviets to catch up?

Bradlee explained that our story was about an operation, Ivy Bells, that had been compromised by Pelton five years earlier, and nothing more. Graham said the President was worried about much more, and she hoped Bradlee would be extra careful.

Casey felt that he had the cards—Ronald Reagan and Katharine Graham.

The morning of May 19, when jury selection in Pelton's espionage trial was to begin, NBC correspondent James Polk said on *Today,* "Pelton apparently gave away one of the NSA's most sensitive secrets—a project with the code name 'Ivy Bells,' believed to be a top-secret underwater eavesdropping operation by American submarines inside Soviet harbors."

Bradlee called Casey, who had not heard of the NBC broadcast, and asked, "Here you've been telling us not to publish this. What are you going to do?" That afternoon Casey issued a statement saying he was referring NBC's broadcast to the Justice Department for possible prosecution.

It was now clear that we had to run our story, even if in truncated form. Headlined "Eavesdropping System Betrayed, High-Technology Device Disclosed by Pelton Was Lost to Soviets," the story ran on May 21. It said that Pelton had compromised "a costly, long-running and highly successful U.S. operation that used sophisticated technology to intercept Soviet communications." The operation, it said, used submarines and the device was retrieved and in the hands of the Soviets.

Casey issued a mild statement that our story was being reviewed to see whether prosecution would be initiated.

Pelton's trial began the next day. Tyler and I began dropping more and more details about Ivy Bells into stories; the first day we identified the location of the Ivy Bells operation in the Sea of Okhotsk.

Five days later, Casey and Odom issued a joint public statement that "cautioned against speculation and reporting details beyond the information actually released at trial. Such speculations and additional facts are not authorized disclosures and may cause substantial harm to the national security." This was quickly and universally hooted at; the notion of the government waging a war on "speculation" was absurd.

Casey told the Associated Press on May 29, in an effort to lower the noise level, "I think that certainly the press has been very hysterical about the thing, saying we're trying to tear up the First Amendment and scuttle the freedom of the press. We're not trying to do that.'' As for his caution against ''speculation,'' Casey said, ''If I had it to do over again, I might not use that word. I might use 'extrapolation.' ''

Casey called Bradlee. This was nearly their twentieth conversation so far that year.

The DCI said, ''I don't want a pissing match.'' *

* On June 5, after thirteen hours of deliberation, the jury convicted Pelton on two counts of espionage, one of conspiracy and one of disclosing classified communications intelligence. He was later given three life sentences in prison plus ten years.

24

WHILE PUBLICLY Libya occupied the Reagan Administration that winter and spring, behind the scenes it was Iran which dominated the foreign-policy agenda in the White House and the CIA.

McFarlane sat at the desk in his suburban Washington home. It was after 9 P.M. on March 10. He turned on his computer link-up with the White House and punched in the code that allowed him to receive his classified messages. The light was on, indicating that a computer message called a PROF note was waiting. Probably Ollie. He pressed the key and read: "Per request from yr old friend Gorba [Ghorbanifar], met w/ him in Paris on Saturday. He started w/ a long speech re how we were trying to cut him out, how important he is to the process and how he cd deliver on the hostages if only we cd sweeten the pot w/ some little tid-bits—like more arms etc.

"Bob Gates has assembled a nice amt of intel on Soviet threat . . ."

North also asked for some personal advice: Wasn't it time for him to return to the real Marine Corps?

McFarlane missed the White House; the "outside" was not what it was cracked up to be. He thirsted for a role even now, just three months after his departure. He started a note back to Ollie. Yes, the two should discuss North's future. "Frankly," McFarlane typed, "I would expect the heat from the Hill to become immense on you by summer. Consequently, it strikes me as wise that you leave the White House. At the same time, there will be no one to do all (or even a small part of what) you have done. And if it isn't done, virtually all of the investment of the past five years will go down the drain.

"How's this for a self-serving scenario: North leaves the White House in May and takes 30 days leave. . . . (North joins same think-tank as McFarlane). . . . McFarlane/North continue to work the Iran account as well as to build other clandestine capabilities so much in demand here and there."

North realized the Iran initiative was by no means over. He was not about to leave his power base, which he had expanded dramatically with a private communications system. Earlier in the year he had been given fifteen KL-43 encryption devices from the NSA that allowed him to transmit classified messages to and from those assisting him in counterterrorist and hostage-release efforts. He also chose to use it for the contras. One device was given to General Secord. Another went to the CIA station chief in Costa Rica, who operated under the pseudonym Tomas Castillo and had been of great help to the contra effort.

As a demonstration of presidential backing, Reagan in late March met in the Oval Office for a brief picture-taking session with Castillo, North, the Costa Rican Minister of Public Security and Poindexter.

By April, North had fully integrated the Iran and contra operations. He told McFarlane on April 7, "Per request of JMP [Poindexter] have prepared a paper for our boss which lays out arrangements" for the next Iran arms shipment. North's paper, "Release of American Hostages in Beirut," said that a major portion of the $15 million expected to be paid by Iran for arms could be set aside for the contras. Poindexter had approved the diversion. The Administration and Casey were again trying to get Congress to approve weapons and direct military assistance for the contras, but it was going slowly, the usual legislative confusion. ". . . $12 million will be used to purchase critically needed supplies for the Nicaraguan Democratic Resistance Forces . . . to 'bridge' the period between now and when Congressionally-approved lethal assistance . . . can be delivered."

Under "Recommendation," North wrote: "That the President approve."

On April 8, the Intelligence Oversight Board, a presidentially appointed in-house review group set up after the intelligence abuses of the 1970s to monitor propriety and legality, gave Poindexter a legal analysis. It said that under the "communications" and "advice" finding, any U.S. agency could "provide basic military training" to the contras. The only restriction was that such training could not include "participation in the planning or execution" of military operations.

Messages flowed in from the private communications network to North from Secord about ammunition "drops." On April 12, the CIA man Castillo informed North about a successful "air drop" to the contras and his plans for the coming weeks: "My objective is creation of 2,500 man force which can strike northwest and link-up . . . to form solid southern force. Likewise, envisage formidable opposition on Atlantic Coast resupplied at or by sea. Realize this may be overly ambitious planning but with your help, believe we can pull it off.''

North enlisted McFarlane and asked by computer link-up: ''We are trying to find a way to get 10 Blowpipe launchers and 20 missiles. . . . Dick Secord has already paid 10 percent down on the delivery.'' The crucial end-user certificate had been acquired.

McFarlane replied: ''Could you ask the CIA to identify which countries the Brits have sold them to. I ought to have a contact in at least one of them. How are you coming on the loose ends for the material transfer? Anything I can do? If for any reason, you need some mortars or other artillery—which I doubt—please let me know.''

The walk in the Old Executive Office Building from Room 302 to Room 345 around the corner took less than a minute. More and more Lieutenant Colonel North found himself making that short trek from his own office to Casey's. Casey was not a boss but a soulmate. The DCI had evolved into a father figure, an intimate and adviser. He had become a guiding hand, almost a case officer for North. When the Colonel had arranged the secret supply operation for the contras in 1984, it was Casey who had almost drawn up the plan, instructing North to set up a private entity to be headed by a civilian outside the government. It was to be non-official cover for a covert operation that was as far removed from the CIA as possible. Casey had recommended General Secord for the task, and had explained to North how he could set up an ''operational account'' to be run out of the NSC for petty cash, travel and special anti-Sandinista activities inside Managua.

As North's activities became increasingly risky and compartmented, Casey was one of the few who knew. North found Casey's advice invaluable; he knew how to get things done and did not hesitate. He warned North that his calls into Central America on open telephone lines were probably being intercepted by the KGB at a Cuban listening post. So North obtained the KL-43 encoding devices from NSA. Casey provided the latest intelligence on the contra arms brokers and recommended that two of them be dropped because of questionable activity and associations; one was suspected of transferring technology to the Soviet bloc.

North explained to the DCI that he and the Israelis had devised the diversion scheme to funnel the profits from the Iranian arms sales to the contras. Casey was effusive, immediately grasping the irony. Iran had earlier tried to ship arms to the Sandinistas and had provided them with some $100 million in oil credits over the years. To get the Ayatollah to fund the contras was a strategic coup, a "sting" of unimagined proportions: having an enemy fund a friend. The DCI labeled this "the ultimate covert operation."

North's world became more and more confined. The most secret System IV channel for NSC intelligence documents was not considered safe, his paperwork was "non-logged," he dealt with "out-of-system" documents. But he could talk freely with the DCI, who was the Godfather of both the Iran and the contra supply operations.

Casey warned North that Ghorbanifar was almost certainly an Israeli intelligence agent. That meant they had to be extra careful, not that they should stop using him. Just realize who you're dealing with, Casey admonished. When it looked as if North was going to make a preliminary secret trip to Tehran, Casey told him he could be taken hostage himself. He had to prepare for the possibility of torture. Only one way to deal with that, Casey said. North had to have with him the means to take his own life.

Soon it seemed that North's whole life was "off-line." It existed only for the few who knew. Even Poindexter's deputy was kept in the dark. North was the deniable link. Casey said that someone had to fill that role, be willing to take the hit if the secret NSC operations were ever exposed. North replied that he knew his job. He would take the spears in the chest.

To North, Casey was an enormously attractive figure. The DCI was an intellectual of sorts; he would read an entire book on a plane trip; he seemed to know everyone who had accomplished anything of importance. North realized that Casey was the driving force behind the efforts to support the various anti-Communist resistance movements in the world. He had a world vision of how to reshape the world in the interests of United States foreign policy. He was a conceptualizer, an idea man.

And, North saw, Casey was the one in the Administration who thought the most beyond tomorrow. The DCI spoke with some conviction about having a stand-alone, off-shore, self-financing entity that would operate independent of Congress and its appropriations. It would operate in real secrecy, either alone or jointly with other friendly intelligence services. Apparently he had in mind the Saudis and Israelis. Plausible deniability would be reestablished. In the best tradition of capitalism, this would be a revenue producer, "a full-service covert operation," Casey called it.

Not just the ransoming or rescue of hostages; not just counterterrorism but other operations; North had given code names to some proposals, TH-1, TH-2, TH-3. From their experience, Casey and North knew they had to have the ability to instantly move into action. As Casey said, "You want something you can pull off the shelf and use on a moment's notice."

• • •

Poindexter, keenly aware of North's all-fronts effort, sent him a private computer message on May 15 entitled "Be Cautious." He warned: "I am afraid you are letting your operational role become too public. From now on, I don't want you to talk to anybody else, including Casey, except me about any of your operational roles. In fact, you need to quietly generate a cover story that I have insisted you stop."

North reported to Poindexter that he had more than $6 million immediately available for the contras. "This reduces the need to go to third countries for help. It does not, however, reduce the urgent need to get CIA back into the management of this program.

"Unless we do this, we run increasing risks of trying to manage this program from here with the attendant physical and political liabilities. I am not complaining, and you know that I love the work, but we have to lift some of this onto the CIA so that I can get more than 2–3 hrs of sleep at night." He mentioned that there would be more money soon and more visibility; this would surely rouse the anti-contra Democrats in Congress.

"While I care not a whit what they say about me, it could well become a political embarrassment for the President and you.

"The President obviously knows why he has been meeting with several select people to thank them for their 'support for Democracy' in CentAm."

A few days later North proposed to Poindexter that they have a quiet meeting without papers, to be attended by the President, McFarlane, Casey, Shultz and Weinberger. McFarlane and he were about to depart for Tehran carrying arms. "I don't want a meeting with RR, Shultz and Weinberger," Poindexter replied on May 19.

Casey was being pressured by General Secord, who came by to see him. "Mr. Director, you and I are both too old to waste time beating around the bush," Secord said. "I've come here to complain about your organization. . . . I'm not getting any support. I wanted intelligence information, guidance. Whatever support you can give us, I want . . . But instead, what we're getting is a lot of questions about the nature of our organization. How is it organized? Who owns it? Who's got the shares? What's Secord doing? Just like an investigation of our organization . . . I don't need to be investigated. I need to be supported."

Casey promised to look into it. Soon after that, Casey was over at his Old Executive Office Building office talking by phone with North and asked him to walk over. North showed up with Secord.

"Good to see you again, General," Casey said.

North informed him that donations to the contras were trailing off. There was a shortage of funds once again.

Casey said that some people in the Administration were optimistic about getting new direct military contra funding from the Congress that summer. But he admitted that he didn't agree and was pessimistic.

North asked Secord for an assessment.

Secord said he was short of funds and needed expensive, advanced navigation systems and weather radars.

"How much money is needed?" Casey asked.

"Well, that depends on what period of time you're talking about," Secord said. "Unless the U.S. government gets back into the support of the contras, we're not going to make it." That was the central point he wanted to impart.

Secord estimated they then would need another $10 million.

"Ten million dollars," Casey repeated. "Ten million dollars." The Saudis might come up with that. "But I can't approach them." The current law said that the State Department could solicit for the contras, and in that case only for humanitarian purposes. Casey looked at the General. "But you can."

"But, Mr. Director, I'm not an official of the U.S. government. I don't think these people are particularly interested in solicitation from private citizens. I think that would be very foolish."

"Well," North interjected, "somebody damn well better start looking into this thing right away, because it's a rather desperate situation."

Casey said that Shultz could make the approach, and he would speak to the Secretary about it.

The State Department did not go to the Saudis. It was later able to obtain a secret $10 million contribution from the Sultan of Brunei, a small oil-rich state on the island of Borneo. This followed a three-hour meeting between Shultz and the Sultan. The previous year the CIA had provided the Sultan with head-of-state security services under an omnibus covert action finding allowing the agency to expand its efforts to protect pro-U.S. leaders and forge closer ties.

North provided the number of the Swiss bank account in which the Sultan was supposed to deposit the money. His secretary, Fawn Hall, transposed two digits in the account number, with the result that the $10 million went into the wrong account and was not received by the contras.

In late May, McFarlane, North and several others, including George Cave, a former CIA station chief in Tehran who spoke Farsi, went undercover to Tehran with the weapons in the hope of getting all the hostages returned. But McFarlane and North returned emptyhanded. One of Cave's reports to Casey said that Ghorbanifar had suggested using the extra funds from the arms sales for the contras and the Afghanistan resistance.

McFarlane expressed his worries about North to Poindexter on June 10: "It seems increasingly clear that the Democratic left is coming after him with a vengeance in the election year and that eventually they will get him." McFarlane recommended that North be sent to Bethesda Naval Medical Center for a disability review so that he could retire from the Corps. "That would represent a major loss to the staff and contra effort but I think we can probably find a way to continue to do those things."

There had been a subtle shift against the Sandinistas, and on June 25 the House approved, 221 to 209, a Senate-passed bill giving $100 million to the contras. The CIA would be back in business when this aid began in October.

The House Intelligence Committee interviewed North over the summer, and he denied that he had given military advice to the contras or that he had ever known of specific contra military operations. After Poindexter received an account of North's denials, he forwarded a "Well done" message to him.

With final passage of the new $100 million in contra aid from the United States, North realized he would soon be out of business. He had dubbed his private network "Project Democracy," and on July 24 he wrote to Poindexter that it was time for the CIA to buy out these assets. North estimated the total value at over $4.5 million, including "six aircraft, warehouses, supplies, maintenance facilities, ships, boats, leased houses, vehicles, ordnance, munitions, communications equipment, and a 6,520 foot runway" in Costa Rica. "All of the assets—and the personnel—are owned/paid by overseas companies with no U.S. connection . . . It would be ludicrous for this to simply disappear just because CIA does not want to be 'tainted' with picking up the assets and then have them spend $8–$10M to replace it—weeks or months later."

Poindexter agreed it should be phased out and directed North to speak with Casey about this, but Casey wanted the agency to keep its distance.

Ghorbanifar learned that he was going to be cut out of the Iranian arms operation by a new secret channel the United States had developed through the nephew of the powerful Iranian Parliament Speaker, Rafsanjani. So Ghorbanifar pushed his contacts in Iran to the limit, and on July 26 Father Lawrence Jenco, an American hostage held for eighteen months, was released. Casey wrote a top-secret memo to Poindexter: "It is indisputable that the Iranian connection actually worked this time, after a series of failures. . . . In summary, based on the intelligence at my disposal, I believe that we should continue . . . I am convinced that this may be the only way to proceed, given the delicate factional balance in Iran."

Casey and Shultz were determined to finish what had been started in Libya. The CIA gave wide circulation to intelligence on the seven main residences that Qaddafi used, perhaps hoping it would leak to the colonel to remind him that he was being watched. It didn't get out. A sensitive source report came in saying that Qaddafi had acted so bizarrely in a meeting with Yemeni officials that he might be on the verge of a nervous breakdown. Casey felt that they had Qaddafi on the ropes, that the United States had to keep up the pressure, and jar him, cause him to lose confidence in himself, create a centrifugal force so that his regime would fly apart and he with it. The Pentagon could send planes just off the Libyan coast to break the sound barrier, generating sonic booms. "Humiliate him," Casey said. The seventeenth anniversary of Qaddafi's revolution was coming up on September 1. As usual, Qaddafi was to speak. Suppose they could frighten him into not appearing. He had already moved his military headquarters from the coast hundreds of miles inland, away from the easy access of U.S. bombers.

Casey dispatched his DDI Richard Kerr and Tom Twetten (Tom and Dick, as they were known) to the White House to explain what the CIA could do to apply psychological pressure on Qaddafi. Twetten, a twenty-five-year veteran of the DO who had served in the Libyan city of Benghazi in the 1960s, said it would be no problem for the CIA to plant false stories in publications abroad to unnerve Qaddafi. The coup de grâce was just around the corner.

It was summer. There was comparatively little to do. Qaddafi could be Ronald Reagan's victory. Though there was no crisis, a sub-Cabinet Crisis Pre-Planning Group was set for the afternoon of August 7 in the Situation Room. The State Department sent around a seven-page TOP SECRET/VECTOR memo to the eleven participants from the White House, State, Defense and the CIA.

State called for "closely coordinated covert, diplomatic, military and public actions aimed at precipitating Qaddafi's overthrow by Libyans . . . a sequenced chain of real and illusory events.

"Possible Next Steps. The goal of our nearterm strategy should be to continue Qaddafi's paranoia so that he:

—remains preoccupied, off balance

—believes that the Army and other elements in Libya are plotting against him (possibly with Soviet help). Believing that, he may increase the pressure on the Army, which in turn may prompt a coup or assassination attempt.

"Working with the exile groups is not likely to bring the downfall of the regime, although we should enhance their image in Qaddafi's mind. We therefore must increasingly take direct covert action, which will require increased [Defense] support. Overt [Defense] actions will be required to contribute credibility to rumors that the US is planning further actions."

State recommended sending a special emissary to Britain, France and Italy to brief "on the need to step-up pressure on Qaddafi now—but not going into all the details of our strategy. . . . The dialogue would also fuel rumors in Libya of another US attack."

The memo proposed that the U.S. government "background[s] media on 1) three-ring circus in Libya with in-fighting among groups jockeying for post-Qaddafi era, 2) threat of resurgent terrorism and threats to Libya's neighbors, and the need to continue to deter Qaddafi, 3) likely Qaddafi successors, and 4) the plight of Libyans under Qaddafi."

A senior Defense official's "trip to Chad later this month provides an opportunity for disinformation to reach Qaddafi that the U.S. and France are developing contingency plans of a 'Chad option.' " Another Defense official's visit to Tunisia and other Libyan neighbors would provide "similar opportunity for disinformation."

The memo proposed signals intelligence "deception" to make it appear that U.S. planes were flying over Qaddafi's line of death; that a maritime notice of intent to operate carrier battle groups should be issued and then not followed up on.

"Foreign Media Placements. Articles should be placed to show the following: Libyan military dissent; the existence of an underground in the Libyan Army; combined operations planned against Libya; Soviets planning a coup; Libyan intelligence should be provided photography of Libyan dissidents meeting with Soviet officials in Paris, Baghdad etc.; U.S. coup planned with senior Libyan help.

"Deception Operations. Use Clandestine radio. Caches Discovered. Using U.S. submarine and planes, send in or drop equipment such as rubber rafts, into Libya or on beaches to make it appear that a coup is planned or underway."

Howard R. Teicher, the director of the NSC's political-military office, proposed in a top-secret memo that the Administration "shame" France into joining in some action to oust Libyan forces from Chad. He suggested that the White House might have to go around the civilian government of President François Mitterrand and rely on "military to military channels and not through the political channels which failed earlier this year. . . . given the stated desire of some general officers to cooperate with us against Qaddafi, we might actively encourage them to sell the proposal to their civilian leadership."

On August 7, ten sub-Cabinet officials met in the Situation Room to consider the papers and lay out a plan. Lieutenant General John H. Moellering, the personal representative of the Chairman of the Joint Chiefs of Staff, could not believe that they were considering a policy of pretense. What if the papers ever got out? he asked.

"Don't we trust each other?" someone else asked.

Several days later, Casey received a TOP SECRET/VECTOR memo from Poindexter to prepare him for an upcoming NSPG meeting with the President on Libya. He read, "Qaddafi's aura of invincibility has been shattered, his prestige is badly tarnished, and his grip on power seems precarious.

". . . Our actions should encourage internal dissidents to act, increasing Qaddafi's fears by convincing him that further U.S. actions are underway . . . more direct covert action. . . . Overt DOD [Defense] operations will also be required to give credibility to rumors that the U.S. intends to take further military action . . . fueling rumors of military action . . . unilateral and joint [military] exercises designed to deceive, overburden and 'spook' Libyan defenses. . . . Deception operations . . . foreign media placement should focus media attention on in-fighting among Libyan groups, jockeying for position against Qaddafi, speculation about successors to Qaddafi, the general plight of Libyan society, and rumors of foreign planning for renewed actions against Qaddafi.

". . . an auspicious opportunity to promote an enduring change in Libyan support of terrorism and contribute to the downfall of Qaddafi."

Casey liked this.

Poindexter also sent a memo to the President:

"TOP SECRET/SENSITIVE

"Most intelligence estimates conclude that in spite of new tensions and Qaddafi's own shock, depression and impaired performance following the April 14 raid, he is still firmly in control in Libya.

"OPPORTUNITIES. There is interagency consensus that a U.S. policy that succeeds in further pressuring and isolating the Libyan regime could have a significant impact stimulating internal forces that would ultimately force a change in regime.

"There is also consensus that *any* alternative leadership to Qaddafi would be better for U.S. interests and international order.

"During the NSPG you will be presented with a plan developed by State and CIA in which a series of closely coordinated events involving covert, diplomatic, military and public actions is proposed. One of the key elements of the strategy is that it combines real and illusionary events—through a disinformation program—with the basic goal of making Qaddafi *think* that there is a high degree of internal opposition to him within Libya, that his key trusted aides are disloyal, that the U.S. is about to move against him militarily.

"Forces within Libya which desire his overthrow will be emboldened to take action. . . . demoralize him and energize those who would seek to replace him.

"Although the current intelligence community assessment is that Qaddafi is temporarily quiescent in his support of terrorism, he may soon move to a more active role."

At 11 A.M. on August 14, Reagan met with Shultz, Weinberger, Casey, Poindexter and Admiral William J. Crowe, Jr., the Chairman of the Joint Chiefs of Staff.

Poindexter lavished praise on Defense, saying that the April 14 raid had been technically impressive, that it had deterred terrorism, weakened Qaddafi at home, and contributed to an enhanced image of America in the world. But it was now time to back this up with a massive disinformation program, to create a sequenced chain of events that would lead to Qaddafi's downfall.

Admiral Crowe was visibly disturbed, and he asked to speak. Was this an appropriate use of military resources, to execute a psychological "fly-by"? Would it be effective to make it appear that something dramatic was in the works and then not deliver? Might not this plan lessen the deterrent value of the April 14 raid, make the United States once again a paper tiger?

But the wheels were grinding. The CIA and State were ready. It seemed to be a comparatively cost-free exercise. The President was comfortable. Noting Qaddafi's proclivity for ostentatious and strange costumes, Reagan quipped, "Why not invite Qaddafi to San Francisco, he likes to dress up so much."

Shultz retorted, "Why don't we give him AIDS."

The others laughed. Reagan nodded. Policy was made.

One participant later said, "They even signed on to the flaky ideas."

Nearly every conceivable harassment technique was adopted. The meeting had not considered terrorism or military action.

On August 16, the President was presented a two-page NSDD to sign. It specified that the deception and disinformation program could be carried out under the previous finding on Libya. The objectives: "dissuade Qaddafi from engaging in terrorism; bring about a change of leadership; minimize the possibility of Soviet gains in Libya."

Reagan signed. The classification was top secret, the code word VEIL.

Nine days later, *The Wall Street Journal*'s main lead began: "The U.S. and Libya are on a collision course again." The story said Qaddafi was plotting new terrorism and the U.S. was readying a new air-raid plan. The Chad disinformation opportunity was presented as fact. The next day Poindexter embraced the *Journal* story publicly, and White House spokesman Larry Speakes called it "authoritative."

Other news organizations, including *The Washington Post,* also bit on the Administration's disinformation, publishing stories that a new confrontation was looming. Over the next several days, Administration officials both affirmed and attempted to knock down the stories.

At the CIA and the Pentagon, some of the Libya experts were aghast. The Administration was poking a stick into Qaddafi's cage, doing precisely what stirred him by placing him at the center of world events. Though there had been no specific plan to spread the Libyan disinformation into the U.S. media, the White House had leaked it. Even if it hadn't, such disinformation was certain to have spilled over or "blown back." The experts were astounded that the White House had failed to contemplate the consequences.

Soon there were reports that Qaddafi was planning new terrorist attacks in response, perhaps, to the much-publicized planned U.S. confrontations. An attack on a U.S. base was thwarted secretly, but on September 5 four men shot up a Pan American plane at the Karachi airport, leaving twenty-one persons dead. An Arab with a Libyan passport, Salman Taraki, was intercepted as he phoned the Libyan People's Bureau in the Pakistani capital to say that he had been on a "special mission" of the Libyan Intelligence Service. He was later arrested and, along with the four hijackers, subjected to intense interrogation.

Casey, always delighted to attend any gathering of OSS veterans, went on September 19 to address their convention at the Mayflower Hotel in Washington. "Fellow survivors," he called to them, "thank God we are all here." The audience was small and old. Helms and Colby were both there. Sophia listened intently to the hour-long speech from the front row, signaling to someone at the head table to get her husband to speak closer to the microphone. Casey made two central points: their founder General Donovan's vision was that "psychological and irregular warfare could be the spearhead of covert war"; and during World War II the most "devastating" problem for the OSS had been the White House staff. "Anyone with access to the President could get a charter for himself."

Five days later, I told Casey that we had seen some top-secret memos, code words VECTOR and VEIL, about a disinformation campaign against Qaddafi. He stared at me fiercely. "I don't know what you are talking about," he said and turned away.

On October 2, we ran a long story on the memos, headlined "Qaddafi Target of Secret U.S. Deception Plan, Elaborate Campaign Included Disinformation That Appeared as Fact in American Media."

President Reagan and Poindexter met with news columnists that day at 11 A.M. in the family theater of the White House. The President said, "Well, I challenge the veracity of that entire story that I read this morning with great shock.

"Yes, there are memos back and forth about that and what the information is, and so when I challenge the veracity of that whole story, I can't deny that here and there, they're going to have something to hang it on.

"We would just as soon have Mr. Qaddafi go to bed every night wondering what we might do."

The President added, "I've come to the conclusion that Mr. Woodward is probably Deep Throat."

That evening Shultz took a different approach. "Frankly, I don't have any problems with a little psychological warfare against Qaddafi," he told reporters at a press briefing.

"If I were a private citizen, reading about it, and I read that my government was trying to confuse somebody who is conducting terrorist acts and murdering Americans, I'd say, 'Gee, I hope it's true.'

"If there are ways in which we can make Qaddafi nervous, why shouldn't we?

"There's a wonderful book which you might read that was written about World War II. And the title of it is a quote from Winston Churchill, who said, 'In time of war, the truth is so precious, it must be attended by a bodyguard of lies.' "*

* The book, *Bodyguard of Lies,* by Anthony Cave Brown, is about military intelligence operations and the efforts to deceive Hitler before D-Day, 1944.

The next day, *The New York Times* carried five stories on the disinformation operation, three on the front page, and raised questions about Administration credibility.

North wanted to take a polygraph test to prove he had not leaked anything on the Libyan disinformation campaign. In a computer message to Poindexter, he asked, "PLEASE authorize us to be polygraphed re this Woodward mess. You, the President, WE need to find the person who is doing this."

On Saturday, October 4, Poindexter's deputy, Alton Keel, had me over to the White House to explain that there was no intent or policy to lie to the American media, no authorized leaks, no planting of stories, and that the use of the word "assassination" in the State Department memo was "unfortunate phraseology," but it was used because assassination by others in Libya could not be ruled out, he said.

Casey was having more serious trouble that fall with the Senate Intelligence Committee, which for over a year had been investigating the various spy cases. The committee had done a devastating postmortem on the Year of the Spy. Casey had a copy of its top-secret report, which the committee wanted to declassify and make public. Focusing on four major cases, the report said that in each the U.S. intelligence agencies had been tipped to potential espionage, often years before, and that the bizarre personal behavior of those eventually caught should have triggered investigations.

- Pelton's bankruptcy while at the NSA, and a previous disciplinary problem while he was in the Air Force, could have alerted his superiors. There were indications also that his departure from the NSA in 1979 had been forced on him. He had traveled to Vienna several times; his phone calls to the Soviet Embassy had been tapped by the FBI. But most alarming was a top-secret code-word Navy report done in 1982 on the Ivy Bells compromise; the report concluded that the Soviets had discovered the cable tap in 1981 because they must have had a human spy. It ruled out coincidence or luck and showed that the Soviets knew where to go and what they were looking for. This report and any suspicions about a human spy had been kept from the Senate and House committees because the Navy and the NSA clearly didn't want to have

Casey had suggested that Brown also write the biography of General Donovan and helped him gain access to the Donovan and OSS papers. The book, *The Last Hero,* was published in 1982.

to answer questions, fearing that the Congress would cut out funds for high-risk submarine espionage.

- The CIA man Howard's unacceptable personal behavior was well known. But, again, the Moscow station chief's 1984 cable saying that the compromises of sources and operations could have come only from a human source had been ignored. The committee had interviewed the station chief, who explained that Moscow was a hard environment, that all operations, human and technical, were risky, 50-50 propositions. He had said it was possible to have bad luck, for example, get ten "heads" in a row during the toss of a coin. There was a premium on taking hits, and agency people feared being declared PNG, persona non grata, and expelled for espionage. For the covert operators being "PNG'd" was the intelligence equivalent of landing on "Go to Jail," a professional screw-up and disgrace. Past cases of expulsions going back ten years were remembered. The operators preferred to live with the probability of compromise.
- Jonathan Jay Pollard, a civilian intelligence analyst with the Naval Investigative Service who was a terrorist expert, had been arrested in 1985 and charged with spying for Israel, carrying away suitcases of classified documents. Pollard had, for years, claimed to casual acquaintances, including a senior deputy in the service, that he worked for the Mossad, but no one had believed him or raised questions. The Israelis had been so plugged into U.S. intelligence publications that they provided Pollard with lists of National Intelligence Estimates on which they wanted the updates. Pollard had claimed to the Israelis that he could gain almost unlimited access to the Navy computers; though no absolute evidence was developed that this was true, the contents of the Navy computers to which he had access had to be considered compromised in their entirety.
- The espionage of Navy men John Walker and Jerry A. Whitworth was perhaps equal to Pelton's in terms of damage to the United States. Senior Chief Radioman Whitworth had been paid $300,000 by the Soviets for delivering between twenty-five and fifty rolls of Minox film two to four times a year between 1976 and 1985. Whitworth had once rented a white Rolls Royce. Yurchenko had said the KGB regarded the Walker/Whitworth operation as the most important in KGB history. The KGB officers who ran the operation were heralded, one winning the Hero of the Soviet Union award, and two others receiving the coveted Order of the Red Banner. Yurchenko said that the operation yielded information that would have been "devastating" to the United States in time of war and would have had war-winning implications for

the Soviet side during a conflict. Whitworth had been the Registered Publications System Officer on the nuclear-powered aircraft carrier *Enterprise,* in charge of all of the most sensitive cryptographic documents, including repair manuals, wiring diagrams and daily "key" setting on the code machines. His spying allowed the Soviets to read a full year of operational-message traffic from *Enterprise.* The Soviets had been able to decipher more than one million messages and learn about the advanced cryptographic equipment used by the other U.S. military services and intelligence agencies.

- Back in the late 1970s, Admiral Isaac C. Kidd, the commander of the Atlantic Fleet, had been alarmed about what the Soviets were doing with their submarines, reacting to U.S. exercises as if they were reading the message traffic. Kidd had his intelligence officers do a report. It concluded that there was a leak and that it was probably a radioman with broad access to crypto material. The NSA examined the report, but there was no follow-up. It was not until seven years later, in 1985, that Walker and Whitworth were exposed, when Walker's wife tipped the FBI.

The committee report detailed the security problems at the Moscow embassy; bugs had been found in typewriters, and the new U.S. Embassy building was riddled with every imaginable eavesdropping device. Most references to Moscow were deleted, because Casey didn't want the Soviets to have any idea what the U.S. knew. The rest of the report was declassified, but with virtually all the details removed.

Casey still wasn't happy. He sent a letter to Senator Durenberger saying that he agreed there was nothing classified in the report but that in its totality it was classified. The two had some hard words. The references to Howard and Pelton had each been reduced to two short sentences summarizing what was on the public record. Casey still resisted, wondering why this blood had to be drawn in public. Durenberger said that the problem had to be faced, and that if Casey wanted to get his budget through the Senate he had better let the declassified version be published. It finally was, in October 1986, but the 156-page document, "Meeting the Espionage Challenge: A Review of United States Counterintelligence and Security Programs," dealt only in generalities when it came to anything sensitive, and it broke no new ground.

Casey was still determined to achieve some breakthrough in Iran. This did not involve merely selling arms to open the door to Khomeini or to deprive the Soviets of unchallenged influence, or even to obtain the release of the American hostages. There were long-established, ambitious CIA covert operations in support of an effort to oust Khomeini, and to bring about Iran's defeat by the Iraqis.

Since 1982, the CIA had been supporting the main anti-Khomeini Iranian-exile movement, the Paris-based Front for the Liberation of Iran (FLI, pronounced "flea.") at $100,000 a month. Casey had no realistic expectation that the group could ever mount a coup, but their contacts did provide some sketchy intelligence.

Another $20,000 to $30,000 a month went to support Radio Liberation, which broadcast anti-Khomeini programs from Egypt to Iran for four hours a day.

Two months earlier, in August, the CIA had established a direct top-secret Washington–Baghdad link to provide the Iraqis with better and faster intelligence from U.S. satellites. Casey had met with senior Iraqis to make sure the new channel was functioning and to encourage more attacks on Iran, especially against economic targets. In mid-August, Iraq executed a surprise bombing attack on the Iranian oil terminal at Sirri Island, which had been considered immune from Iraqi raids because of the distance.

The previous month, September, the CIA had supplied a miniaturized television transmitter for an eleven-minute clandestine broadcast to Iran by Reza Pahlavi, the son of the late Shah. "The baby Shah," as he was known to his critics, had declared, "I will return."

Concerning intelligence information that was being provided to Iran as part of the secret arms/hostages meetings, Casey agreed that a little disinformation could be served up. In a memo to Poindexter, North said that Casey, Twetten and Cave "recognized that the information need not be accurate. . . . we believe that a mix of factual and bogus information can be provided at this meeting which will satisfy their concerns about 'good faith' . . ."

Casey was impressed that new secret channels into Iran had been developed. One was Speaker Rafsanjani's nephew, the other was the Revolutionary Guard intelligence director in the Prime Minister's office. When the nephew visited Washington secretly to meet with North, an electronic "surveillance package," as North called it, was authorized so that the meetings could be surreptitiously taped.

"Talks going extremely well," North reported by computer to Poindexter. "Sincerely believe that RR can be instrumental in bringing about an end to Iran/Iraq war—a la Roosevelt w/Russo/Japanese War in 1904. Anybody for RR getting the same prize . . . ?"

25

CHARLIE ALLEN, THE senior CIA analyst on the Iran project and the counterterrorist NIO, was increasingly troubled as the operation spun out of control. NSA coverage was so complete that Ghorbanifar, the Israelis and other middlemen could hardly make a move without something being picked up, and Allen began noticing an incredible price markup on the Iranian arms. Millions of dollars were missing or unaccounted for: $3.5 million left over from the first 1985 shipment; $24 million left in one Swiss account from December 1985; $3 million in interest for one thirty-day period. A covert operation was normally controlled down to the nearest fifty cents. In this operation, there was an enormous profit pool of extra cash. Allen examined the intercepts; there were lots of complaints from the Iranians and those who had put up some of the money, such as Khashoggi. The same people, General Secord and his team, were directly supplying both the contras and the Iranians. Allen went to see Gates.

"I'm deeply concerned," he said to the DDCI. "The creditors are demanding payment. This is going to be exposed if something isn't done. Perhaps the money has been diverted to the contras. I can't prove it."

Gates said he didn't want to hear any more. He didn't want to know about funding for the contras; it was illegal for the agency to be involved; the less he knew, the better.

Allen said it was not a rumor, but an analytic judgment based on the intercept material.

Disturbed, Gates said they better get this information to Casey. It didn't happen for six days.

On October 7, Allen told Casey about the possible diversion to the contras. Casey said he had just talked with an old friend and client, Roy Furmark, a New York businessman and lawyer for Khashoggi. Furmark had told him that the investors who had assisted Khashoggi in putting up the "bridge" loan of some $10 million were very, very unhappy; they were feeling cheated, threatening lawsuits and publicity. The United States would be brought into the transaction.

Allen agreed to put all his concerns down in a memo.

On October 9, North drove to Langley to lunch with Casey and Gates. In the subdued and controlled setting on the seventh floor, he summarized recent meetings he had had with new Iranian contacts. He was optimistic, as usual. They could get at least one hostage. Not, sadly, the body of Beirut station chief William Buckley, who was now presumed dead. The Iranian contacts said there was a 400-page interrogation report of what Buckley had given up under torture. Maybe they could get a copy.

Casey expressed concern about operational security; their old channel, Ghorbanifar, was obviously very unhappy and was about to blow.

Gates said that maybe he had been reading too many novels, but the fact that there was only one piece of paper—the January 17 finding on Iran—on the arms-sales/hostage operations, and the fact that it was sitting in John Poindexter's safe made him very nervous. Should that piece of presidential authorization disappear, a lot of people, including the three of them, could be in a lot of trouble.

Casey agreed. He would insist that Poindexter supply him with a copy of the finding, and North said he would facilitate that.

The discussion turned to Central America. Four days earlier, a contra-supply plane had been shot down in Nicaragua and Eugene Hasenfus, a cargo handler, had been captured by the Sandinistas. He had appeared that morning at a press conference and said that he believed he worked for the CIA.

Gates asked whether any CIA people, assets, proprietaries or anything, direct or indirect, were involved in the private funding and supply operation for the contras.

"Completely clean," North said. He had worked hard to keep Iran and the contras separate.

At the end of the lunch, North mentioned something about Swiss bank accounts and the contras.

He was not specific, and neither Casey nor Gates pursued the matter, but after lunch Gates went back in to see Casey. "Could you make heads or tails what the hell he was talking about?"

Casey said he couldn't.

Should we be concerned about it? Gates asked.

Casey waved him off.

Two hours later, Casey and Gates went to the Capitol to assure the chairmen and vice-chairmen of the Senate and House intelligence oversight committees that the CIA was not involved in the Hasenfus plane or in any weapons-supply operation.

Back at his White House computer, North sent a note to McFarlane: "We urgently need to find a high-powered lawyer and benefactor who can raise a legal defense for Hasenfus. . . . There will be a fair bite of history made in the next few weeks. . . . By Tuesday, a Swiss lawyer retained by Corporate Air Services should be in Managua. We should not rely on this person to represent the whole case since he is supported by covert means." North said he had located $100,000 from a donor for another attorney for Hasenfus. "Believe this to be a matter of great urgency to hold things together. Unfortunately RR was briefed that this plan was being contemplated."

North spoke with Casey. "Get rid of things, clean things up," the DCI said. North then began a massive housecleaning, attempting to shred all the memos that referred to the contra diversion. Casey said someone had to be ready to take the fall, but North probably was not senior enough to be a credible sacrifice. Maybe it would have to be Poindexter.

On October 14, Charlie Allen provided Gates with a seven-page memorandum that contained three recommendations. First, he urged that they set up a planning cell in the NSC immediately, bring in someone like Kissinger or Richard Helms to make a hard, outside program review, and subject the secret initiative to real questions: What are the true objectives, the options, the motives of the players?

Second, Allen said, the White House and the CIA had to get ready for public exposure. Ghorbanifar was about to go to the media or to court; he was a very unhappy former agent alleging that the United States government had failed to keep several promises. Third, they had to decide how best to shut down the Ghorbanifar channel in an orderly and systematic way. On page six Allen said, *"The government of the United States along with the government of Israel acquired substantial profit from these transactions, some of which profit was redistributed to other projects of the U.S. and of Israel."*

After he had read it, Gates bounded through the connecting door to Casey's office. Look, he said, and Casey read. This was dynamite, Casey agreed. He called Poindexter to set up a meeting at once. It could not be arranged until the next day, October 15, when Casey and Gates went to Casey's office in the Old Executive Office Building next to the White

House. The national-security adviser had squeezed in a half hour for the Director of Central Intelligence and his deputy. Casey presented the Allen memo to him.

"Get the White House counsel involved right away," Casey advised him. It was unraveling, allegations of impropriety and shabby conduct were about to fly unsparingly. Poindexter should consider having the President lay the project bare before the American public before it leaked in dribs and drabs.

Poindexter put them off.

Back at Langley, Casey and Gates summoned Allen. Casey wanted Allen to talk to Roy Furmark at once, assemble all the details and write up a full memo. Furmark again that day had contacted Casey to stress the urgency of resolving his clients' financial claims.

After Allen saw Furmark the next day, he reported by memo that Furmark had recommended another arms shipment to Iran "to maintain some credibility with the Iranians . . . and to provide Ghorbanifar with some capital so the investors can be repaid partially and so that Ghorbanifar can borrow money to finance additional shipments."

Furmark wanted to keep the process rolling; he thought it could result in the release of additional hostages. And Ghorbanifar had told him that North had indicated that the $10 million could be paid back from the $100 million in contra aid that was now available from U.S. funds.

They were about to have an incredible mess on their hands, Allen said.

On October 22, Allen went to New York and met again with Furmark, who told him that Ghorbanifar would allege that the bulk of the $15 million from the earlier May arms shipment "had been diverted to the contras."

At 9 A.M. the next day, October 23, Allen laid it out for Casey. The DCI ordered a memo to Poindexter prepared for his signature reflecting this allegation. The memo was drafted and placed in Casey's in-box.

North continued to sell arms. Using the new channel with Rafsanjani's nephew, Iran had paid $7 million into the Swiss account, and $2 million was drawn to pay for five hundred TOW missiles which were delivered to Iran at the end of October. That left $5 million. North reported to Poindexter that the United States was assured of getting two hostages back "in the next few days."

On November 2, David Jacobsen was released. The next day, the Lebanese magazine *Al-Shiraa* reported that the United States had been secretly supplying arms to Iran, and that McFarlane had secretly visited

Tehran earlier that year. Shultz was on his way to Vienna for arms control talks with the Soviets as the story broke. He sent a cable to Poindexter recommending that they now go public and attempt to explain. Poindexter replied by cable that Bush, Weinberger and Casey agreed on the necessity for remaining "absolutely close-mouthed."

When the President met with Jacobsen at the White House that Friday, November 7, he told reporters that the story out of Beirut had "no foundation."

Jacobsen, freed after seventeen months, bristled at questions about how his release had been achieved. Raising his arm to caution reporters, he said, "In the name of God, will you please just be responsible and back off."

Even though the whole thing was unraveling, Furmark again told Allen that day that his clients would soon up the ante. They would disclose the siphoning of Iran arms money to the contras.

Casey and Gates went again to see Poindexter. Casey recommended that White House counsel Peter J. Wallison look over the whole matter.

"I don't trust Wallison to keep his mouth shut," Poindexter replied.

Casey now despaired that there was a way to keep the lid on, and the situation was aggravated by disunity at the top. Personal feuds that had simmered for years within the Administration were at the breaking point. Shultz, who had long opposed the Iran initiative and was resentful that the NSC had run it, began to signal his disagreement in public. The Pentagon leaked Weinberger's opinion that selling arms to Iran was "absurd." Don Regan and Poindexter got into a tense dispute in front of the President about whether to offer some public explanation; the President sided with Poindexter, who felt that they still could get some more hostages out if secrecy could be preserved.

On Monday, November 10, Casey went to the White House to join the President, Bush, Shultz, Weinberger, Meese and Poindexter. The President told them that rumors and press reports were endangering what they were doing. He felt he was not dealing with terrorists in Iran, but with moderate factions, and that the arms shipments were not ransom payments. A basic statement needed to be made, the President said, a statement that would avoid details and specifics of the operation. Shultz learned, for the first time, that the President had signed the January 17 finding for the Iran arms shipments. Despite the unease, a statement was released saying that all the top advisers were "unanimous" in supporting the President; it condemned "speculative stories" and said that the United States government's "policy of not making concessions to terrorists remains intact."

Word was spreading within the U.S. intelligence agencies that there was big trouble with the money on the Iran arms sales. On November 12, Senate Intelligence Committee investigators went to the CIA and attempted to obtain the NSA intercepts on the Iran project. Casey blocked this, claiming that the project was still close-hold.

The White House realized that the President was going to have to go public to put the best face on the Iran project, so a televised speech was scheduled for the evening of November 13. Beforehand, the leaders of Congress and the intelligence committees were invited to the White House for a briefing by Poindexter and Casey. The national-security adviser began by reading the January 17 finding that ordered Casey not to disclose the operation to the committees. The leaders from the Hill were beside themselves with rage and disbelief.

Afterward, Casey asked Pat Leahy whether he needed a ride. Leahy said he was going to Georgetown to meet his family for dinner and accepted. The two had been at each other's throat for more than a year. Back in October 1985, just after the *Achille Lauro* hijacking, Leahy had gone on television to say that U.S. intelligence knew that Egyptian President Mubarak had been lying. Leahy had said, "When Mubarak went on the news yesterday and said the hijackers had left Egypt, we knew that wasn't so. Our intelligence was very, very good." The clear implication was that Mubarak's phone calls had been intercepted. Casey had sent the Senator a stern letter, charging him with a gross breach of security and virtual treason. In fact Leahy had said no more than Administration spokesmen had already said, but Casey held that the statement from the Senate Intelligence Committee vice-chairman carried more weight.

Leahy had won reelection by thirty percentage points the previous week, but no thanks to Casey. Days before the election, *Reader's Digest* had published an article, "Congress Is Crippling the CIA," that cited the alleged Leahy security breach in such a way that Leahy concluded it had come from Casey.

"I know you're pissed off," Casey told Leahy as they settled in the back of his car.

Leahy said it was improper for the DCI to meddle in the political process and attempt to defeat unfriendly senators. But real hell is now going to have to be paid on this Iran project, he said. The Senate committee was going to conduct a genuine investigation with subpoenas and sworn testimony, no more informal, friendly chats. The failure to inform and consult with the committee violated every promise, pledge and understanding.

The Democrats had won control of the Senate in the previous week's election, and Leahy said he might stay on the committee, moving into the chairmanship.

We've got to work together, Casey said as the car pulled into Georgetown. Leahy hopped out, and Casey followed, grabbing the Senator's arm. It was the height of the evening rush hour, and the car had stopped in the middle of the street, backing up traffic.

We believe in the same things, Casey said, patting Leahy's arm, and he hinted that the CIA wanted to give Leahy a medal for his work on the committee.

An hour later, the President delivered his television speech. He said he had not paid "ransom" for the hostages, but was seeking "access and influence" in Iran. The weapons were "defensive"; he likened the secret Iran initiative to Nixon and Kissinger's 1971 opening to China.

"We did not—repeat, did not—trade weapons or anything else for hostages. Nor will we."

He added that it was all legal, "and the relevant committees of Congress are being and will be fully informed."

Poindexter took the January 17 finding on Iran from his safe, had a copy made, and sent the copy to the Senate Intelligence Committee. Now there it was in black and white. Senators Durenberger and Leahy still thought it inconceivable that the President had ordered Casey "to refrain from reporting this finding to the Congress." It was ten months old. But Casey was comparatively clean: he was following orders, though they were sure he was party to the policy and the orders. Durenberger and Leahy were struck by the enormity of the transgression: the whole notion of congressional oversight had been undermined, the clock had been turned back a decade or more. The President had said simply that he could deal them out at will. Most glaring was the line in the finding that notification was being withheld because of the "extreme sensitivity and security risks."

The bellboys at the Tehran Hilton, where McFarlane and North had stayed six months earlier, knew something was up. So did key Israelis, Saudi arms dealer Khashoggi, and the Iranian middleman Ghorbanifar. These people could be trusted, but not the United States senators who shared all the other intelligence secrets? What else didn't they know?

As part of the White House effort, Poindexter visited *The Washington Post* for lunch on Friday, November 14. Puffing calmly on his pipe, he said the operation was a reasonable risk. The President was not going to be bound by conventional notions of what could and could not be done in foreign affairs.

Two days later, Poindexter made a rare appearance on NBC Television's *Meet the Press*. While he waited for the show to begin, I asked him about his twenty-eight years as a naval officer, particularly his time commanding a destroyer in the mid-1970s.

"Naval officers," he said, gently extracting his pipe from his jacket's side pocket, "are better equipped because of command at sea. You have to make decisions; you learn there is nobody else out there in a pinch. You learn to be cool, whether on the bridge of a destroyer or here. They're the same."

On the air, Poindexter said that the Administration was going public with the Iran initiative "because of all the speculation and the leaks." He said the initiative "was basically an intelligence operation," and accordingly Casey, not he, would present the facts to Congress.

That day Casey left for Central America. It never hurt to be out of the country when explanations were due. But he wanted to keep his eye on the ball, which was still the contra war. He had his hunting license back. The $100 million in congressionally approved contra aid had been available for a month, and he was supervising the renewed effort; $70 million of the $100 million was for the CIA, almost triple what had been provided in any previous single year by Congress.

On Monday, November 17, Casey received a call from Gates urging him to return to testify before the intelligence committees at the end of the week. The next day Poindexter called Casey on a secure phone. The CIA taped the call as an operational message.

"I got to thinking about the hearing on Friday and the coordination that the two of us need to do," Poindexter said. "If you can get back on Thursday so we could meet . . . I think it would be very useful, so we make the best possible presentations on Friday, and try to lay as many of these questions to rest as we can."

"Are you going to have a lot of people at the meeting—uh State and uh Defense?" Casey asked.

"I'd like to spend some time just the two of us," Poindexter said. He added that Meese wanted to be helpful and would like to be in at least one of the meetings.

"Ah," Casey replied, "you, you set whatever time you'd like for us to get together and have a little talk ourselves, then I'll have, I'll handle a meeting any time you set it."

• • •

Relations between Casey and Shultz finally snapped. That same Sunday, the Secretary of State had gone on television and had made no effort to disguise his disagreement with the Iran arms policy. He said that Poindexter was the "designated hitter" on the operation. Asked whether he had authority to speak for the Administration on the issue, Shultz replied firmly, "No."

Shultz had come to loathe Casey. It was clear that the DCI had set up an alternative foreign policy, not just in Iran. His influence had been too great. First he had used his analysts and other CIA officials for intelligence-gathering to find out what was going on around town. Then the CIA apparatus had been used as a policy-planning service for the DCI, and finally it had become an implementing agency through its own operations officers or now through the White House. There was no better illustration than when Casey had shamelessly peddled the first Graham Fuller paper on Iran all around town the previous year. Rejected by State and Defense, he had sold it at the White House.

Shultz was also aware that Casey had effectively sabotaged arms control agreements over the years. The DCI had a back-channel alliance with the hard-line Assistant Secretary of Defense Richard Perle. In retrospect it was clear to Shultz that the intelligence agencies had produced a never-ending stream of reports that cleverly undermined arms control. Playing to the President's predisposition, Casey had argued that arms control talks were simply another tool of the Soviets, who designed their positions around two calculations: first, they made up their minds on what new weapons they wanted to build; second, they determined what the United States wanted to build that would be most dangerous to them. This was often calibrated by the Soviets down to the kind of fins they wanted to put on their missiles six years in the future. Of course, this was logical for the Soviets. All nations involved in negotiations, including the United States, made similar evaluations. But Casey's "evidence" had been presented to demonstrate that the Soviets were not serious and were manipulating the negotiations.

Casey had added immeasurably to the hesitation in the White House on arms control, Shultz felt. Perhaps the job of DCI had become too big. Intelligence had too much money. The DCI had his hand in the multi-billion-dollar satellite hardware decisions ten years off, setting the priorities. He controlled the analytical process and the estimates. He controlled covert action and counterintelligence. With an activist like

Casey, the DCI had a policy role. Somehow these responsibilities were too great and perhaps needed to be divided up, Shultz felt.

Casey was old. It was probably his last job. He was wealthy. He had little or nothing to lose. In pursuing his goals, he had created a general feeling of distrust in the agency's objectivity, not just in the Congress but even within the Administration, Shultz felt. In some sense Casey had lost his integrity. He had been a shadow Secretary of State.

The evening of November 18, at about six, I went to the White House to meet with Poindexter's deputy, Al Keel. He wanted to argue that we should not publish a story about the covert efforts to support the anti-Khomeini exiles that had been proceeding alongside the initiative to sell arms to the Khomeini government. Keel was tired and overwrought. "There is an absolute frenzy out there in the press on this story," he said, sitting at the desk in his cubbyhole office. "We got behind the power curve; we've been ten days behind it."

A youthful, bearded man who spoke with conviction, Keel rolled a pencil on his desk and said that they had had no choice but to trade in arms, the chief "currency" in the Middle East. "We had to establish our bona fides. And we frankly didn't trust them, didn't trust Iran, didn't trust the channels we were dealing with. They didn't trust us. There was no mutual trust. We're the Great Satan. So how do you establish your bona fides? Do you try powdered milk? Do you try bandages? That's something they can get at the local drugstore. You have to try arms."

He said that it would be "devastating" if a story were published that said, or even implied, that the United States was dealing not only with its channels to the Iranian moderates, but with the exiles, those associated with the Shah's regime. He paused and looked up. "There's no way that Tehran can ignore it."

I replied that the Iranian government regularly accused the CIA of supporting the exiles and pro-Shah forces. They said it in their newspapers and on their radio. And the exiles knew they were getting money from the CIA; they acknowledged this to reporters in their offices in Paris.

He agreed, but said that the stories about these things had been in the back of the paper, not on the front page, and that the references had been oblique. "There will be a real threat to lives, lives will be at risk if this story runs. . . . It will sever our channels. Give me a minimum of twenty-four hours, hopefully seventy-two hours, so we can contact our channels in Tehran, our moderates, to tell them a bad story is coming. Frankly, to tell them, 'Cover your ass.' "

Back at the *Post* we decided that this claim was not very credible; White House assessments didn't have much weight anymore. The President was scheduled to appear for a press conference the next day, and we suspected the White House did not want a story about embracing Khomeini with arms all the while the CIA was supporting Iranian exiles, and the backers of the baby Shah, who wanted to overthrow Khomeini. We decided to run the story.

That night North, McFarlane and several other NSC aides attempted feverishly to put together a chronology of events that would distance the President and blur his role, particularly on his initial approval of the first Israeli shipments in 1985. North summoned his assistant, Lieutenant Colonel Robert Earl, to the office by computer message: "Let's get our little-nipper in here and find out wtf is going on." In Marine jargon, "wtf" means "what the fuck."

At his press conference, the President defended the Iran project. "I don't think a mistake was made. . . . I don't see that it has been a fiasco or a great failure of any kind." He denied four times that he had "condoned" the Israeli shipments, or that any other country was even involved. Twenty-five minutes after the press conference, however, Reagan issued an unusual correction, saying that he had in fact condoned such a shipment by another country.

Casey and Gates went to the White House the next day to attempt to resolve a dispute with North, who was claiming that it was not he who had requested CIA assistance back in November 1985 for the Israeli shipment. Poindexter and North finally agreed that it had been North. That night, Casey was back at the White House, attempting to put together his testimony for the intelligence committees the next day. He met with Poindexter, Shultz and Meese. He was planning to say, in his testimony, that the CIA thought the 1985 Israeli shipment was "oil-drilling equipment," not arms.

Later that night, Shultz went to see the President in the White House living quarters. In a tense meeting, the Secretary of State told the President that the Director of Central Intelligence was about to lie to the intelligence committees, and that something had to be done. Statements were being made that would not stand up even to the most superficial scrutiny. Shultz was boiling. He'd never thought he'd have such a conversation, almost scolding the President of the United States. But he told Reagan he had to face facts, that anyone looking at the record would see arms-for-hostages.

Meanwhile, Casey chaired a meeting at Langley with a large group of CIA officers who might know something about what had happened. He had met with North and they deleted the description of the 1985 Israeli shipment as oil-drilling equipment, fixing the problem with an omission.

The next morning he rose early and continued to revise his testimony, scaling it back, molding the information to fit what was already out and what could not reasonably be expected to stay secret. At 9:30 Casey appeared in a top-secret closed-door session before all fifteen members of the House Intelligence Committee. There was much unhappiness. After Casey read his ten-minute summary, Chairman Lee Hamilton unequivocally challenged Casey's view that notification of covert action could legally be delayed some ten months. Casey responded coolly, "We are talking about a constitutional prerogative which presidents have claimed." Care and caution required nothing less, he said, and time got "chewed up" as the Iranians attempted to exert their limited influence on those holding the American hostages in Lebanon. "I think it was a bona-fide attempt in which the things we committed were rather small and certainly proportionate to the magnitude of the things we were trying to achieve." The weapons passed out were insignificant.

"You got to take those risks, or sit and let the world go by. I personally was in favor of taking the risks in a cautious and prudent way.

"I wouldn't now be willing to say I wouldn't take the risk if I could do it over again."

Some Republicans jumped in, defending the President's decision, and arguing that the committee leaked. Dave McCurdy, the Oklahoma Democrat, asked, "Who managed the operation, Mr. Casey?"

"I think we were all in it. It was a team."

"Who headed the team? Who called the shots? Was it Poindexter or Casey?"

Casey replied, "I think it was the President."

At 11 A.M. Casey was due at the Senate committee and left, saying he would return to the House committee at 1:30 P.M.

He went to the Senate Intelligence Committee's secure hearing room and sat at the long witness table where a special microphone stood like a praying mantis poking in his face. It was to aid the senators in deciphering the Director's legendary mumbling. Clair George sat beside him. After six years of dodging and ducking, this was a moment of reckoning. All the members of the committee sat around a white horseshoe-shaped table. Senate Minority Leader Robert C. Byrd, a West Virginia Democrat and an ex officio member of the committee, was also present.

"Excuse me, Mr. Chairman," Byrd inquired, "but is the witness under oath?"

It was an awkward moment. Durenberger responded that with the exception of confirmation hearings, the committee did not swear witnesses. This promoted an atmosphere of "free exchange," he said. Its proceedings were not adversarial, but if any senator wanted the witness under oath, it could, of course, be done. No one, including Byrd, spoke up.

Casey sat silently, and then began reading from his prepared statement. He attempted to present the operation as routine covert action. He did not mention the absence of a finding before the CIA assistance for the 1985 Israeli shipment; nor the existence of the finding drawn up by Sporkin that had the President retroactively approve the CIA role in the Israeli shipment. He referred to Iranian middleman Ghorbanifar as a "representative of Iran" and not by name.

Several senators pressed for the "representative's" identity and his relationship with the CIA. Casey evaded the question, but it was then directed to Clair George, who referred to Ghorbanifar as a highly sensitive source whose name should not be used.

"Wasn't it Ghorbanifar?" a senator asked.

"Well, yes, Senator," George said, "but we would be very concerned for his life if that ever got out."

Ghorbanifar's failure to pass a series of lie detector tests was not disclosed.

When asked whether General Secord had played any role in the Iran arms shipments, Casey said he had heard the press reports and tried to leave it at that. He was questioned further.

"We are aware of Mr. Secord's activities and we do not approve of them," the DCI said.

In references to the meetings with the Iranians, Casey referred to an "NSC official." When asked who that was, the DCI said, "I'm not sure," and passed the question to George. The DDO said he too was not certain. He turned back and passed the question to his executive assistant, who was sitting behind them. The assistant said he did not know for sure.

Lieutenant Colonel North's name was not mentioned.

Casey tailored his briefing to extend an olive branch but no new facts. He did not bring up the troubling money problems, the missing $10 million, or the possibility that some money from the arms sales had been diverted to the contras.

At 1:50 Casey was back at the House committee saying that he did not think it was a good idea to have the NSC conduct operations. He said that it first happened with "this Central America business." Given the congressional restrictions placed on the CIA in the Nicaragua operation, the NSC became operational, he said, acknowledging what the Administration had previously denied. "The NSC has been guiding and active in the private provision of weapons to the contras down there," Casey volunteered. "I don't know all the details. I have kept away from the details because I was barred from doing anything. I knew that others were doing it."

Asked about the "nameless ex-patriot" (Ghorbanifar), Casey said he was untrustworthy, "a kind of dubious guy." Pressed, Casey said, "In this kind of thing you don't get the purest souls to do what you want them to. You usually take those people that have a checkered career or checkered record."

"It is just a matter of degree as to how much of a rascal he is?" one Democrat asked.

"Yes," Casey said, "I think that is fair."

To a difficult question, Casey said, "It is hard to be precise on that," or "I don't have it at my fingertips," or "That is above my pay grade." This was all true, but no member really pushed him or followed up as the DCI slid off the questions. Much of the time was spent as the congressmen debated each other. Pages of the transcript show Casey uttering not a word. Casey did remind them that the project obtained the release of three hostages.

Hamilton said, "I just think you are going to have a lot of trouble explaining your policy on terrorism now."

"You don't have to be a great prophet to figure that at this point," Casey replied. By 3:05 P.M. he was released.

Attorney General Meese went to the President that morning and suggested to him that no one had the story straight. There were too many contradictions, too much they didn't know, too many gaps, too many inconsistent recollections. They're all going to look silly when Congress looks into the matter, he said. The President authorized the Attorney General to begin his inquiry.

Meese contacted Poindexter and asked that he assemble all the relevant documents. In the West Wing, Poindexter asked his military assistant, Navy Commander Paul Thompson, who was also a lawyer, to bring in the covert action findings from the safe. The first Iran finding, dated December 5, 1985, portrayed the Iran initiative as a straight arms-for-hostage deal. This was precisely what Reagan was denying.

"They'll have a field day with this," Thompson said, handing the finding to the Admiral.

Poindexter saw that it would be a significant political embarrassment. Like the skipper on the bridge of his destroyer, he decided to act. He tore up the finding and, turning in his chair, he placed it in the burn bag behind his desk. The bags were burned as part of the routine destruction of excess classified material. The Admiral also found other computer notes and unfinished documents—private, frank communications that were no longer needed. He ripped them up and placed them in the burn bag also.

That afternoon, Meese called McFarlane at home. "Bud," he said, "I have been tasked by the President to put together an accurate record of events in this matter and I would like to talk to you."

McFarlane arrived at the Justice Department in midafternoon and laid out his recollections for an hour.

Meese had questions about the President's involvement and the role of other Cabinet officers. That took another half hour. Meese's assistant left the room, and Meese started to follow him.

"Ed, wait a minute," McFarlane said. "I want to talk to you about this. You know, as you may have seen in this morning's papers, I gave a speech last night, and I have taken on responsibility for every bit of this that I can and I shall continue to do that."

"Yes, that's been noted."

"But I want you to know that from the very beginning of this, Ed, the President was foursquare behind it, that he never had any reservations about approving anything that the Israelis wanted to do here."

"I know that," Meese said, "and I can understand why. And, as a practical matter, I'm glad you told me this, because his legal position is far better the earlier he made the decision." He said that if the President had made an "oral finding" or even a "*mental* finding" instead of the normally written one, that put them all the more in the clear because the President had the authority to order covert action. He added, "Bud, whatever you do, don't try to shave the truth or make what you think is best for yourself or the President. Just tell the truth and don't try to figure out what's going to be helpful or hurtful to the President."

Meese then spoke with FBI Director William Webster, who offered the services of the FBI in Meese's inquiry. Meese said he didn't see any criminality, and he felt that to bring the FBI in would open them to the criticism that the Bureau was being used for political purposes.

About 6:30 that evening, North went to his office. He had more or less made up his mind to be annihilated. Instructing his secretary of four years, Fawn Hall, to assist him, he began removing documents, memos and messages from his safe and files. Cool, weary but intent, he piled them in a large stack. Everything was to be shredded. It took an hour. He also asked Hall's assistance in altering four memos, removing troubling references.

• • •

Saturday, November 22, was warm. A busy weekend was ahead. Meese took two assistant attorney generals to the White House with him. He met first with Shultz and then with Sporkin. His assistants went to work in the files. At North's office they found an undated memo on Iran, unaddressed: *"$12 million will be used to purchase critically needed supplies for the Nicaraguan democratic resistance forces."*

Meese later took his assistants to lunch at the Old Ebbitt Grill two blocks from the White House. They described the diversion memo they had discovered in North's office. Meese uttered an expletive, but felt it could be legitimate, or perhaps the memo only reflected one of North's pipe dreams.

Casey was in his Old Executive Office Building office and called down to Poindexter, "Why don't I come over and we'll have a sandwich together." For nearly two hours, the two men who knew the most ate and talked alone. North joined them near the end. Among other issues, they discussed the second channel with the Iranians. The big play was still an option, a hope. Casey always believed that one of the best tactics was to cover an emerging problem with a visible success. Instead of the dubious services of Ghorbanifar, they now had a direct channel through Ali Hashemi Bahramani, a nephew to the Speaker of the Iranian Parliament, Rafsanjani, and the Revolutionary Guard intelligence director in the Prime Minister's Office named Samaii. For some time Bahramani and Samaii had been sending messages to North with an Israeli-manufactured secure communications device. But for the last week Bahramani had said he felt threatened and possibly under surveillance, so his messages had come through his bodyguard.

The lunch ended at 3:20 P.M. At 3:40, North called Meese to set an interview for the next day. Then at 3:46, Casey called Meese to say he had something to tell the Attorney General. "Why don't I drop by on my way home this evening," Meese said.

Casey offered the Attorney General scotch or beer, it was all he had. Meese, not a scotch drinker, took a beer. Casey said that his old friend Roy Furmark had been passing messages from those who had put up the money for the Iran arms sales. They were saying, "Either pay us the money we're owed or else we're going to try to make it look bad."

Both lawyers recognized blackmail. But, by Meese's account, neither shared the most troubling information they had. Casey did not mention Furmark's charge that money had gone to the contras, and the Attorney General did not mention the undated North memo they had found several hours earlier suggesting the diversion.

Meese had made an early appointment with North for the next day, Sunday, but North asked that it be postponed until 2 P.M. so that he could go to church with his family. North called McFarlane and asked to meet him at 12:30 P.M. at an office McFarlane had at the Old Executive Office Building. They talked for fifteen minutes. North said he was going to have to lay the facts out for Meese about the diversion of Iran arms sale money to the contras. As McFarlane knew, North would not do anything that was not approved. In this case, it was a matter of record: there was a memo that North had done for Poindexter.

At 2 P.M., Meese arrived with his two assistants.

North said yes, money had been diverted; three accounts had been opened in Switzerland and the numbers given to the Israelis. The money had been deposited in those accounts, and the contras were appreciative. About $3–$4 million from one arms sale had gone in that direction. The $12 million mentioned in the memo, North said, was not U.S. money and it was not Israeli money. It had sounded fine to him.

"Did you find a cover memo?" North asked.

"Should we have?" inquired Meese.

"No, I just wondered."

Casey, meanwhile, wrote a classified letter to the President suggesting that Shultz be fired. Using the baseball terminology Shultz had used the previous week for Poindexter as "designated hitter," Casey said that at State the President needed a new "pitcher."

On Monday at 11 A.M., Meese explained to the President and Don Regan that he had uncovered a diversion of money to the contras. Meese went to see Poindexter in the national-security adviser's office. "I assume you're aware of the memo we found in Ollie's files." Poindexter said he knew and realized that he would probably have to resign.

Before lunch, Poindexter found a computer note from North. "There is that old line about you can't fire me, I quit . . . I am prepared to depart at the time you and the President decide. . . . We nearly succeeded. Semper fidelis. Oliver North."

"Thanks, Ollie," Poindexter typed. "I have talked to Ed twice today on this and he is still trying to figure out what to do. I have told him I am prepared to resign. I told him I would take the cue from him. He is one of the few besides the President that I can trust. If we don't leave, what would you think about going out to CIA and being a special assistant to Bill? This would put you in the operational world officially. Don't say anything to Bill yet. I just want to get your reaction."

During a photo session at the White House, the President was asked whether he should have acknowledged mistakes in the Iran arms shipments. "I'm not going to lie about that. I didn't make a mistake," he replied. Pressed about others, he said, "I'm not going to fire anybody."

Casey had Furmark out to Langley and attempted to learn about the money used in the Iran operation. He called North.

"There's a man here who says you owe him $10 million," the DCI said.

North said there was only $30,000 left in the Swiss account. "Tell him the Iranians or Israelis owe him the money," North said.

Casey tried to reach Meese and failed. He tried Don Regan and left a message saying he urgently needed to talk to the Chief of Staff. It could not wait. Regan agreed to stop by Langley on his way home for dinner. Up on the seventh floor, Casey betrayed little, and with hardly a facial reaction asked what was going on, what was on the President's mind.

Regan blurted out that a diversion of funds to the contras had been discovered.

"What are you going to do about it?" Casey asked. He was stolid, unreadable.

All along, Regan continued, he had thought the arms transactions with Iran were, as they used to say on Wall Street, NPH, "No Profit Here." Given the information about the diversion, the plan was to make it all public the next day.

"Well, do you realize the consequences?" Casey asked sharply, and then ticked off the impact of such a disclosure. "You're going to blow the whole Iranian thing, and possibly blow the lives of these hostages." Iran would be enraged at being overcharged for the arms. Congress would be beside itself, uncontrollable, and would likely cut off the contra funding, the DCI said.

"Be that as it may," Regan replied. "How the hell can we sit on this stuff any longer? I mean this thing is an absolute disgrace. . . . We have this possible criminal act."

"I hope you realize that, you know, this is going to cause quite a few upsets and it's going to be a major story," Casey replied.

Regan indicated that irrevocable decisions had been made; there was no turning back, no choice.

Casey was late for dinner at the Metropolitan Club, where he was to meet Bernadette, his daughter, and Edward Hymoff, an OSS veteran and writer who wanted to write Casey's biography. They had a handshake agreement that Casey would provide access to the CIA and to senior Administration figures, including the President.

When Casey arrived at the club, Hymoff, Bernadette and her husband were waiting. Aware of the current flap, Hymoff said, "You know the shit is going to hit the fan."

"We can handle it," Casey said confidently, and turned to the proposed book. He was staying until the end of the President's term, but he would work something out so that Hymoff could spend the last six months of 1988 at the agency gathering information. Until then, they should focus on the rest of his life—OSS, investor, author and the SEC. He was anxious to get going. He was going to spend the Christmas holidays at his Palm Beach house, and they agreed that Hymoff could come and tape some interviews.

"Bill, what are you going to do after the Administration?"

"I'm not going back to lawyering," Casey said, "but venture capital." Government had again convinced him that a small private enterprise could move faster, better. He also said that he was thinking of doing his autobiography.

"Daddy," Bernadette said, "you must do a book."

At 6:30 A.M. the next day, Tuesday, November 25, Casey called Meese and asked him to stop by on his way to work. The Attorney General's car pulled up at Foxhall Crescents at 7 A.M. Casey wanted to know what was going on.

Meese explained: Poindexter is going, it's all going to be announced.

Casey said he would pull all the memos together and send them to Meese.

Next Meese reached Poindexter's car by phone and asked that the Admiral meet him at the Justice Department. Once Poindexter arrived, the Attorney General had one message: "You should resign today." Meese volunteered that he didn't think North had done anything illegal.

Poindexter went back to his West Wing office and ordered breakfast brought to him on a tray. He sat at the end of his conference table and calmly told his military aide, Commander Thompson, that he would be requesting reassignment in the Navy that day. There were no jitters, no flash of emotion, no doubt. Thompson later said, "Of all the people in the world who might have to take a fall, the Admiral was probably the most qualified in history."

Don Regan soon arrived in Poindexter's office. He was on fire. "What the hell happened here?"

Poindexter adjusted his trifocals, dabbed at his mouth with his napkin, and put it aside. "Well," he said, "I guess I should have looked into it more, but I didn't. I knew that Ollie was up to something. I just didn't look into it."

"Why not?" Regan demanded. "What the hell. You're a Vice Admiral. What's going on?"

"That damn Tip O'Neill," Poindexter said, "the way he's jerking the contras around. I was just so disgusted."

"Well, John, I think when you go see the President at 9:30, you better make sure you have your resignation with you."

"I will." *

At Langley, Casey called for Charlie Allen. Where was the goddamn month-old memo he had sent to Poindexter about the possible diversion of money? They found it, in Casey's in-box. Nearly hysterical, Casey drafted an immediate top-secret, "Dear Ed" letter to Meese explaining what had happened: he and Gates had told Poindexter several times about these allegations, had given him a memo in mid-October, but the memo that laid out the possible diversion most starkly had somehow, inexplicably, never gone forward to the White House.

That morning the President gave the congressional leaders an early warning about the diversion. They were called to the White House and

* Eight months later Poindexter testified under oath that he thought North's contra diversion scheme was a good idea and that he approved it but never informed or sought the approval of the President. Since 1981 the President's policy of aiding the contras had not changed, Poindexter testified. He said that a diversion of Iranian arms sales profits to the contras would be similar to third country support. Instead of the Saudis giving, it would be the Iranians, or it could be considered a private Iranian contribution. This was a matter of implementing the President's known policy. Poindexter claimed he felt he had the authority to approve the diversion, that he knew it would be politically explosive and that his job was to deliberately insulate the President from the decision. "On this whole issue," he testified, "you know the buck stops here with me." He said that the President would have "absolutely" approved of the decision and would have enjoyed knowing about it, but that Poindexter's plan of total deniability required that it never be mentioned to Reagan, tempted as Poindexter was on several occasions. North's secretary, Fawn Hall, testified under a grant of full immunity that the one diversion memo that Meese's investigators had discovered had been revised by Poindexter at one point, suggesting that it was intended to be forwarded to the President. North testified that, in total, he prepared five memos that referred to the contra diversion for Poindexter to forward to the President, but that he believed he had shredded them. Poindexter testified that he did not recall these other memos. When the detailed financial records were finally deciphered, investigators established that only about $3 million eventually reached the contras from all the Iranian arms sales profits, and an excess of $8 million remained in various bank accounts in Switzerland.

the President told them that Poindexter was "not a participant," but had volunteered his resignation in accordance with Navy tradition which held that the skipper is responsible for everything that happens in his command. Reagan defended his National Security Council system and said it had "served this country well."

"Without condoning" the diversion scheme, the President said, "it wasn't contrary to policy."

At a noon press conference, the President read a brief statement and introduced Meese, who announced that between $10 million and $30 million had been diverted to the contras. Shaken and grim, the President said he had not known earlier. He announced that Poindexter had resigned, and that North had been fired.

Later that day, Fawn Hall smuggled a half-inch-thick stack of documents from North's office by concealing them in her clothes and boots. She took them to North and said their defense would be "We shred every day." In the evening a security officer sealed the office.

The next day, I reached Casey on the telephone to ask how the Administration had got into the arms sales to Iran.

"The Israelis, in '81, were telling us to work with the Iranians, for the purpose of getting close to the military," Casey said. "It seemed credible to us, based on the future, post-Khomeini era."

Why were there profits that could be diverted to the contras?

"Iran was willing to pay more," he said, and suggested that any "illegality" found would be on the part of others.

Who?

He paused. "Poindexter just got caught."

Did you know about the diversion to the contras?

"The law said I had to stay away," he said, reiterating what Meese had said at his press conference, that no one at the CIA knew, including the Director.

The contras are your boys, you must have had a clue that they were getting $10 million to $30 million?

"Gossip," he snapped. "I learned yesterday of it for sure from Meese."

You didn't know what North was doing?

"Goddammit—no one will go to jail . . . inside the Beltway." He hung up.

A few days later, Stansfield Turner's former deputy, Frank Carlucci, was appointed the national-security adviser; an independent counsel was sought to conduct the criminal investigation of the Iran-contra affair; the President appointed a three-member commission headed by former Senator John Tower to investigate the NSC; and the Senate Intelligence Committee began a full-scale investigation. Poindexter's only other conversation with Casey was to ask the DCI's advice on selecting an attorney.

About 1 P.M. on December 3, I called Casey again. A number of Administration and congressional leaders were saying that he was finished at the CIA. He was eating his lunch as we chatted.

"The chairman and vice-chairman say we'll come out smelling like a rose," he said between bites, referring to Senators Durenberger and Leahy. "We were barred by law from supporting the contras, and we didn't."

The CIA had made two trivial mistakes on the Iran arms sales, he said. The first was the assistance rendered to the White House on the November 1985 Israeli shipment of arms to Iran before Reagan had signed a finding. The assistance was to put North in touch so that a "routine commercial flight" could be found. "It's not a Supreme Court case."

Second, he said, some "dumb" low-level employee at the agency had used the same Swiss bank account for the Iran arms sales as was used for the joint U.S.-Saudi covert support operation to the Afghan rebels. So some of this Iran money and the $500 million for the Afghan operation had been commingled, he said. "But all the money is accounted for."

Was this whole thing a big sting operation by the Iranians to get U.S. weapons?

"Bullshit—the President said woo them and we did."

I asked another question.

"Goddammit, don't needle me. I don't know why I take your calls."

I said that there were a number of unanswered questions.

"I expect you to exercise the normal restraint of an adult."

Well, others, many others, are saying that you knew more, had to be involved, et cetera.

"That's why I wouldn't have your job for all the money in the world," the DCI said, a crispness and clarity rising in his voice. "You're destined to be right only a part of the time."

The legal department at the CIA, still trying desperately to keep all agency activity within the boundaries of law, attempted to determine precisely what contact was permissible between CIA officers and the private airlift and donors to the contra cause. An associate counsel issued an opinion on December 5 to Clair George that "contacts with the benefactors, although contrary to policy, were not contrary to law."

With Poindexter and North gone, Casey singlehandedly had the task of pulling something out of the foundering Iran initiative. For an upcoming meeting with the second Iranian channel in Frankfurt, Germany, on Saturday, December 13, Shultz had won White House agreement that there would be no more arms sales to Iran and that the CIA representative at the meeting would not talk policy. Casey called Don Regan to persuade the President to reverse himself, and a top-secret message was dispatched to Frankfurt, authorizing the State and CIA representatives to have "policy and intelligence discussions."

After the Frankfurt meeting at the Park Hotel, Shultz received a secure telephone call from the State Department representative. The Secretary was stunned after he heard his report and he called the President to say they needed to talk at once. The President invited Shultz to the White House the next morning.

At the White House on Sunday morning, Shultz said that the Frankfurt meeting illustrated how much out of control everything was. Poindexter, North, Casey and the CIA had been negotiating on matters about which there could be no flexibility. Iran's representative in Frankfurt had referred to a nine-point agenda, previously agreed on by North and the CIA. Among other things, it said the United States would work to win the release of 17 prisoners who had been convicted of the 1983 truck-bomb attack on the U.S. embassy in Kuwait. In the long battle against terrorism, the United States had regularly and vociferously backed Kuwait's refusal to release the 17 prisoners. The 17 were members of Al Dawa or "The Call," a radical fanatical Muslim fundamentalist group tied to those who had killed the 241 U.S. servicemen in 1983 in Beirut and other terrorist attacks. These were the suicidal fringe; some were related to the Lebanese faction Hizbollah and its leader, Fadlallah. Kuwait's steadfastness had become a symbol of a united front of antiterrorist toughness. But the CIA was off in Germany saying this issue was negotiable. Accustomed to operations founded in expediency and subterfuge —not consistency—the agency was making a mockery of the President's principles and doctrine, undercutting the President's personal pledge that terrorists could run but not hide. This NSC-CIA attitude was at the root of the whole current mess. Shultz said he found it sickening.

The President's eyes flashed and his jaw set. In that single meeting, the Iran argument that Shultz had been waging and losing since mid-1985 was finally over.

The next morning, Monday, December 15, Casey was in his seventh-floor office at Langley preparing for another appearance before the Senate intelligence committee when he suffered a seizure. An ambulance was summoned and he was rushed to Georgetown Hospital. He had another seizure, but was speaking and moving normally. On Thursday at 7:40 A.M. he was taken into surgery, and a three-member team operated until 1 P.M., removing a cancerous soft tumor called a lymphoma. It was scooped out from the inner side of the left brain, the area controlling movement of the right side of the body. In a statement, his doctors said they expected that the seventy-three-year-old Casey would be able to resume his normal activities.

Gates took over as acting DCI, and spent much of January resisting White House pressure to suggest a replacement for Casey, who was seriously ill and virtually unable to speak. Forced to come up with some names, Gates proposed former Senators John Tower, Paul Laxalt or Howard Baker. None of them would come in and tear the place to shreds, he hoped.

After six weeks, Casey improved dramatically. On Wednesday, January 28, Gates was allowed to visit him in the hospital.

He was sitting by the window. He never had much hair, so the hair loss from radiation and drug treatment was not that noticeable. Gates had a list of subjects to cover and he began. Casey was lucid, making short comments or grunting as Gates moved down the list.

"Time for me to get out of the way," Casey finally said, waving his left arm in the air, "make room."

The next day Gates arranged for Don Regan and Meese to visit the hospital. Casey couldn't write, so Sophia signed his resignation letter. He had served six years and one day.

I took a list of persisting questions, added some from the previous years, and drove over to Georgetown Hospital. Two unusually heavy snowfalls had blanketed Washington during the latter part of the month, and the traffic was thin. I didn't have to wait long in the lobby to see one of the telltale CIA security men with his walkie-talkie earpiece stroll through. He went down a long corridor, turned left into a new wing, and took the elevator. It stopped at the sixth floor. I went up. In a small room, four CIA security men were watching afternoon television.

Casey was in Room C6316, registered under the alias "Lacey." The door was closed, and after I identified myself, the lone security man declined to let me in.

Each time I had interviewed Casey over the previous three years, I had written out my questions on sheets of yellow legal paper. I had saved all these sheets and now had a thick packet of many folded and old pages. Some questions—asked, answered by Casey and verified elsewhere—now only prompted more curiosity. As I spent several hours reviewing what I might want to ask, I attempted to condense it to one page: "Key unanswered questions for Casey." More than ever it was evident how preeminent this man had been to the Reagan Administration's aspirations and predicaments. As much as anybody's, even the President's, Casey's convictions, fierce loyalties and obsessions were behind the contra operation, the Iran initiative and the range of other secret undertakings and clandestine relations. His view of the law—minimum compliance and minimum disclosure—had permeated the Reagan foreign-policy enterprises. His ambition had been to prove that his country could do "these things," as he once had told me. He meant covert actions conducted in true, permanent secrecy. It was part nostalgia. It was also part a demonstration of willfulness.

"We could win," he had once said longingly to one of his top assistants. He felt his big accomplishment had been to prevent Central America from going Communist, much like America's post–World War II achievement in saving Western Europe from the Communists. Sophia said to me in a phone conversation, "From the head and the heart, Bill was a born patriot."

Was he? Was that what it was about? His country at any cost? What price had been paid? Now that the game was about over, I realized that I could not escape making a judgment. I had scrupulously avoided that for the three and one-half years I had known him. It was easier and safer for me that way. For some reason we had formed a partnership over secrets. In entirely different ways, we were both obsessed with secrets. During this game, secrets were the exchange medium. What were the secrets? What was their value? What was their use?

The previous year Casey had told me that he had read a review I had written of John le Carré's *A Perfect Spy*. Casey said he agreed with my interpretation of the le Carré view of espionage, that the better the spying, the better the deception. I had quoted him one of my favorite lines from the book: *"In every operation there is an above the line and a below the line. Above the line is what you do by the book. Below the line is how you do the job."* Casey just took it in, an intense, almost gloomy, look on his face. He could be so distant. What did he think? I had asked. No response. Did he agree? Nothing.

Casey had been an attractive figure to me because he was useful and because he never avoided the confrontation. He might shout and challenge, even threaten, but he never broke off the dialogue or the relationship. Back in 1985 when we had exposed the covert preemptive teams to strike against terrorists he had said to me, "You'll probably have blood on your hands before it's over." That was, I later learned, after Casey had worked secretly with the Saudi intelligence service and its ambassador in Washington to arrange the assassination of the arch-terrorist Fadlallah. Instead of Fadlallah, the car bomb had killed at least eighty people, many innocent.

How did he square that? I imagined, and hoped, he felt the moral dilemma. How could he not? He was too smart not to see that he and the White House had broken the rules, probably the law. It was Casey who had blood on his hands.

The institutional questions about the White House, the CIA, Congress, the political temptation of covert action, the war-making authority, the awful fakery of "plausible deniability" would be addressed by the investigations. I kept coming back to the question of personal responsibility, Casey's responsibility. Events, disclosures would not take him off the hook but would more likely put him on it more firmly.

For a moment, I hoped he would take himself off the hook. The only way was an admission of some kind or an apology to his colleagues or an expression of new understanding.

Under the last question on "Key unanswered questions for Casey," I wrote: "Do you now see that it was wrong?"

Several days later I returned to Casey's hospital room. The door was open. Scars from the craniotomy were still healing. I asked Casey how he was getting along.

Hope and then realism flashed in his eyes. "Okay . . . better . . . no."

I took his hand to shake it in a greeting. He grabbed my hand and squeezed, peace and sunlight in the room for a moment.

"You finished yet?" he asked, referring to the book.

I said I'd never finish, never get it all, there were so many questions. I'd never find out everything he had done.

The left side of his mouth hooked up in a smile, and he grunted.

Look at all the trouble you've caused, I said, the whole Administration under investigation.

He didn't seem to hear. So I repeated it and for a moment he looked proud, raising his head.

"It hurts," he said, and I thought he was in physical pain.

What hurts, sir?

"Oh," he said, stopping. He seemed to be saying that it was being out of it, out of the action, I thought. But he suddenly spoke up, apparently on the same track about the hurt. "What you don't know," he said.

In the end, I realized, what was hidden was greater. The unknown had the power, he seemed to be saying, or at least that's what I thought. He was so frail, at life's edge, and he knew, making a comment about death. "I'm gone," he said. I said no.

You knew, didn't you, I said. The contra diversion had to be the first question: you knew all along.

His head jerked up hard. He stared, and finally nodded yes.

Why? I asked.

"I believed."

What?

"I believed."

Then he was asleep, and I didn't get to ask another question.

A few weeks later Sophia took him home, but he was soon back in the hospital. She finally took him to Mayknoll to die. He contracted pneumonia and was hospitalized on Long Island. There, the morning of May 6, the day after Congress began its public hearings on the Iran-contra affair, Casey died.

CENTRAL AMERICAN COVERT-ACTION CHRONOLOGY

March 4, 1981—President Reagan signs a finding authorizing money for political backing to moderate Christian Democrats and military officers in El Salvador.

December 1, 1981—President Reagan signs a finding providing for the first lethal assistance to the contras to oppose the Sandinista government in Nicaragua; $19 million is to be spent to train and arm a 500-man paramilitary force in conjunction with Argentina. The finding is outlined to the congressional intelligence committees as an effort to save El Salvador by interdicting arms shipments from Nicaragua to the leftist rebels in El Salvador.

March 10, 1982—First public disclosure that President Reagan had authorized the covert support to the contras.

December 1982—President Reagan signs into law the first Boland Amendment, which prohibits the expenditure of funds "for the purpose of overthrowing the Government of Nicaragua."

September 20, 1983—At the urging of the intelligence committees, President Reagan signs a second finding on the Nicaragua operation, declaring that the covert program is designed to induce the Sandinista government to negotiate and pressure them to cease support to the Salvadoran rebels. Congress finally authorizes $24 million for the next year.

April 1984—The CIA's direct role in the mining of Nicaraguan harbors is publicly disclosed. Congress refuses to authorize another $21 million sought by the Reagan Administration. Secret funding from Saudi Arabia, at the rate of $1 million a month, begins in July 1984.

October 1984—Congress cuts off funding to the contras and bans any support, "directly or indirectly," until December 1985. The Saudis secretly contributed another $15–$24 million.

December 1985—Congress partially lifts the ban and authorizes limited assistance to prevent the contras from being decimated; the CIA is allowed to provide intelligence "advice" and communications equipment and training. President Reagan signs a finding January 9, 1986, authorizing this limited assistance, which costs $13 million. In addition Congress authorizes $27 million in "humanitarian" contra assistance, including food, medical supplies and some transportation. The State Department was authorized to solicit additional "humanitarian" aid from third countries.

October 1986—Congress lifts the ban, and $100 million is authorized for the contras.

ACKNOWLEDGMENTS

The flexibility and patience of Benjamin C. Bradlee, the executive editor of *The Washington Post,* and Richard E. Snyder, the chairman of Simon & Schuster, Inc., have permitted me to weave my way through the dual existence of newspaper reporter and book author. I doubt if anywhere there are more formidable believers in independent inquiry or the printed word than these two. I owe them both an extra debt for their backing and friendship. This project was initially begun with my *Post* colleague Charles R. Babcock in the fall of 1984. It was to be a series of articles for the *Post.* Instead, we published a number of news articles on covert operations. I owe him special gratitude for his efforts. Though he bears no responsibility for this book, I thank Chuck, one of the most careful and thorough reporters, for the information, suggestions and insights he unselfishly shared with me.

The *Post* provided me with immense support and guidance. In particular I thank the managing editor, Leonard Downie, Jr. No one cares more about the *Post* or devotes more attention to the quality of its daily product and professional standards. Assistant managing editor for national news Robert G. Kaiser and the deputy projects editor Steve Luxenberg—two of the wisest and most talented newspapermen anywhere—both spent days reading this manuscript and advising me. I owe much to other *Post* colleagues: in particular Ferman Patterson for his eternal good nature, competency and research skills; the *Post* library staff who often chased and located what we thought was lost or unobtainable; the telephone operators who fielded the calls and separated the essential from the non-essential.

For the complicated legal review, special thanks to John Bender and Eric Rayman of Simon & Schuster, Inc.

At Simon and Schuster, much appreciation to Joni Evans, who has always been a source of great support. Also to Henry Ferris and David

Shipley for a thousand assists. Many thanks to Sophie Sorkin, Eve Metz, Frank Metz and Jeanne Palmer. Greatest respect and appreciation to Vera Schneider.

Alice Mayhew, my editor at Simon and Schuster on now my fifth book, is, like the best of book people, someone concerned with the truth. She wields a relentless red pen, and has the intellect, backbone and stamina of a team of editors. She is a true collaborator.

No work about intelligence can be pieced together in a vacuum. I acknowledge the many books and newspaper and magazine articles that added background or detail to my own work: especially the articles that have appeared in the *The New York Times, The Los Angeles Times, The Wall Street Journal,* on the Associated Press wire and by *Post* colleagues Patrick Tyler, Benjamin Weiser, George Lardner, Walter Pincus, Dan Morgan, Joe Pichirallo, Lou Cannon, David Hoffman, Don Oberdorfer, John Goshko, George Wilson, David Ignatius, Michael Getler, James Conaway and Rick Atkinson. Extra thanks also to William Greider.

Tali and Fe are thanked for moral support and understanding. Carl Bernstein, my friend, colleague and sounding board, provided several critical and most helpful readings.

My greatest thanks go to the sources for this book. Many sat with me for days, endured repeated requests for more information, recollection, explanation and documentation.

And to Elsa Walsh for daily counsel and love.

INDEX